A PRIMER
FOR FILM - MAKING

A PRIMER FOR FILM-MAKING

A COMPLETE GUIDE TO 16 MM AND 35 MM FILM PRODUCTION

KENNETH H. ROBERTS AND WIN SHARPLES, JR.

PEGASUS

A Division of
Bobbs-Merrill Educational Publishing
Indianapolis

LINE DRAWINGS BY JACK FISCHER

PHOTOGRAPHY BY MALCOLM KNAPP

RICHARD C. TOMKINS

MEL WITTENSTEIN

The Bobbs-Merrill Company, Inc.
4300 West 62nd Street
Indianapolis, Indiana 46268

First Edition
Seventh Printing—1978
Library of Congress Catalog Card Number 70–91620
ISBN 0–672–63582–8 (pbk.)
ISBN 0–672–53582–3

DEDICATION

TO MY WIFE, SANDRA.
K.H.R.

TO MY FATHER,
WHO BEGAN MY
EDUCATION IN FILM;
AND TO MY STUDENTS,
WHO ARE CONTINUING IT.
W.S. JR.

ACKNOWLEDGMENTS

We would like to gratefully acknowledge the invaluable contributions of the following people who served as consultants, contributed illustrative material, and made available to us motion pictures for study. We extend to them our gratitude and our thanks.

Capturing the Image. . . . . . . Daniel Bourla, Richard C. Tomkins

The Tools of Cinematography . . . Robert Kaplan, F&B/Ceco, Inc.

Lighting the Image. . . . . . . Joseph Tawil, Berkey-Colortran, Inc.

Developing and Printing the Image . . . . Harold J. Freedman, Deluxe Laboratories, Inc.

The Image in Flux and Juxtaposition . . . . . Ezra Baker, Ed Cullen, Richard Matt, Frank Post, Donovan Thesenga

The Cutting Room . . . . Irv Pivovar, F&B/Ceco, Inc.

Opticals and Titles . . . . . Richard Rauh, The Optical House, Inc.

The Sound Mix. . . . . Alex Alden, SMPTE; Gus Mortensen; Sam Platt, Townsend, Production Service, Inc.

Contributors of Illustrative Material

Arriflex Corp. of America; Audio Film Center (Martin Bresnick); Bach Auricon: Bardwell & McAlister, Inc.; Bell & Howell; Cargill, Wilson & Acree, Inc.; Cinema Beaulieu; Cinema 5; Columbia Pictures; Contemporary Films/McGraw Hill (Nancy O'Rourke); DeLuxe General, Inc. (Harold J. Freedman, Edwin Riester); Eastman Kodak Company (Phillip Perkins); Eclair Corp.; Embassy Pictures (Ted Spiegel); F&B/Ceco (Irv Pivovar); General Enterprises, Inc.—Steenbeck (William Engstler); The Mario Ghio Production Group, Ltd; Hollywood Film Company (Lillian Kaye); The Intercraft Corp.—KEM Division (Robert Rowen); Janus Films (Bill Frantz, John Waxman); Kenyon & Eckhardt Advertising, Inc. (Bruce Andrews); Lincoln-Mercury Division, Ford Motor Company; Magnasync/Moviola Corp. (Garey Lundberg); Magna-Tech Electronics Co., Inc.; Manhattan Audio Co. (Melvin Gold, Tony Roberts); Mattco Associates (Bill Fraser); Mitchell; Movielab, Inc. (Fred Koevari); National Recording Studios, Inc.; The Optical House, Inc. (Richard Rauh); Paillard, Inc.—Bolex; Pelican Films (Jack Zander); Photo-Magnetic Sound (John Arvonio); Precision Laboratories (Irwin Sheldon); SOS Photo-Cine-Optics; State of Georgia Department of Industry & Trade; Storer Studios (Bob Bates); 20th Century-Fox (Norman Steinberg); United Artists Corp.

Frame blow-ups by Dick Sawicki, Photographer, and The Optical House, Inc.

Motion picture research courtesy of:

Audio Film Center (Martin Bresnick, Wally Dauler, Michael Kerbel)

Brandon Films (Walter Zilka)

Contemporary Films (Nancy O'Rourke, Harry Bohrs)

Continental 16 (Andrew Sager, Eileen Teitler)

Grove Press (Kent Carol)

Janus Films (Bill Frantz)

Films Inc. (Ray Ettore, Douglas Patterson)

Leacock-Pennebaker (Peter Hansen)

Museum of Modern Art Study Center (Regina Cornwell)

University 16mm (Kirk Karhi)

CONTENTS

PREFACE

One must learn to understand that editing is in actual fact a compulsory and deliberate guidance of the thoughts and associations of the spectator.
— *V. I. Pudovkin,* Film Technique

Our purpose in this book is to make known to the reader the tools of film-making. Only by thoroughly understanding the wide range of tools available to him—and the variety of ways in which they can be utilized —can the film-maker fully appreciate the enormous creative potential open to him. He has under his control an infinite number of variables which can affect the presentation of his subject: the type of camera and type of film, the camera lens, the lighting of the subject, the ultimate assembly of the units of filmed material into a cohesive whole, the optical effects, the elements of film sound. Each of these offers him seemingly unlimited choices. However, something must guide and determine his choice.

Certainly a choice should not be made from less than the full range of available tools; too often a camera is used because its operator has a general familiarity with its operation rather than because it is the best possible camera to accomplish the particular requirements of a particular film. But equally important, a choice should never be made arbitrarily. The relationship of the camera to its subject—the "set up"—may often be chosen for convenience, or simply as the best way to comfortably include the required material, rather than because it will offer the most meaningful interpretive presentation of that subject for that precise moment in the film. Later, the shots may be joined together with little awareness of the new meanings and emotions which their juxtaposition will evoke in the spectator. In each case tools have been chosen and choices made governing their use—but the choices are arbitrary because the film-maker has no clear idea of an overall theme or purpose which must be fulfilled in his film.

Pudovkin's simple statement is the essence of our theme. Editing, and the many other facets of the art and craft of the film, are a means for "compulsory and deliberate guidance" of the spectator. Having this potential, it is essential that they be utilized by the film-maker for a purpose. It is only when he has defined the overall theme of the film that the director can properly judge the significance of each shot and its unique contribution to the film as a whole. Only when he knows the significance and purpose of each shot can he determine the way in which he wishes first to film it and then to place it in its special relationship with the film's other images, both audial and visual. The use of these tools, then, is determined by the director's purpose and certain aesthetic principles which he may then apply.

In attempting to set down these aesthetic principles we may at times declare that there is a "way" to perform a particular aspect of the film production process. Carried away by our enthusiasm, we may even declare that there is an "only way," or, worse still, that a particular way is "not the way" to do something. There is never, of course, "one way." What is true, however, is that each "way" chosen will have its own unique effect upon the spectator, and this must be planned for.

The aesthetic principles—and, for that matter, the practical techniques offered in this book—are a kind of consensus. They are patterns in which we and many others have worked in performing our jobs in film-making. That they have in many cases been successful is obvious. But they are only a starting point, and the reader can and must discover his own way to utilize them. Breaking rules will have its own affect, as real and as important as the following of these same rules. The initial task is to establish these patterns and principles as a base from which to work, a stable springboard from which to vault a creative imagination.

This brings us to something which we consider of paramount importance: the proper budgeting of the enormous cost of film-making. If one thinks he can drop down to his neighborhood camera store and pick up one or two pieces of equipment and a few rolls of film and then skip blithely off into the wilderness to create a cinematic masterpiece in three days, he is due for a shock when he faces the realities of the situation. In spite of Claude Chabrol's whimsical statement that "all you need to know to be a film director can be learnt in four hours," the fact is that film is a frighteningly complex and expensive medium.° It is essential from the start that one know the wide variety of crafts and services involved in the process and the expense that each will entail. Certainly the total amount of money available for production must also be known so that it can be properly apportioned among these essentials. If the budget can only handle three days of location shooting, then this must be considered in the planning of the film and the shooting *must* be accomplished in this period of time. If this is impossible, then other budget cuts will have to be made; it does the film-maker little good to have shot a wealth of marvelous material if he has no money to pay for his lab work, sound, and opticals at the end of production. Even the unpredictable can be predicted in budgeting; human beings do tend to make errors and are eternally optimistic. The wise producer always budgets for his blunders, politely if euphemistically called "contingencies" in his budget.

Actor George Segal tells a story about the shooting of a film in which he was acting. Segal was invited by the director to see a screening of the "dailies," the unedited results of the previous day's filming. There were five different takes of one particular shot in which Segal and other actors were involved and he watched each carefully. Afterward, the director asked Segal for his opinion. He replied thoughtfully that if it were his own choice, he would personally prefer the third take to the others. "But George," the director replied, "Frank fell down during that take."

It is inevitable that each contributor to the total film will see his own contribution from his own point of view, often exaggerating its importance. Only the director can conceive the overall balance of the

*It is of course true that many initially free creative talents have been stifled by the very process of learning to cope with the complex technical requirements and resulting enormous cost of film-making. This has been so in other forms of art, including the art of politics, and their history is filled with the accounts of imaginative and courageous attempts by the artist to avoid this entrapment. This would seem to be what Chabrol, Truffaut, Godard and the others of the New Wave of French film-makers have been attempting by their calculatedly off-hand approach to the film. Yet there would seem to be a very real question as to which is the better way to avoid this problem—whether to ignore the danger or to master it. Obviously we believe the mastery of the technical complexity of the film process to be the route to ultimate creative freedom. But it is a route, not a goal; a means, not an end.

film, properly relating each separate element to the whole. This is perhaps his most important job: to provide the inspiration and discipline that welds the vast complexity of contributions into a unified, artistic whole.

It is beyond the scope of this technical work to deal with the evolution of a directorial style, a personal approach to a film. Not the art, but the technical craft of film-making is our subject. The director's choice of subject, his interpretation of it, his desire to communicate it are very much his business. The evolution of a personal style and an individual process of film-making—the stylistic use of film techniques and tools—is also the individual's business. What we hope to offer is a choice of the technical means by which he may accomplish this.

K.H.R.
W.S., Jr.

CHAPTER 1

THE BUDGET

Most every facet of film-making is distinguished by its lack of predictability. Not only is film-making a complex technical medium—a factor that contributes greatly to its uncertainty—it is also a medium which places the film-maker at the mercy of his abilities and frailties, as well as those of his associates, not to mention the mercy of the weather and a plethora of other contingencies which multiply in proportion with the complexity of the film. We shall have occasion to repeat throughout this book that the one possible protection for the film-maker is adequate advance preparation.

The one area where such protection is vital is the financial structure of the film. Therefore, once the film's idea has been determined, the first step is the preparation of a budget. Regardless of the type of film, someone—the instructor of the student film-maker, the sponsor of the industrial film, the producer of the theatrical film—will be concerned with how much that film will cost. As clairvoyant as it may sound, the budget should encompass all of the foreseeable expenses that will be incurred in putting the idea on film.

The ability to prepare a comprehensive budget is as vital to film-making as the ability to use the tools of the medium creatively and imaginatively. Everyone, from the novice making his first film to the professional making a feature-length film, no doubt has a limited amount of capital to spend on a production, whether that limit is $100 or $50,000. Common sense, therefore, dictates that the apportionment of the capital be planned so that *all* of the costs of the film are met through completion. Frustration and disappointment can result for the fledgling, and disaster for the professional, if the project remains uncompleted because the money has been exhausted. The budget, composed from a knowledge of a number of ascertainable facts and the possession of a fair amount of intuition, can be helpful in the avoidance of such an eventuality. However, the budget can not serve as a guarantee that the money problems are solved; it can serve only as a basic plan and guide to be followed as the film moves through each step of production. The worth of the budget becomes apparent when the film-maker finds that the cost of one phase of production exceeds the amount allocated, and that he must determine where and how a later cost can be trimmed.

THE APPROACH TO THE BUDGET

The first step in preparing the budget is to compile an *all-inclusive* list. Leaving out an expensive item obviously destroys the purpose of the budget. This list may include salaries, raw stock, shooting costs, laboratory expenses, post-production fees, insurance, and screening expenditures.

SALARIES

The novice or student making a film will probably utilize the services of friends, classmates, and acquaintances to serve voluntarily before and behind the camera. A thoughtful gesture on the part of the film-maker would be to take into account the various expenses, such as travel and food, which will be imposed upon his volunteers and set aside some money to reimburse them. Although these expenses are not wages in the precise definition of the term, such a disbursement of the film's funds can be listed under this classification and thus get the novice or student into the habit of considering this item.

A procedure frequently followed by the advanced film-maker producing a film without financial backing but desiring to use experienced people to staff his production is to collect a cast and crew who will agree to work "on speculation." An agreement is usually arrived at between the maker and his personnel which stipulates that the cast and crew will be paid a specific wage or a percentage of the profits realized from the film should it be distributed.

The film-maker who has secured financial backing for his project usually prefers to acquire the services of experienced personnel. These associates may or may not be members of the various professional unions. In the matter of a crew, it is sometimes difficult to find first-rate people without using union members. The use of union people affects a film's cost in two ways: the wage scale, and the union requirements concerning the number of people who must be hired (although the latter is, to some degree, negotiable). One important fact to remember is that the film-maker need not be a member of the union to direct union personnel if he is a principal in the company producing the film.

RAW STOCK

In order to determine the raw stock cost, it is first necessary to decide whether the film will be shot in 16mm or 35mm and whether it will be in color or black and white. These decisions may be dictated by where the film is to be exhibited—theater showings almost invariably require 35mm, television almost invariably requires color.

The key figures needed to finally determine the cost of the raw stock are the *proposed length of the completed film* and the *amount of stock that will be exposed.* These two figures make up the film's shooting ratio —the amount of film exposed compared to the actual length of the completed film. If the completed film is to be ten minutes in length, it will contain 360 feet of 16mm or 900 feet of 35mm film. (16mm runs through the camera at 36 feet per minute and 35mm at 90 feet per minute at sound speed or 24 frames per second.) It is an established fact that more film will have to be exposed than will be actually used in the edited film; therefore, the shooting ratio will never be 1 to 1, but rather it will usually vary from a 5 to 1 to a 20 to 1 ratio for a "normal" film. As a result the amount of raw stock that may be used to shoot the ten minute film can range from 1,800 feet (16mm) or 4,500 feet (35mm) to 7,200 feet (16mm) or 18,000 feet (35mm). A 10 to 1 ratio is generally a safe guess for budgeting. Needless to say, the ratio can be as low as 2 to 1, but the lower the ratio the less footage the editor has to choose from when piecing the film together.

SHOOTING COSTS

A number of questions must be asked in order to determine an estimate of the shooting costs. Are stock shots to be used? Will there be any animation? Will the film be shot on location and/or in the studio? Will special equipment be required? Will travel and accommodations have to be provided for the cast and crew? All of these questions propose shooting costs that will have to be budgeted.

The one basic cost for both studio and location shooting is for equipment. But the use of a studio additionally involves studio rental and sets, whereas location shooting involves travel, food, power supply, and sometimes sets, permits, rental, and additional equipment in order to maintain control over picture and sound quality. These costs are usually based on a per day figure, so they must be multiplied by the estimated number of days required to complete the shooting. The film-maker should also budget in the possible cost for any needed retakes.

Finally, the necessary equipment must be determined and the cost budgeted. It can usually be rented on a daily or weekly basis. If the equipment is rented by the week, the fee charged by most suppliers is five times the daily rental cost.

LABORATORY EXPENSES

1000 ft. exposed	$47.50	$47.50
X.0475	X .03	+ 1.43
$47.50	$1.4250	$48.93 Total Cost

The first laboratory cost to be computed is the fee for the developing of the raw stock and the printing of a timed or one-light print (dailies) to be used as a work print by the editor. This fee is generally a specific price per foot (e.g., $.0475 per foot), and the total cost is arrived at by multiplying the number of feet exposed during shooting by the price per foot. The laboratory generally charges a nominal fee (usually 3 percent) for threadage waste, and this should be added to the final figure. All exposed film must be developed, but some film-makers cut costs by having only specified takes printed for the work print.

Next the film-maker must decide whether or not he wishes to follow a process that will protect his camera original—such as an internegative or interpositive (see page 485). Such a procedure is wise if more than one or two release prints are to be made. A protection procedure is also a per-foot cost, but this final figure is computed times the final edited footage. (A ten minute film = 360 ft. (16mm) × the cost per foot for an internegative.) Threadage waste must also be computed. Professional contracts usually require the producer of the film to supply the sponsor with only an answer print of the edited camera original, an optical sound negative, and the matched camera original (original cut to match the edited workprint). If the producer is to supply an internegative, interpositive, optical reduction or blow-up, or if he is required to supply release prints, the cost of these items are added to the budget. The cost of any desired fades and dissolves must also be computed.

The first print struck from a master—whether the master be the edited original, an internegative, an interpositive, a reduction, or a blow-up—is called an *answer print*. It is imperative to take this into account when budgeting because any answer print must be allocated in the budget at its appropriate cost, which is approximately double the price of a release print.

A final reminder: The length of the edited film will be the length of an answer print, optical sound negative, music and sound effects track (if needed), an interpositive or internegative, and the release print. The length of the film exposed during shooting will determine the cost of developing, the printing of the dailies, and the cost of edge numbering.

When faced with the decision of whether to shoot in 35mm or 16mm, some quick arithmetic often helps with the decision. Since a film-maker needs almost three times as much 35mm stock (90 ft. per minute) as 16mm (36 ft. per minute) for a comparable length film, and since lab and stock prices are approximately twice as much for 35mm, the final cost for stock and laboratory services will be around six times as much for 35mm as for 16mm.

POST-PRODUCTION FEES

EDITING Editing costs can involve either the hiring of an editor, the rental of a cutting room, or simply the rental of editing equipment. If the first alternative is followed, the film-maker should attempt to include any necessary voice editing in the editor's fee. An additional editing cost that should not be overlooked is for matching the camera original with the edited workprint. The matching fee is usually computed by the reel (ten minutes), as is the general editing fee.

NARRATION   If the film requires narration, a reasonably accurate computation should include the cost of the narrator and the recording studio's fee, which will be based upon the approximate amount of recording time required (determined by the amount of narration to be recorded), the type of stock used (quarter-inch tape and either 16mm or 35mm sound film), the transfer time (re-recording from the quarter-inch tape to either 16mm or 35mm), and the editing of the quarter-inch tape. If the cost of voice editing has not been included in the general editing fee, it should be figured into the budget here.

MUSIC AND EFFECTS   In arriving at the music and effects costs the basic decisions will be whether to use stock music or to have an original score composed and recorded, or whether to employ stock sound effects or to have live effects recorded on location. If an original score is required, the budget figure should include the costs for composing, arranging, copying, and recording. The recording costs will include the payments for the musicians, studio time, special instruments, and recording stock. When negotiating with a professional composer, it is possible to reach an agreement which will include in the composer's fee all of the above costs. This is the most satisfactory arrangement.

If the decision is to use live effects, the cost of the recording technician and the recording equipment should be figured into the budget.

The final computation will be for the editing of the original music and effects into the picture.

If stock music and effects are to be used, a music house can provide a complete quote which includes the license of the music, the selection and editing, any stock needed, and the supervision of the mixing session.

SOUND MIX   The cost of the sound mix is dependent upon the amount of time needed in the mixing studio. A re-recording studio can estimate this time on the basis of the complexity of the job and the length of the film. Costs will include the mix time; the stock, including a quarter-inch tape for a protection tape; a music and effects track (m&e) if required; an optical negative, including stock and developing; and any needed transfer.

DUBBING   The film-maker will have to decide whether all sync dialogue will be recorded during shooting or whether it will be dubbed later in a recording studio. If the decision is to dub, the cost estimate will depend upon the amount of dialogue to be dubbed. This cost will include the technique of looping and the laying-in of the recorded voices—unless, of course, the studio has the special equipment that skips these steps, but naturally this increases the cost of the dubbing session itself. An important factor to remember concerning dubbing is to reach an initial agreement with the actors that will include the dubbing sessions at no additional fees.

Even when a film is dubbed in a studio, it is essential that a true recording be made of the dialogue at the time of the shootings. This recording can be either a stenographic record or, preferably, a "scratch track" which is a less-than-perfect reference recording of the spoken dialogue made by a sound recordist with the appropriate equipment during the shooting.

OPTICALS AND TITLES   This budget figure will include all of the titles and any needed optical effects—freeze frames, optical reversals, shot duplications, traveling mattes, or any of the other innumerable effects available.

INSURANCE

The vital item of insurance can easily be overlooked when planning a production budget. It may be as indispensible as film stock to the professional production and, in fact, is generally required of the producer by many sponsors and by all equipment rental services. Laboratories assert responsibility *only for the cost of the replacement of any stock they may damage.* The film-maker will find little comfort in being handed a check for the cost of his film stock alone if he has just completed six months of filming in the Gobi Desert.

Several insurance companies are listed in the Motion Picture Enterprises handbook which specialize in film production insurance, and F&B/Ceco, Incorporated the equipment sales and rental company, offers the following comprehensive list of policies:

EQUIPMENT INSURANCE   Available at a cost of 10 percent of the rental bill; $250 deductible for cameras, $150 deductible for all other equipment.

NEGATIVE INSURANCE   The cost is also 10 percent of the rental bill. It is an all-risk policy covering physical loss or damage of raw stock and/or exposed or developed film, including masters, fine grains, work prints, sound tracks, and tapes. It covers loss by fire, theft, or disappearance.

FAULTY STOCK AND CAMERA INSURANCE   This policy also costs 10 percent of the rental. It is a $1500 deductible policy that provides insurance against faulty stock, faulty camera, or faulty developing or processing of exposed or developed film, sound tracks, or recordings.

CAST INSURANCE   The policy provides for the reimbursement of expenses incurred due to an accident or the sickness of a performer which delays production.

PRODUCER'S LIABILITY INSURANCE   This policy provides insurance against lawsuits for invasion of privacy; copyright infringement; libel; slander; and unauthorized use of titles, formats, ideas, characters, or plots.

PROPS, WARDROBE, AND SETS INSURANCE   This policy provides for the replacement and/or repair of props, wardrobe, scenic drops, and sets which become lost or damaged.

EXTRA EXPENSE INSURANCE   Coverage is provided for unforeseen delays caused by the loss of or damage to sets or scenery, including the cost of overtime needed to repair such damage.

THIRD PARTY PROPERTY DAMAGE   This policy covers the damage or loss claims of owners of property used in production, such as losses incurred in museums, private homes, department stores, and borrowed private property.

RAIN INSURANCE   This insurance covers all expenses incurred when exterior shooting must be postponed because of rain. Reimbursement includes salaries for the cast, crew, musicians, equipment, and location rental.

SCREENING EXPENDITURES

If a projector is not readily available to the film-maker, the cost of renting one should be included in the film's budget. If the film is 35mm, this may require the hourly rental of a projection studio. Such a studio can also provide interlock services—running of the picture synchronized with the separate sound tracks—which may be necessary during the post-production stage. Screenings should be made of the dailies initially, of the work print as often as possible, of the interlocked picture and tracks, of the answer prints, and of the release prints.

PRODUCER'S FEE

Since the budget can include only estimated costs, the film-maker may find himself in trouble when the inevitable problems crop up and add to the cost of the film. The process of making a film is highly complex and errors are likely, so the film-maker producing a financially-backed film should have some safety margin within the budget. One solution to this dilemma is to include in the budget a 15 percent *producer's fee* to cover contingencies. This figure is computed by estimating the total production cost and then adding to it 15 percent of the figure.

GATHERING THE INFORMATION

Budgeting is basically a matter of common sense combined with a modicum of intuition. Anyone with a telephone, pen and paper, and the MPE handbook can collect cost quotes on every aspect of film-making from film services and suppliers. The film-maker must first determine what he will require of these services and suppliers (this is where the intuition enters) and then contact them with information on his requirements. The services and suppliers will then be able to provide him with an estimated cost. For example, when contacting the laboratory, the film-maker must inform them of the type of film stock that will be used; the amount of stock that will be exposed, developed, and printed; the proposed length of the completed film; and any special requirements such as internegatives or blow-ups. The laboratory will then furnish the film-maker with appropriate prices with which he can then figure his budget estimates. The same procedure is followed with the equipment companies, optical houses, music houses, and any other services required by the production. A comprehensive breakdown of the budget is included in the Appendix.

Whatever the intended cost of a film, it is a good idea to get into the habit of budgeting. It is the first of many organizational steps that can be followed by the film-maker to bring some order to a complex, and sometimes seemingly chaotic, medium.

The following are hypothetical examples of production budgets for two ten-minute films:

SALARIES	
Director	$ 1,500.00
Talent	4,000.00
Script	1,000.00
Director of Photography	500.00
Unit Manager	500.00
Gaffer	250.00
Camera Operator	250.00
Camera Assistant	250.00
Script Girl	250.00
Grip	250.00
Props	250.00
	$ 9,000.00

STOCK	
9,000 ft., 35mm	$ 2,100.00

LABORATORY	
Developing	$ 620.00
Work Print	1,400.00
Edge Numbering	80.00
Answer Prints (2)	1,100.00
Internegative	550.00
Dissolves and Fades	500.00
	$ 4,250.00

POST-PRODUCTION	
Editing	$ 1,000.00
Editorial Assistant	300.00
Music	500.00
Sound Effects	150.00
Matching	150.00
Opticals and Titles	800.00
Mix	400.00
	$ 3,300.00

INSURANCE	
Negative Insurance	$ 500.00
Equipment Liability	120.00
Producer's Liability	50.00
	$ 670.00

EQUIPMENT	
Camera & Accessories	$ 800.00
Lighting	400.00
	$ 1,200.00

PRODUCTION EXPENSES

Location Scouting	$ 500.00
Costumes	500.00
Props	250.00
Stock Shots	500.00
Transportation	160.00
Meals	250.00
Miscellaneous	250.00
	$ 2,410.00
Subtotal	$22,730.00
Producer's Fee	3,400.00
TOTAL	$26,130.00

SALARIES

Director	$ 500.00
Cameraman	250.00
Talent	250.00
Assistant Director	250.00
	$ 1,250.00

STOCK

4,000 feet, 16mm, Color	$ 325.00

LABORATORY

Developing	$ 225.00
Work Print	400.00
Edge Numbering	100.00
Answer Prints (2)	220.00
Internegative	170.00
Dissolves and Fades	300.00
	$ 1,415.00

POST-PRODUCTION

Editing	$ 500.00
Music	300.00
Sound Effects	150.00
Matching	150.00
Opticals and Titles	800.00
Mix	400.00
Narrator	150.00
Recording	150.00
	$ 2,600.00

INSURANCE

Negative Insurance	$ 270.00
Equipment Liability	100.00
Producer's Liability	100.00
	$ 470.00

EQUIPMENT

Camera & Lighting	$ 750.00

PRODUCTION EXPENSES

Studio Rental	$ 500.00
Costumes and Sets	900.00
Transportation	250.00
Meals	100.00
	$ 1,750.00
Subtotal	$ 8,560.00
Producer's Fee	1,280.00
TOTAL	$ 9,840.00

CHAPTER 2

THE TOOLS OF CINEMATOGRAPHY

THE CAMERA

The basic tool and the primary instrument through which the film-maker funnels his impressions and depicts the world around him is the camera. It is a delicate instrument with a limited vision of the actual world, yet it is a highly flexible instrument once the film-maker has learned to look at his world through its visual limitations.

The camera's vision resembles that of the mythical Cyclops, who had only one eye in the middle of his forehead. The camera also has only one eye, and that eye has a fixed and narrow range of vision.

The camera had been on the drawing board for centuries, but before the camera itself could be invented other contributing inventions and principles had to be born. We can trace the beginnings back to the camera obscura of Leonardo da Vinci, who theorized that an image of reality could be transmitted to the back wall of a darkened box by means of light passing through a tiny hole in the front of the box. It was the principle of the camera obscura, combined with the development of the lens, that led to the first still camera in the 1820s.

In 1824, Peter Roget (of *Thesaurus* fame) advanced his theory of "The Persistence of Vision with Regard to Moving Objects." This theory, and the already existing still camera, provided the necessary ingredients for the invention of the moving-picture camera. Roget realized that there is a mental carry-over, prolonging for a fraction of a second the image that the eye is seeing. Thus if a new image were to be brought before the eye while the old image still persisted, the two would merge.

The film exploits Roget's principle by rapidly presenting a succession of images to the eye, each within the period of persistence. Since each image blends with its neighbor, there is an illusion of flow between them. If the images chosen were to represent frozen aspects of successive stages of a continuous movement, the illusion would be of a flow of movement. Film animation also works on this same principle, presenting the eye with photographed drawings of successive stages—the arm at the side, slightly raised, raised a bit more, half raised, three-quarters raised, and finally fully raised. Present these images rapidly, within the time of persistence, and we see the illusion of continuous motion.

While inventors were soon turning out parlor toys that utilized Roget's theory (the Zoetrope and the Praxinoscope to name two) no one could invent a practical machine capable of projecting the images from the glass plates utilized in photography at this time. The final necessary ingredient for the motion picture camera was a flexible film. The breakthrough came in 1888 when the Eastman Company announced the commercial availability of celluloid film. Within the year came the first motion picture cameras. The early cameras were extremely crude compared with the sophisticated instruments now available. They were bulky and heavy and were powered by a hand crank that drove the film past the lens aperture.

How the Camera Operates

Actually there has been little change since the earliest cameras in the basic principle of how the camera works. Some camera movements in the instruments which recorded the works of Griffith and Chaplin have never been excelled. Yet great advances have been made in the sophistication of the camera.

THE MOTOR

Every camera must have some type of motor driving the mechanism that moves the film. In the first cameras it was a hand-crank. Today our cameras are driven either by an electric motor or a spring-wind motor.

The spring-wind motor eliminates the need to carry batteries for a power supply and, therefore, can be more convenient in some location work. Without the need for an electric motor, the weight of the camera is greatly reduced, making location assignments easier to handle. But in general the spring-wind camera is a less desirable camera to use for most filming operations. One of the major disadvantages of this type of motor is that it limits the length of any take. Depending on the camera, the maximum amount of footage this motor is capable of driving without being rewound ranges from 16½ to 22 feet in 16mm and is approximately 50 feet in 35mm. At sound speed of 24 frames per second—there are 40 frames per 16mm foot, 16 per 35mm foot—the film-maker must limit all of his takes to a duration of approximately 35 seconds. Such a limitation can be most inconvenient, the camera motor invariably going dead in the middle of an unrepeatable action shot. A second major disadvantage of the spring-wind motor is that the accurate control of the speed of the camera is reduced. Sound shooting and a number of other instances where precise control of speed is essential are impossible with this motor.

Most professional cameras are driven by an electric motor (Fig. 2.1), which is more efficient and solves the disadvantages of the spring-wind. True, the electric motor adds weight to the camera and necessitates either a 110 volt power source or the carrying of a battery, but reasonably portable batteries (Fig. 2.2) are available, and they are a minor inconvenience when compared with the additional control they afford the film-maker.

The electric motor has been developed so that it operates the camera mechanism at a constant and accurate rate with a minimum of effort. This factor is imperative for a high quality and steady exposure of the film.

There are four types of motors available for most electric drive cameras: Synchronous Speed, Constant Speed, Variable Speed, and Time Lapse/Animation (Stop Frame).

Fig. 2-1 A synchronous motor

The Synchronous and Constant Speed motors are calibrated to run at a constant speed of 24 frames per second (fps) with a nearly instantaneous start-up at this calibrated speed. When one is double-system sound filming, these motors are capable of running the camera in exact synchronization with the motor running the sound recorder.

From the above description it would appear that both the constant speed and the synchronous speed are identical for sound filming, but this is not so. The constant speed motor, which is powered by a D.C. battery, is used with a sync-pulse generator (see page 172). An "umbilical" cable is run between the sync generator and the recorder. This generator sends out through this cable an impulse of 60 cycles which is also recorded on the tape and which is later scanned by the reproducer when the sound on the tape is transferred to perforated stock. The 60 cycle impulse thus ensures our being able to reproduce ("transfer") any number of copies of the original sound, all of them "in sync" with the picture. The synchronous speed motor allows the camera to run in synchronization with the recorder without the need of the "umbilical" cable or the sync generator. If an A.C. powered synchronous motor is used, both this motor and the recorder are powered by the same source, thus establishing synchronization through the A.C. source's 60 cycles. Synchronous motors are now available equipped with either a crystal or tuning-fork control system, and this motor operates off of a D.C. battery. However, the tuning-fork system is not as proficient as the crystal system. The crystal system requires matched crystal-based reference frequency sources, either attached to

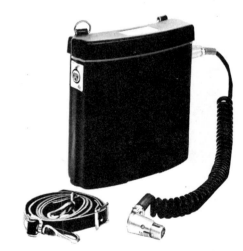

Fig. 2-2 A portable camera battery

or incorporated in both the camera and tape recorder. The camera's source controls the speed of its motor; the signal from the recorder's source is recorded on the tape and used during transfer in the same manner as the conventional sync-pulse described above.

The Variable Speed motor does not run at a constant speed. It is equipped with a rheostat which regulates the speed of the motor from a minimum of 4 frames per second to 50 or more frames per second. The camera operator is usually able to set the speed by the use of a tachometer which registers the speed in fps.

These variable speed electric motors are separate units from the camera, are easily mounted, and are interchangeable on most camera models. They operate with either single, two- or three-phase, A.C. or D.C. The voltages vary according to the make and model of the motor. They range from 8, 12, 16, or 24 volts D.C. from a battery; or 90, 100, 220/230 volts from an A.C. source.

Time Lapse/Animation motors are available which allow some cameras to operate at very low speeds. For time-lapse photography they can be attached to a timer that operates the camera at pre-set time intervals. These motors will run either forward or reverse and operate at speeds of 1, 2, 3, 4 or more frames per second. They are also capable of running at a continuous speed. Time Lapse/Animation motors are powered by a 110 volt A.C. source and have a remote control starting switch.

THE FOCUSING AND VIEWFINDING SYSTEM

The major concern of all film-makers is the image recorded on the film. The lens, of course, is the instrument that produces the recorded image. Every camera needs some kind of system which allows the camera operator to frame the image that will be recorded and some method that will facilitate the focusing of the lens producing the image. In some cameras both tasks are accomplished by the same system, in others by separate systems.

SEPARATE VIEWFINDER The simplest and, generally, least expensive cameras are equipped with the latter of the two systems. These cameras are equipped with a viewfinder that is separate from the taking lens. It is mounted on the camera next to the taking lens and supplies an image with an optical system made up of small separate lenses, called objective finders, or one lens and a series of insertable mattes. These objective finders or mattes correspond in size to the lenses mounted on the camera turret. This system allows the camera operator to see approximately the same picture as the lens. The picture is only approximate because of parallax, which is the displacement of the image observed because of the viewing positions of the viewfinder and the taking lens.° Some cameras with this system are equipped with a parallax adjustment; the viewfinder is affixed so that it can be displaced along a calibrated scale. Other cameras, however, are not so equipped, and therefore the camera operator must adjust for the parallax when framing his image. The closer the shot the more acute is the parallax problem.

°To better understand parallax, extend your arm with your thumb in an upright vertical position. Close your left eye and sight with the right eye. Line the thumb up with some object, then close the right eye, and open the left. You will note that the sighted object seems to jump to your left. The jump is the result of parallax.

Focusing the lens with this viewfinder system is accomplished either by measuring the distance between the lens and the subject to be photographed and setting the lens according to this measurement, or through a separate focusing system, a critical focuser, operative only when the camera is not running. This system cannot be used for framing since only a portion of the frame is visible.

MONITORING VIEWFINDER AND THROUGH-THE-LENS FOCUSING The need for the camera operator to be able to frame the image and focus the lens by being able to see exactly what the lens was viewing led to this system, which was perfected by the Mitchell Corporation for the Mitchell NC, BNC, Standard, and High Speed cameras. This system operates by displacing the camera body to one side so that a ground-glass screen is positioned directly behind the taking lens. The image on the ground glass can be magnified from five to ten times and viewed through a focusing microscope. The displacement of the camera body is accomplished by constructing the camera in two parts. The camera base with the lens turret is attached to the tripod, or whatever mount by which the camera is being supported. The camera body, which includes the film drive, magazine, and viewfinder, is attached to a track which is a part of the camera base. The body is displaced by twisting the rackover handle. This displacement allows the focusing microscope to be placed directly behind the taking lens, thereby allowing the operator to accurately frame and focus the image to be photographed. This displacement process is commonly called "rackover." Before shooting, the operator must shift back the body of the camera so that the shutter is behind the taking lens. During the actual shooting, the image cannot be viewed through the lens. The operator must follow the action through the monitoring viewfinder—attached to the camera body next to the taking lens —and must adjust for parallax.

THE REFLEX SYSTEM From the disadvantages seen in the first two viewing and focusing systems, the obvious solution would be a system that would allow the camera operator to view and focus entirely through the lens, even while the camera is operating. In 1936, the German company Arnold and Richter introduced the reflex viewing and focusing system on their Arriflex camera.

The reflex system provides through-the-lens viewing and focusing, so that the operator is always seeing an image identical with the one being exposed on the film. The Arriflex system works in an ingenious way. The front surface of the shutter blades, which revolve between the lens and the film and are mounted at a forty-five degree angle to the plane of the film, are silvered and thus serve as a mirrored surface that reflects the image back through an optical system which magnifies it and, because of a prism, turns it upright (Fig. 2.3). The image is reflected to the operator during the time that the shutter is closed, and passed through the shutter to the film when it is open. The shutter moves so rapidly that the image and brightness are relatively constant in the viewfinder. This system is so superior that most of the newer camera designs

Fig. 2-3 The Reflex system. (1) Lens
(2) Mirrored shutter blade (3) Prism
(4) Ground glass lens (5) Eyepiece
(6) Film (Jack Fischer)

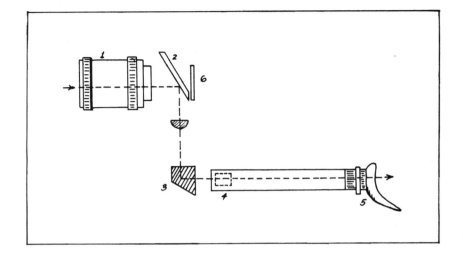

have incorporated it, and similar conversion systems have been developed to incorporate in those models which did not originally utilize reflex viewing.

Not all reflex systems, however, follow the same technique as the Arriflex system. The Bolex and several other makes utilize a prism that is inserted between the lens and the shutter at a forty-five degree angle to the optical axis. This prism splits the beam of light, reflecting part of the light to the viewing system and allowing the remainder of the beam to pass on to the film.

Fig. 2-4 Bayonet turret lock

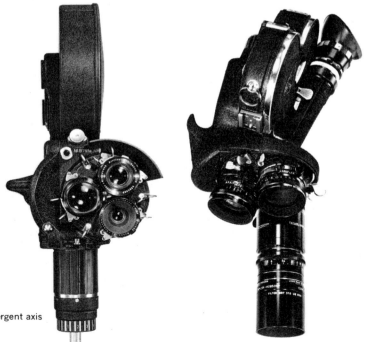

Figs. 2-5a and 2-5b Front and top view showing the divergent axis

With a few exceptions most professional cameras have their lenses mounted on a revolving disc on the front of the camera, called a lens turret. The very large studio cameras and the Arriflex 16BL are equipped with a single lens mount to facilitate soundproofing. In the case of the Arriflex 16BL, this lens is generally a zoom lens which, within the limitations of a zoom lens, allows for the flexibility of a multiple lens mount. Most lens turrets provide for the mounting of three or four different lenses. The lenses are attached by threads (C mount), by clips, or by bayonet mounts (Fig. 2.4). Some lens turrets, such as those on the Arriflex models, are designed with the lens axis divergent (Fig. 2.5). With this design no lens interferes with another lens' field of view.

LENS TURRET

This device is a very important lens accessory. Its main functions are to protect the lens from light reflections and to provide the camera with a receptacle for filter holders containing glass or gelatin filters and mattes for special effects. It contains a boom which attaches to the camera and an adjustable bellows, plus the matte box which holds the filters.

MATTE BOX AND SUNSHADE

Some professional 16mm cameras accept 100 foot daylight load spools within the body of the camera. The film spool and a take-up spool are mounted on spindles within the camera body.

FILM SUPPLY SYSTEM

All 35mm and nearly all 16mm professional cameras accept a light-tight chamber which stores the raw and exposed stock. This chamber is called a magazine. The magazine for most cameras is mounted on the top of the camera with the raw stock on a spindle at the front of the magazine and a take-up spindle for the exposed film directly behind it. Some camera designs utilize the coaxial magazine, which has the raw stock and exposed film mounted side by side on the same drive shaft. This type of magazine is found particularly on cameras designed primarily for handholding, with the magazine mounted on the back of the camera rather than on the top. This arrangement provides better balance and allows the operator to rest the magazine on his shoulder for additional support.

Many of these magazines are powered by their own torque motor. Other camera designs have part of the film drive mechanism included in the magazine and thus operate off the camera motor.

The film passes from one compartment through a slot in the base of the magazine that is attached to the camera, into the camera body where it is threaded through the gate system, up through another slot in the magazine base, and onto the take-up spool. The film is protected in its passage from the magazine to the camera body and back again by some form of light trap.

Fig. 2-6 A 100 foot load 16mm camera with its door removed showing the film spindles, gate, and film drive sprockets

THE INTERMITTENT MOVEMENT

The intermittent movement is the most critical element of any camera body's design; the only other part of the camera of comparable importance is the lens. It is the device that carries the film through the gate, a frame at a time, and positions it behind the aperture for exposure. At sound speed the movement must position the film twenty-four times every second. This movement, if the picture is to be steady and of high quality, must be extremely precise. The intermittent movement must operate in conjunction with another mechanism which feeds the film from the spool into the gate and from the bottom of the gate onto the take-up spool. The latter mechanism drives the film by means of sprocket wheels which have teeth that penetrate the perforation holes of the film and allow it to move smoothly and continuously. Since both mechanisms—the intermittent movement and the film drive sprockets—operate at different motions (one is continuous and one is intermittent) it is necessary to loop the film above and below the gate to prevent the rapid downward thrust of the intermittent movement from tearing or mutilating the film.

As mentioned above, the function of the delicate intermittent movement is to carry the film down a frame at a time and position it for exposure. This function is accomplished by the coordinated movements of several parts of the mechanism. One or more claws penetrate the perforations of the film and pull the film down. At the bottom of the claw's movement, the frame to be exposed is directly behind the shutter. At this point the claw retracts from the perforation and moves upward. During the claw's upward movement the film is exposed. At the top of its movement, the claw again enters the film perforation and starts the cycle over (Fig. 2.7–1).

Fig. 2–7 (1) The claw enters the film's perforation, pulls the film down one frame, retracts, and moves up to begin the process again. (2) A. The Claw [1] retracts from the film [3] perforation as the registration pin [2] enters the perforation next to the aperture. B. The registration pin holds the film steady for exposure as the claw moves up. C. The registration pin retracts and the claw enters a perforation hole. D. The registration pin holds as the claw moves the film down one frame, and the process begins again. (Jack Fischer)

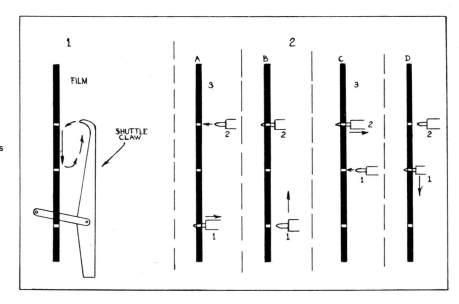

Coupled with the intermittent movement, some cameras have another mechanism which ensures an exact registration of the photographic exposure by holding the film absolutely steady during the time it is motionless. This mechanism is the registration pin (pilot pin). At the time the claw reaches its downward movement and begins to withdraw from the film, one or two pins enter the film perforations next to the aperture and remain there during exposure. As the claw again enters the film perforation, the pin retracts, allowing the film to move down again (Fig. 2.7–2).

THE SHUTTER

The movement of the shutter mechanism of a camera is synchronized with the intermittent movement. The shutter must shield the film after a frame has been exposed to light and is being pulled down by the claw so that the next frame can take its place. In simple form, the shutter is a disc with openings in it. It is placed between the film and the lens. The disc rotates and this rotation is synchronized with the intermittent movement so that an opening in the disc arrives at the lens at precisely the same time the claw has completed its downward pull, thus exposing the stationary film to light.

The angles of the opening of the shutter vary with different cameras. Some cameras have a separate variable shutter so that the opening can be adjusted by a control mounted on the outside of the camera. This provides the camera operator with an additional control over the film's exposure.

SELECTING A CAMERA

One of the first major decisions you must make as a film-maker is the selection of the camera or cameras that you will use in your production. The selection of the camera is important because you will have to consider what the camera will be required to do and then proceed to select one that will meet those requirements. You will have to consider such things as: (1) Where will the film be shot, on location or in the studio? (2) Will the camera be mounted on a tripod or dolly, or will you have some scenes that will require handholding? (3) Will the film be shot in 35mm or 16mm? (4) Will there be any long takes, or will the film be shot basically in short takes—in other words, will 100 foot loads be sufficient or will you need a camera with a magazine? (5) If you are shooting on location, will the site be readily accessible, or will it be difficult to reach? One final point to consider, and one frequently neglected, is: (6) Is your cameraman familiar and comfortable with the camera selected? No competent and conscientious cameraman will ever use a camera with which he is not completely familiar. So be sure to discuss with your cameraman the selection of the camera.

These are only a few of the questions that will have to be answered. Consider these questions seriously and thoroughly, for the selection of the wrong camera for the job could hamper and limit the effectiveness of your filming. There are many fine cameras available for rental to the film-maker and any of them are usually available for purchase through one of the major equipment suppliers or manufacturers. We have selected the most commonly used models in 35mm and 16mm to discuss here.

35mm Cameras
ARRIFLEX IIC

Fig. 2-8   Arriflex IIC

This model is the basic 35mm Arriflex (Fig. 2.8). There are other variations of this basic model: (1) 35–IICV which has all the features of the IIC plus a variable shutter which can be adjusted from a completely open 165° to a completely closed 0° or set at any position in between. (2) 35–IICGS which again has all of the features of the IIC plus a factory-installed Electric Clapstick System and Combination Tachometer/Generator. This makes this camera ideal for use with Rangertone/Pilotone quarter-inch tape sync sound. (3) 35–IICHS which is the basic IIC with a specially balanced movement for high-speed filming up to 80 fps. (4) 35–IICT which is again the basic IIC but with a special gate and ground glass for filming in Techniscope. (5) 35–IIC/B which is the most recent modification of the IIC model. It has a three-lens turret in which two of the mounts utilize the standard Arriflex clip lock, and the third, a heavy-duty bayonet-type lock. There is a complete range of models with this modified turret: 35–IICB/V, 35–IICGS/B, 35–IICHS/B, and 35–IICT/B.

The basic Arriflex IIC has over the past years become a universally used camera. Even Hollywood, which has been dominated for over thirty years by the Mitchell camera,° is using the Arriflex as a second camera. The Arriflex is probably the closest to an ideal camera for use on location shooting. An outstanding expert in Hollywood on location shooting, Fouad Said, who was Director of Photography on the widely-traveled television series, "I Spy," uses the Arriflex camera exclusively. The major argument against the Arriflex over the Mitchell is that the Arriflex does not photograph as steady a picture as the Mitchell. Not long ago a well-known cinematographer conducted an experiment along the lines of this argument. He shot some footage with both cameras and then edited the footage together. This footage was screened for some film experts, and they were asked to select the takes shot by each camera. No one could do it.

DESCRIPTION   The Arriflex 35–IIC is the basic 35mm camera manufactured by Arnold and Richter. It contains the Arriflex mirror shutter reflex viewfinding and focusing system. Some of the camera's main features are an interchangeable eyepiece, precision film movement, a three-lens turret, the Arri quick-change magazine (200, 400, and 1,000 ft.), and a complete system of accessories for professional filming.

INTERMITTENT MOVEMENT   This mechanism involves the use of only a single claw which is activated by a special cardiod cam. The movement of this claw, however, has a unique feature that contributes to an extremely steady picture and to precise film location. When the claw reaches the bottom of its pull-down, it goes through a long horizontal

*A friend of ours recently completed shooting on a feature-length film in Puerto Rico with an Arriflex. On the first day of shooting, the leading actor, a Hollywood veteran, insisted that they could not shoot a feature film with an Arriflex. The actor contended that the only camera to use was a Mitchell.

pull-out. The latter movement serves to improve the location of the film and the steadiness of the picture. Another feature of this mechanism also contributes to picture steadiness: the exceptionally long rear pressure plate. The filmgate is stainless steel and chrome-plated with cross-stages to prevent "breathing."

SHUTTER   As mentioned earlier, this camera has the mirrored shutter that revolves at a 45 degree angle between the lens and the filmplane. The shutter opening is 180 degrees, which provides a 1/48th second exposure at 24 frames per second.

VIEWFINDING AND FOCUSING SYSTEM   This camera has the Arriflex reflex system that provides through-the-lens focusing and viewing. The viewfinder image is brilliant since all of the light (intermittently) reaches the viewfinder. The system is installed on the camera door. The eyepiece is adjustable for individual eyesight. To prevent light leak when the operator is not using the viewfinder, an available system has the eyecup attached to a diaphragm that automatically opens when the cup is depressed and closes when the pressure is removed. The image in the viewfinder is upright and is magnified 6½ times.

LENS TURRET   The camera has a three-lens turret which has code marks that can be read from the back of the camera by the operator so that at a glance he can see which lens is in the taking position. It has the Arriflex clip-lock lens mount, except, of course, the IIC/B models.

MOTORS   A variety of motors is available for this camera and in most cases serve also as a handgrip for the camera. The variable speed motor operates off of a 16 volt D.C. source or a 24–28 volt D.C. source. The motor contains a rheostat which can adjust the speed from 8–40 fps. There is a built-in tachometer that is scaled from 0–50 fps. For sound shooting a 16 volt or 24 volt D.C. constant speed motor is available. When the power source is 110 volt A.C., a synchronous motor can be obtained.

FILM SUPPLY   A 200 ft., 400 ft., and 1,000 ft. magazine is available for this camera. These magazines contain a film drive sprocket so that the film is prethreaded in the magazine with a fixed loop. Both magazines contain loop protectors.

OPTIONAL ACCESSORIES   Sound blimps are available for 200 ft., 400 ft., and 1,000 ft. magazines. The blimp that holds the camera and the 1,000 ft. magazine converts this camera—primarily used on location—into a very capable studio camera.

MITCHELL NC AND BNC

Both of these camera models (Figs. 2.9 and 2.10) have been for over thirty years (and still are) standard equipment in the film industry. Probably the major reason for the Mitchell's success is its rock-steady registration in the intermittent movement of the camera. The high quality maintained in the manufacture of their cameras has gained for the Mitchell Corporation a reputation for accuracy control. Both the NC and BNC

Fig. 2–9 Mitchell NC

Fig. 2–10 Mitchell BNC

are alike with certain exceptions in the BNC: (1) a sound insulated casing; (2) one-lens mounting; (3) automatic parallax correction of the monitoring viewfinder; (4) automatic dissolve control; and (5) several focusing controls.

DESCRIPTION Both the NC and BNC are constructed in two parts to allow for the rackover process. The camera base contains the matte box and sunshade, the lens turret on the NC and the lens mount on the BNC, and the rackover mechanism. The camera body is made up of the mechanisms for driving the film, the controls, the motor, the focusing tube, the monitoring viewfinder which is attached to the side of the camera body, and the magazine which is attached to the top of the body.

INTERMITTENT MOVEMENT The intermittent movement of this camera is excellent; it is one of the chief reasons for its overwhelming success. The mechanism makes use of two forked pull-down claws and two registration pins. The claws engage four perforations simultaneously for the pull-down movement. The dual registration pins register the film at the time of exposure. The movement is constructed so that it can be easily removed from the camera for cleaning. The speed of the movement is adjustable from 1–32 frames per second.

SHUTTER These cameras contain a variable shutter with a 175 degree maximum and a 0 degree minimum. The shutter is variable in 10 degree calibrated segments. The cameras also contain an automatic pre-set mechanism that carries out 4 foot fades in or out by manipulating the shutter. On the back of the camera body is a miniature shutter indicator that visually shows the position of the shutter blades in relation to the camera aperture.

VIEWFINDING AND FOCUSING SYSTEM These cameras contain the rackover system that was discussed earlier in this chapter (see page 15). When the rackover mechanism is operated the camera body is displaced to the right so that the focusing microscope is placed behind the taking lens. The focusing microscope then provides through-the-lens ground-glass critical focusing and framing. This critical focusing is enhanced by the variable magnification control on the focusing microscope. Interchangeable ground glasses are available with any of the various aspect ratios sketched onto the ground glass. The eyepiece can be adjusted for individual eyesight. The focusing microscope also contains built-in contrast viewing filters for color and black-and-white emulsions. Once the focusing and framing are complete, the camera body must be racked back into position so that the aperture is behind the taking lens.

The viewfinding is accomplished by means of a separate monitoring viewfinder that is attached to a special mounting at the left side of the camera body. The camera includes a special accessory that provides for parallax-free viewing. On the BNC, parallax is automatically controlled because the parallax adjustment is attached to the lens focusing control by a system of cams.

LENS TURRET The NC model contains a four-lens turret with the lenses held in position by bayonet-type locks. The turret is a heavy-duty rotary type that can be easily rotated and locked in position with a locking pin. The BNC has a single-lens mount in which the lens is positioned in place with the bayonet-type lens lock.

MOTOR   Two variable speed motors are available for these cameras. One operates off of a 12 volt D.C. source and has a speed range of 8–24 fps. The second operates off of a 110 volt A.C. or D.C. source and also has a speed range of 8–24 fps. Synchronous motors are available that operate off of a 110 volt, 60 cycle, one phase A.C.; or a 220 volt, 60 cycle, three phase A.C.; or a 220 volt, three phase interlocking A.C. source.

FILM SUPPLY SYSTEM   Both the NC and the BNC can be supplied with either 400 ft., 1,000 ft., or 2,000 ft. double compartment-type magazines that are insulated for silent running. The magazines are the same for both cameras.

REFLEX CONVERSION OF THE MITCHELL NC AND BNC   F&B/Ceco, Inc. has devised a system for converting the Mitchell BNC (Fig. 2.11) and NC models to reflex through-the-lens focusing and viewing. Their system accomplishes the conversion by placing a beamsplitter/prism in front of the shutter. The prism reflects the light to the viewing optical system. The light loss with this system is only one-quarter of a lens stop, and it certainly makes the camera easier and quicker to use. The system necessitates a modification of the filter system, but the intermittent movement and film drive sprockets are undisturbed. The monitoring viewfinder is also undisturbed and can be used should the camera operator so desire.

Fig. 2–11 Mitchell BNC Reflex Conversion

ECLAIR CAMERETTE (CAMEFLEX) CM–3–T (ALSO 16/35MM)

This camera design is the result of several years of research into the features camera operators most wanted in a camera. The task finally was to design a camera that was lightweight with a shape that contributed to handling ease, high precision, fast loading, and adaptability for taking different drive motors. The 16/35mm model won an award from the Hollywood Motion Picture Academy because of its versatility and capabilities. This camera obviously can be used with either 16mm or 35mm film stock.

DESCRIPTION   The most unique feature of this camera is its magazine system. The film is actually threaded in the magazine itself where the film drive sprockets and film loops are included. This system, of course, allows for extremely rapid camera loading.

INTERMITTENT MOVEMENT   This movement has two sets of ratchet-type pull-down claws on each side of the 35mm film. When 16mm stock is used only one centered claw is used. The claw stroke can be adjusted for either normal four perforation pull-down or two perforation pull-down for Techniscope, and, as noted, it can be adjusted for single perforation pull-down for 16mm. The registration principle of this camera provides a very steady image. Registration is accomplished by a double rear pressure plate and very long side rails. The top plate holds the film flat in the focal plane, and the bottom plate holds the edges to keep them aligned for the pull-down claws.

SHUTTER   The Cameflex has a variable shutter with a 200 degree maximum and a 35 degree minimum. The shutter has a mirrored front surface for the reflex system and rotates at a 45 degree angle between the lens and filmplane.

VIEWING AND FOCUSING SYSTEM   This reflex system works on the same principle as the Arriflex. The viewfinder itself is of the full 360 degree rotating type so that framing and focusing can be carried out from any camera position. A special shutter prevents any light leak.

LENS TURRET   The Cameflex contains a three-lens divergent turret. Lenses are held in position by bayonet-type lens mounts.

MOTOR   The motors for this camera are mounted on the right side of the camera and may also serve as a handgrip. The motors may be changed in a matter of seconds. The basic motor is a variable speed type operating from a 6/8 volt D.C. source. It is rheostat-controlled. Variable speed and constant speed motors that are transistor-controlled are also available for 6, 12, and 24 volt D.C. sources. The constant speed motors have a 50 or 60 cycle sync-pulse output. Synchronous speed motors for 115 volt, 60 cycle, A.C. and 220 volt, three-phase, 60 cycle, A.C. sources are also available for sound shooting. One unique addition is a hand-crank that can supply speeds of 1, 8, or 16 frames per turn.

FILM SUPPLY SYSTEM   As mentioned above, the magazines for this camera provide one of its most unusual features. 200 ft., 400 ft., and 1,000 ft. prethreaded magazines are available for the camera.

OPTIONAL ACCESSORIES   A lightweight magnesium tripod, a quickly operated sound blimp, and an Aquaflex underwater housing can be obtained for this camera.

16 mm Cameras

Not too many years ago the majority of all professional motion picture production was carried out in 35mm. Combat photography in World War II, the showing of training films and feature films to the GIs in 16mm, the advent of television and its news coverage, and special documentary shooting brought 16mm into popular acceptance and popular use. One of its major advantages was the reduced cost of production.[*]

Technical developments in the 16mm field over the past fifteen or so years have provided film-makers with cameras that are every bit as sophisticated as the 35mm equipment. Manufacturers are now providing us with cameras that are lightweight, high in precision, sturdily constructed, and easy to operate. These same manufacturers are constantly redesigning their products to include the most recent technological developments.

[*]Motion picture production and TV series production has remained in 35mm, but recently one TV dramatic series began producing in 16mm. This could be an indication of a new trend.

The number of makes and models of 16mm cameras is large, so again we have selected those cameras most commonly used in professional 16mm production.

When the Arnold and Richter Company designed their first 16mm camera, the Arriflex 16S, they incorporated all of the outstanding features of their 35mm cameras plus something new in the intermittent movement—the registration pin.

ARRIFLEX 16S, 16S–GS, 16M, 16 S/B

Fig. 2–12 Arriflex 16S and 16M with 400 foot magazines

DESCRIPTION   The basic model is the 16S (Fig. 2.12), but the 16S–GS is basically the same camera with the addition of a factory-installed electric automatic clapstick and 60 cycle signal generator for use with all Ranger-tone/Pilotone sync sound quarter-inch tape recorders. The 16 S/B contains the same modified turret as the 35–IIC/B. The 16M model (Fig. 2.12) has all of the features of the 16S and 16S–GS, but has no internal film capacity or film drive sprockets. The 16M employs prethreaded magazines which contain the film drive.

INTERMITTENT MOVEMENT   All three models utilize a single cam-driven pull-down claw plus a single registration pin. The claw enters the perforation from the front of the film (the emulsion side), and the registration pin enters the perforation from the back of the film (the base side). The filmgate is extra long, and the rear pressure plate and side guide rails extend the entire length of the filmgate. All of the features combine to ensure a rock-steady exposure.

SHUTTER   The shutter of the 16mm models is the same mirrored reflex shutter rotating at a 45 degree angle between the lens and the filmplane as the 35mm models. The shutter opening is 180 degrees. The shutter speed at 24 fps is 1/48th of a second.

VIEWFINDING AND FOCUSING SYSTEM   All models offer the reflex through-the-lens focusing and viewing which gives a parallax-free, upright image in the viewfinder. The manufacturer insists that since the light reaches the film and viewfinder intermittently, the image in the viewing system is bright even when the lens is stopped down, but experience has shown that this is not exactly so. The eyepiece gives a 10× magnification and can be interchanged for a prescription spectacle lens.

LENS TURRET   The turret takes three lenses with the Arriflex clip-lock mounting found on the 35mm cameras (in fact lenses for the 35mm camera can be used on the 16mm). The 16 S/B, of course, has two Arriflex mounts and one heavy-duty bayonet mount. The turret is designed with 21 degree divergent lens axes so that there is no physical or optical interference from wide-angle to extra-long lenses mounted simultaneously.

MOTOR   The standard motor is a variable speed motor that is driven by an 8 volt D.C. source. This motor is rheostat-controlled for speeds ranging from 5–50 fps. This motor also operates either forward or reverse. The constant speed motor is also powered by an 8 volt D.C. source and runs the camera at a constant 24 fps or 16 fps. A synchronous motor is available for either 110 or 220 volts, either 50 or 60 cycles A.C. for running at 24 fps. A 110 volt time-lapse motor can be obtained for animation filming.

FILM SUPPLY SYSTEM   The 16S, 16S–GS, and 16 S/B will accept 100 ft. daylight loading spools within the camera body. 200 ft. and 400 ft. magazines, powered by a separate torque motor, can be attached to the 16S, 16S–GS, and 16 S/B. One very important procedure to remember when using a magazine with the 16S is before each take to twist the take-up spindle of the magazine until the film is taut. If this is forgotten, a malfunction can occur in the camera threading when the film slack is rapidly pulled taut by the starting camera. The 200 ft. magazine will accept 100 ft. daylight spools or 200 ft. darkroom core loads. The 400 ft. magazine will accept 200 ft. daylight spools or 400 ft. darkroom core loads. These magazines have a footage counter that records the unexposed film footage.

The 16M has available for it 200 ft. or 400 ft. magazines which contain the film drive sprocket. A 1,200 ft. coaxial-design magazine is also available for the 16M model. None of the magazines for the 16M model require a separate torque motor.

BOLEX (ALL MODELS)

Fig. 2–13   Bolex H-16 Rex 5

The Swiss-made Bolex (Figs. 2.13 and 2.14) has a reputation for being rugged and dependable and for providing high quality and steady exposures. It is lightweight and easy to operate, making it perfect for one-man filming operations. One of the outstanding features of the various Bolex models is the automatic threading due to the interlocking of the film drive sprockets and the intermittent movement. This makes threading the camera fast, easy, and foolproof.

DESCRIPTION   All of the models are precision-built and designed mainly for hand-held operation. They have been used extensively in Europe for news coverage operations. They include several convenient features: (1) the aforementioned automatic threading; (2) a filter slot behind the lens for the insertion of gelatin filters, so the same filter can remain in place when lenses are changed; (3) reflex viewing on all of the later models as well as a separate viewfinder which can be mounted on the camera door; (4) an elaborate system of counters that indicate used footage as well as the number of exposed frames; (5) a variable shutter for greater exposure control; and (6) a spring-wind motor plus a device that allows for the use of an electric motor.

INTERMITTENT MOVEMENT   A single trailing claw pull-down system assures picture steadiness. This movement is interlocked with the film drive sprockets to provide automatic threading.

SHUTTER   The shutter has a 130 degree opening that can be varied by means of a sliding lever. The shutter, when completely open, gives a

1/64th of a second exposure at 24 fps and 1/640th of a second when three-quarters closed. The shutter can be locked at full open, half closed, and three-quarters closed.

VIEWING AND FOCUSING SYSTEM   All of the later model Bolex cameras have a reflex viewing system that operates on the beamsplitter principle. A prism is inserted between the lens and the aperture which splits the light beam, sending part to the viewfinding system, and part to the film. The manufacturer says there is no need to compensate for the light loss; however, experience has shown that an adjustment of one-quarter to one-half a stop should be made. A separate viewfinder called the octameter—providing eight focal ranges from 10mm to 150mm—is provided and can be attached to a mounting on the camera door.

LENS TURRET   All of the models with the exception of the H–16 M–5 have a three-lens turret. The H–16 M–5 has only a single mounting for use with zoom lenses. The H-16 REX requires special lenses suggested by the manufacturer.

MOTOR   The spring-wind motor will expose 16½ feet of film before needing a rewind. The spring motor can be disengaged and a compact, lightweight electric motor attached. This motor operates off batteries or an A.C. source with a transformer. The camera speed range is from 12 to 64 fps. A constant speed motor is available for the H–16 REX 5 and H–16 M–5 models. The constant speed motor contains a built-in sync generator for synchronous sound filming.

FILM SUPPLY SYSTEM   All models will accept 100 ft. daylight loading spools within the camera body. A 400 ft. magazine with an attachable take-up motor is also available.

OPTIONAL ACCESSORIES   An automatic fading device is available for the H–16 REX 5.

Fig. 2–14   Bolex H-16 M-5

The basic design of this camera is one of the oldest (some forty years), most rugged, most dependable and most popular lightweight 16mm cameras on the market (Fig. 2.15).

DESCRIPTION   The camera has maintained its original basic design principles; however, several details have been modified over the years. The 70 Design comprises a series of six different models: DA, DL, H, DR, SR, and HR. The common name applied to all of the models is "Filmo."

INTERMITTENT MOVEMENT   This mechanism contains a single cam-driven pull-down claw that enters and withdraws from the film perforations at a right angle. This assures a steady image in the exposure without a registration pin.

SHUTTER   The Bell and Howell Filmo has a fixed shutter with an opening of 204 degrees, except the very early models which have an opening of 216 degrees.

BELL AND HOWELL 70 DESIGN (FILMO)

Fig. 2–15   Bell and Howell 70HR with magazine and electric motor attached

VIEWING AND FOCUSING SYSTEM   Viewing and framing are accomplished by use of a separate viewfinder fixed to the left side of the camera. The viewfinder has a small turret to which can be attached objective finders corresponding in size to the lenses mounted on the camera's turret. Matched gearing on the lens turret and viewfinder turret of the DR, SR, and HR automatically positions the correct objective finder for the taking lens. This viewfinder has an adjustable eyepiece with a parallax correction to 3 ft. For focusing the taking lens, a critical focuser is built into the camera on the right side and just behind the turret. The focuser provides an inverted and greatly magnified circular portion of the center of the frame. The diaphragm of the lens must be opened completely and the turret rotated 180 degrees in order to place the taking lens before the focuser.

LENS TURRET   The camera has a three-lens turret that accepts any lens with a C type mounting. This camera has a safety device that prevents any shooting until a lens is correctly seated in place in front of the aperture.

MOTOR   The basic motor for the Filmo is a spring-wind governor-controlled mechanism that exposes between 19 and 22 ft. per winding. This mechanism will run the camera at seven different speeds: 8, 12, 16, 24, 32, 48, and 64 fps. The speed is controlled by a dial on the right side of the camera. The 70 SR model operates only at 128 fps, but it is no longer manufactured, although secondhand models are often available. The 70 HR model can be adapted for an electric motor drive. One variable speed motor is powered by a 12 or 24 volt D.C. source and another by a 115 volt A.C./D.C. source. A synchronous motor is available that operates off of a 115 volt, 60 cycle A.C. source.

FILM SUPPLY SYSTEM   All models accept 100 ft. daylight loading spools in the camera body. The 70 HR and 70 SR can also be equipped with external magazines that hold 200 ft. daylight loading spools or 400 ft. darkroom core loads.

BEAULIEU R16ES

Fig. 2-16   Beaulieu R16ES

The Beaulieu is a relatively new French-made camera that has become quite popular in Europe and the United States. There are two models: 16ES and 16ES Automatic (Fig. 2.16).

This camera is extremely lightweight (only four pounds—six pounds with its 200 ft. magazine) but delicate. Its popularity is due to the weight feature plus its compactness and ease of operation. The most unique feature of the Beaulieu R16ES is its built-in "electronic-electric" light meter that provides the exposure setting of the lens. The 16ES Automatic model automatically sets the lens diaphragm at the correct opening.

The camera has a reflex viewing system that incorporates a new "divided grain" ground glass and mirrored guillotine (up and down) sliding shutter that operates at a 45 degree angle to the filmplane. Due to this system the image through the viewfinder is very bright.

The lens turret will accept three C mount lenses. Long-focus lenses can be mounted without additional support if the rear thread at infinity does not exceed 3.8mm.

Recent developments by the manufacturer include a 200 ft. daylight load magazine and a transistorized speed-controlled motor that is powered by a 7.2 volt battery. This motor can operate at speeds ranging from 2–64 fps and has a special constant speed control. The Beaulieu sync generator is custom calibrated to the Uher 4000L tape recorder with Rangertone and the Uher 1000L with Pilotone for sync sound filming. It may also be used with the Nagra tape recorder. The camera also contains a footage/frame counter and a tachometer.

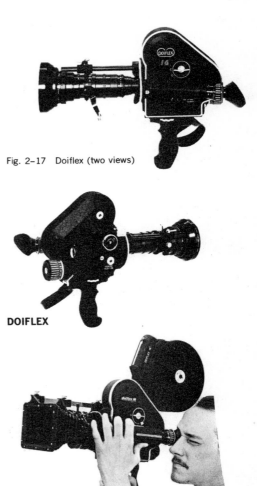

Fig. 2–17   Doiflex (two views)

DOIFLEX

One of the newest cameras on the 16mm market is the Japanese-made Doiflex (Fig. 2.17). The Japanese have long been famous for their still cameras and 8mm cameras, but this is their first design of a professional 16mm camera. Its design and characteristics resemble the Arriflex. The camera contains a reflex viewing system, an intermittent movement that contains a single pull-down claw and a single registration pin, a three-lens turret for C mount lenses, a built-in tachometer calibrated from 0 to 50 fps, an 8 volt variable speed motor for speeds from 2 to 48 fps, and a fixed shutter with a 1/57th of a second exposure at 24 fps. At present the camera can accept only 100 ft. daylight loading spools; however, a 400 ft. coaxial magazine is being developed (Fig. 2.18). Other developments promised for the future are constant speed and synchronous speed motors.

Fig. 2–18   Doiflex equipped with coaxial magazine

CANON SCOOPIC 16

The Canon Scoopic 16 is the second Japanese-made camera to gain popularity. It is a rugged, compact camera that weighs only 7 pounds, 5 ounces. The Canon Scoopic 16 accepts 100 ft. daylight loading spools of 16mm single or double perforated film. Loading the camera is a simple operation because of its automatic self-threading system. The camera contains a 13–76mm Canon Zoom Lens with a manual zoom control.

The Scoopic 16 incorporates a fully automatic exposure control system that contains a cross-coupled CdS cell located above the lens mount. The cell can be programmed for ASA speeds from 10–320, and it automatically controls the diaphragm opening of the lens in relation to the camera's running speed. Should the cameraman choose to over- or underexpose the image, a manual control device is included that overrides the automatic system.

The Canon Scoopic 16 is powered by a small 12 volt interchangeable, rechargeable battery that fits into a battery compartment located in the top of the camera body. It is also possible to power the camera from an external battery. When fully charged, the small 12 volt Canon Nickel Cadmium battery will run the camera through approximately 800 ft. of film. A special Canon Scoopic Charger is optional and necessary for recharging these batteries. This charger can recharge two batteries at the same time.

The motor of the Scoopic 16 will operate the camera at 16, 24, 32, and 48 fps. The shutter speeds at these running speeds are 1/43, 1/64, 1/86, and 1/128 of a second, respectively.

The Scoopic 16 contains a reflex viewing system that incorporates a beamsplitter prism. Since its lens is a zoom lens, focusing should be accomplished with the lens set at its longest focal length (76mm).

A complete range of accessories is available, including lens hood, external battery box, close-up lenses, compensating filter for the CdS meter, and Canon 72mm exclusive screw-in lens filters.

16mm Blimpless, Silenced Cameras

Until recently, when a film-maker was planning to shoot a scene that required synchronous sound recording he was forced to rent or purchase a sound blimp into which he could place his camera. The blimp was necessary in order to deaden the sound produced in the camera by the intermittent movement and the slap of the film loop. These noises could be picked up by the microphone and thus destroy any sound take. However, the moment the film-maker had to use the blimp, one of the major advantages of 16mm filming—mobility—was hampered, for inside the blimp the camera was considerably more cumbersome to handle. Recently, however, several cameras have been designed that are practically noiseless and so retain their valuable mobility while shooting sync sound.

ARRIFLEX 16BL

Fig. 2–19   Arriflex 16BL

This camera is the latest design in the Arriflex 16mm line (Fig. 2.19). Its design and construction make it an excellent selection for either double-system sound filming (with a separate sound recorder) or single-system filming (with a magnetic sound head in the camera and magnetic striped film). A magnetic recording module which contains the magnetic recording head is an optional accessory for the 16BL and simply plugs into the basic camera. With this module you have the most versatile of sound filming cameras. The basic design of the 16BL combines the characteristics of the 16S and 16M with several new design elements which make the 16BL a noiseless camera. The intermittent movement of the 16BL is identical in concept with that of the 16S and 16M, but all of the moving parts of the movement in the 16BL are housed in a special sound insulating housing. The camera body itself is built with an effective noise deadening material. As a result the amount of noise emanating from the camera is practically nil.

The 16BL has been designed to take only a single lens. Generally this camera is provided with a zoom lens; however, short-focus Arri lenses are also available. Whatever the lens, it is mounted in a special blimped housing that limits any noise radiation coming from the camera. Angenieux zoom lenses available are: 12.5mm to 75mm, 9.5mm to 95mm, and 12mm to 120mm. A Zeiss Vario Sommar 12.5mm to 75mm is also available.

Four hundred foot magazines with special acoustical construction are supplied for the 16BL. This magazine accepts a 400 ft. darkroom core load or a 200 ft. daylight loading spool. A 1,200 ft. coaxial magazine of acoustical construction is also available.

In addition to the regular Universal and synchronous motors, the Universal motor can also be supplied with a tuning-fork control system that allows double-system Rangertone/Pilotone sync sound recording *without* the usual "umbilical" cable connection between camera and recorder. The Universal motor also contains a control that allows it to operate as a variable speed motor.

One final difference between the 16BL and the 16S and 16M is in the viewfinding system. Instead of the fixed viewfinder tube of the 16S and 16M, the 16BL has a periscope finder that permits viewing in any camera position. The periscope permits a 360 degree vertical and a 15 degree horizontal rotation.

ECLAIR NPR (NOISELESS PORTABLE REFLEX)

The design of this Eclair camera also provides the noiseless running without sacrificing mobility. The physical appearance of the camera is quite different because the designers have abandoned the traditional top-mounted magazine and have attached the coaxial magazine of the NPR at the rear of the camera (Fig. 2.20). As with the Eclair Cameflex 35, the magazine can be rapidly attached to the NPR, even when the camera is running. The rear-mounted position of the magazine allows it to serve as a shoulder support of the camera when a take is being hand-held.

The viewing and focusing system is of the reflex type. A high reflectance front-surfaced mirror shutter reflects the light to the viewer optical system. The image in the viewer is magnified 12× and is very bright even at low light levels or with a stopped-down lens.

The standard motor for the NPR is a 12 volt D.C. transistor-controlled constant speed type. This motor generates a 60 cycle sync pulse. A variable speed motor and two synchronous speed motors are available for the NPR; one is heavy-duty.

Fig. 2-20 Eclair NPR

16mm Sound-on-film Cameras (Single System)

The need for a camera that would record both sound and picture on a single strip of film was felt mainly in the television industry and its news departments.

Until the advent of magnetic recording tape, all film sound was optical sound. This could take the form of either single system (sound and picture on the same piece of film) or double system (sound and picture on separate pieces of film). Today magnetic sound is universally used for double-system sound and, in the use of magnetically-striped film, can be used for single-system sound as well. Optical sound is used exclusively for single system. In normal film production the sound is initially recorded in double system, thereby giving the editor a maximum flexibility in handling it, for he can cut either sound or picture independently. Release prints (composite prints) are invariably single-system.

The sound-on-film camera has been around the industry for some time, but mainly in 35mm. These cameras were much too heavy and complex. Television's needs spurred the manufacturers to design compact, portable units. We shall now discuss three of the most popular cameras.

AURICON CINE-VOICE II

This camera is the smallest and most portable of the cameras manufactured by Berendt-Bach (Fig. 2.21). The Cine-Voice II accepts only 100 ft. daylight spools. However, F&B/Ceco, Inc. has a conversion system that utilizes specially made 200 ft. magazines or Mitchell 400 ft. and 1,000 ft. magazines.

The Cine-Voice has a sinusoidal-type intermittent movement which utilizes a single claw pull-down. The film is guided over a system of stainless steel balls to guarantee an in-focus, scratch-free picture.

The camera's separate viewfinder is mounted on the side of the camera and is equipped with a parallax adjustment device. This viewfinder provides a 13mm wide-angle lens field, and amber-colored plastic mattes must be inserted to indicate 17mm, 25mm, 50mm, or 75mm fields. Focusing must be accomplished with a measuring tape.

The Cine-Voice II is available with either a three-lens turret accepting C mount lenses or a singe-lens mounting for use with a zoom lens.

The manufacturer can supply either variable area or variable density optical recording instruments. A "Filmagnetic" magnetic recording head can be installed for use with pre-striped film.

A 115 volt, A.C. constant speed motor is standard equipment, but a 115 volt, A.C. synchronous motor is also available. A recent development is a tuning-fork control system synchronous motor that provides double-system sound filming with battery power.

Fig. 2–21 Auricon Cine-Voice II

AURICON PRO–600

This camera is actually a more sophisticated version of the Cine-Voice II (Fig. 2.22). The intermittent movement and film drive sprockets are identical to those found in the Cine-Voice II. The body of the camera is a larger version of the Cine-Voice. The lens turret takes three C mount lenses and matching objective finders are also mounted on the turret. A single-lens mount version is also available.

Four different viewfinder systems are available for the Pro–600: (1) the standard viewfinder that is found on the Cine-Voice II; (2) a studio viewfinder with an automatic parallax control; (3) a telefinder system that utilizes objective finders mounted on the lens turret and has a 10× magnifying eyepiece; and (4) Model CM–77 which has a C mount for a zoom lens with its own reflex viewfinder.

Focusing with system 1 and 2 must be accomplished by measuring tape and lens calibration. System 3 has a ground-glass focusing eyepiece on the right side of the camera. The lens must be revolved 120 degrees from the taking position to the focusing position and then revolved back to the taking position for shooting.

Fig. 2–22 Auricon Pro-600

The Pro–600 is equipped with a 600 ft. double compartment magazine that has an independent magazine drive—the Electromatic torque-motor take-up. This independent drive begins operation at one-third speed the moment the camera is connected to power, whether the camera motor is on or off. As a result, this drive provides a constant tension on the film take-up and prevents the film from slacking off when the camera is not running.

This camera is supplied with a 115 volt, 50 or 60 cycle A.C. synchronous motor. Optical sound pick-up can be carried out by either a variable density or variable area galvanometer. The "Filmagnetic" sound head is used for magnetic recording on pre-striped film.

AURICON SUPER–1200

This Auricon model, although basically the same as the preceding two, is a much heavier camera with the characteristics of a studio camera. It too has a sinusoidal movement with a single pull-down claw. But instead of the film being guided over a series of steel balls, the film is guided over a jewel-hard sapphire filmgate surface that prevents emulsion pickup and guarantees an in-focus and scratch-free picture. This system also contains an external push button that retracts the claw for easier threading.

The viewfinder system employs an optical rackover system. A mirror is shifted into a 45 degree angle between the lens and the aperture for framing and focusing, but before shooting this mirror must be withdrawn from its focusing position. The viewfinder then functions as a separate finder utilizing matched objective finders that are mounted on the camera turret.

The Super–1200 can be equipped with either a 600 ft. or 1,200 ft. double compartment magazine with the same Electromatic torque-motor take-up found on the Pro–600.

The Auricon Super–1200 is so silent in running that it is equipped with a safety switch that stops the camera and activates a buzzer alarm, warning the camera operator that something is wrong in the take-up system.

CAMERA ACCESSORIES

In addition to the camera, the film-maker must also select various accessories that will be necessary for the filming of his particular production: (1) camera supports; (2) a means for moving the camera during a take; (3) sound deadening devices; (4) filters; (5) exposure meters; and (6) lenses.

Camera Supports
THE TRIPOD

First developed for the still camera, the tripod was quickly adopted for the first motion picture cameras and still is the most commonly used form of camera support. The tripod actually comes in two parts—the legs and the head. The three legs are made either of metal or wood. Wood is the most commonly used because of its strength, flexibility, and light weight.

Fig. 2-23 Pro-Junior friction head for tripod

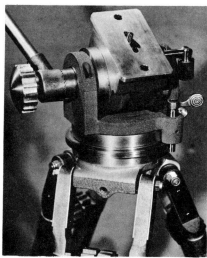

Fig. 2-24 Pro-Junior fluid head for tripod

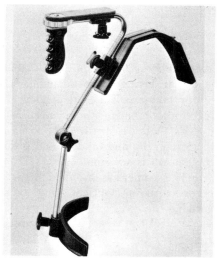

Fig. 2-25 Arriflex body brace

Four different types of heads are available: (1) the friction head (Fig. 2.23); (2) the fluid head (Fig. 2.24); (3) the geared head; and (4) the gyro head. The friction head is very common although it is the least satisfactory on movement shots. The fluid head is the most recent in design and is quickly becoming the most popular because of its great performance. The gyro head also performs smoothly on movement shots but is a noisier and costlier mechanism. The geared head is used almost exclusively with studio cameras to control the bulk of this equipment. This head is very heavy but performs smoothly and easily. In conclusion, for most camera work, unless you are using the very large studio camera, we would recommend wooden legs and a fluid head.

THE TRIANGLE (SPIDER)

This is a necessary device that is used with the tripod. The triangle is made of wood or metal (generally aluminum) and consists of three adjustable arms which open up to form a "Y" shape. The legs of the tripod are placed into grooves on the ends of the triangle arms. Some triangles are equipped with clamps which keep the tripod legs in place. The triangle is a necessary base for the tripod when the tripod is being used in any location where the ground or flooring is hard and smooth. Without the triangle the legs of the tripod will slide because of the lack of any footing.

HI-HAT

This is a camera support that is used when you wish to place your camera near floor level. The Hi-Hat is a metal device with three legs and stands approximately eight inches high.

**THE SHOULDER POD
AND THE BODY BRACE**

Both are forms of camera supports that either attach to the camera operator's body or brace against some part of the operator's body (Fig. 2.25). Both devices are used to give additional support and control of the camera during a hand-held shot. Some cameramen prefer the pod and some prefer the brace. The brace is a bit more cumbersome, but generally provides a steadier support.

Fig. 2–26 Moviola crab dolly (two views)

If the film-maker is to make full use of his camera, he must have some means of moving that camera, and these movements must be smooth. For such takes the film-maker must have some type of dolly. The range of possibilities runs from the large studio dolly that rents for approximately $25 or $35 per day to several very low-cost improvised methods that, if handled properly, can be as effective as the studio dolly.

THE CRAB DOLLY   This type of dolly (Fig. 2.26) is a rather elaborate moving platform that allows for a wide variety of movements. It contains a hydraulically-operated boom on which the camera is mounted and seats for the camera operator and an assistant. This camera-vehicle can be used to carry out a wide variety of movements because the pneumatic-tired wheels can be turned in any direction. Therefore, with the camera mounted on the dolly and with a camera assistant to steer and push the dolly, the film-maker can turn curves or right angles, move in diagonals or just about any other direction, including up and down.

THE ELEMAK DOLLY   This dolly is a compact dolly of Italian design. It has a hydraulic center-post for the camera and a seat for the operator, but it has no platform. It is a highly versatile vehicle, easy to handle even in tight corners or narrow spaces. The Elemak will move in any direction. In locations where the floor is smooth, it can be used like a crab dolly.

THE COLORTRAN HYDRAULIC DOLLY   This is the latest addition of compact, versatile dollies (Fig. 2.27). It comes in parts which fit into two carrying cases and can be assembled in minutes. Its two carrying cases fit into the trunk of a standard automobile, making this an exceptionally easy dolly to transport (Fig. 2.28). It is the smallest professional-quality dolly available. The ColorTran dolly has a 27 × 39 inch platform that is mounted on eight wheels that can be steered in any direction. It contains a hydraulic post that will accommodate both large and small cameras. This dolly is capable of smoothly carrying out a wide variety of movements.

THE DOLLY

Fig. 2–27 ColorTran hydraulic dolly

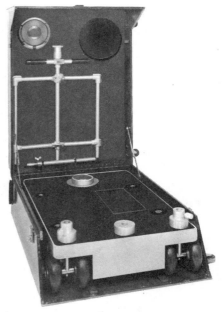

Fig. 2–28 ColorTran dolly in carrying case

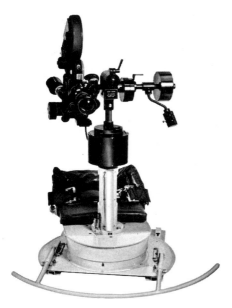

Fig. 2-29 Aero-Vision

IMPROVISED DOLLIES   There are several improvised arrangements which can be used to accomplish camera movements. Just about any four-wheeled vehicle capable of supporting the camera and its operator can be used for effective moving shots. A child's toy wagon has been used more than once. A wheelchair with the camera operator in a body brace and sitting in the chair is a highly effective way to move the camera. Warehouse dollies that have a flat platform, baggage trucks, or carriers used in hospitals to move bedridden patients can all be used as dolly-type vehicles. When the camera movement is to take place over a large area, an automobile can be a very effective dolly. The best type of automobile is a convertible because it allows more freedom; another possibility is one of the mini-buses having a flat roof. These can work quite well with the camera mounted on the roof or inside the bus. You can move the automobile under its own power; however, this tends to add a jerkiness and a vibration which can affect the steadiness of the shot. Perhaps the smoothest shot can be accomplished by pushing the automobile. You will need, of course, two or three strong backs for this operation. If the terrain is uneven, decrease the air pressure in the tires so the movement will not be as affected by the bumpy surface. A less strenuous means of assuring picture steadiness when shooting from a moving car, train, plane, or boat is the utilization of one of the gyroscopic devices available. These range from the small gyros that can be attached directly to a hand-held camera up to elaborate devices consisting of a frame to which the camera is attached and on which is placed the gyro and a seat for the cameraman. Examples of this device are the Tyler Vibrationless Mount and Aero Vision (Fig. 2.29). With such a device the cameraman can be perched in a helicopter, on the deck of a boat, on the tailgate of a station wagon, or on a golf cart, ensuring in all cases the elimination of the vibrations caused by the moving vehicles.

Sound Deadening Devices
CAMERA BARNEYS

Barneys of two types are available. One is a camera parka that allows filming in temperatures as low as –60° F. and is called a Heater Barney. It contains heating pads that are powered by a 115 volt, A.C. source. This same parka can be used in extremely hot climates as well for it not only heats and insulates in cold weather, it insulates and keeps heat out in temperate climates.

The Sound Barney is the same parka without the heating pads. Obviously it is used in sound filming in an effort to deaden the sound of the running camera.

THE BLIMP

The sound blimp (Fig. 2.30) is the most satisfactory sound deadening device for use with the camera. It is constructed of either metal or plastic and is lined with some form of soundproofing material. It has doors which provide access to the various parts of the camera. However, the blimp is so constructed that nearly all of the camera operation can be

Fig. 2-30 Arriflex Blimp

carried on from the outside of the blimp. Generally one needs to open the blimp doors only when changing the film supply. As a sound deadener, the well-built models are perfect.

THE CHANGING BAG

The changing bag is used for loading magazines which accept the darkroom core loads. With the changing bag this operation can be carried out even in bright sunlight. It functions as a traveling darkroom.

THE SLATE

The slate (Fig. 2.31) is used to record important data during shooting. The data is marked on the slate, which is then held before the camera and photographed before each take: Such data as the number of the scene and take; the date; whether the shot is an interior or exterior; the number of the sound take; the names of the film, director, and cameraman. This information is vital for the editor who will later cut the film. On top of the slate is the clapboard, a hinged portion that can be opened and then closed suddenly to produce a loud noise. This sound serves as a reference mark or sync mark when the editor is synchronizing the soundtrack with the picture.

Fig. 2-31 Slate

CAMERAMAN'S EQUIPMENT

Camera tape, a measuring tape, cotton swabs, and a set of tools which can be used for maintaining the camera should be taken along on any filming assignment. The camera tape has an unlimited variety of uses. The measuring tape is used to measure the distance from the camera to the subject so that proper focus adjustments can be made. With a reflex camera the measuring tape is not so vital. The cotton swabs and the tools are necessary items for cleaning and maintaining the camera and should always be a part of the basic equipment.

Filters

Just as the human eye is sensitive to certain colors of the spectrum, so is film emulsion. Since film is also affected by the intensity of light that reaches its emulsion, a second major function of the filter is to provide the film-maker with a control over the light intensity in addition to that offered by the lens diaphragm.

Filters to be used in cinematography can be categorized into three basic types: (1) filters for use with black-and-white film; (2) filters for use with color film; and (3) filters used for special effects in either black-and-white or color filming.

FILTERS FOR USE WITH BLACK-AND-WHITE FILM

As we mentioned earlier, all film emulsion is sensitive to the colors of the spectrum. Black-and-white film, however, is oversensitive to blue, so much so that this oversensitivity tends to overpower the emulsion's sensitivity to the other colors of the spectrum. If a natural reproduction of an exterior scene is to be filmed, some type of filtering is necessary to control this oversensitivity to blue. These filters will absorb some of the blue light thus achieving a photographic balance with the other colors.

For every color of the spectrum there is a complementary color or opposite. Red will absorb green, green absorbs red, yellow absorbs blue, and so on. We therefore utilize the complementary colors to control the colors that reach the film's emulsion. If you were shooting an exterior scene in which some expanse of the sky were visible, you would see the blue sky and the white puffy clouds because the human eye tends to be more sensitive to yellow. If you filmed this scene without a filter, you would be disappointed to find that the sky is merely a mass of white, and the faces of your actors are dark gray or black. The problem, of course, is simply that there is too much blue light. If you had filmed the scene with a yellow filter, a portion of the blue light would have been absorbed, and the scene would have photographed much closer to the way you saw the scene. These filters are called correction filters because they change the film's response so that it records all colors at the approximate brightness value as seen by the human eye.

Filters are also used in black-and-white filming for penetrating haze in long shots of distant landscapes. Be careful that you do not confuse haze with mist or fog, since the latter two are composed of water droplets and are, therefore, basically white. Atmospheric haze scatters mainly blue light and a large quantity of ultraviolet light. As a result, if such shots are taken without filtering, the film will record more haze than is visible to the human eye. The amount of haze decreases as stronger yellow, orange, and red filters are used. The greatest haze penetration is accomplished with a heavy red filter. These filters are called haze filters.

Still another important use of the filter in black-and-white filming is to change relative brightness values. If two colors, for example, are photographed without filters and thus recorded as being nearly the same, and are then photographed with filters, their brightness will be changed and their difference in color will be discernible. By use of these filters, we can increase the contrast between colors. To decrease the contrast, you shoot either without any filtering or with neutral filters or green filters. The filters used to increase the contrast are called contrast filters.

In using any filters, there is one vital element that must be considered—the filter factor. Since the task of the filter is to absorb part of the light that would otherwise contribute to the exposure of the film, an exposure correction must be made that corresponds to the amount of light that has been absorbed. The amount of times the exposure must be increased over the exposure reading without a filter is called the filter factor. Be careful, however, that you do not confuse the factor with the stops the lens must be opened. A filter with a factor of two means that the lens must be opened an additional one stop. Each time a factor is doubled another stop is required. Therefore, a factor of four requires a two stop compensation, and an eight requires three, and so forth.

The uses for filters with color film differ considerably from their uses with black-and-white film. With color film the chief concern of the film-maker must be with the color quality of the light source, a factor that is almost nonexistent with black-and-white film. The concern stems from the fact that different light sources emit an illumination of different color qualities. Daylight has a predominantly blue quality, as we found when discussing black-and-white filters, but tungsten illumination (incandescent light) emits a light which is predominantly yellow. The human eye tends to perceive all colors as they appear in daylight. When we see a color illuminated by tungsten light, we mentally compensate for the "yellow" of the tungsten source. Color film is unable to compensate, unless it is made with the compensation built in, so to speak. The film is *balanced* for use with a particular light source. Color film manufactured for use with a tungsten source will produce colors that the human eye will perceive as having a daylight quality. One of the main uses of filters with color film is to compensate for a film that is exposed by a lighting source for which it is not balanced. When a piece of color film balanced for use with a tungsten source is exposed to daylight, the developed image will have an overall blue cast. The film, after all, has been balanced so as to compensate for the human tendency to see more blue in tungsten light; to expose it to a source possessing large quantities of blue will, therefore, lead to an over-balance of blue. To correct this problem, the film-maker merely places an orange filter (Wratten 85) before the lens, which absorbs the excess blue and thus exposes an image balanced for human vision. Should the film be balanced for daylight and the film-maker finds he must expose it with a tungsten source, he must now compensate for the additional yellow in the light source. He merely places a blue filter (80A filter) before the lens, and this filter absorbs the excess yellow. Thus once again, an image is exposed similar in color to what the human eye perceives. This discussion is an over-simplification of the problem and the principle, but it will be discussed more fully under Color Temperature of Color Film (see page 55).

In color cinematography, the film-maker is making use of a film that has a color-sensitive emulsion. He is, therefore, limited tremendously in his use of colored filters. He can use them for technical purposes, such as balancing the light source which we just discussed, or he can use these colored filters to create unusual effects in the color of his photographed images. Such effects have a very limited use. There are examples of such uses; the unusual color effects were created in the film *South Pacific* in this way. But the film-maker must be careful of such effects for they do add an extremely unreal quality to the film.

Color correction filters are available to the film-maker to be used to change the overall color quality of a scene. We would recommend, however, that the film-maker refrain from their use. Such color correction can be carried out more competently by the laboratory, since their color printers are also equipped with these same filters. The laboratory will have to compensate anyway for the differences in color sensitivity

FILTERS FOR USE WITH COLOR FILM

of the different rolls of film the film-maker has exposed, as well as exert a color control over duplicate negatives or prints struck from the original stock so that there is an overall quality to the finished product. Working with the laboratory and their timer will produce much better results than if the film-maker attempts this control during the production stage of the film (see page 488). Such an attempt at color control in the filming stage could result in an overall color cast that would be difficult to correct in the laboratory.

Color film, like black-and-white, is overly sensitive to ultraviolet light rays. We noted that when the film-maker is faced with penetrating an atmospheric haze when shooting in black-and-white, he uses a filter that absorbs the ultraviolet rays. The same procedure is in effect when shooting in color. Special ultraviolet filters are available. They are practically colorless and so have little or no effect on color quality; but these filters do absorb ultraviolet rays, thus allowing the camera to penetrate the atmospheric haze. Such a filming problem is found in shooting long landscape shots or in aerial photography.

FILTERS USED FOR SPECIAL EFFECTS

Filters that are used to obtain special effects are generally neutral and so do not affect color values. As a result, they can be used for both black-and-white and color film. These filters are used to diffuse the light so as to soften hard lines, particularly in close-ups of the face (diffusion filters); to create fog effects (fog filters); to reduce the intensity of a light source in a specific manner (neutral density filters). All of these filters are used to control and modify the light before it reaches the film.

DIFFUSION FILTERS Diffusion filters are not filters as such since they do not absorb light. Instead they modify some of the light by refracting many of the rays and thereby displacing the focus of the light rays before they strike the film. Diffusion filters come into particular use when filming close-up shots of faces in order to beautify the face. Since the filter refracts the rays and displaces the focus, it can be used to soften hard lines or blemishes as much as possible without being obvious. Most non-theatrical 16mm film production will make little use of diffusion filters, since such production is seldom concerned with beautifying the face of a glamourous star. However, should you ever be faced with such a problem, be careful that you do not combine such soft close shots with close shots of sharp focus, for the soft focus will be much too noticeable. In such cases, add a slight diffusion to the close shots to be intercut with the soft-focus shots. A special sliding filter is available for use with moving shots which begin with a long shot and move in to a close-up shot of a face. To diffuse the entire shot would be out of the question. Therefore, sliding filters are used which vary the diffusion. The filter is graduated from one end, which is clear glass, to the other end, which is heavily diffused. As the moving shot travels from the long shot and sharp focus into the close shot and soft focus, the filter slides past the lens and varies the diffusion. This same procedure is followed when the camera remains stationary and the subject moves toward the camera.

FOG FILTERS   These filters are based on the principle that fog creates a bluish halo around any bright object because of the defraction and dispersion of light by the small droplets of water making up the fog. Surely you have witnessed this effect when you have been in foggy weather and have seen a street light or automobile headlight through the fog. This is the effect created by the fog filter. The illusion is more complete when combined with lighting that is flat and nondirectional. Be careful in their use, especially on moving shots, for it can become obvious that it is not fog at all but something over the lens. These filters are made of optical glass that has been sprayed with a special laminate. Fog filters are available which duplicate fog conditions from light to heavy.

POLARIZATION FILTERS   Polarization filters are especially useful for reducing or eliminating reflections from any shiny surface such as water, glass, sand, metal, etc. Generally, however, you should not eliminate reflections, for this will cause the picture of the subject to be flat. Leave some reflection to give dimension. These filters are also useful for obtaining dark blue sky effects in color; this effect is best achieved when the sky is clear, not overcast. Polarization filters are also convenient for increasing the reflection in a glass window when such reflections can be used effectively. By positioning the filter differently you can also eliminate such reflections when they are not wanted.

These filters polarize by eliminating all light vibrations but one. You can visually observe the effect by revolving the filter. They have limited use in exterior shooting because they function only within certain conditions of camera angle, sun angle, and sky color. As a result, panning or moving the camera is impossible because the conditions will not match throughout the entire movement. Since at least half of the reflected light is absorbed by the filter, an increase in the exposure setting is necessary.

NEUTRAL DENSITY FILTERS   Neutral density filters are helpful in reducing exposure when using high speed film in daylight and for increasing the lens aperture for a reduced depth of field when shooting in bright light. These filters are especially useful in filming in color because they do not alter the color, but do help control exposure and contrast. They do not affect color because they are gray, and, therefore, the gray absorbs all color rays in an equal proportion.

These filters can be ordered in combination with other commonly used filters to facilitate their use. For example, if a film-maker is color shooting with high-speed tungsten film in daylight and wishes to reduce the exposure, he could use an 85 filter combined with a .30 or .60 neutral density filter. Neutral density filters are available from .10 density to 4.00 density.

We would suggest that all film-makers obtain a copy of the *American Cinematographer Manual* and carry it with them at all times during shooting. The manual contains a complete breakdown of filters for black-and-white and color film, including charts of make and number, uses and effects, filter factors and stop compensations, and light balancing facts.

Consulting these charts is the most practical, easy, and foolproof method of proper technical use of filters. No person can store all of this information in his memory.

Exposure Meters

The most fundamental concern of the film-maker is the control of the intensity of the light rays that pass through the lens to the raw film stock. The intensity of this light must be adjusted to match the rather narrow limits of the film. Control is achieved through the use of the exposure meter, one of the most useful tools of the film-maker. However, the information is not automatically obtained from the meter. The proper use of the meter requires considerable judgment on the part of the film-maker.

Three factors must be combined to determine the correct f/stop of the lens: the intensity of the light, the sensitivity of the film, and the exposure time. The meter measures the first—the intensity of the light. The sensitivity of the film is provided by the manufacturer. This sensitivity is standardized according to its exposure index value (see page 54). The exposure time is determined by the number of frames per second and the degree of the shutter opening. These figures are generally 24 fps and a 175 degree shutter opening which gives an exposure time of 1/50th of a second. The light meter then combines all of the foregoing factors and provides the film-maker with the lens aperture setting in f/stops.

The light meter, like the lens and the human eye, has a certain field of view. It accepts the light emanating from the field of view. Instead of forming an image as it does in the lens or eye, the light falls onto the surface of a photoelectric cell. This photocell generates a current that is proportional to the light that has fallen on it. The size of the measured current is indicated on the ammeter of the exposure meter, generally in footcandles (see page 66). The main reason any light meter requires considerable judgment on the part of the film-maker is that the field of view of the meter is never equal to that of the lens; generally it is larger. You must consider this fact and compensate for any additional light entering the meter which is not entering the lens.

Light meters are of two types: the reflected light meter, which measures the light reflected from the images to be photographed, and the incident light meter, which measures the incidental light illuminating the subject to be photographed.

REFLECTED LIGHT METER

The reflected light meter is pointed at the scene to be photographed, and its ammeter records the amount of light that is reflected from that scene. The major factor to remember with this meter is that the light picked up by the meter will vary according to the angle of the meter and its field of view. You should attempt to match the meter's field of view with that of the taking lens. Flesh tones are extremely important in both black-and-white and color filming. In order to maintain a consistent brightness of these tones from shot to shot, without undue shifting from light and dark, the most common method is to use the meter close up on the subject's face or on your own hand.

In the 1940s, Don Norwood introduced a newly designed exposure meter which measured the incident light falling upon a subject to be photographed. Until this time the only meters available were reflected light meters. The "three-dimensional" incident light meter was so accurate that it soon became standard equipment in cinematography.

This meter is used at the location of the subject to be photographed. It is pointed either at the camera or the light source. It measures the incident light intensity and it takes into account the three-dimensional factors of front, side, and back light sources. The meter combines these two factors and its answer gives a lens setting that is appropriate for all of the light illuminating the subject.

Spot meters are of recent design. They measure reflected light within a narrow field of view. The spot meter is most useful as a second meter with an incident light meter. When shooting with available light in situations where there is a great deal of contrast between bright and shaded areas, and where it is difficult if not impossible to get to the location of the subject to be photographed, the spot meter can be a valuable item to have along. With its narrow field of view it is possible to easily read the various elements of the scene and arrive at a compromise setting without having to move away from the camera's position. The spot meter is also invaluable when shooting a subject that is far off, especially if light at the camera's position is different from the light falling on the subject. By pointing the spot meter at the subject, you can get an accurate reading.

An electric-eye exposure control system has been available for some time for amateur 8mm motion picture cameras, but until recently a system accurate enough for professional use did not exist. An electric-eye system must be capable of "looking" at the scene to be photographed and either indicating the correct setting for the lens aperture or automatically adjusting this aperture for the best possible exposure of the scene. Experts in this field have estimated that a cinematographer may encounter any one of twenty-seven different types of situations affecting exposure control. Therefore, any electric-eye system acceptable for professional work must be able to solve any of the twenty-seven situations. Such a system has been recently designed.

The new system contains a CdS photoelectric cell that receives its light through the taking lens of the camera. The optical and photometric system has two fields of view—one for the main subject of the scene, and a second for the background. The system weighs both fields of view, taking into consideration the photographic importance of each with over 50 percent influence coming from the smaller main subject, and less than 50 percent influence from the larger background area. The system then integrates these weighted values and gives a single setting that will produce a balanced exposure of professional quality.

THE LENS*

The lens on your camera is the most important tool with which the cameraman will work. The lens supplies the eye to your camera, and it is through the lens that you will funnel your impressions. Therefore, an understanding of the lens is vital to the success of your filming.

To better understand the basic functions of the lens, let us return for a moment to Leonardo da Vinci's camera obscura. Da Vinci observed that when light reflected from an image passed through a tiny hole in the front of a black box, the image was formed onto the back wall of the black box.

This principle is the basis of the workings of any camera. The light enters through the tiny hole, crosses, and forms an inverted image on the back wall where the film has been placed with the emulsion facing the hole. The tiny hole of da Vinci's camera obscura suffices for the making of photographs, but the exposure time required is much too great. Because of the small amount of light entering the box, an exposure could take minutes. In motion pictures we must allow enough light to enter so that the exposure can be made in at least 1/50th of a second. For this speed of exposure, a lens is needed. Basically the lens serves the same function as da Vinci's "tiny hole," but the lens is much more efficient.

FOCAL LENGTH

The focal length of a lens is the distance from the optical center of the lens to the filmplane when the lens is focused at infinity (a distance of over 50 feet). If the optical center of a lens is located three inches from the filmplane, the focal length of the lens will be three inches or 75mm. If another lens's center is one inch from the film, its focal length will be one inch or 25mm. Since the size of the picture itself never changes in a film camera, but rather remains at the size of the frame, the focal length determines the size of the image that will be formed within the frame. Thus the focal length determines the field of view of the lens and the amount of effective magnification within the frame. In the case of our examples, the one inch lens will form a wider field of view than the three inch lens, so it will be our wide-angle lens. The three inch lens will form a field of view one-third the width of the one inch lens, or rather, it will exclude three times the amount of area of the one inch lens. Therefore, the three inch lens will be our long-angle lens because of its longer focal length.

*For a complete study of the lens we would suggest a book on optics. Due to the scope of this book, we must limit discussion to the fundamentals.

Actually the terms wide-angle and long-angle are relative because the application of these terms is dependent upon the size of the picture frame. In an 8mm camera the picture frame would be small, so a one-inch lens would be a long-angle lens. When used with 16mm film with its larger frame area, the one-inch lens becomes more of a midrange or normal-angle lens. Only when used with 35mm and its large frame area is the one-inch lens considered a wide-angle lens.

APERTURE

The size of the hole in the lens determines the amount of light admitted through the lens. This hole is the aperture, and the size of the aperture is regulated by the iris or diaphragm, or iris diaphragm. Unfortunately, the simpler the construction of the lens, the less the aperture can be regulated. In a simple lens, the larger the aperture is opened, the more the image will be distorted. The simplest lens would consist of a convex or converging element, but it would have no photographic usefulness because it cannot control distortions or aberrations caused by the light rays and their different points of focus. In order to control these aberrations or distortions, a motion picture lens consists of a series of elements of converging and diverging types (convex and concave, respectively). This compound lens overcomes many of the aberrations by better controlling the points of focus of the light rays because of the different types of elements. Such a lens, however, does not eliminate all distortions; this is impossible.

LENS CONSTRUCTION

Some of the elements of the lens are separate, some are cemented together, and all are mounted with great accuracy inside a metal barrel that has a matte-black inner surface. The iris is mounted between the elements and is controlled from outside the lens barrel. The iris control is calibrated in f/stops alone, some in f/stops and T-stops, and some only in T-stops.

In order to decrease any unwanted light reflections off the surface of the lens elements, they are coated with a thin transparent film of magnesium fluoride which serves as an antireflection coating. This coating will resist abrasion and moisture rather well, but great care should be taken never to touch it with the fingers or to roughly clean it since the coating is extremely thin.

USING THE LENS

A camera lens accepts the light reflections from an image, and through the combination of lens elements bends the rays of the light reflection so that they come together or cross. When all the rays come together at the same point, we are provided with a photographic image sharp in detail and outline. We say that the image is in focus. If a lens had to accept only the light reflections from a flat surface, the precise point of the interception of light rays could be more easily calculated and achieved. Such a lens would have to be concerned with only a two-dimensional object. However, the camera lens must accept the reflections of a three-dimensional scene. No lens has yet been constructed that can accept the rays reflected from objects at different distances and bring all of these rays together at the same point.

DEPTH OF FIELD

The question is, how can the lens focus objects that are in more than one plane of distance from the lens? Just as in the case of persistence of vision, the human eye has what Raymond Spottiswoode has called a "spatial tolerance" that allows us to see blurred images as sharp points. A point in the photographed image is considered "in focus" because it has been registered by the lens as a point on the film. This is called *critical focus,* and all of those points that are in critical focus compose the *plane of critical focus.* A point outside this plane is registered on the film as a circle. This circle is called the *circle of confusion.* Here is how the eye's "spatial tolerance" affects what we see: If this circle is far enough away from the viewer or is small enough, the eye perceives it as a point. Hence there is an area on either side of the plane of critical focus in which we will accept some amount of blur as being of reasonably sharp focus (circles small enough to be perceived as points).°

The depth of field of the lens is the distance from the nearest and farthest point within which objects will be of acceptable sharpness when the lens is focused at less than infinity. The depth of field of any lens is affected by the f/stop, the focal length of the lens, and the distance of the object from the lens. The shorter the focal length of the lens, or the smaller the aperture, the greater the depth of field. In reverse order, the longer the focal length or the larger the f/stop, or the closer the object to the lens, the narrower the depth of field. A take that must be focused over a wide range of depth will require either a short focal length lens or a small aperture, which means an increase in the amount of illumination.

One other remedy for the depth of field problem is to utilize the hyperfocal distance of a lens. When faced with the problem of photographing a take that must keep an object relatively near the camera in focus as well as an object that is distant from the camera, you utilize split-focus. The split-focus is the hyperfocal distance which is a special type of depth of field. The focus of the lens is set at a compromise distance so that both near and distant objects are in reasonable focus. For example, you are filming a scene in which you must have an object twenty feet from the camera in focus, as well as a building in the background at infinity in focus. You are shooting with a 25mm lens stopped down to f/2.8. Instead of setting the lens at infinity, you set the lens at

*The film-maker should remember that the size of the circle of confusion is also governed by the conditions under which the film will be viewed. The degree of image magnification, the size of the film to be projected, the distance from the projector to the screen, and the amount of illumination can all affect the size of the circle of confusion in the final screened image. For example, a 16mm film projected over a long distance will tend to "come apart" and lose its sharpness because of the long throw.

its hyperfocal distance of twenty-eight feet, ten inches, and everything from nineteen feet, six inches to infinity will be in reasonably sharp focus. Again we recommend the use of the *American Cinematographer Manual* and its hyperfocal charts to find these variables.

As we have seen, one of the most important settings in the lens is the size of the aperture, which we have found is calibrated in f/stops, T-stops, or both. So we say the light-admitting capacity of the f/stop calibrated lens is measured in f/numbers. The f/number corresponds to the ratio of the focal length to the diameter of the lens opening. Basically, it is a smaller number indicating a larger aperture diameter and, therefore, a smaller exposure time. When a lens is set at f/2, this means the focal length is two times as great as the diameter of the diaphragm opening, at f/4 it is four times as great, and so forth. Therefore, when a 50mm lens is set at f/2, the size of the diaphragm opening is 25mm. Most film lenses are calibrated in a series of stops: f/1.4, 2, 2.8, 4, 5.6, 8, 11, 16, 22, and 32. With equal illumination, each of the stops will give inverse degrees of exposure in a geometrical progression. This means —depending upon whether you are opening or closing the lens—that each stop is either double or half the exposure of the preceding stop.

F/STOP AND T-STOP

Many film lenses, particularly zoom lenses, are also calibrated in T-stops. The T-stop number is the true f/number when the lens is free from reflection and absorption loss. As we have seen, the f/number is purely geometrical and, therefore, does not take into consideration any of the loss of light resulting from reflection or absorption, thus making the f/number imperfect. The T-stop number (the T means transmission) represents the f/number of a lens opening with 100 percent transmission of the light rays. No fixed ratio between T-stop and f/stop can be applied to all lenses in general. The differences in the two calibrations represent the light loss that takes place within the elements of any given lens. Therefore, the T-stop is variable and cannot be incorporated into a light meter since the meter must function for many different lenses.

T-stop calibration for zoom lenses is very important. The construction of the zoom lens is much more complex than a fixed focal-length lens. Therefore, the light loss due to the large number of optical elements will be much greater than in a conventional lens. The T-stop calibration is essential to compensate for the loss of light transmission.

The *American Cinematographer Manual* tells us that "exposure tables are generally based on 'effective' f/stops—which are, in fact, T-stops. Small variations in emulsion speed, processing, exposure readings, etc. tend to cancel out."[1] However, for the best possible results, a film-maker should run tests using their particular lenses, light meter, light, and film.

The main function of the calibrations of a lens is to control the diaphragm so that it acts as a variable *stop* to decrease the amount of light admitted to the film. We, therefore, *stop down* the lens mainly to prevent overexposure of the film. We have also discovered during our discussion of the depth of field of a lens that stopping the lens down provides us with a larger depth of field and, therefore, increases the distance within which objects can be brought into acceptable sharpness. You must remember, however, that no cinema lens, with the exception of telephoto lenses, operates at maximum efficiency when stopped down below f/16. Below this stop the optical quality of the image is reduced. When you must reduce the light below this point, use filters or the adjustable shutter of your camera, if it has one.

EQUIPPING THE CAMERA WITH LENSES

Selecting the lens to use on the camera is the next decision the filmmaker must make after having made his camera selection. Generally any filming assignment will require a wide-angle lens, a normal-angle lens, and a long-angle lens. In addition to these basic lenses, the film-maker may need extremely wide-angle lenses of varying sizes, telephoto lenses of varying sizes, or a zoom lens which also is available in varying sizes. Basic photographic needs in conjunction with script and aesthetic need will determine exactly what lenses to select.

DEPTH OF FIELD

WIDE-ANGLE LENS   The size of the picture area (size of raw stock: 8mm, 16mm, 35mm) of your frame will determine what focal length lens will function for you as a wide-angle lens. If you are working in 35mm, a lens of 25–35mm is considered to be a wide-angle lens. If you are filming in 16mm, a lens of 12½–17mm is considered to be a wide-angle lens. A lens that falls in the middle of this range will probably provide you with the most pleasing results—a 15mm lens for 16mm, and a 30mm for 35mm.

Your wide-angle lens will be the lens of lowest magnification; it will provide you with the widest field without distortion and it will give you the greatest depth of field unless a wide f/stop is used. When you are shooting in a small cramped area, the wide-angle lens is the one that will do the required job. However, do not expect the wide-angle lens to see what your own eyes see. Human vision takes in a view of approximately 120 degrees. Your wide-angle lens will "see" a field of less than 50 degrees.

Besides providing you with the widest possible field, this lens can also add a sense of drama to your set-ups. With a wide-angle lens perspective will be increased, movements toward or away from the camera will be accentuated, and separation of objects, people, and the background will be more apparent.

Suppose you were to shoot a scene from a relatively low angle with a 25mm lens in 35mm or a 12½mm lens in 16mm. The camera would seem to be near floor level and the walls of the room would seem to curve outward. This linear distortion would provide a macabre, eerie feeling to the scene.

The wide-angle lens tends to increase any movement toward or away from the camera. An automobile racing toward the camera can have a tremendous visual impact when photographed with a wide-angle lens.

As mentioned earlier, this lens is invaluable when shooting in cramped quarters. Because of the lens's exaggeration of perspective, the wide-angle lens will also provide a sense of separation between the people in the scene and the background, particularly if the shot is an interior shot with the lens set at a small aperture. The walls will not seem to bear down on the people so much as they would with any other lens.

Should you widen the aperture of the wide-angle lens when shooting within an in-depth setting, part of the image in the picture will be blurred or will be in soft focus. Such an image can also have dramatic value when used in the proper place.

Dolly shots, when made without a track, or hand-held moving shots are much more effective when made with these short focal-length lenses; the short focal length decreases the amount of movement necessary to achieve the desired effect. Particularly in the case of the hand-held shot, the short focal-length lens will also decrease the amount of unwanted jiggle of the camera as it moves.

Remember, however, when shooting out of doors, the shorter the focal length, the more the amount of foreground that will appear in the picture. When this excess foreground is unwanted, lower the camera and tilt it up a bit.

NORMAL-ANGLE LENS This class of lens is also known as the standard lens or the middle lens. With a 35mm camera this lens would range from 35–50mm. With a 16mm camera, the range would be from 17½–25mm. This lens is referred to as the normal-angle lens because it is supposed to correspond to the focal length of the human eye and, therefore, provide an image identical in space perception with that seen by the human eye. We should note here that the 17½mm lens is a much better focal-length lens for the 16mm camera and 35mm for the 35mm camera for use as the normal-angle lens. However, most 16mm cameras are equipped with a 25mm lens. The 25mm lens is a compromise lens falling between a wide-angle and a long-angle lens. The 25mm is a reasonably good lens for use with close shots and long shots—when you can move the camera far enough back. If you must shoot with only one lens, that lens should be a 25mm. However, when you can have a three lens complement, select a 17½mm as your normal-angle lens. The fact that most 16mm cameras when sold are provided with a 25mm lens has led to the use of this lens as the normal-angle lens.

The 35mm lens or the 17½mm lens as the normal-angle lens is best because of the compositional force it can provide pictorially. Chances are that under normal circumstances you will make more use of this midrange lens than either the wide-angle or long-angle lens. So you will want a lens that provides the sense of perspective of the human eye, as well as a lens that will have a variety of uses. The 35mm or 17½mm will maintain an illusion of three dimensions, provide better modeling of the subjects before the camera, and allow more compositional force because of the shorter focal length and increased depth of field than a 50mm in 35mm or a 25mm in 16mm.

LONG-ANGLE LENS (LONG-FOCUS LENS) This lens will be your lens of greatest magnification, unless you must utilize longer focus lenses for special effects. Normally you will equip your camera with a lens of 75–100mm for 35mm and 35–50mm for 16mm.

When a script calls for a close-up, the reaction of the novice film-maker would probably be to move the camera in closer and shoot it with a normal-angle lens. The novice should take a lesson from Hollywood, where it is standard practice to shoot close-ups with a 75mm or 100mm (35mm production) lens. A long-angle lens used on a close-up will provide a much more flattering picture of the face, and it will also allow the camera to be farther away from the shot, which can facilitate the positioning of lights. This farther distance can also be less trying on the actor. Try giving a relaxed performance with a camera lens practically sticking down your throat!

Certain problems are also inherent in using the long-focus lens. One of the major problems is the tendency to reduce the space between objects and thus "clutter" the shot. This problem can be turned to an advantage in some situations. Traffic moving slowly on a street, a crush of pedestrians walking down a sidewalk, a rank and file of marching soldiers can all be made to appear more impressive when shot with a long focal-length lens.

TELEPHOTO LENS Certain special effects are often required of the film-maker which can best be achieved with the use of the more sophisticated telephoto lens.

The telephoto lens is used primarily to bring distant objects into close view. They cover a small angle of vision and increase the "cluttering" effect discussed earlier. In fact, with a 500mm lens in 35mm production a shot covering several different planes of objects will record the objects so that they appear to be all in the same plane or side by side. This distortion of the lens when properly used can be quite effective (see page 101). This compression of space can also be employed to good advantage when it is necessary to bring the background closer to the main subject. One final advantage is the shallow depth of field of this lens. It allows the lens to isolate a subject from the background. By sharply focusing on the main subject, the background is blurred, thereby making the main subject stand out in sharp focus.

Perhaps the chief advantage of this lens is its ability to bring objects close to the camera without the camera being physically near the main action. This ability can be of tremendous use in filming a documentary subject, or in filming sports, news, wildlife, and even dramatic films.

Burnett Guffey, Director of Photography for *Bonnie and Clyde*, utilized a 400mm lens in shooting a scene showing two men sitting inside a restaurant talking. The camera follows these two men as they rise, leave the cafe, and walk down the street. Such a shot necessitated the use of a telephoto lens. The major problem to be faced with this shot was the lack of depth of field, which in this case was about one foot. Expert follow-focus through a reflex viewing system was a must.

EXTREME WIDE-ANGLE LENS Any size lens under 30mm in 35mm and 15mm in 16mm production can be considered an extreme wide-angle lens; however, you should understand that the more extreme the desired effect, the shorter the focal-length lens you must use. The 25mm in 35mm and the 12½mm lens in 16mm production are not infrequently used as standard wide-angle lenses. The extreme wide-angle lens is used to achieve a greater width and to force the perspective. Again Burnett Guffey utilized a 9.8mm lens while filming location interiors in order to gain more width in small areas and to force the perspective.

The shorter the focal length of the lens, however, the more linear distortion is produced in the picture (Fig. 2.32). Such distortions do have their uses. A recent deodorant commercial has made effective use of the extreme wide-angle lens. In this commercial several characters walk up to the lens and smile; they look as though we are seeing their impression reflected from the surface of a glass ball. Such strange and eerie effects can be most useful.

Fig. 2–32 (In Cold Blood, Columbia Pictures)
Linear distortion caused by
extreme wide-angle lens

Great care should also be taken in panning a shot that is utilizing an extreme wide-angle lens. The horizontal movement of the camera further exaggerates the linear distortion of the lens. Parallel lines in the center of the shot become increasingly curved as they approach the edge of the frame. Therefore, the movement increases the warped effect of the scene. Such shots are extremely unrealistic and should be used sparingly.

ZOOM LENS   The zoom lens is a special assembly of lens elements whose variable focal length can be manipulated during shooting, and, due to the increased or decreased magnification, thereby create the illusion of movement while keeping the image in continual sharp focus. This lens is probably the most useful optical development for cinematography in recent years. It can be used with great advantage in nearly every area of motion picture production, both theatrical and nontheatrical. Perhaps the chief advantage of the zoom lens is that it replaces the need for a film-maker to carry a full complement of lenses, but instead, to use the zoom lens set at different focal lengths. Until recent years most zoom lenses were not as optically correct as fixed-focus lenses and therefore could not be used in this manner. Today they display excellent sharpness throughout their zoom range.

The zoom lens does possess certain optical characteristics the film-maker should be aware of. For one thing, as the focal length is varied from short to long, there will be a gradual compression of subjects on different planes. Should a zoom lens lose its focus during a zooming movement, refocusing is impossible. (Of course, if the lens is focused properly this will not occur. If it does, have the lens adjusted by a specialist.) To keep the subject centered during a zooming movement from short to long focal length will require a slight pan and lift of the camera to compensate for the side-drift and slight drop that develops in the framed image.

In focusing the zoom lens, the film-maker should move it to its longest focal length, open the aperture completely, focus, and then move back to the desired focal length. In short, *always focus the lens at its longest focal length.*

CARE OF THE LENS

Consider the lens as an exceedingly delicate instrument and treat it in a way that befits such an instrument. It may look simple and tough, but looks are deceiving. Use only a fine camel's-hair brush to clean a lens and never touch the optical surfaces with your fingers, a rag, or a piece of tissue paper. Fingerprints contain acids which can permanently etch the magnesium fluoride coating. Should you find a fingermark or a grease spot on the lens surface, clean it off with a cotton swab and lens cleaning solution.

Lens caps should always be placed on the lens when filming activity has ceased or when the camera is being moved. If the lens is removed from the camera, a lens cap should be placed on both ends of the lens. If you are filming during a windy day, it is wise to place a filter over the lens to protect it. If no filter is required in the filming, place a clear optical glass over the lens. A filter is less expensive to replace than a lens. Always protect the lens from any shocks which might jar loose the elements. Lastly, removal of the lens elements except by an expert can cause irreparable damage.

After deciding upon the choice of equipment, the film-maker must then make a decision as to what film to use. Aesthetic considerations will, of course, play a part in your final selection as to film choice, but here we shall be concerned only with the practical aspects of your selection. **FILM**

The speed of the film is your first practical consideration, so the first matter to determine is the amount and type of illumination available during production. High-speed films and emulsions which must be pushed have a much greater granularity than the medium and slow-speed films. Excess grain should be avoided at all cost, unless used for some particular effect, because it can diminish the effectiveness of your film. Likewise, never push an emulsion if film of the proper speed is available. The film selected, therefore, should be of no higher speed than will be necessary for a proper exposure. It is senseless to use a fast emulsion if a slower one is sufficient. When you find it impossible to predict the lighting conditions you will encounter, have both a quantity of moderate and high-speed film available for use.

Since filtering will have an effect upon the speed of your film, we suggest that you select film that will require the least filtering. If you know you will be shooting in bright sunlight, it would be foolish to use a high-speed film which will require you to use a heavy neutral density filter to prevent overexposure. The filter will have an unnecessary effect upon the quality of your picture. On the whole, the best practice is to select a color emulsion that will need little filtering instead of one that will require heavy filtering to convert or balance it to a light source for which it was not designed.

The next major consideration is whether to employ negative or reversal film. Theatrical films shot in 35mm use negative exclusively for both black-and-white and color. The use of negative is best generally, especially if a number of prints will be struck. Yet in 16mm production, the general practice is to shoot reversal film. Prints are then made from the original onto reversal duplicating film; or, the original is printed onto an internegative from which the positive prints are struck. When negative film is used in the camera, the 35mm method is to print a master positive from the camera original, then the master positive is used to make a dupe negative from which prints are struck. Such a method is not practical in 16mm because the 16mm film will become much too grainy, hence the reason for employing reversal stock. We do not say that a 16mm film-maker cannot use negative film, but consult your laboratory first and ask their advice. If you do shoot 16mm negative, be careful in your handling of the original. Sixteen millimeter negative scratches very easily, and these scratches will show up on prints as highly magnified white marks.

Exposure Index

Until recent years no one standard was available for judging film speed and its measurement. At different times and in different countries, various standards were utilized, making uniformity impossible. In recent years, the American Standards Association with the cooperation of the Eastman Kodak Company devised a uniform standard that has been put to use—American Standard Exposure Indexes.

"The Exposure Index is a number associated with the sensitivity and latitude of the emulsion, its development, its intended field of use, and the spectral quality of the light which illuminates the subject."[2] Obviously all film production takes place under a variety of conditions and with a variety of equipment; so to ensure acceptable results, safety factors are included in the exposure index.

The exposure index values are arrived at through practical tests, but should not be regarded as absolutes. These values are not fixed and can be changed when your own repeated tests show the need for a change. These values should be used as a starting point or a guide.

Black-and-White Film

The various black-and-white negatives available range from very slow to very fast film. The basis for their choice by a film-maker is the intensity of the light available. The slow films can be exposed out of doors when there is good sunlight. The moderate speed films can be exposed out of doors or indoors when a fair amount of light is available. The high-speed films can also be used out of doors and indoors and are necessary when light conditions are poor. The ultrafast films must be used when lighting conditions are the poorest, both outdoors and indoors. The high-speed and ultrafast films will have to be considered when the film-maker wishes to do his shooting with a very small aperture or is planning for high-speed cinematography.

The reversal films are of a slightly slower speed than the negative films, but they still provide speeds ranging from relatively slow to high-speed. The reversal process will generally produce positives that are less grainy than negative materials. However, reversal materials are more effective when only a small number of prints are needed.

Although several manufacturers produce a wide range of black-and-white and color films, we have selected as examples the products of one particular company, Eastman Kodak, because they are the most universally-known products.

XT NEGATIVE   This is a very fine grain low-speed negative that should be used only when there is a high level of illumination. Its main use is for prints for rear projection but it is also an acceptable exterior film. ASA/Exposure Index: Daylight—25; Tungsten—20.

PLUS-X NEGATIVE   This is a moderate speed film of fine grain that is suitable for exterior and interior use under average lighting conditions (640 footcandles at f/5.6). This film is probably the most popular film for general production work. ASA/Exposure Index: Daylight—80; Tungsten—64.

DOUBLE-X NEGATIVE   This is an exceptionally fine high-speed film that is useful for exterior and interior shooting under adverse lighting conditions. It is also a fine selection when a greater depth of field is desired without an increase in the level of illumination. ASA/Exposure Index: Daylight—250; Tungsten—200.

4x NEGATIVE   This film is an ultrafast stock but of medium graininess. It has the same uses as Double-X. ASA/Exposure Index: Daylight—500; Tungsten—400.

PLUS-X REVERSAL   This is a moderate speed reversal-type panchromatic (sensitive to all of the colors of the spectrum) film that is quite suitable for exterior and interior work when ample light is available (1000 footcandles at f/5.6). This film yields a positive with good contrast and exceptionally low graininess. ASA/Exposure Index: Daylight—50; Tungsten—40.

TRI-X REVERSAL   This stock is high-speed, reversal-type, and panchromatic. It can be used for interiors or daylight conditions and it is especially useful for weak light or shooting that takes place late in the day. It yields a positive of good contrast and graininess characteristics. ASA/Exposure Index: Daylight—200; Tungsten—160.

4x REVERSAL   This is a relatively new high-speed stock that yields a positive of excellent grain. Use 4X when lighting conditions are poor and may necessitate pushing the film. Its speed can be doubled by pushing it during the first development stage with little loss in quality. ASA/Exposure Index: Daylight—400; Tungsten—320.

Color Film

On the whole, color-film cinematography in 35mm utilizes negative stock, and 16mm, reversal stock. However, the Eastman Kodak Company has recently developed a new color negative that is now available in 16mm as well as 35mm (Type 5254–35mm. Type 7254–16mm). This new color negative is also twice the speed of the old 35mm color negative (Type 5251).

COLOR TEMPERATURE

Most color film is produced by combining three emulsions, each one sensitive to one of the primary colors on one base. This color film is able to record an image in color, and this film is also made to balance with the particular hue of a particular light source. (You will remember that this fact was first presented in our discussion of filters.) The various sources of light do not all emit the same tint of light—daylight is bluish and tungsten light is yellowish. As mentioned earlier, the human eye is able to adjust to the differences of tint and see both as a white light. Color film cannot adjust, and this is the reason color films are manufactured so that they will balance the color quality of a particular light source. The differences in the color quality of the various light sources are referred to as *color temperature* and are measured in *Kelvin degrees*. Tungsten film is balanced for 3200 degrees Kelvin.

Color temperature is based upon the colors of a perfect radiator or black body. To better understand this concept, picture if you will a black poker immersed in hot coals. As this "black body" draws heat from the hot coals, it gradually begins to change colors. The higher the temperature of the poker, the closer the color of the heated portion of the poker moves toward white. When the temperature of the poker reaches 3200 degrees Kelvin, it will emit a color of light that matches the color quality of incandescent light, and when it reaches 6000 degrees Kelvin, it will emit the same color quality as the light of an overcast day. Thus, when the light source matches the emission of the black body in color, it is said to have a color temperature that is equal to the actual temperature of the heated black body. The Kelvin degree scale is obtained by adding 273 to the actual temperature in degrees Centigrade ($0°$ K = $-273°$ C.).

As a result of color temperature, color film can provide us with an accurate color reproduction of a scene only when the color temperatures of the light source and the film balance. When daylight film is used with an incandescent source, the scene will contain an overall reddish hue. When tungsten film is used with daylight as the light source, the scene will possess an overall bluish tint. As we mentioned earlier, the most common practice is to employ filters to balance the color temperature of film and light. In the case of the former example, a blue filter is used, and in the case of the latter example, an orange filter. The problem with filtering, however, is that it reduces the light due to absorption. Color film, in general, is much slower than black and white and consequently requires a fair amount of light. Having to use filters can be most inconvenient. Therefore, when selecting color film, always keep in mind the light sources you will be employing and make your selections to fit with those light sources.

COLOR NEGATIVE TYPE 5254 (35MM), 7254 (16MM)   This film is a recently developed color negative stock and is the first available for 16mm cinematography. It has now taken the place of Type 5251 which for years has been the favorite of 35mm production. Its higher ASA rating makes the new stock acceptable for use in below-normal lighting conditions. This film is balanced for 3200 degrees Kelvin, so it must be used with an 85 filter when filming in natural light. ASA/Exposure Index: Daylight (with 85 filter)—64; Tungsten—100.

EKTACHROME COMMERCIAL TYPE 7255 (16MM)   This film has been the standard color stock used in 16mm color production when prints are needed. The original is low in contrast so that the prints will possess good contrast characteristics. It is a reversal film that is balanced for 3200 degrees Kelvin. ASA/Exposure Index: Daylight (with 85 filter)—16; Tungsten—25.

Light Sources and Color Temperature

Sources	Color Temperature
Sunlight—sunrise or sunset	2000
100 watt tungsten lamp	2865
500 watt tungsten lamp	2960
1000 watt tungsten lamp	2990
Photoflood and Reflector Flood lamp	3400
Sunlight—early morning	4300
Sunlight—late afternoon	4300
Daylight Blue Photoflood	4800
Carbon Arc	5000
Sun Arc lamp	5500
Direct midsummer sunlight	5800
Overcast sky	6000
Summer sunlight plus blue sky	6500

EKTACHROME EF (DAYLIGHT) TYPE 5241 (35MM), 7241 (16MM) This is a high-speed reversal-type stock that is balanced for daylight. It has exceptionally fine grain and sharpness despite the fact that it is a high-speed film. It has an exceedingly wide latitude and can be pushed as much as three stops with only a slight increase in graininess and a slight loss in color quality. ASA/Exposure Index: Daylight—160; Tungsten (80A filter with a 3200K source)—40, (80B with a 3400K source)—50.

EKTACHROME EF (TUNGSTEN) TYPE 5242 (35MM), 7242 (16MM) This is a high-speed reversal-type stock that is balanced for a 3200 degree Kelvin source. This stock, like the above EF film, can be pushed with little loss in quality; however, the latitude is not as wide as the daylight stock. When pushed beyond an ASA of 250, there is some loss in color quality and an increase in grain characteristics. ASA/Exposure Index: Daylight (with 85 filter)—80; Tungsten—125.

LIGHTING THE IMAGE

Lighting is one of the most important single elements of cinematography, and yet it is the phase of production that is most often overlooked by the nonprofessional film-maker. The best camera and lenses in the world, combined with the best effort, is wasted and useless when not combined with imaginative lighting. After all, lighting is the medium that is employed by the film-maker to mold each of his compositions and to add psychological impact. Its main purpose is *not* just illumination. How painful it can be to sit through the efforts of the uninformed film-maker, his subjects lost in the shadowed abyss of the scene shot with available light, or lost in what seems to be a violent snow storm because the film has had to be "pushed" to its capacity in processing due to the lack of light during production, or appearing as flat cardboard cut-outs because the lighting that has been employed has been used without a hint of imagination—merely flooded onto the scene to provide enough illumination for exposure. Falling into these traps is not only senseless but unnecessary. The film-maker who thinks he can produce a successful film without lighting does not merit the title of film-maker.

We are the first to admit that most of us are continually beset with budgetary problems and that lighting equipment can be an expensive addition to our production plans. But this is not the area where we should try to save. At the same time we do not need all of the elaborate equipment of a major theatrical film. What we do need in large quantities is imagination, for even the simplest of lighting set-ups when carried out with imagination can provide a quality to the final image that has no comparison in dollars and cents. Likewise, the most elaborate equipment can be used without imagination and provide an image that looks cheap when finally viewed on the screen.

Lighting your film should be just as much a creative endeavor as any other phase of your production, but, as with any successful creative effort, your lighting should not scream at your audience from the screen. To be successful it must be unobtrusive. Never let your "technique" show. Your lighting can be invaluable in setting the mood and effectively illuminating the subjects to their best advantage, but it must be carefully thought out and planned *before* the shooting begins. Do not wait until everyone is ready to begin and then discover that you have forgotten to plan and set up the lights. Good lighting must be planned and built up, not just flooded onto the scene. You must know where to throw highlights and where to leave shadows. You must know where to build up important details and where to play down less interesting details. You must know how, where, and when to give objects in the scene dimension with modeled lighting. And finally, you must know how to provide character and emotional key to each scene through the use of lighting. The film-maker uses lighting in the same way that an artist uses color and tone: to express mood and to create an atmosphere, to reveal the character of a person, to unify the structure of his painting, and to create a surface reality through a sense of depth.

Fig. 3–1 *In Cold Blood*, Columbia Pictures

Fig. 3–2 *The Firemen's Ball*, Cinema V

Generally speaking, the film-maker will use dark illumination to set a somber, tragic mood, bright illumination to establish a happy, gay atmosphere, or any variation of these two extremes to fit a variety of moods. Such uses of light will invest the scene with emotional tone that will affect the spectator and evoke in him the proper feelings for appreciation and understanding of the film-maker's purpose. Look, for example, at the somber, tragic emotional tone of the lighting throughout Bergman's *The Seventh Seal* or the sense of tragic foreboding in the lighting of Lumet's *The Pawnbroker* or Brooks' *In Cold Blood* (Fig. 3.1). On the other hand, consider the bright, happy atmosphere provided by the lighting for a comedy like Forman's *The Firemen's Ball* (Fig. 3.2), or the romantic atmosphere created by the lighting in *Elvira Madigan*. Without this valuable production element, the effectiveness of any of these films would have been lost because they would have lacked the realism and vivid drama that was contributed by the lighting.

The lighting of *The Seventh Seal, The Pawnbroker,* and *In Cold Blood* was predominantly what is called *low-key lighting* in film parlance. This type of lighting creates a mood by contrasting dark areas with light areas, thus casting a greater depth of shadows and providing the spectator with a harsher illusion of reality. The lighting of *The Firemen's Ball* is what is referred to as *high-key lighting.* In general, when the script calls for lighting that compliments a gay, buoyant mood, a high-level illumination is used with only a few shadowed areas and with brilliant highlights emphasizing various elements within the scene.

We do not mean to say that such formulas are stringently adhered to at all times. What is here presented is only the general rule, and all rules are made to be broken when they do not fit with your purpose.

Fig. 3–3 Light coming from below the subject's face (Mel Wittenstein)

Fig. 3–4 Light coming from the side (Mel Wittenstein)

Fig. 3–5 Light coming from directly in front of the subject's face (Mel Wittenstein)

We said that the painter reveals character with color and tone; the character of a face can be greatly changed or probed in film through the use of lighting. Generally, by aiming the light down onto the face, a quality of youthfulness is given to it. But aim the light from below the face (Fig. 3.3) and that angelic appearance is changed into one that seems wicked and unearthly. Aiming the light from the side will give the face solidity or reveal the depth of character by outlining the lines and crevices of the face (Fig. 3.4). Throw the light on the face from the front and it is beautified by blurring away the faults (Fig. 3.5); however, front lighting takes away its character at the same time. Direct the light from behind, and the face is spiritualized or etherealized by creating a halo around it. Through the imaginative use of light more can be done for the expressive quality of the face than the best work of the make-up artist.

By utilizing lighting to stress what is important and to shade what is unimportant, the film-maker, like the painter with color and tone, unifies the structure of his scene. By illuminating the important and allowing the unimportant to fall into shadows, he controls the concentration and attention of the spectator.

Lastly, the film-maker and his light, unlike the painter, can create an illusion that goes beyond the surface of his "canvas." Although, like the painter's canvas, the film-maker's screen is a two-dimensional surface, he can, with the use of lighting combined with camera angle and lens, create a sense of depth that is far beyond the capabilities of the most proficient and creative painter. Lighting *is* the third dimension.

The painter deals with a static creation, whereas the film-maker deals with images that are constantly in a state of movement—movement from shot to shot, movement of the subjects within the composition, and movement of the camera. Therefore, the lighting must be adapted to this movement. As the film cuts from shot to shot within a scene, the lighting must provide sufficient illumination and yet generally must match the mood of the preceding shot. As the subjects within the frame of the composition move, they must be seen by the spectator, but at the same time the previously established ambiance must be maintained. And as the camera moves, the lighting, in a sense, must move but still maintain that ever-present atmosphere.

Beyond the physical movement that takes place, there is the dramatic movement of the film. Do not for a moment think that dramatic movement is an element only of the theatrical film. No matter what the subject of the film, if it is to capture and hold the attention of your audience, that film must have dramatic movement. Combine the physical movement and the dramatic movement, and the film-maker and his lighting are faced with yet another problem—tempo. The lighting must suit the tempo as well as the mood and atmosphere of the film. Basically, tempo is the degree of fastness or slowness of a particular scene or sequence, and that fastness or slowness can apply to the physical movement and the dramatic movement, or both. The tempo of the physical movement, then, is the swiftness or slowness with which the actions are carried out, while the tempo of the dramatic movement—a less tangible element—is the speed with which the dramatic narrative is brought forth to the audience. Generally, in suiting the tempo to the mood, we say that a low-key mood, and thus a low-key lighting, suggests slow physical action, while a high-key mood and its matching illumination suggest a fast tempo of physical movement. In much the same manner, slow dramatic movement will be best suited with low-key lighting, and fast-paced dramatic movement with high-key lighting.

Let us return first to the problems inherent in the tempo of physical movement. Quite obviously the swifter the physical movement of a scene, the less the time that will be devoted to that movement on the screen. Conversely, the slower the movement, the greater the amount of screen time that will be devoted to it. As a result, in a fast-paced scene the audience must perceive and understand the action at a comparable swift rate. Therefore, the main task of the lighting is to assist in this quick perception, while maintaining the ambiance of the scene whether it be low-key or high-key. This means that the scene or shot cannot be brilliantly lit when the emotional atmosphere is low-key, but rather the scene must be rendered in highlights and shadows that will simplify the action and make it readily perceivable by the spectator. In Stanley Kubrick's *Paths of Glory* there is a short scene in which three men are sent out on a night patrol to scout the enemy stronghold. As the three men make their way across no man's land, its barbed-wire fences and shell holes, the audience can easily perceive the action because of the highlights and shadows falling across the terrain. At the point where the spectator's keen perception is paramount—when the leader turns coward, throws a grenade that kills one of his own men, and runs away deserting the third—Kubrick adds brilliant light to the scene by having a flare explode overhead. Thus the ambiance of the scene is maintained and sufficient light is provided for the audience to witness and grasp the action.

On the other hand, the problem of immediate audience perception is not so acute in the slow-paced and somber scene. What we might call the lighting "tempo" can likewise be slowed down and thus become more complex. A scene in F. W. Murnau's *The Last Laugh* is an excellent example of this lighting concept. An old man returns late at night to the lavish hotel where he is employed to return the doorman's greatcoat which he has stolen. He makes his way to the long darkened hallway leading to the offices and storeroom of the hotel. The lighting of this hallway is extremely low-key and the movements of the old man are in silhouette. The old man hears a noise and flattens himself against the wall. A slowly swinging beam of light comes into view at one end of the hallway. Back and forth the light swings as it comes nearer and nearer to where the old man is hiding in fear of discovery. Finally, the swinging light comes to rest on the face of the old man, and we see that the beam of light is from the flashlight of his friend, the nightwatchman. Murnau has not only preserved but heightened the atmosphere, movement, and composition while using a more complex pattern of lighting that is compatible to the physical tempo of the scene. The swinging light beam punctuates that tempo.

But what if the film-maker must maintain a low-key atmosphere while at the same time creating a sense of rapid and precise movement? The low-key would seem to cancel out any projection of precision in the movement and would tend to make rapidity impossible. If the film-maker employs parallel planes of light and shadow across the scene, he will not only maintain the low-key but also accentuate the movement and thus heighten the tempo. Examples of this solution abound in war films, adventure films, and Westerns. The hero and his band are making a night attack on the enemy. As they move through the forest or the jungle, the beams of light from the moon pass through the branches of the trees, creating those necessary planes of light and shadow so that the audience can perceive their maneuvers as they approach the enemy. When the attack begins, the moonlight is then aided and abetted by the light from fires and bomb blasts of the attack to again create the planes of shadow and light. Thus the film-maker has created the mood and enhanced the tempo, as well as provided enough illumination for the witnessing of the action. Scenes with an atmosphere that require high-key lighting create few perception problems for the audience. The bright illumination can only contribute to the physical tempo, unless it is static. When this is the case, the dramatic tempo is usually of prime importance.

Fig. 3–6 *Paths of Glory*, released by United Artists, © Harris-Kubrick Pictures Corp., 1957

Fig. 3–7 *In Cold Blood*, Columbia Pictures

Let us look at the problems inherent in lighting for dramatic tempo. Since, as we have indicated, dramatic tempo does not necessarily correspond to physical tempo, it would not be inconceivable to have a scene overflowing with dramatic movement and have only a minimum of physical movement taking place, or vice versa. In such cases the film-maker would generally design his lighting to heighten the dramatic tempo.

To exemplify our case of rapid-paced dramatic action and a minimum of physical action, let us return to Kubrick's *Paths of Glory* (Fig. 3.6). The court-martial scene has a swiftly-paced dramatic tempo. Following the general rule cited earlier, the lighting should be bright, high-key. What does Kubrick do? He bathes the entire scene with sunlight flooding through the great glass windows lining the walls of the enormous room of the castle. Yet the movement of the scene is nearly static; the officers defending and prosecuting the three soldiers being unjustly tried for cowardice in battle carry out what movement there is. High-key lighting has also provided a heavy, dramatic mood when necessary. An identical procedure is used in the courtroom scene of *In Cold Blood* (Fig. 3.7).

In conclusion, we can best suit the physical tempo of a scene by manipulating the brilliance of parts of the predominant visual key, and we can suit the dramatic tempo by manipulating the overall tone of the visual key.

However, we hasten to point out that none of the effects lighting of which we have been speaking should be incorporated into a film if it might destroy the visual unity and coherence of the production. Any type of lighting must be chosen for its place within the scope of the whole film. The truth of the matter is, some scenes do lend themselves to effect lighting, and it can be tempting; we repeat, however, you cannot think only of the individual scene but of how that scene will fit with what comes before and after it.

LIGHTING TERMINOLOGY

Have you ever found yourself in a situation where you had to buy or rent technical equipment without knowing the technical terminology? Too many film-makers have not the slightest acquaintance with lighting terminology. The President of the Berkey-ColorTran Corporation has told us that one of the most difficult problems he has to contend with is the lack of understanding by clients of simple lighting terms.

LAMP   This is the element placed inside a lighting instrument to create the light rays. It is *not* a "bulb." The bulb is the glass casing that surrounds the filament.

CANDLE   The candle is the fundamental unit of light intensity. It is used as the measure of the ability of a source to radiate light. A source that can cast illumination on an object at a given distance to the same degree as would a standard candle is said to have an intensity of one candle. A standard candle is a ⅞ inch sperm candle.

FOOTCANDLE   This term is applied to an arbitrary standard measure of light intensity. It measures the amount of light that falls on a surface that is one foot from a source of one candlepower.

CANDLEPOWER   Candlepower is also a term used in the measurement of light intensity. It is that intensity expressed in candles. A certain instrument, for example, may have a candlepower of 60,000 candles. Essentially, it is the light-emitting power of a source.

LUMEN   The lumen is the measure of an amount of light. It measures the rate at which light is emitted or received. One lumen is equal to one footcandle of light covering an area of one square foot. Therefore, the lumen measures the flow of light from the source of one candlepower to the area of one square foot. To find the total lumens covering a certain area, take the measure of the illumination in footcandles (given by your light meter) and multiply it by the area measured in square feet.

BRIGHTNESS   When determining the light-emitting power per unit of area, we are measuring the brightness of a source. Two different sources can have the same candlepower yet differ in size. The smaller of the two sources is then said to be brighter. The brightness of a source is expressed in "candles per unit area." When we measure both the candlepower and the brightness of a source in all directions, together they will provide us with the complete specifications of a particular light source.

FOOT-LAMBERT   The foot-lambert is very important for it is the measure of reflected light seen by the camera lens. The foot-lambert is a unit of photometric brightness which is usually used to render the amount of light per area reflected from an object, or, in the case of projection, the light per area that is reflected from the screen. A perfectly reflecting surface that reflects light at the rate of one lumen per square foot is said to have a brightness of one foot-lambert in every direction.

LUX   Lux is the photometric term that is used internationally in place of footcandle. It represents a meter-candle. 10.764 lux equal one footcandle, but the number is usually expressed in round numbers, so one footcandle equals 10.8 lux.

TUNGSTEN-HALOGEN   This is a new term slowly coming into general use as the name for the recently developed type of light source (Fig. 3.8) that is commonly called quartz-iodine or tungsten-iodine. When this new source was placed on the market it employed a quartz envelope with a small amount of iodine gas inside—hence, quartz-iodine lamp. However, today tungsten-halogen is a better term because elements other than quartz and halogen gases other than iodine are now being used. These new sources are more compact and a great deal more efficient throughout their life because of the new tungsten-halogen cycle. A halogen gas—chlorine, bromine, fluorine, or iodine—is sealed inside of an envelope made of a substance that has a high melting point and a low coefficient of expansion, such as quartz, so that the heat does not cause it to crack. The filament, because of the qualities of the envelope can be positioned closer to this bulb wall and, therefore, can permit a hotter filament in a more compact envelope. The lamp is more efficient because it is self-cleaning through a regenerative process which eliminates the blackening of the bulb wall which reduces the efficiency. The tungsten particles which evaporate from the filament, and would be deposited on the glass wall and cause blackening, are combined with the halogen gas. The particles are then redeposited back on the filament and the halogen gas is then released. As a result of this regenerative process, the lamp has good lumen and color temperature maintenance throughout its life.

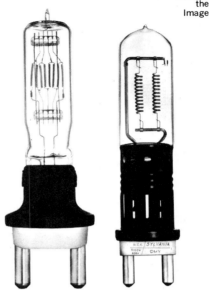

Fig. 3–8   Bardwell and McAlister's 2000w and 500w tungsten-halogen lamps

LIGHTING THE SCENE

To say that on the following pages we can provide you with a foolproof process to follow consistently in setting your lights would not only be an error, it would be most presumptuous on our part. The first thing you must learn is that there are no hard and fast rules for setting lights. What you do will not only be different for each film, it will be different for each shot. The only true rule, if it can be called that, is to know what you want to express visually and utilize the lights to enhance and contribute to that visual expression.

There are basic elements that the film-maker should master and utilize, just as there are specific tools—the lighting instruments—that you should experiment with and learn to use properly. We can provide you with the basic elements, but the experimentation and proper usage will come only from the experience of doing.

Generally, the lighting you will be involved with need not be highly elaborate or complex; however, this does not mean that it can be passed over. People have become conditioned to the technical excellence of the theatrical film and they expect to see the same excellence in any film they view. You cannot achieve any semblance of this excellence without the use of first-rate lighting.

The equipment you need is readily available from any equipment rental service, but how you use it is dependent upon your grasp of certain basics and your creative ability. If you choose your equipment carefully, utilize your imagination, and take care to balance the lighting, you should end up with results that will satisfy the expectations of your audience.

Until a few years ago, the problems of lighting for the nontheatrical film were sizable, mainly because of the bulky, complicated equipment necessary. Since the development of the tungsten-halogen light source, lighting units are more convenient to handle, more compact, mobile, and simplified, but high in output. At the same time, better light controls and accessories are also available. These developments are of particular importance to the nontheatrical film-maker for they allow him to be more flexible and effective. The nontheatrical producer tends to utilize real places in making his films. These new light sources are most compatible with this practice. In fact, the trend of making films in real places seems to be growing rapidly in the area of theatrical films also, a development made possible by the invention of the tungsten-halogen lamp.

Lighting "Rules"

The first "rule" that any film-maker should learn, remember, and put into practice is *never state what you can imply*. This applies to lighting just as it applies to every other aspect of production. James Wong Howe, the noted cinematographer, has said, "I think that sometimes we should merely suggest things, rather than to say directly. Then you make the audience work a little harder—try to see a little more—and I think they appreciate it."[1] Mr. Howe further provides us an example of this philosophy in what he calls "lost and found lighting." In lighting an object such as the head, Mr. Howe does not always light it fully, providing a complete view of the face and the outline of the head. Instead, he lights enough to partially illuminate the object and provide clues as to its total shape, and lets the audience fill in the remainder of the shape in their imaginations. (An example of this technique can be seen in Conrad Hall's lighting in Fig. 3.1.)

A second "rule" to put into practice when lighting for realism is that the lighting for every shot should look natural to the situation and be in key with the subject. The lighting should be set so that the illumination of the scene is coming from the apparent light source in the setting—sunlight or moonlight through the window if the scene is an interior, a chandelier from overhead, a table lamp sitting nearby, a streetlamp. This "rule" is based upon good old-fashioned common sense. The lighting source of the scene should be the first consideration of the film-maker in planning his lights.

The best source of knowledge in determining the lighting of a scene is nature itself. Observe is the key word in learning to light. Observe how light falls from the chandelier, the table lamp, the sun, the streetlamp. Then attempt to duplicate these patterns, while at the same time providing enough illumination for a proper exposure and for the perception of the action by the audience. The sun provides the key, for most of our artificial illumination in life is patterned after the sun. Are not our lamps, chandeliers, streetlamps, etc., placed above us so that their rays fall in a pattern similar to that of the sun? If we observe the light from the sun, we will see that as the rays of light reach the earth's atmosphere, part of the rays are diffused and part of them will continue on and strike the object we are viewing. The diffused rays will provide the light that surrounds the object and fills in many of the shadows. When we utilize manmade light, that illumination should simulate the light of nature. If the sun's rays are strong enough, they may be sufficient for our purposes. When they are not, we provide additional direct sun rays and additional fill light in the way we set our lighting units. In doing this, we must then consider the angle and the elevation of the main source—the sun in this case—and duplicate this angle and elevation in the positioning of our instruments. The same procedure follows with any light source other than the sun.

Since no light source in the world emits its rays in a constant, never-changing pattern, by following nature and duplicating its lighting, we have an endless variety of lighting patterns from which to choose. We must consider the object to be lighted, the general mood of the scene, the psychological implications of the scene, and then turn to nature for the patterns to employ as the basis of our lighting plan.

The third "rule" to follow is to plan the lighting of the film well in advance of production. The need to plan fully in advance cannot be overstressed. Such planning facilitates the speed and efficiency of filming by bringing up aesthetic and technical problems at a time when they can be efficiently overcome.

Each scene of a film will have a prevailing mood and tempo. As we have already discovered, the light can provide invaluable assistance in the capturing of this mood and tempo, but this assistance is more certainly achieved if the lighting is planned in advance. Even more important, the mood and tempo of the lighting of each scene must be compatible with the overall production style of the film. The lighting of each scene must fit with that of the scenes that come before and those that follow. In short, the film must have visual and dramatic unity. Hence the plan of the lighting must be compatible with that unity. Again, only lighting planned in advance can assure the film-maker of such unity.

Since film is predominantly a visual medium, the ability of our audience to perceive the action is of paramount importance. When the film-maker can compare his plan of the actions of the film with the plan of the lighting, he will be able to adjust one to fit the other for the best possible visual expression for the purpose of his film.

The best of creative ideas can be ruined because the film-maker has neglected to plan out the technical aspects involved in bringing the ideas to fruition. Since the lighting is one very important factor in accomplishing this, it must be pre-planned. Too many technical considerations are involved to leave it until the last minute.

Since the film-maker will more than likely be renting most, if not all, of the equipment he will need, he must have a light plan revealing just what his needs will be. Do not wait until you are on your way to

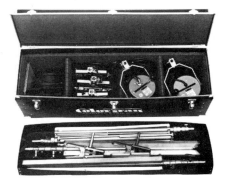

Fig. 3-9　Compact lighting equipment in travel case

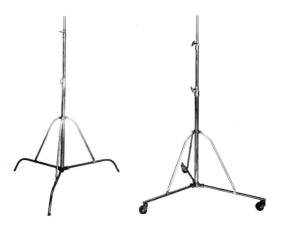

Fig. 3-10　Stands and (below) stand and boom arm

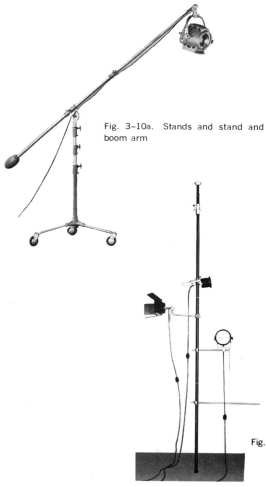

Fig. 3-10a.　Stands and stand and boom arm

Fig. 3-11　ColorTran's Pole King

the filming location to stop and rent your lighting equipment. Reserve this equipment in advance so that you will not be disappointed at the last moment because it is not available. To be involved in shooting and discover that you do not have the piece of equipment that you need to light the scene can be frustrating. Only with thorough pre-planning will you know in advance the type and quantity of equipment that is needed to achieve the visualization of your script and expose the type of film you have selected.

Most professional cameramen prefer to work at a certain f/stop, particularly when filming indoors. They select the most effective diaphragm opening of the particular lenses they will be using, and the diaphragm opening that will provide the depth of field required. This necessitates sufficient equipment to maintain the proper light level for that opening. For the best exposure results and the best matching of takes, we recommend you follow this lead of the professionals and adopt this practice also. Therefore, this is another aspect to keep in mind in drawing up your light plans.

Pre-planning the lights will also indicate to the film-maker the size of the crew that will be necessary. Select too many people and you have wasted valuable money in wages and cluttered the set with unnecessary personnel. Hire too few, and you will have to hold up filming to set the lights. This can be far costlier in time and money than the wages of one more lighting assistant. Many professionals do not appreciate it when they must do the work of two. Thus the effectiveness of this person is greatly reduced because he is mentally upset and because he is physically tired from having to do too much.

Knowing the filming location and the lighting requirements, the film-maker can determine the amount of floor space needed for his lighting equipment and whether he will have that floor space available. Do not wait until you are at the location to discover that if you set up the necessary equipment, you will have no room for the camera or the action that is to be photographed. Your lighting plan should take these factors into consideration. If the floor space is inadequate, different arrangements may be possible, but they may require additional equipment that must be planned for. Can you imagine the frustration of planning to place your instruments on floor stands and finding that there is no room for them? Other means of support—such as a Pole King (Fig. 3.11)—are available, but they must be included in your equipment needs.

All lighting equipment requires some type of power supply in order to operate. The film-maker must know if there is a power source available to him, what type of source, and the location of that source. If none is available, he must supply his own. I know of a film-maker who was to shoot a sequence on a street corner in New York City. He scouted the location and discovered that there was a shop on that corner from which he could run a power cable that would provide him with A.C. power. He then selected lighting equipment, sound equipment, and a camera motor that would run off of A.C. power. He arrived at the site with equipment, crew, and cast to find that the shop was closed for vacation. That wasted day was quite costly. This was a foolish mistake that could have been avoided had he thought to talk to the shop owner while scouting the location. This foolish film-maker would have avoided his mistake also had he brought along an A.C. generator, or had he selected battery-powered equipment. At the same time the film-maker discovers what power supply he has available to him, he should discover the location of that source so that he can determine his cable requirements. What good is the power supply if it is too far away to reach?

Lastly, by knowing the location and its requirements, the equipment and its requirements, the script and its requirements, the film-maker will be able to determine what lighting controls he will need. Will the aesthetic and technical requirements necessitate the use of a dimmer board? If so, he will need the board, the power to run it, the cable to connect it, and a crew member to operate it. Knowing what he will require of his instruments will tell him what accessories he will need to control their light, such as scrims, barn doors, cookies, dots, flags, etc. Knowing the location and the instruments to be used in lighting the site will tell the film-maker what he will need to control the light of that environment—overhead scrims to control sunlight, sheets of filter to control color temperature when filming color, antireflectance spray to tone down light bounce from objects within the environment (Fig. 3.12), Windex to clean a dirty window, etc. Without pre-planning, the film-maker will be prepared for none of this.

Fig. 3-12 Applying anti-reflectance spray to the background to tone down unwanted light bounce (Richard C. Tomkins)

Setting the Lights

When at the filming site, the lighting plan will serve as the basic guide as to the aesthetic requirements of the scene—whether the lighting should be basically low-key or high-key. Generally, whoever is setting the lights (in professional production this falls into the bailiwick of the cameraman) will familiarize himself with the lighting plan, the action that has been blocked out by the director, and the camera angle. The proper atmosphere must be created and the action must be properly recorded by the camera—very important considerations in how to set the lights. A run-through of the action of the scene should be carried out so that the lighting man will have a full picture of the demands to be made of the lighting. Now the lights can be set. Their setting-up should be directed from the viewpoint of the camera.

KEY LIGHT

As we mentioned in the beginning of this chapter, the light must be built up for a scene. The key light is the first to be set for it is the *key* to our plan. This key light provides the illumination that is supposedly coming from the principle source in the environment. The basic exposure setting will be determined from the key light, no matter how much other light is thrown on the setting. As the names suggest, high-key and low-key determine the effect strived for; therefore, the key determines the f/stop. Once the intensity of this light is determined, it remains the same throughout the sequence within that setting. This intensity is usually determined by the mood of the scene, the size of the setting, and the ability of the subject or the cast to work under lights for an extended period of time.

The position and angle of the key light is important. The most favorable angle of light for facial features is from three-quarters front, one side or the other. Normally the key light is placed at that angle unless the main source or some other factor dictates another angle. The key can be positioned, if so dictated, from straight in front to directly behind the subject. It is not uncommon to place the key light directly in front of the subject's face on close-ups—especially when the subject is female—in order to smooth out and beautify the face. However, the shape of the face should be considered before this approach is used.

The next step is to measure the footcandles by placing an incident light meter in front of the subject's face, pointing toward the key light. If the lamp is too bright, it is flooded the necessary amount (if the unit has a flood control), or the lamp is backed away the necessary distance, or a scrim is placed in front of the light until the desired reading is achieved. If the light is not bright enough, any of the above procedures is reversed.

When shooting outdoors during daylight, the key light will come from the direct sun rays. On overcast days, it may be necessary to supplement the sunlight with artificial light. In such a case the lighting unit is placed at the same angle as the sun, and its intensity is controlled in the same way as outlined above. Another technique that may be used is to position reflectors which will bounce additional sunlight into the places desired.

How large an instrument to be used as the key light will be determined by the mood of the scene, the brightness indicated by the source, the working aperture favored by the cameraman, and whether the production is being shot in black-and-white or color. Various types of key lights are available in a variety of sizes. They are a form of spotlight and produce a strong highlight that creates well-defined shadows. For small-scale production, close-ups, small settings, or low-key scenes, the smaller units are sufficient. The greater the intensity or the larger the area to cover, the larger the instrument needed. Never try to increase the intensity by using two smaller lights. The main source of illumination in any normal locale comes from only one source. Use two spots and you cast double shadows, a very unnatural phenomenon.

FILL LIGHT

The fill light is the next to be set. The fill light is the illumination that sets the mood of the scene and controls contrast by filling in the shadowed areas created by the key light. The intensity of the fill light is determined by the dramatic effect desired and is in direct proportion to that of the key light. The fill light is a diffused light that is placed at the subject's eye level. This placement will allow the light to fill in any harsh shadows that might exist about the eyes, nose, and throat.

The lighting ratio is the relationship of the key light plus the fill light to the fill light alone. The lighting ratio must be computed in this manner because the brightest area will be where the key and the fill overlap. The film-maker establishes his lighting mood and controls the contrasts of light and shadow by adjusting the lighting ratio. If the key light and the fill light are equal in intensity, this is a ratio of two to one (2 = key + fill 1 = fill alone). Such a lighting ratio is very bright and is what we have classified earlier as high-key lighting. The scene is nearly devoid of shadow. High-key does not, of course, necessitate this low a ratio. It merely requires less contrast between key and fill. Filming with color film also requires a low lighting ratio. Generally, color film is not exposed with a lighting ratio exceeding three to one, unless special effects are required or the filming takes place under unusual circumstances.

Obviously low-key lighting requires a much greater contrast ratio. An eight to one ratio, for example, creates a very dark, nightlike atmosphere. Naturally, the higher the ratio the more contrast there will be in the scene due to the lack of fill light to illuminate the shadowed areas. This ratio also determines the brightness range that the film will reproduce—one other reason why higher ratios are impossible when shooting color. Color film has less latitude than black-and-white, and, therefore, in high ratio scenes the highlights are burned out and the shadows are black.

In order to be accurate in determining the overall contrast of a scene, the reflectance ratio of the subject as well as the lighting contrast ratio must be considered. The reflectance ratio is dependent upon the physical nature of the subject or subjects being photographed. A woman in a white blouse and a dark skirt can reflect as much as six times the amount of light off the blouse as off the skirt. Therefore, the reflectance ratio is six to one. The lighting contrast, therefore, must be governed by the subject contrast. Generally, if the subject contrast is low, a higher lighting ratio can be used. If the subject contrast is high, the reverse is in order.

The lighting ratio may be measured in footcandles, when artificial light is used, or in f/stops. Place an incident light meter where the key and fill overlap, and take a reading. Then adjust the fill light until the desired ratio is reached. If, in achieving the desired ratio, the fill lights are greatly changed, it may be wise to recheck the key-plus-fill reading since it may differ from the first reading.

Obviously indoors it is a relatively easy matter to arrive at a lighting ratio because of the control over the intensity of the lights. In exterior shooting such contrast lighting is frequently ignored. It can be achieved through the use of reflectors or booster lights. The key reflector or booster is positioned in the same angle and direction as the source light, and the fill reflector or booster is placed in the same position that it would be placed on an interior set—at eye level. It is wise *not* to ignore the lighting ratio for exterior shooting if you are to obtain consistent results throughout the production of a film.

Special lighting units are available for use as fill lights, such as ColorTran's Mini-Lite. Such units should project a broad, diffused beam

Fig. 3–13a   Key light only

Fig. 3–13b   Fill light only

Fig. 3–13c   Key and Fill light

of light. "Softlights," scoop lights or pan lights fitted with diffusers generally work best as fill lights. Size again depends upon the intensity that will be required of the instrument.

BACKLIGHT AND KICKER LIGHT

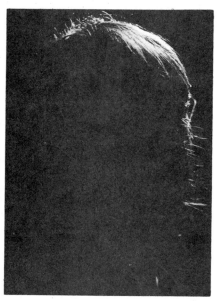

Fig. 3–13d Kicker light only

If your lighting is going to aid in providing a three-dimensional image on the screen, you will need to place instruments that will provide depth to the lighting. The backlight and kicker are used to highlight the subject and to provide the necessary depth. These lights and their modeling effect will also serve to separate the subject from the background.

The backlight is positioned opposite the camera and above and behind the subject. The kicker is placed directly opposite the subject from the key light. Spotlights are mostly used because their beam can be controlled.

These sources require considerable control because of their position, and because without control they interfere with the key and fill lights due to the shadows they throw. Their position places them—especially the backlight—in direct line with the lens, so care must be exercised to shadow the beam out of the lens. Therefore, careful barndooring and goboing is essential. With these control devices the lens can be shielded from the light and the shadows thrown by these units can be shaded off by limiting the light to the subject, allowing none of it to spill onto the floor. The only shadows that can be allowed are those from the key light because it represents the natural illumination in the environment. At the same time, allowing the backlight and kicker light to spill onto the floor might illuminate the floor brighter than the subjects in the frame. This, of course, would be most distracting and must be avoided.

BACKGROUND LIGHT

Fig. 3–13e Background light only

Special illumination of the background is generally necessary, although there are times when the lighting for the subject will provide most of the illumination of the background also. Background lights are separate instruments set up for the express purpose of lighting only the background. The advantage of using separate background light is that careful control of the contrast ratio between the subject and the background is possible. If the key and fill lights serve this function, it is difficult to control the value of the background. The use of such instruments also allows for visually interesting treatments of the elements that make up the background. These instruments are set in their patterns and then usually remain in these positions throughout the shooting in that environment.

The brightness of the background will depend upon the mood and the general key light that is already established for the scene. In high-key scenes the background is often brighter than the key light falling on the subjects, while in low-key scenes it may be barely discernible, limited to lighting which accents only certain elements of the background, letting the rest go dark. The basic purpose of any type of background light is, of course, to make the set look realistic and to provide an interesting pattern behind the subject of the scene.

Background light is usually provided by instruments set up out of the camera's range. However, with the development of the tungsten-halogen lamps, it is possible—because of the compactness of these units and their high intensity—to secrete these instruments within the setting that is within the range of the camera's view. They can easily be hidden behind furniture and such elements when the scene is located within very close quarters. In the studio the background lighting is generally mounted above and aimed down at the set. Such an arrangement is naturally beneficial since it eliminates instruments within the set that can clutter needed floor space and, because the light is aimed down from above, unnecessary shadows are eliminated. Wherever the background lighting is positioned, it should appear to originate from a natural source, such as light through a window, or any normal illumination visible to the camera's view, like a lamp. For example, if an illuminated table lamp is in view of the camera, the background behind the lamp should be lighted with a spot light to simulate the effect on the wall of the burning lamp. Care should be taken after the background lights are set to tone down any reflectance from objects within the background that might be distracting to the viewer. A special aerosol spray is available which works most efficiently and is unharmful to the finish of any object.

Fig. 3–13f All lights (Mel Wittenstein)

The key, fill, back, kicker, and background lights, when properly placed and adjusted, provide the illumination necessary for the scene, help in establishing the mood, provide a sense of depth to the scene, and allow for the movement that is so vital to film. Such a lighting arrangement should not only affect the appearance of the subjects but keep them lit throughout the movements they will carry out. When a character, for example, turns his face away from the key light, the kicker will take over the illumination of the face and the key will serve as a modeling light. Thus the mood, etc., is maintained as is the necessary illumination of the subject. Great care must be taken to achieve the proper balance of the various instruments. By losing the preconceived balance of the lighting plan through over-lighting in one area, you can change the emotional effect of the lighting. Remember, each light used must have a value and a function in the scene being shot. Never turn on a light and leave it on without justifying its function in each scene in which it is used.

Fig. 3–14 ColorTran Quartz King spotlights—650w, 1000w, 500w

Control Devices and their Use

Even in the most routine film assignment, the need to control the light that is projected from the instruments is vital. As we have mentioned earlier, this control is of particular importance in the setting of the backlight and the kicker light, but it can also be most important in the handling of the fill, background, and key lights.

BARNDOORS

With the older fresnel lens-type of spotlights, barndooring was an effective means of controlling the edges of the light beam emitted from the instrument. Barndoors are still useful with the new tungsten-halogen

Fig. 3-15 Bardwell and McAlister's
Baby Keg spotlight

Fig. 3-16 Bardwell and McAlister's
Tiny Mac spotlight

units but are not quite as effective. Barndoors are hinged wings mounted onto a frame thin enough to slip into the gel-holder flanges which are a part of the front assembly of lighting instruments. They are available with two and four doors. When slipped into the gel-holders, they control the edge of the beam of light by the opening or closing of the hinged doors. The edges of the light beam will, of course, strike these doors and thereby cast a shadow, since these doors serve as an obstruction for the light beam. When these barndoors are used with the old fresnel spots, they control the beam by casting a definite, soft-edged shadow. In actuality, there is no sharp change from one light level to shadowed light level; instead, there is a relatively narrow area in which the light level changes from one level to the other. Of course, the narrower the flood setting of the spot, the more precise this region becomes. Therefore, by widening the flood setting so that the beam is more diffused, the more effective the barndoors will be because the shadow edge will be softer, more diffused. As a result of this effect, barndoors have little or no use when an instrument is focused at "spot."

The main purpose of the barndoor is to control the extraneous, unneeded light. This is a needed control, since in the lighting of a scene the act of not lighting is just as important as the act of lighting. Generally then, barndoors are used to achieve the following effects: (1) to limit the area illuminated by a specific instrument or, to be more specific, not lighting part of the area; (2) to prevent the light beam from a unit from passing into the lens—the problem mentioned earlier in regard to the backlight; (3) to eliminate a microphone boom shadow by shading out the boom shadow through the elimination of the light causing the shadow; and (4) to control the light beam by forming a light-shadow line that will blend with scenery or some other architectural element.

SNOOTS

Snoots are another device which can be mounted on the front of a spotlight in order to concentrate the light and eliminate spillage. They resemble a top hat with a square brim and with a hole in the top. It is a tubelike shape that allows for the control of the light beam. Snoots are made in a variety of sizes from about a one-inch diameter to an eight-inch diameter or more.

FLAGS, DOTS, GOBOS

These are devices of varying sizes and shapes which are employed to control the beam of light. Generally these devices provide sharp light-to-shadow transitions and should be used when this is the effect desired. The type and degree of control they provide is very limited.

DIFFUSERS

A variety of diffusers are available which are mounted in the flanges on the front of spotlights. Spots, as we have said, project a focused beam of light that casts a sharply defined shadow. Diffusers are used to modify the beam and thus break up the sharp shadows. They are available in a variety of materials. Some are made of silk, others of celloglass or frosted gelatin. This type of diffuser breaks up the beam from the filament radiating over the surface of the material of the diffuser, and it is projected as a diffused light that casts a much softer shadow line. Other diffusers are made of scrims or nets and have no altering effect on the beam from the source but merely reduce the amount of light from the lighting units.

Fig. 3-17 Bardwell and McAlister's Big 10kw spotlight

CUKALORIS

The cukaloris is more commonly referred to as the "cookie" and is a shadow device that is used to break up the flat light that can fall across large masses of wall area, etc., making it a valuable device for controlling background and set lighting.

The cookie is a panel that usually measures approximately sixteen by twenty inches. It can be made from any rigid or semirigid material that is opaque or at least semiopaque. Such materials as cardboard and hardboard have been used but cast very definite shadows. Panels of celloglass or fiberglass create a much softer pattern of light and shadow.

When you have decided upon the type of shadow pattern, definite or diffused, the proper material is selected and then perforations or cut-outs are made in the material irregularly. Above all, refrain from any established pattern. If you do not wish to make your own cookie, commercially-made die-cut units are available.

The cookie is used by placing it some distance between the light unit and the object being illuminated. The light and shadow pattern can be regulated by moving it nearer to or farther from the lighting unit. The type of instrument with which it is used will also have some effect upon the pattern of the cookie. A spotlight and its sharply focused beam will cast a much more sharply defined light and shadow pattern than will a flood lamp. The cookie is a more aesthetically pleasing way to tone down large expanses of wall, for example, with its mottled effect than merely giving the wall an overall dark tone.

Fig. 3-18 Bardwell and McAlister's Foco spot

SCRIMS

Scrims of various sizes are generally carried when shooting on exterior location; they are used to subdue light. Black scrim is sometimes placed over objects which reflect too much light into the lens. Still other scrims —blue scrims—can be stretched behind the foreground of a scene to create an atmospheric haze in the distance. This practice will diminish the background and create a sense of greater distance. White scrims are used in the same manner to create fog or mist effects. Some sort of backlighting is used in either of the above cases to control the desired effect.

Large overhead scrims can be used to subdue the intensity of sunlight hitting the subjects of the scene. These scrims soften the effect of the harsh light on the faces of the subjects. The scrim is stretched onto a frame that can be placed onto a large stand or, in the case of the smaller ones, can be attached to a pole that is held by some member of the crew.

Fig. 3-19 Bardwell and McAlister's 2kw, 5kw, 10kw spotlights

Fig. 3-20 ColorTran's softlight

In the studio, large scrims are seldom required; instead, smaller versions, usually two by three feet, are used. These are called suitcases and again are used to control the density of the light or to soften a light pattern. These suitcases are also generally placed on stands and interposed between the light source and the subjects.

The main function of the scrim is to cut the intensity of the light by 30 percent (single scrim) or 50 percent (double scrim). A scrim tends to diffuse the light slightly but not effectively. Again, its prime function is to cut intensity without the use of a dimmer or without changing a spot light to "flood" position.

Any of these scrims should be constantly checked for their condition. They tend to burn or discolor when placed too near a light source. This same sort of discoloration results with age. When in this condition they will affect the color of the light and should be replaced. In the case of the metal scrims, they tend to discolor and rust, especially in the center, where they have been chiefly exposed to the heat of the light beam.

GEL

Colored gelatin is used to alter the color quality of a beam of light from an instrument. It is available in sheets and can be cut to fit into special gel frames that slide into the flanges found on the front of lighting units.

UMBRELLA LIGHT

This is an arrangement made up of an actual umbrella and a tungsten-halogen light. The umbrella is made of a white mylar base material and is stretched over an aluminum frame. It is the same weight and construction of a normal umbrella, except its handle is adjustable and is constructed so that it can be mounted on some type of support. A tungsten-halogen lamp is mounted on the handle with the lamp pointing up at the inside of the umbrella.

The major use of this arrangement is to provide a soft light, a north sky quality, or a shadowless light source. It is frequently used to simulate a window light source because the light projected from the umbrella has a "wrap-around" quality.

CAMERA-MOUNTED FILL LIGHT

By attaching a metal bar to the top of a camera, a fill light can be mounted onto the camera and moved with that camera. This is a practice that has been followed in Hollywood for many years and is slowly finding its way into other areas of film production. Its use is similar to that of the camera-mounted flash bulb in still photography. The light emitted serves the same purpose as any fill light, namely to wash out shadowed areas, but this camera-mounted fill can be especially useful with close-in shots or with moving camera shots. To set up floor lamps that provide satisfactory illumination is virtually impossible when the camera must move; the camera-mounted fill solves the problem because the light travels with the camera. Care must be exercised in the use of this type of fill light also. When fill light is overdone, the contrast between the highlights (key lighted) and the shadows (fill lighted) becomes so negligible that the result is a flat picture.

The dimmer board came to film with the advent of sound. After sound became a part of film production, the use of multiple cameras on the set to cover the action from different angles became widespread. As a result of this practice, takes were longer and the subjects moved much more freely within the setting. At the same time, sound brought stage-trained actors to film, and they were accustomed to more freedom of movement. Therefore, because of these new factors, dimmer boards were incorporated for a more precise and flexible control of lights.

By attaching the instruments lighting a scene to a dimmer board, the light intensity of each instrument can be individually controlled by an operator manipulating the controls of the dimmer board. Take for example a scene in which a subject at the back of a room slowly walks toward the camera. It is essential that the key light falling on this character remain approximately at the same level of intensity on the subject. However, without dimmer control, as the subject walks toward the camera, the closer he comes to the key light the more intense the light on the subject will become. When a dimmer is attached to the lamp, the intensity can be decreased accordingly, keeping the intensity on the subject the same. However, dimmers can be a problem when shooting color film for the dimmer affects the color temperature of the lamp. When the dimmer setting is lowered the light gets redder.

DIMMERS

Fig. 3-21 Bardwell and McAlister's Indirect Light

REFLECTORS

Reflectors are used not only to control light, but also to provide light in exterior shooting. Many cameramen dislike the look of obviously artificial light when filming in natural locations so they resort to the use of reflectors. When reflectors are used as the source of lighting, they are placed in approximately the same positions as are artificial lights. Elevated reflectors are used for key and backlights and reflectors positioned at a lower angle are used as fill light.

The normal use of reflectors is to fill in unwanted shadow area with light reflected from the surface of the reflector. However, never place these reflectors on the ground since light seldom originates from the ground.

Reflectors can be purchased or constructed by the film-maker. The simplest form of reflector can be made of a frame with oilcloth or white paper tacked to the frame. A reflector can be constructed by cutting a piece of quarter-inch plywood and painting it white or by covering it with a special reflector paper that is available. The most useful reflectors can be constructed using metal foil to cover the reflecting surface. One side can be covered with silver foil, and the other side with gold foil, since there are situations—because of color temperature—when the yellow light from the gold foil is needed.

Fig. 3-22 Colortran's Mini-Lite "6" with integral four leaf barndoor

SUN GUNS

Frequently the cameraman must use more than reflectors when shooting on location. He may find the use of artificial light necessary to accentuate or reduce the contrast of light and shade, or he may wish to highlight an important detail that might otherwise be unobserved by the audience. Perhaps one of the most useful lighting instruments for these purposes is the battery-powered Sun Gun. These units operate off of a nickel cadmium battery, are relatively lightweight and small in size, and are very versatile. They contain a beam control that permits adjustment of the beam from flood to spot or any position in between.

When shooting with available light, the use of either reflectors or artificial light or both is advised. Available light varies constantly, and the film-maker must take care to avoid an impossible problem when it comes time to match the various takes in the editing room.

USE OF LIGHT WHEN SHOOTING COLOR

Lighting for color film can be a highly complex process. When the light is flooded all over the scene, the results frequently resemble the pictures of a picture postcard—devoid of any style. This is generally not the impression the film-maker wishes to create. The pictorialist era in film-making is over. The matter of prime importance is to provide pictures which visually express the dramatic elements of the film, no matter whether the film be theatrical or nontheatrical.

One of the major contributing factors to the complexity of lighting for color is the low sensitivity of its emulsion to light. As a result, a greater amount of light is required to expose the film. The more light that is used, therefore, the less contrast that is possible. As mentioned earlier in this chapter, color film also has a narrow latitude between light and dark. Because of the narrow brightness range, care must be taken in lighting the scene to see that highlights are not burned out and shadows allowed to go to black in the final image recorded on the film. As a result, more fill light is generally used in color filming.

Fortunately, color itself is a contrast factor. The film-maker is concerned with contrast because it provides the modeling of objects in the picture, but color can serve the same purpose as light and shadow. Whenever the film-maker has a choice as to color, the right choices can help greatly in producing the necessary contrast. Michelangelo Antonioni, the noted Italian director, has been known to exercise his choice of color to the point of painting grass a different shade of green and altering the natural colors of other elements within a certain environment, and many "industrial" film directors paint walls and floors of subject factories.

Nature itself can cause problems that add to the complexity of shooting in color. The light that comes from the sky has a bluish tint, light reflected from the ground can have a brownish cast, and light reflected from leaves and foliage can have a greenish quality, and so on ad infinitum. The film-maker must control these problems caused by nature. James Wong Howe has told of the problem he faced when shooting the white-washing-the-fence sequence in *Tom Sawyer*. The white fence looked blue at the top and brown at the bottom when shot outdoors because it was reflecting the earth and sky. He felt that the whiteness of the fence was so important that the set was constructed in a studio, and the scene was shot where the color could be controlled.

Generally, however, the film-maker need not be so accurate in his color rendition. Faithful reproduction of the colors of a scene is not necessary. The audience need not see the colors as the film-maker sees them during filming, unless those colors are vital to the believability of the scene. The only things that must be reproduced faithfully are the colors of readily recognizable objects, such as the American flag, and flesh tones. Great care must be taken to shield these objects and the skin surface of the human body from unwanted color reflections.

Separating the main subject from the background is one of the major functions of lighting for black-and-white film. Many film-makers carry over this concept when shooting in color. This separation is not so vital in color filming, for as color can provide contrast, it can also provide this separation which is, to a degree, a form of contrast. As a result, less backlighting is actually necessary when shooting in color. Instead, the proper selection of colors is more important. Contrast the color of the background with the color of the object that is to be photographed in front of it, or the object will blend into that background. The value-reflectance or brightness of the background should be kept darker than the subject's skin tone.

Perhaps the most complex matter to deal with in color filming is the problem of color temperature. As we have said before, the only time color film will provide a reproduction of the scene as the eye sees it is when there is a balance in the color temperature of the film and the light source. The proper use of filters can bring about this balance.

The problem of color temperature is not so severe when shooting exteriors. Colors outdoors are constantly changing because of weather, the seasons of the year, the time of the day, and we do not expect them to constantly have the same appearance. As a result, faulty color renderings on the screen, unless too extreme, will generally go unnoticed by the audience, with the exception of the aforementioned flesh tones and recognizable objects. Reflectors are constantly used to provide or control light. If the bluish tint of skylight is needed to maintain color temperature, a reflector with a silver surface should be used. However, if it is necessary to warm the color of the light, then a reflector with a gold surface must be employed to add a yellowish tint.

The major area where color temperature control is more difficult is when shooting actual interiors. Most actual interiors contain windows which admit sunlight. Generally, however, that sunlight is not sufficient to provide the film-maker with necessary illumination for a proper exposure of the less sensitive color emulsion. Therefore artificial light must be used to provide a high enough degree of illumination. The color temperatures of sunlight and incandescent light do not match. The easiest solution to the problem is to shut out the sunlight from the windows. Notice the next commercial you see on television that is staged inside an airplane. The standard practice is to shut off the light from the windows of the aircraft by closing the sliding blinds of those windows. These small windows will normally go unnoticed by the viewer.

But how does one solve the problem when it is necessary to the believability of the scene or the action of the scene to have these windows open to the sunlight? One procedure is to use a painted flat outside the window that shuts off the light. The flat has a view of the outdoors painted on it, and lighting units are set up to simulate light coming through the window. A more satisfactory procedure is to use tungsten film and to place over these windows large sheets of 85 filter, available in thin gelatin sheets and lately in rigid plastic sheets. When the thin sheets are used, a wise procedure is to place the gel between two sheets of glass, which eliminates the crinkling of the gel. A colored dye is also available that can be sprayed onto the glass of the windows, but reports are that it is not very satisfactory because of its tendency to streak and go on uneven.* To reduce the light volume when following this procedure of covering the windows with gel, it may also be necessary to use neutral density filters with the 85 filters.

Another procedure to use to correct this color temperature problem is to use either daylight film or tungsten film with an 85 filter on the lens. Do nothing to the light coming through the windows, but instead place blue filters (MacBeth filters), or the new dichroic filters which are more efficient, over the lighting sources. The blue filters absorb a great deal of light (64 per cent), and this can cause a great deal of difficulty because of the low sensitivity of the color film. Instead of incandescent units, one could carefully use the blue (daylight) corrected photofloods that are available and thus do away with the need for filters.

Shooting inside of an automobile can cause the same problems as the previously mentioned interiors. Sunlight is flooding through the windows, yet it may not be sufficient to illuminate the action. The same choices are available. Cover the windows with 85 filter and utilize a Sun Gun or Mini-Lite inside for the extra illumination. Of course, if this procedure is followed, all of the windows of the auto must be closed. Burnett Guffey, in filming *Bonnie and Clyde*, solved the problem by ignoring the windows and using a Sun Gun with 26-Blue gelatin filter attached. This filter—though flimsy and with a tendency to fade rapidly —produces much less of a light loss than glass filters.

Another color temperature problem is faced if it is necessary to use dimmer control when shooting color. Altering the voltage of an incandescent lamp will affect the color temperature. A change of ten volts will result in a change of 100 degrees K. in the color temperature. Therefore, dimmers could be used to control color temperature, but cannot be used for effect lighting.

When a mismatch in color temperature is suspected but is not as certain as the above examples, the film-maker may find it necessary to use a color temperature meter to measure the color temperature of his light source. Such situations can develop when the accuracy of the voltage is uncertain. These meters measure the proportion of red and blue radia-

*Berkey-ColorTran is working on some new products that may soon be on the market.

tions from the light source. Several such meters are on the market and should be part of the film-maker's equipment when shooting in color.

A film-maker may find himself with a night scene. One procedure is to use high-speed film and shoot at dusk. However, using this procedure allows little time for filming and makes it difficult or impossible to achieve any balance of illumination from take to take.

SHOOTING DAY FOR NIGHT

A second, more controllable way, is to shoot day for night. Professional cinematographer Conrad Hall *(In Cold Blood, The Professionals, Cool Hand Luke)* usually employs a combination of pola-screen and graduated neutral density filters in color photography and underexposes the film 2½ stops. The pola-screen acts as a variable depth filter for that portion of the sky which is at right angles to the sun and, therefore, darkens the sky. If a great deal of panning is necessary in the scene, the pola-screen is not possible; the neutral density filter will reduce the volume of the light. He then uses backlight to separate the faces from the background. He uses little or no fill light except on close shots, and then only on the faces.[2]

Charles G. Clarke, also a professional cinematographer, puts forth a different procedure, basically for black-and-white film, in his book, *Professional Cinematography.* Mr. Clarke underexposes the film only two stops. On long shots he utilizes a red filter that turns the sky darker. However, on close or medium shots in which faces are seen, he employs a light red filter and a light green filter in combination. The light red filter produces the necessary overall correction and darkens the sky. The light green filter prevents the skin tones from being chalky white due to the light red filter. The light green filter produces very good skin tones. These two filters together have a filter factor of 10, but Clarke compensates for only a factor of 6 and thereby takes into account the necessary underexposure. Clarke further suggests the use of booster light or reflected light onto the face to reduce the contrast.[3]

Another color process of shooting day for night is to utilize tungsten film without the 85 filter, thereby providing an overall bluish tint, and underexposing 2½ stops, utilizing silver reflectors for highlights from the "moon" and gold reflections for highlights supposedly originating from fire or incandescent light of some sort. Whenever it is possible, select a location that is deep in shadows and reveals little or no sky—and shoot on an overcast day.

CHAPTER 4

INTERPRETING THE IMAGE

Throughout the ages, man has sought a means of capturing the reality surrounding him. In so doing, he proves to himself that he is in control of his chaotic environment. The caveman painted on the walls of his cave images of the beast that rivaled him for control. Even the primitive caveman realized that the beast had life and movement, and that to truly capture it he must render it in motion. His aboriginal imagination prompted him to paint the four-legged beast with eight legs, an interpretive device still used by the small child to indicate motion.

As man's science and technology grew, his need for control of life's chaos also increased, for his science and technology contributed more and more to his confusion. The same technological development provided him with what has seemed by many to be the ultimate tools for this control—the camera and its lens, the microphone, and film.

This obsession with the control of reality has led some theoreticians to erroneously look upon the camera as some kind of magic box with the power to reach out and snatch parts of the world to objectively freeze onto the emulsion of its film. But how can the camera be objective and unsullied by human hand? What it sees and records is under the total control of the one who operates it, and the operator must sift through a multiplicity of subjective choices in determining the camera's view. This operator's brain, emotions, taste, and understanding of artistic and optical principles tell him the lens, the film, the speed, the angle, the action to be selected, and even the moment the camera is to be activated. These subjective considerations deny the camera any true objectivity. The camera becomes a tool like the painter's brush to be used by the film-maker to capture and communicate his interpretation in two-dimensional sight and sound of a three-dimensional microcosm of reality which is normally measured by sight, sound, taste, smell, and touch.

Film practitioners, like these theoreticians, have been goaded by the same obsession and have sought, and still seek, to bridge the gulf between film and reality by moving the camera into "real" places to view "real" people engaged in "real" action, seemingly believing that in so doing they are truly capturing life. But to follow such a path, striving to imitate nature, is to confine oneself within enormous restrictions. The power of the film is not in its *similarity* to reality; the power is in the *differences* that exist between the two. The film world and the real world are two completely different things, and it is the differences which free the film-maker creatively. What is captured by the film-maker is something totally new. And this newborn reality is faithfully accepted by the film-viewer, who has willingly chosen to suspend his disbelief, as the true reality. It is due chiefly to the ability of the camera to isolate and enlarge small details of the real world which might otherwise be missed, to establish visual relationships between elements within the real environment so that new and deeper understanding is possible, and to control the emotional response to this reality through its limited yet limitless vision that the film-maker can re-create and communicate what he sees and feels in a way that is more meaningful than "reality."

THE MEANS OF INTERPRETATION

The film-maker must learn to use reality as a filmic device, to take elements from the real world and, by manipulating and combining them with the unique features of the film medium, give these very elements a new existence. This new existence will have the power to express and communicate not only the physical state of the real world but also the emotional and psychological implications of the subjective world.

Time and Space

Two of the most constant factors of the physical world are time and space. Space is three-dimensional and immobile. Time is measured in a never-ending chronology. But time and space share a double existence for us—the uncompromising existence of the physical world and the free existence of the mental world. Physical time-space forms a frame of reference and identification for us and has been conditioned by our physical being, our vision, and our experiences. We are imprisoned within this framework. The man standing on a street corner, faced with arriving at a certain place at an appointed time for a vital meeting, knows that he must find some means of getting to this place, for it cannot come to him. On the other hand, he also knows that the appointed time will arrive no matter what he does. He thinks, "Wouldn't it be great if I could close my eyes, concentrate on the place, and suddenly be there. But, of course, that isn't possible." He rushes into the street to flag down a taxi, reasoning that he can cover the necessary space in less time this way. But no taxis are in sight, and time is irretrievably passing. In his mind something begins to happen to the restricted space-time of his physical world because of his mental state. "How can I possibly cover all of the distance in the length of time I have?" He starts to hurry along the street, but he feels that he is moving on a treadmill, as in his mind the length of the street begins to grow and the speed of the clock increases. Thus, to him, space has expanded, while time has compressed. He quickens his pace in an attempt to overcome the restrictions imposed upon him and begins to wish that the distance he has to travel were shorter and the time longer. He begins to think, "I didn't say I would be there at exactly eleven o'clock; I said 'around' eleven." He notices a familiar landmark, and begins to convince himself that he is almost at his destination. The more he convinces himself of this, the more he fulfills the wish in his mind, until, miraculously, he begins to feel that the space is decreasing and the time expanding. Now the spatial expansion and temporal compression have reversed in his mind, but in actuality not a thing has changed—he still has the same physical space to travel in the same span of physical time. Who is to say which is more "real," the actual time and space or that in his mind?

Should the film have to function within the physical limitations of our hurrying gentleman, its power would be lost. The film's greatest asset is its ability to transcend the confines of the physical time-space continuum. So, in a sense, the time-space of the film world is artificial. Film space is two-dimensional, lacking weight, depth, tangibility, and a continuous presence, but, at the same time, it is mobile and capable of alterations that are impossible in our physical world. Time can be compressed, extended, broken, and frozen. We have seen such spatial and temporal freedom in the mind of the gentleman rushing to his appointment. This freedom is possible because time and space have that second existence mentioned earlier—the liberated existence of the mental world. The film must function within the latitude of the mental concept. In our minds, thoughts, and dreams, time and space are bent to our whim and we are whisked on some kind of magic carpet from place to place by our imagination.

The same magic carpet carries us through the space of the film world as the film-maker cuts from shot to shot or moves his camera from place to place. In the wink of an eye the film-maker, by joining two pieces of film together, carries the spectator from one environment to another, or from one location within a particular place to another location within that same place. By cutting from a long shot to a medium shot or a close shot, the film-maker whisks you through space just as the spectator compresses the space of his mental world as his own attention "zeroes in" on some important particular of an observed action. The film simply does it better. Or the film-maker, by utilizing the focal length of a particular lens, can compress the planes of space of the physical world into one plane of space in the world of film. One of the most fascinating aspects of film space is its ability to take portions of physical space that may exist miles apart and re-form them so that they appear as a new space. How often we have seen a character walk to a window, pull back the curtain, then a cut in the film and we see the street outside of the window. Chances are the interior was shot in a studio somewhere and the street somewhere else, but they suddenly are re-formed into a new and unified space.

The film-maker obviously must use the space of the physical world to create his artificial, but freed, space. He is limited by the frame lines of his picture only in the amount of the physical world he can include in his image. It is this limitation that has, since the early stages of film development, motivated experimentation in wide screen, 3-D, Cinerama, and multiple screens surrounding the audience, seen by many at the various world's fairs. A program on the Columbia Broadcasting System's "The 21st Century" forecast that films of the future would employ the imaginative forms experimented with in these world's fair films. This is certainly an understandable assumption, for the more film can duplicate the sense of physical space without its physical limitations, the greater will be the involvement of the audience.*

At the same time that the frame is a limitation, it is also an asset. Nature's space is in a state of chaos, and man, through the frame of his vision, gives meaning and beauty to this chaos. When we stand on a high hill and look out on the sky, trees, hills, grass, flowers, it is the frame of our vision that isolates the various elements and composes them into a meaningful, beautiful view. So it is with film, only in this instance the meaning can be more profound and the beauty more vivid. The frame of the lens is far narrower than the frame of human vision, so it selects a much smaller fragment of this chaos. The narrow frame of filmic space isolates and intensifies this fragment, and the film-maker can give meaning to those elements that might otherwise be lost to the human eye. Through his arrangements of these elements within the frame lines —his compositions—he provides beauty as well as meaning. Without the valuable frame lines, compositions in space would be impossible and the film-maker would be left with nature's chaos.

The film-maker employs his temporal freedom to accelerate time, to slow it, to freeze it, and at times to disregard it in his quest to create the illusion. Time, like space, takes on a new dimension, a new meaning, and becomes another element in the film-maker's "bag of tricks." By changing the dimension of time in film, the film-maker is afforded a vital element for his interpretation and illusion of reality.

*A strong sense of involvement was created by one of the film exhibits at the New York World's Fair. The screen was the huge domed ceiling of the theater, and the audience lay back on reclining seats as it took a filmed journey through space. The spectator, with the picture 180° around him, felt as though he were floating through the void of outer space.

Time is plastic and can be freely modeled, but it takes precision to control it. To achieve his purpose the film-maker must plan shot by shot and action by action, thinking always of how it will be assembled. He manipulates not only the physical action, but also his and his audience's emotional feelings about time and the compression or expansion of the time necessary for the dramatic purposes of his film. The physical time, which is the time that it takes to record or later to project any action carried out in the film, is altered, of course, the moment the camera records it because of the camera's artificial reproduction of it. But far more opportunities of alteration are open to the film-maker. Normally within the shot, time is fixed; the time it takes to carry out the action determines the time of the shot. But in moving from shot to shot, the film-maker has the freedom to alter time to suit his purpose. Although he generally chooses the fixed time within the shot, the film-maker can also choose to alter it by recording it in slow motion or accelerated motion or to freeze the action or reverse it.

Such manipulations of time, when used properly, can underline the meaning and the emotional content of the action without destroying the audience's acceptance of the illusion of reality. The end of Truffaut's *The 400 Blows* provides us with one of the most poignant images in film by stopping time and freezing on the face of the young boy when he finds himself at the sea and unable to run farther. Or Arthur Penn's use of slow motion in the death of Bonnie and Clyde makes their doom a macabre dance of death, drawing the audience into this violent action by drawing out time to the point of being unbearable.

Although accelerated motion is most commonly used for its comic effect, it can be used for other purposes. Frequently it is employed to make action seem more exciting: the stampede of cattle, the wild chase sequence of cars careening along the curving mountain highway, the fast draw of the hero or villain, the fist fight on the edge of a cliff. It can also be used to underline meaning or emotional content; but it must be used sparingly no matter what the reason, for the tendency of an audience is to laugh when movement is accelerated. For example, in *The Informer*, John Ford utilizes accelerated motion in the scene where Gypo finds his girlfriend about to sell herself to a dandy in order to have money to eat. Gypo grabs the man, lifts him in the air, and throws him to the street. This action was filmed at a slower than normal speed, and thus appears faster when projected normally. Whether Ford did it for psychological reasons or to make the action more exciting, it comes dangerously close to eliciting laughter. Like the magician, the film-maker must never reveal his tricks.

In dealing with the emotional state of time the film-maker is also bringing to his work the feelings his spectators have had toward time when caught up in situations like our gentleman rushing to his appointment. Emotional reactions to time can be most beneficial to the film-maker in communicating to his audience, as well as in creating the illusion of reality. By utilizing these reactions, the film-maker can induce the proper mood within his audience to fit with a particular scene—

happy and exhilarated for a comedy, excited for adventure, suspenseful for mystery. The film-maker can achieve these emotional reactions by expanding or compressing the film time.

The emotional image of time is closely allied with rhythm. Just as the actual world is influenced by a regulated beat of time—minutes to hours to days, seasons of the year, the time necessary for the creation of life, the heartbeat that sustains life—so is the illusion of the world that is placed on film. Every film, depending upon its overall mood and dramatic purpose, has a basic rhythm. The film-maker must be aware of this rhythm, for each shot and its length, the duration of the action, or the movement of the camera must be considered in relation to the part it will play in the establishment of this rhythm.

To suit the purpose of his film, the film-maker must compress time. The Greeks told us that drama had to have a unity of time, that what happened on stage should take no longer than it would take in actuality. But since the time of the ancient Greeks, man has sought to expand his dramatic horizons by compressing time. Although some film-makers have utilized actual time—Andy Warhol in *Sleep,* Fred Zinnemann in *High Noon,* Agnes Varda in *Cleo From 5 to 7,* Alfred Hitchcock in *Rope*—for the most part, films span a much longer period of time than the time it takes to view them. Therefore, the film-maker has the freedom to deal with time as it suits the purpose of his script. Stanley Kubrick in *2001: A Space Odyssey* deals with a time span of better than four million years. Usually too great a time span can be injurious to a film because it is simply too great a problem to distill such a time period. Kubrick's attempt to solve this problem° is to cover the major portion of the four million years in a matter of seconds. At the end of "The Dawn of Man" sequence, the ape-man has learned to use his first tool, the bone club. In his exhilaration he throws it into the air. Kubrick's camera catches the bone in close-up as it rises and then falls through the air, then match dissolves to a shot of a space ship falling through space, à la Eisenstein's "intellectual montage." The space ship, of course, is a more advanced tool of man, and so by matching a symbol of the past with a symbol of the future Kubrick compresses the time.

If the film-maker is to best serve himself and the purpose of his film through his use of compressed film time, he must decide how much can be left out, and what is essential and must be left in. Jean-Luc Godard revolutionized the contemporary concept of film time in *Breathless (A Bout de Souffle)* when he decided that various elements, heretofore considered essential, could be omitted, following Eisenstein's lead in the "ruthless suppression of the inessential." He broke the established time sequence by eliminating anything that was routine, believing that it was unnecessary to provide these things since the audience would know their logical course. Consequently, Godard provides us with the beginning of a conversation of small talk and then cuts to the end of the conversation, believing that it is a waste of time giving us the entire discussion, or, as at the beginning of *Breathless,* he reduces an action to only the essential parts when he depicts the slaying of the policeman by the hero in

*We should mention, however, that one of the major criticisms of this film was that it attempts to cover too great a span of time.

three or four quick shots—the policeman climbing off of his motorcycle, a close-up of the gun in the hero's hand firing, and the policeman falling dead. As a result, his jump cuts from the beginning to the end of familiar occurrences provide us with an abstract, a metaphor of the real world. Godard and his concept of film time have gathered many disciples. But not everyone is a Godard, and if a film-maker leaves out too much, his film runs the danger of being difficult to follow. Generally time is more effectively compressed between scenes, rather than within scenes. While Godard is perfectly willing to compress within a specific conversation, jumping from the beginning to the end, even he is not always successful; in less capable hands, such a practice could be disastrous. The transitions between sequences are the ideal places to compress any great lengths of time because they will bridge not only the gap from one place to another, but also from one time to another. This does not mean that every action and conversation must be shown in toto. On the contrary, the ability of film to express a whole through the presentation of parts of the whole is the bulwark of filmic expression. But the film-maker must take care to present *all of the essentials* so as not to confuse his audience.

Contrarily, the film-maker may find situations in which it is necessary to expand time to suit his purpose. For a classic example, Eisenstein, in *Potemkin,* expands the real time that it takes to carry out the slaughter on the steps of Odessa. This expansion is necessary to project an impression of the horror of the event and to give it the dramatic emphasis that it requires. Further, it is justified as being close to the way in which the participants might have experienced the event. Earlier in this same film, Eisenstein adds dramatic meaning to a single action by expanding the time required to carry it out. A young sailor, angered and near mutiny because of the treatment afforded himself and his shipmates, is in the mess setting the tables. He looks at one of the dishes; written on it is "Give us this day our daily bread." He smashes the plate on the table. Eisenstein expands the smashing of the plate by shooting the action from a number of angles and overlapping these various shots in the editing. The opening of the bridges in *Ten Days that Shook the World* is another example.

Some films have been built around the idea of expanding a brief period of real time into the running time of the entire film. A good example of such an expansion is Robert Enrico's *An Occurrence at Owl Creek Bridge.* The period is the Civil War. A saboteur has been sentenced to hang. The scene of the hanging is a bridge over Owl Creek. As the doomed man drops, the rope breaks, and he escapes by swimming underwater. He makes his way to his wife and his home. But as he reaches to embrace his wife the scene cuts back to the bridge. The body of the saboteur is hanging lifeless at the end of the rope. The majority of the action of the film has taken place during an expansion of the fraction of a second that it took the body to fall the length of the rope. What the audience has witnessed is the thoughts that flashed through the mind of the man in the instant before his death.

The Camera, Lens, and Film

Although the camera is mechanically limited in what it can do, the lens optically limited in what it can see, and the film chemically limited in what it can record, these implements are the film-makers chief means of projecting his illusion of the real world *plus* his subjective impressions of that world. By manipulating what the camera, lens, and film can do, as well as utilizing in a positive way their limitations, the film-maker can provide an objectification of the physical and mental which not only communicates to but also involves his spectator. Let us see how we can use the limitations of our tools as well as their assets as counterparts of our own mental and emotional powers.

THE FRAME

The frame is as vital an element for interpretation and expression for the film-maker as the frame that is placed around the work of a painter. It allows the film-maker the opportunity to circumscribe only those elements that are mentally and emotionally necessary for his purpose. The irrelevant can be cleared away, allowing the camera to concentrate on the essential. This border also serves to draw attention to what is within, for the tendency of human vision is to stop its movement when it reaches a defined boundary, thus keeping the gaze of the audience centered within the frame lines.

Generally the center of the action occurs within the frame of the picture, but tension and suspense can be created by shifting the center outside the lines of the frame. Such framing is frequently employed in cases of violence; by centering the camera on a reaction to violence, we create tension without having to show the violent action itself. This technique dates back to the practice in ancient Greek drama of having violence take place off-stage. The use of this type of framing can also be used to arouse the curiosity of the audience. By having the action take place outside the frame, the spectator becomes anxious to see what is happening; he wants to be able to see what the character or characters within the frame are seeing. Then when the camera pans or the film cuts to the out-of-frame action, the spectator's anxiety is resolved. Thus the film-maker has built suspense.

FRAME AND COMPOSITION   Normally the film-maker stages his action within the lines of the frame, and the shape of that frame dictates to him the shape of the action. Effective framing involves the use of effective composition (see page 159). The manner in which the film-maker utilizes line, mass, form, and movement to create an aesthetically pleasing and a dramatically purposeful picture is prescribed by the borders of the picture created by the frame.

OBLIQUE FRAMING   One additional use of the frame is the concept of oblique framing (Fig. 4.1). The camera is positioned at an angle to the action taking place in front of it, but when the recorded image is projected onto the screen, the spectator has the impression that it is the image that is at an angle. Such framing is useful in adding dynamics to a certain action or is commonly used to show a mental or intoxicated

Fig. 4–1   Oblique framing (Mel Wittenstein)

state by giving the audience the impression that they are seeing the distorted view through the eyes of the intoxicated or distraught character. The "Batman" television series used this technique ad nauseum, but a selected use can be very effective, particularly with figures against a neutral background, as in Eisenstein's *Ten Days* and Orson Welles's *Mr. Arkadin.*

CAMERA ANGLE

One of the most powerful devices for aiding the film-maker in expressing the emotional and psychological content of a scene is the position from which the camera views the action: the camera angle. The placement of the camera determines the area and viewpoint of the lens. Effective use of camera angle must be combined with effective framing and composition, and its practical aspects are discussed at length in the next chapter. What we are concerned with here is its use as a tool of interpretation and expression by the film-maker.

A major concern of the film-maker is the attempt to delve below the surface of reality, expressing what is happening within the minds of the characters, to affect the spectator psychologically and emotionally. Camera angle can be one of the most useful devices for accomplishing this. Shooting from below an object can make it appear powerful and imposing, thus making the audience feel this power at the same time the film-maker is expressing the psychological state of the character. Stanley Kubrick, in *Doctor Strangelove,* not only makes his audience feel dominated by General Ripper, but also expresses the mental state of this character through the use of an exceedingly low angle (Fig. 4.2). General

Fig. 4–2 *Dr. Strangelove,* Columbia Pictures

Ripper, who has just sent SAC bombers to strike Russia, tells Captain Mandrake that the trouble today is that war is not left to the generals and goes on to outline the rest of the problems of the world. The speech is obviously the ravings of a deranged mind and is frightening in itself, coming from the lips of a man in a position of great power. Kubrick makes it almost unbearable by dropping his camera to the floor and having it shoot straight up at Ripper. The audience is given the impression that this powerful lunatic is in command of their destiny and they are totally at his mercy. Combined with the speech, it is enough to frighten the audience to death, which obviously was Kubrick's purpose.

Sidney Lumet, in *The Pawnbroker,* utilizes a low camera angle when he first introduces the three hoodlums who will later rob and kill in the pawn shop. They first appear at the shop with a stolen lawnmower, and Lumet places the camera in front of the mower and on the floor looking up past the lawnmower at the forbidding trio. In this manner, Lumet foreshadows the importance to the story of these three and creates a psychological impression in the minds of his audience.

Placing the camera above and shooting down on an object will provide an effect that is the reverse of the low-angle position. A high-angle shot will communicate an impression of insignificance or inferiority. Joseph Losey makes excellent use of both high- and low-angle in projecting the relationship of the two main characters in *The Servant* (Fig. 4.3). The servant is shot from a high angle, creating the impression of his inferiority and dominated position in relation to his master, whereas

Fig. 4–3 *The Servant,* Audio Film Center (Dirk Bogarde, the servant, on the left; James Fox, the master, on the right)

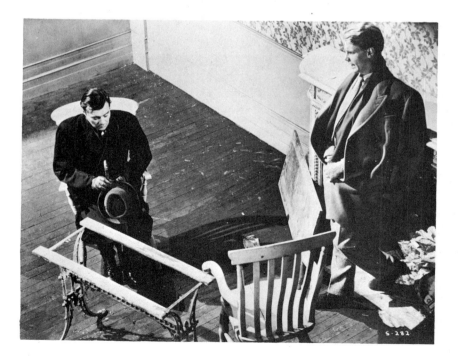

the master is shot from a low angle, which sets up his position of command. As the story progresses the positions of the two men slowly reverse to where the servant is the one in command and the master is the subservient one. To aid in this progression and regression, Losey slowly adjusts the camera angle until finally the servant is shot from the low angle and the master from the high. Thus Losey has depicted visually the psychological changes in the two men.

The use of the subjective angle, so that the action is seen through the eyes of one of the characters, is a most effective means of expressing the state of mind of this character. Using the subjective angle as the eyes of the audience makes the spectator a participant, and the film-maker evokes the spectator's emotions through his involvement in the action. By letting the spectator see the world through the eyes of the character, the film-maker can show the audience what the character feels about that world. Carol Reed utilizes a number of shots from the viewpoint of a twelve-year-old boy in *The Fallen Idol*. In so doing, Reed supplies the audience with a view of a familiar world but at the same time an abnormal view because it is the world seen through the eyes of a child. Through the interpretive employment of both subjective and objective camera angles, the film-maker has the opportunity of showing the audience the character's impressions of actuality.

A very important function of camera angle is the proper identification of objects. By placing the camera at eye level and directly in front of a building, the spectator will see the building as a two-dimensional object because the angle eliminates the depth factor. However, by placing the camera in a position where it records not only the front, but also the side, the spectator is given an impression of depth and three-dimensionality. Such camera angles can aid in the audience identification of the nature of the object. Positioning the camera so that it emphasizes the broad shoulders and thick neck of a character can express the brutality of the person. Or shooting at an angle that stresses the weak chin and frail body of a character can indicate the inner weakness of the individual. Therefore, when positioning the camera, the film-maker should be concerned with more than just presenting an *external view* of the object, but rather he should let the angle express the *inner nature* of the object too.

Since the view of the camera is limited by its position, camera angle can also be used to mislead an audience for a later effect—a useful technique for comic business. At one angle the character seems to be doing one thing, and then by shifting the angle the audience sees that he is doing something else.

The film-maker must remember that the position of the camera is a vitally important tool which can be utilized to project his interpretation of the real world and a tool that can be used to arouse emotional responses within the audience. Careful thought should be exercised in determining the proper angle of the camera. Mistakes in the camera placement can elicit feelings and project impressions that can hamper or counter the meaning and effectiveness of a film. This use of the interpretive camera is particularly effective because it is a wordless communication with the emotions, not with the spectator's intelligence.

CAMERA SPEED

Normally the speed of the camera is set at twenty-four frames per second, referred to as "sound speed," and is the speed at which all projectors operate. This speed reproduces movement on the screen that corresponds to what the audience sees as normal movement. At times, however, the film-maker may wish to alter that normal speed and use that alteration as an interpretive tool. He can then either slow the speed of the movement or accelerate it. With slow motion the film-maker adjusts the camera so that it takes pictures faster than the constant speed projector projects them, and thus the movement on the screen is slowed down. For fast motion the film-maker sets the camera to take pictures slower than they will be shown, and as a result they appear accelerated on the screen.

Such variations of film speed can be highly effective as means of expression. Until recently these variations were seldom used, but lately film-makers have rediscovered their value and found that they can be as valuable as the variations of camera-angle and image size.

Slow motion is particularly effective in a tragic situation. In *Elvira Madigan*, the slow motion sequence at the end of Elvira chasing the butterfly draws out the time as the audience awaits the gunshot that will end the life of this beautiful girl, so in love with life.

In a number of television commercials—Pepsi Cola, Clairol, Maybelline, Coppertone, etc.—slow motion is used to draw out the grace of movement of lovely girls and young lovers.

Slow motion is also frequently employed to express a dream state or a narcotic condition. It serves these purposes most effectively by softening the reality of the situation, giving it an aura of the unreal or imaginary. This technique has been employed quite frequently to depict the narcotic effect of drugs.

Fast motion is a useful tool of expression unless, as we mentioned earlier, it becomes an obvious technique which evokes laughter. The earliest of film comedies and farces abound in the use of accelerated motion, and the increased pace brings a brilliance to the action that could not be achieved in any other way. Contemporary examples of this use are *Morgan* and the Beatles' movies.

Variation of shooting speed also has its technical purposes in filming. By reducing the speed of the camera, less light is needed for an exposure. This has less practical value in motion picture photography than still photography because of the distortion of the action; however, in shots without distinct movements the film-maker can utilize this technique to compensate for a lack of light.

DOUBLE EXPOSURE

One of the most common problems with which the novice still photographer is plagued is double exposure. He has neglected to wind the film in his camera and so exposes one picture on top of another. Yet in the proper hands, double exposure can be an effective and expressive technique (Fig. 4.4).

A type of double exposure is commonly used as a transition; it is referred to as a *dissolve*. By blending one picture on top of another, the dissolve expresses a change of locale or a change in time. It is generally accompanied by a change in the content of the sound track.

For dramatic purposes double exposure was first used as a means of depicting the supernatural. By overlaying the picture of the ghost or demon onto a scene in a real environment or setting, objects within that environment could be seen through the image of the ghost, thus establishing its unreal, ethereal state. There is a fine example of this in *The Uninvited*, a superlative ghost movie.

Double exposure is also used to show the inner life of a character, his thoughts, feelings, or dreams. An early example of this technique is in Edwin S. Porter's *The Life of an American Fireman*. The dream of the Fire Chief is shown at the same time we see the chief sitting asleep in a chair. The same effect is used in contemporary film, usually in a more sophisticated manner. Porter felt that it was necessary to place the dream inside of a balloon in the corner of the frame. Today the inner life may be shown by superimposing over the character's face what is going on in his mind. If the dream or thought is of an extended nature, it is normally superimposed over the face where it is held briefly, and then the face close-up is dissolved away, placing the audience fully within the thought or dream.

Double exposure is also frequently used to introduce a symbol or visual metaphor. John Ford, for example, uses double exposure in a scene in *The Informer* to contrast the early friendship between Gypo Nolan and Frankie MacPhillips with Gypo's treacherous thoughts of turning in Frankie for a twenty pounds reward. Gypo is shown looking at a "Wanted" poster for Frankie which offers the twenty pounds reward. This reward looms in close-up, and then over the picture of Frankie that is on the poster appears a shot of Frankie and Gypo singing and drinking in a pub. Later, when the two are together again, the poster returns to force itself on Gypo's mind, even though he struggles to wipe it away.

Double exposure is also a phenomenon that can occur in nature, for example, when the reflection on a glass is seen at the same time that we see the objects on the other side of the glass. Use of such a phenomenon can occur in film and is most expressive. The scene in *In Cold Blood* between Perry and the prison psychiatrist just before Perry's execution is much more effective because of the use of the raindrops on the window reflected onto Perry's face, so that they appear as tears running down his cheek. This "double exposure" adds great poignancy to what Perry is saying about his relationship with his father.

Fig. 4–4   A double-exposure

SOFT FOCUS

Soft focus is a clear-cut example of the use of a defect as a tool of expression. It is the use of a lens aberration in which all of the objects except the main subject are blurred or out-of-focus, or in which the entire picture is out-of-focus. The latter is accomplished by either putting the lens out of focus over its entire depth of field or by placing gauze or Vaseline on an optical glass over the lens. The former case of soft focus is achieved by using a lens with a short depth of field so that the main subject is in focus and everything else is not, or by smearing Vaseline on an optical glass placed over the lens so that it covers everything in the shot but the main subject. Obviously the Vaseline is never placed directly on the lens.

Soft focus stylizes nature and changes it into something new, an abstraction that frees the imagination. The effect on the screen resembles an impressionist painting. *Elvira Madigan* uses soft focus as a means of evoking the feeling and appearance of an impressionistic work by blurring out the surroundings, such as leaves of trees and flowers, so that they appear as dabs of paint (Fig. 4.6). These images create a highly romantic atmosphere. Undoubtedly impressionist painting influenced this film-maker as it likely influenced those who first incorporated soft focus as a means of visual expression.

In the beginning, soft focus was used to provide a supernatural aura around the heroine or the saintly. Film-makers soon learned that it could

Fig. 4–5 *In Cold Blood*, Columbia Pictures

Fig. 4–6 *Elvira Madigan, Cinema V*

be used to focus audience attention by blurring out the unimportant and keeping the center of attention in sharp focus; to soften sharp lines, blur the shape, and in general beautify the image; and to separate the image from the background, emphasizing depth. Soft focus is also another means of expressing subjective states of mind, such as fainting, drowsiness, intoxication, or narcosis. Finally, it can be used as a transition into a flashback, being the visual equivalent of a disturbance of the emotions when a memory of the past begins to invade our thoughts.

DEPTH OF FIELD

As we discovered in our discussion of the lens, depth of field is the distance between objects in the foreground and those in the background that are of acceptable sharpness of focus. It can be manipulated by the use of lenses with different focal lengths (shorter focal length, greater depth), by adjusting the aperture of the lens (the smaller the opening, the greater the depth of field), and by the positioning of objects in relation to the camera.

In the 1940s the development of faster film and more powerful lighting made it possible for the film-maker to use a much smaller aperture, even in interior shots, and thereby keep a greater depth of the scene in focus. This process was called *deep focus*. From this point on, excellence in cinematography was synonymous with having the sharpest image and the greatest depth of field. Deep focus was a valuable means of visual expression in the Welles-Toland *Citizen Kane* because of the film's con-

Fig. 4–7 *Citizen Kane,* Janus Films

cern with a materialistic society. It provided the film-maker with the means of emphasizing and contrasting the dramatic actions within that vividly realized materialistic environment (Fig. 4.7). For example, the enormous size and opulence of Kane's castle could be emphasized and contrasted with the prosaic and emotionally empty activity that took place within its ornate walls.

Despite the fact that the human eye does not see everything in sharp focus, deep focus is now commonly used for a depiction of reality. Selective focusing is frequently employed for a state of semireality with dramatic overtones. The contrast between the two is a most effective means of objective and subjective expression.

The film-maker can also increase the effect of depth with:

LIGHTING   The use of side- and backlighting creates a greater sense of depth by separating the subject from the background and by modeling or giving shape to the subject.

FOCUS   A sense of greater depth can be achieved by allowing the foreground or the background to go out of focus. This technique duplicates human vision.

COLOR   By utilizing colors in the background different from those of the subject, the two are separated, thereby creating the effect of greater depth.

MOVEMENT   The action within the frame of the picture or any movement of the camera can create the illusion of greater depth.

PERSPECTIVE   Using a wide-angle lens or placing objects closer to the camera will force the perspective and create a sense of greater depth.

PERSPECTIVE

Simply stated, perspective is the convergence of parallel lines and the progressive reduction in size of objects as the distance from the viewer is increased. According to mathematical principle, the farther an object is away from the point from where it is being viewed, the smaller the image appears, its size decreasing in proportion to the square of the distance from the point of viewing. An object that is twenty feet away is four times smaller than one ten feet away. However, human vision makes a mental correction so that the differences in proportion in the size of objects are reduced. The lens is incapable of this mental correction and so renders perspective objectively, determined basically by the lens-to-subject distance. Since the lens does not have the stereoscopic vision of the human eye, the effect is created by the changes in size that are produced by changes in lens-to-subject distance. When the film-maker's chief concern is the presentation of a realistic impression, he must create a screen image that is in line with the audience's way of seeing things. Therefore, that image must include the subjective interpretation of perspective, or in other words, the film-maker must compensate for the mental correction. Distort perspective and you distort reality. At other times, however, the film-maker may be more concerned with communicating the state of mind of his characters to his audience rather than communicating actuality and in such situations the distortion of perspective may be a useful means of visual expression. Mike Nichols, while filming a sequence in *The Graduate,* was concerned with expressing in some way the state of mind of Benjamin, his hero. Benjamin has run out of gas, but he must get to the church in time to prevent his love from marrying someone else. He jumps from his car and starts running to the church, which is still some distance away. Nichols obviously observed that at this point the hero and the audience feel that he will never make it, that he is running but not getting anywhere. To communicate this feeling to the audience, the shot of the hero running to the church was shot with a 500mm telescope lens which compresses the compositional planes, distorts perspective, and creates the impression that poor Benjamin is running on a treadmill. This shot is a considerable change from the way we would normally see this event, and the film-maker can employ it effectively to communicate a subjective state.

Perspective need not violently change the realistic view to be an effective tool for the film-maker. Due to the fact that perspective in film is governed by the increase or decrease in size as an object is nearer or farther away from the camera, it can be used to develop or maintain a contrast between two objects. Earlier in this chapter we mentioned that Joseph Losey used camera angle to indicate the relationship of the two men in *The Servant.* In this same film, and frequently in the same previously cited shots, he also utilized perspective to establish the contrast between the two characters (Fig. 4.8). In the beginning, the master is generally closest to the camera, therefore increasing his size and dominance; but as the change in relationship between the two takes place, Losey moves the servant closest to the camera, and thus increases his size and dominance over the master.

Fig. 4-8 *The Servant,* Audio Film Center

Certainly distortion of reality through a distortion of perspective combined with other elements can be utilized by the film-maker to stylize his film. By forcing perspective or reducing it, the film-maker can create effects that will give an individual style to the work.

CAMERA MOVEMENT

In the proper hands movement of the camera can be a powerful means of visual expression, but the secret to its success is in the ability to move without calling attention to the movement. This can be achieved by having the camera's movement resemble the physical and mental experiences of human vision. When the camera is moved so as to capture these experiences, the spectator will accept such movement because he is unaware of it. But when that movement jars or disturbs, makes the spectator overwhelmingly aware that he is watching the camera move—unless, of course, that is the specific effect desired—such "flexing of the muscles" reduces the expressive qualities of the film. In a sense, the spectator is, of course, always aware that he is watching a film. This is essential if he is to have an aesthetic experience. But at the same time, if the film is to be successful, the spectator must also be emotionally involved in the experience taking place on the screen. When a camera movement impinges on that involvement, it frustrates and disturbs the spectator, he "breaks out," and the illusion of reality is destroyed. When a spectator can say, "Hey, look at the way the camera pulls back," the shot has lost its usefulness to the film and exists only for its own sake.

PANNING   Panning (either horizontal or vertical movement, although the vertical is usually referred to as tilting) was the first camera movement to be discovered by the film-maker and came with the development of the flexible tripod head. Panning the camera does in some ways resemble the movement of the eyes, although everything in a pan shot is in focus, a thing not possible for the eye. Actually, when we shift our attention from one point to another, the process closely resembles a combination of "cutting" and "panning." The eye is naturally selective, and the material that lies between the points of interest passes in an unnoticed blur as we shift our attention. This can readily be observed when watching a person's eyes "roam" (the eyes "flick" rather than pan) over a room or a landscape, or when you yourself do the same. The human eye pans when following a moving object on which it has focused, maintaining focus throughout the movement. To some degree we also "pan" in looking over a panorama stretched out far below us, standing on the top of a high hill. Or when we are looking at a tall building, we tend to start at the bottom and follow the building up to its top. Seldom do we look at such scenes in "cuts." By duplicating these human experiences in filming such situations, the film-maker accomplishes the task of showing his audience the various elements of environment and doing so in a natural way. Such pan shots are frequently used to establish the locale of a scene.

When the film-maker must follow an action, such as a moving vehicle or person, he has basically two choices. He can cut to different points of view as the action progresses, or he can move his camera and follow the action. When the shot is from a subjective or a point-of-view angle, and when the character from whose position the audience sees the action is in a stationary position, the pan is a useful movement to employ, for when not moving with the action the spectator does tend to move the eyes with the continuous flow of the action. If the complete action is not a continuous flow, but rather is made up of a combination of isolated incidents, the cut can work quite well, for in life we tend, in viewing such an action, to "zero in" on the isolated incidents.

In the treatment of a scene of continuous action of great excitement —a chase, an Indian attack, an automobile race—since the excited participants (and the spectator *is* a participant!) would tend to see the action as a series of isolated, vividly realized incidents, the montage technique is the more effective. By cutting, the director moves the spectator rapidly about and projects him into the action, in contrast to the more detached observation the pan offers him. Pan shots of reasonable length are usually included as part of the montage, as are tracking shots, but the basic technique used is the cut to a short, static shot of a portion of the action. Tony Richardson's *Charge of the Light Brigade*, or *Grand Prix* and *Bullitt*, offer interesting examples that are worth studying.

At the end of the trial in *The Caine Mutiny Court Martial*, both the cut and the pan are used effectively. The spectator, as well as the entire court, has been staring as if hypnotized at Captain Queeg's breakdown on the witness stand. Finally Queeg himself seems to come to his senses, realizing what he has done; the defense lawyer, by causing Queeg to reveal himself under pressure as an extreme neurotic, has won his case. As awareness dawns on Queeg he slows down, finally coming to a halt, looking hesitantly around him. At this point the camera cuts to the defense attorney, the prosecuting attorney, and the defendant, and then repeats the cuts. Although each man's feelings are complex—the victors are far from proud of what they have done—it is unmistakable by the expressions on their faces that Queeg has destroyed himself. Then the camera pans down the row of judges and the inexorable roll of the camera is a devastating condemnation of Queeg, the grim impassive face of each judge visually voting against him. A pan would have been unthinkable for the shots preceding, and to cut from judge to judge would have been ludicrous; nor would either technique have the same appropriateness in the other context. The cuts allow an instantaneous shift from one point of attention to another without the distraction of the extraneous material over which the camera would have had to pass to reach each point. The pan along a row of parallel faces, quite close to each other, with no intruding material in between, works perfectly and lends the measured, inevitable pace that is needed here.

The pan can be used in a highly interesting and expressive way to indicate a transition in time and/or place. One of the most vivid examples of this technique is the 360° pan employed by John Frankenheimer in *The Manchurian Candidate*. A squad of American soldiers has been captured by the North Koreans and flown to a Communist headquarters where the GIs have all been subjected to brainwashing. One of the soldiers is the key to a Communist plot. He has been conditioned to be an unknowing assassin. In a scene in which he is made to "perform" for an audience of Communist specialists and leaders by killing one of his fellow countrymen, Frankenheimer employs the transitional pan shot. The scene begins as the recurring dream of another of the soldiers, who had been a member of the captured squad and who, therefore, had undergone conditioning. We see the captured soldiers sitting on a stage surrounded by plants, listening to a lady speaker discuss the hydrangea. The camera cuts to an angle from the point of view of the stage and begins to pan along the ladies seated in the audience drinking tea, gossiping, and smoking. The shot continues its panning movement along the audience and returns to the stage as an objective view from the audience so that the soldiers, the stage, and the speaker are visible. Only now the stage is different. It is the stage of a lecture hall, and the background contains huge photographs of Communist leaders. The speaker too is different; she is now an Oriental male, and he now tells his audience (and the audience of the film) that the soldiers think they are in a small hotel in New Jersey listening to the weekly meeting of the Ladies' Garden Club. In this 360° pan shot Frankenheimer has shown a change in time and place, as well as a transition from the subjective dream-state to the objective view of this happening in the past.

A derivative of the transitional technique is to rapidly pan the camera (called a *swish pan*). This type of pan is highly stylized and tends to whisk the spectator's eye along with it. Because of the unnaturalness of it, the swish pan should be used sparingly and only when a jarring effect is desired. *The Man From UNCLE* used the swish pan repeatedly as a transition device.

Finally, the pan can be used to tie different elements of the environment or action together. An example of such a use can be found in Marcel Camus' *Black Orpheus.* At the end of the film the camera pans up from the dead bodies of the lovers to the beautiful view of the hills of Rio, the sea, and the sky. The pan seems to say to the spectator, "Here we see the dead lovers and here we see nature in all its beauty; both are completely different, and yet both are of the same world." Nothing but a pan shot could say it as well.

The film-maker must also be aware of the problems presented by the pan shot. The movement, with the exception of the swish pan, is slow-paced,* and unless that slowness is desired and fits with the rhythm of the film and the tempo of the scene, the shot is likely to be left on the cutting room floor. Once the pan is begun in a shot, the film must stay with the movement to the end because it is difficult to cut or dissolve in the middle of the camera's movement. Therefore, if it does not fit with the rhythm and tempo, it cannot be used.

Alfred Hitchcock's *Rope* is an experiment in making a film without a cut. Each reel is filmed in a single shot, the camera finishing on some stationary object such as a door frame, the next shot beginning unnoticeably at the same point. While a fascinating experiment, the film fails precisely because it does not choose to take advantage of the power of the cut in the elimination of the unessential. At several points the disadvantage of the pan shot becomes obvious.

One point, cited by Karel Reisz, is the climactic moment of the film. Two boys who have murdered a fellow student are confronted by their teacher with evidence of their crime, the rope with which they have strangled their victim. The camera in a close shot watches the teacher, his back to the boys, remove the rope from his pocket and suddenly turn to them, revealing at once the rope and the fact that he knows what they have done. At this point the spectator is intensely eager to see how the boys have reacted, a classic moment for the direct cut. Working within his self-imposed restrictions, Hitchcock must pan, and as the camera swings from the rope to the stunned murderers, we are subjected to details of the room, a picture on the wall, a window with a neon sign outside. Never has there been a more dramatic illustration of the power of the direct cut than this example of *not* using it.

Reisz correctly observes that even if the desire was to prolong the wait until the boys are revealed, it would be far better to hold the shot on the rope in the teacher's hands than to drag us over the clutter of meaningless insignificant detail. Be certain in your use of the pan that you fully intend the presentation of the detail of the shot at the leisurely pace of the pan; if not, the direct cut is called for.

THE TRACKING SHOT   The tracking shot came into use when the camera was given wheels, the movement carried out by mounting the camera on a wheeled device that moves the camera bodily. The term "tracking"

*As anyone who has ever attempted a panning shot knows, too quick a pace to the movement of the camera will result in a stroboscopic effect, rendering the shot useless. Therefore, the pan is, by definition, a slow movement. That is its strength, and that is its weakness.

has come into use because the earliest devices had to be mounted on rails or tracks so that the movement would be steady. Today, however, these vehicles are equipped with pneumatic tires, and the use of track is rare. Tracking movements can be toward, away from, or parallel to the action being photographed.

The motion picture screen has a two-dimensional surface, and the picture projected onto it is also two-dimensional. The real world is three-dimensional, so the film-maker is always concerned with creating an illusion of the three-dimensional. The fact that the tracking shot penetrates the depth of the environment, proving its solidity, makes it a valuable tool for the film-maker in the creation of this illusion.

The film-maker, in employing the tracking shot to penetrate, may begin the shot from a long angle which provides a view of the general area, then move into that area, coming to rest at the end on a specific object; or he may begin with the close shot and pull out to reveal the general view. The former movement will establish the locale in the mind of the spectator and then take him by the hand and lead him into that locale, eliminating the unessential as the movement progresses, until finally pinpointing the central element. The latter movement, unless the spectator is already aware of the general locale, can disorient the viewer and intrigue him, making him wonder where he is until the camera begins its movement. Both of these impressions can be created through cutting, but cutting is sudden and creates a much more dramatic impact. The beauty of the pull-back is its gradual revelation, and the strength of the track-in is its relentless pursuit of the heart of the matter.

By moving parallel to the action, the shot will create the impression that the spectator is also moving. If such a factor is established before the movement, the impression will resemble the human optical experience and will, therefore, be readily accepted by the viewer. One of the prime dangers of the tracking shot is the feeling engendered that the spectator is floating alongside the action, or into or out of the action, a most unreal experience. Handholding the shot, when it is feasible, creates less of the unreal sensation because the spectator feels that he is walking rather than floating.

There are several fine tour-de-force examples of the tracking shot in the Russian film, *War and Peace*, directed by Serge Bondarchuk. The camera sweeps along beside a cavalry charge for an incredibly long time; then, caught up by the force of a countercharge of cavalry, sweeps back along the same path. Tracking shots are an important part of any chase on horseback, infinitely superior to process shots with the hero flogging some stuffed mount while a wind machine whips his tresses. *War and Peace* also abounds with tracking shots in its ballroom scenes, as the camera rolls unendingly down the ceiling over the mass of dancers or along the side of the ballroom through the adjoining rooms. Like the pan, the tracking shot must be carefully chosen for the spot where it is appropriate; but when it is, it's unbeatable.

The tracking shot, like the pan, can be useful in expressing the subjective state. In this case the spectator has the impression that he is seeing the action through the eyes of a participant and is made aware of the subjective state of that participant. The camera then becomes a force in the action, not merely an objective device recording the action. This same impression is created when the camera is used as the eyes of the audience and makes the audience a participant in the action. F. W. Murnau used this type of subjective movement of the camera most expressively in *The Last Laugh* to express the drunken state of the leading character. Wanting his audience to feel the same drunkenness as the protagonist, he employs the camera as the eyes of the drunken audience; spinning and weaving its way around the scene. A film in the 1940s, Robert Montgomery's *The Lady in the Lake*, made the camera the eyes of the leading character, and the entire action of the film is revealed to the audience through his eyes. The audience sees the leading character only when he is reflected in a mirror, or some other shiny surface. This extreme use of the subjective camera was only partially successful. An extended use of the subjective camera can become dull if prolonged. The tracking shot, like the pan, may call attention to itself through its slow movement and its dissimilarity to human vision.

THE ZOOM SHOT   The zoom shot is a form of camera movement, although the camera never moves—the impression of movement being created by increasing or decreasing the magnification of an object in the scene. Like the tracking shot, it can be used to move into or out of the center of interest. However, unlike the tracking shot, the zoom shot seems to pull the center of interest toward the spectator or to push it away. Whereas the tracking shot creates the impression of moving the spectator toward or away from the interest point. The impression created by the zoom lens has also been interpreted as one in which no movement takes place, but rather the center of interest enlarges or reduces in size.

   Many cameramen have not yet gotten over the novelty of the zoom lens and are forever subjecting us to inappropriate uses of it. Since the cut from the establishing shot is always available to us, we must be absolutely certain that the particular effect of the zoom is called for before using it. Obviously the cut renders the significant detail instantly and the zoom inexorably, so the desire to move in on the subject must at once be very powerful and yet demanding of a slow tempo for the zoom to work. Quick zooms have their place, but they are gimmicky and attention attracting. It makes much more sense to use the zoom as a pullback, starting on the disorienting and intriguing detail (a man perched strangely on a piece of metal), pulling back to reveal where this detail is located in its surroundings (the metal is part of an enormous skyscraper under construction, and he is high in the air). The desire to know where this intriguing detail is located is powerful and yet gratified by the act of gradual revelation, and thus the pull-back works far better than a cut to an establishing shot.

Probably the film-maker's most powerful tool of visual expression is the close-up. It gains its power from its ability to select and concentrate. By   **THE CLOSE-UP** means of the close-up, the film-maker exercises complete control over what the spectator will see, excluding all of the unessentials and concentrating the spectator's attention on the one vital element. In a sense then, it derives its power not only from what it shows but also from what it excludes. As a result, the film-maker has the opportunity of communicating with complete accuracy and unmistakable clarity, since his spectator is prevented from seeing anything but what the film-maker has chosen to show, in the order he has chosen, and for the duration he has chosen.

Since the close-up is such a powerful device, it should be used for the presentation of the most vital elements of the film.° The properly chosen and executed close-up can add dramatic impact, as well as control of attention and clarity. But when it is improperly used it can confuse and destroy attention.

THE FREEZE FRAME

The freeze frame (stopped motion) creates the impression of arrested time, holding the subject in suspended animation. In so doing, the film-maker preserves the image throughout time much as a vivid image is seized and hauntingly held by one's memory. This provides the spectator with the time to savor the image and to respond to it. The frozen images of Elvira Madigan, of Jeanne Moreau in *Jules et Jim* (Fig. 4.9), of the boy

Fig. 4–9 *Jules et Jim,* Janus Films

*An editor friend described cutting a cinema-verité film in which he was forced to use facial close-ups for cut-aways since he lacked suitable neutral material. He observed that the close-up called disproportionate attention to the cut-away at a time when he sought what we call the "neutral intercut," as an unobtrusive bridge between important shots.

in *The 400 Blows,* of the young Natasha in *War and Peace,* leave us with the feeling that these people have been preserved forever from the passage of time.

The freeze frame also has validity as a means of controlling attention and concentrating that attention on a particular detail. However, the film-maker must be cautious in his use of this device. The image can appear awkward and ridiculous when frozen in the wrong position, so the frame used must be carefully chosen on a projection machine such as a Moviola which allows the editor the opportunity of studying each individual frame.

The freeze frame is used frequently behind the titles of a film, and is often seen this way on television. Sometimes when a subject film is assembled, it is discovered that a shot which would make an excellent title background is not long enough for the title to be contained. The freeze is both a practical device for lengthening the shot and an effective aesthetic device in rendering a particular portion of the shot significant to back up the title. The usual method used is to freeze a few frames before and unfreeze a few frames after the title is on screen.

THE NEGATIVE IMAGE

Since a film is made up of positive images, the sudden appearance of a negative image—one in which the light and shade values are reversed—can be a most startling effect (Fig. 4.10). Until recent years the use of the negative image was rare and so had even greater impact when it was used. In its earlier uses it presented an image that not only turned shade to light, and vice versa, but also eliminated color. Such an image was most unreal. Recently the technique has been to utilize the reversal of light and shade and to add color in a manner which heightens the unreality. The colors appear to wash over the image. Stanley Kubrick uses the technique in *2001: A Space Odyssey* at the end of the much-discussed "psychedelic" journey of the astronaut in the last portion of the film.

The fact that the negative images produce a feeling of nonreality indicates its possible uses. The preponderance of use has been to evoke an illusion of fantasy or a dream world. An early example appears in *Blind Alley* which dealt with a psychologically disturbed killer and a psychiatrist. The killer reveals to the psychiatrist that he has been bothered throughout his adult life by a recurring dream which the psychiatrist says is at the root of his desire to kill. When the killer finally reveals the dream, it is presented in negative images with the voice of the killer telling the dream to the doctor. In this same manner the negative image has also been used to depict the confused thoughts, as well as dreams, of a mentally disturbed individual.

The negative image functions quite well as a reproduction of the other world, a spirit world that is the opposite of the real world. Several science-fiction television series have made ample use of this device for such illusions, including the supposed demonstration of the effects of imaginary weapons of the future.

Fig. 4-10 A negative image (Mel Wittenstein)

Recently the negative image has also found its way into the production of television commercials. A recent series of commercials for an automobile manufacturer employs the negative image and the color wash. Undoubtedly the purpose of its use is the visual impact it provides as a unique attention-getter.

Finally, the negative image has been used as a symbol. Godard uses it this way in *Alphaville* and *A Married Woman*—a symbol of death or the void that exists beyond modern civilization's inhumanity.

FILM STOCK

A major artistic decision every film-maker must make is whether color or black-and-white film will best suit what is to be expressed in his film. Neither, as we discovered earlier, presents a completely realistic impression of life. Since color exists in nature, black-and-white, with its lack of color, presents a stylization of nature. Color is also stylistic to a degree because its reproduction of nature's colors is not entirely accurate and tends to beautify. Because black-and-white film is an obvious stylization, it frees the film-maker to create a filmic reality resembling the real world and yet different. The film-maker is able to get closer to the inner reality of his subjects. It is like stripping away part of the façade and revealing the true nature or the true condition. Utilizing only light and shade, the film-maker is able to interpret without the conflicting implications and sensations of color; he has begun his interpretation beneath the surface of reality. Yet, the use of black-and-white film does not mean that the film-maker forsakes beauty, for there is a unique beauty in the chiaroscuro world of the black-and-white film (Fig. 4.11).

In a strictly practical sense, black-and-white production is less expensive and less complicated technically than color production, but such considerations should not be the basis for artistic decisions.

Since the earliest days of the medium, film-makers have been aware of the need for color or have considered its lack a serious drawback. Color existed in reality, and if an illusion of that reality was to be created, the lack of color was seen as an obvious disadvantage. To belie this disadvantage the early film-maker took to "tinting" and to "toning" their black-and-white film: red for fires and violence, green for landscapes and seascapes, blue for night, amber as an overall tint for smoothness and body for the "weak" black-and-white image. Pathé and others even followed the extraordinary practice of hand-coloring the individual frames, achieving some remarkably beautiful results. Finally, years of research later, a workable color process was discovered.

Color film is admirably suited for comedy, romance, farce, and the spectacular because the beauty and richness produced is a valuable and necessary asset. On the theatrical or nontheatrical level of production, it suits well any film that deals primarily with the surface of reality: the travelogue, the subject film, the commercial. In these instances, color enhances the beauty of the picture or adds a beauty that might not be fully present, thus providing production value to the film.

Color does have its uses below the surface of reality, for it contains emotional values that can contribute to the dramatic or symbolic effects of a film. In recent years much research has been going on concerning the emotional values of color. How do certain colors affect the emotional reactions of the viewer? By utilizing these values, and thus by utilizing the meanings of color, the film-maker can contribute to the meaning of his film.

Many film-makers have found themselves faced with a dilemma. Their film necessitates an accurate rendition of reality and, therefore, color; but, at the same time, the beautification presented by the color process could also be a detriment to the needed illusion. Some have given up and

Fig. 4-11 *The Seventh Seal,* Janus Films

grudgingly used either black-and-white or color. Some have employed a combination of the two, as in *The Wizard of Oz*, in which the drab actuality of Kansas is rendered in black-and-white and the glorious Aladdin's-lamp world of Oz inevitably in full color. Others have selected color film and devised some means of modifying and subduing the colors reproduced. Arthur Penn felt that a more convincing effect of realism was needed for *Bonnie and Clyde*, so he employed color film but attempted to subdue the color mostly in the handling of the sets—dirtying the walls, selecting old buildings, using earthy and dull colors within the environment and in the costumes. John Huston, however, chose to change the actual reproduction of the color for *Reflections in a Golden Eye*. He chose to render all colors but pinks and reds in an almost monochrome sepia, thus accenting the pinks and reds. The production was actually filmed utilizing normal color-filming techniques, but a "double printing" process was utilized in the laboratory, producing the desaturated effect. In a sense, Houston's film was similar to a tinted black-and-white film only with the reds produced as true color. This same process can be used to accentuate any other color of the spectrum and can be used for the entire film or for only portions of it.

However, Houston's use of desaturated color in *Reflections in a Golden Eye* met with a great deal of controversy. Critics agreed and disagreed. Many patrons were furious because the film had been billed as a color film, but because of the desaturation they felt that it was not. There were rumors that after the film completed its initial run in New York City, it was released in a full color print. If this is the case, it is a shame, for the desaturation was an important dramatic plus for this particular vehicle. While it is true that this effect is not appropriate for every film, the film-maker should remember that the laboratory, just as with this process, can often make a valuable contribution to his attempts at artistic expression.

There is frequently a conflict between the director's certainty that his film is a black-and-white film (Olivier said this quite correctly about his *Hamlet*) and his realization that a color film is in many ways better box office. This is particularly true today when every film is a potential television special. Thus the director sincerely trying to choose what is artistically best for his film is often forced by financial considerations to work in color. An interesting compromise, comparable to that used by Huston in *Reflections*, was that of Richard Brooks on *In Cold Blood*. The film, which Brooks insisted was a black-and-white film, was in fact *shot* in black-and-white, but *printed* on color stock, thus giving a slight tone to the print, relieving some of the harshness of the original. Both Brooks and Huston have come fascinatingly close to the silent film techniques of tinting and toning with these "modern" methods they have employed.

COLOR TEMPERATURE

The fact that color film renders color differently when exposed to a light source for which it is not balanced can be utilized by the film-maker as

Fig. 4-12 *In Cold Blood*, Columbia Pictures

a means of rendering colors in a non-literal way. Should the film-maker desire to change the effect of a scene by giving it a cold, harsh, bluish tone, he need only intentionally raise the color temperature by using tungsten film with daylight or by raising the color temperature of the light source. Conversely, if he desires a warm, reddish tone to the scene, he need only lower the color temperature by employing daylight film with a tungsten source, or by lowering the color temperature of the light source.

LIGHTING

Since an entire chapter has been devoted to the uses and techniques of lighting, it should only be necessary here to remind the film-maker that one of his most important tools of visual expression is his lighting of the scene. Effective and expressive film production is dependent, in part, upon sufficient lighting to gain the exposure desired and upon the proper use of lighting to create an atmosphere which suits the dramatic mood of the film (Fig. 4.12). Film lighting must harmonize with an image that is constantly moving in time and space.

LOCATION

A most important plus for visual expression is the setting within which the film will be photographed. Throughout the history of film, the film-maker has been torn between the control afforded him in the studio and the quality of reality he gains when shooting in real locations. The post-Revolutionary Russians and the neo-realists in Italy following World War II forsook the studio because they felt in so doing they were shunning artifice, and, as Eisenstein had said, were going "away from realism to reality." No one can deny the sense of reality that is achieved by filming in real places. If this strong sense of reality is necessary to proper visual expression, there can be no substitute.

On the other hand, the studio affords the film-maker complete control of such vital elements as lighting and sound. Imagination and attention to detail can combine to create a sense of reality. As a result, many film-makers have found that they can create the necessary illusion as well as maintain complete control, and thus gain greater freedom by working in the studio.

RHYTHM AND TEMPO

A misconception abounds that the rhythm and tempo of a film are fully determined in the editing process. Actually, rhythm and tempo are determined in a general way by the material itself, and not only the editor but the director, cameraman, actor, and soundman must be aware of the basic rhythm and tempo and function within it. The composition and duration of a shot must be determined by the visual and dramatic content of the shot. A simple, uncomplicated composition will require less time for the audience to grasp than a complex composition. A close-up demands less time than a long shot. A moving shot demands more time than a static one. A shot that is vastly different from the one that came before it will require a longer duration. The line and mass of the composition, the movement of persons and objects, the movement caused by a change from shot to shot, the movement of the camera are all contributory to the rhythm and tempo of a film and obviously must be considered long before they reach the editor's table. As vital as the editor's contribution is, in many ways it is a carrying-out of an artistic conception that began in the first stages of production. The film must be conceived, planned, shot, and directed overall with the final editing assembly and rhythm firmly in mind.

Rhythm and tempo are intangible elements that cannot be achieved through the reasoning process but are arrived at primarily through intuition or feel. The film-maker "feels" that a short take will project excitement and a long shot deliberation. His intuition tells him whether the movement should be covered in one long take or broken up into a series of short takes. Rhythm is capable of precise control, but the film-maker must realize that it is not neglected until the editing stage; that every facet is planned, directed, and shot with the knowledge that each of these facets will play some role in the establishment of the rhythm and tempo of the completed film; and that the rhythm and tempo must be appropriate to the material and purpose of the film.

A sense of rhythm is the one indispensable asset for the director. This is probably true of any artist, for the actor, film editor, composer, comedian, conductor, dancer, sculptor, and painter all deal in their own way with rhythm. There is probably no way in which one can create in himself a sense of rhythm he does not possess, but an awareness of its importance and a consciousness of its use can go a long way toward helping the film-maker to develop this innate talent to the fullest.

CHAPTER 5

CAPTURING THE IMAGE

I can only say that I feel that every director should know as much as possible about the camera and what can be done with it. Without the camera there is nothing. . . . I believe that the motion picture camera has been used too passively for the most part. It should be the most creative thing about the entire business of film-making.[1]

—Gillo Pontecorvo, Director, The Battle of Algiers

A creative film stems from the individual who has something to say and the creative freedom to say it. The European film-makers have, for some time, accepted this and even taken it for granted, but such thinking has been slow in coming to America. For too many years the individual has been stifled by restrictions imposed by enormous crews, an assembly-line process that has divided the responsibilities among an unending procession of "chiefs," and a money-making mania which guaranteed a steady stream of pap that was, with a number of magnificent exceptions, high in technical value but artistically bankrupt.

THE PRODUCTION UNIT
The Creative Team

As the Europeans have known for some time, there must be one guiding force to the film—the director. Ideally, he chooses the subject of his film; works on the preparation and scripting from the beginning, seeing that it evolves in the way that he wishes; chooses the cast of performers; selects the cameraman who can best photograph his film; actively directs the film and supervises the use of the camera; and finally, controls the editing, music, opticals, and all other aspects of the making of his film. The film is the product of his imagination, talent, and exhaustive effort.

The major creative forces on any film, besides the director, are the cameraman, the script writer, and the editor. (The role of the script writer will be discussed shortly and a later chapter is concerned with the functions of the editor.) Most directors consider the cameraman to be their alter ego during the shooting stage. A good cameraman understands composition and optics and knows the tools with which he works and of what they are capable. He must fully understand the practical and creative use of lighting, and it is helpful, if not mandatory, that he know color and the psychology of color. And the cameraman, like the director, needs the ability to work with other people and to motivate them.

The cameraman's basic functions are to determine the exposure settings, to conceive the lighting of each shot, to designate the filters or any other needed photographic controls, and, in some instances, to select the composition of each shot. The latter responsibility is dependent upon the relationship between the director and the cameraman. In some relationships the director sets the action and determines the compositions; in others, the director blocks the action and the cameraman determines the composition; and in still other relationships the compositions are arrived at through the mutual efforts of the director and the cameraman.

Many problems can be solved and much time saved if the cameraman and the director pre-plan together before the actual filming begins, working out the photographic treatment of the film. By discussing the style, the mood, the type of action, any special effects, any known problems, etc., they can diminish many of the problems that can surface during the production stage. The ideal situation, particularly when filming a dramatic script, is to call together the cameraman and all other top members of the production staff, plus the major performers, for a rehearsal period. This will provide everyone with a grasp of the production and a chance to anticipate some of the "bugs" before the costly phase of actual filming begins. In professional production this is not always possible because of the cost factor and the unavailability of those involved. If the film-maker is not faced with these deterrents, such a rehearsal period can be most beneficial to the film.

Besides the cameraman, the director must establish a close relationship with those who will be performing before the camera, whether they be actors, models, students, company presidents, or people recruited at the filming location. These people are under the control of the director, and he must elicit from them what is necessary for the purpose of each shot. The story form presents the greatest problems, for the characters that are outlined in the script must be fully created. Therefore the director must have a firm concept as to the personalities, traits, and relationships of these characters so that he can inspire and guide the actors in their creation. The *subject-film* form generally calls for the subjects to portray themselves, but even here the director's careful and patient guidance is vitally important.

The director must strive to achieve from the performers an intimacy and subtlety of performance. The keen eye of the camera, especially in the close-up, can pick up the twitching of an eyelash, so that twitching must contribute something meaningful to the character or situation.

The tendency of many when they get in front of the camera is to "do" something; the problem is that they often over-do. Like people speaking to foreigners, they seem to feel that they must exaggerate to communicate to their audience. On film, when the purpose is to communicate a realistic interpretation of a situation, this exaggeration is unnecessary and distracting. When the subject exaggerates, his "stagy" performance signals the unreality of the scene, thus breaking the involvement of the audience. We have seen how the meaning of the film's images can be communicated to the audience in the way the director uses his camera and the way in which the editor juxtaposes the images on the pieces of film. This condition reduces the need for explicitness on the part of the camera's subject. The fact that the director has various ways of controlling the audience's attention also reduces the need for the performer to "do" things. The Mosjukhin° experiment illustrates that the actor need do nothing but that which is low-keyed and sincere. The fact that he does not have to "do" a great deal to put across his point does not mean that he need not be skilled in his work. On the contrary, it takes a great deal of skill to provide the casual subtlety of a Bing Crosby or Gary Cooper.

The Technical Team

Supporting the creative efforts of the director, cameraman, and script writer are the sound crew and camera crew.

THE SOUND CREW

The sound recordist and his crew are a necessary addition if the film being shot contains lip-synchronous dialogue—movement of the lips in the picture visibly synchronized with the voice. The *mixer* is in charge of the sound reproduction and so must be concerned with acoustics and the elimination of extraneous noise. Depending upon the conditions, he may have to devise some means to deaden or liven the sound on location so that the recorded sound will be acoustically suitable. His major problem, generally, is to deaden sound. He does this by hanging sheets, rugs, blankets, or some material that will reduce the reverberations of the sound. The problem of controlling extraneous noises can be more difficult since there are noises that defy control. Substandard sound is the chronic fault of the low-budget production.

°An experiment was carried out in Russia in the '20s by the Kuleshov Workshop in which a close-up of an actor, Mosjukhin, that had been shot for an earlier film, was inserted into another film in three different places. The result was the audience attributed three different expressions of emotion to the same shot after viewing the latter film.

The mixer should have a crew of one or two assistants. He will have to have an assistant to handle the microphone which generally will be placed on a *boom* or *fish-pole*. The fish-pole contains various controls which allow the assistant to move the mike in and out and turn it to change its angle. By moving the fish-pole and manipulating the controls, the assistant is usually able to keep the microphone in the proper position for a good pick-up of the sound. If the mixer has a second assistant on his crew, this second person is generally assigned to the tape recorder; his task is to make certain that the recorder is operating on cue, in the proper way, and at the proper level. The mixer then monitors the sound fed into the recorder so that he is always aware of the quality of the sound and the existence of any unwanted sound. Without the sound assistant the mixer must serve as recordist as well.

THE CAMERA CREW

The size of the camera crew can vary from one man to four or five, depending upon the budget, whether the crew is union or non-union, and the type of film. Ideally the size should depend upon the complexity of the film and, therefore, the work that must be accomplished. It is possible to utilize a crew of one—the cameraman—and he must set the camera and lights and operate the camera. For high-quality cinematography it is unwise to foist all of the work onto one person. Ideally the cameraman should have at least two assistants if the shooting assignment requires much in the way of lighting. One assistant functions as a *gaffer*

Fig. 5–1 Director, cameraman, and camera crew shooting a take (Richard C. Tomkins)

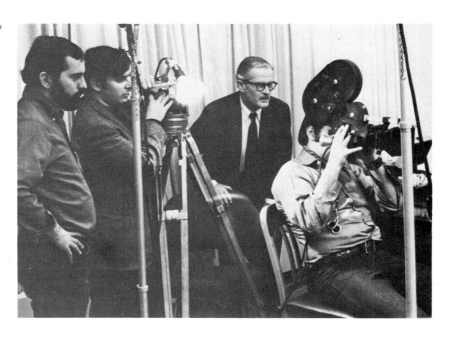

and assists in the setting of the lights. The second assistant aids in the *operation of the camera*—loading magazines, operating the dolly on moving shots, following focus when necessary, etc. On union productions with a sizable budget, the crew can consist of a gaffer, and three camera assistants. One of the assistants functions as the *camera operator,* for on such productions the director of photography rarely operates the camera. The second assistant *follows focus and operates the dolly.* The third assistant carries out such odd jobs as *loading the magazines, "slating the takes,"* and *keeping the camera report.* Whether a production has one or five assistants, someone must be assigned the job of slating and keeping the *camera report.* The editor of the film will be at a disadvantage if each take is not marked at the beginning with the slate, indicating the scene and take number so the editor will know its position in regard to the script.

Fig. 5-2 Assistant cameraman shading the lens (Richard C. Tomkins)

When the take is for sync sound, not only should the scene be identified with the slate, but the *clapper,* which is part of the slate, should also be utilized (unless the camera is equipped with an *electric clapstick*) to provide a reference point for the editor when he syncs the picture and sound. In shooting a take the director tells the recordist to start the tape. He then directs the cameraman to roll the camera. When both the tape and the camera are *running at speed,* the director instructs the assistant to *"slate it"* or *"mark it."* The assistant steps into the shot, holding the slate in clear view of the camera. He lifts the clapper and speaks the scene number and the take number, then slaps the clapper down. The noise made by the clapper is recorded on the tape, and the action is recorded on the film. Thus the editor has his needed reference points; in the cutting room, he can sync the voice and picture by matching the sound clap to the visual. Next, of course, the assistant steps out of the scene and the director calls "Action." This is the standard procedure when shooting a scene of controlled action. If it is impossible to control the action and therefore to identify the start of a take, the assistant holds the clapboard upside down at the *end of the take,* rather than the beginning. If the take is a sync sound take, he of course bangs the clapper at that time.

Fig. 5-3 Assistant cameraman changing lenses (Richard C. Tomkins)

Fig. 5-4 Assistant cameraman taking a light reading (Richard C. Tomkins)

The *slate,* itself, is a small blackboard with spaces for the title of the production, the scene number, the take number, the cameraman's name, the director's name, and the name of the production company producing the film. Generally the only information that changes between takes is the scene and take numbers. All of the material can be written in chalk on the board. Or the information can be written on tape with a black flow-pen, and the tape stuck to the front of the board. Some camera assistants make up tapes of a selection of the numbers so that they can change the material more rapidly. They usually stick the numbers to the back of the slate for easy access. When the tape method is used, the writing and the numbers are easier to read in the editing room.

The camera report will provide the editor with a full description of the take and whether it is the approved take of the director.

Fig. 5-5 Assistant cameraman slating a take (Richard C. Tomkins)

UNIT MANAGER

If a production requires much in the way of location shooting, hiring a unit manager can be money well spent. Whoever functions in this job can be given the administrative responsibilities of going ahead of the production unit and selecting the locations; making all of the necessary arrangements for shooting; checking for adequate power to run the lights, camera, and any other equipment; foreseeing any sound problems; and in general making all preparations so that the unit can move in and start work immediately. If a unit manager is not used, these responsibilities will have to be carried out by the director or the script writer.

ASSISTANT DIRECTOR

If the film is being shot in a studio, an assistant director is usually substituted for the unit manager. The assistant director relieves the director of the administrative duties so that he can be free to concentrate upon the more artistic elements.

SCRIPT GIRL

Once the complicated procedure of filming begins, it is not uncommon for the script itself to be neglected, except for an occasional glance by the director, now more concerned with the visual images than the words on a page. Yet it is important for someone to keep track to see that all elements of the script are covered properly. The script girl—although it is not mandatory that this function be handled by a female—takes over the responsibilities of recording all changes in the script during production, informing the director concerning continuity problems, and in general seeing that no changes occur in the appearance of objects or persons when they are shot at different times but are to be edited together in the completed film. It can be frustrating in the editing room to find that in two different shots of the same scene a subject is wearing two different ties.

GRIP

One final optional member of the production unit is the grip. His services can be most helpful whether the film is being shot on location or in the studio. His main responsibility is the props that will be used to dress the set or be handled by those appearing in the action of the scene. He must see that all props are present and in their proper place for each shot. Someone in charge of these minute details can add greatly to the efficiency of the production unit.

Recording the Take

The process of filming, which the director oversees, is a slow, painstaking procedure. The director has the greatest control over the filming when he is shooting controlled action from a prepared script. When this is the case, the director generally goes over each take with the cameraman and the sound mixer (if lip-sync is required) before the shot is recorded. A run-through of the action may then be helpful for the cameraman and the sound mixer so that they can determine the positions of their equipment in order to record what is desired with the best results. Once the director and/or the cameraman has placed the camera, and the sound mixer has located the microphone and any other sound controls, the lighting set-up must be resolved. Preliminary consideration of the camera, sound, and lighting set-ups may have occurred in the pre-planning of the director and the cameraman, but the final decisions cannot be made until the actual filming begins. Frequently the director will rehearse the action that is to be performed during this set-up period.

When the equipment is ready and the action thoroughly rehearsed, a "dry-run" can be carried out. Any deficiencies noted in the dry-run are corrected and, if deemed necessary, other dry-runs are performed. Finally, when everyone is satisfied with the set-up and what must be performed within the shot, the take is recorded.

Frequently the take will have to be repeated. The filming process is complex, and the coordination of all factors may not come together on the first try. Everyone must be at the peak of performance for that one take, and to reach that peak on the first attempt is not always possible. If changes are necessary, they are made, and all try again. This process is followed—as long as time and the budget permit—until the director is satisfied that the best possible take has been recorded.

Seldom are scenes shot in sequence, and this serves to make the director's work even more difficult. The shooting schedule is broken down into the easiest and least costly program. Scenes that occur in the same location, for example, no matter where they will appear in the completed film, are generally filmed at one time. This eliminates the necessity of having to return again to the location once these scenes are completed, unless retakes are necessary. The same procedure is often followed in the grouping of the scenes in which certain individuals appear.

Such scheduling solves economic and logistic problems, but it creates headaches for the director. He must have a complete grasp of his entire film from the first day of shooting so that he can do any scene of the film at any time. The grasp must be so thorough that if the beginning of a scene is filmed at one time, and the middle and end a month later, all of the shots will fit together, each shot matching emotionally and pictorially with the other shots, as if they were shot in sequence at the same time. A director with an excellent visual memory has the advantage for then he can carry every shot—the action, the camera angle, the emotional peak, the lighting, etc.—in his head until the film is completed. If the director is unable to do this, there is a strong danger that the film will be inconsistent and undershot (not enough material for the editor).

This sort of procedure, however, works only when the director is dealing with a tightly-scripted, controlled action. In certain types of production, such control by the director is not possible. Many documentaries and "industrials," for example, or any scenes of uncontrolled action cannot be filmed in this stop-and-go process. In such cases, the director will have to depend upon his staff and crews to be keenly aware of what is needed and to get this material on film when it happens. The director's responsibility is to communicate his concept of the scene to those who will be operating the camera and microphone so that they will view the action with this concept in mind and capture the necessary materials to bring the concept to fruition. In some cases the director may be with the crew, instructing them as to what and how to shoot. But frequently such scenes are shot with several crews, and it is not always possible for the director to be with all of them when they are shooting. Therefore, the director will have to leave the decisions to the heads of these crews. Directing such a film can, perhaps, be more frustrating than directing one in which the director has supreme control, but if the director is accurate in his instructions and if he can later cull from the exposed footage the proper pieces of film to build his conception, the film can be as disciplined as the tightly-scripted film.

THE SCRIPT

The writing of a film script is an art in its own right and is beyond the scope of this book. It is impossible, however, to discuss the techniques of film production without first considering the basic concepts of writing for the film. Our purpose will not be to teach you how to write a good script; we can no more accomplish that than we can teach you how to make a good film. All we can do is provide you with a general survey of some theories and procedures which have been used by many script writers and have been useful to us.

The script will not, of course, spring fully developed from your imagination, but rather will have to pass through stages of development. The first stage undoubtedly will be the basic idea or theme—what you wish to say or want to accomplish in your film. It can often be a help to sum up that idea in a *statement of purpose* for that will force you to consolidate the idea into a simple concrete statement. This statement can provide you with a reference point in selecting from a multiplicity of events those elements which will best express the idea and serve the purpose of the film. The next step is to arrange the selected events in their most effective order. When this step is complete, you have a *synopsis* of the film. Now you will probably wish to enlarge upon the synopsis— to provide a more detailed description of the events and to indicate how each of the events will be tied together so as to establish and maintain a unity and coherence. Your script has then developed into a *treatment* (Fig. 5.6). The treatment can then serve as your guide in the development of a *shooting script* (Fig. 5.7) which will contain specific ideas concerning the visual treatment, transitions from scene to scene, plus any dialogue, narration, and sound effects to be employed to add depth, meaning, and understanding to the visual images, the story, and the characters and their relationships.

The writer should always keep in mind that he is dealing with a means of expression that is first and mainly visual. The script should never be a work of literary effort with a list of visual ideas thrown in as an afterthought to the precious words. If the film is predominantly visual,

IRELAND ON THE GO!

IRELAND ON THE GO!

PICTURE	SOUND

The film opens on an up-angled view of the balcony overlooking the great banquet hall in Bunratty Castle. It is a dark scene, illuminated by two flaming torches. Immediately a man in 15th Century dress steps onto the balcony from the doorway behind, and looks directly at the camera. He is the man who welcomes the diners at the Bunratty banquet - but his words are changed somewhat as he welcomes our theater audience. As he speaks - there is a bit of a twinkle in his eye,

> "Noble Lords and Gracious Ladies, I bid you welcome! In fact, in the ancient Gaelic language, 'Cead Mille Failte' - one hundred thousand welcomes! A land of tradition and beauty awaits your pleasure.
>
> "Come Noble Lords and Ladies, join me in the emerald isle that is Ireland. I invite you to come and see what is happening today in our ancient land."

The scene fades quickly to black, accompanied by a trill on an accordian. Then, the accordian begins to play a traditional Irish jig - a bit slowly at first, gradually increasing in tempo - over a series of scenes that appear behind the titles and visually set the theme for the film.

PICTURE

NOTE: Numbers after each scene description refer to location on specially-prepared map of Ireland.

FADE IN

1. EXTERIOR - BUNRATTY CASTLE (1A)

Begin with up-angled scene featuring flags on the parapets, against an Irish sky. TILT DOWN to reveal the castle itself.

2. SAME - BUT CLOSER

of doorway to castle. MAN from Bunratty appears in doorway, with Irish wolfhound. He is the man who welcomes the visitors to the Medieval Banquet. He is dressed in Medieval costume.

3. MCU - MAN

from Bunratty, speaking directly to camera.

SOUND

EFX - TRUMPETS BLOWING, as if an important declaration is about to be made.

CONTINUE TRUMPETS

STOP TRUMPETS

MAN FROM BUNRATTY - SYNC: "Noble Lords and Gracious Ladies, I bid you welcome. In fact, in the ancient Gaelic language of my country, 'Cead Mile Failte' - one hundred thousand welcomes! A land of tradition and beauty awaits your pleasure.

(continued)

Fig. 5-6 An excerpt of a treatment

Fig. 5-7 The material in Fig. 5-6 realized as a shooting script

the dialogue and sound will reinforce, perhaps counterpoint, the visual images. Thus when the script is completed, it should consist of words describing visual impressions, words which are then translated back into visual images by the director.

The script the writer produces will serve as the blueprint from which the film will be built. Unlike the stage play or the novel, the film script is never a finished product but rather undergoes constant change. These changes are rendered principally by the director and, to a lesser degree, by the editor and cameraman as they convert the words on a page to visual and auditory images on film.

The Basic Elements

The film script is built step by step, the basic unit being the *shot*. The shot is one single image from camera-start to camera-stop, even though the composition of the image may be changed by the movements of the subjects of the shot or the camera. The writer plans and describes each shot in his script as he conceives of it in his imagination. Shots are manipulated and strung together to build a *scene*, although there are single-shot scenes also. The scene is a continuous action that takes place in one time and one place. A series of closely related scenes that form a dramatic segment like the chapter of a novel or the act of a play are then joined together in a predetermined continuity to form a *sequence*, and a progression of sequences composes the total film. The writer has complete freedom to use these elements in the way that best expresses his basic theme.

Let us now look at the more specific aspects of scripting the film. For convenience we feel it is necessary to divide the all-encompassing term *script* into two categories—the story film script and the subject film script. We fully realize that any categorization is unrealistic and abstract and of course the story film may contain factual information and the subject film may tell an interesting story, but these categories do seem to indicate a basic stylistic and procedural difference.

The Story Film Script

The story film, whether factual or fictional, places its emphasis on the story and the characters within that story, allowing these elements to communicate the theme and purpose of the film. For years the story film has been strangled by Aristotelian precepts laid down over 2,000 years ago—for the theater! When sound came to film with those prophetic words of Al Jolson in *The Jazz Singer*, "You ain't heard nothin' yet," the film-maker changed his emphasis, which until that time had been, correctly, on the visual image, and the motion picture entered into a phase tyrannized by talk. Story films began to resemble recorded plays.

Today the style of storytelling is changing. Many of these changes were brought on most dramatically in the 1950s by the works of Bergman, Kurosawa, Fellini, Antonioni, and the French "New Wave," with Godard, Truffaut, and Resnais in the forefront.

Characterization and story are still the "meat and potatoes" of the story film, but the well-made play script is fast becoming as outdated as the waltz. A "cinematic" story form, uniquely suited to the film, has evolved. Audiences today see faster and see more, and so the film-maker is beginning to give the audience more to look at—and fewer words to listen to.

Not only has the dependence upon dialogue ceased, but other literary values such as the conventional plots of the past, sequential narrative, and dramatic choice seem to be losing favor with contemporary audiences and film-makers. The contemporary audience, weaned on television commercials which employ rapid pace and visual excitement to tell their "stories" in sixty seconds, has been prepared for something else.

Form alone could not change; content, too, has had to change with changing times. The new visual forms cannot be superimposed upon the old conventional, well-plotted stories, for they are forms meant to convey today's stories to today's audiences. The contemporary spectator is not content to see stories with the familiar patterns relived vicariously by the spectator of the past, who promptly walked out of the theater to forget them. The pat little plots with the happy-ever-after endings no longer suffice. The conventional story film is, of course, still with us, and probably will be for some time, but it is the contemporary Cinematic Cinema which provides the writer with the greatest latitude in using the film as a means of personal and meaningful expression.

The communicative artist, whatever the form in which he practices, must be concerned with capturing and holding his audience; this is particularly so in the art of film, where the nature of the spectator's experience is such that his attention must be powerfully held throughout. There is nothing better to hold the spectator enthralled than a great story, involving fascinating characters—characters about whom the spectator cares. His desire to know how it comes out must be exploited by the film-maker. Yet this in no way implies that conventional theatrical plotting must be followed in telling the story and presenting the characters; the film has far more diverse and effective ways for accomplishing this than does the theater. A perceptive critic recently commented that television, with its constant interruptions by commercials (not to mention the inhabitants of the viewer's household) demands not the painstaking step-by-step building of the plot associated with the theater, but rather a series of powerful attractions presented individually to the viewer over the course of the program. Thus it is recognized that it is impossible to hold the viewer's attention from start to finish, that it must be recaptured anew throughout the film. This is precisely what today's Cinematic Cinema does to its spectators, with its abandonment of conventional continuity and its planned disorientations. Nevertheless, these are devices used to present stories and characters.

Despite all of the contemporary changes wrought on the story film script, certain basic ideas still have validity. Characterization remains one of the most important dramatic tools of the writer, and he should still determine precisely what characters he needs to tell his story and communicate his purpose. Even a contemporary audience finds unnecessary characters irrelevant and confusing and wants every character introduced to serve some purpose. The writer should be concerned also with the relationships between his characters and with the delineation of his selected characters so that each becomes a distinct and consistent personality. Perhaps today it is even more important that the writer take pains to see that characters not remain static, for the contemporary audience wants something exciting to happen to the characters, and not something they have seen a dozen times before.

The writer will probably always be concerned with the discipline of time. A basic "rule" that is often followed is to limit every scene to no more than three minutes. The feeling is that what must be told can be told within that time limit, and any scene beyond that length might slow the pace of the film. Most writers judge film time by figuring a minute a script-page.

The script should still possess a form of continuity so that the visual and auditory images join together and flow as a unified and coherent whole.

The Subject Film Script

In scripting the subject film the most important attribute of a good writer is his ability to gather, organize, and edit information, for facts are his stock-in-trade. This information, generally, is not difficult to locate, but the quality of the script will depend upon the quality of this information. The best sources are, of course, primary sources—where and to whom the events have happened—and not necessarily the public library, although this does not mean that some information in initial stages of preparation cannot be gathered from books.

We would also recommend the use of a tape recorder in gathering information. Talk with the people involved in the subject with which you are concerned, place their impressions, ideas, and knowledge on tape. The scriptwriter might take along a Polaroid camera so that he can also gain a visual record, which may prove valuable in the later planning of the film's visual images. Perhaps an even better suggestion would be the use of an 8mm motion picture camera. In this way the scriptwriter is capturing the primary material in motion; he will later be able to re-view the complete story. He will have for his use a kind of 8mm storyboard that may later be most useful in the synthesization of the material, for these motion pictures might indicate what has or has not visual potentialities. This technique could prove most valuable to the novice who may not as yet have developed his visual memory to its peak.

Once the gathering is completed the writer is left with a stack of notes, tape recordings, still photographs, and, perhaps, rolls of 8mm film. His Herculean task is now to make sense out of all of this material, to pull it together in some semblance of order, for no part will seem to have any connection with the other bits and pieces. The writer needs some kind of framework and that framework must suggest itself from the material on hand. In going over the collected materials the writer may find that it fits into a time sequence (past, present, future), a space sequence (one place to another place), or a logical sequence (cause to effect). At this stage the writer may find that the material does not fit with the concept or idea that was first decided upon. If this is the case, and the writer does not feel that the material can be molded to fit the preconceived idea, the idea will have to be revamped. One of the great dangers to a film-maker is stubborn preconception. Such a revamping will not be unique, for the production of a subject film is a constant revamping.

One final word of advice: The scriptwriter must organize, organize, organize. No doubt the best procedure to follow is the very old and very tried-and-true technique of making an outline. Nothing works better in bringing order to the chaos of the writer's research and imagination.

Now the writer must embark upon the task of editing his material, selecting the cinematic realities that will be suitable for the film, and scrapping those that will not befit the film's purpose. He should use actuality as a guide, but he should remember that the writer's purpose is to make a contribution to the creation of a unique filmic reality which is something new and different, and, above all, visual.

THE SHOT BREAKDOWN

One of the first decisions that will have to be made each time that the camera is set up concerns the shape and content of the image that will be recorded. This decision will be based primarily upon what the film-maker wishes to communicate in the shot. Closely allied with the question of the shape and content of the image will be the decision as to the choice of the action that will best communicate the meaning. There is no "one" way to shoot a subject, but there certainly must be a "best" way, and the best way is dependent upon the shot's context within the film.

The director cannot think in terms of one shot at a time, for he knows that the impact and meaning is dependent upon how these shots will join together. Each shot must augment and fulfill the shot that came before. The film is in a constant state of movement—the movement of the subjects within the frame, the movement of the camera which alters the picture continuously and constantly changes the point of view, and the sense of movement that comes from editing as the picture changes from one view to another. No shot can be conceived statically for its isolated content, but rather must be conceived for its part in a constantly changing flow of images, emotions, and rhythms.

Once you have determined the content and purpose of a scene, you should break down that scene into its separate shots, taking care that each shot will contribute to the rapport with your audience that we have already deemed so necessary. Basically, two different procedures can be followed in preparing the shot breakdown.

Master Scene

A frequently used procedure in the production of theatrical feature films, especially for scenes of complicated action, is the master scene technique; this technique also has validity in other film genres. All of a situation that occurs in a single setting is recorded in one continuous take; the action and the dialogue from the beginning to the end of the event are filmed with one camera, which may or may not remain in a stationary position. Portions of the action are selected for filming from different camera angles or at varying degrees of closeness, so these portions of action are later repeated and shot to be used during the editing stage as cut-ins within the master scene. This technique is particularly useful when the action is controlled and can be repeated almost identically a number of times to secure the cut-in shots.

The master scene can also be shot with multiple cameras; in this instance one camera records the master scene and the other camera or cameras record the cut-in shots simultaneously. When filming a sequence over which the film-maker has no control of the action, this is the only feasible technique to employ to get more than a long-shot coverage of the event.

The master scene technique does provide certain advantages. With one camera filming the entire action from beginning to end, the film-maker is covering himself. He can be certain that he has captured the entire event for the editor. Then, if he has properly covered the important points of the action with cut-ins, he has provided his editor with a variety of choices in the way that the scene can be cut, as well as the all-important opportunity of controlling the filmic time of the scene. If the cut-in is unsatisfactory for some reason or other, the action of the scene is still intact in the master scene. The wise film-maker, when utilizing the master scene, will shoot a supply of *reaction shots, reverses,* or *cut-aways*—shots that show a reaction to the main action or shots of a secondary course of action occurring simultaneously with the main action. Then the editor will be supplied with ample appropriate material to use to heighten the interest value of the scene, to increase or decrease the tempo of the scene, to improve the performance of an actor by being able to cut away to a reaction at a weak point in his performance, or to compress the action and the time of the scene—to mention only a few uses.

Trained actors seem to prefer the master scene because it affords them an opportunity for a sustained performance of some duration. Since filming is done in bits and pieces with little continuity of story line maintained, it can be difficult, particularly in highly dramatic moments, for an actor to give a performance that sustains the emotional feeling when the filming is done by a single shot process. The master scene allows the actor an opportunity to build a sustained performance, even though portions may have to be repeated later for the cut-in shots. Actors find it easier to repeat portions of the scene and maintain the emotion than trying to reach a certain level of emotional build for each shot of the single shot technique.

The master scene technique also has its disadvantages. One of these is cost, and this can be a major factor in how a film will be shot. The master scene technique utilizes a great deal of film that may never be used because of the double coverage of parts of the action. The film-maker may be wasting time and money in following the master scene approach if he has a clear picture in his head of how he wants the final edited version of the scene to look.

As the editor cuts from the master scene to the cut-in and back to the master scene, he frequently *cuts on action.* As a result, the actions of the cut-in shots must match perfectly the action in the master scene, or the editor may not be able to make his cut. Let us say, for example, that A crosses to the telephone, picks it up in his left hand, and dials with the right hand. The director has also shot a close shot of this same action. The editor decides to use the master scene to the point where A reaches down and picks up the phone and then to cut to the close shot for the remainder of the action. But in looking closely at the two shots, the editor discovers that in the close shot *A* picks up the phone in his right hand. The desired cut is impossible because the actions do not match and the phone would seem to "jump" from one hand to the other if the two shots were cut together. Trained actors can generally match the action precisely any number of times, but the untrained actor frequently has difficulty when faced with having to remember exactly how he has carried out an action, particularly if the scenes are shot days apart.

The untrained actor may also have difficulty in shooting the master scene if required to memorize lines, move correctly, and remember to stop exactly at spots pre-marked on the floor during a run-through. The film-maker can have his troubles with the trained actor, let alone the untrained. When using untrained personnel in front of the camera, the single shot approach may provide for the best results. It is probably significant that the "father" of montage, Eisenstein, dealt almost exclusively with untrained actors.

If you are improvising the action, camera placement, and angle, the master scene technique is not recommended, since this procedure will obviously work best when the action and camera work have been thoroughly planned and rehearsed. Without such planning and rehearsal, you may find it impossible to remember the bits of action during specific points and how they were carried out, thus making accuracy in the filming of the cut-ins impossible. D. W. Griffith's answer to this was to shoot his masters first and then plan his close-ups after screening the dailies; he was notoriously unsuccessful.

Lastly, the repeated use of the long shot of the master scene can become visually repetitious. With the camera in the same position and angle, cutting back and forth to it can, after a while, become quite monotonous unless the action in the scene or the movement of the camera offsets the repetitiveness of the shot. Also, as we have learned, the shot-in-depth, with its visual complexity and increased illusion of three-dimensionality, offers the film director the same opportunities enjoyed by his stage counterpart in placing his actors in significant relationship with each other and their environment. Welles can hold a master shot for an extraordinary length of time, moving the actors about in a giant chess game which continuously holds the interest of the spectator.

Single Shot

If you choose not to break down your film into master scenes, the alternative procedure is the single shot technique. This means that each scene of the film must be broken down into a series of single shots that will be joined together to form the action of the film. Generally a long shot is included at some point in the opening of each scene so that the geography is established; then the remainder of the action is broken down into closer shots for which the camera position and angle have been changed. The major task in using this technique is assuring a proper continuity of shots. The beginning and ending of each separate shot made of a *continuous action* must contain an overlapping of the action of the shot that will come before it and after it in the edited version, so that the editor will have a choice of cutting points and be able to cut on the action if he so wishes. The scene is made up of a series of shots that are usually quite different from one another; there is generally little repetition of positions and angles of the camera since one of the major advantages of this technique is the opportunity it affords for visual variety. Each shot in the sequence is a separate entity with its own dramatic purpose.

This technique adapts itself well to improvisational shooting, as well as to shooting with a complete preconceived concept of the scene and every shot in it. However, improvisational filming is not recommended for the beginner. In such a highly complex field there is nothing so valuable as thorough planning. Great care must be exercised to make certain that the entire action is adequately covered and that each shot will cut with the shot that is planned to come before it—whether this be according to a preconceived plan or whether the shooting of the scene is improvised on the spot.

This technique does tend to limit the editor and what he can do creatively. Since the scene is shot with a preconceived notion as to how the scene will be cut together, the editor will have little leeway in editing the film. This technique, perhaps even more than the master scene, is helped when you film a quantity of cut-away shots that will grant the editor more creative opportunity, as well as provide him with "pad" material in the event shots will not cut together properly. If such a situation does happen, the editor may be able to cut to a reaction shot (cut-away), snip off the "no-good" (N.G.) portion of the shot, and then cut back to the next action shot without any noticeably disturbing effect. Without the reaction shot to cut to, you are stuck with a bad take in your film.

Since this method requires filming the entire action in bits and pieces which will be joined together later for a full expression of the entire action, you must be able to stop and start at will any part of the action to be filmed. But try not to think a shot at a time. If continuity is to be maintained you should "think in threes." Each shot must be considered in relation to the one before it as well as the shot that will come after. Thus all movements at the end of shots showing a continuous action will be overlapped in the beginning of the following shot. Going back to our earlier example: A picks up the telephone at the end of a long shot. The next shot is a medium shot of A using the phone. The beginning of the medium shot should contain the action of A picking up the telephone, and in precisely the same way that he picked it up in the long shot.

The great advantage of the single shot technique is the freedom it affords the film-maker in breaking the action down into small parts (which, if necessary, can be improvised on the spot), allowing the film-maker the chance to incorporate a high degree of visual variety since *the position and angle of the camera may be changed for the filming of each shot.* There would be no sense in breaking the action into small parts if you filmed the action from the same position and angle. Every time you complete a shot, move the camera or change the angle, or both. Let each shot have its own appropriate dramatic purpose and interpret it with your camera according to that purpose.

The single shot technique may involve less duplication of footage than the master scene method, so from a budgetary standpoint it should be less expensive. Generally, a greater portion of the film exposed is utilized by the editor than is with the master scene method.

Although the subject before the camera does not carry out the entire sustained scene, the scene may be shot in sequence; this can be a great advantage when working with untrained subjects, who must perfect and remember only a small portion of the overall action and, therefore, should make less mistakes.

The single shot technique has its disadvantages. For one, you can become so wrapped up in getting the overlapped action for continuity that you pay less attention to what goes on within the shot, and so you end up with a fine continuity of dead shots. Since the major advantage of this technique is that each shot can have its own dramatic purpose, the film-maker must take full advantage of this. Achieve both the dramatic purpose of your shots and the continuity between them. While making a complete shooting plan may be difficult under certain circumstances, some basic concept of how the action will be shot should be predetermined. Any plan may change due to unforeseen circumstances when filming begins, and you must be prepared to improvise, but the general plan worked out beforehand can serve as a guide to ensure meaningful camera angles, matched action, proper selection of placement, and an adequate coverage of the action. It is difficult, if not impossible, to achieve these goals shooting off the top of your head.

One final disadvantage of the single shot technique is especially prevalent when filming interiors with artificial light. If your lighting is to be useful and meaningful, it should be set for each shot; with the action broken down into small parts, and the camera moved about repeatedly, the lighting will have to be changed often. This takes time, so the entire filming process will no doubt consume more time than the master scene approach. However, the photographic quality should be consistently higher because of the necessity to adjust the lighting to each shot.

To conclude, we would suggest that you select the master scene approach with a single camera if the following conditions exist:

1   filming from a shooting script;
2   using trained before-the-camera subjects;
3   desiring greater variety for editing;
4   having sufficient film available;
5   utilizing controlled action.

Use the master scene with multiple cameras when:

1   filming uncontrolled action;
2   the script involves action that can be staged only once;

3   more than a long shot of the action is desired.

The single shot technique normally is best if:
1   visual variety and a dramatic purpose to each shot is desired;
2   the action is completely controllable;
3   untrained before-the-camera subjects are being used;
4   the budget is tight, necessitating a firm control over the amount of film used, but extra shooting time is available;
5   improvisation is necessary.

Obviously you do not have to use one or the other of these techniques for the entire film. The technique employed should be selected because of the advantages it offers for any given situation, whether it be the entire film or only a scene or sequence. You may select the master scene for a portion of a scene that involves some very complex action and then go to the single shot technique to complete the scene. When to use each technique will be dictated by each situation for there is no overall rule one can or should follow.

PUTTING THE CAMERA TO WORK

Before we turn our attention to the technical aspects of the use of the camera, you should first be made aware of the basic purpose the camera must serve. When deciding how and what the camera will record, consider first your interpretation of the subject of the film, and then how the projected shot can convey that interpretation to the audience. The shot will probably never convey to the audience the full implications of the meaning it communicates to you (unless your film is instructional and must communicate specific information). But the shot should say something to the spectator if he is to become involved mentally and emotionally with the film. You will use visual symbols to carry the meaning and emotional involvement to the audience. But if the symbols are to have a chance to accomplish their task, you must control the attention of the audience, project the mood of the scene, and establish an emotional climate. The symbols visually project your interpretation of the scene and the film, and the manner in which the camera is used will contribute greatly in controlling attention, projecting the mood, and establishing the emotional climate. Above all, the symbols, not your camera technique, should reach the attention of the spectator. You want the audience to see, understand, and be affected by the symbols, not the clever way you manipulate the camera; but unless the camera is used properly, it will call attention to itself. One basic function of the camera is to imitate or replace the physical and mental controls of the spectator over his optical system. It becomes, so to speak, a second optical system for your audience, a mind's eye, and we control its attention to see only what we wish it to see.

In life we control our own attention through both a physical and mental process. The eyes physically focus on an object; the physical action of the eye is triggered by a mental process. Mentally we fix our whole vision onto an object, and thereby that object receives our full attention. The mind says that we must see only that object, although physically the view of the eyes takes in other objects, but the mind ignores them. No actual change in the scale of the object takes place, but there is a mental change in scale, for the mind has caused the object to fill the entire "screen" of our mind.

When something happens in film that warrants the spectator's full attention, the film-maker will duplicate this mental process. However, in film the scale of the object is actually changed and the entire screen is filled with a close-up.

In life our eyes often first wander over many nonessentials until they come to rest upon an object that then catches their complete attention. This state can be duplicated on film in several ways:

1 By panning the camera to the essential article and then cutting to a close-up.
2 By panning the camera to the object of attention and then zooming into a close-up.
3 By tracking into a close-up of the object.
4 By zooming into a close-up of the object.
5 By duplicating the physical focusing of the eye by focusing the lens. We have already learned that the eye brings the essential details into sharp focus, allowing the nonessentials to blur out. We also know that the lens is capable of duplicating this exact process when the proper focal length is employed.
6 By setting up certain situations that allow the spectator to use his own mental and physical controls as he normally would:
   (a) A moving subject in contrast with static objects will catch our attention in life; so will it on film.
   (b) A figure, because of its importance to an action, will catch the spectator's attention in the real world; this figure holds the same power on film.
   (c) Any contrasting object or person gains our attention, and we can contrast by color, size, height, or spatial distance.

The camera can capture the attention of the audience by duplicating or replacing the human system of focusing attention, in many ways even improving upon it. The use of any one of these techniques is dependent upon the degree of attention you desire and the situation in the scene. When the technique is too emphatic or too far removed from the spectator's daily use of his own vision, it calls attention to itself. You have committed the sin of overacting with your camera. The audience should be more concerned with the action, not with a virtuoso performance of the camera. This in no way inplies that your camera work must be prosaic and ordinary. On the contrary, it must be highly imaginative if it is to unobtrusively control the attention of the audience, help maintain the mood of the scene, and create the proper emotional climate. It must accomplish all of this while being consistent with the physical and mental powers of the spectator's vision.

Moving the Camera

Film gained its freedom and became a unique and fascinating art form when the camera became mobile. The first step toward mobility came with the realization that it was possible to cut between shots, but camera movement was always on the outskirts, looking on at the action from afar. Griffith supplied the next step in mobility when he transported the camera into the action, removing the camera from its seat in the orchestra and allowing it to witness the action at close range. Even with these developments the film was hobbled; it served mainly the function of a recording device. It was Murnau who finally unshackled the film by allowing the camera to operate as a separate force. Murnau gave the camera movement within the shot, and now the camera could move within and participate in the dramatic action. Now the film-maker could achieve a sense of movement by cutting from shot to shot, through the action happening within the frame, and in the movement of the camera. It is the latter which probably creates the greatest sense of movement because such movement carries the spectator along with the camera.

BASIC TYPES OF MOVEMENT

The camera can *pan* to the left, to the right, up, or down. The movements up or down are sometimes referred to as *tilting* the camera. A pan movement is a turning or tilting of the camera so that its view takes in the horizontal or vertical panorama of an area without, however, moving from its axis. When the camera is either mounted on some kind of vehicle or is hand-held, the camera can engage in a *tracking* movement. Such a movement of the camera occurs when the camera is transported through space toward, away from, parallel, or diagonal to the course of action being photographed. Another movement of the camera is the *crane* shot, made possible by utilizing a special vehicle that has a counterbalanced arm on which the camera and its operator are placed. The arm, and therefore the camera, can be raised, lowered, swung to the right or left, or any combination of these movements. A shot that resembles the crane shot, but is less restricted, is the *helicopter shot.* The camera is mounted inside of a helicopter which can rise, drop down, or move in any direction in relation to the action being photographed.

These movements can also work together within a shot. By mounting the camera onto a crane, you have the capability of tracking and panning, as well as moving the arm of the crane. Such flexibility of movement can be extremely tempting, but at the same time the results can be quite grotesque. Your decision as to what movements to make use of should be guided by the purpose the shot is to serve. If you have reason to think that a movement or combination of movements will take away from that purpose, you should rethink the movement, and find the one that will be completely subservient to your purpose. Remember, the spectator's concentration must be on the focal point of the shot, not the shot itself.

Too often we ignore the potential of camera movement, except for panning, because we feel it will be too expensive. The rental of a crab-dolly to be used for tracking the camera *is* expensive—approximately $35.00 per day plus some means of transporting it to where it is to be used—but it is not necessary to go to such expenses. We have mentioned several substitutes that may cost nothing that can be used in place of the dolly (see page 36), and more than likely you can think of devices we have not mentioned.° If you can spend the extra money or put your ingenuity to work, the ability to move the camera can add a smoothness of continuity and a flexibility of expression that is usually associated with the best cinematography.

You can find many who are against movement of the camera per se; they feel it creates too unreal an experience for the audience. Yet if movement is properly employed, this need not happen. People with this attitude are a bit behind the times. This was why the Russian filmmakers, in the silent era, devised the montage, seeking to achieve greater expression without moving the camera. We are in an era in which the prime concern is what happens within the frame of the shot, rather than in the relationship of the frames to one another. If our concern with the concept of the frame is to be fully voiced, the camera must move. We will admit that movement of the camera has lately been carried to extremes. Dwight MacDonald, the former film critic of *Esquire*, has justifiably complained that in some cases the talkies have become the walkies. But we are not advocating excess. We are advocating the use of movement when it adds meaning to and/or aids in emphasizing the content of the frame.

Removing the camera from the tripod and holding it in the hands is a method of shooting that has been standard procedure for some time with newsreel and combat cameramen, and, in such action scenes as fights and dancing, it has been a technique used on feature films as well.

The influence of the *nouvelle vague,* cinema verité, and the underground film movement in the United States has established hand-holding as a technique, and it can be found in most every type of film production today. It offers freedom and fluidity in the following of an action and at the same time creates a unique feeling of subjectivity, for the movement of the camera operator can be seen and the spectator has the sensation of participating in the action. For this reason, unless the shot calls for a subjective impression, hand-holding should not be used. There is an example from Mike Nichol's *The Graduate* that we consider to be excellent usage of the hand-held camera. One scene of the film takes place at the birthday party for the hero. He has been given a complete scuba diving outfit by his father and has been goaded by the father into demonstrating the outfit in the family pool. We first see the hero ludicrously encumbered by the wet suit, air tanks, face mask, flippers, and carrying a spear gun. As he begins to move out of the house and walk to the pool, the camera becomes subjective so that we see the short journey through the hero's eyes, including a view of the flippers protruding ahead, as he takes each step and the sound of the breathing apparatus is in our ears.

THE HAND-HELD CAMERA

Fig. 5–8 Hand-holding the camera

°One student felt that he needed some sort of dolly, so he borrowed his little sister's tricycle and mounted the camera on it. The tricycle worked quite well.

In this instance the subjective experience is not only useful, it is vital to the scene. The shot was accomplished, of course, by mounting a face mask on the camera to simulate the real framing of the mask. The camera operator wore flippers and hand-held the camera as he stomped his way to the pool.

The hand-holding technique is not as simple as it might seem. The camera can be held in one of several ways, depending upon the camera and the movement that is to be carried out. Some cameras—Bell and Howell Filmo and Eyemo, Doiflex, Bolex, etc.—are held by a handgrip located beneath the camera. The standard grip on the Arriflex 35IIC is on the side, but many cameramen hold both the side grip and the motor, which is on the bottom, for maximum control. The operator's wrists and forearm carry the weight of these cameras. *Body braces* and *shoulder pods* are available, and they help relieve the weight of the camera considerably. Other cameras, especially those with a rear-mounted magazine (the 16mm Eclair, for example), can be supported partially by the shoulder, with the wrists and forearms providing the remainder of the support. These cameras are also generally used with a body brace. This manner of handholding affords greater steadiness to the picture. No matter what technique is employed, handholding requires great stamina on the part of the cameraman.

The camera operator needs to work out a method of moving with the camera so that the resulting picture will not look as though the operator were bounding along on springs. For a steady picture the best lens to use is a short focal-length lens. If you attempt the shot with a long focal-length lens, anything that causes the slightest movement of the camera will be magnified ten-fold—a slight breeze, the breathing of the camera operator, even the operator's heartbeat. A student film-maker destroyed a beautifully composed shot that psychologically and emotionally projected exactly what he was seeking. The shot was taken with a 75mm lens. It consisted of a long view of a gently sloping snow-covered hill, backed by a line of evergreen trees, and broken only by a flight of stone steps. Into this tranquil setting comes one tiny lone figure who descends the stone steps. Within the framework of the film, this shot depicts the movement of a character who feels lonely and alienated from everyone around her. The shot, as conceived, worked perfectly in projecting just such an impression. But the director destroyed the effect by handholding the shot. The weather was cold and so was the camera operator, and to make matters worse, the director chose to move the camera parallel to the movement of the subject. With the long lens taking the shot, the movement of the camera left one with the distinct impression that the operator was moving along ground zero of a bomb blast as the frame of the picture violently bobbed and danced around.

In conclusion, one usually handholds only if:

1   the task is a moving shot;
2   the subjectivity of the hand-held movement is desired;
3   a short focal-length lens can be used;

4 the weight of the camera can be supported so as to insure the best possible picture steadiness.

Never set out intentionally to shoot a film without a tripod. You will be constantly hampered and severely limited in what you can shoot. The tripod will give you a firm support that will produce steady pictures and also assure you smoother panning movements because of the flexible tripod head.

Camera Angle

You have an infinite variety of choices as to where to place the camera to view the scene. The selection of a particular position should never be based upon a haphazard decision, for camera angle is a useful and powerful factor in audience comprehension of the action and audience involvement. Camera angle specifies the position of the spectator in relation to the action being carried out. It can also determine the extent of the spectator's view of that action, and it can communicate to him the psychological implications of the view—like the high- and low-angle shots utilized by Losey in *The Servant*.

However, the spectator must also be placed in a *possible* position. The "creative" director who has placed his camera inside of the fireplace to view the action taking place in front of the fire has certainly not selected a "possible" position. How many people sit inside a fireplace? Who wants a burned backside? As a result, the impossibility of the camera angle signals to the audience the unreality of the action taking place in front of the camera, and the unwelcome knowledge that contrivance is present.

By controlling the extent of the spectator's view of the subject, camera angle also serves the film-maker as a means of controlling the spectator's attention and of indicating to the viewer the point of dominant dramatic emphasis in the action.

BASIC TYPES OF CAMERA ANGLE

Should you reach the decision that you wish to place the spectator outside the action, viewing it through the eyes of an unseen, omniscient eavesdropper, you would select *objective camera angles* (Fig. 5.9). The camera is used as an unseen observer. The angles are more neutral and impersonal. The scene takes place oblivious to the camera and no one within the scene must ever look into the camera lens. Most films are shot utilizing a majority of objective angles.

Should your decision be to place the audience within the scene, you would employ *subjective camera angles* (Fig. 5.10). The subjective camera can serve as the eyes of the spectator actually being involved in the scene, or as the eyes of an involved participant through which the audience sees the action. It is not inconceivable that a scene might employ objective angles as well as both types of subjective angles. The film *Bullitt* utilizes both of these types of subjective angles interspersed with objective angles in a most exciting automobile chase sequence. The

Fig. 5–9 An objective camera angle
(*Paths of Glory*, released by United Artists, ©
Harris-Kubrick Pictures Corp., 1957)

Fig. 5–10 A subjective camera angle

spectator is placed at times in the seat next to the driver, viewing the action through the windshield of an auto involved in the chase; at other times he actually sees the action through the eyes of the driver of this same car; and at still other times he views the action from outside, watching the chase objectively, from the sidelines.

The drunk scene in *The Last Laugh* is another example of the involving of the audience in the film's action; the camera's spinning and stumbling as in a drunken stupor here serves as the eyes of the audience. The example given earlier from *The Graduate* shows the use of the camera as if it were a participant in the scene—we see the walk to the swimming pool through Benjamin's eyes. Remember when using the subjective angle that any subject in the scene relating to the subject represented by the camera *must* look directly into the lens of the camera. This is essential for the proper subjectivity. Sudden shifts from an objective angle to a subjective angle can have great shock value, for such a shift tends to disorient the audience. Be certain that such a shock and disorientation is desired before using this technique. The subjective angle can be an interesting way of treating an action and involving your audience, but be especially careful in what you involve them and for how long. Carried too far, the subjective angle can alienate the spectator who may not wish to be involved in the action in that particular way for that length of time. In other words, the involvement is not left to the choice of the spectator, and so it is important that the director act for the spectator as the spectator would wish him to.

The final classification of camera angle falls somewhere between the objective and subjective angles. This camera position is called the *point-of-view angle.* This angle views the scene or action from the viewpoint of a particular participant, but is not a subjective angle because it does not show the action directly through this participant's eyes. Rather it is objective and views the action as though the camera were standing next to the participant as an unseen observer seeing the action from this participant's point of view. As a result, the spectator gets a closer view of the action without becoming involved as a participant.

A common practice when filming a scene between two or three people is to gradually bring the audience in closer to the action by first utilizing over-the-shoulder shots and then cutting to point-of-view angles. In the point-of-view shots *the subject does not look into the camera,* for that would mean the shot was from a subjective angle and that we were seeing one participant through the eyes of the other. The camera, you will remember, is next to the subject, so the other person looks to the side of the camera lens; which side of the lens is determined by the *imagainary line* (see page 149).

Another conventional use of the point-of-view angle is to show the audience what a subject is seeing when he looks off-camera. This is commonly referred to as a *reverse angle* (Fig. 5.11). In the first shot we see the subject look to the right or left frame of the picture and we realize that he sees something beyond the range of this shot. The camera then steps to the side of the subject, so to speak, and looks in the direction the subject is looking, and so the audience sees what the subject was seeing off-camera. Again, the film-maker must not allow anyone to look into the lens or the shot will become one of a subjective angle. This must be of vital concern because the subjective angle has an impact which may not be desired.

Fig. 5–11   A point-of-view camera angle. In the first shot we see the subject looking off-camera; and the next shot shows us what he sees (Mel Wittenstein)

Cutting from an objective angle to a point-of-view angle creates no difficulty because both shots are in a sense "objective" angles. But by utilizing the two, you move the audience from its position as unseen observer on the sidelines into the center of the action, but still as an unseen observer.

Camera angle involves several decisions on the part of the film-maker: the *size of the image* desired, the *angle at which the image is viewed,* and the *height at which the camera is placed.*

THE COMPONENT PARTS

IMAGE SIZE   The size of the image desired will determine the type of shot that is selected. Shots are divided basically into three categories. The *long shot* (Fig. 5.12) gives us a wide view of an area, but the objects are small in scale. When we wish to orient the audience and familiarize it with the locale, the people, and the objects located within that locale, we employ a long shot. Entrances, exits, and movements from place to place which have a dramatic purpose are also generally depicted in long shot. The long shot used as an establishing shot generally appears at

Fig. 5–12 A long shot

Medium shot

Close shot (Mel Wittenstein)

Fig. 5–13 A 2-shot: profile

Angled (Mel Wittenstein)

or near the beginning of a scene in order to orient the audience. Then the camera's view is moved closer into the action, focusing on the most important parts of the whole action. Normally the film-maker might move back to a long shot after the scene has progressed for a time in order to reorient the audience to the geography of the scene, and then again at or near the end of the scene. These long shots add a sense of scale to the scene, allowing the audience to refamiliarize themselves with the location and the positions of the subjects within that locale. Yet often we hesitate to go back to a long shot because it reduces the size of the subjects and because the action gets lost in the clutter of objects and people. The long shot lessens our control of the audience's attention. The long shot should normally be kept on the screen for only a short time, unless it serves some definite dramatic purpose, and should never be employed when important action is taking place that could be viewed better at a closer range.

The *medium shot* presents a midrange in both the extent of the view and the scale of the image (Fig. 5.12). The subjects are generally shown from above the knees or from just below the waist. The medium shot can include more than one subject, viewed from a closer range so that the spectator will be able to see facial expressions, movements, and business.

One of the most useful shots of the medium range category is the two-shot in which two subjects carry out dialogue or action, or both. A two-shot can be staged with the two subjects in profile, or it can be angled, an important variation giving a sense of depth to the shot and increasing its dynamics (Fig. 5.13). The major problems with the profile are that it is not a particularly interesting shot since the subjects are in an obviously symmetrical composition, and it is difficult to give dominance to either of the subjects. To provide interest and dominance when needed, you must rely on lighting, action, dialogue, or color, when applicable.

When the two-shot is staged by angling the shot and creating a sense of depth, the major problems with the profile shot are eliminated. With this type of medium shot the subject nearest the camera is usually closed to (turned away from) the camera to whatever degree desired, and the other subject is generally seen in a three-quarter open position—three-quarters of his front visible to the camera. Obviously the subject that is more open to the camera receives dominance and the different positions of the bodies create a more interesting composition. If you wish to then switch the dominance you only have to reverse the preceding shot.

The *close shot* encompasses a narrow, constricted view with the objects seen in a large scale (Fig. 5.12). Several variations of the close shot can be employed. The *medium close shot* shows one person from the mid-chest and up. A *close-up* will reveal just the head or head and shoulders. The *extreme close-up* includes only some portion of the subject's face. All of these close shots naturally fill the entire screen with their image. The close shot is an extremely powerful shot and so normally is used only when we wish to add emphasis to some detail. It is such an important filmic device that we will discuss it at some length shortly. Of course, the close-up can be used with great effectiveness in presenting objects and portions of the body other than the face.

Although the above types of shot are the basic choices in determining the image size and range of the scene, a wide variation of these basic shots exists. These variations range from the *extreme long shot* (Fig. 5.14) that shows a large expanse of area, to the extreme close-up that fills the screen with a view of the human eye (Fig. 5.15). To provide you with rules or procedures to follow in determining when you might use each particular shot would be foolish. The selection must be based upon considerations of the complexity of the action, the importance of the action, the rhythm of the scene, and the visual style, to name only a few. Generally a film is composed of a predominance of medium range shots with the long shots and close shots being used for orientation and emphasis, respectively.

Fig. 5–14 An extreme long shot (Mel Wittenstein)

SUBJECT ANGLE   The main thing to remember in establishing the angle at which the subject will be photographed is that you are preparing a film dealing with a three-dimensional world to be projected onto a two-dimensional screen. Therefore, to achieve this sense of depth the subject must be viewed so that two sides are shown, and, when possible, either the top or bottom. For example, viewing a building from a straight front position gives a flat appearance; it has no solidity (Fig. 5.16). The human subject is also best viewed at a three-quarter angle rather than straight on. The use of proper angling of the image in the creation of depth is further strengthened by lighting, movement (camera and subject), use of short focal-length lenses, color, etc. Always strive to achieve the three-dimensional; it not only creates a greater sense of reality, it is more aesthetically pleasing.

Fig. 5–15   An extreme close-up (Mel Wittenstein)

CAMERA HEIGHT   The height at which the camera is placed is a very important factor in the effective quality of the camera angle, and yet it is a factor that is frequently neglected, especially in nontheatrical subject film production. Too often the camera height is determined by the position that is most comfortable for the camera operator or by the position that provides an "interesting" picture. Both of these elements can be considerations, but the height should never be arbitrarily arrived at without some concern and consideration of the aesthetic, dramatic, and psychological implication which are part of the effectiveness of a shot. As we discussed in Chapter 4, the height of the camera can have a considerable effect upon your audience, especially in shaping its reactions and involvement in the film.

Fig. 5–16   Subject angle: flat

When filming at a *level angle* the camera is placed at the eye-level of the subject or at the level that corresponds to the eye-level of a person of average height. When employing the *objective camera angle* and shooting from a level angle, always select the eye-level of the subject being photographed whether he is sitting or standing. Too many cameramen consider eye-level to mean their eye-level (or rather, normal tripod level) and not the subject's. When the subject is sitting, the camera should be

In-depth (Mel Wittenstein)

dropped down to the eye-level of the sitting subject and not placed at the eye-level of the cameraman. The latter would be a case of a high-angle shot looking down on the subject, not a level angle.

When the *point-of-view angle* is being used, the level is determined by the eye-level of the one from whose point of view we are seeing. If one subject is standing and one is sitting, the camera will look down on the sitting subject and look up at the one standing.

The *subjective close shot* is generally placed at the eye-level of the person being photographed, unless some psychological factor dictates otherwise. For example, the subject through whose eyes we are seeing the person may feel dominated by that person; therefore, we project our subject's feelings by shooting the close shot of the person from a slightly lower angle rather than the eye-level of the subject.

A *high angle* is achieved when the camera is pointed downward at the subject being photographed. The high-angle shot has practical, as well as aesthetic and psychological, uses. On the practical side, the high angle can make it easier for the audience to orient to the area of the scene. A common practice is to open a scene with a high-angle long shot of an area, such as a city, a factory complex, a village nestled in a valley, etc., and then to drop down for a level angle as we move into the area. Remember the superb opening to Olivier's *Henry V*, as the camera sweeps in over sixteenth-century London, or *West Side Story*, with a similar descent into New York on a summer morning. First, the audience is provided with an aerial map of the region, and then it is moved into the location, thus allowing the viewers in the audience to orient themselves fully.

Another practical consideration occurs when we must film an action that takes place over a large depth of field. Filming the action at a level angle or a low angle will record in sharp focus only the action taking place in the foreground, but by shooting the same action at a high angle we can provide a view of the entire action that is in sharp focus. Actually, level or low angles could not record the entire action even if sharp focus over the complete area could be achieved because the action in the background would be blocked by the action in the foreground (Fig. 5.17). This is, of course, the main reason why sporting events are filmed from a high angle.

Fig. 5–17 The level angle shot:
a limited range of view because objects in the foreground block objects in the background
The high angle shot is free of these obstructions (Mel Wittenstein)

Aesthetically, high angles are much more pleasing in presenting areas with a complex pattern. In a travel film on Peru produced by the authors, we opened the sequence in Lima with an aerial shot of the city at night and then dissolved from this to a moving shot through the streets of Lima. This combination was aesthetically pleasing because of the fascinating patterns of lights in the opening high angle and the multi-colored neon lights of the street rushing by in the moving shot.

One important point to remember about the high-angle shot is that it tends to give the impression that the speed of the action is slowed down because of the large area encompassed in the camera's range. An excellent example of the use of a high-angle shot to purposely slow the action, so as to achieve a particular psychological reaction in the audience, occurs in a Japanese film entitled *The Island*. This film deals with the hardships and struggles of a Japanese family living on a tiny island off the coast of one of the main Japanese islands. Near the end of the film one of the children becomes seriously ill and the father races for the doctor. He must first row across the expanse of water that separates the small island from the main island. The father must then run to the doctor's house, which is some distance from the dock. To psychologically expand the distance and slow the speed of this life-or-death race, director Kaneto Shindo shot the father running down the road to the doctor's house in extreme long shots at a high angle. The audience sees a large expanse of the countryside including the doctor's house and the road leading to it. The tiny figure of the father running as fast as he can appears to be moving at a snail's pace.

However, if the action you are filming is fast-moving, and you wish to project that accelerated pace, you must take care in filming the action from a high angle. As illustrated in the above example, your action will be slowed down considerably and you will lose the impression you wish to project.

When the camera is tilted upward to view the subject from below, it is called a *low-angle* shot. This angle can range in height from just below eye-level downward to an extreme worm's-eye view of the action.

The low angle is useful in establishing emphasis or dominance in a scene (Fig. 5.18). That piece of action or subject you wish to emphasize is placed in the foreground with the camera at a lower angle looking up at the action or subject. This will cause this action or subject to appear to be towering over anything that is going on in the background.

The low-angle shot has practical uses as well. One way to eliminate unwanted background or to obtain a previously missed close-up, is to drop the camera to a low angle and isolate the subject against the sky or any other nondescript background. Many of the effective close shots of athletes in Reifenstal's great film of the 1936 Berlin Olympics were made in this way. Practically speaking, too, the low angle will also tend to indicate a separation between persons or objects. Lastly, if a wide-angle shot contains too much unwanted foreground the camera level can be dropped down a bit and the camera tilted up, eliminating the unwanted material.

Fig. 5-18 The low angle provides dominance for the subject in the foreground (Mel Wittenstein)

A useful procedure to follow is to change camera angle every time you record a different take of a continuous action that will later be cut together in a series. If such a practice is not carried out, grave problems can arise in the editing room. Before-the-camera subjects may be able to duplicate their actions, but chances are the duplication will not be exact. Without the changes of angle to cover the discrepancies in the action, no matter how slight, jumps in the movement will result when the pictures are joined together. Some film-makers only change the lens, or use a zoom lens and merely change its focal length. In some cases this is a necessary practice, such as in switching from an over-the-shoulder shot to a point-of-view shot. In this instance the over-the-shoulder shot is preparing the audience for the close shot, and therefore the close-up should be from essentially the same camera position. Many times this procedure of changing lens and not changing camera position is used because of lack of time. Every time the camera is moved the lighting must be changed to adapt to the new position, and this does take time. The practice of changing the lens is quite common in nontheatrical production, but too frequently it is used because the film-maker is lazy, uninformed, or unimaginative. The tendency to follow this technique seems to be particularly prevalent when the film-maker is using a zoom lens. On the whole, unless some particular purpose dictates otherwise, we suggest that you change both the lens, when applicable, and the position of the camera when recording a new take. Change of scale alone will not insure a continuity which is able to be smoothly edited.

The camera angles which you select should be based upon consideration of a number of factors. Many of these considerations may be carried out intuitively, and all may not apply to each shot. But all should be given some thought when you are preparing your shot breakdown before production begins.

First of all, technical considerations may affect the types of camera angles you will be able to employ. Limitations in lighting or camera equipment may make the use of some angles impossible. Time can be the film-maker's greatest enemy. Certain camera angles consume a great deal of time to set up. We recently made a film that had to be completed within a ridiculously short time, on an even more ridiculously short budget. It was impossible to use any difficult camera angles, no matter how tempting they were. Being aware of the time limitations, the shot breakdown was prepared utilizing straightforward angles with the visual style created in the editing and optical effects. This is not the best procedure to follow. But if such technical problems are not considered beforehand and solutions worked out, the film-maker may find himself in a ticklish situation.

Editorial considerations also play an important role in the selection of camera angle. The action as a whole must be considered, then determinations made as to whether parts of the action when joined together in the editing room will project a true impression of the whole action. If this is not possible (or if this is not the effect desired), angles must be determined which will present the action as a whole, with close-ups to be inserted within these angles to provide emphasis for the most important facets of the action. The effectiveness of either of these techniques in capturing the action will depend a great deal upon the angles chosen.

Consideration of the *light in nature*—determined by the weather, the natural features of the location, etc.—can be very important factors when determining camera angle. For the best photographic results, the key light (direct sunbeams) should strike the scene from the side or from three-quarters front. Even with careful planning this factor limits your choice of camera angle or necessitates the time-consuming use of booster lights or reflectors. Certain natural features of the location may be unwanted, so camera angles will have to be selected which eliminate the unwanted features. Recently while filming a historical piece, we had to continually employ camera angles which would eliminate telephone wires and any other contemporary structures which would have destroyed the illusion.

We have repeatedly stressed the *aesthetic, psychological,* and *dramatic* considerations that must always be applied in determining camera angle. While it is true that technical and practical considerations often make it impossible to employ the angles we wish for aesthetic, psychological, or dramatic reasons, prior consideration of all of these factors will allow us to make compromises. You may not always be able to get exactly what you want, but by knowing what camera angle can do, and by including these considerations in selecting the angle, you can only improve your work. Camera angle is a vitally important tool of the film-maker and must *never* be selected haphazardly or whimsically.

Continuity of Shots

Earlier we stressed the necessity of preparing a shot breakdown for your film. One of the major reasons for making this shooting plan is to increase the chances of success by increasing the possibilities that your film will have a lucid continuity. As we have already pointed out, the film is made up of a series of scenes which are in turn composed of a grouping of shots. Someone has, somewhat simplistically, likened the construction of a film to the writing process whereby the shot is the word, the scene the sentence, the sequence the chapter, and the film made up of a group of sequences as a book is made up of a series of chapters. Just as words must fit together to form the sentences that make up the chapters of the book, so must a film have continuity of construction. Each shot must fit with the last on through to the completed film; they must be visually and logically unified. We have compared the film to a jigsaw puzzle; continuity is one element which assures that the pieces will fit together to create a realistic impression of the action.

The film-maker must consider the overall action of the scene and how it can be joined to the next scene, allowing the action to flow smoothly. Without continuity a film would be a series of jumbled images lacking meaning and purpose. As each shot came on the screen, the audience would have to be concerned anew with what the action was, where the action was taking place, what the relationship of each image was to the one preceding, and what the particular image meant to the film as a whole. Continuity answers such questions easily and instantly.

CONTINUITY OF TIME AND SPACE

We have already discovered that both time and space are entities which can be molded to fit the situations in a film. The quickest way to distract a spectator is to make changes in the normal time patterns without leading him through these time changes by means of familiar film conventions. A common manipulation of the time pattern is the use of *flashbacks* (or *"flash forwards"*), which carry the spectator from the present into the past (or future). Unless the spectator is taken by the hand and led carefully through the time change, he can become lost. Resnais' *Last Year at Marienbad* is one of the most confusing films ever made because of the director's disregard for physical time. The majority of the audience is lost in this film because there is no attempt to maintain a continuity of time. The film does not make it explicitly clear to the spectator whether what he is seeing is happening now, has happened in the past, will happen in the future, or is happening only in the mind of one of the characters, and such a lack of time perception disorients and confuses. The implication of this film is that the motion picture can present time as the mind experiences it, and we know that the mind may experience recollections of the past, projections into the future, and even imaginary desires far more vividly than the prosaic, "actual" present. Whether each member of the audience is willing to accept this implicit premise is another matter!

The less visually sophisticated audience of the past required an optical effect, such as a fade or dissolve, any time that there was a transition from one time period to another, whether it was a change of a few minutes or a year. Today, audiences are far more acclimated to filmic time, and as a result they will accept many time changes without these traditional visual transitions. The film *Bullitt*, for example, contains only one dissolve; *Dr. Strangelove* also contains only one optical time transition, and today film after film proves to us that the slavish dependence upon these transitions is a thing of the past. Our basic contention is that a controlled and deliberate disorientation is both an effective means of leaping the film forward in time and a valuable device for holding the spectator entranced and involved in the film of today.

The cameraman must know from the start whether he is filming material which will utilize traditional time changes or which will depend upon impact editing for these transitions. The film adage that the cameraman must be an editor by second nature is never more true than in this instance; if you think you can leave to the cutting room the imposition of the transitions of Cinematic Cinema you have a surprise in store for you. This is a complex subject, and we can only present to you the fact that you must begin with an awareness of its importance and devote your own taste and imagination to solving its complexities. In the simplest terms, the cameraman must prepare for the requirements of the film, utilizing dissolves and fades by shooting the necessary footage on the ends of his shots. For the film using the *flair cut*, it will be particularly important that the shots planned to begin each new scene have entrance points which are at once filmicly intriguing and immediately indicative of the setting to which the film has leaped.

The film has long had the right to transport the viewer instantaneously from place to place. Yet, with rare exceptions, this right was granted on the condition that the spatial transition was accomplished with a temporal continuity binding the shots. When Griffith cut from the train station to the onrushing engine or from the beleaguered defenders of the cabin to the hard-riding rescuers, the implication was that these events were happening simultaneously in separate locations and that each event continued to unfold while we observed the other. Whenever we lept forward in time, whether within the same setting or during a transition from one locale to another, the traditional optical transition was obligatory. The reason that this convention was allowed the film was simple: All forms of art, particularly communicative forms, reserve for themselves the right to eliminate the inessential as a means of gripping the attention of their audience. This has in no way changed today. What the Cinematic Cinemaker has finally caught onto (and this is the particular contribution of that nose-thumbing iconoclast Godard) is that it is unnecessary to telegraph this elimination of the inessential to the audience. The transition dissolve is as outmoded as courtly manners; since we all know what we are after, let us skip the preliminaries and get down to the essentials. This is precisely the implication of Godard's *jump cuts*. The film-maker has two shots in his hands showing police motorcycles at two stages along a road; he wishes to show that they have moved forward. The film-maker knows that he wishes to do this and his audience knows this also. Why not cut the two shots together, instead of laboriously dragging out the time-honored cut-away to the fleeing car to bridge the jump, since everyone knows that it is a convention that has nothing to do with the real meaning of the scene? This is a powerful argument, and the films of Godard, Antonioni, Fellini, Richard Lester, Tony Richardson and their contemporaries, with a graceful acknowledging nod to Eisenstein, present it eloquently.

The fact is that contemporary audiences are accustomed to the manipulation of filmic time and space, so long as it is done with flair and communicative intelligence. If a character is leaving his home to drive to a destination, it is simply not necessary to subject the spectator to the tedious details of his journey; he will accept a cut from the slamming car door to the front wheel of the car spinning up to the front door of the destination. We need only show what is necessary for the film's dramatic purpose and the intelligent spectator's perception of the scene. In a sponsored film, the authors' once compressed a whirlwind sightseeing tour of New York City into some two minutes of film time, linking some eleven different locations with nothing more than flair cuts and whirling swish pans and a driving musical background. Needless to say, the audience had no regrets at not seeing the girls trudging from place to place, laboriously boarding buses, or scrambling for cabs. The audience knew as well as we that the presentation of the girl's awe and excitement and the bustle and glamour of New York was all that was needed.

The film-maker has also the opportunity of enlarging space by overlapping an action and thus expanding the time it takes to move in the space, as Eisenstein did in the opening of the bridges sequence in *Ten Days*. For example, let us suppose that you must show someone walking down a circular staircase and you wish to expand the length of that staircase. A series of shots at different angles can be taken and then overlapped in the cutting. The staircase may consist of only twenty steps, but by overlapping the action you can enlarge them to any number you wish. You could even create the impression that the person is descending into the bowels of the earth.

It is well not to wait until you are in the editing room to have some idea as to how you will show transitions in space. Like time changes, they can be planned beforehand so that there is a consistent visual style throughout the entire film. Consistency requires either pre-planning or a great deal of luck. There is some evidence that pre-planning is a safer factor on which to rely.

CONTINUITY OF DIRECTION OF MOVEMENT

One of the knottiest problems with which you will have to deal is the achieving of a continuity in direction of movement in an action. If the film were not composed of a series of shots put together, but rather was one long shot, movement direction would not be a problem. When a film subject moves in one direction in one shot he should be moving in that same direction in the shots that follow, unless a change of direction is shown or indicated by some transition in a succeeding shot. If an unexplained change in direction takes place, the audience can become disoriented and confused, just as they would if cameras were used from both sides of the field in covering a football game. The same is true of a subject looking or pointing in one direction, the succeeding shots should be consistent with the direction first established. This problem of maintaining consistency of direction accounts for more mistakes than any dozen other factors. It is not a simple matter and should be planned before shooting to prevent these mistakes. Let us say we are going to show a portion of an auto trip. We show the car moving out of the left side of the frame, so we have set up its direction to be from right to left in the picture. Every succeeding shot should show the car moving in that same direction; if we suddenly show it moving from left to right the audience may get the impression that the driver is returning home. Once you establish a direction for a movement, it should be consistently maintained throughout the sequence no matter if the action is shown in consecutive order or in single shots interspersed in the film. Camera angle may be changed, different types of shots may be employed, but the direction should not vary, unless the moment at which the direction is changed is shown.

If you are required to move from an exterior to an interior of a moving object, such as the above automobile, the movement seen through the window should also indicate the same direction or the audience may have the impression that the automobile is suddenly traveling backward.

However, if in our example we must show the man going and returning we should change the direction for the return trip. If we show him moving from right to left going to his destination, we would naturally show him moving left to right on the return trip. Both directions should be decided upon before the scenes are filmed to maintain a consistency.

Contrasting directions can be used to show subjects moving toward one another. Let us add another ingredient to our example. The man leaves his home, driving from right to left. In the next shot a small boy rides off from his home on a bicycle, moving from left to right. Cut to the car still moving in its established direction. Cut to the boy moving left to right. The audience will immediately sense a connection between the two subjects. A few more cuts back and forth are shown; then a shot reveals the boy and the car moving toward each other, and the boy is struck by the car (Fig. 5.19). By maintaining these two directions we are consistent with the travel of the two movements while suggesting the meeting of the two, building suspense, and adding dramatic impact.

At times in our sequence we may wish to cut in shots that are *neutral* in their direction; for example, a shot of the car which does not indicate direction. In this case we could either employ a view that shows the car moving directly at the camera or directly away from it (Fig. 5.20). However, care must be exercised to keep the car centered in the frame; the minute one side of the car is favored it will indicate a specific direction. If the car in the straight-on shot must exit the frame, it should pass out on the side of the camera that is consistent with its movement. In the case of our example, the car moving right to left should exit the frame on the left side. If the car is shown from the rear, and we are shown the entrance into the frame, this entrance also should be consistent with the direction; the car should enter on the right side of the frame if supposedly moving right to left.

Shots can be employed which show the subject walking directly into the camera until the picture is blacked out, or which begin with a blacked-out picture which opens up as the subject walks away from the camera. These shots also have neutral directional value, but should be used sparingly or they will lose their impact.

Shots of a neutral direction can be used to provide visual variety. If a number of directional shots must be shown, especially in consecutive order, they can become monotonous. The monotony can be broken up by inserting the shots of neutral direction. Straight-on shots have a greater dramatic impact on the audience than a three-quarter angle or profile shot of a specific direction. These neutral direction shots can also enable you to change directions. They will distract the audience momentarily so that you can then come back in the next shot with the car moving in a different direction without confusing the audience.

THE IMAGINARY LINE   A useful tool that the film-maker can employ in order to maintain a continuity of direction is to draw an imaginary line along either the right or left side of an action and to always keep the camera positioned on whichever side was selected. The direction of the action will be established in the opening shot of the sequence and that direction will be dictated by the side on which the camera was positioned when it photographed the action (Fig. 5.21). Any subsequent shots of that action will necessitate that the camera be on the same side. The camera, of course, can be positioned anywhere within the 180° degree radius of that side.

Fig. 5–19 Contrasting screen directions suggest the eventual meeting of the two subjects (Mel Wittenstein)

Fig. 5-20   Neutral directions (Mel Wittenstein)

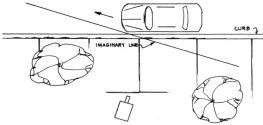

Fig. 5-21   The imaginary line drawn on the left side of the action establishes the screen direction of the subject from right to left (Jack Fischer)

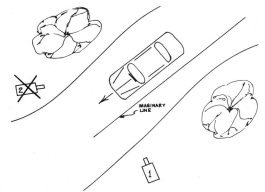

Fig. 5-22   All subsequent shots should place the imaginary line on the left of the action; camera position 2 crosses the line and reverses the direction (Jack Fischer)

To exemplify the imaginary line, let us return to our earlier example of the automobile. We established in the opening shot that the car was moving from right to left. This was determined by the fact that the camera was positioned on the left side of the automobile (Fig. 5.21). In all subsequent shots of the automobile moving toward its destination (Fig. 5.22), the camera *must* be on the left side of the automobile, unless a change of direction is indicated in a shot. If the camera is always placed on the left side, the car will always be moving in the frame from the right side to the left. In Fig. 5.22 we see the car moving along the highway. Camera position number 2 is incorrect, for that is on the right side of the car and will record the car moving from left to right. Position number 1 is the correct position to maintain continuity.

However, a film-maker is continually beset by technical problems—the direction of the sunlight or the proper background for the shot. In the above example, what if some technical factor forced you into selecting position number 2 for the camera? As long as you redrew the imaginary line you would have no problem, for the redrawing would indicate to you to reverse the direction of the movement of the car in order to keep the camera on its left side. If, for some reason, reversing the car's direction were not possible—you must show the car coming down a mountain, for example, and reversing the car's direction would have the car going up the mountain—you would have to solve the technical problem (wait for the sun to move!) or change the locale. The camera *must* be on the car's left side if you are going to maintain the original direction.

Remember, *you must always redraw the imaginary line each time that you change scenes*, and as long as you *draw the line on the same side of the action established in the initial shot*, you will have no continuity of direction problems. Whenever a cut to another shot shows the subject in a different locale with a different background, the shots should include entrances into or exits out of the frame, so that a sense of progress is depicted. If the shots are taken without these entrances or exits, it is traditionally impossible to edit the shots together without a jarring effect unless a dissolve or a cutaway is placed between each shot. This solution is not particularly desirable. A good practice to follow is to film all movements with both entrances and exits, then the editor can decide the best way to utilize them. Start the camera before the subject enters the frame and keep it running until after the subject exits the frame. If a character exits the frame close to the camera, and the shot is to be a straight cut to the next shot which has the subject entering, that succeeding shot should have the subject entering close to the camera (Fig. 5.23). If this practice is not followed the shots will not cut together well, despite the consistency of direction, because the differences in the distance from the camera will be distracting.

Many times we must film a reaction to a movement in close-up. This can be particularly confusing. The subject of the close-up should follow the action as though it were happening behind the camera. The confusion concerning this reaction shot stems from the fact that the camera is shooting a reverse shot so the movement in the reaction close-up will be from left to right when following a man moving from right to left! This seems so illogical to many film-makers that they film the close-up reaction moving in both directions, leaving the decision as to which to use for the editing room. Just remember to tell the subject that he is seeing the movement occurring behind the camera, and there will be no need to shoot the reaction moving in both directions.

Fig. 5-23 A subject exiting the frame close to the camera should then be shot . . . entering the frame close to the camera if the two shots are to be cut together (Mel Wittenstein)

CHANGING DIRECTION OF A MOVEMENT   When at all possible, the established direction of a movement should be maintained. However, situations do arise which necessitate a change. Whenever possible this change should be shown on the screen. If this is not possible, some device should be used to eliminate the confusion that would result if the change were arbitrarily included.

One solution to the problem of executing a change in direction would be to shoot across the imaginary line on a corner or curve so that the object exits the frame on the "wrong" side, reversing the direction (Fig. 5.24). Another solution would be to employ a reaction close-up in which the subject in the close-up indicates the directional change by the way he follows the movement change or in the way he indicates the new direction. A third method would be to shoot a straight-on shot in which the object exits the frame on the "wrong" side of the camera. This shot would then be cut with a shot of the object entering the frame near the camera moving in the new direction.

TRAVEL DIRECTION   Many times our audience is aware that a subject is traveling from one specific place to another—New York City to Chicago. In this example the audience would be aware that the subject was traveling in a westerly direction. Because of conditioning from looking at maps, the mind conceives of a westerly movement as one from right to left and an easterly movement as the reverse. Therefore, our subject traveling to Chicago from New York City should be shown moving from right to left. Northerly and southerly movements are not as easily established since up and down movements will not work well on a horizontal screen. Therefore, northerly movements are frequently shown by showing the subject moving from the lower left of the frame to the upper right, and southerly movements are indicated by moving the subject from upper left to lower right.

INTERIOR DIRECTION   If you are required to film in a number of different rooms and hallways of what is supposedly one house or building, maintaining consistent direction can be a difficult matter if the action moves from room to room. If such is the case, the best practice to follow is to make all of your camera set-ups on the same side of the building. This way the imaginary line is constant. When this is not possible, straight-on or moving-away shots can be taken with subjects entering or exiting the frame from the side of the camera consistent with the pre-established direction.

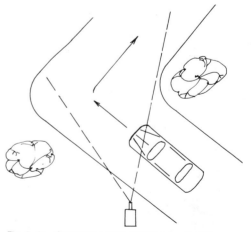

Fig. 5-24 Changing screen direction by shooting across a curve (Jack Fischer)

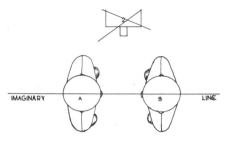

Fig. 5-25   The imaginary line in a static
scene (Jack Fischer)

STATIC DIRECTION

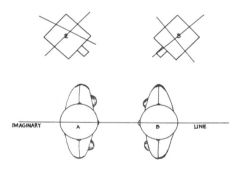

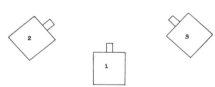

Fig. 5-26   Close-ups must also be shot from
the same side of the imaginary line (Jack Fischer)

Camera position 1 (Fig. 5-26)

Camera position 1 (Fig. 5-25)

Camera position 2 (Fig. 5-25)

The principle of the imaginary line can be just as important for static shots as it is for shots possessing movement. Within the static shot we should be concerned with the direction in which the subject faces the camera or looks past the camera so that the shots can be match-cut.

The imaginary line should be drawn through the center of the two nearest subjects which are on opposite sides of the picture (Fig. 5.25). The camera can be placed anywhere within a 180° semicircle on one side of the line, but if the camera is placed across the imaginary line (Fig. 5.25, Camera Position 2), the positions of the subjects are reversed. This can be distracting when the two shots are cut together. The camera can be moved anywhere: right or left, near or far, as long as it *does not cross the line.* If the camera must move in for close-ups (Fig. 5.26), the imaginary line must still be respected or the subject's look in the close-up will be in the wrong direction—away from, rather than toward, the other subject.

Camera position 2 (Fig. 5-26)

Camera position 3 (Fig. 5-26) (Mel Wittenstein)

However, one can cross the imaginary line to shoot subjects or action in the background of the previously established line. In this case the line moves with the camera, or rather, you redraw the line so that it runs parallel to the old line (Fig. 5.27). In essence the line has moved deeper as the camera has probed deeper.

Difficulty frequently arises in shooting close-ups of subjects facing one another in a previously established two-shot. When moving in for the close shots from a point-of-view angle, care should be taken to assure that the subjects are looking to the correct side of the camera. The trick on the close shot is to keep the camera on the correct side of the imaginary line. To aid you we would suggest that either you place the other subject in the two-shot next to the camera on the correct side, or that you stand there and instruct the subject in the close shot to look at you. If you are shooting dialogue, it is best that you use the subject who speaks his lines from his off-camera position (Fig. 5.28).

One exception to the rule of never crossing the imaginary line should be mentioned. If you are employing a moving camera on a shot, it can cross the line, or the subjects within the shot can cross the line. This is permissible simply because it happens at a time when the audience sees it happening. The only time you should not cross the line is *between* shots; anything can happen within the shot, for the line is simply redrawn at the end of the shot in preparation for the shot that will follow.

Innumerable static situations can arise during the filming of a scene that will have to match-cut with other shots in order to give a continuous view of an action. The main thing to remember and carry out is the drawing of that imaginary line in the proper place—through the nearest opposing subjects. Doing this and keeping your camera on the correct side should ensure that you do not face problems in the editing room later when you will have to match-cut these shots to give a continuous flow to the action. Having thoroughly absorbed the vital importance of maintaining continuity of direction, go out and see Godard's *Breathless*, a film that violates this principle with gleeful regularity.

When D. W. Griffith developed the close-up he provided a unique and powerful means of selecting and isolating the essentials to be shown to the audience. Many writers explain Griffith's development of the close-up as a great artistic revelation, but another story says that the development of this device, like most every other technical and aesthetic advancement of the film, stemmed from the need to solve a very practical problem—how to cut costs. Money problems have been a cross to bear for even the film greats. The production technique when Griffith entered film-making was to show the full set and all of the actors involved in the action. Griffith determined that he could reduce the costs of filming if, instead of breaking the film down into shots that showed all of the actors and all of the set, he broke the film into close shots and group shots. In this way, he could first film all shots involving groups of actors, then film shots involving individuals. By following such a plan he could reduce

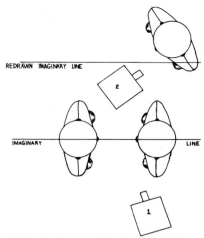

Fig. 5-27 To shoot a subject in the background, redraw the imaginary line parallel to the old line (Jack Fischer)

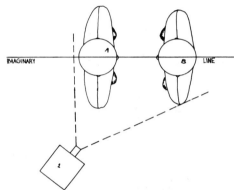

Fig. 5-28 To keep the look of the subject in the correct direction in a POV close-up, the director or the other subject should stand at the side of the camera that is compatible with the previously established imaginary line (Jack Fischer)

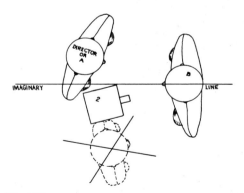

The Close-up

his payroll considerably after the first days of shooting when he no longer needed all of the actors. Although the reason behind the close-up may have been practical, Griffith immediately grasped the aesthetic strength of this device.

. The close-up is, as film director Mark Robson has stated, "the cornerstone of greatness of the film." But to achieve that greatness it should be properly filmed and effectively edited into the film. As with any powerful device, its improper use can reverse its power and it can work against the efforts of the film-maker by confusing and distracting the audience.

The size of the image of the close-up can vary, and the size is in direct proportion to its impact. The *medium close shot* provides a view of the subject from mid-chest to above the head, the *close-up* shows the head and shoulders of the subject, the *head close-up* reveals just the head, and the *extreme close-up* discloses some small portion of the head or any other object. The closer the shot is, the more the magnification of the subject, and therefore the more impact that shot has on the audience. As a result, the extreme close-up gains its power from all that it excludes, as well as what it includes. It should be used only rarely to express intense emotion, a moment of highly dramatic significance, or an extremely important facet of an action.

TYPES OF CLOSE-UPS

Fig. 5–29 Cameraman shooting an over-the-shoulder shot and the resulting shot (Richard C. Tomkins)

OVER-THE-SHOULDER SHOT   One of the most common close shots is the over-the-shoulder shot which serves quite well as a transition from an objective angle shot to a point-of-view angle (Fig. 5.29). In a sense, we move the spectator from the sideline position of the objective shot to a midway point in the over-the-shoulder shot, and then finally into the center of the action with the point-of-view close-up. Of course, the over-the-shoulder shot need not be employed if the camera is kept in a purely objective state. In that case we would move the spectator from a distant sideline of the action to a closer sideline, but not into the center of the action.

The over-the-shoulder close-ups of a pair of subjects should be set up so that they have a similar appearance generally—the same camera positions in relation to subject, same subject positions, and approximately the same image size. If they are recorded in this way, the back-and-forth editing of the two can be carried out unobtrusively.

In any over-the-shoulder shot, the subject over whose shoulder the camera is sighting is generally placed in a three-quarter back position so that his back and side are visible and the side of the face is seen, except for the nose. If the two subjects are facing one another, the opposing subject—the center of attraction of the close shot—is usually seen in a three-quarter front position. Of course, the camera can also be in closer, so that only the head and shoulders of both parties are seen; however, the overall positioning mentioned above remains the same. And remember, the over-the-shoulder shots of each of the two characters remain on the preestablished side of the imaginary line.

CUT-IN CLOSE SHOTS   These shots are used to magnify subjects or parts of the main flow of action of a scene. The close shot continues the flow of the main action but gives us a magnified view of the selected portion, whether it be a dominant person, object, or action. These cut-ins can be filmed from either an objective, subjective, over-the-shoulder, or point-of-view angle. Naturally the objective angle is from the viewpoint of an unseen observer, while the subjective angle is from the viewpoint of either a participant in the action or the spectator as a participant, with the subject of the shot looking directly into the lens. The over-the-shoulder and point-of-view close shot have already been discussed, but we should add that when these shots are of two players engaged in dialogue or intimate action, they are usually filmed in matched pairs so that the editor will be able to cut back and forth in the action and/or dialogue if he so desires. Before you move into over-the-shoulder and/or point-of-view shots, you generally establish the physical relationship of the two subjects in a two-shot. Again we remind you not to forget the imaginary line, taking care to position the camera on the proper side with the subject of the point-of-view shot looking at the correct side of the lens. We repeat, the best procedure to follow is to place the opposing subject off-camera on the proper side or stand there yourself to ensure that the subject of the shot is looking in the right direction. When the height of the subjects in point-of-view shots is different, have the lower positioned subject look to the proper side and above the lens, and the higher positioned subject, to the proper side and below the lens.

The cut-in close shot, as with any close shot, is usually used to add emphasis and increase the audience's attention, but in the case of the cut-in, it provides emphasis and added attention to some facet of the overall main action. We can isolate some participant in the action, some object that plays an important role in the action, or some small portion of the overall action and, therefore, stress its importance to the flow of action or provide clarification if it is so small it might be missed without this isolation.

The cut-in close shot can also be used to enable you to compress time. By cutting from the overall view of the action to an isolated portion, and then returning to the overall view, it is possible to eliminate the unwanted portion of the action contained in the overall view. For example, we must follow a subject as he walks across the street. The complete cross takes too long filmicly and so is unnecessary, but how can we shorten the action and maintain continuity? We begin with a long shot or medium shot as the subject begins to cross the street, cut to a shot of his feet walking or to a shot of his face. We can then cut back to the long shot as he reaches the other side (Fig. 5.30). He has progressed farther than he would have actually during the time of the cut-in. The continuity has remained intact, but the close-up of the face or feet has allowed us to compress the time and, in this case, the space as well.

The use of such close-ups has come into wide use as transitions in time and place. In the past the audience would have been distracted if too long a time or too great an expanse of space was covered by a relatively short length close-up, but in recent years the use of a close shot for such a deliberately disorienting transition has been more and more

Fig. 5–30 Use of the *cut-in* close shot
to compress time and space (Mel Wittenstein)

accepted. The authors recently completed a film in which we used a series of close-ups of a girl in her room applying make-up. The last close-up reveals the application completed, but when the camera pulls back we discover she is not in her room but in a restaurant with a group of people. A great deal of time and space is compressed without disturbingly disorienting the audience. This cut-in close-up, like any cut-in close shot, works because a long shot is included at some point in both scenes to orient the audience to the environment and the position of the subject within the environment. This procedure should always be followed no matter what the purpose of the cut-in close shot.

You may, in the making of a film, find yourself with the problem of having to show a subject involved in an action that cannot be placed on film for physical reasons—the subject is performing a medical operation or injecting a hypodermic needle into someone's arm, to mention a pair of frequently faced examples. The cut-in close-up is, of course, a solution to this problem. By cutting to the close shot of the doctor's face we exclude the unfilmable action.

Finally, the cut-in close shot can be used to cover up mistakes not discovered until we are in the editing room and cannot obtain retakes. Should you find yourself with a mismatch between two shots that are to be cut together, the mismatch can be corrected by inserting a cut-in close-up as a "neutral intercut" between the two shots. The audience will then accept the changes that caused the mismatch as happening during the time of the close shot. A mismatch exists in Figure 5.30, but the close-up of the feet serves as a "neutral intercut."

CUT-AWAY CLOSE SHOT   This shot presents an image that is related to the main flow of action but not a part of that main action. The cut-away may present a secondary action happening at the same time as the main action *or* a reaction to the main flow of action. They can be filmed from the same angles as the cut-in, with the exception of the over-the-shoulder angle, and selected for the same basic reasons—to keep the spectator as an unseen observer, to involve him fully, or to involve him while keeping him out of the action as a participant.

The cut-away close shot allows the film-maker to show his audience the reactions to the main flow of action by subjects who are off-camera and not involved in the action being recorded in the previous shot or shots. More can often be said by showing someone's reaction to the action, than showing the action itself. An act of violence can be more horrifying, for example, by showing the reaction of someone viewing it than actually showing the violent act. Many times the film-maker may not wish to show the action for one reason or another—it would be too violent, too personal, too expensive—and his solution may be the cut-away that is a reaction to the unseen main action.

By cutting away to a reaction to an action, we can also initiate a similar reaction in our audience. The makers of horror films capitalize on this technique by cutting to a player's reaction to the unseen monster which triggers a similar reaction (generally) in the audience.

The cut-away, close shot or otherwise, can also be used by the film-maker to comment upon the main flow of action being shown. In his first film, *Strike*, Eisenstein shows the massacre of a group of striking workers by the Czarist troops. In the midst of the massacre he cuts away to shots of a cow being slaughtered in a slaughterhouse.

Finally, the cut-away can be used for the same editorial purposes as the cut-in, only the cut-away is more versatile since it is not restricted to the main flow of action as the cut-in is. When a mismatch occurs—a change in the direction of a movement or some other factor that would have a jarring effect upon the audience if the two-shots were cut together—the editor can insert a cut-away close shot either of a reaction to the main action or a secondary action, if such exists in the script (Fig. 5.31). This cut-away will bridge the gap between the two shots. We highly recommend that you always shoot a number of cut-away close shots, whether you plan to use them or not, as a back-up in case of editorial problems. These isolated shots can be used when a cut-in close shot can not, because the subject of the cut-away does not have to be established in a long shot previously as is the case with the cut-in (see Chapter Seven). While filming a sequence on Fifth Avenue recently, a firetruck came racing down the street. We turned the camera on the firetruck and caught its movement on film. Later in the editing room we discovered that we had inadvertently allowed a change in direction by our subjects walking down the street. We pulled the shot of the firetruck, placed it between the two shots of mismatched direction, included the sound effects of the firetruck over all three shots, and so solved our editorial problem. A cut-in would not have solved the problem as well.

On the whole, however, a cut-in close shot is preferable to the cut-away because the subject of the cut-in is involved in the main action and, therefore, has more direct interest value. The cut-in also tends to move the audience into the center of the action, whereas the cut-away moves it farther away from the main action and thereby reduces the audience involvement. Unless the cut-away contributes something to the purpose of the film, it should not be employed. Even when used to cover a mistake, it is best if the shot can contribute something besides the distraction. Our firetruck, for example, covered our mismatch in direction, but also contributed an exciting and colorful dimension to the environment.

Fig. 5–31 Use of the *cut-away* close shot to compress time and space (Mel Wittenstein)

Several technical factors should be considered when shooting close-ups. When movement occurs within a close-up, it should be deliberately slowed down. The action is so greatly magnified that without deliberate slowness the movement will appear greatly accelerated and seem to flash by on the screen. Yet the tempo of the action cannot be too out of line with the tempo of the action in a wider shot if you are planning a matched cut between them. You could not, for example, match-cut a medium shot showing a man quickly reaching for an object on a table with a close shot showing the hand slowly entering the frame and clutching the object. The mismatch in tempo would prevent you from cutting

SHOOTING THE CLOSE-UP

the two shots together. Therefore, the tempo within the medium shot would have to be slowed down somewhat so that it would cut with the slower close-up or you simply would not use the close-up.

Often we wish to use a close shot of a subject before or after that subject has made a movement in a long or medium shot. In these instances, the movement should be *overlapped* in both the close shot and the wider shot. The editor will then have the choice of making the cut on the action or after the action. Unless the action is overlapped the editor has no choice. Generally an editor will prefer to *cut on the movement* because the movement covers the cut and makes the cut less noticeable. Your movement patterns, as a result, will flow much better if you overlap the action in all shots that are to be cut together to show a continuous action, whether close or wide. Let us return to our example of the man reaching for the object on the table. Let us say in this instance he reaches out and places his hand on the object and leaves the hand there. We should shoot the medium shot with the complete action. Then we should shoot the close-up, duplicating the action of placing the hand on the object and letting it stay on the object. The editor can then use the medium shot until the hand is near the object and cut to the close shot as the hand reaches the object and then, if he desires, cut back to the medium shot after the hand comes to rest. In this instance the editor has cut on the action and the cuts will probably be less noticeable. However, if he chooses, the editor could use the medium shot of the full action and cut to the close-up after the hand has come to rest, using only the part of the close shot that shows the hand on the object.

When filming a scene, the quickest procedure is one involving the movement of camera and lights as little as possible. Therefore, when it is at all possible—when you are filming controlled action—we would recommend that you group your shots rather than shooting in sequence. This will, of course, necessitate the preparation of a shot breakdown. Shoot first your long shots and medium shots that require several subjects perhaps, then film the close shots which require only one subject. This procedure will reduce the number of lighting changes and will eliminate all but those subjects required for close-ups upon completion of the wider shots, thus reducing the number of personnel who may get in the way and who, going back to Griffith, may have to be paid another day's wages.

But if you must shoot in sequence—showing the construction of something, for example, when saving all close-ups until the last is impossible—mark with chalk or tape the positions of your lighting instruments for the wider shots so that you can return them to their original position as quickly as possible. Such a situation would also require that the action be broken down into a single-shot plan.

Whenever it is possible, the background of a close-up should be chosen with care so that distracting objects, designs, surfaces, etc., can be avoided, unless, of course, such a background is desired for some specific reason. Generally it is best if the background is indistinguishable, with a surface that contrasts with the subject of the close-up. We use the close shot to control attention and provide emphasis, so the subject of the close-up should be the only thing the audience sees distinctly. Some frequently used techniques are to throw the background out of focus, to isolate the subject with light, or, in color filming, to contrast the color of the subject with the color of the background. When such techniques cannot be employed, the positioning of the camera and/or the subject becomes the only solution. If the background is wrong, change the angle of the camera or, if possible, move the subject so that the background is neutralized.

Composition

Composition is the artistic and meaningful positioning of all of the pictorial elements within the frame of the shot. It should be aesthetically pleasing to the eye—proper balance, proper use of line, mass, color, and movement—and it should visually provide the proper dramatic emphasis, significant relationships, the mood and meaning of the scene. Film composition is the responsibility of the director and/or the cameraman, depending upon the relationship between the two people and the ability of the director to communicate what he is attempting to achieve. To whomever the responsibility falls, it is still one of the most important visual elements of film production. Rarely neglected in theatrical films, it is all too often neglected in nontheatrical subject films. Through a fresh and imaginative use of composition the most prosaic things can be made interesting and can psychologically control the audience's emotions and attention. The ugliest of scenes, through the way in which it is composed, can elicit an aesthetically pleasing response from an audience. The composition—combined with effective use of lighting, lens setting, focal length, etc.—can give even ugliness a strange kind of beauty. Consider, for example, the strange beauty of the shots of the factory dump in Antonioni's *Red Desert*. Of course, the use of composition and its associated techniques can also accomplish the reverse. It is an extremely powerful device that should not be neglected.

Despite its power, composition is one of the most flexible of the film-maker's tools. The rules of composition can be bent to fit the film-maker's purposes, but before you begin to bend them, you should know the basic rules of composition. The overwhelming majority of your film's scenes will utilize the basic principles; so when you do manipulate these principles the results will be unusual and, therefore, have unique impact and meaning.

Properly used, an important function of composition is to focus the attention of the audience on the point of the shot where we desire emphasis. It can contribute greatly to the projection of the meaning of the film's purpose, and it can glamourize or deglamourize the material. Composition can aid in setting the emotional climate and the mood, as well as indicate the psychological implications of the environment and the relationship between the environment, the people in the film, and the film's purpose. Finally, it can serve the purpose of unifying all of the diverse parts into a meaningful and harmonious whole.

The static arts, such as painting, sculpture, and still photography, also utilize composition, but their subjects are frozen in time and space, even though the work may suggest movement. Therefore, the use of composition by the static arts is concerned only with spatial relationships. Motion pictures are far more complicated, for they deal with subjects in motion. Thus the requirements of film composition more closely approximate those of theater and dance because composition for the film must consider both time and space. What may be a startling static composition can be totally useless and ineffectual when the subjects in the scene or the camera begin to move, or the film begins to cut from angle to angle.

The film-maker employs the same compositional principles as do graphic artists, but his compositions are chosen for their suitability to the types of movement that will occur. However, he cannot compose simply by following the rules of static composition when plotting a camera movement, since that movement as it is carried out will consist of an infinite series of compositions. But he can begin with meaningful composition and end with another; this is well within his power.

The first compositional consideration is the choice of *what is to be shown* in each shot. This choice will be defined by the frame of the picture and the angle of that frame. This frame is a rectangle with an aspect ratio (ratio of height to width) of generally four to three for normal film size and five to two for wide screen. The angle at which the frame is set and the elements which fall within the frame lines will be the basic ingredients of the composition. The fundamental problems are the best angle for the frame for each shot and how the elements included within the frame can best be arranged. For the possible solutions to these problems we must turn first to the rules of composition.

RULES OF COMPOSITION

One can learn the basic rules of composition, but they alone will not be enough. You must learn the rules and how to use them, and this knowledge plus your own artistic taste, likes and dislikes, experience, emotional sensitivity, and frame of reference will combine to provide you with the solution to your compositional problems. Even though the basic principles are not an end in themselves, they can be a means to that end.

THE ELEMENTS OF COMPOSITION   Every picture contains basic elements which, when properly combined and employed, can serve the film-maker as the symbols of a universally understood language to nonverbally communicate meaning and emotion.

The compositional *lines* of a picture are provided by the outlines of objects, people, buildings, trees, hills, roads, etc., and by the lines our minds form as our eyes follow the movement of an object, or as we trace over the picture looking from object to object. These actual and mental lines can be vertical, horizontal, curved, straight, diagonal, jagged, or combinations of any of these. Each of these lines has a universal psychological implication. A straight line projects a sense of strength or masculinity, while a gently curved line projects the opposite—femininity, gentleness, or fragility. Vertical lines of some height will also suggest strength. But horizontal lines tend to communicate peace, solidity, tranquillity. Diagonal lines are dynamic and can communicate violence or force. Whenever it is possible, incorporating the lines appropriate to the mood and meaning of a scene in the arrangement of objects in the picture will provide your film with useful emotional stimuli and will back up the emotions displayed by the actors.

Compositional *forms* can be actual physical forms or forms created through the positioning of objects causing the spectator's eye movement over objects to circumscribe mentally the outline of the form. The most common compositional form is the triangle (Fig. 5.32) because it can control the spectator's attention, leading it to the apex of the triangle and thus contributing dominance to the person or object at that apex. The triangular form also possesses psychological stimuli, for it projects a sense of stability or solidity, probably because many solid objects in nature—rocks, mountains, trees, etc.—have this form. The triangular form allows us to arrange objects with a great deal more variety than any other form because the apex need not always be at the top. The apex can be placed to either side or at the bottom of the frame.

Fig. 5–32 A triangular grouping (Mel Wittenstein)

Compositional *mass* is the pictorial weight of an object, a figure, an area of space. The mass can be composed of one element or a group of elements. A building or a mountain is a mass, likewise a group of soldiers gathered around an artillery piece is a single mass because of the closeness of the grouping.

Mass can be a strong attention-getting device because its pictorial weight will tend to draw the eyes of the spectator to it. Since more than one mass generally appears in a picture, the one that must receive dominance is given greater weight. This additional weight can be added to a mass by giving it greater *light value* so that psychologically it is heavier. The human figure can possess greater pictorial weight than an object of much greater proportions by keeping the object dark and lighting the figure, or vice versa. Through light contrast, by color or some other means, a mass can be isolated from its background and thus attain greater pictorial weight. The actual size of a mass can give it dominance in a scene, and this size can be increased by camera angle, focal length, or its position in the picture. Should we desire to increase the emphasis on a single figure so that he dominates over another mass composed of a group of figures, we need only to place the single figure near to the camera, to angle the shot so that he appears larger, or to use a focal length that will magnify his size. Light and color can be extremely important aids in increasing pictorial weight, for a greater light intensity or a more vivid color will psychologically increase the weight of a mass. It is important to remember that the weight of a person or object is a matter both of physical and aesthetic valence. *Physical valence* is determined by the object or person's actual physical size, whereas *aesthetic valence* is determined by the emotional and psychological weight. Thus a small man of strength, intelligence, and intensity will possess a higher aesthetic valence than some fat and lumbering lout, and a short vicious revolver higher aesthetic valence than a benign haystack.

In many ways aesthetic valence is an attribute carried into the part by the actor, but the part itself is certainly a contributor to this quality also. Would you accept as examples of high aesthetic valence George C. Scott, Lee Cobb, Marlon Brando, Charlton Heston, and John and Robert Kennedy, and of low aesthetic valence, Truman Capote, Troy Donahue, Billie Burke, and Connie Stevens? Since the essential quality of the person of higher valence is that our eyes are drawn almost hypnotically to him, it is obvious that such quality must be considered in determining the balance of the screen, for focusing lines of sight is a powerful means of increasing the weight of the compositional object.

Because of the importance of *movement* to film, it too can be a vital force in composition. Movement like the other components of composition may possess psychological and aesthetic powers which can be utilized by the film-maker to convey emotional stimuli to the audience. These powers can be attributed to mental conditioning. For example, a movement from left to right is easier for the spectator to follow because he reads from left to right. As a result, a movement in the opposite direction, from right to left, possesses greater strength because it is "moving upstream," so to speak. Therefore, when a feeling of relaxed, peaceful action is desired, the movement of objects in the shot or the movement of the camera should be from left to right. Ascending movements may obviously suggest growth, a sense of lightness, or hope. But a downward movement, in contrast, may intimate despair, heaviness, or doom. Diagonal movement is the strongest and, therefore, the most dramatic. It can signify strength, opposition, power, or stress. For the most impact, an ascending movement is normally carried out on a diagonal from the lower right corner of the frame to the upper left and a descending movement, from the upper left to the lower right.

BALANCE Every composition should be balanced; a sense of equilibrium should exist. When a composition is unbalanced, the spectator is vaguely disturbed, like looking at a picture hanging crooked on the wall. Movement, of course, makes balance extremely difficult to achieve at times. However, movement, if it is active, will tend to distract the audience and make them less aware of any compositional imbalance.

Actual balance is achieved by equalizing physical weight, but pictorial balance is attained by equalizing psychological weight, taking into consideration aesthetic valence. Emphasis, intensity, or importance may provide greater psychological weight to the object receiving it. Therefore, the moving object in contrast to the static, the lighted object in contrast to the unlighted, the speaking character in contrast to the silent, or the brightly colored object in contrast to the object of subdued color may have greater psychological weight. The position of an object within the composition can affect its psychological weight. Think of balance as a teeter-totter: The closer an object is toward the center, the less its weight, and conversely, the closer to the edge, the greater the weight. As a general rule, elements of greater weight are placed near the center to equalize their weight and prevent them from visually "tipping up" the picture. Thus if one is attempting to balance a single man against a mob, the man would be placed far over to the side of the frame and the mob close to the center, for the same reasons that daddies sit near the center on see-saws and kids out on the far end. Of course, if your lone man in the frame has a high aesthetic valence and is playing the role of the heroic protagonist against the mob his weight is proportionally increased. In a certain sense this might imply that we could adjust the balance and move him nearer to the center of the frame in recognition of his "weight." Theoretically this is quite true, but as a practical matter, the director will use everything within his power to lend strength to the character, and the isolating of the man against the balance of the mass is an effective means of accomplishing this. So rather than thinking of high aesthetic valence as a reason for avoiding the means open to you for lending weight and strength to the character, think in terms of using every means at hand to increase his valence, whether these means be physical, aesthetic, or part of the mechanical contrivance of the film.

TYPES OF BALANCE   The least visually interesting type of balance is *symmetrical balance* (Fig. 5.33). Symmetrical balance exists when a center line can be drawn through the middle of a picture and both sides of the picture have an equal distribution of mass. Such balance tends to be static and lifeless and to lack contrast or conflict. Look to either side of the picture's center, and you see approximately the same arrangement. The dominance is also equalized, for the emphasis is equally split between the two sides of the picture. An example of symmetrical balance is the two-shot in profile when we see both figures equally. The dominance switches back and forth as the characters speak. Symmetrical balance is best used only on static, quiet, tranquil scenes.

The type of balance that receives the predominance of use is *asymmetrical balance* (Fig. 5.34). If the same center line were drawn in an asymmetrically balanced picture, each side of the picture would contain a mass or masses, but the weight on one side would be unequal to the other side. We can balance the unequal weights in the same way balance is achieved on a teeter-totter. The object of heaviest pictorial weight is placed nearer the center while the lighter weight is moved closer to the edge. The two things that make asymmetrical balance possible are the element of aesthetic valence and the concept of the teeter-totter. Since two objects of comparable physical mass can have vastly different aesthetic valences they can be set off against each other in a *seemingly* asymmetrical balance by moving the person with the heavier aesthetic valence closer toward the center of the frame. And, by choosing two persons of different *total* valence (both physical and aesthetic) and placing the lighter farther out from the center of the frame, you also gain the appearance of asymmetrical balance. Naturally the object with the heaviest pictorial weight will have dominance in the picture and will be the focal point of interest. Asymmetricality is achieved in single subject close-ups by placing the subject slightly off-center, balancing the picture with the

Fig. 5–33 Symmetrical balance (Mel Wittenstein)

Fig. 5–34 Asymmetrical balance (Mel Wittenstein)

greater space on the other side of the picture which now takes on pictorial weight. The space should be provided on the side to which the subject is looking for it is the subject's look that adds the greater weight.

Remember that it is not just actual physical valence that must be considered in determining the greater pictorial weight of a subject or object, but also its aesthetic valence, its position in the picture, its brightness, its color, whether it is moving or static, and whether it is speaking or silent. An object small in size can pictorially outweigh another object of larger scale because it is moving or speaking, because it has more light falling on it, or because it is of a bright contrasting color.

The dominant subject is usually higher in the horizontal planes of the picture than the opposing subject or subjects, although lowness, if it provides a dramatic contrast, can also lend weight to the subject. This can be accomplished by the actual positioning of the subjects, or it can be accomplished in depth by placing the dominant subject either nearer the camera for the higher position or farther away for the lower. The higher position should be the preferred one because the difference in height alone may command the attention of the spectator. When such positioning is not practical, the lower position can be employed equally well if it is reinforced by better lighting, by throwing focus to the dominant subject by having the other subject or subjects look at him, by angling the subjects so that the dominant one is more open to the camera, or by providing the dominant subject with action or speech while keeping the others static or silent.

Imagine the frame broken into vertical thirds and horizontal thirds. Where these four lines cross are considered to be the four strongest compositional points in the picture (Fig. 5.35), but remember, utilizing these positions is only one way of providing weight to a subject. Never try to employ these points slavishly in every composition unless you want those compositions to be dull and monotonous.

Using the imaginary horizontal and vertical lines can be helpful. The line of the horizon is generally placed in the lower or upper third of the frame, contributing to the asymmetrical structure of the picture. The picture will also be more interesting if the horizon position is varied constantly. The vertical lines can also aid in your asymmetrical positioning of objects—particularly when you have only one character or subject in the picture. When that subject is moving, leave him with approximately two-thirds of the picture area, for this satisfies the desire of the spectator who wants to feel that there is sufficient space ahead of the moving object so that it will not collide with some element unseen by the spectator. These lines can also be useful in the staging of angled two-shots. The subject facing the spectator is generally given two-thirds of the screen space. Mentally drawing the vertical lines can aid in employing this principle.

FRAMING   As we indicated in the beginning of this discussion on composition, the angle or position of the frame lines can be of particular importance to our composition. By manipulating the framing of a pic-

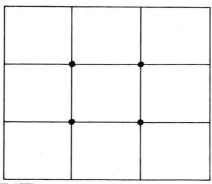

Fig. 5–35 Frame divided into thirds establishing the compositional points (Jack Fischer)

ture, we can choose, isolate, or limit the elements that will be employed in the picture. The frame forms the conceptual structure for our compositions. However, there are no rigid rules that must be adhered to. Your artistic taste and judgment should be in command. There are, however, useful general hints that can be passed along:

1 Frame the moving character so that he has more space in the direction toward which he is traveling (Fig. 5.36).
2 Frame the static subject so that there is more space in the direction in which he is looking (Fig. 5.37).
3 Allow sufficient head room above the subjects or they will appear crowded into the frame.
4 Do not allow too much head room by framing the subjects too low in the picture, for this will make the resulting picture appear bottom heavy.
5 Subjects should not be framed so that they stand or sit on the bottom frame line, nor should they be lined up exactly with the side frame lines.
6 The bottom frame line should never cross a subject's joints, but rather should be positioned between joints.
7 The dominant subject of the picture should be positioned on the left because that is the strongest area; if, however, it must be placed on the right, additional factors such as light, body position, contrast, etc., can be employed to compensate.

Fig. 5-36 Frame a moving subject so there is more space in the direction in which he is travelling (Mel Wittenstein)

Fig. 5-37 Frame the static subject so there is more space in the direction in which he is looking (Mel Wittenstein)

Fig. 5-38 When the main subject is in the background, try to frame the object in the foreground to accentuate the depth (*The Island*, Audio Film Center)

8 Whenever possible, do not position large masses, unless they are to be dominant, on the left side of the frame for it can be extremely difficult to compensate and render dominant a figure on the right.

9 Generally the subjects should be framed with an adequate amount of space.

10 Avoid symmetry in your framing and attempt to balance asymmetrically.

11 When the main subject is in the background, try to frame some object in the foreground that will accentuate the depth (Fig. 5.38).

PERSPECTIVE Since the film-maker is working in a two-dimensional medium but attempting to create a three-dimensional effect, his compositions should be arranged in depth. His control of perspective is essential for in-depth compositions. He can control perspective with his lens selection combined with his positioning of the subjects in relation to the camera, or, in exteriors, by utilizing atmospheric conditions.

Parallel lines appear to come together or converge at the horizon. Renaissance painters discovered that they could create a sense of depth by diminishing the size of their subjects as the distance increased, duplicating this natural linear convergence. The film-maker, by composing in depth, sets up this same linear convergence. The farther a subject is from the lens, the smaller it appears, and so the farther away it seems, especially when contrasted with an object in the foreground. When working outdoors, the film-maker has the additional control provided him by a phenomenon in nature—atmospheric haze, which tends to make distant objects appear lighter and softer. A sense of depth is created when these distant objects are contrasted with the darker and more sharply-focused objects in the foreground of the picture.

For the control of perspective and the use of it as a compositional factor, you may follow certain staging and technical principles that have been discovered to be quite useful:

1 Scenes shot with a short focal-length lens will have a stronger perspective. This lens need not be a wide-angle lens, but rather should be the lens that records the perspective of the scene as it would appear to the eye if it were viewing the scene.

2 Camera angle can contribute to the perspective if it is chosen to reveal the greatest number of planes of the object to be photographed. Show the front and side of a human figure or the front, side, and top or bottom of an object.

3 Move your subject and the camera so that they cover and uncover other subjects or objects in the picture. You can convey to your audience a sense of depth by moving the camera so that it shoots through or past objects in the foreground or by moving the subjects through or between other subjects or objects in the picture, so that at times they are covered and then uncovered.

4 Position the subjects and objects in your scene so that there is a partial overlapping. Isolating and separating these subjects or ob-

jects reduces the sense of depth, because the spectator's poor depth perception will not allow him to discern which is closest and which is farthest away. Overlapping them reveals this to the spectator.

5 Movements toward or away from the camera are far better than movements across its view. The movements toward or away will increase or decrease the size of the subject and, therefore, impart a feeling of depth. The movement across maintains a constant size. Only rarely do we have objects move directly at the camera or away from it; generally we angle the movement. In that way we make the movement less powerful, but still maintain the sense of depth by providing some image-size change. When it is mandatory that a movement be across the scene, angle the camera or stage the movement so that some change in image size takes place, no matter how slight.

6 One important factor in providing perspective is *modeled lighting*. It produces light and shadow areas that add depth to the scene. Flat lighting that produces shadowless illumination reduces the sense of depth.

CONCLUSION   An aesthetically satisfying picture should be balanced, it should have a singleness of purpose or be unified, and finally, it should be simple—containing only those elements which contribute to the purpose of the shot, and those elements arranged so that they project meaning.

Common Faults in the Use of the Camera

In light of what has been previously discussed concerning the proper use of the camera, we here provide you with a check list of the most common camera faults found in the work of beginning film-makers.

FAILURE TO ESTABLISH A CONTINUITY OF SHOTS   The most common procedure for maintaining continuity is to first record in a long shot the action and locale in order to orient the viewer, then to move into the medium range and finally into the close-up for the most important elements. This procedure duplicates, to a degree, the way a spectator would see the action. It is possible to reverse the procedure, but only when the action close-up has impact and importance.

FAILURE TO COVER AN ACTION FROM A VARIETY OF CAMERA ANGLES   One important factor in maintaining interest is variety, and in film this applies to a variety of angles. Every time a new phase of the action is photographed, there should be a change of camera angle.

FAILURE TO OVERLAP THE ACTION SO THAT SHOTS OF CONTINUOUS ACTION CAN BE SMOOTHLY EDITED TOGETHER   The overlapping of the action should be carried out in conjunction with a change in camera angle so the editor can effect a smooth transition from shot to shot.

OVER- OR UNDEREXPOSURE OF THE PICTURE   The picture is washed out when overexposed and dark when underexposed. Generally this mistake is due to inadequate knowledge about the light meter.

A LACK OF SHARP FOCUS   This is a common fault particularly with cameras not equipped with a reflex focusing and viewing system or when using lenses with a narrow depth of field. The overall image of the picture is blurred and useless.

FAILURE TO USE A SOLID, STEADY SUPPORT FOR THE CAMERA   This produces an unsteady picture that, except for situations in which this specifically is desired, is difficult to watch. The beginner seems particularly fascinated with hand-holding the camera. Use a tripod.

OVERABUNDANCE OF CAMERA MOVEMENT   This is a general error among novice film-makers. The camera should be moved only when it accomplishes a specific purpose, otherwise it attracts attention to itself.

DIFFICULTY IN PANNING THE CAMERA WHEN FOLLOWING AN ACTION   When following an action, it is wise to frame the action so that there is more space ahead of the moving subject than behind it. The camera leads the subject. And the panning movement should always be in the same direction as the action. This difficulty with the panning movement also involves the composition in the beginning of the shot and at the end. Both compositions should be interesting, and the movement between should be smooth. The beginning film-maker invariably pans too fast, causing the image to "strobe."

FAILURE TO ALLOW A SUFFICIENT AMOUNT OF FOOTAGE AT THE BEGINNING AND END OF A PAN SHOT   This can cause problems if, in the editing stage, it is necessary to eliminate the pan movement. If the footage on the compositions at the beginning and end is long enough, it may be used as separate shots.

LACK OF UNDERSTANDING OF THE PRINCIPLES OF GOOD COMPOSITION   This fault affects the quality of any film-maker's work. Film compositions are not static compositions, but compositions in motion. They must be aesthetically pleasing and meaningful.

FAILURE TO MAINTAIN A CONSISTENT FLOW OF SCREEN DIRECTION   Such a mistake can be most confusing for an audience. When a subject moves across the screen from left to right and passes out of the frame on the right side, he must enter the shot that follows from the left side unless some indication is given that the subject has changed directions.

FAILURE TO USE THE CLOSE-UP TO ITS FULL ADVANTAGE   This failure to use one of the film's most powerful devices mars the work of many novice film-makers. The tendency among beginners is to film in long shots and medium shots.

FAILURE TO UNDERSTAND THE COMPLEXITIES OF THE CAMERA   The camera is a complex instrument requiring a number of adjustments. Failure to make the adjustments can affect the image recorded. To list the most common errors:

1   the film incorrectly threaded;
2   lenses not securely mounted;

3   speed control improperly adjusted;

4   failure to correct for parallax when using a camera with a separate viewfinder;

5   failure to charge the battery before using a power-operated camera; or,

6   forgetting to wind after every shot the spring motor of cameras powered by this type of source.

LOCATION SHOOTING

Throughout its history, the film has passed through periods that decried the artifice of the studio and demanded the return of the film to the street and "reality." After a time the film would pass into a period that censured the sordid reality of the street and would move back into the studio. The contemporary film, due partly to the contemporary search for meaning and truth in our lives and, perhaps, due equally to the development of more compact and portable film equipment, is on its way back to the streets and their "reality." As a result, many film-makers are faced with the unique problems of location shooting with its comparative lack of control, in contrast to studio shooting.

The Background

One of the strongest advantages in location shooting is the utilization of authentic backgrounds, but the effort required is wasted if these backgrounds are not utilized properly. When the action is staged and the camera angles chosen so that the background contributes to the meaning and atmosphere of the scene, when the background is more than just a backdrop in front of which the subjects move, the increased cost, extra effort, and loss of precise control of sound and light may well be worth it.

When the background is integrated into the action of the scene, it can establish not only authenticity and provide us with a functional environment for the action, it can also contribute psychologically to the viewer's perception of the emotional and intellectual content of the film. For proof of this one need only look at the works of Michaelangelo Antonioni. In each of his films the backgrounds play a vital role: the barren and rocky island in *L'Avventura*, the house under construction in *L'Eclisse*, the factory district of northern Italy in *Red Desert*, mod London in *Blow-Up*, and the desert in *Zabriskie Point* are all powerful contributors to the climate of the film. Man is conditioned by his environment, so how can one present a view of man without considering that environment and using it so that the audience understands its effects upon the motivations of the subjects?

At the same time, however, the action of the film is the most important element and the background should never be allowed to intrude upon that action. By separating the subjects of the scene from the background so that they do not blend into it, flattening the visual effect of the picture, the background is kept from intruding upon the action. Camera angle and the positioning of the subjects will aid in this separation, as will the proper use of light and color.

Location versus Studio

Some film scripts require that they be filmed on location; other scripts would make it impractical and unreasonable to even consider location shooting. When the script necessitates utilizing the real environment, you have no choice; but when there is choice, you should consider several practical factors.

The first consideration should be *cost*. Constructing a set on a sound stage is not cheap by any stretch of the imagination. You should decide how many days it will take you to shoot, find out the rental and construction costs, then add them up. Location costs can also be considerable, depending upon the subject and location required. Then cost may include the transportation of equipment and personnel; perhaps the rental of additional equipment; perhaps the need for a larger crew; the amount of time wasted in getting to and from the location site, which can lengthen your shooting schedule and thus increase the portal-to-portal wages to crew and cast, increased rental costs of equipment, and increased insurance costs. Compare the costs of studio and location shooting. If the difference between the two is slight, you will then have to decide whether you need the control offered by the studio, or the realism offered by the actual location.

Your second consideration should be *time*. Building a realistic set in the studio does not happen in a day. Yet, once you begin to shoot, the control over light, sound and other technical elements can contribute speed to the production. On the other hand, when shooting on location there is no necessity to take time to create the set; it is there. But all of the equipment will have to be unpacked and set up at the beginning of a shooting day and then broken down and packed up each night. As mentioned earlier, you may also have to add the time necessary to travel to the location. A thousand and one different things can happen on location because of your lack of control. It can even rain! These things can slow down production, so you must make an allowance for such possible contingencies in the planned production time of location shooting.

Third, you should consider the *availability of the set*. If you rent a studio and construct a set, it is there for the next day's shooting or for retakes. If you are utilizing a location setting, you are at the mercy of the owner of the site. He may seem excited at first at the prospect of having a film shot on his property, but as the time drags out and your interruption of his normal day continues, he may begin to question his initial permission. He may gradually become anxious to see the last of you. This can create pressure on the film-maker who already has more than his share of pressures.

Lastly, you should consider and decide *how much control over light and sound is required by your script*. Undoubtedly the studio is far superior in this respect. After all, it was constructed for this purpose. Both light and sound can be critical to your film, and the effort to achieve top quality in each is time-consuming, even more so on location.

Consider thoroughly each of these factors before you decide. Do not rush off to the studio or to the actual location without looking at your alternatives. It could be costly in money and quality to your film. Be sure to check out and keep abreast of the latest in equipment. Every day film equipment seems to improve, making location shooting less of a monumental problem of control.

Over the years light-weight cameras, like the Arriflex and Eclair, have been developed which are compact and portable yet produce results that are comparable to those of the giant monsters of the studio, like the 285 lb. Mitchell. At the same time, more portable equipment has been developed that allows mobility of the camera on location; the new ColorTran dolly packs into two carrying cases which can be loaded into the trunk of an automobile. One of the major filming problems has always been the difficulty of finding proper lighting instruments, but the development of the tungsten-halogen unit has contributed greatly to the solution of this problem. The matter of sound has been affected greatly by the development of compact tape recorders, directional mikes, and wireless microphone pick-up.

An excellent example of the things that are possible on location now as a result of the new equipment is demonstrated in one scene in *The Graduate.* The location for the scene was outside the "Whisky à Go-go" on Sunset Strip. On the night selected for shooting the street was teeming with hundreds of people. To film amidst all of this chaos would have been impossible, yet the atmosphere which would be created by this environment was essential to the film. A camera with a 500mm lens was hidden in a service station on the opposite side of Sunset Strip. The normal lamps in the marquee of the club were exchanged for the more powerful tungsten-halogen ones now available so that enough light could be flooded onto the scene to expose the film. The actors wore wireless microphones concealed in their clothing. The picture and the dialogue of the scene, plus the indispensable authentic sounds and sights of the environment, were suitably recorded. The scene has a much more realistic feeling than could ever have been captured on a set in the studio and it was possible only because of the development of compact equipment that allows such flexibility and yet produces first-rate reproductions of picture and sound.

SOUND FILMING

When embarking upon a project requiring the recording of sound synchronous with the picture, you theoretically have two choices as to the procedure to follow:

1 You can film with a double-system in which the picture is recorded on film with the use of a silent camera and the sound is recorded on tape with a separate tape recorder that is running "in sync" with the camera.
2 You can film with a single-system in which both picture and sound are recorded on the same piece of film. The sound is either recorded on a magnetic stripe that runs along one side of the film, or is recorded optically along one side. This necessitates the use of a special camera equipped with sound pick-up head, either optical or magnetic.

For the majority of sound projects we would recommend the use of the double-system. It will necessitate the use of more equipment, perhaps a larger crew, and a more complex set-up for each scene. But the results that can be obtained are far better.

Double-system Sound Filming

The first thing we should consider is the basic equipment you will need to do the job and then, secondly, how to use that equipment.

EQUIPMENT

The element of major concern as far as your camera is concerned is the motor that will run it. You have several choices when shooting sound. The camera motor can be a D.C. governor-controlled (constant speed) motor, an A.C. synchronous motor, or a battery-powered synchronous motor equipped with a crystal control system. The D.C. motor is lighter, but you are limited in the movement of the camera by the length of the necessary "umbilical" cable between the camera and recorder. The D.C. motor operates the camera at a constant twenty-four frames per second. A small A.C. generator, used with the D.C. motor generates a sixty cycle signal to the tape recorder through the connecting cable so that synchronization between camera and recorder can be maintained. This generator—commonly called a *sync generator*—is either installed in the camera or attached to the motor. Should the D.C. motor operate at other than twenty-four frames per second, the frequency of the sync signal generated to the tape recorder will follow the changed speed of the motor in direct relationship, keeping the two in sync; if the speed drops to twenty-three frames per second, for example, the sync pulse changes to 57.5 instead of sixty cycles per second.

The A.C. motor is used mainly for studio shooting. However, some film-makers still use them on location, despite the fact that they require a converter, a motor control, and several storage batteries in order to operate. The major advantage of the sync motor is that its speed is in direct relationship to the frequency of the A.C. source. If the frequency of the source changes, the camera speed follows in step with the change. The tape recorder also operates off of the A.C. source so that its speed too is controlled by the frequency of that source. If you are shooting in a location where A.C. wall power is available, the A.C. sync motor is a good choice.

The newest and most versatile motor is the battery-powered, crystal-controlled synchronous motor. The speed of this motor is regulated by reference to its attached or built-in crystal frequency source. This motor and crystal control system is used with a tape recorder containing an attached or incorporated matching crystal-generated reference signal source. The signal source of the recorder generates a crystal-based reference frequency that is recorded onto the tape like a conventional sync pulse. This recorded reference frequency signal controls the transfer of the sound from quarter-inch to sprocketed magnetic film in the same way as the conventional sixty cycle pulse. Synchronization is achieved through the identity of the signal controlling the camera motor with the signal being used as a sync signal by the tape recorder.

Undoubtedly the most important technical improvement in sound filming was the development of the *magnetic tape recorder.* The earliest sound films were made by recording the sound onto recording discs that were played back on a phonograph interlocked with the projector. The next step was the recording of optical sound, which had to be developed and printed (an overnight procedure) before it could be heard. This recording technique continued until the development of the magnetic tape recorder. The composite printing of the sound track optically is still the predominantly utilized method; however, until the composite print stage, all elements of the sound are printed magnetically.

The recorder you should select is, of course, determined by what you will require of the machine. For a simple operation you may require only a one-speed recorder with an automatic volume control, a single recording head, and a limited tape load. On the other hand, you may need a machine with a large capacity tape load, a playback head, fast forward and reverse action, two or more microphone inputs, a frequency meter, or any of a number of other features which give you greater control of the quality of the recording. The first step, then, is to determine what your project will require and make your selection accordingly.

Most recorders that record two tracks can be adapted for sync recording. A small amount of sixty cycle A.C. power is fed into the "B" channel, and it thus records a sync pulse that can later be scanned in the transfer process. The "A" channel then records the sound. If you own a two track machine and wish to adapt it for filming purposes, we would suggest that you have a qualified electronic technician make the modifications. This machine must then be used with a camera equipped with an A.C. synchronous motor that operates off of the same A.C. source as the recorder. Anyone interested in this adaptation of a two track recorder can consult the June 1963, issue of the *American Cinematographer,* and an article by Phil J. Fladd, Jr., entitled "Hitch-Hike Sync."

Several of the more popular recorders used in film sound recording are:

NAGRA III   A quarter-inch tape machine with speeds of 3¾, 7½, and 15 inches per second. It holds a five inch reel with the lid closed or a seven inch reel with the lid open. It measures 12½ × 8¾ × 4½ inches and weighs 13 lbs. 13 ounces. The Nagra can be monitored with earphones from either a direct or reproduce circuit while recording and contains a two-watt speaker system for small group listening when not recording. It contains a normal microphone input and a low-level line input for use with an accessory microphone pre-amp or 3 mike mixer. The Nagra is powered by twelve standard "D" size flashlight cells or a nickel cadmium rechargeable battery. This Swiss-manufactured machine is one of the best on the market and is highly recommended. The new Nagra IV series is also now available.

PERFECTONE   A quarter-inch tape machine with a speed of 7½ inches per second. It holds a 600 foot reel which provides sixteen minutes of sound with 1½ mil tape. It measures 5 × 9 × 13 inches and weighs 19 lbs. The Perfectone contains two microphone inputs plus one line input that can be used as an additional mike input. The machine has earphone and speaker monitoring. The operator may listen to either a direct or reproduce monitor. The Perfectone is powered by twelve standard "D" flashlight cells. Nickel cadmium cells are also available.

RANGERTONE   A quarter-inch tape recorder with speeds of 7½ or fifteen inches per second. This machine holds 4,800 foot reels providing one hour of sound at 15 i.p.s. or two hours at 7½ i.p.s. The Rangertone measures 22 × 30 × 36 inches and weighs 230 lbs. It contains six inputs of 100 omh impedence; a separate microphone amplifier is available with three microphone inputs. Earphone and speaker monitoring is possible. It is powered by a 110 volt, 60 cycle, A.C. source.

MAGNASYNC X-400 SERIES   A 16mm magnetic film recorder that operates at sound speed (36 ft. per minute). The Type 1 has a 400 foot capacity or a 1,200 foot capacity with extension arms. The Type 15 has a capacity of 1,200 ft. The Type 1 measures 15½ × 19 × 7½ inches and weighs 27 lbs. The Type 15 measures 18 × 20 × 11 inches and weighs 48 lbs. The Magnasync X-400 contains a single microphone input. It is powered by a 110 volt, A.C. source.

MAGNASYNC 602 (16MM) and 135 (35MM) SERIES   The 602 series is a 16mm magnetic film recorder and the 135 series is a 35mm magnetic film recorder with speeds of 36 ft. per minute and 90 ft. per minute respectively. Both series have a capacity of 1,600 ft. They measure 12 × 23 × 23 inches and weigh 79 lbs. They have a single microphone input. Both series are monitored by a 4 inch VU meter that registers the input signal. They also contain a 6 × 9 inch dual speaker for playback. They are powered by a 110 volt, A.C. source, unless equipped with a D.C. motor which is available.

Of the recorders listed above, three utilize quarter-inch tape, two use 16mm magnetic film, and one employs 35mm magnetic film. The vast majority of professional soundmen agree that quarter-inch tape is the best for all production and music recording. The equipment is more portable. The tape is much less expensive and can serve as a sound master for your protection after the sound has been transferred to sprocketed medium for editing. We recommend that you use 1½ mil tape of the "low print" variety. The base can be Mylar, acetate, or polyester. All tape should be bulk erased before it is used; you should never depend upon the erasing mechanism of your tape recorder. While 7½ i.p.s. is adequate for voice or sound effects recording, 15 i.p.s. is essential for music.

The *uni-directional* and *ultra-directional microphones* are generally used for film production. The uni-directional is generally preferred because it rejects unwanted sounds at the sides and rear of the direction at which it is pointed. The ultra-directional mike (generally called the "shot-gun" mike) narrows down the pick-up even more than the uni-directional. In a particularly noisy location the "shot-gun" may be the best choice.

Wireless microphones are especially useful in situations where mike booms or fishpoles are impossible, such as in extreme long shots that zoom into close shots and in which dialogue must be çarried on throughout the shot. The major problem in their use is the picking up of interference in the receiver from power sources or other transmitters. One should be careful to select only the more sophisticated crystal-controlled transmitter and receiver designs for the best results. Many companies manufacture a so-called wireless microphone, but the quality of the sound is extremely poor in many of these models.

HOW SYNCHRONIZATION IS ACCOMPLISHED

The basic problem is that the sound accompanying each frame of picture must be recorded so that when projected both picture and sound are reproduced simultaneously "in sync." Therefore the mechanism that reproduces the sound must start, come up to speed, and operate at the same rate of speed as the mechanism recording the picture.

There are several different systems for achieving synchronization with quarter-inch tape—Pilotone, Neo-Pilotone, Rangertone, and Perfectone. All operate on the same basic principle, the difference in the systems being the way the fundamental principle is carried out. Basically, synchronization is accomplished by generating a synchronizing pulse or wave from the camera which is recorded onto the tape. This sync signal serves as a measurement of each frame of the picture, providing, in a sense "magnetic sprocket holes." When the quarter-inch tape is transferred to editing stock, the sync signal is scanned by the reproducer, thus keeping any second generation of the sound also in perfect sync.

SOUND FILMING TECHNIQUES

For the best results, in recording dialogue, your tape recorder should be set either at 15 or 7½ i.p.s. Start the recorder and then start the camera. Let them run at least five seconds before the clapboard is used. DO NOT FORGET THE CLAPBOARD!! If you do, you will have no reference point with which to later sync the picture and sound track. If you are using a camera with the electric clapstick, again start the recorder first and then the camera so that you will be certain to record the electric "bloop" which will be used in conjunction with the flash frames on the film as your sync marks. If your camera is a considerable distance from the tape recorder it may be impossible to pick up the shot of the clapstick descending. Sometimes a zoom lens will do the trick. If not, the tape recorder should be equipped with a device that can flash a light as the syncing noise is produced for the recorder. A light can be picked up by the camera at a considerable distance and you will then use the light to sync up voice and picture tracks.

Keep the recording and playback heads of the tape recorder clean.

They can be easily magnetized and thus cause noise and distortion on the sound track, so keep tools, pliers, screw drivers, etc., away from the heads.

The microphone should be placed in relationship to the picture being recorded. In a long shot, for example, the mike should be farther away from the source of sound than in a close-up if the sound is to be properly related to the picture. For the best results the mike should be placed on a boom of some kind. The most versatile boom is the *fishpole*.

When placing the mike keep it approximately an arm's length in front of the speaker and slightly above his head. It should be pointed directly at him unless he has difficulty with sibilance or there is too much harshness in the voice. These qualities can be reduced by pointing the mike to the right or left of the speaker. If it is at all possible, use only one mike for dialogue recording and move it into its proper place by means of a boom. If you must use more than one microphone, they must be *phased*, and if they come within close proximity of one another, the volume should be lowered on the one farthest from the action.

Tests can be run to determine the best placement for the microphone. Place it where you think it should be. Then move it closer and farther away, move it up and down, move it to the left and right of the speaker until you find the spot with the best quality. When recording in an interior, you should test the reverberation of the area in the same manner to find the best position for the mike. An excellent way to determine in what parts of the room the reverberation is the liveliest and the deadest is to walk around clapping the hands. The fluctuations in the reverberation of that sound will indicate the live and dead spots. If the reverberation is too great, you may wish to correct the condition by hanging sheets of sound-absorbing material, such as blankets. The ceiling may also require such treatment. The floors can be covered with carpeting.

The uni-directional or ultra-directional mike can help greatly in the reduction of ambient noises not wanted on the sound track. Moving such a mike closer to the speaker contributes tremendously to the reduction of these noises. Of course, this microphone should not be facing the source of the noises, nor should it face a wall that can reflect them. Take care, however, that you do not place the mike too close to the speaker or the quality of sound will be reduced considerably. Again, test for the right placement.

A major reason for poor quality sound recording is recording the sound at too high a level. Learn to recognize this poor quality and the boundaries on the volume indicator within which the needle should stay for good quality recording. These boundaries can be determined by running tests with the recorder from low to high level, playing them back over a good playback system, and listening for the points where the sound becomes distorted. Once you have established within the boundaries the proper recording level on the VU meter and through your earphones, maintain it. Do not change it. Instead, move the mike until you are getting the proper reading.

Remember as a general rule, that it will always be your purpose to record at the maximum level possible without causing distortion. We will discuss the subject of recording in more detail in the sound chapters.

A good practice when you are recording sound on location, exterior or interior, is to make *presence loops*. This involves letting the tape recorder run for a minute or two with no noise other than the background presence of the room or exterior locale. If the scene should later have to be partially dubbed or even if the voice track has to be edited, this "presence" can be made into a continuously running *loop* which will fill the gaps in the sound track. The need for presence loops is based on the fact that there is no such thing in nature as silence, and that when we actually hear a sound track in a film go dead, the effect is disturbing and noticeable. The presence loop fills this dead space.

The major problem encountered in employing the single-system technique is the twenty-eight frame advance of the sound track, caused by the necessary placement of the sound head in the single-system camera. If the original film is cut, it must be cut to the sound rather than the picture. If we were to cut the picture where we might wish it cut, we would cut off twenty-eight frames of the sound which would be more than a second of the sound.

The single-system is undeniably a faster means of sound production, and that is the major reason it is used for television news work. But even here the cutting problem is most noticeable. This basic problem is the reason why we see lips moving in a TV interview but hear no sound, or we hear sound continuing after the picture has gone from the screen.

We recommend that you rule out the use of single-system sound for any kind of film work. Even though the transferring of the sound from

Single-system Sound Filming

Fig. 5–39 Shooting on location (*In Cold Blood,* Columbia Pictures)

Fig. 5–40 Shooting in the studio
(*Dr. Strangelove*, Columbia Pictures)

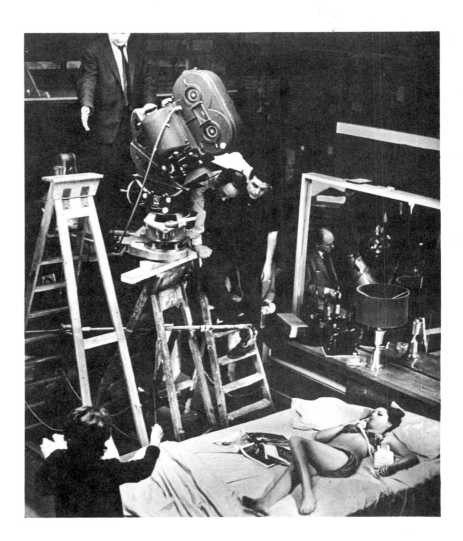

magnetic striping to sprocketed medium is possible, single-system is rarely, if ever, used for any type of sound filming today other than interviews because the sound quality is below double-system standards. However, if you find yourself in a situation where you must use the system and then cut the original, we would suggest that you utilize the following approach. Do not expect this method of using single-system to give you results comparable to those that you can obtain with double-system production.

The best procedure to follow is to adapt a television studio approach to your filming. You will have to use two sound-on-film cameras that run synchronously. This is possible if you use sync motors on both cameras and operate them off of the same A.C. source. Both cameras will record the complete sound track of the scene, but the picture will differ with each camera. Let us suppose that we are filming the following interchange of dialogue:

A: *Excuse me, sir.*

B: *Yes, what can I do for you?*

A: *I seem to be lost. Could you tell me how I can get to 46th Street and Seventh Avenue?*

B: *Sure, that's pretty easy from here. Walk up to the next corner. It's a bus stop. Take the 104 bus to 46th Street. Then walk east one block. That's 46th Street and Seventh Avenue.*

A: *Oh! That's all there is to it? Thanks a lot.*

B: *That's okay.*

This scene is taking place on a street corner. Set up your cameras as in Fig. 5.41 so that they each cover a different view of the scene. Suppose we wish to shoot the first two lines in a medium shot as A walks into the scene, stops B, and they speak the lines. The next shot we want is a close-up of A which will be followed by a close-up of B. We then return to a medium shot of the exchange. The cameras will both begin at the beginning. Camera 1 will be positioned so that it shoots the opening medium shot, and Camera 2 will follow A into the scene and zoom in for a close-up. When A speaks his second line Camera 1 zooms in for a close-up of B, and while B is delivering his directions for A, Camera 2 zooms back to a medium shot and holds it to the end of the scene.

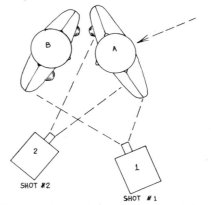

Fig. 5–41 A single-system technique (Jack Fischer)

Since the film from both cameras will have an identical sound track, we can cut back and forth in editing the film together without worrying about the twenty-eight frame difference of picture and sound. The zooms in and out are, of course, not wanted and so will be cut out as we follow our pre-planned shot breakdown. If the cameras are placed on dollies, they can also be moved around during filming if greater visual variety is desired. If you wish the movements of the camera to be a part of the scene, they are carried out while that camera is "on the air." If the movements are to be used only to reposition the camera—just as we used the zooms above—they are carried out while the camera is "off the air."

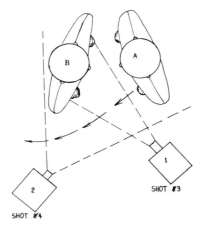

By employing this method you will be able to cut the original film by picture since the sound tracks will match. But the method is doubly expensive since you must utilize two cameras and crews and must use double the amount of film. It also necessitates that the staging and shot breakdown be completely preconceived before filming begins. Before the cameras roll you will have to thoroughly rehearse the cast and all of their movements for they will have to sustain the scene from beginning to end. The camera crews will also have to be rehearsed in all of their movements and what parts of the action they are to record. The actual filming will require split-second timing on the parts of the cast and crew. The complexities of this method will also limit you considerably in what you can do with the scene visually. This same procedure can be used for uncontrolled action with both cameras rolling from beginning to end, and one camera recording a master scene, while the second records the cut-ins. However, we can only repeat, do not use single-system if you have any choice in the matter.

One last important point. In filming location voice sync scenes, you must decide whether you intend to try to make sound tracks of acceptable professional quality to be used in your final sound mix "as is," or whether you wish only to make a *scratch track*, which is simply a record of the scene to later guide you in *studio dubbing*. We will discuss dubbing later; suffice it to say that the dubbing of pictures *in the same language in which they were shot*, particularly by the actors who actually filmed the scene, is a universal professional practice, and should not be compared with the abomination of dubbing in a foreign language. There is nothing more characteristic of the low-budget production than rotten location sound, for it is extremely difficult to control the location situation to enable you to pick up the sound at the quality level you need. However, don't make the mistake of wandering into the dubbing studio with high hopes that you or the actors will remember what they have said months before, or hours before, for that matter. You will require either a *stenographic record* of the lines or a scratch track to guide you; the latter, of course, is preferable.

It is our personal preference to make a scratch track on location and dub the actual tracks later in a studio. To this end, you should always include in your contract with your actors the right for you to use them to dub the picture later, at no additional fee to you. You will waste far more money in monkeying around on location with massive quantities of equipment trying to get first-rate professional sound than you will in using a dubbing studio later. And you may never get the level of sound on location that you require anyway. So give some serious thought to the scratch track/dubbing method for location sync dialogue work.

CHAPTER 6

DEVELOPING THE IMAGE: THE DAILIES

Once the film has been exposed in the camera, it passes on to the next vital member of the production team—the laboratory. The film laboratory plays an essential role in the transition from a vision in the film-maker's mind to the finished film. It is the laboratory that accepts the film with its latent image and transforms it into a visible image that can be projected onto the screen. Obviously the quality of that image is mainly in the hands of the film-maker and his cast and crew, but the laboratory and its equipment and processes can be counted on to contribute greatly to that quality of the exposed image. If the laboratory is to be a contributor to the finished product, the same teamwork that existed between the film-maker, the script writer, the cameraman, the cast, and the crew must exist with the laboratory.

The laboratory should contain and utilize the latest and most modern equipment and techniques for processing and printing. The selection of the laboratory to be used should be made by the film-maker before production begins. The laboratory's advice on the film to be selected and the proper way to expose the film can be most important to the successful outcome of the film. The film-maker should be careful in his selection of a laboratory and make certain that the one chosen has seen fit to advance with the field. The budget-minded film-maker may select a certain laboratory because of its lower prices, but this should not be the criteria considered. A dollar can be saved in many places, but the laboratory is not one of those places. The most important consideration for the film-maker is whether the laboratory can provide him with the highest quality of work.

The film-maker must then look upon the laboratory as the expert in its area of film production, and, just as he listened to the cameraman, for example, during the production stage, he must listen to and accept the advice of the laboratory in regard to its functions in the production of the film. But again, the film-maker knows what must be accomplished with the visual image, and so he must communicate his desires to the laboratory. Only if the laboratory comprehends the purpose of the film-maker can it provide the film-maker the services he requires.

Therefore, in dealing with the laboratory it is vital that the film-maker employ terminology which means the same for both parties. Several years ago the American Standards Association devised a "Nomenclature for Motion Picture Film Used in Studios and Processing Laboratories" that was adopted by the Association of Cinema Laboratories. We recommend that this terminology be employed in all communications with the laboratory, especially if it is a member of this association (see Appendix). The variations in terminology and technology which exist in any industry as broad and varied in scope as film-making must be eliminated if the film-maker is to receive what he needs from the laboratory.

DEVELOPING THE EXPOSED FILM

Most film-makers, upon the completion of each day's shooting, deposit their exposed footage with the laboratory for developing and the printing of the *dailies*, sometimes called *"rushes."* Film should be processed as soon as possible after exposure, and most laboratories can provide dailies for the film-maker overnight, i.e., on a "daily" basis. In this way, the film-maker can view the results of the previous day's shooting and determine whether or not any retakes will be necessary before the company strikes its equipment from a location or dismantles a set in the studio.

Depositing the Film with the Lab

If you are hand-carrying the film to the laboratory or shipping it via the mail, you must provide the laboratory with the following facts:

1 complete description of the film materials;
2 amount of footage;
3 title of the production;
4 what services you desire;
5 your delivery requirements; and
6 shipping instructions if the order is not to be picked up.

The film should be on a camera spool or on a core, put in a black paper bag, and placed in a can. The can should always be taped around the edge. Usually the tape that is around the can when the film is purchased is carefully removed and saved, generally by sticking it to the surface of the camera case. This tape may then be reapplied to the can when the exposed footage is returned to the can. The can should then be labeled "exposed"; the type of film that is enclosed, the approximate footage, the process that is desired of the lab, and the ASA rating at which the film was exposed is included on a label on the can. Never punch or scribe the film that is being sent to the laboratory because these marks may weaken the film and cause it to break in the developing machine. When it is necessary to mark your film during shooting—for example, to indicate start marks or frame lines when making double exposures in the camera—do so with India ink which will not be removed during the developing.

If you do not wish the laboratory to print everything on the roll of exposed film, but instead to print only specific takes, you must provide the lab with a copy of your camera report with the takes desired plainly marked. This also necessitates the slating of each take—a practice that we have already stated is necessary for the editor. Your camera report should identify the shot, indicate the footage where these takes can be found, and how long the takes are. Circle the required takes on your camera report if your report sheet does not have a "print" column and inform the laboratory to print only these circled takes (Fig. 6.1). By printing only selected takes you will save some lab costs and lessen the amount of material through which your editor must wade. However, any take not printed will never be seen, so you must be certain that the unprinted takes are absolutely worthless. It is surprising how often a take that was not considered good enough during shooting turns out to be the best take; also, many times one or two feet from an "out take" can be utilized, sometimes for an entirely different purpose than the shot was meant for. Print selected takes if you wish, but be certain to print any take that might have the slightest possibility of use.

The Developing Procedure

Although the exposed material from which you will print is invariably called "negative," in certain cases it is actually a positive image, and hence properly called "camera original." This is so in the case of reversal film, and until the quite recent development of 16mm color negative film, all 16mm color film was reversal. There is one very important aspect to this. When the lab sends to the cutting room the camera original and the dailies, the inexperienced editor, picking up the first roll he sees and noticing that it contains positive images, assumes that the *other* roll is the precious "negative." This poor editor may be moving toward disaster. The camera original must never be handled by anyone not fully trained in "negative handling" techniques. Any damage to the original—and it is highly susceptible to scratches—will be passed on to every print made from it, which is exactly why dailies are used for editing. The

MATTCO ASSOCIATES, INC., McHenry, Illinois   JOB# J-138

DATE SEPT 19

Production Department Camera Log
Order No. ___J-138___   Title ___IRELAND ON THE GO___
Film Stock ___5251___   Type of Camera ___ARRI___ Mag# ___1 + 2___
Location ___BUNRATTY CASTLE___   Director ___MATT___
Cameraman ___OLSON___   Sound Engineer ___FRASER___
Assistant ___P___   Magnasync # ___
Production Mgr. ___FRASER___   Script Girl ___

SCENE#	TAKE#	SOUND	CAMERA FOOTAGE	N.G.	HOLD	PRINT	REMARKS
Roll # 8 —							
1	1	MOS	320			✓	EXT. CASTLE
	2	''	260			✓	" "
2	1	''	200	✓			M.S. MAN IN DOORWAY
	2		120			✓	" " " "
	3		70			✓	" " " "
Roll # 9 —							
3	1	1	360			✓	MED. SHOT. MAN AT CASTLE
3	2	2	310	✓			" " " "
3	3	3	260	✓			" " " "
3	4	4	200			✓	" " " "
3A	1	5	140			✓	C.U. MAN AT CASTLE
3A	2	6	80			✓	" " " "
3B	1	7	10			✓	VCU. MAN AT CASTLE
		8					" " " "
Roll # 10							
3B	1	8	340			✓	VCU. MAN AT CASTLE

Fig. 6-1

standard practice for labs is to head the original with white leader for thread-up on the processing machine; the dailies will have clear film on the head of the roll. Check with the lab before you touch your material if you are uncertain. A simple way of avoiding this potential problem is to have the lab keep your original and send you just the dailies; in fact, since we strongly recommend that a professional do your negative matching, you should consider letting the lab perform this service for you. Then the material can remain in protected environs. Negative matching is the last place to try to save money by doing it yourself.

The process whereby the laboratory develops your camera original is basically the same as the process carried out by any amateur still photographer, only the motion picture process is considerably more sophisticated. The still photographer places his film in a series of trays of solutions, the first being the developing solution where the film is sloshed back and forth. The film is then rinsed in water, next placed in a fixative, rinsed again, and dried.

Motion picture film is threaded into a large developing machine that contains areas corresponding to the still photographer's trays. The film is attached to leader film that is threaded throughout the machine and thus pulls the exposed film through the machine. It first pulls the exposed film through an area where a constantly recirculating developing solution is sprayed onto the film through a series of jet sprays. The older method—still used by some labs, but now more sophisticated—pulls the film through a series of tanks, and the film is immersed into the agitated solutions. If the machine does not provide sufficient turbulence it is not nearly as satisfactory a procedure, for the tanks are like a series of stagnant pools containing the waste removed from previous film that has passed through and so do not provide the quality control of the jet sprays.

To understand what happens to the film when the developing agent is sprayed onto it, you should first know that the film itself is a celluloid base coated with an emulsion made up of silver halides suspended in gelatin. The silver halides are metallic silver combined with one of the halogens. When the silver halides are exposed to light, a change takes place in them, this change is not visible to the human eye, but the latent image has been produced on the film. Certain chemicals, or developing agents, which have no effect upon the silver halides that have *not* been exposed to light can be sprayed or washed over the film. Those silver halides that *have* been exposed are reduced to an opaque black metallic silver by releasing the halogen, which then combines with the other ingredients and is washed away. The exposed image is now formed in this black metallic silver on the celluloid base. The reason the developing process is carried out in darkness or in a red light is because at this point if the film were exposed to light the unexposed areas of silver halide would be exposed and the developer would attack them as well and reduce them to silver.

In order that the film can be exposed to light, the developing machine then pulls the film into an area—after a rinsing stage—where a chemical is sprayed onto the film. This chemical attacks the silver halides that have been unexposed to light and washes them away. This solution, which is also constantly recirculating, is the hypo. Now the celluloid base contains a black metallic silver image that is suspended in gelatin. Since the hypo would gradually bleach out the image, the film is next pulled through a rinsing stage where water is sprayed onto the film, rinsing away the hypo solution. The film is now pulled into the dry end of the machine where jets of warm air dry the film. Finally, at the end of the machine, the film is wound onto reels. What is now suspended on

DEVELOPING PROCESS

the celluloid base is a negative image—the reversal process which provides a positive image will be discussed shortly.

What has been described above is a simplification of the process of developing black-and-white negative. In the first solution are other ingredients besides the developing agent, although the agent is the most important element. The other ingredients—preservatives, accelerators, restrainers, and antifoggants—provide the conditions which allow the developing agent to work properly and produce high quality results. Time and temperature are two other important factors in the resultant quality of the developing process. The solutions are maintained at a temperature that is compatible with high quality fine grain results. The time or rate of development is dependent upon the speed at which the film was exposed in the camera, hence the necessity for the laboratory's knowing the ASA rating at which the film was exposed. Of course the graininess of the image is also affected by the rate of development. The emulsion of the film contains the light-sensitive grains which are affected when the film is exposed to light. They do not all lie on the same plane in the emulsion; some are near the surface, others are deeper in the emulsion. The more intense the light that strikes the film the deeper it penetrates into the emulsion and thus affects the grains that are positioned in the deeper plane. The developing agent will, of course, first attack those sensitized grains on the surface, but the longer the agent is allowed to work, the deeper into the emulsion it will penetrate. Therefore, if the agent must be allowed to penetrate to achieve the proper image with its contrasts of light and shade, the rate of development must be adjusted.

THE REVERSAL DEVELOPING PROCESS

As mentioned earlier, in 16mm production it is possible to utilize a film that, when processed, yields a positive rather than negative image. This film stock is called *reversal* film, and the camera original is not a negative but a positive.

Reversal film was developed by the Eastman Kodak company in the 1920s and allowed the film-maker to record an image on 16mm film, thus sparing him the cost of having a positive print made, because the image that he obtained with his camera was developed as a positive. This, of course, revolutionized the amateur market because of the reduction in the cost of filming—the same type of film is used today in 8mm. When 16mm production became popular professionally, reversal film was still utilized a great deal in black-and-white because of its excellent picture quality and was used always in color filming because, until recently, all color film in 16mm was reversal film.

The first stage of the developing process of reversal film is to provide a negative image—the *exposed* silver halides are attacked by the developing agent which releases the halogen and reduces the exposed silver halides to an opaque black metallic silver. The *unexposed* silver halides also form an image, but one opposite from the exposed halides—a *positive* image, since the exposed silver halides form a negative image.

At the completion of this first stage the film is in the same state as at the end of the first stage of the negative process. But the desire now is to form a positive image, not a negative one. To form this positive image on the celluloid, the negative image is bleached so that the metallic silver is oxidized. Then the film is exposed to light for a period of time sufficient to expose fully the previously unexposed silver halides. This new image is then developed in the same way as negative film, only what emerges from the machine is film with a positive image. The reversal process has added a bleaching stage, a reexposure period, and a second development.

COLOR DEVELOPING PROCESS

Color film contains basically red, green, and blue recording emulsion coatings superimposed on a single film base. The blue emulsion layer is blue sensitive and records the blue components of all colors in the scene. The green recording emulsion is green sensitive and records the green components. The red layer is red sensitive and carries out the same function for all red components in the exposed scene.

The processing of color film is too complex for a satisfactory simplified description. The process that is followed is dependent upon whether the stock is negative or reversal and upon the type of film—Kodachrome, Ektachrome, Gevachrome. In the developing stage color developing agents are used, and in a subsequent stage substances are employed to convert the reduced silver into silver salts that are removed in the fixing stage. Water washes, as in black-and-white processing, are used between each step of the processing so that there is no chemical carry-over from the previous stage. When the processing has been completed and the film dried, all that is left in the film emulsion are the dyes in the gelatin, for all of the silver salts have been removed.

PUSHING THE EMULSION SPEED

Situations will arise in which the film-maker must photograph a scene that does not have sufficient illumination to properly expose the film at the Exposure Index recommended by the manufacturer. The first thing you should be aware of is that the manufacturer knows what his film can do best and has assigned an Exposure Index that is the most effective speed of the emulsion. However, it is possible to increase that speed—also called "pushing the emulsion speed," "forced developing," "longer development," "extended development," and erroneously, "using a higher ASA"—within limits, without too much loss in quality.

In the production stage the cameraman deliberately underexposes the film, simply because he does not have sufficient light for a normal exposure. Many films today have a great deal of latitude. But you should remember that some films do not respond well to pushing. First check with the manufacturer of the film you are planning to use; he will advise you as to which film can and cannot be pushed and how much pushing can be tolerated without a loss in picture quality.

The *American Cinematographer Manual* suggests that you take an incident light reading and then use the "Incident Light Foot Candle" table on page 329 of the *Manual* to find the ASA Exposure Index necessary to shoot at the desired f/stop. Shoot the scene as if the film were actually rated at this ASA Exposure Index. Place the film in a separate can and instruct the laboratory to process it at that speed.

Black-and-white film offers the laboratory more flexibility for extended development than color film. One full stop increase is quite easily obtained by a longer development stage. However, when black-and-white film is developed longer there is generally an increase in the graininess of the image and an increase in the contrast. This increased contrast, however, can be reduced when a *master positive* is struck from the original, an example of the lab's flexibility mentioned earlier.

Color film and its slower emulsion speeds, even more than black-and-white with its higher speeds, may necessitate pushing the film in processing. The cameraman has fewer choices in color filming in the selection of color emulsion. In 16mm filming your choice is mainly between low-speed and high-speed reversal stock, and now the relatively fast color negative manufactured by Kodak. Extensive tests have been carried out on these films which show that they can be pushed satisfactorily if underexposed. Movielab, one of the industry's major laboratories recommends the following:

Film	EI	1 stop	1½ stops	2 stops	2½ stops
ECO 7255 Daylight w/85 filter	16	ASA 32	ASA 48	ASA 64	—
ECO 7255 Tungsten	25	ASA 50	ASA 80	ASA100	—
EF 7241	160	ASA320	ASA480	ASA640	ASA960
EF 7242	125	ASA250	ASA375	ASA500	ASA750
7254 Daylight w/85 filter	64	ASA128	—	—	—
7254 Tungsten	100	ASA200	—	—	—

The film that has been generally used in all 35mm production has been Type 5251 (see page 55) which is a color negative film. However, the recent addition by Kodak of Type 5254 and its higher Exposure Index will undoubtedly lead eventually to its exclusive use.

Film	EI	1 stop	1½ stops	2 stops	2½ stops
5251 Tungsten	50	ASA100	—	ASA200	—
5254 Tungsten	100	ASA200	—	—	—

Again we must remind you that for the best possible picture quality you should follow the recommended exposure index of the manufacturer. Force the emulsion speed only when you have no other recourse.

PRINTING THE DAILIES

At the completion of the developing process of *negative* film, there is a negative image on the film. This must now be printed onto a suitable *positive* stock to provide the film-maker with a positive image. This positive image print will be his daily. Whether you are using negative or reversal film as your camera original, it is wise to have a positive daily printed for screening and for turning over to the editor for his work print. Camera originals should never be used for anything but print material if you wish to retain the film.

When the camera original is negative, this negative is threaded emulsion to emulsion with a positive stock onto a continuous contact printer. On this printer a light is shined through the negative image of the original onto the positive stock which is held in contact with the original. Opaque portions of the negative image will stop the light from the printer from exposing the silver halides behind them on the positive stock, and so those halides opposite the transparent portions of the negative will be exposed to the light. When the positive has been exposed, it is then developed and fixed. But this time, of course, the parts that have been exposed (and are, therefore, converted into the opaque black metallic silver) are those parts opposite to the negative image. A positive image is the result.

A reversal original is printed in contact with reversal stock. This print stock is then developed in the same way as the original, providing the film-maker with his positive image daily.

When filming in black-and-white, the film-maker has but one choice as to his dailies—obviously a black-and-white copy. But when filming in color the film-maker does have a choice: color *or* black-and-white dailies. The main advantage in ordering black-and-white dailies is that they are cheaper—about half the cost of a color print. But in our opinion the disadvantages far outweigh the advantage. Black-and-white dailies are colorblind so that you are unaware of the tonal values of your color film. It is impossible for your editor to know if he is cutting scenes together of different color tone, and flare may not show on a black-and-white print but will be immediately apparent in a color print. Unless it is budgetarily out of the question, always order a color print rather than black-and-white.

Timed versus a One-light Print

A one-light print is one that is run through the printer without any compensatory changes in the printer's light from beginning to end. A timed print is one in which the printer's light intensity is changed to compensate for the different densities of the camera original.

The film-maker has a choice of whether to order a one-light or a timed print. Most laboratories lean toward a timed print. A timed print will show what can be done to the camera original through laboratory skills. Producers who utilize a timed print generally do so because they feel that they will have a better-looking edited work print to show to their sponsors or any other production critics, and thus have a better chance, perhaps, of receiving early approval of the project.

The proponents of the one-light print argue that the timing employed by the laboratory may not be the timing that will be required when the film is finally edited together, and therefore the timed print will be in error, which could tend to confuse. They further argue that it is erroneous to think that a timed work print will garner early approval—for the edited work print will still be only an approximation of the final film since it is without opticals, sound track, titles, etc. Lastly, these proponents believe that a one-light print will reveal to the film-maker exactly how the original take appears, and so the editor can better judge how to best cut the takes together. One final consideration: A one-light print is much less expensive than a timed print. Therefore, if you wish to evaluate the camera exposure of your camera original or you are operating on a tight budget, order a one-light print. If you wish to provide the client with the best quality work print, order a timed daily.

Edgenumbering

Upon completion of the editing of the film—which is done with the dailies, although they are called the *work print* once the editor makes his first cut—the edited work print must be matched to the camera original which is then utilized in the printing process. This "negative-matching" is discussed in full in Chapter 13. In the early days of film production this matching was accomplished by visually matching the action of the original and its print. This was not the most reliable method since it was slow and tedious and was dependent upon the eyesight of the person editing the original. In the mid-1920s a new method was devised whereby footage numbers were applied to one edge of the original film during manufacture. These numbers were printed through when a print from the original was made, so that the editor could now match the work print and the original by matching these numbers.

Today these *print-through edgenumbers* can be satisfactorily printed through from 35mm negative. However, these edgenumbers are generally difficult to read when printed through from 16mm original.

The major problem with edgenumbers, aside from the fact that they are impossible to read easily on 16mm film, is that there is no serial order of the numbering, and serial ordering facilitates filing and identification of film cuts and film sections. Today the film-maker can have the laboratory apply *ink-printed edgenumbers* to both the original and the dailies. These edgenumbers can be maintained in some serial order.

The printed edgenumbers are generally available in six digits. The first two digits are letters—the letters A through K with the letter I omitted are available—and these letters are followed by four numbers (see Fig. 8.2). The two letters can be used to identify the production in some way. These edgenumbers can be printed either every forty frames or every sixteen frames. The sixteen-frame type is preferable, particularly if you are going to have fairly short cuts in your picture; this will insure there being at least one edgenumber on each shot in the work print. The laboratory keeps a record on edgenumbers so that the film-maker can specify the letters he desires for his production and request that all dailies and original for that particular production be numbered in sequence. If he sends the laboratory each day's shooting instead of holding the film and sending it all at once—a system we do not recommend—the laboratory enters each day's order in the record and maintains the same serial numbering roll by roll until shooting is completed. The first roll of dailies may read GE0000 to GE0399, the next roll would then begin with GE0400 and so on. By maintaining his own record of the numbers assigned to each roll, the film-maker can locate any take he might desire very quickly and easily. Before the editor cuts the dailies into his work print, the film-maker should first check the edgenumbers for readability and sync on both the dailies and the camera original at the head and tail of each roll.

The main advantage of the printed edgenumbers is that they are numbers in a continuing series, roll by roll. The print-through numbers, when they can be seen, are not in a roll-by-roll series, but rather each roll will have a different series of numbers. This business can be complex enough without unnecessarily adding to the complexity. Edgenumbering is relatively inexpensive, so is within even a tight budget.

VIEWING THE DAILIES

When you receive the dailies from the laboratory, you will, of course, wish to screen the footage to find out whether you have captured what you hoped to capture on film and to check the quality of the photographed images. Some people screen their dailies on a Moviola. We prefer to screen the dailies on a projector. This latter method will provide you with a much bigger and brighter image, and your analysis of the material will be much more accurate.

STORING THE ORIGINAL

When the dailies are picked up from the lab, the camera original will also be returned to you. Make sure that you have thoroughly identified the original footage, then put it away in a safe place. (Remember, the original will be the roll of film with the white leader on it.) Ideally the original should be stored at a temperature of approximately 70°F., and at about a relative humidity of 50 percent. As long as the temperature is not over 80°F., and the humidity not over 60 percent or below 25 percent, the original should be safe until you need it to match with the edited work print. Upon completion of the film you will, no doubt, wish to store the original and any masters in the laboratory vault. This will be discussed more in Chapter 13. Raw stock, if it is to be stored for any length of time, should be stored under refrigeration. However, it must be returned to normal room temperature eight hours before exposure.

PAYING THE LAB BILL

Be sure that you discuss with the laboratory the payment procedures required of you. They may be willing to extend credit to you, but be sure that you determine the amount of credit. We have known film-makers who neglected to determine the extent of their credit. They contracted the laboratory to carry out services that totaled, say, $2,000. When they went to the lab to pick up their materials, they were told, much to their chagrin, that the lab was extending them only $500 of credit. Before they could receive the materials, they had to pay the laboratory $1,500. This can be a ticklish situation when you have not planned to pay out this much capital at this time and may or may not have that much on hand, especially when the sponsor of the film is waiting to view or receive these materials.

If you have not established credit with the laboratory, you will have to pay for each job order before the materials can be released to you. There are many stories in the industry about film-makers who have been unable to collect their materials from the laboratory because of inadequate financial arrangements. Do not fall victim to this trap. The laboratory provides the film-maker with a service, but not a free one.

CHAPTER 7

THE IMAGE IN FLUX AND JUXTAPOSITION:
THE AESTHETICS OF FILM EDITING

The potential of music as a form of art must date from the moment when a lonely shepherd first perforated his simple reed pipe. From the potential of pitch rises the creative complexity of all music. So must the potential of film as an art form date from that moment when the primitive film-maker first understood that the film was to be constructed from a multiplicity of shots.

Initially this infinitely productive insight must have stemmed from the simple need to include properly within the limiting frame the varieties of filmic action. The frame must always be kept alive and filled—alive with motion and filled with the importance of the filmed material. By its nature, the camera inevitably moves in on its subject, closer and closer, until the frame is filled. To remain at a distance which enables the fixed form of the frame to include the entire length of the body is seldom satisfying; the body's form cannot fill the squat frame, whose side portions remain unused and lifeless. To render the trivial extremities of the body faithfully is meaningless; it is to the face and to the eyes, those "mirrors of the soul," that we turn for understanding, driving the camera in until the essence of the subject fills the screen and all that is inessential is eliminated by the frame's choice.°

°It was Charles Chaplin who first freed the comedic camera from the requirement of portraying the human form in its entirety, from head to toe, a relationship of camera to subject insisted upon by all other comic performers of his day. It was D. W. Griffith who instinctively first sensed the aesthetic potential of the close-up, using it to present to the spectator the *meaningful* portion of the body. Griffith did this over the outraged cries of his fellow film-makers, distributors, and exhibitors, the latter reporting instances of their audiences rushing screaming from the theaters at the sight of huge disembodied faces floating hideously about on the screen. Years later, Fred Astaire would insist that the now selective camera return to the portrayal of the entire human form for his dance sequences, believing that the grace and intricacy of his art required this.

But the film does not consist wholly of a series of such soul-searching close-ups. When a second person joins the scene, the camera must pull back, searching for a proper grasp of this new subject, again filling the frame with all that has meaning and importance. When the need arises to relate these people to each other or to their world, a new relationship of the camera-subject is dictated. Finally, the subject in motion has its own unique demands of the camera, which must flow with the moving image, still filling the frame with the essential life of the shot.

Soon, from this instinctive response, the film-maker senses that the camera's relationship to the subject is potentially interpretive. If the camera gazes up toward the subject, the subject's strength and importance are increased proportionally; peering down, the camera dominates the diminutive subject, as the king dominates his subjects, kneeling in homage. A full, rich range of dynamics is open to the camera—its position, its angle its tilt, its focus, its framing, its distance—all contribute to the camera's *opinion* of the subject, and *our* opinion of the subject, for it sees as we, the spectators, do.

To accomplish this *the camera must constantly change its relationship to its subject, rendering the continuity of the film as a succession of varied shots.*

THE UNITY OF THE TRADITIONAL FILM

But the film must have form, unity, inevitability, as must any art. From any given note, there are a limited number of notes to which traditional music may turn; each note sets up an expectation—an expectation which must be fulfilled, and which, being fulfilled, provides form and inevitability. So does each shot in the film set up an expectation—an expectation derived from the basic content of the shot, the cutting point at which the shot ends, and the rhythm of the cuts themselves. This too must be fulfilled. Something must bind together the potential disunity of the film, "a visual medium which is, by its very nature, continually in danger of falling apart." This is the function of editing.

Yet, editing is more than an unobtrusive, self-effacing cementing of the bits and pieces of the film. We know that the juxtaposition of two shots can create new and unexpected meanings. We know that the rhythm of the change of shots can reach deep within the spectator. Further, we know that the cut itself can "explode," driving the film far beyond the original intrinsic meaning of the joined shots. This, too, is the function of film editing, and this raises a disquieting question of a potential conflict with its cementive function. We must learn to distinguish between *invisible* and *visible*—at times, *flamboyantly visible—cutting.*

The film—eagerly, joyfully and wrongly welcomed since its inception as the certain imitator of life, the sure purveyor of actuality—has placed principle demands upon the cementive editor, particularly since the coming of sound. Having superbly freed the film from the limitations of the single cold and distant shot, the film-maker will now expend his energy on disguising this technique. The film will be made to appear as the continuous flow of a single shot. As the imitator of actuality the film must maintain the *illusion of temporal continuity.* Of course, other forms of art—the symphony, the novel—have made use of the device of *transition,* bridging the temporally complete segments. The symphony has utilized the resolved pause between its separate movements, each movement having a kind of temporal unity within itself. The chapters of the traditional novel, while containing certain unobtrusive compressions and expansions of actual time, are also assumed to maintain a temporal continuity. Transitions—the skipping forward of time—are accomplished in a whisk of words, but they are unmistakably stated. The traditional film, borrowing from its sister arts, made use of its own stated transitions: the fade, the dissolve, the wipe. Only upon the use of such devices did the film skip forward in time.

We have seen a vital function of the editor as that of unobtrusively cementing together the various portions, shots, of the film, with a second important function being the rendering of certain shot juxtapositions visibly, with flair and impact. To this we must add the function of rendering the *transitions* of the film with clarity and logic. Let us see how these various functions work within the traditional form of the film.

It is within the scene in continuity, where the illusion of temporal continuity must be maintained, that the cut must be rendered unobtrusive. It is here that the fact of a multiplicity of shots traditionally must be disguised, and contrivance masked from the spectator. What this means, basically, is that in cutting from one shot to another, *any material simultaneously present in both shots must match.* The smiling actor, hands in pockets, puffing on a half-smoked cigar, dressed in a red shirt, and needing a shave, must appear just so in both shots. What is more, if he is beginning to rise at the very end of the outgoing shot, he must continue that rise in the incoming shot, and continue at what appears to be precisely the same point at which the spectator saw him last.

The editor in the cutting room will be presented with two shots of this action, perhaps one from the actor's right in close shot and one from his left in medium shot. If his choice is to cut at the precise point at which the actor's bottom is four inches from the chair, he must find this point in each shot. He will maintain the first shot until the actor's bottom reaches this point and then cut the shot. He will now remove the beginning of the second shot up to this four-inch point, splicing the remainder of the shot on to the selected beginning portion of the first shot. If he has selected carefully, the flow of action will proceed from shot to shot, and the cut will be unobtrusive. He will have *cut on action.* If he has additionally proceeded from the medium shot to the close shot at a point where the actor's rise has *stirred the interest of the spectator,* he will have further strengthened the "rightness" of the cut and rendered it almost completely unobtrusive.

All this would be quite simple if the two shots have been made *by two cameras simultaneously,* since the action in each shot would be

CUTTING WITHIN THE SCENE: THE CEMENTIVE FUNCTION; THE UNOBTRUSIVE CUT

identical. In practice, this is infrequently done, the shots generally having been made *by the same camera consecutively.* If, in such a case, the repeated action has been performed exactly the same in each shot, his task of matching will be as simple as with simultaneously filmed shots. If not, the editor has his work cut out for him.

In such a case, the procedure of *cutting on action* and the *placing of the cut at the point of spectator expectation* are equally important. The editor might, on the other hand, prefer to *cut at a point between actions,* when the limbs are in momentary repose—in this instance, just before the rise. This, in its place, is equally effective. If he utilizes the device of *within-the-scene anticipation*—a second character provoking the chair-sitting person and then turning to look at him just before the cut—he has further contributed to the cut's invisibility. Perhaps most important, if he has made a *major, meaningful change of camera relationship to the subject*—both *positional* and *scalar*—this will serve both to disguise any mismatch in action and to make meaningful the cut itself. Finally, as a practical matter, he will assure himself that the *elements of continuity*—position of hands, length of cigar, clothes worn, facial appearance—*will be consistent* between shots; or, if this is not possible, *that they not be comparable* by the spectator at the moment of cut.

CUTTING WITHIN THE SCENE: PARALLEL EDITING

Parallel editing, a technique evolved by D. W. Griffith to heighten the climactic excitement of his famed "last-minute rescue," is the direct cutting between an action and one or more simultaneously occurring actions in another locale. The actions are connected by an idea; that is, they are associated actions. A classic example is the ubiquitous wagon-train-under-attack scene in which repeated cuts to the cavalry riding to the rescue are intercut with the main action.° Such a scene—and it is, in a sense, a single scene with more than one locale—possesses a temporal, but not a physical, continuity. When we return to either element of the scene, we will expect the action within the scene to have progressed by the length of time we have been absent from it.

Although this is technically a type of within-the-scene cutting, the techniques used by the editor lie between those normally employed in within-scene cutting and those utilized in flair and impact cutting; in fact, they are closer to those of the latter. Although the cuts are within the plane of temporal continuity, there are obviously no simultaneously present elements to match between shots. Important to the success of the cut is the editor's choice of *an effective exit* and *an effective entrance point* for his shots. To exit on the *completion of an action*—an arrow thuds into a wagon, an Indian spills from his horse in a bursting cloud of dust—and to enter on the *impact* of an *exciting, immediately graspable image*—pounding hooves, a whipping cavalry guidon—will render this cut effective. The requirements of cut invisibility are not necessary here; it is precisely the impact of the cut that is so effective. Yet, in a sense, such a cut is not obtrusive, not calling disproportionate attention

*An interesting aspect to this intercutting is the fact that merely by progressively shortening the length of each succeeding shot of the parallel action the editor will create the impression that the action is increasing in tempo—even if its pace is precisely the same throughout.

to itself, for its visible technique is lost in the driving excitement of the scene.

In handling transitions there is no need for a "matching" of the shots by the editor in the sense of the exact duplication required in the within-the-scene continuity cutting. Here it is a matter of an aesthetic match, a match with flair. This can be particularly effective in the image matching of the *dissolve*, the gradual blending into each other of the juxtaposed images. Too often editors use a uniform length of dissolve, invariably a second or two, and pay little attention to the flowing together of the two images, an effect which can be quite beautiful and deeply moving.[6] The use of the dissolve and other transitional devices—including the contemporary use of the *direct cut*—will be discussed in detail later in the chapter.

The word "montage," the French word for the editing process, literally "mounting," was used by Eisenstein to refer to the process of editing. Through the influence of his films, particularly the famous Odessa Steps sequence from his masterpiece, *Potemkin*, the term became associated with a particular kind of rapid shock cutting which Eisenstein did supremely well, but which represented only a portion of the full range of editing processes he employed. Such "montage sequences," representing the acme of "the ruthless suppression of the inessential," evolved strangely into the familiar dissolve-ridden sequences of the Hollywood films of the 1940s, in which drifting calendar pages, floating railroad station signboards, and churning train wheels are used to depict the rising career of a young singer or in which a variety of scenes of training camp activity are used to show in one or two minutes the young recruit's first weeks in the army. The rationale behind such a sequence is the presenting of a selected impression of material, the full presentation of which would burden the film. It represents a careful gauging of the event's relative importance to the film and can be considered a rendering in *filmic time* rather than actual time. Extraneous material is eliminated with the willing consent of the spectator. The selected material makes the filmic point; anything more would be superfluous. A useful tool to the filmmaker, the dissolve montage is far from Eisenstein's use of the device, more closely resembling the collage-like juxtapositions of material in the German films of the twenties. However, dissolve-less, direct cut montage sequences rendering a series of rapid, essential impressions of the total material, utilizing many of the specific editing techniques evolved by Eisenstein, are a familiar part of many of our contemporary subject films. They represent one of the most individually creative tasks of today's editor.

The montage sequence is also a vital part of many story films. Since the editor depends upon the involved desire of the spectator to deal only with the essential, it is important to use the montage in the right place. Essentially, it is the *state of mind of the scene's participants* which justifies this treatment. Thus an attack on a wagon-train, a frenzied dance, a cavalry charge, or a wild bar-room brawl are ideal subjects, just as was the massacre on the Odessa Steps. Such scenes which demand full emotional involvement by the spectator and by the participants in the scene—scenes of deep emotion and high action—are the meat of montage.

The essence of the montage sequence is the impact of the cuts and the new sensations evolved by the juxtaposition of these images in collision; (obviously there is little impact of image in a dissolve). Here the editor will seek the meaningful cut, with little consideration for the unobtrusive cut. Still, he will avoid any obvious and distracting "jumps" in the temporal continuity caused by a careless mismatch. Since the mismatch is observable only when material is simultaneously present in both of the shots involved in the cut, the editor can avoid this by cutting from one segment of the action to another, entirely different segment. Scenes of mass action lend themselves to this. If some element must be present in both shots—a cut from a group of dancers to one member of the group—then the editor must match only that one element. If he cannot match it, then he must disguise the mismatch in some way. Two effective methods are *changing radically the angle and/or scale of the camera's approach* to the subject and utilizing the *cut-away*, the intercutting of a shot containing no elements in common with them between the two mismatched shots.

In the montage sequence the editor is much more concerned with an *aesthetic matching* of the cut shots. By the essential rightness of this matching he will ensure that vital unity of the scene which it is his responsibility to create.

As discussed above, the *completion of an action* and the *forceful, intelligible beginning of the next action* are important criteria in making the cut. Another important consideration is the *matching of image position* between the shots; the eye must not be distractingly jerked about from one portion of the frame to another at the cut. Nothing helps the montage cut so much as a *flow of action* within the outgoing shot, which directs the spectator's attention into the expectation of the cut. Such *directional cutting* can occur either as a wholly motional device—the flow in the outgoing shot runs left to right and then is either continued or smoothly reversed upon itself in the incoming shot—or a combination of motion and position—the flow directs the eye to that portion of the frame at which the incoming image appears. Also useful as a device is the *continuity of idea* between images, even if their form is dissimilar—the cutting from an ocean liner to a toy boat. *Cutting on form* is one of the most useful methods of lending unity—cutting from a fountain to a burst of fireworks, a spinning car wheel to a rolling hoop, from a lamp to the sun. *Tonal cutting* is also used, with a gradual progression from sharp to soft focus or light to dark image creating a sense of progression. And certainly, today, the understanding of the range of *complements of color* can be used in joining together the images of the montage. It is of course essential that the lighting key between shots not offer any glaring mismatch—sunny day to cloudy day, well-lit room to the same room in deep shadow—and that any clashing of color between shots be avoided.

Film editing, then, is essentially a process of fitting together the separate pieces from which the film is to be built, pieces supplied by the cameraman. But editing is more than just a matter of finding a snug fit. The basic content of the shot may be affected both by its juxtaposition with other shots and by the rhythm to which it is cut. The editor's job, then, is to: *choose the shots to be used* (the others become *out-takes*); *choose the portion of the shot to be used* (the remainder becomes *trims*); *determine, within certain limits, the order in which the shots shall occur;* and, *determine the length of time the shot shall run,* taking into consideration the factors of intelligibility, mood, pace and rhythm.

"THE SECOND DIRECTOR"

The stage director rehearses his actors over a period of time, guiding them in the creation of character and helping to mold the interaction and rhythm of their performances; however, he then must send them out on their own, hoping that his patient work will bear fruit but prevented himself from any intrusion into the actual performance. The orchestral director has one further advantage over the stage director: He may participate fully in the actual performance, determining its rhythm and the subtleties of its dynamics.

The film director goes far beyond even this. Once rehearsal is complete, the director can immediately set about to permanently capture the performance on film, free from any necessity of establishing a performance that can repeat itself, with "the illusion of the first time," night after night.° Once he has recorded the performance he can proceed through editing to control absolutely the elements which are to be seen and to be emphasized and the tempo and rhythm of the whole and its specific parts. And so the editor is the "second director," an extension of the director. Many film directors are reformed actors, former and present writers, ex-cameramen; all of these experiences are of help, but not essential. It is difficult to see how a director can function in film without a firsthand knowledge of editing, and, in fact, many film directors are editors.

CHOOSING THE SHOT APPROPRIATE TO THE FILM'S PURPOSE

If the editor's job is the building of the film's continuity, we must first consider whether this continuity differs in different films, and even in different scenes within the same film. Obviously, it does. A shot of a motorboat would be handled in a particular light and leisurely way within a vacation-land travelogue; a motorboat in a race sequence would be treated quite differently, the shots chosen for their excitement and cut in a rapid and building tempo. In a mystery, the boat should have a quality of menace about it, reflected in the way the shot is selected and handled by the editor. In an instructional film, a straightforward, objective shot of a boat might be left on the screen for thirty seconds or more, while a narrator explains in detail a complex operating procedure. Yet

*Performing on the stage while intoxicated is unthinkable, especially in drunk scenes, for the performer must be controlled, and errors become a public matter. On the other hand, I have heard both actors and directors advocate the use of a drink or two for the film actor (**not** the director!) to "loosen up" the performance, particularly in drunk scenes. Specifically, I heard Elia Kazan say that he took James Dean out for a pizza-and-beer lunch after they had wasted the morning unsuccessfully trying to shoot a scene in *East of Eden*. Kazan said that after a few beers, Dean had "no trouble" with the scene in that afternoon's shooting. Thus George Stevens' firing of the blank pistol off-stage to capture the look of fear on the faces of the actors in *Diary of Anne Frank* is a cinema director's trick. All the film director need do is make the moment happen *once*, and capture it, and it lives forever.

Fig. 7-1A Cutting before the completion of an action: cutting on position; cutting on direction; cutting on idea; cutting on impact
(last frame of outgoing shot, vehicle moving from right to left)

Fig. 7-1B First frame of incoming shot, vehicle in motion right to left and toward camera, camera panning right to left with vehicle

DETERMINING THE LENGTH OF THE SHOT

Fig. 7-1C Last frame of incoming shot, vehicle exiting frame at left, camera now stationary (Instant Holland, distributed by Paramount Pictures Directed by Richard Matto)

*Metric cutting, a series of cuts determined by tempo alone, would seem to represent an ignoring of shot content, but this is not so. Shots chosen for metric cutting invariably are chosen because their content lends itself to this: for example, facial close-ups or shots of continuous motion, as a running machine or turning wheels. Shots portraying segments of action with a beginning and end are avoided.

there is a consistency in this, for in each case the shot is selected and treated in a way appropriate to the film and its purpose.

Thus the absolutely essential first step in editing is for the editor to determine *the purpose of the film,* its intended *mood* and *style,* and its *theme* and *subject.* To a great degree this will be evident from a screening of the *dailies,* for, as we know, the camera is interpretive. But it is also vitally important that the editor seek out the director, as well as the material itself, to determine this. The editor is an *interpretive,* not a *creative,* artist. He may interpret creatively, but he still must interpret the supplied material and not impose his own ideas. His work must rise from the material and the director's intent. As there is the documentary film's "found story," so there is "found editing." On the stage the director is essentially an interpretive artist, the playwright alone being creative. In the film, this order is reversed, the writer supplying basic material to the director, who then creates the film. To know what the director wants, to effect it, to carry it out creatively—this is the editor's job.

We have discussed the importance of juxtaposition. What about rhythm, which is determined by the length of the shots? The editor must always cut every shot *as short as possible.* Of course the catch is, "as possible"; what determines that is the real question.

The success of any performing artist rests on his ability to hold the attention of his audience. He must constantly manipulate this attention, holding it and extending it to the last possible instant before releasing it, then quickly changing to a new device for holding and building attention anew.

ROBBER: *Your money or your life!* (A pause, a *long* pause.) *Well?*
JACK BENNY: (Very quickly) *I'm thinking, I'm thinking!*

If the artist waits one second too long, he has lost, irrevocably. But the great performer carries this pause to its absolute, unbelievable limit and then breaks off one split second before it is too late.

In an essentially visual scene, such as a montage sequence, the accumulative tempo of the cuts sets up an *expectation of the next cut,* and the editor must utilize this expectation. A good idea is to use the Moviola to run the sequence you are cutting, absorbing the rhythm. Since rhythm is an essentially auditory sensation, the visual cuts are translated into a palpable rhythm in the editor's mind. He may actually voice this rhythm, or listen to the sound of the taped splices thwicking through the Moviola gate. Once he discerns this rhythm, the next cut becomes absolutely determined, the editor slamming down on the Moviola brake at the right instant, then marking the film for his cut.

Remember, however, that the *content* of the shot is never ignored.* The editor quickly discovers that the shot content sets up its own expectation of cut, which may be different from that of the repeated cuts themselves. This is both a matter of *intelligibility* (it is disturbing to the spectator to have the shot snatched away from him before he can grasp it; the more complex the ideas or images presented, the longer the shot needed) and a matter of the *completion of an action* (it is equally disturbing to be denied the chance to follow an action through to completion). The cut on an incipient action, an action that has just begun and run only for a few frames, is particularly annoying.

However, this offers an excellent example of how an "inviolable" film rule can be broken deliberately, in this case either for the purpose of gaining a sense of disturbance or to drive forward the pace of the film. A skillful editor knows how to use cuts a *moment before the completion of an action*, depending upon the fact that the spectator, knowing how the action will complete, will accept the quick cut as a means of getting on to the business at hand. This is another example of the elimination of the inessential in editing. It is a technique used within the montage sequence, particularly the arbitrary montage of the subject film where a compilation of images is used to give an overall impression of a general subject. Two examples are shown from the Paramount short subject, *Instant Holland*. In the first, (Fig. 7.1 A–C), a direct cut is made to a beer wagon moving rapidly toward the camera. Note that the preceding frame (Fig. 1A)—the last frame of the outgoing shot—is still almost wholly filled by a moving horse-drawn coach. It is also significant that the beer wagon (Fig. 1B), is intercepted in action; there was no need to open on an empty frame and allow the wagon to "enter the stage." This cut also represents an example of *cutting on position* (both images, and hence the spectator's attention, are centered in the frame), *cutting on direction* (both vehicles are moving from right to left), *cutting on idea* (horse-drawn vehicle to horse-drawn vehicle), and *cutting on impact*. The third frame illustrated, (Fig. 1C), is the last frame before the next cut (the camera has panned left with the moving vehicle); note that the wagon still fills one-third of the frame. The frame is still "alive," and the spectator is thrown forward into the next action by the cut.

The second example, from the same film, (Fig. 7.2 A&B), was used as a transition cut to a new subject of entirely different mood. The first frame illustrated, (Fig. 7.2A), shows a group of children running from right to left; the camera pans with them and simultaneously tilts down to their feet. They are not allowed to exit the frame, the cut being made with the last frame, (Fig. 7.2B), still alive, one-third filled with motion. The incoming shot was the tranquil interior of a museum—an example of *cutting on idea*, since a group of children are shown in the museum—and the cut worked perfectly as a transition, without any need for a dissolve between these two dissimilar moods.

To repeat, we cut every shot as short as we can, once its essence has been grasped by the spectator, because we can never push beyond his limit of interest and lose his attention. On the other hand, it could also be said that we cut each shot as long as possible, at the point *just before we would lose the spectator*, as in the Jack Benny example. This holds true in the slowest-paced scene as well as the fastest.° Shot content affects the cutting point because the spectator's normal restlessness to move

Fig. 7-2A Cutting before the completion of an action: cutting on idea (first frame of outgoing shot, children running right to left, camera panning right to left with their motion and tilting down)

Fig. 7-2B Last frame of outgoing shot, children exiting frame to left, camera now stationary (*Instant Holland,* distributed by Paramount Pictures)

*Stage actors and comedians, familiar with the technique of "riding a laugh," will also understand this observation. When the audience begins laughing, belief is suspended; the actors simply hold in position until the laugh reached its climax. The moment the laugh peaks and begins to lessen, the next line is thrown, and the scene continues. Obviously the line would not have been heard if thrown during the beginning of the laugh; but it is equally important that it be quickly picked up at the precise instant that the laugh lessens, for this is an indication that the audience has lost interest in that joke and is now looking forward to the next one. If they are allowed to grow restless, the actor is in trouble. Likewise, a good stage manager always cuts short the curtain call before the audience grows restless, at the very first hint of a lessening of applause. "Always leave them wanting a bit more" is a golden rule of the performing arts.

on is suspended so long as he is concentrating in an attempt to fully grasp the subject at hand. This is one reason why a gripping story and an engrossing performance have great importance to a film, demanding the spectator's intense involvement in the film experience. The editor functions just as does the superlative comedian. The editor, like the comedian, holds the shot—and the audience's attention—for just as long as he can, and then cuts. This, in a very real sense, is cutting as quickly as possible.

CHOOSING THE SHOT AND THE PORTION OF THE SHOT: THE LIFE OF THE SHOT

The editor invariably sees several takes of the same shot, and he and the director must determine which is the best take for the purposes intended. Often, if the camerawork is less than ideal, the editor must choose a shot for *technical considerations*—it is the only one in focus, or properly lit, or capable of being matched in continuity to its neighbor—rather than because it is the best shot aesthetically. This is unfortunate, but it is also a part of the editor's job; he functions as a technician of the practical as well as an artist of the ideal.

Once the shot is selected, the choice is made as to what portion of the shot is to be used, a procedure we shall go into in specific detail in the following chapter. Basically, the editor seeks out the *life of the shot,* that sometimes minute portion of the shot which contains its essence, and gives attention to *suitable entrance and exit points* for his cuts. Since, many times, a very small portion of the shot is actually used in the assembled work print, the editor must be constantly alert while screening his material in order to detect these vital fragments, scattered like uncut diamonds throughout the mass of unusable material. Later, the exact portion and length of the shot to be used will be determined by the scene's tempo. Haskell Wexler's *Medium Cool,* a film directed by a first-rate cinematographer, utilizes a great deal of documentary footage. It offers many superb examples of a choice of the life of the shot—a policeman tying his shoe or scratching his chin, a young soldier grinning, a cameraman being removed from a roof by police—and a number of excellent examples of direct cut impact transitions.

DETERMINING THE ORDER OF SHOTS

While the determining of shot order is an editing function, it need not necessarily be performed by the editor himself. Certainly the director must have some definite shot order in mind when he plans his continuity and while he is shooting, and, in fact, the writer of the dialogue film has taken over much of the responsibility for continuity that once belonged to the silent film editor. Yet to think that the editor has abdicated complete responsibility in this important area would be an error. Since the editor will receive material in which he will have varying degrees of flexibility of shot arrangement, his guiding rule must be to remain constantly on the alert for inventive ways to rearrange the order of shots differently from that which was anticipated for them. This applies both to the editor himself, who may see an imaginative use for the material entirely unforeseen by the writer or director, and to the director and writer functioning as editors, who may break with the "traditional" arrangement of shots to achieve new and exciting effects.

Conventional shot arrangement has dictated the beginning of a scene with the *establishing long shot*, an overall orientation of the geography of the scene from a comparatively objective, at-a-distance viewpoint. This is then followed by a medium two-shot, then by alternating over-the-shoulder shots, and then by comparatively subjective alternate close-ups of the characters involved (Fig. 7.3). The basic rationale to the long shot–medium shot–close shot progression is quite sound. Generally, one wishes to get the lay of the land before moving on to significant details, which can later be related back to the whole. Certainly their significance can often be fully understood only in relation to the whole. The movement from objective distant shot into subjective close shot follows the wish of the spectator, who inevitably wants to draw closer to that which interests him. This traditional shot order is a sound means for involving the spectator more deeply in the scene, proven through constant and continued use.

There is, however, an intriguing alternative to this traditional sequential treatment of the scene. Why not begin with the attention-catching detail, "hook" the attention of the spectator, and then satisfy his desire to know more of the general significance of this detail in relation to the whole? Not only is such an approach as psychologically sound as the traditional arrangement, but it also can offer one important further effect, much sought after by today's film-maker: The momentary, *planned disorientation* jolts the spectator into awareness and forces him to think, to work for understanding. Many contemporary film-makers have rejected the silver-platter approach to the audience—a technique unhappily prevalent in the work of many film directors who dealt with "meaningful" and "significant" subjects, and revelatory of an inherent distrust of their audience. Today's directors take for granted that the spectator is willing to expend effort for a more rewarding film experience. The success of the work of Ingmar Bergman has had incalculable effect on his contemporaries in this area, as have the films of Fellini, Antonioni, Richardson, Resnais, Lester and Godard, each in their own way This confidence in the spectator's willingness to work for his film experience, to strive with alert intelligence to think and interpret for himself *Marienbad, The Seventh Seal, Petulia, Weekend, L'Avventura, 8½, Blow-Up)* is a foundation-stone of contemporary Cinematic Cinema.

However, it must be pointed out that this is an instance of the editing function as practiced by the director and cameraman; such arrangement must inevitably be pre-planned, particularly in the story film. The brilliant cut in *The Graduate* of Dustin Hoffman leaping up from the pool toward a rubber float and landing on Mrs. Robinson in a hotel bed in a matched flow of action is perhaps the essence of Cinematic Cinema. Such editing can "happen" in the cutting room through the alert reaction of the editor to his material, but the director is advised to plan and shoot with such juxtapositions firmly in mind.

Fig. 7-3 Six photos illustrating the classic coverage of a conversational scene; establishing two-shot, medium two-shot, respective over-the-shoulder shots; respective close-ups

ACTION SEQUENCES

Where the editor functions most fully as a creative determinant of shot order is in the handling of action sequences. Only in such scenes does he retain the creative sway he held in silent film days.

Here the editor has full range of control over the order of shots and the length they are to run; thus he controls the emphasis of material and the tempo of the scene. The content is largely predetermined; after all, the writer has decided who will win his screen battles and the cameraman has supplied the basic material at the director's request. Yet even if the climactic moment of the scene is predetermined, the peaks and valleys and the length and tempo of the journey on the route to the summit may be arranged and controlled in an infinite number of ways. This is particularly true of the more active sequences and/or sequences shot with a variety of camera angles and usable cut-aways. In such sequences the mundane work of finding acceptable matches between successive shots is simplified, and this enables the editor to make his determination of shot order on the basis of aesthetic rather than practical considerations.

MONTAGE SEQUENCES

Of all action sequences, montage sequences offer the editor maximum opportunity for creative rearrangement of material and control of tempo. We have said that the rationale behind the montage is the basic cinematic fact that the spectator is forever willing to skip the inessential and move on to the meaningful. If we are to convey through montage the essence of a sightseeing tour of New York, we would begin by photographing our actors in a variety of filmicly interesting settings about the city. Once we come to examine this material in the cutting room, the actual order in which the shots were made, and, for that matter, the actual geography of the city, are meaningless to our purpose. The geography of the montage will be created from the filmic material itself. We might choose to begin with a particularly bustling shot for an introduction to the city and to end with a shot that can be savored long after. The actual order of places visited between these opening and closing shots can be chosen to give a sense of progression of color and excitement (or the opposite if that were our purpose), and this sense rises from the quality of the shots themselves, not from the scenes actually filmed. Nor would we care in the slightest if we find ourselves transporting our character from one end of Manhattan to the other in a split second, rather than laboriously moving him along like a chess pawn, one stumbling square at a time. The montage character is to be moved like a queen in a chess game, with great sweeping leaps and not like the pawn, severely limited in its power and imagination.

Not only would we consider *content* in striving for a continuity of progressive idea between shots, but also the *form* of the images themselves as it affects the cut. A cut from a tall building to a tall tree or from a strolling soldier to a toy soldier in a shop window (cutting on form, cutting on idea) can be used; or we can match the flow of motion from one shot to the next, just as Nichols did in the pool-to-bedroom cut in *The*

Graduate. By matching a shot of a playful monkey in a zoo cage to a shot of our characters laughing, we can show them having a relaxed good time, even if such a juxtaposition never occurred during the filming. We might create small sub-groupings of shots within the scene, scenes of eating in various locales, scenes of walking, or asking directions, or laughing. Since all of these considerations rise from the filmic material itself, we are truly creating a filmic reality and practicing aesthetic editing.

Note that one important implication will govern our work throughout: At all times we will avoid the mundane and the inessential. As artists we have the privilege—in fact, the responsibility—of *selecting*. It is not necessary to show that our characters paid checks, stumbled over curbs, argued with cab drivers, or visited toilets—unless, of course, these actions are to our particular purpose. In the lighthearted, carefree tour of a flamboyant city we shall choose only lighthearted images to present, just as our memory would retain only such images from a joyful tour of this city. Yet this does not imply that small details cannot be used with great effectiveness, for they too can be a vivid part of memory. We have listed what we need not show; yet chosen filmicly, these very images may be just the thing for our purpose. We have all seen shots of pissoirs used effectively in films of Paris, where the toilets are charming (if that's the right word) and certainly an essential part of Paris. A coin dropped into a bus collection box, a traffic light flashing WALK—DON'T WALK, a quick flight of pigeons, an old man sunning himself in the park, a sidewalk hotdog man—all are a part of New York too. Selectivity does not eliminate the inadvertent and fortuitous image. The trivial is not without significance.

To see some of the finest editing of this type, one has only to watch television, particularly feature film trailers and travel commercials. We think immediately of the marvelously edited commercials for the Province of Ontario, the Jamaican Tourist Board, virtually all of the airlines, particularly those of TWA, Eastern, and Pan Am, Parliament Cigarettes' series filmed in London, and some excellent montage commercials by the French and British Tourist Boards. We are not the first to observe that the one-minute commercial, stripped ruthlessly of the inessential, is close to the essence of the cinematic.

TEMPORAL AND SPATIAL CONTINUITY

The film transition is a device for maintaining the illusion of continuity while allowing the director to compress time. The editor deals with within-scene continuity which is, with a few deliberate exceptions, a believable temporal continuity. Since the time of D. W. Griffith, the spectator has accepted an *instantaneous spatial change*, so long as the illusion of temporal continuity has been preserved. Thus when we have cut from the speeding train to the station and back, we have expected the train to have moved a distance along the track comparable to that which it might actually have traveled while it was unseen. This is the essence of continuity cutting. Note that we have said a "comparable" distance; the spectator can seldom determine this distance with perfect accuracy, nor does he care to. So long as we have not shattered his belief in temporal continuity, he has willingly suspended his disbelief to allow the film-maker a good deal of flexibility in such matters. In today's Cinematic Cinema, we see daily the pushing forward of the limits to which the film-maker can go without encountering disbelief.

Whenever the conventional film has been called upon to leap forward or backward in time a distance which could not be willingly accepted by the spectator within the illusion of continuity, the use of some form of transition was called for.

Transitions

There are several transitional devices available to the film-maker, each with its own particular effect.

THE FADE

The fade out/fade in has long been the transitional device utilized to express a complete sense of change between the bridged sections, a calm, resolved pause before continuing the film, (Fig. 7.4). The outgoing image is progressively faded frame-by-frame into black, held momentarily, and the incoming image then faded up to its full strength, the shot continuing.

Fig. 7–4 The fade-out: six successive images from a six-frame fade-out (Television commercial for the State of Georgia, Department of Industry and Trade: conceived and directed by Cargill, Wilson, and Acree; production by Storer Studios, Inc.; opticals by Optical House, Inc.)

The length of time of the fades out and in, as well as the length of the pause between images, can of course be varied, although usually the fade out is the same length as the fade in. (It is possible to fade out, hold for a moment, and then cut directly in.) Titles are invariably faded in and out when they are superimposed over a filmed action background (when they fade in and out very quickly—often in ⅓ or ½ a second— they are said to "pop" on or out), and virtually all films end with a fade out, the sense of resolve being felt essential at that point.

However, the fade in is much less frequently used today to open a film, the film-maker usually choosing to open on the impact of the full, sharp image. As a transitional device, the fade is seldom used in the contemporary film, somehow seeming to conflict with today's notion of what the film must do. Perhaps we are too impatient for even such a momentary, unfilled pause, too anxious to push forward to the next excitement of the film. At any rate, the fade, both as a reminder of the technical contrivance of the film and as a slowing of its driving pace, is out of tune with today's cinema.

The dissolve, although in declining usage today as a means of transition, is still an effective filmic device. In contrast to the fade out/fade in, in which the scene goes momentarily into black, the dissolve is a gradual blending of the adjacent images, (Fig. 7.5 A–C). In a twenty-four frame (one-second) dissolve, the outgoing image fades out in twenty-four equal steps, at the same time that the incoming image fades in in twenty-four equal steps, the images superimposed. Thus at the twelve-frame midpoint, each image is at equal strength. In theory, the outgoing image should dominate up to that point, the incoming from that point on. In practice, the incoming image, by virtue of its newness, usually takes on our interest about one-third of the way into the dissolve, a point to remember when starting a sound cue over a dissolve. The sense of the two locales blending in the dissolve is quite effective; it is essentially filmic (the dissolve, invented by the magician-film-maker Georges Méliès, was the first truly cinematic device discovered), and is particularly effective in scenes of gentle transition. In the traditional, "realistic," film, it has been the most common means of indicating a passage of time; the contemporary cinema no longer requires this.

In *The Loneliness of the Long Distance Runner*, directed by Tony Richardson, there is a scene in which a young boy and girl walk on a deserted beach. Their conversation continues through the scene, implying temporal continuity, but Richardson has chosen to dissolve between the visual images. As a practical decision, this allows him to choose his images for their visual effectiveness, without regard to the technical consideration of whether they can be cut in continuity. Nor is it necessary to disguise a potential mismatch with a mood-shattering cut-away to the ubiquitous sea gull of such beach scenes. But more important there are aesthetic gains. The effect is quite wonderful; there is a gentle implica-

Fig. 7–5a The dissolve: the last frame of full image of the outgoing shot just before the beginning of the dissolve

Fig. 7–5b The dissolve midpoint, 12th frame of a 24-frame dissolve, both images equally dominant

THE DISSOLVE AND THE SUPERIMPOSITION

Fig. 7–5c The first frame of full image of the incoming shot just after the end of the dissolve (*Weekend in Peru:* director, Kenneth Roberts; editor, Win Sharples, Jr.)

Fig. 7–6a The swish pan: last frame of shot before camera begins swish pan

Fig. 7–6b Second frame of swish pan: image of two girls from center frame in Fig. 7–5a is visible at far right

**THE SWISH PAN,
THE RIPPLE DISSOLVE,
THE WIPE,
THE TURNAROUND,
THE IRIS, AND THE MASK.**

Fig. 7–6c Fifth frame of swish pan: image totally unrecognizable appearing as a horizontal blur *(Weekend in Peru:* director, Kenneth Roberts; editor, Win Sharples, Jr.)

tion that the things we say in life are a part of a continuing conversation that goes on and on wherever we may be—the setting may change, but the words are the same. The genius of this use of the dissolve, and it is an important creative innovation of the Cinematic Cinema of today, is that it frees the dissolve from its limited use as a temporal transition device and makes of it a means for creating the mood and rhythm· of the scene. The dissolve used as a mood-creator is an integral part of some quite lovely cosmetics, bathing suit, and diet cola commercials, particularly effective when they are shot with an interpretive camera using a soft-focus lens and atmospheric lighting. The slavish use of the dissolve in adhering to the illusion of temporal continuity is unnecessary today; its full potential as a filmic device lies ahead. The *superimposition,* an overlapping of two simultaneously present images and hence first-cousin to the dissolve, can be similarly freed from its restrictive use as the creator of on-screen ghosts and goblins and utilized with equal effectiveness as a creator of mood and atmosphere. The death scene in John Huston's *Moulin Rouge* uses supers effectively.

There are a number of attention-getting transitional devices available to the film-maker. The *swish pan* is a gimmicky whirling of the camera to the right or left at the end of a shot, (Fig. 7.6 A–C). When the next shot is cut against the end of the swish pan the two locales seem to flow quickly into each other (the spectator is unable to detect the cut at the end of the pan and so the effect is as if the camera actually whirled from one locale directly to the next). The television series *The Man From Uncle* was obsessed with swish pans; they are appropriate only in films requiring a jazzy, off-beat transition. Contrary to the name, there is nothing particularly effeminate about the swish pan.

The *ripple dissolve,* a wavy blending of the adjacent images as if oil were pouring over the screen, was a much beloved means of transporting the spectator in and out of a flashback or a dream in pre-Resnais, pre-Fellini days. There are good examples in *The Running Man* and *Cat Ballou.*

The *wipe,* an extremely common transitional device of the American films of the nineteen-forties, is related to the dissolve in that the two images are simultaneously present, (Fig. 7.8 A–B). In contrast to the dissolve, the wipe's images never are superimposed over one another, but are present side by side. The incoming image wipes across the outgoing image, it does not push it out of the frame. In a left-to-right straight wipe, at the midpoint one sees the left half of the incoming image filling the left half of the screen and the right half of the outgoing image filling the right half of the screen. There are an infinite variety of wipes (see Fig. 9.1) but the most common are top to bottom, bottom to top, diagonal, and sideways. As another attention-getting device the wipe has specific and limited use today. However, a particularly effective use is being made in the contemporary multiple-image film, in which the side-by-side images may be made to wipe in or out in a variety of contrasting ways. (Fig. 7.9 A–D, 7.10 A–D).

Fig. 7-8 The wipe: illustrated are the 2nd and 15th frames of a bottom-to-top wipe; at this rate the wipe would be completed in 28 frames (note that the incoming image does not "push up" the outgoing image nor does it "slide up" from the bottom: it is as if the outgoing image were imprinted on a scroll which rolls up, revealing the incoming image already in place beneath it)

Fig. 7-10a Successive frames from a multiple-image film; a cut from one 4-frame field to another —only the upper-right image has "cut"; the others run continuously past this point (Television commercial for the State of Georgia, Department of Industry and Trade: conceived and directed by Cargill, Wilson, and Acree; production by Storer Studios, Inc.; opticals by Optical House, Inc.)

Fig. 7-9a The wipe in a multiple-image film: the illustrated images move simultaneously inward onto a black field in the 15th frame

Fig. 7-9b The wipe in a multiple-image film: in the 43rd frame the two images are entirely visible still moving toward the center of the field

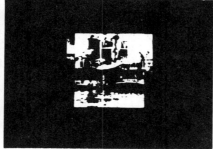

Fig. 7-9c The wipe in a multiple-image film: in the 50th frame the two moving images have met in the center and a third image is wiping out from the center toward the edges

Fig. 7-9d The wipe in a multiple-image film: in the 62nd frame the incoming image has almost completely wiped out the two outgoing images: the total effect lasted for 64 frames

(Television commercial for the State of Georgia, Department of Industry and Trade: conceived and directed by Cargill, Wilson, and Acree; production by Storer Studios, Inc.; opticals by Optical House, Inc.)

Fig. 7-10b Successive frames from a multiple-image film: in the outgoing shot, the frame is presented isolated against a black field; at the "cut," this image continues as the black field changes to a full-field image (there is an interesting counterpoint of image between the player crouched at the sidelines out of the action and the violent activity of the full-field image)

Fig. 7-10c Division of the screen into 4 images of similar content and contrasting form.

Fig. 7-10d Division of the screen into 9 images: 7 of the images are of flowers, 2 of a child; the upper right image dominates our attention because of its contrast to the majority of images present and by the nature of the image itself.

Inviting me to dinner?

Fig. 7–11a The iris (*Shoot the Piano Player,* Janus Films)

Fig. 7–11b The mask (a first-cousin to the iris): the illustration of two successive frames shows a direct cut in the "background" material while the mask remains the same

THE (FRAGMENTED) IMPACT DISSOLVE

*In the sound optical the images are "blended" by the overlapping sound; the incoming image is audially present while the outgoing image is visually present.

The *turnaround,* or *flip wipe,* also a product of an earlier era, is a flipping of the on-screen image to reveal the incoming image on its reverse side.

The *iris,* invented by Billy Bitzer and D. W. Griffith, is a progressive circular narrowing (the iris out) or expanding (the iris in) of the image, usually against a black background, (Fig. 7.11 A&B). It can be used, as Griffith himself used it, either as a means of fading in or out or to emphasize one portion of the screen, functioning as a kind of close-up. The iris is associated with the silent film era, and as such has been used by such contemporary film-makers as Truffaut, Godard, and Richardson as a kind of homage to the silent film. The *mask* is an arrested iris; its most common use is to create the effect of a subjective view through fieldglasses, a periscope, or a keyhole. Illustrated, (Fig. 7.12), is a particularly effective use of side-by-side masked images from *Shoot The Piano Player.* In the same film, Truffaut makes an excellent aesthetic use of the iris in, (Fig 7.13), intruding the presence of the impressario between the couple whose marriage he will ultimately shatter. This might more accurately be termed a wipe, since two images are present simultaneously, rather than one image against a black background. However, the spirit of the film and a realization of Truffaut's enthusiasm for the silent movie—as well as the presence in the film of other irises and other silent film devices—would seem to justify calling this too an iris. Again, specialized use of the iris is obviously called for, for it is extremely attention-getting and essentially dated.

The swish pan is accomplished with the camera; the fade, the dissolve, the ripple dissolve, the wipe, the turnaround, the iris and the mask are all created optically, although it is possible to execute dissolves and fades in the camera itself, as was done originally until the invention of the optical printer.

In Dennis Hopper's *Easy Rider* there is an interesting use of a transitional device which must be added to those available to the contemporary film-maker. It combines attributes of several other transitions, yet it is unique in offering an overall effect none of the others possesses. It promises particularly interesting prospects for development of imaginative applications transcending its use merely as a means of getting from one scene to another. Most transitional devices involve a blending of the juxtaposed images, the impact cut being the obvious exception; the images are simultaneously present—superimposed in the dissolve, side-by-side in the wipe.* The quality of blending in these transitions is precisely their limitation—there is an inherent softness to them. The beauty of the device used by Hopper is that it achieves a blend, but a disorienting blend with harsh impact, slightly ginmicky and attention-getting, quite appropriate to this film, which is itself a troubled blend of Wyatt's sometime serenity and the aimless, frenetic quest of the other people portrayed. We can best describe this transition as an impact dissolve.

The technique involves the use of flash cuts—probably four frames, one-sixth of a second long—in alternation. Following a flash cut of the incoming scene the film returns to a flash cut of the outgoing scene, back to the incoming, back to the outgoing, incoming, outgoing, finally ending on the running shot incoming. The flash cuts can be all the same length or can become progressively shorter, ending with a vivid whirr of impact. Because of the phenomenon of persistence of vision, the images appear to overlap and so are actually "simultaneously present."° The key to the success of this technique is in the choice of *contrasting images;* contrast can be tonal (the most strikingly effective impact dissolve in *Easy Rider* involves a day-to-night transition), formal (the basic shape of the juxtaposed images cannot be too similar), or positional (the effect achieved by Eisenstein through his contrastingly tilted shots of the machine gun). The images should be static and essentially simple and easily grasped—close-ups work well—but this is not absolutely necessary.

The author used an extension of this device in a contemporary short made by the Mario Ghio Production Group for distribution by United Artists, *Inland Sea Odyssey.* We had material on a Japanese festival, covering both the afternoon "warm-up" and the full-scale dancing and parading at night. We began with the afternoon preparations, showing the two young couples in the film being instructed in dance steps, enjoying the laughter of the crowds, lifting each other up on their shoulders for a better glimpse of the excitement. During this afternoon sequence, flash cuts of the night activity were cut in at spaced intervals, initially four-frame cuts, then six and eight and eventually twelve frames long. The flash cuts were chosen for their contrasting deep blue color, instantly conveying the sense of night. They occurred with increasing frequency until close to the actual transition point. At that time we chose two contrasting faces—a close-up of one of the women dancers in the parade and a close-up of another young girl (a member of one of the couples) learning the dance—and began to alternate back and forth between them, the shots shorter and shorter until finally ending in a blur of two-frame cuts leading to an impact cut of the street at night. During the ensuing festival-at-night sequence, we continued to intercut flashes of the afternoon images. The sight of a young boy carried on his father's shoulders triggered a return to the similar afternoon scene; our protagonists' dancing cued a return to scenes of their dancing instruction, and scenes of enjoyment returned us to similar scenes of laughter in the afternoon. The fun of the afternoon naturally leads us to anticipate the dramatic excitement of the full-scale festival at night, and our presence at the night activities reminds us of the expectant joys and the particularly vivid memories of the afternoon. We are dealing in filmic time and space, for the film is memory and anticipation. That this technique may not be instantly comprehensible to the spectator is a risk we are willing to take, as are so many contemporary film-makers. The spectator is expected to experience the film, accepting his momentary disorientation, and to solve its riddle to his own ultimately greater satisfaction.

Fig. 7–12 The mask (*Shoot the Piano Player,* Janus Films)

Fig. 7–13 The iris (*Shoot the Piano Player,* Janus Films)

*The first use of this I can recall is in Eisenstein's *Ten Days that Shook the World.* He alternates flash cuts of a machine gun firing, the shots low-angle and strongly tilted and chosen for their contrast to each other. I was certain upon first viewing that the shots were actually supered but upon examination on a Moviola they proved to be adjacent flash cuts; it was persistence of vision that caused the illusion of superimposition. Not used as a transitional device, the technique was striking and one of those moments when the silent film can convey a powerful sense of having actually heard a sound which has been presented visually.

THE SOUND OPTICAL

Fig. 7–14a The sound optical; impact cutting
(last frame of outgoing shot 1)

Fig. 7–14b First frame of incoming shot 2:
leap in temporal and geographical continuity

Fig. 7–14c Last frame of shot 2 (camera has
tilted up) now the outgoing shot

Fig. 7–14d First frame of incoming shot 3
(*Darling*, distributed by Embassy Pictures)

In Alfred Hitchcock's 1935 film, *The Thirty-nine Steps*, the protagonist has fled his rented room, leaving behind a corpse. The landlady enters the room, discovers the body and screams; at this instant a shrieking train whistle wipes out the scream and the film cuts directly to the train on which the lodger is fleeing. An identical device is used by Richard Brooks in the 1967 film, *In Cold Blood*. Having taken the two men we know to be murderers up to the house of their intended victims, Brooks fades out. The next scene is the following morning. Has the murder of the family taken place, or have the men turned back at the last moment, perhaps to return the next night? The house is perfectly peaceful, calm and secure on a small-town Sunday morning. We enter the house with a family of friends who have come to accompany the occupants to church; our tension mounts. The young girls run up the stairs as the camera tracks back with the father into the kitchen, tilting down as he off-handedly picks up the telephone. We still are in doubt. Then, in a sickening jolt, we see that the phone wire has been cut. We know. At this precise moment, a young girl screams upstairs, her voice is almost immediately wiped out by a police siren, and the picture cuts to the whirling tires of a police car, slamming us forward into the action of the film.

In each case the director has used sound imaginatively to aid an abrupt transition; the sound has helped the director to make a dramatic, almost flamboyant cut, perfectly appropriate to the momentary mood of the film he is creating, something a dissolve or fade would simply not do. Yet the sound has lent to this abrupt transition the same clarity and precision of purpose that the optical effect would have offered; the director has used a *sound optical* to "blend" the juxtaposed images just as the traditional optical visually blended the images.

The aiding of a film transition by the use of sound need not always be executed with such impact. John Schlesinger's *Darling* is a film which uses a wide variety of direct cut transitions, temporal leaps which are perfectly appropriate to this illusion-less story of a restless, disoriented girl. At times the sound optical uses the actual sound of one of the two juxtaposed scenes, overlapped into the second to blend the two just as the dissolve does. The sound of a running train backing a shot of the lovers kissing in one of the train's compartments is carried over a direct cut to a baggage cart in a station; the camera pulls back and pans left to reveal the lovers in a phone booth as the sound dies down into the natural sound of the station. (The lovers, on their way to a hotel room, are calling their respective wife and husband in order to excuse their not returning to their homes that night.)

The sound optical can also be effective without any overlapping, the sound creating a kind of cutting on idea, the cut answering the sound. In another scene from *Darling* the dry, cynical wit of the film is expressed perfectly in such a cut. The girl returns to their London apartment from an afternoon with her new lover; they have, in fact, planned a trip together to Paris. Questioned by the justifiably suspicious first lover, she explains that her car had been towed away, delaying her return. Obviously not believing her, he sarcastically hands her some money, "For the tow." "Where would I be without you," she replies charmingly, and the film answers by cutting to her driving happily through Paris with the new lover, a considerable temporal and spatial leap.

In another example of an overlapping cut on idea, a phone rings over a street scene and we cut directly to the phone in a room; the girl runs into the room to answer it, pulled into the scene just as we are. Later in the film a jet plane intrudes over the girl lying tearfully on a bed in her Italian palace, the film cutting to a notice in the hands of a British customs inspector in the London airport; the camera tilts up to the official's impassive face and then cuts to reveal the girl standing before him, (Fig. 7.14 A–D). The jet noise, swelling throughout, is now the actual background of the scene. Although no traditional optical device has been used to assure the spectator of the leap forward, the sound overlap and the imaginative cutting (the interposed shot of the customs official avoids a disturbing jump from the girl lying half-undressed and crying on her bed to the same person fully composed and clothed in the airport) make this direct cut transition work.

Darling offers a variety of other examples of sound opticals. The two lovers realize their afternoon together must end. The man announces he must leave "My wife." The girl replies, "My husband," and we cut on idea directly to the husband in their apartment, seeing him for the first time. Later, we see the girl being shown an apartment by the landlord who is describing its virtues to her. As his voice continues, the film cuts directly to the lover carrying his suitcase out of his own home—he has obviously left his wife—and the camera tilts down to the farewell note he has left; there is a cut directly to a jumbled pile of newly unpacked books and a tilt and pullback to reveal the man entering the new apartment with his suitcases, another temporal and geographical leap perfectly suited to our interest in the story, (Fig. 7.15 A–D).

There is a particularly effective transition later in the film using *commentative*, rather than *actual*, sound. The girl is standing at a telephone crying, "For God's sake, who is it?" She hangs up dispiritedly and her voice over (the film is narrated in the first person by the girl) tells us that she had "No one to turn to." The film cuts directly on idea to a shot of her walking in the rain beside a priest. The phrase "No one to turn to" is repeated and echoes in "No one to fall back on" as they continue to walk. They approach a church and the idea cut is directly to a crucifix, the camera tilting down to reveal her kneeling in prayer, (Fig. 7.16 A–E). The crucifix has clearly been interposed to avoid a jump from the girl entering the church to the same person kneeling in prayer at another time, in another place; yet, the cut from the room to the walk in the rain is perfectly acceptable and *does* jump. It works because there is a major change in locale and because we do not immediately recognize that a jump has occurred, since the girl's back is to us, but it works primarily because the continuing narration—a sound optical—has bridged the scenes intelligibly and inevitably. This inventive handling of the scene enables Schlesinger to deal with this parenthetical sequence in a very

Fig. 7–15a The sound optical; cutting on form, position, and idea (outgoing shot a few seconds from the end)

Fig. 7–15b Last frame of outgoing shot (camera has tilted down): leap in temporal and geographical continuity

Fig. 7–15c First frame of incoming shot

Fig. 7–15d A few seconds later in incoming shot (camera has trucked back and tilted up as man from outgoing shot has entered) *(Darling, distributed by Embassy Pictures)*

Fig. 7-16a The sound optical, cutting on idea; tonal cutting (mood between shot matches); the disguised jump cut (last frame of outgoing shot 1)

Fig. 7-16b First frame of incoming shot 2

Fig. 7-16c Last frame of outgoing shot 3

Fig. 7-16d First frame of incoming shot 4

Fig. 7-16e A few seconds later in incoming shot 4: camera has tilted down (*Darling*, distributed by Embassy Pictures)

short time. Its significance is that it represents a short-lived spiritual period which anticipates the girl's marriage to an Italian prince; it has been presented in perfect *filmic time*, gauged at precisely the right length for the importance it has to the film's story, rather than in anything like its *actual time*, which would have no relation to its importance to the film. Each one of these transitions has been made acceptable to the spectator—and perfectly intelligible—by imaginative cutting and a use of some sort of overlying sound optical. This is an excellent example of editing as practiced by the director and his representatives, the writer and the cameraman, for none of these precise and skillful transitions could have been made to work without careful planning.

An interesting comparable use of overlapping voice as a sound optical—in this case, the sync voices of the on-camera characters—is found in Welles' *Citizen Kane*. The sequence—a montage of successive breakfast table scenes between Kane and his wife, Emily—is beautifully analyzed in a frame-by-frame treatment in Karel Reisz' fine book, *The Technique of Film Editing*, to which the interested reader is referred. Welles uses the previously discussed *swish pan* (Reisz calls them "fast flick pans") to bridge temporal leaps. Overlapping the transition in three instances is the speech of Emily: (1) "Charles—" (swish pan) "—do you know how long you kept me waiting last night?" (2) "Sometimes, I think—" (swish pan) "—I'd prefer a rival of flesh and blood." (3) "Really, Charles—" (swish pan) "—people will think—" In the fourth transition, Kane is answered by Emily following the swish pan. In each instance, the characters are wearing different clothes *after* the pan than they were wearing *before*, indicating that time has passed, considerable time, during which their marriage has crumbled. The scene is another classic example of the perfect gauging of filmic time.

Tony Richardson's *The Loneliness of the Long Distance Runner* is a moving and effective story of a young boy committed to a Borstal reformatory. Knowing that his natural skill at cross country running— "If I could run as fast as you I'd be out of this place"—and servile cooperation with the staff offer him his only way of gaining a release (his situation is much like that of Pruitt in *From Here to Eternity*, for the school's head, like Pruitt's company commander, is obsessed with the need for a sports victory), he nevertheless chooses to become his own man. He wins the climactic race decisively but stands aside at the finish line to let his opponent pass him, facing down the furious headmaster and ignoring the pleading crowd as the events of his bitter past flashing before him cause him finally to answer his friend's question, "Whose side are you on?"

Of great importance to the story is the environment that has sent the boy to the reformatory, seen in a series of six flashbacks, the film beginning with the hero being driven in a van, shackled to several other boys, already on his way to the Borstal house. It is appropriate to the theme and setting of the film that the transitions in and out of these flashbacks are all accomplished by direct, momentarily disorienting cuts, invariably aided by the sound, both commentative and actual.

A piece of free jazz—the music is by John Addison—played on a soft clear trumpet reminiscent of Beiderbecke or Hackett, is used to back the hero's first unsupervised run through the nearby woods and fields. It is the only sunny day in the film, and the swinging, joyful music, the subjective moving shots of the sun through the trees, and a particularly stunning tracking shot of the hero windmilling along, all knees and elbows, his Buster Keaton face floating grimly and serenely along above his galloping body all combine to express the unquenchable spirit of the boy. This music becomes identified with the present tense running sequence and effectively signals the transitions between these scenes and the flashbacks. For example, as the hero stands in his darkened room, the jazz sneaks in behind this flashback scene, anticipating by a moment the direct cut to the present tense, the hero asleep in his barracks. As he begins his run past shining rain puddles on a frosty morning, the trumpet breaks into the full theme, then begins to slow and echo over a travelling shot of his reflection in water; the noise of a busy cafe in the next flashback intrudes into this scene a second or two before the picture cuts directly to the hero's friend, immediately panning left to reveal the hero and their two girls sitting at a table in the cafe. An actual jump cut has been avoided by interposing the friend between the two views of the hero, and the sound optical has made the transition seem precise and intended. Later, rock and roll music and the girls' laughter overlap a direct cut from their train compartment to the four now walking up the stairs of a week-end rooming house, the now asynchronous laughter and music dipping under the landlady's first words. The flashback ends on a shot of the wet sand of the beach, a woodwind variation of the jazz slows and then picks up with the trumpet, up tempo over a travelling shot of the rain puddles; the film cuts to him running past the puddles and we are back in the present.°

Long acceptable as a means for effecting geographical leaps, the direct cut—often, as indicated above, aided by the inventive use of a sound optical—is today used for temporal transitions as well. Having learned his lesson from the iconoclastic efforts of Resnais, Richardson, Godard, and Fellini, the contemporary film-maker is eager to dispense with the laborious convention of the dissolve as a transitional device. It is particularly important that the incoming image carry us forward with instant intelligibility, that the cut be accomplished with flair and precision, and that the film deal with a subject and a time—inevitably contemporary°°— for which this style is appropriate. The audience is quite willing to expend the additional effort that is required to keep up with these leaps in the continuity, and the effort itself is used to involve the spectator more deeply and more meaningfully in the film experience. It is a technique that the late André Bazin, editor of *Cahiers du Cinéma* and mentor of the *nouvelle vague* of French film-makers, would undoubtedly have approved, for it is very much in tune with his expressed desire to see the spectator render his own interpretation of the film's implications.

The direct cut used for temporal transitions is often called an *impact cut,* indicative of its technique. An interesting example, (Fig. 7.17 A&B) occurs in *Darling,* aided by a sound optical. The sound of a child's voice

Fig. 7–17a Impact cut; cutting on position; cutting on form (last frame of outgoing shot)

Fig. 7–17b First frame of incoming shot (*Darling,* distributed by Embassy Pictures)

THE DIRECT CUT

°While we have dealt with the contemporary use of the sound optical, the technique is not new, occuring, long before its use in the famous breakfast table scene of *Citizen Kane,* in the early sound films of Fritz Lang. Interestingly, Lang used the sound optical in precisely the ways we have seen Richardson and Schlesinger use it. In *M* (1931), Lang uses the basic technique of blending together direct-cut adjacent images by overlapping their sound. In the same film he introduces illustrative visual images to back up continuing descriptive dialogue, comparable to Schlesinger's technique in the scene from *Darling* in which the lover's departure from his home and arrival at the new apartment is shown while the voice of the landlord showing the apartment to his prospective tenant continues throughout. (In *M,* when Inspector Lohmann makes his report, Lang cuts to the broken-open door and unopened safes Lohmann is describing; when the police superintendant reports by telephone to the minister, we are shown the teams of detectives carrying out these described investigations.) In *The Testament of Dr. Mabuse* (1931), Lang follows the statement "I'd like to get my hands on the man responsible for this fellow's madness" with a shot of Dr. Mabuse, who is indeed the man responsible; the remark "Woe betide anybody who tries to rat on him" is immediately followed by a shot of Kent, who attempts to do precisely that. Both examples anticipate Schlesinger's "My husband" and "Where would I be without you" cuts in *Darling* (and Truffaut's "May my mother drop dead" cut from *Shoot the Piano Player* and Lester's "I swear on my mother's life" cut in *The Knack,* each to varying shots of dead mothers). It was Lang, along with Josef von Sternberg, René Clair, and Alfred Hitchcock, who first understood the creative potential of film sound, using it contrapuntally and asynchronously at a time when most film-makers were still floundering in the swamp of the "100% talkie."

°°The recent (1970) *Battle of Britain,* an historical film (1940), used direct cut transitions effectively. One example, a classic sound optical: "See you in Berlin," followed instantly by a shot of a Nazi eagle on a building in—Berlin.

Fig. 7–18a Impact cut; cutting on form; cutting on idea (last frame of outgoing shot)

Fig. 7–18b First frame of incoming shot (*Breathless*)

THE DISORIENTATION CUT

saying, "Bang, Bang!" intrudes over the girl writhing in self-pity in her hospital bed following an abortion, and the film cuts directly to a rubber monster mask worn by the child. The scene then reveals the girl playing with her nephew as she convalesces at her sister's home. Once again we note that the jump in continuity of image has been avoided—this time by interposing the child between views of the girl, but here the image has been deliberately chosen for its impact. Like the sudden emphatic note of Hayden's *Surprise Symphony*, the impact image seems to have been inserted here deliberately as a means of shocking the possibly dozing spectator into increased attention to the business at hand. That he must expend some thought to figure out just where he has suddenly been transported is all to the good.

Jean-Luc Godard's *Breathless (A Bout de Souffle)* uses a direct cut from a shot of a newspaper story of a policeman's murder to a shot of his murderer, an excellent example also of *cutting on idea,* and *cutting on form* and *position.* (Note the similarity of body size and position), (Fig. 7.18).

The impact cut is also used with great effectiveness in contemporary subject films, as these examples from Richard Matt's *Instant Holland* show. The direct cuts to the close-up of the puppet and the about-to-be-kicked soccer ball each immediately transports us into the action, excitingly and intelligibly, (Fig. 7.19 A&B). To introduce a scene at an antique shop, Matt chose to cut to the intriguing, momentarily disconcerting close-up of the vase, *then* to offer us the traditionally first-used "establishing shot," hooking our attention with the intriguing detail, then offering us a fuller explanation of its meaning, (Fig. 7.19 C&D). In the same film, a ground-level shot of what seemed to be a modern jet landing at the Amsterdam airport suddenly was revealed to be that of a toy airplane, as a toddler trotted toweringly into view above the plane, and a similar shot of a speeding train revealed grinning children peering through the windows of what was actually a toy train.° The impact cut might well be called a *flair cut,* since an important attribute of such a cut is its execution with a sense of style, with "flair."

It is obvious from our discussion that the direct cut transition often causes a momentary shock and confusion in the spectator. Even though

Fig. 7–19a Impact cut (First frame of incoming shot)

Fig. 7–19b Impact cut (first frame of incoming shot)

we stress the importance of intelligibility of the image, there is still an inevitable split second of disorientation before the spectator adjusts to the sudden leap forward. Many times the director makes deliberate use of this and executes a *disorientation cut;* the monster mask cut in *Darling* (Fig. 7.17).—and the direct cut to the monster movie in Kubrick's *Lolita*—are used in this way. Both Richardson (*Long Distance Runner*) and Resnais (*Last Year at Marienbad* and *Hiroshima Mon Amour*) do this deliberately and repeatedly, in a kind of calculated risk designed to pay rich dividends, provided the spectator is willing to expend the required effort to follow the film. This technique is especially appropriate in films like *Darling, Runner,* and *Marienbad,* for they all deal with disoriented people; the technique thus draws the spectator subjectively into the world of the film.

There is a particularly interesting use of this technique in *The Angry Silence,* (Fig. 7.20 A–E). A young boy, son of a factory worker who is being ostracized and harassed by his fellow workers for opposing their strike, has been humiliated by a group of children. His father enters the bedroom to talk to the boy. A two-shot of the father leaning over his son is followed by an individual close-up of the father, who asks the boy what is wrong. We cut to the boy, who reveals that he has been told his father is "a scab." The instant direct cut to the father catches his hurt recoil from the word, but startlingly, when the camera pans and pulls back with the turn of his head, it reveals him to be in an entirely different setting—the factory cafeteria. The effect is quite disconcerting. It has been achieved by cutting the shot of the father in the new setting directly to the shot of the boy in the bedroom—at exactly the point where we *expect* another shot in continuity in this bedroom setting. The spectator automatically supplies the expected background to this shot—even though, upon careful examination, we can see that the background has, in fact, changed (see Fig. 7.20B and 7.20D). This is a classic disorientation cut. The spectator is caused a momentary shock and perhaps experiences a sudden flash of awareness of the filmic trick played upon him —a reminder that he is watching a film, contrived and controlled by someone. However, the moment that the spectator exerts himself, the transition becomes clear and he moves ahead with the film, subliminally

Fig. 7–20a The disorientation cut (two-shot of father and boy, establishing the geography of the scene)

Fig. 7–20b Following close-up of father (note wallpaper)

Fig. 7–20c Following close-up of boy; last frame of outgoing shot

Fig. 7–20d Following close-up of father; first frame of incoming shot (note wallpaper)

Fig. 7–19c Impact cut (first frame of incoming shot)

Fig. 7–19d Establishing shot (first frame of incoming shot, second shot in sequence) (*Instant Holland,* distributed by Paramount Pictures)

Fig. 7–20e Later in the incoming shot; camera pulls back and pans to reveal new locale (*The Angry Silence*)

aware that the director has counted upon the spectator's quick perception to enable the film to skip forward to the essential. The device is particularly appropriate at this point in *The Angry Silence*, since the protagonist is being driven to a breaking point, to a "disorientation" of his own.

The authors employed a disorientation cut in a subject film, following a series of close-ups of two girls applying make-up in their dressing room with a close-up of one of the girls which pulled back to reveal that they were at dinner later that evening. Our sound change, which normally would have occurred at the change of locale, was also deliberately held until the new scene was established. This device enabled us to move forward with flair from the dressing room to the actual results of the girls' Herculean efforts at the make-up table, exemplified in their appearance at dinner. It also enabled us to skip their departure from their rooms, their travel and arrival at the restaurant—scenes which we did not happen to have shot.°

The Evolution of Temporal Continuity in Films

It is interesting to trace the evolution of film convention regarding temporal continuity. Since the time of Edwin S. Porter and D. W. Griffith, the film has had the right to make *geographical* transitions by the use of the direct cut, but traditionally has used some form of optical effect whenever a *temporal* transition occurred. This would imply that a strict temporal continuity was maintained, with the elapsed time of the film between such optical transitions exactly paralleling the amount of time such action would actually take.

ILLUSIONS OF ACTUAL TIME AND GEOGRAPHY

Such rigid adherence to actual time would negate one of the film-maker's most effective devices, the compression and expansion of time, and, in fact, from the very first the film merely maintained the *illusion* of actual time.

Utilizing the spectator's willing suspension of disbelief, the film-maker often skipped forward a few imperceptible seconds to give a flow and furtherance to the action. Note in even the traditional "realistic" film how often an actor is seen entering a door and then, following a cut, emerging from the door a bit farther on than he would actually have been in the time elapsed. Such skips of time always occur around mundane activities, such as the emerging from and entering of automobiles and houses. Typically, the actor is shown taking the first step or two at the bottom of a flight of stairs, the film then cutting to a shot from the top of the stairs as he finishes the last few steps. If we stop to think—which is precisely what we do *not* do when we watch a film—we would realize that we have not seen the actor climb the middle portion of the stairs; and after all, why should we! (There are uncountable examples of this specific technique; one that comes to mind immediately occurs in Antonioni's *Blow-Up*, when the photographer climbs the stairway in the park).

°Probably the finest and funniest disorientation cut in the history of cinema occurs in Russ Mayer's *Cherry, Harry and Raquel* in the cut from the gynecologist's poised finger to the open end of an automobile jack just as a rod is slammed into it.

Another effective use is made of this technique by cutting from an actor exiting a car—or mounting the front step of an apartment—to someone waiting within the apartment. When the knock on the door occurs in a far shorter time than would have actually been required for the person to traverse the distance we accept it willingly. The mounting of the stairs or the ride in an elevator is simply not important to us—the story is, and so we are quite willing to get on with it. One reason why this sequence works is that the cut has been made on the *spectator's expectation*. The exit from the car naturally makes us look ahead—the cut to the apartment answers this expectation. Now we anticipate the arrival of the visitor—the coming together of the two elements—and the visitor's entrance supplies the answer to our wish once again. This sort of sequential cutting also allows the editor to control exactly the timing of the actor's entrance.

There is an excellent example of this sort of within-scene temporal compression—also utilizing a cut on the spectator's expectation in *Darling*, (Fig. 7.21 A–C). The girl hears the noise of a party from the apartment upstairs and looks toward the ceiling. There is a direct cut to the hall outside the apartment, a high-angle shot looking down, thus placing the spectator above the girl, in the direction she had been looking, an example of *cutting on anticipation*, the upward look "causing" the next shot. Two men from the upstairs party are just entering the scene; the girl emerges from the apartment immediately with a trash barrel and begins a conversation with them, wrangling an invitation to their party. The scene has progressed quite nicely, and seemingly realistically; yet, if we note carefully the first frame of the incoming shot, we can see that the girl is already opening the door—her shadow is visible through the glass—and has already picked up the barrel, clearly a temporal compression, acceptable at this moment as *filmic time*.

There is another interesting cut in continuity in *Darling* illustrating the normally undetectible geographical and temporal compression that can occur within the realistically treated scene. We observe what appears to be a perfectly normal progression of a couple walking along a line of cars in a parking lot, cutting directly from a shot behind the couple to a reverse shot from in front of them while they continue walking; naturally, the noticeable elements in common to the two shots are perfectly matched, the girl carrying a purse in her right hand, the man a coat in his left, and there (Fig. 7.22 A&B) is an exact matching of their steps, which continue unaltered over the cut. Such a cut must occur dozens of times in almost any film. What we do *not* notice however, and what is blatantly apparent when we examine the individual frames, is that the couple has advanced from a position next to the first car in the line to a position considerably farther along, what appears to be some fifteen cars down the line. This is a classic use of the *shot-reverse shot cut to compress action*.

Schlesinger has done this to move them at exactly the time he wants to their waiting car. By letting either of the shots run longer—the outgoing

Fig. 7–21a Temporal compression within the scene; cutting on spectator's expectation; cutting on anticipation (last frame of outgoing shot)

Fig. 7–21b First frame of incoming shot (note shadow of girl through glass to left of door)

Fig. 7–21c Incoming shot a few frames later (*Darling*, distributed by Embassy Pictures)

Fig. 7-22a Temporal and geographical compression using the shot-reverse shot (last frame of outgoing shot)

Fig. 7-22b First frame of incoming shot (note matching elements of continuity but changed spatial position of people) (*Darling*, distributed by Embassy Pictures)

Fig. 7-23a Geographical compression (last frame of outgoing shot)

Fig. 7-23b First frame of incoming shot (*Shoot the Piano Player*, Janus Films)

shot up to the cut, the incoming shot after the cut—he elongates the action; by cutting either shot shorter, he compresses it further. If the scene had been filmed as one continuous shot, either a pan or a tracking shot or even one overall long shot, there would have been no way Schlesinger could have shown us the action in anything other than the time it actually took—unless, of course he used a *cut-away*, moving them forward while they were off-screen. (For example, he could have removed a five-second portion of the shot and substituted a one-second cut-away to any adjacent scene not visible in either shot, the net gain being four seconds, assuming that we would not notice how far they had moved during our absence.) The shot-reverse shot method avoids the interruption by the cut-away of the spatial flow of the action.

Let us assume that Schlesinger wishes the couple to reach their car in ten seconds of screen time. He has a shot of them walking past the first car on the line, continuing on to the car in, say, thirty seconds. He has the reverse shot of the identical action taking the same amount of time. To achieve the desired ten-second length he will combine lengths of the two shots totalling ten seconds. He might, for example, first choose a point six seconds away from the arrival at the car in the second shot, match it to a point four seconds into the first shot and, presto, a ten second walk! Simple, if the shots match and if they have been planned to offer a major contrast in angle and to present differing views of the background, quietly disorienting the spectator enough to prevent his noticing the conjuring trick the director is practicing on him. This is exactly what Schlesinger has done with the shot-reverse shot technique, an example of pre-planned editing practiced by the director and cameraman.

As an interesting comparison, a cut from one static shot to another in *Shoot The Piano Player*, shows an instantaneous geographical compression, (Fig. 7.23 A&B). The simultaneously present elements—the man's photo and the hero's head—match perfectly between shots, but their relationship to each other has changed radically at the cut, the hero having moved ten feet closer to the picture. Each shot is set up the way it should be; the composition of the close shot with the hero in a close relationship with the photo would not have been as right compositionally for the long shot. By taking advantage of the spectator's inability to compare the juxtaposed images and detect the mismatch, Truffaut has rendered the proper set-up for each shot.

Similarly, realistic films have invariably presented an illusion of actual geography, constructing their own filmic locale from the bits and pieces of actuality, as discussed under Montage Sequences, pages 204–05. This represents an adherence to the appearance of reality, but a reality selected and compressed for artistic purposes. An actor might be shown moving through a city via a succession of widely separated locales, but through the use of clever camerawork and editing, each setting seemed in close juxtaposition with the next.

However, the film-maker, while quite willing to practice temporal and spatial compression and selectivity, expended a good deal of time and energy in the traditional realistic film in disguising this process and preserving an illusion of actuality. Change of camera angle, disguising of the background, cutting on action, and cut-aways, were all various devices used to disguise the bête noire of the editor: the *jump cut.*

A jump cut, aptly named, is one in which an element of the scene appears to jump, that is, to mismatch between shots. A cut from a man with his hands in his pockets to one in which he has his arms folded, a cut from an auto passing a forest to the same car in a desert, a cut from a man wearing a hat and smoking a cigarette to the same man without hat and cigarette—all are examples of the dreaded jump cut. For years editors behaved as though they, or at least, their audience, would vanish in a giant puff of smoke if such a cut appeared in their films. The implication was that the jump cut revealed the mechanism of film-making as much as would the visible shadow of a microphone boom or the back of a painted set. Such precautions were well-founded, *if* it were true that the appearance of such jumps would affect the enjoyment of the film experience. Frequently the editor's choice of a shot was based not on aesthetic criteria, but on whether or not it would cut without a jump. The adherence to these conventions has meant that the Hollywood film gave up a good deal of its potential for creative improvisation in order to insure a smooth continuity. Griffith's films, which contain brilliant innovative editing, are full of the most atrocious jump cuts and glaring technical imperfections for the simple reason that he didn't care about such things. He may very well have been right.

THE JUMP CUT

A few years ago, it became noticeable that certain directors had begun to push forward the bounds of these temporal conventions, still maintaining an illusion of continuity, but depending upon the interest of the scene to enable them to make greater and greater temporal compressions without the use of optical transitions. In a sense, they were demanding more from their audiences, and the spectator's acceptance was instantaneous.

In Carol Reed's *The Running Man* (1963) there is a sequence entirely acceptable within the film's realistic framework, yet proving upon examination to be an example of startling compression. The protagonist takes off in a glider which he is about to deliberately crash; he will then disappear, feigning death, in an attempt to collect upon a life insurance policy. The sequence, for which we have been entirely unprepared by the realistic style up to that point, is presented with absolute clarity and precision, its filmic time beautifully gauged. Taking a total of 112 seconds, the sequence covers a period of time in actuality of at least one hour! More important, this is accomplished without the use of a single optical transition, and, for that matter, without any jump cutting. All temporal compressions are accomplished during *cut-aways*—shots of a subsidiary action which allow the off-screen action to be leapt forward— to the rescue activity at the beach near which the glider has crashed.

TEMPORAL COMPRESSION IN THE CINEMATIC CINEMA

The sequence is as follows:

			Seconds
	1)	Glider takes off, dropping wheels	:10
	2)	*Cut-away:* The pilot's wife watching from runway	:02⅔
	3)	Glider continues take off	:06½
	4)	*Cut-away:* The pilot's wife watching from runway	:03
	5)	Glider over beach, quite high	:08
Continuity	6)	Closer shot, the pilot beginning to strip off his clothes	:07
	7)	Glider approaches and passes camera	:04⅓
	8)	Glider hits water	:17
	9)	*Cut-away:* Kids running on beach	:03½
	10)	Pilot swimming underwater in SCUBA outfit	:03
Continuity	11)	*Cut-away:* Uniformed official points telescope	:02⅔
	12)	*Cut-away:* P.O.V. telescope, glider in water	:02⅔
Continuity	13)	Pilot running along a deserted beach	:07
	14)	Pilot rounds a rock on beach and begins to undress	:07
	15)	*Cut-away:* Launching a lifeboat	:04⅓
Continuity	16)	Pilot walking along street, people running past him	:15
	17)	Pilot climbing stairs to boarding house, where he gives a false name to the landlady	:08⅔

The scene takes fifty-eight and a half seconds for the glider to take off and crash; fifty-three and two-thirds seconds are required for the pilot to escape the glider, swim to shore underwater without being detected, change into ordinary clothes, walk from the deserted beach to the populated beach, walk down a street and enter a rooming house! Of this fifty-three and two-thirds seconds, forty and two-thirds seconds are devoted to the main action; thirteen seconds are devoted to the cut-aways, during which the temporal compression takes place. As noted, four sub-groupings of shots are presented in physical continuity; every other cut involves a cut-away.

We have said that sequences of temporal compression have been common to the most realistic traditional films, often utilizing the device of the cut-away. What is unique here—and representative of an important advance in film technique—is the fact that there is no attempt whatsoever to keep the filmic time at all close to the actual time; the filmic time is directly related to the audience's desire, taking precisely the amount of time that it should in relation to the story. The spectator knows perfectly well that what he is missing is the mundane and inessential and so accepts the compression.

There were four courses open to Reed: (1) He might have made his cut-aways to the rescue activity (not of major importance to the story) longer and therefore approximate more closely the length of time that is supposedly elapsing off-camera; (2) he might have expanded in time and used a variety of camera angles to enliven the character's on-camera activities (again of minor interest); (3) he might have dissolved between each shot instead of direct cutting, which would have been tedious and lacking in the driving impact of the direct cut; and (4) he could do exactly what he quite successfully did. In a sense this sequence is a comparatively slow-cut montage, eliminating the inessential and presenting an effective general impression.

There is a similar example of temporal compression in Hitchcock's *The Birds*. The round-trip crossing of the bay in a small outboard motor boat on the girl's first visit to the hero's house takes only a fraction of the time it would have actually taken, fifty-five seconds to cross over a mile of water. Yet the illusion of temporal continuity is preserved and the obvious jump cut avoided by Hitchcock's clever use of a variety of camera angles which keeps us from exactly comparing the backgrounds against which the boat is traveling in each shot. He is helped of course by the fact that the boat is rather distant from the shore background, making our comparison more difficult. It is quite apparent, if we watch closely, that the boat covers the distance in filmic, not actual, time. It is intriguing to wonder how many members of the audience are aware of this when seeing the film for the first time. Even those who are aware surely accept this temporal compression as a means of getting on with the business at hand.

TRANSITION IN THE CINEMATIC CINEMA

Today there are countless examples of films which make temporal leaps with direct cuts: *Marienbad, 8½, Bullitt, Dr. Strangelove, Tom Jones, Shoot the Piano Player, Darling, Breathless, Contempt, Petulia, The Long Distance Runner, Blow-Up, A Hard Day's Night, The Graduate, Belle de Jour,* the entire Monkees' television series, and a surprising number of short subjects, sponsored films, and all types of subject films. Today's audience accepts this willingly.

You will note from our discussion of *Darling* and *Long Distance Runner* that the jump cut is still cleverly avoided for the most part. If at all possible, the time leap over a direct cut is made between scenes in which the same characters are not involved. If this is impossible, the director will attempt to avoid having the same character on camera at the last moment of the outgoing shot and the first moment of the incoming shot. For example, a director might wish to cut directly from a scene in which two men are talking in a room to one in which they are riding together in a car. He has several options open to him. If he has his camera on Man 1 before the cut, he will probably choose to cut directly to Man 2 in the car, revealing Man 1 in a pull-back or at the next cut. (This, of course, would be a form of disorientation cut.) He might also choose to cut to the wheel of the car or to a subjective shot from the driver's point of view, either of which would avoid the noticeable jump cut. If it is absolutely unavoidable that he must end and

Fig. 7–24a   The disguised jump cut (last frame of outgoing shot)

Fig. 7–24b   First frame of incoming shot (*Darling,* distributed by Embassy Pictures)

Fig. 7–25a   The disguised jump cut (last frame of outgoing shot)

Fig. 7–25b   First frame of incoming shot (*Darling,* distributed by Embassy Pictures)

THE UNDISGUISED JUMP CUT

begin the two shots on either side of such a time-compressing direct cut on the same person, he will choose his camera angles carefully, making certain that the two shots are dramatically dissimilar, making it difficult for the spectator to make a comparison between the two, thus carrying him forward with the flair of the incoming shot and his interest in the story. Examples of this sort of cutting to avoid the distracting jump cut were given earlier in the discussion of the sound optical and the impact cut. The Italian palace—London airport transition in *Darling* avoided cutting directly to the girl in the incoming shot, she being the one simultaneously present element in both shots, and interposed the customs official between the two views of the girl, (Fig. 7.14). Similarly, the same film's "moving in" transition interposed the view of the farewell letter and the unpacked books between the two views of the man, (Fig. 7.15), and the hospital bed—sister's home transition interposed the monster mask between the views of the girl, (Fig. 7.17). In all three instances we discovered the simultaneously present element to have actually been in the shot that was cut to, though it was not revealed until the camera moved.

The religious sequence from *Darling,* (Fig. 7.16), offers another means of avoiding the noticeable jump cut; in the cut from the girl standing by her phone to the same girl walking with the priest the simultaneously present element *is* actually visible in both shots—and from the *start* of the incoming shot. However, the fact that her back is turned at the moment of cutting, together with the previously discussed contribution of the sound optical, prevent the jump from distracting.

Darling offers a huge range of these imaginative avoidances of the distracting jump; three others are worth citing at this time. Two cuts are made from almost identically framed close-ups of the man and the girl to shots in which the same person is present. In a cut from the man riding in a train to a shot of him walking in a park the *major change of scale and angle* in the camera's relationship to the subject makes the cut work, (Fig. 7.24 A&B). In a cut from the girl to a long shot of a docked motor cruiser, we are initially unaware that the girl is actually on the boat; in fact we accept the shot as her P.O.V. until the next cut, in continuity, reveals her presence. Again a major change of scale and angle has avoided the obvious jump, (Fig. 7.25 A&B). The third example uses the interposed object, cutting from the couple in bed to a close-up of a typewriter, tilting up to reveal the same couple present, (Fig. 7.26 A–C). Since the man's hands are visible both in the bed scene and on the typewriter, this is technically a jump cut, but it works perfectly. This cut is particularly interesting in that it establishes from the start the importance of the typewriter to the scene. It is in the girl's reaction to her lover denying her the attention she so desperately needs by working at his typewriter—"There's something about a typewriter," she says, grimly—that we first understand the destructive restlessness that destroys their relationship.

We shall end with illustrations from contemporary films which carry temporal film convention a good deal further. All involve a form of jump cut and all have a hint of iconoclastic nose-thumbing to them. The first example is Godard's landmark film *Breathless.*° A key moment occurs during a chase sequence (Fig. 7.27 A&B) in which two successive shots of a pursuing police motorcycle on the road behind the hero's fleeing car are shown. In the first shot, the motorcycle is seen as it is about to pass a truck on the road; in the second shot, following a direct cut, the truck has vanished—as nice an example of a jump cut as one could wish to see. Why has Godard done this when he could have easily inserted the conventional cut-away between these two shots? Why does his editing repeatedly shatter traditional conventions? Is he simply thumbing his nose at film convention, or are there not implications in this editing style which are entirely appropriate to this subject, today's society, and Godard's theme? Reisz and Millar make an excellent point:

Fig. 7–26a The disguised jump cut (last frame of outgoing shot)

Fig. 7–26b First frame of incoming shot

> *"Thus we get a slightly less connected account of the action, but we get all that is necessary and, we might say, only what is necessary. . . . Successive developments of the action are shown to us as they would strike us if we were spectators in real life. Nothing is prepared or led up to. No 'clues' are laid as to imminent action. . . . We are given no insight, we have no omniscience. We have to accept. . . . The logic of the author who used to share his knowledge with us is replaced, for better or worse, by the logic of the passer-by who knows as little about it as we do. In a way Godard is confessing that he knows as little about this man as we do. We must all observe his behavior in order to find out more. . . . All these things . . . are obstacles to conventional smoothness and logic. Yet they are perfectly efficient in the sense that they create an impression of confusion, flight, fear, restrained violence, imminent danger, etc., while staying within the bounds of possibility. . . . The editor is saying, in fact, 'the habitual idea of screen continuity is merely an illusion which is in any case subsidiary to the communication of the scene's meaning. I am going to take advantage of your admission that it is unreal by rejecting it and substituting this cruder but more direct description of the action.' "*[1]

Fig. 7–26c A few seconds into incoming shot: camera has tilted up (*Darling,* distributed by Embassy Pictures)

This style of iconoclastic editing is particularly appropriate to contemporary films dealing with the plight of modern man in an indifferent and unknowable universe.

Fig. 7–27a The undisguised jump cut: cut in continuity (last frame of outgoing shot)

Fig. 7–27b First frame of incoming shot (*Breathless*)

°The reader is referred to an excellent frame-by-frame analysis of this scene in *The Technique of Film Editing,* by Reisz and Millar.

Fig. 7-28a The undisguised jump cut: cut in continuity (last frame of outgoing shot)

Fig. 7-28b First frame of incoming shot (note mismatch in head position, hands, mirror, and background) (*Breathless*)

Fig. 7-29a The undisguised jump cut: transitional cut (last frame of outgoing shot)

Fig. 7-29b First frame of incoming shot (*Breathless*)

Breathless abounds in similar examples. There are repeated undisguised jump cuts during a sequence in which the hero and his girl are riding through Paris in an open convertible, (Fig. 7.28 A&B). Obviously Godard has cut together the essential moments from a succession of shots without bothering to disguise the mismatch, something he could easily have done by using a cut-away or by changing the camera's approach to the subject with each shot. But the business at hand is the girl's conversation, not the cut-away, something which can itself be intrusive; a change of camera position could not have been accomplished without certain complex technical procedures—and this might well have destroyed the casual, gratuitous quality of the scene which is so essential to the film. (Is it not in exactly such a mood that the heroine denounces the boy to the *flics* at the film's end?) Since we all know that the cut-away is a convention, and a phony one at that, why not dispense with what we know to be meaningless to the essence of the film and concentrate on what *is* important? Of course such a scene is enough to make the hair on the back of a traditional editor's neck stand on end, but Godard may very well have something here.

When Godard wishes to effect a transition from an interior scene to an exterior scene he simply cuts the two scenes directly together, (Fig. 7.29 A&B), ignoring the dissolve or even the sort of ingenious maneuvering through interposed objects or contrast of scale and angle that we have seen Schlesinger use. To remove his hero from a car he simply cuts directly to a shot of him walking away from the car, compressing the time at this point of mundane activity just as did his conventional predecessors but without the traditional disguising conventions, (Fig. 7.30 A&B). There is actually a contrast of image between the shots, but one senses that this is a gratuitous, unplanned result. Godard is clearly saying to us that it is a sham and a pretense to adhere to the usual conventions when we all know they are a trick. The very need to slavishly adhere to them exaggerates their importance. The film—its story, its people, the action and emotion and vitality on the screen—is what is really important.

When Godard must deal with a situation exactly like that considered earlier, the cutting on spectator expectation from a person in the street to another waiting in an apartment, we note a similar advance in technique. As the hero enters a doorway on the street, Godard cuts directly, not to the interior of the apartment with its waiting occupant but to the closed door of the apartment seen from the hallway; the door immediately opens, and the occupant appears, implying that the hero has moved all the way from the street door to the apartment door and had time to knock and await the door opening in the instant of the cut, (Fig. 7.31 A&B).

In *Darling*, Schlesinger shows a similar advance in the handling of a temporal compression by direct cutting from a couple some twenty yards away from the entrance to a building to a shot of them emerging through the door into the interior, an instant leap of twenty yards, (Fig. 7.32 A&B). Typically, the cut shows more contrivance and care than

Fig. 7-30a The undisguised jump cut: cut in continuity (last frame of outgoing shot)

Fig. 7-30b First frame of incoming shot (*Breathless*)

those of Godard—we are kept a sufficient distance from the couple to prevent a careful comparison of the images and to minimize our concentration on the moment—tricks Godard would disdain.

Candy offers an interesting variation of the jump cut. A sequence of Candy's progression through New York is shown against a discontinuous series of backgrounds, jump cut. No attempt is used to cut-away between these obvious changes of locale. Director Christian Marquand has implied that such conventions are meaningless in a film which is illusion anyway. The point of the scene is that Candy is travelling about, which can be conveyed quite effectively in this manner. Nothing else is needed. Somehow this simple act increases the moment's enjoyment as we sense in this editing a breezy freedom from convention which is at the heart of the film itself.

Fig. 7-31a Radical temporal compression; ignoring the traditional disguising conventions (32 frames from cut, outgoing shot)

In American International Pictures' *Three in the Attic,* two youngsters are shown gamboling on the lawn. Deliberate jump cuts are created within a single shot by removing portions of the shot without the use of any cut-away to disguise this. The result, which is rather effective, is to see the images leap forward into new positions, then flow softly for a moment (the scene is in slow motion) before leaping gently on, in a kind of dream ballet. The effect is filmic and entirely acceptable.

This discussion is not intended to show that the traditional conventions of temporal continuity no longer exist for the contemporary film. The majority of today's films—and, for that matter, the major portions of the films discussed—still adhere to these conventions. Indeed, there are subjects which demand the conventional treatment. But the fact that

Fig. 7-31b Seven frames in from cut, incoming shot (*Breathless*)

Fig. 7-32a Radical temporal compression: ignoring the traditional disguising conventions; the jump cut (last frame of outgoing shot)

Fig. 7-32b First frame of incoming shot (*Darling,* distributed by Embassy Pictures)

the contemporary film-maker can take advantage of these developments is important, for many times his subject and theme are far better rendered through the use of the techniques of Cinematic Cinema.

SHOOT THE PIANO PLAYER: THE JUMP CUT AND THE CUT-AWAY

There is a most interesting cut in *Shoot the Piano Player.* The young brother of Charlie Saroyan is seen walking along a city street with his friend, moving toward the camera. Suddenly pursuing crooks pull up to the curb in their car and the boys race off down the street. There is an almost undetectable jump cut, (Fig. 7.33 A&B), the instant before the boys run, yet the two shots are filmed from an apparently identical angle and there seems to be no aesthetic reason for two such separate shots to be used to cover this continuous action. Why, then, does the cut occur?

It would be a pretty fair guess that Truffaut wanted the scene in a single shot and was prevented from doing this by a technical error in filming. Perhaps such a shot was made but with too great a time lapse between the portion in which the boys are first seen leaving their school and the arrival of the car; perhaps the camera ran out of film, or the car arrived on the scene too late to be included in the same shot, so that a second shot had to be made. It is possible that two complete takes of the entire action were made, only to reveal in the cutting room that the beginning of one and the ending of the other did not suit the film's demands, requiring that the suitable portions of each be used. Because the two shots—or portions of the same shot—had been filmed from the same camera angle and distance, an unobtrusive cut was quite difficult to make, particularly since the subjects of the shot were in motion. Even if it had been possible to match the action exactly at a cutting point, a cut between two shots from identical angle and distance would violate a cardinal rule of cutting; there would be no aesthetic purpose for the cut to the virtually identical second shot, making the cut noticeable and disturbing to the audience.

Fig. 7-33A *The Jump Cut* disguised by cutting on action. Last frame of outgoing shot.

Had Truffaut chosen to make the second shot from a different angle—i.e., 90° to the side, or a reverse shot from behind the subject as did Schlesinger in *Darling,* Fig. 7.22,—the cut could have been made unobtrusively. Not only would the contrast between shots have made it impossible for the spectator to detect a mismatch of action, but the difference in the incoming image would have aesthetically justified its use. Even if the cut is made for a practical reason, the spectator's acceptance of the cut depends upon the new shot's serving an aesthetic purpose. It will appear to serve a purpose if it contrasts sufficiently with the adjoining shot and therefore adds something not present in the first shot.

Faced with the lack of contrast between shots, Truffaut could have easily disguised his cut with a cut-away, hiding the jump in action caused by the cut, the spectator assuming that the subject has moved during the cut-away. If a man is shown smoking a cigarette in one shot and this shot is cut directly to a shot in which the cigarette is resting in an ash-tray, a jump cut will occur. If a cut-away to another character is inserted between the shots, the audience will assume that the man has placed his cigarette in the ash-tray during the cut-away. However, the cut-away, like any shot, needs aesthetic justification. Not only must it add a new element, it must make sense within the context and not appear suddenly "from left field."° No matter for what arbitrarily practical purpose the editor has inserted the cut-away, his clever integration of the shot with the other material of the scene is what allows him to get away with its use.°° Simply cutting to a flight of birds because the character happens to be outdoors is not enough; the presence of the birds should be properly anticipated, and a reason for their appearance at that particular moment must be supplied. A sound of a bird call and an upward glance by the on-screen character would accomplish this nicely, for example.

In this particular scene from *Shoot the Piano Player*, proper aesthetic justification of a cut-away would have been difficult, but Truffaut most likely could have gotten away with a shot of someone looking down from a window or even a shot of passing traffic, since the spectator is already aware of its presence. The latter would not be a particularly contributive shot, and would in fact distance us from the action inappropriately, but it would make contextual sense, as, for example, a shot of a wandering Bedouin tribesman would not. That Truffaut did not choose to do this reveals either that no one during the filming thought of making any cut-aways—not inconceivable in view of M. Truffaut's lighthearted statement that "Anybody can be a director"—or that he did not wish, à la his mentor Bazin, to interrupt the flow and unity of the shot. Faced with this situation—the desire to render the complete action in a single shot and no single shot with which to do it—Truffaut handled his problem very nicely. He almost entirely disguises the resultant jump cut by cutting just before a sudden major action; by cutting at the precise instant that the boys break into a run, he distracts the spectator from the mismatch just as the conjurer distracts his audience from his sleight-of-hand.

At another point in *Shoot the Piano Player* Truffaut has cut together two takes of Charlie's wife moving across the room, (Fig. 7.35 A&B). There is a barely discernible jump—the images are almost perfectly matched positionally but the girl's expression changes between shots.

Fig. 7-34a The cutaway: not aesthetically integrated into the scene, used to disguise a jump cut (last frame of outgoing shot 1)

Fig. 7-34b First frame of incoming shot 2, the cutaway (identical with last frame of shot at the point outgoing)

Fig. 7-34c First frame on incoming shot 3 (*Shoot the Piano Player*, Janus Films)

Fig. 7-35a The jump cut disguised by positional matching (last frame of outgoing shot)

Fig. 7-35b First frame of incoming shot (note change of expression) (*Shoot the Piano Player*, Janus Films)

*The cut-away is referred to by some editors as a "sea-gull," a practice obviously stemming from the frequent use of shots of these conveniently occurring animals to cover jumps in any scene taking place near water.

**Interestingly, Truffaut uses a cut-away later in the film without really fully integrating it into the scene, cutting from an interior shot of the hero confronting a bartender to an exterior shot of a poster on the wall outside the bar, back to the interior where we see the two men already struggling. There is no question that the poster is actually on the wall—we have seen it before—but there is a very real question as to whether it is aesthetically appropriate at this moment, since a cut to it distances us from the action at precisely the moment we would wish to be closely involved in it. (Fig. 7.34 A-C).

Faced with the reality of needing the two separate shots to complete the scene, Truffaut is probably right to avoid the distancing cut-away; this is a moment of heightened emotion and the inevitable distancing and interruption of the spatial flow of the scene would be disastrous.

The lessons to be learned from this Truffaut parable are important. The value of the cut on a distracting action is demonstrated, as well as the importance of making usable cut-aways while filming. The need to carefully match action between two shots to be cut together is apparent; perhaps most important, is the need of film shots to be cut together from contrasting angles and/or distance in relation to the subject. Behind all of this is the important lesson that the film-maker must know his intentions for assembling his material when he ventures forth to film it.

Practical Reasons for Cutting

From this discussion we can see that a major practical reason for cutting is to remove a portion of a shot, either because the section is unsuitable, or to compress time. The beginning film-maker is probably unaware of the enormous proportion of cuts which are made for practical—not to say desperate—reasons, rather than aesthetic. This is expressed rather well in an amusing and enlightening remark made by Richard Lester, director of *Help!, A Hard Day's Night, How I Won the War, Petulia.* Lester is discussing his work on *A Funny Thing Happened on the Way to the Forum:*

> *That was the first time, I think, where critics started to attack what they called my style, my technique, which is something of which I'm totally unaware. What I was doing was trying to get out of trouble. One only uses a cut because the take doesn't work. Half of cutting rhythms are not done because of a feeling of your metabolism and of your way of looking at things. It's to try to get rid of your own bloody mistakes, of what's wrong, what's not working, where a line should have been cut beforehand.* [2]

We have said that the "realistic" film, with its supposed rigid adherence to strict temporal continuity between its optical transitions, had actually preserved only an illusion of continuity, skipping forward a few moments whenever possible during certain mundane but obligatory activities which the realistic film-maker had to include. We have seen how such temporal compression was accomplished in the cutting room by cutting between usable portions of a shot and between two different shots. Such cutting, as Lester's quote and our discussion of Truffaut's jump cut imply, is often a matter of after-the-fact decisions made in the cutting room, where the film's tempo is to be finally determined. Since the cameraman and director cannot anticipate all of these decisions, they must shoot in such a way that the editor is covered for all eventualities. The use of varying angles between shots to be cut together, a practice all too often avoided by the lazy cameraman who is loath to move his camera and lights between shots, not only offers the editor maximum freedom in determining his cutting points, but also presents the filmic material as it should be, in a series of varying images chosen for their appropriateness to their subjects. The supplying of cut-aways aesthetically appropriate to the scene will give the editor a further flexibility in handling the material.

Another useful practice would be the filming of shots involving the movement of subjects in such a way that the editor can cut any of these shots next to any other, creating his own filmic geography and tempo. This is a complex procedure and one which the cameraman learns through constant practice. One element involved is the use of *varying camera angles;*° another requires *choosing the setting* so that each shot can be easily matched to the setting of the adjacent shot. Another important element is the filming of such shots *beginning with the subject entering and ending with him leaving the frame,* rather than beginning and ending with him still visible.

For example, if the subject is filmed walking around a corner and out of sight in what we choose to be our outgoing shot, we can then cut directly to him walking toward us, well into the incoming shot, since the audience will assume that he has covered the necessary ground in the pause after he has gone around the corner. If the incoming shot has been made with the subject walking into the frame we could reverse the procedure, leaving the outgoing shot with the subject still a few steps away from the corner, picking up the incoming shot a second before he appears. If the shots are made so that we cannot see what is around the corner in each case, they can be cut together creating an *illusion of adjacency.* Should we wish to slow down the scene's tempo, we could cut the outgoing shot after the subject rounds the corner and cut to the incoming shot a second or two before the subject enters. As a further extension of time, a third shot could be inserted between these two, providing it had been shot following these same criteria.

There are countless examples of this technique to be observed in virtually any film; an outstanding contemporary film to study is Antonioni's *Blow-up.* One simple example from *Shoot the Piano Player* should suffice at this time, (Fig. 7.36 A&B). Note how the radical change in angle and scale between the two shots prevents comparison between the surroundings of the respective shots. The traditional film would be far more careful in such matching—obviously the pattern of the road and the other vehicles present betray the mismatch—but this jump cut works quite nicely within the naive and uncontrived atmosphere which Truffaut creates so well and which is indispensable to this film. This technique works extremely well throughout Hopper's *Easy Rider.*

We have said that the camera must constantly change its relationship to its subject, rendering the continuity of the film as a succession of varied shots. By functioning in this way, it fulfills its interpretive potential; the film "keeps the audience thinking and reacting continuously and never allows the presentation to become a passive record." [3] Editing is a process which lends form and unity to the film by joining together the separate shots which result from the camera's variety of approach to its subject. Essentially, editing is the art of knowing *when* to cut *what.*

Fig. 7–36a The jump cut disguised by radical change of angle and scale preventing a careful comparison of background between shots (last frame of outgoing shot)

Fig. 7–36b First frame of incoming shot (*Shoot the Piano Player,* Janus Films)

CUTTING WITHIN THE SCENE WITH A TEMPORAL CONTINUITY

*This was the practice followed by Hitchcock in the discussed scene from *The Birds.* Not only does the variation in angle allow the editor to match the varying shots of the principal in the scene, it prevents the spectator comparing the backgrounds of the newly adjacent shots. Thus a *filmic geography* is created from the bits and pieces of actual geography.

There are five aesthetic reasons for cutting within the scene to a new shot in continuity. They involve a basic decision that the running shot will no longer suffice; it is essential that the new image serve a purpose not served by the previous image. "To transfer attention, however smoothly, from one image to another, when the previous image would have answered equally well, can serve no useful purpose."[4] We cut to a new shot:

(A) to include an action not visible or capable of being included in the running shot;

(B) to render a closer look at an action or object not readily discernible in the running shot;

(C) to reveal an action, or object in a more meaningful interpretive light than that which the running shot supplied;

(D) to emphasize or underline an action, object or emotion;

(E) to draw back and reestablish the geography of the scene indiscernible in the running shot, especially when some new element is added to that geography.

Cutting is never done in an abstract situation. The editor must comprehend fully the film's purpose and theme; from this, and from a consideration of the material before him, comes his understanding of the purpose of the scene. Each choice of shot, *what* shot to use and *when* to present it, is then affected by the importance of the material to the scene's purpose.

To a great degree the choice of shots within a scene follows the *logic of the interested observer*, the varied aspects of the scene being presented in the order and at the time that the spectator himself would choose to observe them, *if* he were in control. But he is not in control; he has abdicated that right to the film-maker, who must perform these functions for him. To a considerable extent, that is precisely what the film-maker does. It was the great Russian director, V. I. Pudovkin, who most eloquently described how closely the selection of shots in the edited scene parallels the choices the observer would make if he were attending such a scene in actuality. This elementary point is forgotten by many editors, who cut quite arbitrarily, as if the mere volume and rapidity of their cuts and the imaginative extent of their presented views justified their editing. Seeing a great director like John Ford cut to the pounding hooves of a cavalry charge they interpret this as an example of the right to cut to *any*thing at *any* time, forgetting that when Ford cuts to the hooves it is because it is right at that moment, because they are a vital and fascinating essence of the charge. Of course Ford has chosen this image because it is exciting and filmic, but it is far from arbitrary. Underlying the imaginative flair of the choice of image is a certain sense of its inevitable rightness in the particular scene at that particular moment.

We have described earlier how the cut from the man about to enter a building to someone awaiting him in the apartment above is essentially right because it answers the *expectation of the spectator;* in Reisz' terms, it is a "logical cut." The imaginative answering of the spectator's *ex-*

pectation is at the root of great editing, just as it is the basis of great comedy. But *imaginative*, not the slavish following of the wish of the least caring and least creative member of the audience, and certainly not always answering the active or even conscious wish of the spectator. The editor's responsibility as an artist demands that he answer the spectator's expectation—an expectation, we might add, which he himself has often created and controlled—with something which is at once innovative, surprising, creative and yet, in a very real way, inevitable.

There are close parallels in actuality for most of the cuts in the film. Certainly we tend to concentrate, to "zero in," on that which interests us, to the exclusion of the insignificant periphery; thus we *cut to close up* psychologically in life at the moment that we do in the film.° We *pan* in actuality also, particularly in following a moving object—our eyes focus on the object and are pulled along by it, the background blurring—and also in shifting our concentration between two closely adjacent points of interest. However, unlike the film which pans over distant vistas, our eyes are more accurately described as *cutting* between two widely separate points of interest, blurring the inconsequential material lying between them. There is, however, one thing we cannot do in actuality which the film readily accomplishes: we cannot instantly physically transport ourselves from one location to another—we cannot *cut to the reverse shot.*

Let us say that we are driving along a crowded street when suddenly a truck before us begins to weave crazily from side to side. In the film, the editor would invariably cut from this point of view to the reverse shot, a close shot of the truck's cab. Is that not exactly what our mind would do in actuality, the picture of the driver flashing instantly before us: Is he drunk, has he had a heart attack, is he bent on our destruction? Therefore we can say that the editor is following the *psychological* cut, the cut in the mind's eye that the person would make in such a situation in actuality. It is this that the editor must keep in mind in choosing his cuts—and the director in planning his shots, for it is the director who dominantly edits the material by his initial choice of camera set-up. In Reisz' terms, the director becomes an "ubiquitous observer, giving the audience at each moment of the action the best possible viewpoint."[5]

THE UNOBTRUSIVE CUT

Within the scene in continuity an essential rightness of cut implies that the cut will be unobtrusive. "Making a smooth cut means joining two shots in such a way that the transition does not create a noticeable jerk and the spectator's illusion of seeing a continuous piece of action is not interrupted."[6] What makes the cut "right?"

We have already stated the two most important criteria for the cut: (1) that the new image serve a purpose not served by the previous image, presenting in some way, something new; and, (2) that it imaginatively answer the spectator's expectation. It follows logically then, that there must almost invariably be a significant contrast between the juxtaposed images when they are varying views of the same subject. As Reisz correctly points out, a cut to a slightly larger or smaller presentation of the

*As a practical matter, we also provide ourselves with opera glasses and binoculars to physically "zero in" on the intriguing subject, masking off the meaningless periphery in life as in the film.

on-screen image seldom is as meaningful—or as unobtrusive—as the cut to a major scalar change in image.[*]

If the editor cuts from a close shot of the subject sitting in a chair to a medium shot which includes both the subject and a nearby listener, he has followed the spectator's expectation of seeing more of what is happening; he has cut for an aesthetic purpose. A cut from a close shot of the subject sitting to a medium shot just as he rises, the incoming shot now able to present the action in its entirety—something the outgoing close shot could not have done—is also aesthetically valid. Significantly, both cuts are for the purpose of including an action not visible in the running shot. However, to cut from one medium shot of the subject sitting to another of the same angle and scale, merely because the incoming shot is being made by a camera in a position from which it can conveniently pan with the rising and moving subject is not aesthetically justified. The spectator cannot anticipate the practical reason which has dictated the cut—it is not any part of his concern —and so the cut is, at the moment, aesthetically without purpose, obtrusive and distracting. Having a logical, practical reason for making a cut does not necessarily mean that it will be aesthetically right, nor does this practical justification make the cut unobtrusive. If, however, this panning shot is begun from an entirely new angle of approach to the subject—or at least from a new scalar relationship—the resulting contrast of image will offer the needed aesthetic justification for the cut.[**]

Theoretically, such justification should stem from the new image offering a fresh interpretive view of the subject; in practice, the mere change itself is accepted by the spectator. So attuned is he to the fragmentation of scenes employed in most films that he readily accepts these successive varying views, seldom if ever consciously noting the particular interpretive significance of the shots, accepting without question their unconscious effect upon him. Having placed himself willingly in the director's hands, he accepts what the director chooses for him to see, so long as it *appears* to have some purpose.

We can say generally, then, that a significant change of image when one is cutting between varying views of the same subject will render the cut aesthetically valid, *especially* if the change is interpretively meaningful. Such change will also disguise any mismatching of the simultaneously present material in the shots, a condition which often results when the material is shot consecutively.

Let us proceed to consider the criteria which affect the unobtrusive rendering of the cut, drawing from the understanding we have gained from the earlier illustrations discussed in the chapter. First, we must consider the scene shot simultaneously by two or more cameras.

[*]It does not necessarily follow, however, that a major change of image is always correct, for a major change implies that something of major significance has happened. "Emphasizing a dramatically insignificant gesture" (Reisz) is equally inappropriate.

[**]An interesting example occurs in Orson Welles' *The Immortal Story*. Welles, a flamboyant master of the unusual and provocative camera placement, renders a succession of cuts to almost hypnotically interesting shots. Yet, they are invariably unobtrusive. In one scene, the old merchant's accountant accompanies a young sailor to the stairs (Welles never could resist shooting down stairways). We note a distracting cut between shots of almost no image contrast. The cut is logically explained—to an editor, not to the film's spectator—by the succeeding action: the sailor moves off down the stairs on a course which the previous camera position could not have covered.

THE SCENE SHOT SIMULTANEOUSLY BY TWO OR MORE CAMERAS

This is the simplest scene for the editor to cut in continuity, for he is assured that *the action covered in each shot will be identical and hence will match perfectly,* and that *all elements simultaneously present in both shots*—the details of the actors' appearance and of the background—

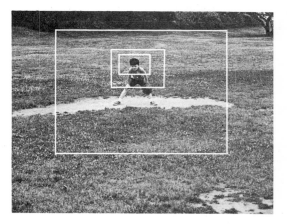

will be identical. In a Paramount short subject, *Miss Smile,* directed by Richard Matt, we had a scene showing the announcement of a beauty contest winner, covered by two cameras simultaneously, one in a high-angle long shot, the other a low-angle medium shot. At one point, wishing to cut to the closer shot as the newly-announced winner stepped forward, we simply located the identical point in each shot at which a still photographer's flash gun had gone off—naturally enough, at the announcement of the winner—cut the outgoing shot one frame before the flash and the incoming shot one frame after, and joined the two at this point. We thus eliminated the distracting flash and gained a perfect match between shots. If all scenes were filmed by cameras simultaneously, the editor's job would be considerably easier. In practice, however, filming is almost always done by one camera, consecutively. This is an entirely different kettle of fish, as we will soon see.

However, while we are considering the simultaneously filmed scene, let us examine the questions of scale and angle as affecting the cut. Since this sort of scene assures us of a perfect match in continuity we can study these criteria unaffected by other considerations. We shall study them separately, although obviously any shot juxtaposition involves questions of both scale and camera angle. Our consideration, in as nearly abstract a situation as we can create, is when to use a shot of a particular scale and at what point within a continuous action it will be effective to cut. In this first hypothetical situation, our only consideration is *scalar.* We shall therefore assume an action photographed simultaneously and from an identical angle, by three separate cameras in long, medium and close shot.

CUTTING WITH A SMOOTH CONTINUITY

SCALAR CONSIDERATIONS   The value of this consideration will be in introducing the editor to an approach to the scene, searching for criteria on which he will base his editing decisions. Naturally, in a real film, it is the editor's understanding of the scene's purpose in relationship to the film's purpose which dominates all such decisions. Yet, even within this abstract scene, we can consider the spectator's expectation as affecting the moment at which a new relationship of the spectator to the material is to be introduced: a cutting point. Only then will the cut be right, and only then will it be unobtrusive.

Since all three cameras are shooting from the same angle we cannot cut between shots of the same scale—close shot to close shot—as of course we could normally with a proper contrast of angle. Our possible cuts, therefore, are: long shot to medium shot, long shot to close shot, medium shot to long shot, medium shot to close shot, close shot to long shot and close shot to medium shot.

Our action consists of a segment from a baseball game, (Fig. 7.37 A–D). A third baseman is seen crouching expectantly, awaiting the ball. As it is hit toward him, he shifts his weight forward just as it bounds into sight, appearing from behind and to the left of the camera, grabbing it as it reaches him. He then looks past the camera to first base, ignoring a runner who appears from his left and rounds the base behind him, finally throwing across the diamond to first base.

Fig. 7-37 A–D

(1) LONG SHOT TO MEDIUM SHOT   If we choose to begin this scene with a long shot, a logical point at which to cut to a medium shot would be at the moment the ball is hit, just before the player moves forward to field it. Such a cut would satisfy the spectator's wish—strongest at that moment—to be involved more closely in the exciting action he anticipates; moving to the closer shot would increase the tension and excitement of the scene. Cutting in the pause before the start of this new segment of action punctuates the scene logically during the pause between its separate sections and portrays the new action in one continuous spatial flow, uninterrupted by a cut. This cut, serving both to *render a closer look at the action* and *to reveal the action in a more meaningful light,* would be unobtrusive and effective, (Fig. 7.37B).

(2) LONG SHOT TO CLOSE SHOT   Such a dramatic scalar leap would probably be used only for strong dramatic effect. If, for example, we wished to show that a shoelace is ominously untied or to emphasize a facial expression, such a cut would be effective. An example of a cut *rendering a closer look at an object* and *emphasizing or underlining an object,* it would probably occur during the pause before the outlined action began, (Fig. 7.37A).

(3) MEDIUM SHOT TO LONG SHOT   This cut goes against the invariable wish of the spectator to draw closer and to involve himself more deeply in the action. Thus it can only be used when its additionally revealed material contributes something of importance to the scene. If such a shot suddenly revealed the base runner bearing down on the fielder, it would be quite effective and would be accepted by the spectator. This is an example of a cut *to include an action not previously visible* and *to reestablish the geography of the scene.* If the latter were its sole purpose, we would never make such a cut once the action had started, for we would tend to dissipate the energy and tension of the scene by drawing back from the action objectively, television baseball coverage to the contrary, (Fig. 7.37C).

(4) MEDIUM SHOT TO CLOSE SHOT   Having begun the scene in long shot and moved to the medium shot at the beginning of the fielding play, a further move in to a close shot would be appropriate to build anticipation of something dramatic about to happen—perhaps just before the fielder is about to bobble the ball. We would lose some clarity by moving in this close, since the spectator would see only a selected portion of the action. Thus such a cut would probably not be made if the play progressed normally; it is justified only for the dramatic urgency of the moment. It is an example of a cut *rendering a closer look* and *rendering an action in a more meaningful light* as well as for the *emphasizing and underlining of an action.* A cut on action—to the fielder's hand as he plucks the ball from his glove and loses his grip on it—might be quite effective, (Fig. 7.37D).

(5) CLOSE SHOT TO LONG SHOT   Again, such a shot violates our rule of driving in closer to the subject to increase interest and excitement and to satisfy the desire of the spectator. It is the least likely cut for us to make

in this situation. However, it is interesting to consider the effect of cutting from the previously discussed close shot of the ball slipping from the fielder's hand to a long shot of the entire infield, base runners racing frantically toward the plate, the catcher shouting for the ball, the other fielders frozen in horror. Such a cut is an example of the *including of previously invisible action,* the *rendering an action in a more meaningful light,* and the *reestablishing the geography of the scene,* (Fig. 7.37C).

(6) CLOSE SHOT TO MEDIUM SHOT   Although the move to the more distant, objective shot might dissipate the scene's energy to some degree, a cut on the spectator's anticipation would be quite logical. Having moved in to reveal the untied shoelace, the bobbled ball, or even a nervous tensing of the fielder's lips, we would create in the spectator a wish to see the outcome of this new revelation—how this significant detail relates to the whole. As the succeeding action begins, we could cut smoothly on action to the medium shot which would show us a clearer overall picture of what is happening, the meaningful segment underlined by the close shot now a significant part of the overall scene. Like the more exaggeratedly dramatic cut from close to long shot, this would represent cutting for purposes of including an invisible action, rendering an action more meaningfully, and reestablishing the scene's geography, (Fig. 7.37 B).

As a general rule, the editor, while maintaining the essential requirements of clarity and intelligibility of this action scene, would tend to push as closely as possible to the subject and action and to utilize as many cuts as possible, recognizing that the rhythm of the cuts themselves will help greatly in building the excitement of the scene.

CAMERA ANGLE CONSIDERATIONS   Let us now examine a hypothetical situation in which angle alone is to be considered in making a cut. Can we determine if certain angles can be more readily cut to than others? We have established another baseball scene, photographed simultaneously by eight cameras, a physical impossibility but assuring us of a theoretical perfect matching of all elements in the scene, (Fig. 7.38). We have drawn through the scene the imaginary line discussed earlier in the book (page 149). Starting from camera position #1 in our outgoing shot, to which positions can we cut for our incoming shot?

We can readily see that cuts to positions #5, #6, #7, and #8, crossing the imaginary line, are disorienting to the viewer; in each case, the umpire—to the left of the batter in position #1—has "jumped" to the batter's right. We note that this is true even in the cut to position #5, a cut to a reverse shot. Although we have seen cuts to the reverse shot made effectively in a sequence involving a *moving subject,* (Fig. 7.22), for example, the parking lot sequence from *Darling,* our present example is a *static subject,* hence the imaginary line is drawn through the two figures rather than horizontally across the camera front or vertically down the center of the image. In such a cut on static shots there are no distracting influences and so the violation of the imaginary line is quite noticeable.

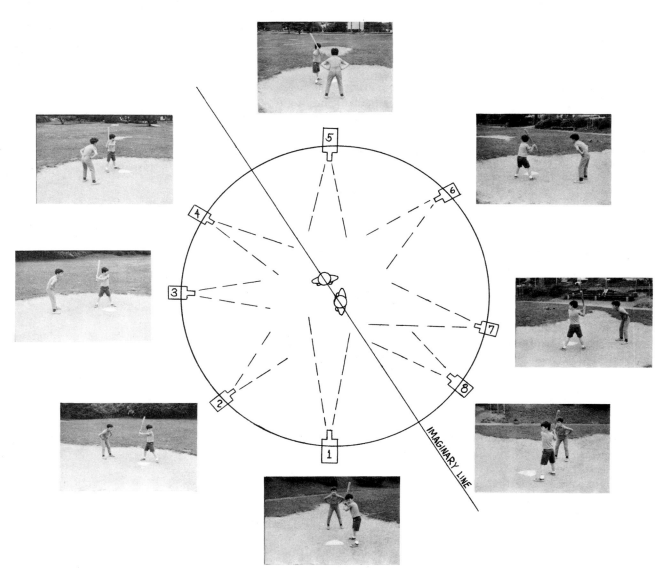

Cuts to positions #2, #3, and #4 are acceptable according to the imaginary line principle; the umpire remains to the batter's left. Is there a relative advantage or disadvantage to any of these? The cut to position #2 would seem to be the least effective; the lack of a major significant change in image raises the question of whether this new image serves a purpose not served by the previous image. A cut representing such a minor angle change invites comparison by the spectator of the relationship between the two figures; the images appear similar, yet the umpire has "jumped" back from the batter in position #2, a disturbing and disorienting leap. In a cut to camera #3, the umpire has again changed his relative position, but the fact that the new image is quite different from the outgoing image causes the spectator to accept such a change as natural. Such a cut would certainly work technically; it's aesthetic justification would depend upon its contributing something new, not offered by the outgoing image. In our theoretical example, with no scalar change on the cut, there is no new purpose served. On the other hand, a cut to camera #4, also offering a major angle change and hence a distinctly new image, reveals a portion of the playing field. (In a real game, the third baseman would be visible in the background.) If such a cut revealed a fielder charging down on the batter in expectation of a bunt it would be aesthetically acceptable; it is probably the most likely cut in this situation.

PRESERVING THE SENSE OF DIRECTION   The editor—or more accurately, the director-as-editor, when he dictates the basic camera set-ups—must preserve what Reisz terms "the sense of direction." There are two aspects to this.

First, such a consideration applies in the filmic treatment of a chase or of a battle between two opposing forces, or even of a subject travelling. In portraying a battle, the director will maintain the opponents facing in the same direction relative to the spectator throughout, the left-hand army facing to the right, the right-hand army facing to the left.° It is for this reason that multiple cameras covering a football game are always placed on the same side of the field, so that any cut between shots from different cameras will maintain the sense of direction. Since football teams change ends of the field at each quarter—football coaches are obviously less concerned with maintaining the football spectator's sense of direction than in equalizing such factors as wind, sun and muddy portions of the field—it is confusing to watch excerpt films of game highlights which cut directly from one quarter to another quarter. I have always felt television directors were missing a bet in not having duplicate multiple camera set-ups for each side of the field, changing between them when the teams "change sides" (reverse direction), maintaining the constant sense of direction throughout the entire game and strengthening the elemental conflict of the game. Present coverage does include an "end zone camera," which of course involves a 90° cut and hence does not violate the imaginary line.

In a chase, or a scene in which the subject is walking, the director will maintain the same direction of movement in each shot of the sequence, which means essentially filming the subject from the same side. Should the story require the subject to reverse direction, this must be shown to the spectator. Naturally this does not mean that the movement be always exactly parallel to the plane of the camera; diagonal movements are perfectly acceptable, so long as the general direction is maintained. One of the few violations of this occurs in Ford's *Fort Apache*, in which a cavalry supply wagon flees right to left while the Indians pursue left to right.

Second, in filming a scene between two people, such as that shown in Figure 7.3, the sense of direction must be maintained by keeping the camera on the same side of the figures as that originally established in the initial shot, insuring that they will face in the same relative direction throughout. When the initial two-shot establishes one person at the left of the screen, succeeding shots will maintain that relationship. Over-the-shoulder shots will show this person over the *left* shoulder—and hence to the left of—the other person; one-shot close-ups will show him looking slightly to the camera's *right*. Obviously the exact opposite holds true for the person to the right of the screen.

*An intriguing sidelight to this is the fact that the eye's dominant flow of direction is left to right, at least among societies which read in that way, causing forces which move from right to left—against the eye's flow—to seem more powerful than forces which move left to right with the eye's natural flow. Armies retreat from left to right and advance from right to left, a practice followed instinctively by most directors, even when not aware of this as a principle. This is also the reason why by far the majority of pans are left to right.

Cutting the scene shot simultaneously by more than one camera is, then, a matter of determining the point at which a significant meaningful image change is to be introduced in response to an instinctive expectation by the spectator, locating this identical point within the shots to be joined, and splicing them together. We have seen a number of criteria which affect our choice of cutting point; we will now see how these same criteria and others affect the cut in consecutively shot scenes.

THE SCENE IN CONTINUITY SHOT CONSECUTIVELY BY ONE CAMERA

Shots made consecutively of repeated—not necessarily perfectly identical —actions present the editor with the task of creating *an illusion of continuity*, a filmic continuity where there has been none in actuality. Initially the director-as-editor is concerned with staging and filming the action in such a way that the cutting points selected in the shots to be joined will contain matchable moments of any simultaneously present material. However, since new shot juxtapositions may be, and invariably are, arrived at in the cutting room, he must also be concerned with staging and filming the material in such a way that the shots will readily lend themselves to these new juxtapositions. It is for this reason that the film director must have a thorough understanding of editing. At this time we will study the criteria which the editor will consider in deciding whether he can make an effective cut within the scene in continuity; the director will be guided by this in planning his filming. Naturally, any technical criteria are in the end subordinate to the specific dramatic reality of the particular film: "All the rules of smooth cutting are subject to the much wider discipline of the *dramatic* as opposed to the *mechanical* demands of the continuity, so they are not to be taken as binding or universally valid." [7]

(1) THE NEW IMAGE MUST SERVE A PURPOSE NOT SERVED BY THE PREVIOUS IMAGE   This has been discussed at length during the consideration of the simultaneously filmed scene; it is the single most important criterion for an effective and unobtrusive cut. An interesting aspect of this is the question of when it may be more acceptable to make a short pan or tilt of the camera from subject to subject instead of cutting. Early films, including those of D. W. Griffith, remained fixed straight forward within the scene, giving today's spectator the sensation of being locked in a neck brace and wearing blinders. Contemporary films move effortlessly within the scene, the gift of the fluid head tripod, the dolly and the camera crane.°

The most important consideration for the use of a moving camera in changing the emphasis and composition of a scene is the precise timing of the camera move. A typical example is a scene in which a single subject is joined by another. If the camera moves back too soon, the empty portion of the frame telegraphs the contrivance of the move; if it lurches back too late, scrambling to adjust to the intruding figure, the move is equally noticeable. What is required is that the camera move back smoothly at precisely the moment that the new character enters, the move, like the cut in a comparable situation, determined by the

*Sometimes the cameraman utilizes a change in focus within the shot, framing the two subjects one in the foreground and one in the background, one in focus and one not, then reversing, causing the in-focus figure to lose focus and hence emphasis while the out-of-focus figure is sharpened and our attention drawn to it. Sometimes the director utilizes the shot-in-depth—a technique eloquently advocated by André Bazin and effectively practiced by such film-makers as Jean Renoir and Orson Welles. Here two or more subjects are included within the framing of the scene, each in clear focus, the decision of where to concentrate his attention being left essentially in the hands of the spectator.

spectator's expectation; such a move will be unobtrusive. Readjusting to a single person when one leaves a two-shot is also to be accomplished unobtrusively by moving in at the moment that the subject leaves; sometimes, if the scene allows it, other figures can be moved smoothly into the gap, filling the dead portion of the frame just vacated. In many ways such subtle moves of the camera are less obtrusive and momentarily distracting than the cut in that situation, especially if the cut is between two images without sufficient contrast. If the director wishes the least obtrusive readjustment of the scene—and particularly if he finds it impossible to offer images of sufficient contrast—the camera move is to be preferred to the cut.

(2) THE CUT MUST ANSWER IMAGINATIVELY THE SPECTATOR'S EXPECTATION
This too has been discussed at length, including the importance of not being slavishly bound to some idea of a "typical" spectator of limited imagination. The importance of this consideration is to insure that we cut with the "shifting emphasis of dramatic action" (Bazin) and not arbitrarily; the cut must be logical.

(3) THERE MUST BE A MAJOR CONTRAST BETWEEN IMAGES IN THE JUXTA-POSED SHOTS   This too has been covered in detail in the study of the simultaneously shot scene. The proposition rises from the first two offered: to serve a new purpose and to answer the spectator's expectation, the new image must offer some significant contrast. Remember, however, a major change does not ensure the rightness of the cut; we must not emphasize the "dramatically insignificant gesture." For this reason, the use of facial close-ups for jump-disguising cut-aways may be technically necessary but aesthetically wrong, the power of the close image and the cut itself creating a sense of strength and importance in the cut-away that the dramatic situation does not require.

Once these major aesthetic criteria are fulfilled, there are a number of more technical criteria which may be applied to insure the unobtrusive cut.

(4) CUTTING ON ACTION   By allowing a consecutive action to bridge two juxtaposed shots—beginning the action in the outgoing shot and picking it up a few frames into the action in the incoming shot—the editor distracts the spectator from the physical cut, utilizing one of the earliest (G. W. Pabst, 1925) and most effective means for disguising the cut in the continuity scene.

Our discussion would imply that the editor matches the movement in perfect sequence, for example, following eight frames of the movement in the outgoing shot with the ninth frame of movement in the incoming. (Remember the "flashbulb cut" discussed under simultaneous camera scenes.) In practice one discovers that this is not always so. There is a slight lag in the eye's ability to adjust to the action presented in the new shot, particularly if there is a major contrast of image. As a technical matter, the editor is advised to make the initial cut with a few frames overlap on either side of the cutting point chosen, (Fig. 7.43). The cut

Fig. 7–39a Cutting on anticipation
(last frame of outgoing shot)

Fig. 7–39b First frame of incoming shot
(*Instant Holland*, distributed by Paramount
Pictures)

Fig. 7–40a Cut serving a new purpose:
answering the spectator's expectation
(last frame of outgoing shot)

Fig. 7–40b First frame of incoming shot
(*Weekend in Peru:* director, Kenneth Roberts;
editor, Win Sharples, Jr.)

can be readily checked on a Moviola. If the overlap is a bit too long, a frame or two can easily be removed; a frame or two can *not* easily be put back—another reason for cutting first with an overlap.

Of course, we are referring to an overlap of, at most, three or four frames. The whole purpose of such a cut is to create the illusion of a continuous flow of action, with the cut unnoticeable. The obvious overlap is as distracting as the jump forward caused by the skipping of a portion of the action between two shots. Nevertheless, it is our observation that the imperceptible overlap is particularly necessary in cuts in which the change of camera angle to the subject between the two shots is limited. Naturally, when a radical angle change occurs, the eye is unable to match action closely, so the inexact cut is almost impossible to detect. An example of cutting on action with an overlap occurred in a film on the America's Cup Yacht Race, directed by Agnew Fisher. We had cut from an aerial shot of the two boats at the moment that their mainsails were raised, catching the action at the precise instant in a closer shot from ocean level. The eye was unable to adjust to the sudden change quickly enough; by the time our attention had refocused, the action had progressed a split second, and so the motion appeared to jump. A slight overlap of four frames corrected this impression.

(5) CUTTING ON THE PAUSE BETWEEN ACTIONS Many editors use the term "cutting on action" to refer to what is actually cutting *between* actions. The discussed jump cut from *Shoot The Piano Player* was such a cut, Truffaut cutting just before the boys ran. This point of cutting was also discussed during our consideration of scalar changes in cutting. Like the cut *on* action, this cut uses the movement in the incoming shot to distract the spectator from the cut itself. In practice it is usually easier for the editor to locate these moments when the limbs are in repose (Figs. 7.40 and 7.44), than to precisely match the cut on action. The advantage of this cut is that it does not interrupt a continuous flowing movement but punctuates the overall action of the scene at the appropriate moment of rest. The flow of movement is thus not interrupted but allowed of its own accord to come to a stop, and the two movements bridged by the cut are each presented as a complete entity.

(6) CUTTING ON ANTICIPATION Another cut used in the beauty contest sequence discussed earlier illustrates another important criterion for the cut, closely related to the idea of spectator expectation. We use the term "anticipation" in this case to distinguish the cut in which a specific physical action within the outgoing shot has "caused" the incoming shot. When the announcement of the contest winner was made, every head in the group whirled in our outgoing long shot; at that precise instant we cut to a closer shot of the delighted winner who rushed forward. Such a cut is truly unobtrusive, for the scene's anticipatory action has created a powerful expectation in the spectator which is immediately answered by the cut. (See also, Fig. 7.21).

Figure 7.39 illustrates another cut on anticipation; the pointing finger of the child creates the cut to the puppet show he is watching. The accomplished editor has known from the film work of Edwin S. Porter and of V. I. Pudovkin that "the meaning of the shot was not necessarily self-contained but derived from its juxtaposition with other shots." It is the anticipation of this classic cut which creates the sense of temporal and physical continuity—a continuity not necessarily present in actuality, for the boy could very well have been pointing to something entirely different at another time, another place.

There are several technical considerations which the editor will follow in choosing his cutting points within the scene in continuity:

(7) CAMERA ANGLE CONSIDERATIONS   Generally, a major change in angle is to be preferred for the same reason that the major scalar change is desired—it renders the cut more significant and meaningful. When the scene is created from shots filmed consecutively by the same camera, cutting between shots of the subject from radically different angles makes it considerably easier to create the illusion of continuity by matching the action of the shots. In *Loneliness of the Long Distance Runner*, Richardson cuts from a frontal shot of the hero with a coffee cup at his lips some 90° to a shot at the side, slightly behind and below (low-angle) the subject, now with the cup held at his waist. The average spectator never notices this jump cut. Had Richardson made a minor change of angle between the two shots, say from a frontal shot slightly to the left of center to another frontal shot slightly to the right of center, the jump would have been so noticeable as to make the cut impossible. This is not to imply that Richardson sought this jump; perhaps a decision in the cutting room after a study of the filmed material required a juxtaposition of two shots not originally planned for adjacency. Since they happened to have been shot from radically different angles the cut was possible; if not, some sort of disguising cut-away would have been called for.

Where Truffaut, in the previously discussed scene from *Shoot The Piano Player*, has used the cut between actions to disguise a jump, Richardson has used a cut on a major change of angle for the same purpose.

We find changes of scale alone, without an attendant change of angle, difficult to match properly and often disturbing to the spectator even when successfully matched. A cut from one shot of a subject to another of the same subject, differing in scale but not in angle, invariably causes the eye to jump, momentarily disoriented, for the image of the subject appears to change position both in relationship to the background and to the edges of the screen.

(8) MATCHING OF SIMULTANEOUSLY APPEARING ELEMENTS   We have noted that the assumed matching of elements present in both the outgoing and incoming shots from simultaneously filmed material must be carefully checked when the shots are made consecutively. This is to include elements of the subject's appearance, elements of the background, and any continuous action between the shots. It is upon this that the illusion of continuity depends.

Fig. 7–41a   Another example of the cut answering the spectator's expectation (last frame of outgoing shot)

Fig. 7–41b   First frame of incoming shot (*Weekend in Peru*; director, Kenneth Roberts; editor, Win Sharples, Jr.)

Fig. 7–42a   A major contrast between images; cutting with camera angle considerations (last frame of outgoing shot)

Fig. 7–42b   First frame of incoming shot (*Shoot the Piano Player*, Janus Films)

Fig. 7–43a Matching of simultaneously appearing elements (last frame of outgoing shot)

Fig. 7–43b First frame of incoming shot (*Darling,* distributed by Embassy Pictures)

Fig. 7–44a Cutting on a pause between actions (last frame outgoing shot)

Fig. 7–44b First frame of incoming shot (*Darling,* distributed by Embassy Pictures)

It should also be noted that this is to include the matching of the lighting key between the shots, whether they are interior or exterior. In the latter case weather and cloud formations become a factor.

Should it be impossible to match simultaneously appearing elements there are ways in which the mismatch may be disguised by the editor. We have noted the use of a *cut between actions* and a *cut on a major angle change* as effective. Additionally there is:

(9) DISGUISING THE BACKGROUND This can be accomplished by shooting the background out-of-focus, by choosing neutral backgrounds (low-angle shots with the subject framed against neutral sky), and by the cut with a major angle change. The crossing-the-harbor sequence in Hitchcock's *The Birds* is an example of the latter. When automobiles are shown en route, consecutive shots showing the car from the front and then from the side are usually juxtaposed. If properly framed, it is impossible to compare minutely the backgrounds of the shots, so long as there is a general similarity.

(10) MOVING THE SUBJECT IN AND OUT OF FRAME We have covered this subject earlier (pages 230–231); the illusion of adjacency between two juxtaposed shots of a travelling subject often depends upon the director having allowed the subject to enter and exit the shots when filming, rather than having started the action with the subject already present. This device also allows the editor maximum control of the filmic time of the scene. Preserving the sense of direction is an important factor in such scenes.

(11) THE CUT-AWAY Should all else fail, the properly integrated cut-away, also covered earlier, (pages 198, 204, 222, 228), can disguise the potential mismatch, so long as the editor is willing to accept the inevitable interruption of the spatial flow of the action.

(12) THE CEMENTIVE FUNCTION OF SOUND CARRIED OVER THE CUT The running of sound over any cut—whether the sound be actual (natural background sounds such as traffic or birds or factory noises or synchronous dialogue) or commentative (narration or musical background)—will invariably make the cut less obtrusive and the continuity more natural.

The following examples of direct cuts within scenes in continuity demonstrate how many different cutting criteria can affect one cut.

Figure 7.40 is a classic example of a cut on a pause between actions, (5), the matching point being the girl's pointing finger. There is definitely a major contrast in the images, (3), and a major contrast in camera angle, (7), although the imaginary line has not been crossed. Since these shots were made consecutively a few minutes apart on a busy street, it is quite obvious that the background elements of the scene do not match between shots; however, the major shift in angle momentarily distracts the spectator and prevents him from comparing the simultaneously appearing elements (8), including the backgrounds, (9), aided in this by the fact that the viewer's concentration is on the girls and, in particular, on the pointing hand. Although this cut was made for a practical purpose—we needed the beginning portion of the outgoing shot and the end portion of the incoming—there is a possible aesthetic justification. The cut reveals the hidden face of the second girl, thus serving a new purpose (1), and might very well answer the spectator's expectation of seeing her face and her reaction (2).

Figure 7.41 is an aesthetically sound cut. The incoming image brings us closer to the three subjects, serving a new purpose (1) and thus answering the spectator's expectation (2) with its resulting contrast of image apparent (3). The cut was aided by cutting on a pause between actions, (5), a puff of steam popping forth from the opened hot-dog tray at the moment of the cut.° We note that a major change in camera angle (7) has disguised the background (9), fortunate in view of the fact that the hot dog man had moved his cart between shots! More important, the major change disguises the fact that the subjects have changed their relative positions and that the simultaneous elements do not match (8). The girls are on the man's *right* in the second shot, instead of his left, they are considerably closer to him, and the girl in the striped dress is on the other girl's left instead of her right. These shots were not originally shot to be cut in continuity; that we were able to do this successfully, creating an illusion of continuity, is the result of these disguising factors involved in the cutting.

Figure 7.42 was a successful cut in *Shoot the Piano Player*. The simultaneous element in common to the two shots is the girl and she does not match (8)—note her head position. However, the shot serving a new purpose (1) with its major change of image and angle (3, 7) answering the spectator's expectation (2) throws the spectator's attention away from the girl so the mismatch is not noticed.

Figure 7.43 offers an interesting example of the cut on action (4) with overlapping frames. Note that the waiter's hand has already extended the wine by the last frame of the outgoing shot; yet, the first frame of the incoming shot begins with his hand starting the action again. The overlap is unnoticeable in viewing the picture and the flow over this illusion of continuous action perfect. The major angle change (7) is not really necessary for any practical reason, for the simultaneous elements— the girl, the waiter, the table decor—appear to be perfectly matched (8). The incoming shot does reveal the girl's face for the first time (1) and so answers the spectator's expectation (2) with its contrast (3).

Figure 7.44 appears to be a perfectly matched (8) cut on a pause between actions (5). The major change of angle and scale (3, 7) serves the new purpose of bringing us closer to the subject (1) and answers our expectation (2).

Figure 7.45, was a successful cut in continuity from *Darling*. The major scalar and angle change (3, 7) serve to disguise the elements which do not match (8, 9). Note particularly the girl's face, the newspaper, the man on her right, and the general relationship to the background, all of which changes between shots, the man, in fact, vanishing. Once again the major image contrast justifies the shot change even though it serves no real aesthetic purpose (1). The cut is particularly helped by a well-executed cut on action (4), for the girl is walking briskly.

°Truffaut uses a similar device in *Shoot the Piano Player*, cutting together two shots of the hero lying in bed. There is a slight mismatch between the shots— Charlie's head is raised a few inches in the outgoing shot, on the pillow in the incoming—but this goes completely unnoticed because of the major angle change between shots and because Charlie lets out a puff of cigarette smoke at the instant of the shot, catching the viewer's attention.

Dialogue Sequences

Fig. 7–45a   A major contrast between images; cutting on action; cutting with camera angle considerations; disguising the background (last frame of outgoing shot)

Fig. 7–45b   First frame of incoming shot (*Darling,* distributed by Embassy Pictures)

Most dialogue sequences are filmed with consecutive cameras. It is the use of *double-system sound* which makes it possible to edit such sequences creatively. This enables the editor to cut sound and picture separately, to run sound over shots other than the one to which it was recorded, to insert a significant reaction shot at a moment not foreseen by the director, and to cut out portions of dialogue at times when the speaker is placed off-camera.

The editor actually has considerable control over the timing of dialogue sequences, provided they have been filmed in a series of separate shots for each line of dialogue. The classic technique for handling dialogue scenes involving two people is to begin with a medium or long establishing shot, cut to a closer two-shot from the same angle, and then begin a sequence of alternating close shots from over the shoulder of the opposite character, climaxing with close-ups for maximum involvement. (see Fig. 7.3). Such a scene then often ends with the camera returning to its previous objective angle. There are other patterns of editing which may be used for the dialogue scene, and certainly many variations of this basic approach; still, it is an extremely useful basic technique. The use of the over-the-shoulder shot and close-up allows the character's face to be presented from the front rather than in profile, a variety in the visual images is obtained, and the editor is able to convey much of the meaning of the scene through the visuals as he should. "Even if the words convey most of the facts and information, the images must still remain the primary vehicle for the dramatic interpretation."[8] In such a sequence the editor has a maximum opportunity for choosing his points of cutting and the particular image he wants to present. And, most important, his control of the timing of the dialogue scene is at a maximum. One good general rule to remember is to time cuts in relation to the dialogue, cutting whenever possible between sentences, or at least between phrases or words. Naturally, a majority of the time the speaking character is seen, but some very effective moments can be realized by the use of reaction shots of the listening character. It was Dudley Nichols observation that the "screen is the medium of reaction," the film's power building through the spectator's identification with the person acted *upon,* the camera turning invariably to the reaction shot in moments of emotional crises.

The dialogue scene can be cut intelligently in a variety of ways, with a considerable amount of control exercised over its tempo and meaning. But the real time for editing considerations to be applied is at the time of writing such a scene. In dialogue scenes, the writer is the primary determinant of the editing; his understanding of its principles is vital.

Action Sequences

Action sequences—fights, dancing, chases, etc.—are the essence of cinema. The familiar plaintive wail that the addition of dialogue to the film has denied the editor his previous range of creativity is simply not applicable in the instance of action sequences. The editor has a wide range of control over the tempo and in his choice and order of presentation of the images. However, he has certain responsibilities of clear communication to the spectator and the fulfilling of these is important to the scene's effectiveness. Let us briefly examine the typical chase sequence.*

THE CHASE

The editor will invariably make use of the technique of parallel editing, alternating the audience's attention from one element of the chase to another, from pursuer to pursued. By keeping both elements constantly before the spectator, the editor keeps the excitement at its peak, reminding us of the closeness of the chase. Through his control over the separate elements, he can vary the fortunes of the pursuer and pursued; by his timing of the length of the shots, he can control the tempo of the chase. (Remember, that several successive shots of an action—wheels turning, a horse galloping, a man running—even if the action is shown at the same speed in each shot, can be used to increase the pace of the scene if each shot is cut progressively shorter.) Invariably, the filmic time of the action is considerably shorter than the actual, the inessential having been suppressed.

As we know, the cut-away can be used to bridge portions of the action, allowing us to compress the filmic time of the sequence. Shots to side-line spectators, a technique used in most auto and horse race films, are extremely useful and particularly appropriate in race scenes. The cut-away to a spectator is useful for a number of reasons other than for simply disguising a cut. The reaction of the spectator will suggest to the film's audience the varying fortunes of the participants in the race; their comparatively static quality makes an effective contrast to the action of the race. However, such intercuts, often close shots, must never be left on the screen for too long a time; their meaning can be more quickly grasped than that of the action shots and so the audience will much more quickly tire of such shots. Note in the climactic cutting of a chase sequence how a succession of varying angles is used, with continuous cutting directly from the pursuer to the pursued, increasing the pace and tension.

You will remember that a proper directional flow of action must be established in the film, and this is particularly important in the chase. Westerns provide interesting examples of this control. The editor must also remember that he has a responsibility to present any film image a sufficient length of time to enable the audience to understand it, or else he risks irritating the spectator. Sometimes this can come in conflict with his desire to cut the image extremely short. This can be remedied by using comparatively simple, close shot images for the quick cuts, and using the complex images for the longer-running shots.

A useful device for conveying to the audience the distance between pursuer and pursued is the use of recognizable landmarks in the scene, another favorite device of the Western chase. The audience will automatically note the length of time between the moment at which the pursued passes this recognizable point and the moment at which the pursuer passes. If this length of time is shortened the next time they successively pass such a landmark, the audience will realize that the pursuer is gaining. Since the film-maker infrequently has the opportunity of showing both

*Many of the observations in this consideration are drawn from Karel Reisz's analysis of Action Sequences, pages 69 through 85 in *The Technique of Film Editing,* an indispensable work to which the authors owe an incalculable debt.

the pursuer and pursued in the same shot, this device is often the only way in which he can demonstrate at appropriate intervals the closeness of the chase.

Montage Sequences

Fig. 7–46 Montage sequences (Zulu, distributed by Embassy Pictures)

*Within the montage sequence of a story film, there may well be cuts in continuity—cuts between varying views of the same subject, cuts between shots in which material is simultaneously present. Such cuts will be made by following the rules of unobtrusive cutting, although their effect may very well contribute to the cutting rhythm set up by the montage sequence.

There is an obvious kinship between the "action sequence" and the "montage sequence," with the montage editor enjoying even greater creative freedom in his choice of juxtapositions and his control of the tempo. The impact of the images themselves and the accumulative rhythm of the cuts determine the form of the montage sequence, probably the most superbly filmic of all scenes. The films of such great action directors as Howard Hawks (*Air Force, Red River, Rio Bravo,* and *Hatari!*) and John Ford (*The Hurricane, Stagecoach, They Were Expendable, She Wore A Yellow Ribbon, The Quiet Man, The Horse Soldiers*) offer marvellous examples of the action montage. An interesting comparison can be made between the B. Reeves Eason-directed classic montage sequence in Michael Curtiz' improbable 1936 version of *The Charge of the Light Brigade* and the stunning contemporary montage edited by Kevin Brownlow in Tony Richardson's bitingly realistic and accurate 1968 version. The major difference does not lie in the evolution of editing technique—Brownlow, author of the wonderfully enthusiastic homage to the silent film, *The Parade's Gone By,* would probably be the first to agree—so much as in the material supplied to the editor, for the developments in cameras, film stock, lenses, and, above all, in the way they are used, have been great.

A personal favorite is the montage sequence work in *Zulu,* the true story of the heroic defense of the mission station at Rorke's Drift against 4,000 Zulus by 105 British soldiers, the film directed by Cy Endfield and edited by John Jympson. The climactic scene, the breaking of the final Zulu charge by repeated volleys of massed rifle fire, lasts for one hundred and ten seconds, and involves forty-four shots, an average of two-and-a-half seconds per shot. The first four shots—an extreme long shot of the start of the Zulus' charge, a slow pan over the waiting soldiers, a travelling shot of the charge and a medium close shot of the officers quietly giving the preparatory commands—last for several seconds each. Of the next 21 shots, all but four are quite short. Two of these four are shots of the three ranks of soldiers firing in succession (Fig. 7.46); the other two show the commanding officer moving to his bugler, readying a signal to his hidden third rank of men. The former are obviously long to allow the action to conclude within the shot, the latter as an effective suspense-building counterpoint to the rapid cuts of the scene. The last nineteen shots of the sequence are extremely short and are cut *metrically,* that is, to a strict, measured beat. Fifteen of the nineteen shots are closeups: heads, a rifle muzzle, a trigger, and a cartridge ejector. Ten volleys are fired in the nineteen shots. When the final "Cease fire" is given and the camera pans slowly over the mound of dying Zulus stretching forth from the men's feet, the effect is stunning, as though suddenly awakening from the powerful grip of a vivid dream.

The flare cut of the montage sequence is in direct contrast to the unobtrusive cut of the scene in continuity.* A number of cutting criteria apply here, but most are not the same as those affecting the unobtrusive cut.

(1) *The state of mind of the participant in the scene* must justify the use of the rapid cutting and fragmented view of the montage sequence. This means that scenes of rapid, mass action and strong emotion are ideally suited for such treatment within the story film. (In a subject film, the use of arbitrary montage is accepted without question as a conscious film technique; the story film, even today, attempts to disguise any contrivance interposed between the subject and the spectator, retaining the illusion of the unaltered.) Any situation in which the participant° might be expected to view the action in a series of vivid, sharply-etched fragments is well suited for montage.

There are a number of technical devices the editor may apply in cutting the montage.

(2) *Cutting on the impact of the new image* has been previously discussed (pages 430–432) as a technique used in effecting direct cut transitions. The impact—and instant clarity and intelligibility—of the incoming image assures the spectator of the intent of the cut and allows the montage to move swiftly forward. The strength of the incoming image wipes out his lingering interest in the outgoing image, essential to the rapid cut montage. Of course, in its place and carefully controlled, a *disorientation cut* (pages 433–434) can work well too; however, the spectator must be able to make a comparatively rapid reorientation, carefully gauged to the tempo of the montage. It is appropriate at this point to recall Eisenstein's concept of *shock attraction,* the observation that the collision of two images can produce a result greater than the sum of their basic contents.

(3) *Directional cutting,* comparable to the cutting on action of the unobtrusive cut, is the use of a directional flow of motion in the outgoing shot to lead the viewer's eye into the incoming shot. The motion can be either that of the camera—panning or travelling—or of the subject within the frame; and the cut can either be directional—the flow the same in both juxtaposed images—or reverse directional—the flow in the incoming image doubling back on that of the outgoing image, (Fig. 7.47 A–C).

(4) *Positional cutting* is a cutting with regard to the positional match of image between the juxtaposed shots, (Fig. 7.48 A&B). This is a particularly important factor in editing the wide-screen film. There is an ease and essential feeling of rightness to the cut which allows the eye to pick up the incoming image at the same point upon which it has focused in the outgoing shot; this is particularly true when the eye has been led to this point in the outgoing shot by following within-the-frame action.

(5) *Cutting on form* is the technique of cutting between similar forms, as from a ball to a sun, from a narrow tree to a candle, or from falling rain to a bathroom shower.

(6) *Cutting on idea* is the cutting between objects bound by an intellectual thought, usually not comparable in form or size of image. Examples are cutting from a full-scale object—boat, car, soldier—to a toy version of the same, from rain on a window pane to tears, from a running tiger to a travelling automobile, or from the statue of a bird to a bird in flight. This is not to imply that the spectator makes a conscious

Fig. 7–47a Directional cutting: the movement of bicycles within the image is from left to right (last frame of outgoing shot 1)

Fig. 7–47b Movement of bicycles within the frame is again from left to right; the direction of flow is matched with that of outgoing shot (first frame of incoming shot 2)

Fig. 7–47c Movement of bicycles within the frame is now diagonally from right to left; matched to the end of shot 2, now outgoing, this gives an example of reverse directional cutting (first frame of incoming shot 3) (*Instant Holland,* distributed by Paramount Pictures)

*The spectator is a participant in the film also, particularly in the montage sequence.

Fig. 7-48a Positional cutting; cutting on form; cutting on completion of action; directional cutting (third frame from last in outgoing shot)

Fig. 7-48b Third frame from first in incoming shot (*Weekend in Peru:* Director, Kenneth Roberts; editor, Win Sharples, Jr.)

note of approval of the cut, merely that he senses a rightness to it and an intent behind it.

(7) *Cutting on the completion of an action* and its corollary, cutting by anticipating the moment of completion, has been covered earlier (pages 196 and 200 and Figs. 7.1 and 7.2). In a quick-cutting montage for a United Artists-distributed short, *Inland Sea Odyssey,* the author used a number of such cuts, cutting on the upward jab of a thumb, the quick double nod of a head, the picking up of a grapefruit, and the slamming of a taxi door, the image adjoining the latter being the landing of a jet plane at an airport. This is an example of *cutting on the impact of a new image,* momentarily disorienting, and a form of *cutting on idea;* it perfectly illustrates Eisenstein's "shock attraction," the viewer making an instantaneous association and concluding that the taxi is on its way to the airport. The essential point to remember is that the audience expects to see the action through and thus is held entranced by the running shot; therefore, if the editor holds such a shot longer than its neighbors in a quick-cut sequence, this will not destroy the fast tempo of the scene. Such cutting with an awareness of the tempo of the cuts but an equal consideration of shot content was termed *rhythmic cutting* by Eisenstein; his *metric cutting,* defined on page 200, is the practice of cutting to a measured length, to a strict tempo, but with the shots carefully chosen for their suitability to this style of cutting.

(8) *Tonal cutting,* another Eisenstein concept, is the procedure of joining together successive images with regard to their tonal progression. In the black-and-white film this was generally limited to gradations toward light or dark or toward sharper or softer focus; the color film offers the prospect of gradations toward warmer or cooler or toward stronger or more subtle hues. In cutting a montage sequence of a working shipyard from the same *Inland Sea Odyssey,* the author found several excellent but slightly diffuse shots of the giant cranes of the yard, shots that would normally have to be discarded. There was also available an excellent extreme long shot of the shipyard, its crane rising out of an enveloping mist. I began the sequence with this establishing shot, cutting in a succession of progressively less diffuse close shots of the cranes ending with a shot of a crane swinging against the sun, its rays spilling over the sides of the frame, then moving into the sharper shots of the scene. The diffuse shots not only became usable but the entire sequence took on an early morning sense of temporal progression which it had not had previously.

(9) *A general awareness of the psychology of color complements* can be used to bind the shots of the color film montage together. Few filmmakers have taken the time to acquire sufficient background in this important area, but the contemporary editor should not ignore this potential.

(10) *The cementive function of sound carried over the cut* is perhaps even more important to the montage sequence with its disparate images than to the continuity scene. Again, both actual and commentative sound can be used. It is invariably amazing to see how the unity of form of accompanying background music can instantly lend cohesiveness to the elements of the montage sequence, making even ill-chosen juxtapositions seem essentially right for the first time.

CHAPTER 8

THE CUTTING ROOM:
THE WORK PRINT

Much of what you have learned of film-making has stressed the importance of editing to the total process. If you have anticipated it as exciting creative work, you are now to learn that it is also a challenging,
laborious, physically demanding job, requiring patience, concentration,
and intelligent organization to perform well. In perhaps no other part
of the film-making process does the gap between your original vision and
the results you actually achieve loom so great. There is much you can
and must do to narrow that gap. One cannot be a film editor without
innate talent, particularly a superb sense of rhythm, a first-rate visual
memory, and a fine compositional eye. But even talent cannot bring you
the results you require without some system of editing. This is something
you must develop for yourself as you work with films and gain familiarity
with them. This book will suggest to you an effective working system,
and from it you can evolve your own system, matched to your special
talents. The essence of our system is organization; its aim is the reduction of the essentially laborious job of editing to make it a free-flowing
creative process.

While editing, one has the constantly infuriating sense of moving against the current, of dancing a graceful ballet in heavy sand. There is a basic contradiction between the tedious practical work of editing and the "free-flowing creative process" you want it so desperately to be. Somehow the editor should be able to choose each required shot effortlessly and in precisely the right order, assemble them instantly, and submerge himself completely in the rhythm of the film that he is, in fact, creating. The realities of editing are quite different. The closer you can come to freeing yourself from this clumsy struggle, the better your chances are of performing creative work.

One suspects that the average movie-goer thinks that a film has been photographed in some magical way in precisely the order intended, with each shot rendered flawlessly on the first take, at precisely the right length, and that this succession of shots rolls effortlessly from the camera to the editor's hands. Of course you now have some grasp of the realities of filming, and know that the shots are actually in vastly different order from that in which they will be finally assembled, that there are many unusable takes, and that even those eventually to be used are not of the length they will finally assume in the completed picture. And so this is the procedure we face: Select the usable shots, arrange them in the proper order, and cut them to the right length.

In general, you may be working in two ways (there are actually many degrees between the two extremes): either from a detailed shooting script and *camera reports* (pages 118–119), or simply from a mass of unlabeled material. In theory, every film should be shot from a shooting script and camera reports kept, and this will make the editor's job a good deal easier. In practice, there are a variety of reasons why this is not done, so the editor must be prepared to receive his material unlabeled. In such a case, it is important that he keep the director on hand throughout the breakout and classification period, so that he can understand the purpose for which each shot was made and the position the director intended for it within the film.

Fig. 8–1a Slate from Cullen Associates production MOS (no sound)

Fig. 8–1b Slate from Cullen Associates production; sync sound requiring use of clap stick

CAMERA REPORTS   At this point you know about the use of camera reports. If accurate reports have been kept, you have before you a record of every shot that has been made in the order made. There will be some notation of what the director thought to be the best take at the time of filming. You will also know where he intends to use this shot within the picture, for the camera reports will assign each shot a scene number to correspond with the shooting script; and, of course, each shot will be *slated* with this scene number (Fig. 8.1A and B). Complete and accurate camera reports are a tremendous help to an editor.

UNLABELED MATERIAL   If there are no camera reports, your initial work is, in a sense, an attempt to create a system of organization which will substitute for them. What this means in practice is that you must go through this material with the director (the assumption being that he knows the purpose intended for each shot) and assign each shot some sort of labeling within the organization of the film. In each case, we are leading to the procedure known as *breaking out,* cutting the mass of material into separate shots so that we can begin to assemble them in the proper order in a coherent rhythm. Before we plunge into this work, let us examine the equipment of the cutting room and its organization. We will begin with film itself.

In the cutting room, the film-maker is to see for the first time the image as it is recorded upon film. The original film stock exposed in the camera has been developed by the lab. In contrast to the usual home movie practice, in which the camera original is projected,° professional procedure today requires that a copy be made from the original, and this copy (called *dailies,* or *rushes* from the universal practice of viewing the results of shooting as quickly as possible) will be the material handled by the film editor and from which he will construct the *work print.* The essence of this work is a constant viewing and reviewing, experimentation and re-arrangement of the material. As you know, the original material, whatever its form, must be handled under carefully controlled conditions, by competent people trained for this work, for it is delicate and easily scratched.

Instead, you will work with dailies, later *conforming* the original to the assembled work print. All subsequent copies—*answer print* and *release prints*—will be made from the conformed original or its copies.

An initial decision has been made regarding whether you wished to receive your dailies *timed* or *untimed (one-light)* and whether or not they will be *edgenumbered,* our recommendation being that they be untimed and edgenumbered every sixteen frames, particularly if you are working in 16mm (see pages 190–191). In addition to the important use of edge-numbering as a means for later conforming the original material to your edited work print, you will find an additional use for them now as an aid to your cataloguing. Should you wish it, a careful record can be made of each shot with its beginning and end edgenumber. Even if your cataloguing is not to be this detailed, you will find the numbers quite useful in locating *trims.* When a portion of a shot is cut into the assembling work print the editor puts aside the trims—the unused beginning and/or end of the shot. Frequently the need comes to locate these trims, either to lengthen the cut-in shot or to use elsewhere another portion of the original shot as it came from the camera. For example, to find a head trim, one has only to note the first number of the cut-in shot and then look for the next consecutive number on the tails of the shots making up the trims (Fig. 8.2). This is particularly helpful if there are several similar shots among the trims. If you are reconstituting a shot and are unsure if you have lost a frame in the cutting process, you have only to count the frames between the edgenumbers on the reassembled shot to see if the sixteen frames are still there; this way you can tell exactly how many frames may be missing.

FILM IN THE CUTTING ROOM
THE DAILIES

Fig. 8–2 Edgenumber BF 8964 is first number on shot cut into work print; edgenumber BF 8963 is last number of head trim to this shot

*Interestingly, this practice also was followed in the early days of Hollywood. In *The Parade's Gone By,* there is a quote attributed to Charles Rosher, cameraman for Nestor, the first motion picture studio established in Hollywood itself, in 1911: "Although we had a developing room, we had no printing machinery. The picture was cut directly from the negative, and we thought nothing of running original negative through the projector. Scratches and abrasions were mere details. When the negative was cut, the completed reel was sent to New York or Chicago for printing."[1]

Because of the importance of these numbers to the negative matcher, it is essential that each shot as cut into the work print have at least one edgenumber on it. With today's editing, shots of less than sixteen frames are not uncommon, so it is quite possible that there would be no number on the cut-in shot. Always check such short shots carefully; if there is no number, check the head trim for the next previous consecutive number and mark it on the numberless shot with the number of frames between it and the first frame of the cut-in shot, e.g. AA1033 plus 4. The matcher can conform the negative exactly to the shot by checking the action carefully; but first he must locate this original from the mass of material he has on hand, and this will be a great deal easier if he has the edgenumber.

THE ARITHMETIC OF FILM

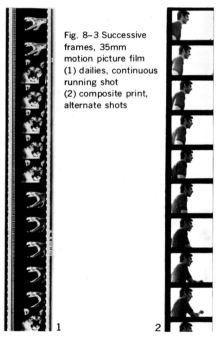

Fig. 8–3 Successive frames, 35mm motion picture film (1) dailies, continuous running shot (2) composite print, alternate shots

1   2

*One frequently hears today of "1:85 projection." This is a method for projecting a normal size film image by use of a special lens, so that it will fill the wide screen often used in movie theaters. This is accomplished by simply enlarging the picture and cutting off the top and bottom of the image in projection. If a feature film is being shown in a wide-screen form, the theater often chooses not to change the screen size for the accompanying short, even if it has been shot in normal 35mm. The 1:85 projection solves their problem. Needless to say, if film is to be projected this way, the cameraman must have anticipated this in advance; otherwise he will lose important material from his film image, including the tops of heads!

This brings us to the film itself, to the study of what Raymond Spottiswoode so aptly calls "the arithmetic of film." We shall confine ourselves to dealing with the most commonly used professional gauges, 16mm and 35mm. From our understanding of the intermittent working of the camera we are prepared for what we see: a succession of images, appearing upright when the film is held vertically, each image a stationary picture (Fig. 8.3). If we could examine them closely enough, we would observe a progression of action from one frame to the next. If, for example, we are looking at a shot of a moving car, we would see a succession of stationary images of the car, the car a bit further along in each frame. One side of the film appears smooth and shiny; it is called the *base*. The other side appears dull, and, if held at an angle to the light so that the light reflects off it, we can detect tiny ridges along the outline of the image; this is the *emulsion* side. The base is of cellulose, and it supports the thin coating of light-sensitive emulsion which registers the image. If the film is 35mm, we find that the image appears backwards if we look at it through the base, correct if we look through the emulsion side. Looking through the emulsion, if one sees a narrow black or transparent band along the left-hand side of the film, offsetting the image to the right the film is *cut aperture;* without the band, it is *full aperture*. In the final *composite print* (called a *married print* in England) which will be projected in theaters, the optical sound track will take up this band. When sound was introduced a method had to be found for including the sound track on the film. A device called an *Academy mask* is used in cameras to cut off this band on the side of the film, and a band between frames, necessary to restore the image to its original proportions. The image is rectangular, 0.868 by 0.631 inches, a ratio of 1 to 1:33, and the film itself is 1.377 inches wide (35 millimeters).°

Along the side of the film are *sprocket holes*. There are four sprockets to each 35mm frame, and the film is *double-perf*, that is, there are sprockets on both sides, (Fig. 8.4).

The purpose of perforations is to engage with pilot pins and sprocket teeth on many film drive mechanisms, thus insuring good steadiness and registration. It is easy to see the importance of extreme accuracy when it is realized that each 4/5 inch by 3/5 inch picture may have to be projected on a screen forty feet wide by thirty feet high, or a magnification in area of more than 300,000 times. Even under this terrific enlargement, there must be no visible wobble of the image. This order of magnification is easier to grasp when the starting area is larger. It is as if a Rubens canvas measuring 12 by 9 feet were to be enlarged to the size of one hundred and seven city blocks.[2]

In the cutting room the film is wound on reels with the emulsion out, so that it winds off the reel with the emulsion up, toward the editor and away from the table. The image will thus appear right-way-to and the easily-scratched emulsion will be kept away from the table and equipment.

In projection, 35mm frames travel past the lens at the rate of twenty-four frames per second, *sound speed*. A slower or faster rate would distort both sound and action.[*] There are sixteen frames to each foot of 35mm film so each 1½ feet of film passes in one second, 90 feet in 60 seconds. It is a simple matter to compute seconds from feet in 35mm since the ratio is always 2:3, e.g., 10 seconds is 15 feet, 20 seconds is 30 feet, 30 seconds is 45 feet.

Thirty-five millimeter film is normally handled in the cutting room on reels with a maximum capacity of 1,000 feet, usually kept to around 900 feet, or ten minutes. Hence the use of the term *one reel* for this length of time, as in "Chaplin one-reelers" and "two-reel shorts." Feature film release prints are handled on 2,000 foot reels; 2,000 foot reels are sometimes used in the cutting room, but they are awkward to handle.

While 16mm film is basically similar to 35mm, there are some important variations due to the difference in size and the varied stocks and printing methods used (Fig. 8.4B). Sixteen millimeter film also has a base and emulsion side. If the film is *"A"-Wind,* the image reads correctly when viewed through the emulsion—it reads "as a print." If the film is *"B"-Wind,* the image reads correctly when viewed through the base—it reads "as an original." An "A"-Wind print is threaded in a *projector* with the emulsion *away* from the lens, in a *Moviola* with the emulsion *toward* the lens. A "B"-Wind print is threaded in a *projector* with the emulsion *toward* the lens, in a *Moviola* with the emulsion *away* from the lens.

Sprocket holes are found one to a frame, and 16mm film may be either *single-* or *double-perf.* Release prints are single-perf, ensuring that they will always be loaded correctly into projection machines, which all have single sprocket drive mechanisms. Dailies, however, are double-perf, so it is possible to put them wrong-way-to on projectors and moviolas, getting a reversed image. The simplest way to ensure always getting a correct image is to establish the correct threading at the start of your work and then splice *single-perf leader* (leader is unexposed film or discarded film used for fill and for heading and titling films) at the head of the work print with the perforations the proper way for threading. No matter what type of 16mm film is being used, the *Moviola* and *projector winds* will be opposite, but since the single sprocket drive mecha-

*"Slow motion" is achieved by filming *faster* than usual, not by projecting slower.

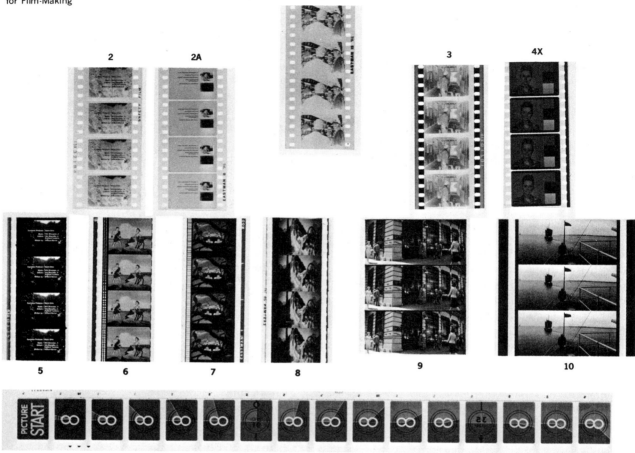

Fig. 8–4 16mm MOTION PICTURE FILM
Camera Films (1) Kodak Ektachrome EF
Film, 7241 (Daylight), Projection
Contrast Color Reversal Original
(2) Eastman Color Negative Film,
7254, Color Negative Original
(3) Eastman Ektachrome Commercial
Film, 7252, Low Contrast Color
Reversal Original; *Duplicating Films* (4) Eastman
Color Reversal Intermediate Film,
7249 (5) Eastman Color Internagative
Film, 7271 (5) Eastman Color Internagative
(6) Eastman Color Intermediate
Film, 7253;

nisms of each are on opposite sides, your single-perf leader will only engage correctly if the film is properly threaded. Frequently an editor splices single-perf leader into the middle of a work print to *slug* (replace) a damaged section, then forgets and starts the double-perf film in a reversed position. When the single-perf leader is reached, the machine naturally rips it to shreds; machines do not think; editors can, theoretically. The single-perf head leader eliminates this possibility, as well as the embarrassing reversed image.

There is no Academy mask used with 16mm, hence no sound band down the side of the dailies. The frame line between frames is quite narrow, in contrast to 35mm. The sound track on a 16mm composite print is on the side away from the sprockets, which are single-perf. The image is also rectangular at a 1 to 1:33 ratio, (0.404 by 0.295 inches) and the film itself is 0.628 inches wide (16mm).

CUTTING ROOM EQUIPMENT

You will find yourself in one of four basic situations. One, you may be part of an organization with a completely equipped cutting room of

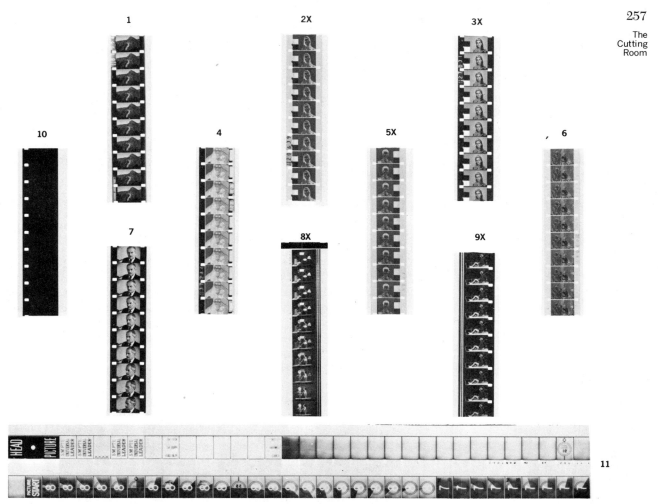

Print Films (7) Eastman Ektachrome
R Print Film, 7389 (Dailies)
(8) Eastman Color Print Film, 7385
(Composite print, variable area
sound track)
(9) Eastman Reversal Color Print
Film, 7387 (Composite print, variable
area sound track); *Leader* (10) Opaque leader
(11) SMPTE Universal Leader (head
portion only illustrated) (Courtesy
of Richard C. Tomkins, Ezra Baker Films,
Eastman Kodak, SMPTE

professional caliber. Two, you may gain the use of such a fully-equipped room by hiring a professional editor to cut your film. In such a case, his facilities are available to you as part of his fee as editor. Three, you may obtain such a facility for your own use by renting a cutting room, by the day, week, or month. It will contain all necessary equipment—naturally you must specify what you will require—and such rooms are available in most major cities where active film work is being performed. Four, you may set up your own limited cutting facility—or obtain access to one through a school—which, while it may not be the ideal set-up, can work as well for you as it has for many other beginning film-makers.

We will describe the variety of equipment available, including all that you might expect to find in the fully-equipped professional cutting room, and give you some idea of what we consider the minimum equipment for setting up your own room. The basic equipment consists of the Moviola, the viewer, the sound reader, the synchronizer, the splicer—both tape and cement—the editing table, rewinds, storage racks, film bins, reels, and a number of miscellaneous smaller items to be found around the cutting room.

The Moviola Editing Machine

Fig. 8-5a Steenbeck Film Editing Machine, Model ST 6000, 6-plate combination 16/35mm (projection screen to the rear, speaker to the right rear, supply plates to the left, take-up plates to the right, film feeding from left to right on cores)

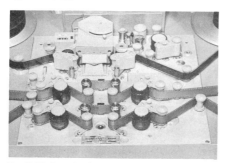

Fig. 8-5b Steenbeck Film Editing Machine, Model ST 6000, 6-plate combination 16/35mm (close view of transport deck showing simple threading and parallel relationship of picture and tracks)

Fig. 8-5c Steenbeck Film Editing Machine, Model ST 6000, 4-plate 16mm

The Moviola must be considered the essential piece of film-viewing equipment in the professional cutting room in the United States. Let us state from the start that there are other devices which can perform the same function (and do, particularly in other countries), among which must be included the Westrex Sound Editor and the Intercine Editing Table. In particular, the recently introduced Steenbeck Film Editing Machine, (Fig. 8.5 A–C), and KEM Universal Editing System (Fig. 8.6 A–G), are considered by those who have used them to be superior to the Moviola in many ways. Still, the fact is that the Moviola is a universal presence in today's cutting rooms. For all its faults—and there are many, in particular its rough handling of 16mm film—it is almost impossible for the film-maker to avoid using one.

We shall attempt to present a thorough grounding in its use and at the same time offer workable alternatives. A film can be assembled using a viewer, and many have been. Several companies offer combination devices of viewer, sound reader, and synchronizer which are able to duplicate the functions of the Moviola at considerably less cost, and we shall discuss these. If you are to work as a film professional in the United States, however, you must know the Moviola, so we will begin here (Fig. 8.7 A&B).

Fig. 8-6a Kem Universal Editing System, 8-plate model, entirely modular in design

Fig. 8-6c KEM Universal Editing System, 8-plate model; editor utilizing quick-wind flange and sound reader for 16mm and 35 mm film

Fig. 8-6b KEM Universal Editing System, 8-plate model, set up to run two pictures and two sound tracks

Fig. 8-6d KEM Universal Editing System; editor winding on front plates at high speed

The Moviola is a device for projecting film. Unlike the standard film projector with which you are familiar, the Moviola projects its image up into a small viewplate which is part of the machine. Technically, the Moviola uses the *Maltese cross movement* to actuate an *intermittent sprocket* to drive the film past the lens. As you know from your study of the camera, film must be viewed *intermittently;* this means that each frame must be held stationary before the lens for 1/12th of a second while it projects its image, and then must be moved on to be replaced by the next image. If this did not occur, the film would appear as a blur. This intermittent action requires an alternate pulling and release of the film as it feeds into the *gate* of the Moviola. If this erratic tugging were passed on the film winding off the *take-off reel (supply reel)* at the bottom of the machine, it would break the film. To prevent this, Moviolas, as well as cameras and projectors, use the device of the *film loop.* As the film feeds from the take-off reel it passes through a *sprocket gate* into which it is locked. The drive on this sprocket runs at a steady motion and so pulls the film smoothly off the take-off reel, and feeds it to the intermittent. Between this sprocket gate and the intermittent gate at the lens of the machine there is a *loop* in the film—that is, the film does not run directly into the lens gate but bulges out in a loop. The size of this loop changes very slightly as the intermittent operates but never interferes with the take-off reel or the continuously running sprocket gate. Above the lens gate is a *second sprocket gate* performing the same function of providing a loop before the film feeds on to the *take-up reel* on top of the machine.°

It is important to use the proper size loop each time the Moviola is *threaded* with film. If the film happens to jam as it feeds through the lens gate it may continue to run but will *lose the loop,* and the film will tighten between the sprocket and lens gates. The Moviola should immediately be stopped, the lens gate opened, and the proper size loop restored, for the film is subject to ripping when it is without a loop. If you need to run a composite print, most Moviola picture heads have an *optical pick-up* head above the top sprocket gate. When the film is being run silently, we bypass the optical pick-up (Fig. 8.8 A&B).

Additionally, there are sets of *rollers* with spring actions between each sprocket gate and the respective take-up and take-off reels, which give a further protection against the film ripping; any quick pull from either reel will work against the spring rather than pulling directly on the sprocket gate. There is a small *focusing knob* next to the viewplate, and a *framing lever* that allows you to properly frame the picture in the plate. Framing refers to centering the running picture in the viewing plate so that the frame lines which divide one frame from another are not visible.

A *footage counter* is attached to the picture head; there are a variety of such counters, also to be found on synchronizers, some counting in frames, some in minutes and seconds, some in 16mm and some in 35mm footage. The usual counter found on the picture head is a footage counter calibrated to the gauge of that particular head, 16mm or 35mm. As the film is run on the Moviola, the counter keeps an accurate, to-the-frame

THE PICTURE HEAD

Fig. 8–6e KEM Universal Editing System; film on cores is easily tabbed with papers or marked with grease pencil

Fig. 8–6f KEM Universal Editing System; removing 16mm picture module from left extension

Fig. 8–6g KEM Universal Editing System; replacing picture module with a 16mm sound module

* Some editors, particularly those who have worked on sync-dialogue-laden feature films and/or in Hollywood, prefer to use the Moviola without attaching the spindles holding the take-up and take-off reels. The film is hand-fed and collected in the bag hung behind the machine. The film is then assembled on the editing table.

Fig. 8–7a
1. Gate
2. Take-off reel (supply reel)
3. Sprocket gate (lower)
4. Loop (lower)
5. Sprocket gate (upper)
5A. Loop (upper)
6. Take-up reel
7. Optical exciter lamp, picture head
8. Spring rollers, upper and lower
9. Focussing knob
10. Framing lever
12. Projection light switch
13. Release switch to gate
14. Rheostat control to picture head lamp
17. On-off switch, picture head motor
19. Brake
20. Rheostat knob, picture head motor
31. Optical-magnetic sound and tone selector
33. Headphone
34. 16mm reel spindle
38. 35mm reel spindle lock

Fig. 8–7b
11. Footage counter, picture head (16 mm, as is picture head)
15. Adjustment nut, on 35mm spindles
16. Picture viewer (LGS–16 large screen twice normal screen area)
18. Forward-reverse switch, picture head motor
22. Flange
22A. Clutch
23. Forward-reverse switch, sound head motor
24. On-off switch, sound head motor
26. Optical exciter lamps, sound heads
28. Volume controls for each optical pick-up on sound heads
29. Volume controls for each magnetic pick-up on sound heads
30. Master volume control (magnetic and/or optical); amplifier off switch
32. Speaker
35. Footage counter, sound head (35mm, as is sound head)
36. Frame counter
37. Volume control for optical pick-up on picture head)
38. 35mm Reel lock

count of the amount of film run, functioning whether the film is run backward or forward. There is a *light switch* on the righthand side of the picture head and a second light switch attached to the film gate. When the gate is opened to insert or remove film, the second switch automatically cuts off the light, restoring it when the gate is closed. The *release switch* on this gate is on the righthand side of the gate. There is also a *control* which allows you to adjust the degree of tightness with which the gate holds the film as it passes through it, a consideration when you are running tape-spliced work prints.

If the Moviola is 35mm, you will note *tension controls* on the spindles on which your take-up and supply reels are to be placed. These are adjustable. If too great a tension is placed on the take-up reel, the film may snap; if too little, it will not take up properly. If too great a tension is placed on the supply reel, there is also a danger of the film snapping; if too little, the film will not feed steadily off the reel but will run down

in a large loop onto the floor. You can gauge the proper tension by pulling the film from the supply reel by hand; get to know what is right and check it each time you use the machine.

The picture head is powered by a variable speed motor; the motor has an *on-off switch*, a *forward-reverse switch*, a *brake* and a *rheostat knob* that varies its speed. The motor can, and most frequently, is, run by a *foot pedal*, the on-off switch being used primarily for long continuous runs of the film. With the rheostat control, the picture can be run at an extremely slow speed to study the film carefully or quite fast (well over sound speed—normal film speed) to get quickly to a particular point in the film. Most important, the picture can be stopped at any given frame (the brake will stop it instantly) in order to pick or mark a precise point in the film for cutting. The lamp does not burn the film when it is stopped, and the image is sharp and bright. The film can easily be turned forward and backward a few frames by hand, or run slowly with the rheostat motor to the desired point. This characteristic of allowing careful examination of the film at any precise point is one of the essential features of the Moviola. There are others.

One other important feature of the Moviola, in contrast to the standard projector, is the ease of putting in and removing film, and this brings us to the method of threading the machine. If a single short piece of film is to be viewed, the film can be run from a roll held in the operator's hand, and need not be taken up on the top reel. All that is necessary is to flip open the lens gate (using the *release catch* on the side), lay the film carefully in the gate so that the sprocket wheel at the top of the lens gate engages the sprocket holes of the film, and carefully close the gate. If the film is single-perf 16mm, note that the sprocket holes *must* be on the operator's *left*. Then open the bottom sprocket gate, loop the film properly, and again close the gate carefully to engage the film sprocket holes in the sprockets. It is not necessary to use the top sprocket gate so long as the take-up reel is not being used. (Actually you can run without the bottom sprocket gate, but the image will be unsteady.) The film will simply feed off the back of the machine as you are viewing the shot and can then be rolled up at the end of viewing. Most machines have a *canvas bag* hung on the back of the Moviola into which the film falls, keeping it from the dirt of the cutting room floor.

If you are running an entire film which requires feeding from the take-off reel and up to the take-up reel, this is the method of threading (Fig. 8.9 A–F). Take the reel of film and place it on the *take-off reel spindle* at the bottom rear of the Moviola with the film feeding off the bottom of the reel. Close the *lock* on the end of the 35mm spindle. Take hold of the film and feed it under the picture head, reach directly up and attach it to an empty reel on the *take-up spindle* at the top of the machine. The film is usually attached to the reel by a piece of *masking tape*, common equipment in all cutting rooms. An alternate method is to feed the film end into the slot provided in the center of all reels. The advantage of this method is to avoid having the masking tape lodge in one of the gates of the Moviola (or projector); however, sometimes

Fig. 8–8a Threading for running 16mm picture without sound

Fig. 8–8b Threading for running 16mm composite print in order to pick up sound from optical sound track

Fig. 8–9a Winding 16mm film onto take-up reel

Fig. 8–9b Placing 16mm film in picture head gate

Fig. 8-9c Seating 16mm film in top sprocket gate with film clamp

Fig. 8-9d Seating 16mm film in bottom sprocket gate

Fig. 8-9e Testing proper alignment of film against top spring roller

Fig. 8-9f Setting film against bottom spring roller

The Sound Head

reels have their slots obscured by previously used tape, making it easier to use tape. Once you have secured the film, either in the slot or with tape, give the reel a spin to wind the film securely (two or three turns will do it).

Now flip open the lens gate and settle the film in it; be sure the sprockets properly engage the sprocket holes. If there is a specific start mark it will be simple at this time to set it directly in the center of the gate so that the film will start on its precise starting point and be properly framed. Now form the proper size loop at both the bottom and top sprocket gates and engage the film; be certain that the sprockets of the film are all properly seated at these two gates also. (To check this after each gate is locked, pull the film above and below the gate; there should be a slight amount of give; if not, open the gate and set the film properly or it will rip when the machine is started.)

To set the film on the top rollers, grasp the film at the point where it feeds from the top sprocket onto the take-up reel, pull it slightly toward you, and slip it around the top spring roller on the machine from which it will run directly onto the take-up reel. If you push this reel forward until the film is taut, you will note that the film pulls against the spring of the roller, which gives a little. This is its purpose, and shows you that you have threaded the roller properly. The bottom pair of rollers are at the back of the machine, just below the take-off reel. Note that the film is now running from the reel under the lower roller and toward the front of the machine and the lower sprocket gate. Take the film just as it comes off the take-off reel, pull it slightly forward and pass it, from the side, in front of the top roller. Again check proper threading by winding back on the take-off reel. You are now fully threaded; set the footage counter on zero, turn on the light (always turn the light off when you are away from the machine; bulbs burn out rather fast on a constantly used Moviola), set the motor switch to "forward," and you are ready to start.

What we have described thus far is only the picture head of the Moviola. It is possible to obtain a separate picture head which can be set on an editing table, (Fig. 8.10A), but by far the most common type of Moviola is one with the picture head and at least one sound head set side by side on a wheeled stand. Moviolas are commonly referred to by the type of heads they contain, starting with the picture head and reading right to left. Thus a 35mm picture Moviola with a 35mm sound track is a 35–35; a 16mm picture Moviola with 35mm sound is a 16–35; and a 16mm picture with 16mm sound is a 16–16 (Fig. 8.10C). There can be more than one sound head; we have a 35–35–35–35 for running completed sound work. If one has a choice, we would recommend as the most versatile machine, a 16–35–35–16 (Fig. 8.7). Such a machine can run 16mm picture, one 16mm soundtrack (the form that voice tracks to 16mm pictures usually take), and two 35mm soundtracks (the form that music and effects tracks most frequently take). Comparatively rare are machines with two picture heads (Fig. 8.10E), and *Preview Moviolas*, machines with large viewers (Fig. 8.10D).

The sound head next to the picture head is powered by a *synchronous speed motor* which will drive it at exact sound speed. This sound head, with its motor, is connected to the picture head on the right side and on its left to another sound head; each other sound head is in turn connected to its neighbor, until the machine ends at its far left in a *flange*. The machine's flange, like the flange used on the cutting table, is used to rewind film; the function of both will be described later in this chapter. Any head can be disengaged from its neighbor in a second by sliding open a simple *clutch* on the connecting drive bar between them (Fig. 8.11). If all clutches are engaged, the entire machine can be run by the synchronous motor at exact sound speed, or by the variable speed motor at a selected speed. The variable speed motor is less powerful, however, and should not be used to run the entire machine for long stretches; that is the function of the synchronous motor. The picture head can be disengaged, and the sound heads run together without it. Also, you can disengage the sound heads starting from the left, so that on a three-sound-head machine you can run tracks 1-2-3, 1 and 2, or 1 alone (numbered from right to left). This motor also has a *forward-reverse switch*, an *on-off switch*, and a *foot pedal on-off switch*.

Each sound head is equipped to pick up both optical and magnetic sound, and so has both an *optical exciter lamp* and a *magnetic sound pick-up*, each with its own *volume control*, located on the front of the machine. There is also a *master volume control* for overall volume once you have balanced the separate sound tracks against each other. In today's film work one almost never uses the optical potential of these sound heads, so the exciter lamps are left turned off. There is a *control* located on the back righthand corner of the right side of the Moviola stand which offers two settings each for "optical" and "magnetic" and one combination optical-magnetic. This setting is normally left on "high magnetic" unless a composite print is being run through the picture head's optical pick-up, in which case it must be changed to "high optical" in order to pick up the optical soundtrack of the completed film.

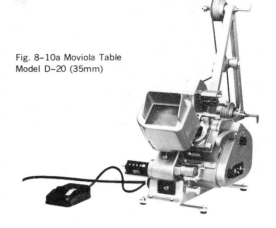

Fig. 8–10a Moviola Table Model D–20 (35mm)

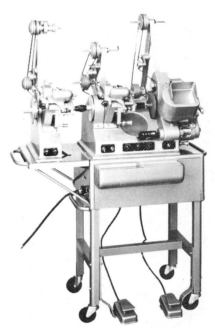

Fig. 8–10b Moviola Model UD–20–S (35mm) with CE–20 cabinet extension and separate sound head

Fig. 8–10c Moviola Model UL–20–CS (16mm) equipped with a composite sound head able to reproduce optical sound recorded on picture film

Fig. 8–10d Preview Moviola Model UDPVCS (35mm) is ideal for multiple-viewer screenings

Fig. 8–10e Moviola Model U2L–20–2S equipped with dual footage and seconds counter and electric brake

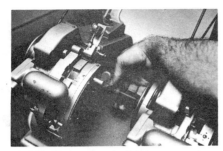

Fig. 8–11 Disengaging clutch between sound heads of a Moviola

Fig. 8–12a Magnetic 35mm film being threaded on Moviola sound head.

Fig. 8–12b Placing film in gate

Fig. 8–12c Forward push against take-up reel pulls against tension roller to see if film is smoothly threaded

One can listen to the sound on the Moviola's own self-contained *speaker* (it has its own amplifier), on a separate, better speaker which could be wired into the machine, or on earphones. The *earphone jack* is on the righthand side of the stand near the magnetic-optical switch.

The magnetic pick-up heads are similar to those in a ¼ inch tape recorder; they can be flipped up and out (see Fig. 8.11) of contact with the sound track running through their particular head, and you should do this when backing up sound tracks for a long stretch. Although one gets used to the sound of three soundtracks being played backward simultaneously, there is no particular reward for such martyrdom, and there is no need to wear out the *shoe* of the pick-up head needlessly. They can be replaced, but are, like everything else connected with the Moviola, expensive.

The quality of sound on a Moviola is, like the picture quality, not ideal; but again, it does the job. It is theoretically possible to wire a separate amplifier and speaker set-up into the pick-up heads, and this would obviously improve the sound somewhat. We have never bothered to go this far, and there is some question as to whether the nature of the sound pick-up might not be a limiting factor even in such a system. The best rule, with Moviola sound as well as picture, is to use it for exactly what it is, an enormously convenient and virtually indispensable tool, and then go to first-rate projection and sound dubbing equipment to see and hear your tracks as they really are. Moviola amplifiers should be left on all day; tubes wear out from being turned on and off frequently. At night, *always unplug the Moviola from the wall.* We once came in on a Monday to discover a cleaning woman had started one up on Friday, panicked, and run out—leaving it running. By Monday, the Moviola didn't smell particularly good!

Our own multiple-head machine is equipped with three footage counters: a *16mm footage counter* on the 16mm picture head, a *35mm footage counter* on the first 35mm sound head, and a *frame counter* connected to the drive of the machine. We use the frame counter because we do a lot of work with animation; the 35mm counter is used for all of our sound footage, and our 16mm counter is rarely used.

The sound heads are easily threaded (Fig. 8.12 A–C). Place the reel containing the soundtrack on the *bottom spindle* and lock it on with the film feeding off the bottom of the reel and the emulsion of the film out and toward you. Take the end of this film, run it *over* the drive bar, and attach it to the *take-up reel* on the top spindle (locked), just as you did the picture, and give the reel a few turns forward until the start mark appears. Open the *sound gate* by its *release catch* and seat the sound film carefully over the sprockets at the top of the gate. Close the gate carefully. Remember to check and see if the sprockets are properly engaged by pulling the film to see if it gives slightly. The sound head has a single *spring roller* system at top and bottom; common sense will show you how the film should thread around it; again, check by tightening the respective reel against the adjoining roller. The spring should give and return when pressure is released.

The Moviola is powered by a belt drive; the belts are made of leather and usually joined by metal clips. Moviolas need fairly constant servicing but there are several things you can do yourself. Purchase a belt-repair tool (Fig. 8.13), (if the film equipment store does not have them, they can be found in some hardware stores), a few extra clips, and a reel of belt leather. When a belt breaks, clip off the end, puncture the new end, and use the old clip to unite the ends. There is an adjustable tension on the belt pulley, so the slightly shortened belt will still work. Check the other head(s) to see how the belt is threaded. Spare lamps should be kept on hand—they are always blowing out ten minutes after the supply store closes—and you can replace them yourself. Finally, you should regularly clean the accumulation of emulsion from the film gate with cotton swabs dipped in acetone (Fig. 8.14); never scrape the gate with metal because it will scratch.

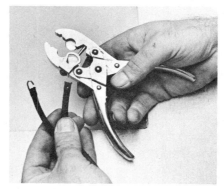

Fig. 8–13 Leather belt repair tool: hole punched in belt by tool and metal clip for joining ends of belt

Check to see if the proper clutches are engaged and the switch of the synchronous motor set on "forward." While remembering our caution about running the whole machine too far on the variable-speed picture-head motor, we suggest a convenient method of operating the machine. Leave the variable-speed motor switch on "reverse" and the synchronous-speed motor switch on "forward"; use the foot pedal of the variable-speed motor for backing-up short distances. This is much more convenient than constantly switching the synchronous-speed motor from "forward" to "reverse" each time you want to back up a couple of feet. However, for long distances, use the synchronous motor on reverse—and do not forget to flip the sound heads up!*

The Steenbeck Film Editing Machine is an outstanding addition to the tools of the editing room (Fig. 8.5). Although its distribution is at present not comparable to that of the universally-found Moviola it can be expected to increase steadily, for it is highly praised by the editors who have worked with it. The Steenbeck offers a number of improvements over the Moviola which more than justify its expense, which is considerable. Its high cost would appear to make it a tool of the busy professional editing room.

Fig. 8–14 Cleaning picture head of Moviola with cotton swab and acetone

A number of models are available, including 16mm 4-plate (picture and one sound track), 16mm 6-plate (picture and two sound tracks), 35mm 4-plate, and 35mm 6-plate (both obtainable in standard screen, Cinemascope, or a combination of both). Of particular interest is the Model ST6000 Combination 16/35mm, offering over thirty various combinations of 16mm and 35mm picture and tracks through the changing of modules, accomplished in less than two minutes without using tools. In addition to the usual composite 16mm or 35mm prints and 16mm and 35mm mag sound tracks, the machine can run 17.5mm mag film, a separate 35mm optical track, and 16mm mag striped prints. It projects a bright clear 8 by 11 inch picture in rear projection by means of an optical compensator, or revolving prism, assuring maxium safety to the film and enabling camera original material to be run without danger of scratching. The sound quality is excellent—the almost completely silent operation of

*The instruction manual supplied with the Moviola will provide important additional information including notes on lubrication, adjustments, and operating problems and their causes.

the machine is a help here—with the sound controlled by slide attenuators; mixes can be simulated on the machine.

The Steenbeck is controlled by a central operating lever or an optional foot switch and has electrical braking which will stop the film motion within one frame. The machine offers three speeds in forward and reverse, 2-4 frames per second, 24 frames per second (optionally available at 25 frames, European television standard), and 100 frames per second, for high-speed search or rewind operation. Picture and tracks are handled on cores in projection wind. Each track can be interlocked or disengaged electrically to the drive system through slide switches located on the table top. Cutting can be accomplished without unthreading, for the tracks all run parallel to each other (Fig. 8.5B); there are three possible sync points, one on either side of the transport deck as well as in the central picture gate and sound heads. The Steenbeck functions as a viewer, sound reader, synchronizer, and rewind in one and enables the editor to perform his work "on the table," the most convenient and efficient place.

If the Steenbeck is used for selecting good takes and outs, the material can be fed from one supply plate to the left of the transport deck alternately on to two separate take-up plates to the right of the deck. At the end of the reel, the editor has one plate of outs and one of good takes, tails out; these can be quickly rewound—at four times sync speed—back to the appropriate supply plates.

The Advance-Retard System is an excellent innovation for syncing tracks to picture. It enables the editor to electrically advance or retard the front sound track in relationship to the picture or central sound track while the sound tracks and picture are in motion. A dial (Fig. 8.5B) indicates the amount of adjustment made. When exact sync is found, sync marks may be applied or punched through sound and picture simultaneously. Also available is an Automatic Start Marking System for "slateless synchronizing."

The KEM Universal Editing System (Fig. 8.6 A–G) is billed as "the world's most advanced editing machine," something it may very well be. It is available in 2-plate (i.e. one track), 4-plate, 6-plate and 8-plate tables; the 6-plate table contains all electronics and controls necessary to make the 8-plate table with the addition of left and right KEM Extensions. The KEM presents a large, clear picture (9½ by 13 inches), excellent sound (from a 12-watt, 15–60,000 cps $\pm$ 3db solid-state amplifier), offers the opportunity of performing all editing work on the table itself, and has the potential of over fifty possible combinations of its instantly interchangeable modular units. The 8-plate table can run one picture with three separate sound tracks,° two pictures with two sound tracks, three pictures with one sound track, or four sound tracks, and it can handle any combination of 16mm and 35mm picture and sound. (Also available are 17.5mm sound and such picture formats as 8mm, Super-8, 65/70mm Cinemascope, and Techniscope. TV modules offer the option of monitoring in the next room or across town and of recording directly

---

*Since the picture heads offer the option of composite sound pick-up, either optical or mag, it is actually possible to run four tracks with picture, so long as one is a composite track.

onto video tape). All can be run in perfect sync, in any combination, electromagnetically interconnected; they may also be instantly uncoupled and manually adjusted. Any of the four transports can be run backward or forward at 4, 24, 48, or 120 frames per second (the editor may set the four speeds at other rates within a fairly large range, if he wishes); they may be run singly or together at the push of a button or with a foot pedal. The front plates can free-wind at high speed, 1,000 frames per second. The film is wound rock-hard on cores—reels may be used, if desired— in projection wind, and the KEM can run camera-original without damage. Splices of any type can be handled, even film held together with masking tape will run.

Material is threaded on the KEM with the base side toward the editor for convenience in marking. Two-thousand foot plates are available in addition to the standard twelve-hundred foot plates. Up to four counters may be mounted on the table and are available in feet, feet/frames, frames, minutes/seconds, and meters. Like the Steenbeck, the KEM offers the option of changing sync between a picture and sound track while they are running; they may be advanced or retarded with a switch while a differential counter tells exactly how many frames and perforations sync has been changed. The KEM will stop within one frame.

With its large picture, high quality sound and noiseless operation the KEM may be used to run a mix rehearsal of multiple sound tracks (three with picture, four blind). A test mix may be made into an external sync recorder, and special "Trans-Edit Extensions" are available for "studio quality" dubbing.

With two pictures and two matching sound tracks, the KEM functions as two interlocked editing machines. If the editor wishes to make a cross-cut assembly from two such sync-sound takes, he may cut directly on the machine, ending up with a finished assembly and with his trims assembled in sync too. The editor will find it invaluable to be able to turn to an examination of his trims, which represent a "history" of the cutting of the film; the editor's knowledge and control of his material is first-rate with a KEM.

With a splicer and an editing chair the KEM is a complete editing system: an editing machine, synchronizer, cutting table, hi- and sync-speed rewinds, and high quality sound system all in one. There is no need to move repeatedly back and forth between the editing machine and the cutting table for they are one in this system. The ordinarily separate processes of editing sound and laying in the tracks (to be discussed later in this chapter) can be performed on the table simultaneously, quickly and efficiently, with leader fed from the available transports. Since sound and picture modules are instantly interchangeable, the editor may run up to four sound tracks in sync for laying in music and effects.

The KEM is an impressive (and expensive!) machine; its unique multiple picture potential and the basic ease and efficiency of its operation make it a highly desirable piece of equipment for the busy professional dealing in sound-with-picture work.

The Viewer

Fig. 8–15 Typical cutting room set-up

Fig. 8–16 Moviscope viewer with magnetic
sound head attachment for reading
16mm magnetic film

In the fully-equipped professional cutting room, the viewer is to be regarded as an additional means for viewing film, lacking the sophistication and versatility of the Moviola but possessing two advantages: Film can be run through it at a high rate of speed, and, because of its small size, it can be placed conveniently on an editing table and used in close approximation with a splicer, synchronizer and sound reader (Fig. 8.15). The quickness with which film can be screened with a viewer makes it the ideal means for running through a large quantity of film to find one particular shot. Its use on the editing table, together with additional items of editing room equipment with which we shall deal in this section, offers you alternative ways of performing several of the basic functions of the editing room at the table rather than on the Moviola. Such practices as syncing picture to voice tracks, laying in sound effects, and even the basic editing of the picture itself can be done this way. Once we have presented the operation of the pieces of equipment individually, you will be given some idea of their operation as units. When we enter into the practice of editing, some coverage will be given to the use of the viewer as an alternative to the Moviola, and, of course, we will deal with its use in performing its own special functions.

There is an *on-off light switch* and a *focus knob* (Fig. 8.16). The viewer projects the film image into a viewplate by means of an *optical compensator*, a device which utilizes a revolving glass prism to refract the entering rays of light so that they keep pace with the film as it passes through the viewer. The viewer itself is not powered; the film is run through by means of *rewinds* mounted on the editing table, and it is the motion of the film itself which turns the compensator, the only moving part in the viewer. The compensator's operating speed is governed by the film speed; film can be moved through a viewer at high speed without danger of damaging the film. Because of the speed at which it will be operated, it is important that the viewer be properly aligned between the rewinds so that the film is not twisted as it runs through. The viewer's image is not as clear or as bright as that of the Moviola, but it certainly is possible to follow the action of the film with a viewer. A major disadvantage in actually editing a film (considering the function of editing as determining the rhythm of a film through the length of shot) is that it is quite difficult to run the film at constant sound speed through the viewer since you are running it by hand-cranking the rewinds. This makes it impossible to properly judge the rhythm of the shot, and there is no means of braking the film suddenly at a particular frame to mark it for cutting, as there is on the Moviola. Add to this the relatively poorer image and one has a pretty fair comparison. Now let us mention that some 16mm viewers cost approximately one twenty-fifth the price of a 16–16 Moviola, and allow you a moment to mull that over.

We rate the viewer as an important item of equipment in the cutting room for high-speed scanning of large amounts of film footage and a useful tool for the performing of several editing functions at the table. We also rate it, in combination with a synchronizer and sound reader, as a definite second choice to the Moviola as your basic editing machine—when the factor of cost clearly prohibits your obtaining a Moviola. Within the last year our company performed sound and editorial supervisory services on the official film of the America's Cup Race, produced and directed by Agnew Fisher. Mr. Fisher made the entire original cut (from an enormous quantity of film material shot in a number of locations over a two-year period) using only a viewer. When it came time for our services, there were only some six or seven cutting changes we were able to suggest in running the film on a Moviola—and this on a subject of sailboat racing, requiring both knowledgeable and precise arrangement of shots and strong pacing of the cutting.

Thirty-five millimeter viewers are rarely used; two which are available are the S.O.S. Ediola Professional 35mm Action Viewer (Fig. 8.17), and the A.C.E. 35mm Rotary Viewer. The standard 16mm viewer is the Zeiss-Ikon Moviscop 16mm viewer (Fig. 8.16), available in the standard left-to-right and also right-to-left feeding models. The Moviscop may be used for running original material, as the image does not come in contact with the machine. Precision Laboratories makes two excellent viewers, the Precision 16mm Sr. Viewer (Model PD–16) (Fig. 8.18A and 8.39), and the Precision 16mm Jr. Viewer Editor (Model S–16) (Fig. 8.31). S.O.S. also carries the S.O.S. Super Pro 16mm viewer (Fig. 8.18B), the 16mm Professional Jr. Film Viewer (Fig. 8.18C), the S.O.S. Ediola Professional 16mm Senior Action Viewer (Model M–16–Sr) (Fig. 8.35 and 8.37), and the S.O.S. Ediola Junior 16mm Action Viewer (Model M–16–Jr) (Fig. 8.18D). The S.O.S. Projectola 16mm Professional Viewer (Model LB–1600), (Fig. 8.19A), is unique in that it projects its image either onto its own 6 × 8 inch screen or onto any other screen, although the image decreases in quality above a certain size. There are also viewers made by Moviola, (Fig. 8.19B), Maier-Hancock (the Professional 16mm Viewer/Editor, Model 1600), (Fig. 8.19C), Craig (Pro 16mm Viewer, Model V–46, and Craig Senior 16mm Viewer, Model V–16), and BAIA (BAIA 16mm Viewer). There is quite a range in price and each has its particular traits, so a statement of your particular needs to a large film supply house like F&B/Ceco, which carries all of these, is in order.

Fig. 8–17 SOS Ediola Professional 35mm Action Viewer

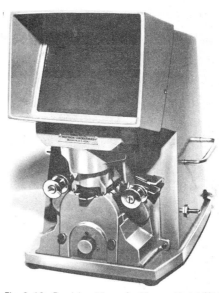
Fig. 8–18a Precision 16mm Sr. Viewer, Model PD 16

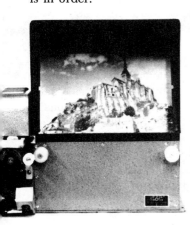

Fig. 8–18b SOS Super Pro 16mm Viewer

Fig. 8–18c 16mm Professional Junior Film Viewer

Fig. 8–18d SOS Ediola Professional 16mm Junior Action Viewer, Model M–16–Jr

Fig. 8-19a SOS Projectola 16mm
Professional Viewer, Model LB-1600

Fig. 8-19b Moviola 16mm Viewer

Fig. 8-19c View-Ed, Professional
16mm Viewer, Model 1600

The Editing Table

The editing table, (Fig. 8.20), comes in a variety of sizes with the usual being 24 to 28 inches wide by 30 to 34 inches high by 60 inches long. Centered in the top of the table—which is made of strong non-scratchable Formica—is a *light box,* a ground glass through which light can be projected from beneath. This is useful for close examination of your film, and the glass is strong enough to place the normal editing table tools directly over it, whether it is in use or not. There is usually a *storage rack* mounted at the back of the table on which small rolls of film can be conveniently stored. Our tables also are mounted with *core dispensers,* 16mm and 35mm, (Fig. 8.15), tall cylinders which contain the plastic cores used as the hub of the *split reels* (described later), and *adjustable lamps* are clamped to each table (Fig. 8.15).

Hollywood Film Company makes a good editing table; so do Neumade, Moviola, Precision, and F&B/Ceco.

Fig. 8-20 Moviola Editing
Table, Model TLRD-1

A rewind is located at the far right and left front edge of the editing table (Fig. 8.15). Their purpose is to wind film from one reel to another, either at high speed or quite slowly as one works on the material. Busy studios have powered rewinds, quite useful in winding vast quantities of material; the ones normally found in a cutting room are cranked by hand. The handle can be engaged or disengaged while the rewind is running at top speed, so it is possible to crank quite hard for several turns, then "coast" until the film slows down, and then engage and crank a few more times. They are geared, of course. One usually winds from the left rewind to the right, using the left hand to continually brake the take-off reel; this ensures a tight wind on the take-up reel and prevents the material from running off the reel, as it will if the take-off reel should run faster than the take-up (Fig. 8.21A&B). Most rewinds can be obtained with a *friction control knob* which can be fitted to the left (take-off) rewind to retard this reel and leave your hand free. Hollywood Film Company has a model with an elbow brake.

There is a shaft protruding from the back of the rewind on which the reels are to be loaded, (Fig. 8.22 A–E). There are models with shafts which can accommodate single reels only, but the most universally useful can handle from one to four reels simultaneously (35mm or 16mm). (The shafts are interchangeable without removing the rewind from the table, by the way.) The base of the shaft next to the rewind body has a protruding piece of metal which engages the slot in the center hole of either 35mm or 16mm reels and locks the reel to the shaft so that it turns as the shaft does. Since this metal piece only extends as far as the first reel, a second reel placed on the shaft would spin freely; subsequent reels are firmly pressed in toward the rewind body by a *spring lock* placed over the end of the shaft after the reels are loaded. *Spacers* (16mm cores can be used as substitutes) are placed between each reel to prevent the sides of the reels from being squeezed together by the spring lock, thus hampering film winding. If more than four 35mm reels are to be handled, a shaft with a *universal joint* is available. When the reels are loaded and the shaft lowered, it rests in a *cradle support* at its far end (Fig. 8.22 B, D).

Fig. 8–21a   Rewinds with multiple and

Fig. 8–21b   single reels, takeup reel on right

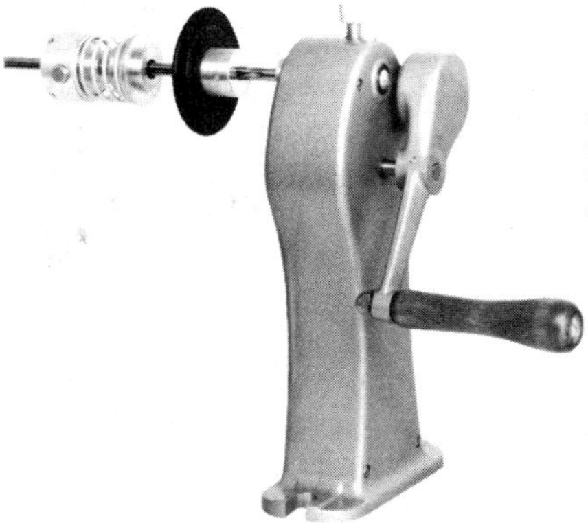

Fig. 8–22a Moviola rewind showing spring clamp and spacer on shaft, friction drag on top of rewind

Fig. 8–22b Moviola rewind with four-reel shaft with universal joint and end support, Model WDUS

Fig. 8–22e Neumade Dynamic Rewinds: left, dynamic geared end with elbow brake, 16mm; right, dynamic geared end, 35mm

Fig. 8–22c Hollywood Film Company Rewind for three 35mm reels

Fig. 8–22d Hollywood Film Company Rewind for four 35mm reels, utilizing universal joint and end support

Fig. 8–23a Hollywood Film Company Rewind with Titewind attachment for 16mm

In order to wind film directly on to a *plastic core,* a technique which allows film to be shipped and/or stored without using a metal reel, a *tightwind* attachment can be placed on the righthand rewind. This is a spring arm with an end roller which guides the film into an even roll (Fig. 8.23 A–C). The plastic core is placed on an *aluminum adaptor* which locks onto the shaft and provides a seat for the plastic core, much as a 45 rpm spindle enlarges the normal spindle of a record player used for $33\frac{1}{3}$ records.

Sometimes, if you are winding at high speed, film starts to spill off, either because it cannot engage properly on the take-up reel or because the take-off reel is running faster than the take-up reel. Prepare yourself for this eventuality by setting in your mind the simple fact that you should, of course, stop the take-up reel *first,* then the take-off. If you grab first for the take-off reel, the film will quite naturally break; sounds simple enough, but it is easy to grab the wrong one in that first moment of panic as the film begins to arch gracefully toward the ceiling. As for "grabbing the reel," we are quite used to stopping reels by pressing them against the rewind which is easy enough to do if the reel has slowed down a bit, (if it's still going top speed, it will burn you, naturally enough). What you must never do is stick your finger into the side of a reel; since all reels are perforated this would compare quite favorably with sticking your finger into an electric fan, and the reel will accommodate you by cutting your finger off.

If you are to rewind a film that has been wound emulsion side *up* onto another reel in which it is to be emulsion side *down,* you can do this either by giving the film a half twist before you attach it to the take-up reel or by turning the take-off reel upside down before feeding the film off. Normally you roll the film off the top of the take-off reel onto the top of the take-up reel (over-over); this suggested method for changing the wind is described as under-over. Incredibly enough, one

Fig. 8–23b Rewinding 35mm film on Moviola Rewind with Titewind and aluminum core adapter

can also wind over-under or under-under, although there is actually no reason for this, unless you are bored with the usual way.

By the way, if you always wind from left to right then you will end up with the film properly loaded on the righthand take-up reel for placing on the Moviola or projector. Some 16mm reels and 16mm and 35mm *split reels* have the interlocking slot for engaging the Moviola or projector spindle on one side only; if you wind to the right rewind, the slot will be properly located when you turn the reel over to load. Sometimes one must wind film that is *"heads out"* off a reel, flip the emulsion, and then wind it back. If you do not want to bother switching reels around between winds, start the take-off reel on the righthand rewind, go to the left and back to the right. Then you will be properly set for Moviola loading.

Fig.8–23c Removing of rewound film from rewind

One last point: There is no difficulty in winding several parallel tracks from take-off reels to side-by-side (and properly spaced) take-up reels, provided you brake *all* of the take-off reels. You will notice that the reels may not wind at the same rate. This presents no problem provided the take-off reels are not clamped together and you place your hand across the top of the take-off reels to hold them all back against the pull (rewinding a bit more slowly than usual). (See Fig. 8.21). If, however, the tracks are running through a synchronizer and the take-up reels are winding up unevenly, film will begin to spill onto the floor and you will have to stop repeatedly to "catch up" the slow-winding take-up reel. This is annoying. Removing the tracks from the synchronizer before rewinding is preferable, but this same problem can occur when you are running tracks forward through a synchronizer. One cause is slippage between take-up reels due to a loose spring clamp; another is a variation in diameter between the center of the take-up reels. To avoid this, always use the same size cores on each reel if using split reels and the same length leader at the head of each track. If you must wind 16mm film with 35mm this problem is almost unavoidable on normal rewinds. However, Hollywood Film Company has a *differential rewind* and "*gimmick*" (that's what they call it!) which can wind up uneven reels of film, even a mixture of 16mm and 35mm (Fig. 8.24A). Moviola also makes a differential rewind (Fig. 8.24B).

Fig. 8-24a Hollywood Film Company differential rewind with "gimmick"

There are some differences between the various makes of rewinds, with Moviola and Hollywood Film Company at the top of the list. Neumade rewinds should also be looked into.

Reels and Split Reels

You should be familiar by now with the film reels that are a part of every cutting room (Fig. 8.24A). In addition to the standard 1,000 foot 35mm size, 100, 500, 2,000, 3,000, and 5,000 foot sizes are available; 16mm reels range from 200 to 2,300 feet. We favor the use of *aluminum split reels*, available in 400, 1,000, 2,000, or 3,000 foot sizes for 35mm, and 400, 800, 1,200, 1,600, and 2,000 foot 16mm sizes. The split reel uses a *plastic core* for its center. (There are a variety of core sizes in both 35mm and 16mm.) One places the core over one side of the reel and winds the other side of the split on. The reel now functions as a normal reel, but after winding film onto it, it can be taken apart and the film removed on its core, thus eliminating the need to use up normal reels (Fig. 8.25). We have found plastic split reels unsatisfactory; the aluminum ones cost more but are indestructible.

Fig. 8-24b Moviola differential rewinds for two reels of either 16mm or 35mm film

If you are handling film on cores, you must be warned against one of the most horrifying (and inevitable) blunders of the cutting room. If you lift up a roll of film on a core without supporting the center from underneath, particularly if the roll is not tightly rolled, a center portion will suddenly drop onto the floor (See Fig. 8.25 A–C). This may not seem like much, but to begin with you will not be able to put the center back. You will then discover that there is no way you can place this separated reel on a rewind, and if you try to rewind by hand, every single turn puts a twist in the film. Once film becomes twisted there is nothing you can do but stretch it out to the end and turn it one turn for each twist, a somewhat laborious task. A friend of ours, a producer of films in Chicago, used to solve this problem by throwing one end of the film out of his sixth floor window and letting it unwind that way—

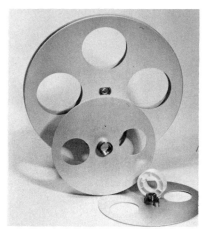

Fig. 8–25a Hollywood Film Company 16mm aluminum split reels

Fig. 8–25b Removing film wound on a core from split reel

Fig. 8–25c Center drop out

until one day the film broke and blew away. Unless you are in a rather high building in a comparatively wind-free city, you are stuck. All you can do is get someone to hold the inner portion and unroll the outside part one turn at a time while turning the roll; if you can break the film into short lengths of one or two hundred feet, it is easier to deal with it. Do not just let the film spill off the outside edge of the roll onto the floor; that's what puts the twist into it. And don't say you weren't warned.

F&B/Ceco carries a variety of reels; Hollywood Film Company also has them. We recommend using steel reels in the cutting room and the plastic only for 16mm release prints.

The Flange

The flange, (Fig. 8.26 A–C), is a device which resembles half a split reel. Its aluminum center core may have a spring tension device for engaging plastic cores. The flange placed on a rewind, is used for wind-

Fig. 8–26a Hollywood Film Company Micarta flanges

Fig. 8–26b Winding film from left rewind spindle to flange on right rewind

Fig. 8–26c (below) Placing film directly on flange without use of core

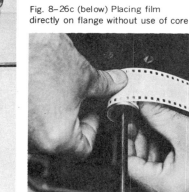

ing film either onto a core or just into a roll with a hole in the center, the way short film and sound film takes are handled. For winding evenly on cores, the best bet is a *companion flange*, or *double flange*, actually a kind of split reel, except that it does not screw together. You can also wind onto a core on the *single flange* if you keep your left hand against the film as it builds against the flange being wound by your right hand. If you are just winding up film on the flange itself, overlap the end of the film by turning it once around the center aluminum core of the flange, hold it firmly, and begin winding, guiding the film against the core with your left hand. Do not wind too fast and watch the film as it approaches the flange; if there is a twist in the film, or a kink or a tangle, stop and straighten it out or the film will break. You can wind up a pretty good length this way, say up to 500 feet of 35mm or 400 feet of 16mm. The roll will simply have a hole in the middle. A number of different-sized flanges are available. For a single flange, we use a 35mm 1,000 foot flange for winding either 16mm or 35mm. Double flanges must be in the appropriate gauge. Neumade makes a variety of flanges with aluminum sides. We have always used the Hollywood Film Company Micarta flange; the side is of a nickproof, indestructible material (Micarta), and contains the spring device so it can handle cored and coreless winding.

Fig. 8-27a Film wound without core

The lefthand end of the Moviola provides you with a *powered flange*. The film is set on the flange just as in the rewinder flange and powered with the foot pedal (*never the switch*) of the Moviola. Use just a touch of the pedal and let the machine coast, then another touch; the same warning holds about watching for any tangle in the film. This is a fast and convenient way of winding up film; however, you cannot wind onto a plastic core for there is no spring device.

Fig. 8-27b Film wound without core

A take wound with a hole in the center can easily be fed into the Moviola, either sound or picture head. Hold the film loosely in your left hand with the center pushed slightly out (Fig. 8.27 A–D) and it will wind out nicely. Do not stick your finger into the middle, because if the center of the film tightens on it the film will not be able to revolve and will pull your hand into the Moviola, which will devour it. For this reason, it is probably best to use the foot pedal rather than the on-off switch when feeding takes in this way. Since even foot pedals have been known to stick (if it does, pump your foot up and down on the pedal in short jabs), set in your mind the fact that the Moviola has a brake on the right-hand side next to the viewplate. Someday you may need to make an instinctive grab for it. *White cotton editing gloves*, which are normal equipment for editors handling negative, are sometimes worn on the left hand when handling film in this way. You can get an occasional burn or scratch from the film, but we handle it this way constantly.

Fig. 8-27c Feeding core-less film into Moviola sound head

If you have played out only a portion of such a roll, you may not want to bother to run it all the way and rewind on a flange. Just poke out the center portion toward your right hand to give you a "handle" (see Fig. 8.27D) and twirl the film back toward you until it is rewound.

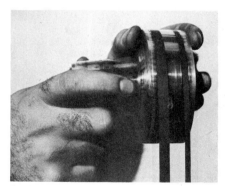

Fig. 8-27d Rewinding core-less film by hand

Synchronizers

Fig. 8–28a Moviola Synchronizer,
two-gang 35mm Model SYB

Fig. 8–28b Moviola Synchronizer,
four-gang 35mm Model SYD

Fig. 8–28c Moviola Synchronizer,
four-gang 16-16-35-35, SYBZB-a

Fig. 8–28d Hollywood Film Company Synchronizer,
four-gang 35-35-16-16, SY235-216

The synchronizer is a measuring machine (Fig. 8.28 A–F). It consists of a *sprocketed wheel* or wheels revolving smoothly in a frame which can be set on an editing table; a *round wheel* is attached to the front end of the drive shaft so that the sprocket wheels can be turned by hand, forward or backward. There is a *brake* fitted next to the front wheel which can lock the entire revolving portion of the machine at a fixed point. On the top of each sprocket wheel is a *clamp* holding two *rollers;* when the clamp is released by the *catch* holding it in place against the sprocket wheel, it springs up. Film is then placed on top of the sprocket wheel, and the clamp locked down, holding the film firmly against the sprocket wheel so that as the film is moved forward or backward the sprocket wheel is revolved. Against the front of the sprocket wheel is a movable *frame disc,* a dial which measures the frames of the film as the roller revolves. The disc contains the number of frames in a foot (forty in 16mm, sixteen in 35mm), so that each complete revolution of the sprocket wheel and its dial counts out one foot of film which has passed through the synchronizer. Most synchronizers read from left to right, that is, film is inserted from the left and winds through to the right. However, they are available on special order reading from right to left. The film having been clamped onto the sprocket wheel, the disc is turned until the "zero" frame lies under your starting point on the film. Attached to the front of the typical machine is a *footage counter.* As each complete revolution of the wheel is made, one foot registers consecutively on the counter.

If one is trying to find particular footage in a film, let us say 80 feet, the reel of film is placed on the lefthand rewind on an editing table and the film fed across to the righthand take-up reel. The start mark is placed in the synchronizer (by releasing and then setting the clamp) and the film moved forward on the take-up reel by turning the righthand rewind. One simply watches the footage counter until 80 feet registers; the film is stopped at this point—the front wheel is turned for exact spotting—with the "zero" frame on the dial straight up under the film. The frame of the film above the "zero" frame on the dial is exactly 80 feet on the film. If you are seeking 80 feet, ten frames (usually written 80′ 10″ or 80.10) the film is then moved forward until the "ten" frame on the dial is at the top; the frame of film above this is 80 feet, ten frames, (Fig. 8.29).

Film can be moved quite rapidly through a synchronizer to locate a particular point in the film quickly and easily. Since the film can be moved at high speed, the synchronizer should always be set in exact alignment with the rewinds and with no twist in the film. Footage counters can be for either 35mm or 16mm, or for individual frames (useful in animation work). There are also high-speed footage counters, combination footage and frame counters, and time counters (hours, minutes, seconds). More than one counter can be mounted on a synchronizer.

Each "channel" of a synchronizer, referred to as a *gang,* will take one reel of film, so the synchronizer is used for running several reels of film in exact sync. If several reels are handled, they will be loaded on the rewinds as discussed previously (page 271). Synchronizers are available for 16mm, 35mm, Vistavision, Cinerama, 65mm, 70mm, 35/32mm, 8mm or videotape, and can have from one to six gangs. Since a multiple gang synchronizer can be used to run a single reel as well as several, the same reasoning we have applied earlier to Moviolas and rewinds holds true here: Select the combination that will give you the maximum possible usage. Probably the most useful single combination would be a four-gang, two 16mm, two 35mm, machine (see Fig. 8.28C). This would enable you to run a 16mm picture with a 16mm voice track and two 35mm soundtracks, a common combination. Such a synchronizer could be mounted with both 16mm and 35mm footage counters and should contain a lever which can disengage the 35mm gangs from the 16mm gangs, enabling them to be run separately as well as together. Since it is not unusual for a film to have more than two 35mm soundtracks which required syncing up, a four-gang 35mm synchronizer is also useful. Our studio also has two-gang 35s and four-gang 16s since these suit our particular requirements.

The synchronizer can also be used for reading sound. For this purpose either *magnetic* or *optical attachments* can be mounted on the gangs of the machine. A sound head mounted on a synchronizer can be plugged in to play through the amplifier of a *sound reader* (to be covered next), or through a *tape reader amplifier*. Should you choose to use the latter, you will be limited to picking up the sound as the track passes through the synchronizer; with the sound reader, you can do this or read your tracks by passing them directly through the reader itself (Fig. 8.30 A&B). Readers cost a good deal more than the tape reader amplifiers. The reader does not have a sprocketed, clamped channel—the film is held on the reader by looping it under rollers—so it is impossible to run the sound film in exact sync with other tracks unless a synchronizer is used in combination with the reader. This is a common practice and you will often see the sound reader set up next to the synchronizer, the track running through the two pieces of equipment consecutively. However, your best bet would seem to be to use the synchronizer with mag-

Fig. 8–28e Hollywood Film Company Synchronizer, single-gang 16, SY–116

Fig. 8–28f Neumade 16mm Showmaster Model SM–161, one gang

Fig. 8–29 Finding 80 feet, ten frames with a synchronizer

Fig. 8–30a Reading sound with the sound reader

Fig. 8–30b Reading sound with the magnetic pick-up attachment of a synchronizer sound reader used as an amplifier

Fig. 8–30c Mixer unit plugged into precision sound reader allowing two magnetic heads to feed sound simultaneously

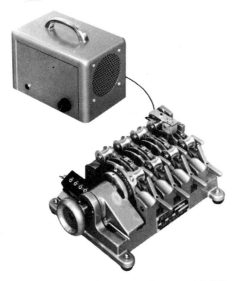

Fig. 8–31a Moviola Synchronizer, four gang 16–SZD

Fig. 8–31b Hollywood Film Company Amplifier/Speaker with magnetic pick-up attachment for HFC Synchronizer

Fig. 8–32 Precision Unitized Sychronizer expanded showing component parts

*Mixing units are available; the separate sound heads on each gang can then be plugged into the mixing unit and the unit plugged into the tape reader amplifier (Fig. 8.30C).

netic and/or optical attachments, feeding into a tape reader amplifier. This is a lot less awkward than the side-by-side arrangement, under which the film keeps slipping off the rollers. Also, you can run as many as three tracks through the synchronizer,° while the sound reader can handle only one at a time.

Moviola makes an excellent synchronizer, available with optical and magnetic attachments, and also can supply an amplifier-speaker into which they can be plugged, (Fig. 8.31A). Hollywood Film Company also makes a first-rate synchronizer and a comparable amplifier-speaker (Fig. 8.31B) but they appear to offer only magnetic attachments for the synchronizer. Neumade's synchronizers offer no sound pick-up attachments. The magnetic heads on both Moviola and HFC synchronizers are identical to the magnetic heads on Moviolas; like the Moviola heads, they too should be flipped up when not in use.

We strongly recommend looking into the Precision "Unitized" Synchronizer (Fig. 8.32). While all synchronizers come in various combinations of gangs, only Precision offers one which can be purchased as a basic unit (one gang, the front wheel, and a counter), and then added to using basic tools in your own cutting room as you purchase more gangs, either 35mm or 16mm. While we have no complaint about Moviola and HFC synchronizers, having used both for years, the Precision synchronizer is a beautiful piece of equipment, and this "add-on" feature is an excellent idea.

Precision has intelligently chosen to add its magnetic sound attachment heads (their optical attachment is similar to Moviola's) reading up instead of down. This enables the editor to run his sound tracks *emulsion down*, thus allowing him to write on the *back* (base) of the film, where grease pencil marks will not come in contact with the sound heads. Writing on sound film with grease pencils is quite common, but should *never* be done where the marks will be scraped off by sound heads, particularly during the sound mix. The grease clogs the head, with an immediate loss of sound quality resulting. One disadvantage of the up-mounted heads is that they cannot be flipped when not in use, but this is not a major problem. Both Hollywood and HFC have left a space in the center of their gangs so that, when the synchronizer is placed over the cutting table's light well, one can see the individual frames clearly when they are in the synchronizer. Precision's gangs do not allow this, so one must examine the frames to either side of the synchronizer. Again, this is not a major problem, but you should be aware of it. By the way, since you may wish to run single-perf 16mm film on a synchronizer, all 16mm gangs are made with single sprockets, usually with the teeth farthest away from the operator. (If you wish it otherwise, you must specify this in ordering.) All companies offer to make up their synchronizers in any combination you wish; remember that you must specify the order in which you wish the gangs. That is, a four-gang synchronizer with two 16mm and two 35mm gangs could have the front two gangs 16mm and the back two 35mm, or vice versa (see Fig. 8.28C). Decide what you want and order it.

You have undoubtedly noticed that the synchronizer with sound reader attachments has begun to approximate the Moviola in function; that is, it can run tracks in sync, measure them on a counter, and reproduce their sound, both optical and magnetic. The only lack is a means of viewing the film in motion and a way of running the film at sync speed, since we are running the film through the synchronizer by hand-cranked rewinds. The former can be accomplished by placing a viewer next to the synchronizer; the latter problem is taken care of by installing a *synchronous drive motor* on the synchronizer (see Fig. 8.33 A&B). This powers the tracks through at sound speed (twenty-four frames per second), the editor having only to take up the slack by slowly turning the righthand rewind. Moviola, HFC, and Precision offer such motors; once again, the Precision motor is particularly fine, easily attached, and runs soundlessly. Whichever you choose, check to see if the film can be stopped easily without tearing it and if the motor drive can be easily disconnected in order to back up the film or run it freely. Precision's drive can be added to the "unitized" machine in your cutting room.

There are a number of "combination units" available for 16mm picture work—various arrangements of synchronizer, sound reader, and/or viewer—best obtained with a base which interlocks the items together securely. Check these out to see which best suits your particular purpose; equipment rental houses carry all of them, so they are an excellent source for comparison. To select properly, you will need some idea of what you will be dealing with.

Film sound is either *double-system* or *single-system:* In double-system the sound track is separate from the picture; in single-system the sound is printed on the picture itself. Virtually all professional film sound is shot in double-system, allowing picture and sound to be edited separately, although single-system is often used for newsreel work, since it allows a simpler equipment set-up. (The release print is made in single-system, since the track is made a permanent part of the picture.) The release print soundtrack is *advanced* twenty-six frames (twenty in 35mm) ahead of the picture. This means that double-system sound pick-up will be parallel to the picture (in what we call *editorial sync*), while single-system sound pick-up will be advanced the appropriate number of frames in front of the picture, in *lab* or *projection sync*. To deal with single-system sound in these combination units, one places the sound pick-up device at the side of the viewing device, spaced the required number of frames ahead. Double-system sound is invariably *magnetic* sound; single-system may be magnetic (some release prints employ *magnetic striping* and "newsreel" filming is done on magnetic single-system also) but is more frequently *optical* sound. What are the conclusions?

If you are concerned with reading composite prints (release prints) you need a unit which can read single-system, almost totally in optical sound.* If you are working on "newsreel" type, *single-system filming* material, you need a single-system unit, probably magnetic. If you are to work with normal *double-system sound,* you need a double-system unit that can pick up magnetic sound; and, you will need to be able to

The Combination Unit

Fig. 8–33a Moviola Synchronizer, four-gang 16SZD with magnetic pick-up

Fig. 8–33b Precision Unitized Synchronizer, two-gang Model S616–2SP with decoupler and Model SYN–1051 synchronizer drive motor

Fig. 8–34 Precision Film Editor consisting of viewer Model S–16 16mm Jr. Sound Reader 800 RL, Base-Model 1100

*Magnetic sound tracks are found on some Cinemascope, Cinerama, M.G.M. 65, Techniscope, Technirama, Panavision, and Todd-AO release prints—all wide-screen systems.

read multiple sound tracks. Occasionally you will have to deal with two pictures with their respective double-system sound tracks (as, for example, in an interview scene filmed with two cameras). Now let's examine the units available.

SINGLE SYSTEM SOUND

Fig. 8–35 SOS Ediola Professional 16mm single system sync viewer-reader

Fig. 8–36 SOS Ediola Professional 35mm Action Viewer with Optical Sounder Reader and base

PRECISION FILM EDITOR   Consists of a Viewer Model S–16, a Model 800RL Optical-Magnetic Sound Reader locked in the proper frame-advance relationship on a base (Fig. 8.34). Fine for single-system, optical or magnetic. Although no synchronizer is a part of this unit, one can be placed on either side for precise measurement of the film.

PRECISION MOVISCOP-SOUND READER UNIT   Very similar to the above; if you own the Moviscop and/or Precision Sound Reader, you need only buy the base and whichever unit you are lacking. Can utilize either the 600RL Optical Sound Reader or the 800RL Optical-Magnetic Sound Reader, depending upon your needs. Like the above, no synchronizer is included, but one could be used in connection with it.

S.O.S. EDIOLA PROFESSIONAL 16MM SINGLE-SYSTEM SYNC VIEWER-READER   Quite similar to the above, but utilizing the S.O.S. Ediola Professional 16mm Action Viewer with a Precision Sound Reader, Model 600RL, 700 or 800RL (Fig. 8.35). Available in Optical Only (Model AO), Magnetic Only (Model AM) or Optical/Magnetic (Model AOM) versions. Again no synchronizer is included, but may be added. It is also possible to purchase components separately.

S.O.S. JUNIOR EDIOLA VIEWER-READER   Exactly like the above, but utilizing the S.O.S. Ediola Junior 16mm Action Viewer. Models BO (optical only), BM (magnetic only), and BOM (optical/magnetic).

S.O.S EDIOLA PROFESSIONAL 35MM ACTION VIEWER WITH OPTICAL SOUND READER AND BASE   The only combination unit dealing with 35mm single-system (Fig. 8.36). Optical only, no synchronizer (but can be added) but can mount a footage and frame counter on the viewer. With the added synchronizer mounting a mag pick-up head, the system can handle double-system sound.

DOUBLE-SYSTEM SOUND

Fig. 8–37 16mm Magniola Model AC/B, two-gang Moviola synchronizer with over-reading mag sound head on first gang—for double system sound reading only

16MM MAGNIOLA DOUBLE- AND/OR SINGLE-SYSTEM SOUND MAGNETIC EDITORS   These consist of (1) a 16mm ground-glass viewer, (2) a two-gang Moviola synchronizer, (3) magnetic sound heads on synchronizer, (4) an amplifier-speaker combination, (5) a base interlocking viewer and synchronizer in projection sync (Fig. 8.37). There are twelve models available, six (1 through 6) with a standard base assembly and six (11 through 16) with a special transistorized base with simplified wiring and a more powerful speaker-amplifier system. All twelve models may be obtained with a motorized base, capable of driving the unit at sound speed. Owners of component parts can purchase just what is needed to complete the unit. The difference in models is between the mounting of the magnetic sound heads on the two gangs; either or both may be mounted reading up or down. Models 1, 2, 11, 12 are for double-system editing only; Models 3, 4, 5, 6, 13, 14, 15, and 16 are for both single- and double-system.

S.O.S. PROJECTOLA-MAGNIOLA HIGH-SPEED EDITING OUTFIT Much like the basic Magniola with two important differences (Fig. 8.38). The Projectola has replaced the ground-glass viewer (meaning an image can be projected for easier viewing) and there is available an optical sound head in addition to the magnetic sound heads. Other than this the components are similar, consisting of a two-gang synchronizer (Precision this time instead of Moviola as in the Magniola) with magnetic sound heads, an amplifier-speaker, and an interlocking base. Also available is the motorized base for driving the unit at sound speed. Models 21 and 22 are for double-system editing only, Models 23, 24, 25, and 26 for double- and single-system editing (with the usual varieties of up and down reading sound heads), and Model 31 is for single- and double-system magnetic and optical editing, the only unit that can do everything. By the way, this unit is made by Precision (their basic unit is called the *Model S616–2SP with Projectola Viewer, amplifier and speaker*), so it could be obtained directly from them. Once again, if you own a portion of the unit, check into buying just what you need additionally.

PRECISION FILM EDITOR MODEL PFE 910 A simpler unit (Fig. 8.39), but worth including, it consists of Model PD 16 Professional 16mm Viewer locked in editorial sync on a base with a Model S616–2S unitized two-gang synchronizer. The synchronizer contains up-reading magnetic heads; a synchronous drive motor can be supplied. Since the viewer is mounted behind the synchronizer it is easy to thread a 16mm picture and two accompanying soundtracks. A sound reader or tape reader amplifier is needed into which to plug the sound heads.

S.O.S. PIC-SYNC A synchronizer with various combinations of picture and magnetic sound pick-up directly from the gangs (Figs. 8.40–42). The viewplate is mounted directly on the synchronizer, and while the image is small, the unit is surprisingly compact. A unique model is available with two viewplates, making it the only unit short of a two-picture head Moviola (expensive and rarely found) capable of handling two pictures and their respective soundtracks simultaneously. Available with single and multiple playback amplifier-speaker and in 16mm, 35mm and 16/35mm combination formats. The Model P–2–F can handle one picture and one magnetic soundtrack; the Model P–4–F will take one picture and three magnetic soundtracks; the Model 2P–4–F will handle two pictures and two magnetic soundtracks. Basically a double-system editor, it can be used with a sound reader for single-system.

You will learn a variety of uses for the synchronizer in the editing room. We will at this time point out only a general idea of its functions. Any editing work requiring the matching of picture to picture or sound to picture can be performed on a synchronizer. Often initial stages of the work will be performed on the Moviola (cuing) and then transferred

Fig. 8–38 SOS Projectola-Magniola High Speed Editing Outfit

Fig. 8–39 Precision Film Editor Model PFE 910

Fig. 8–40 Pic-Sync-Model 35–P–4–F, 35mm four gang: first gang picture; second, third, and fourth gangs magnetic sound film

Fig. 8-41 Four sprocket 16mm synchronizer: permits editing of picture and three sound tracks

Fig. 8-42 Four sprocket 16mm synchronizer: complete editing system permits editing of A and B rolls and two sound tracks

Fig. 8-43a Moviola Sound Reader Model SRC

Fig. 8-43b Closer view of Moviola Sound Reader Model SRC

The Sound Reader

Fig. 8-43c Moviola Sound Reader Model SRM, magnetic sound only in up-reading position

to the synchronizer (laying in). Used in combination with a viewer and sound reader and mounting a synchronous drive motor, the synchronizer unit offers the editor many of the advantages of the Moviola at considerably less cost. Obviously this is true for 16mm work, but this is precisely where it is needed. Chances are it is the 16mm film-maker who needs to keep his costs down; more important, the 16mm Moviola is not a first-rate machine, particularly in its treatment of the film. Some editing functions are better performed on the table with a splicer close at hand. With all of these arguments, we must acknowledge that we still use the 16mm Moviola for most of our own work and that any potential professional film-maker must learn to use it. If budget demands require you to start with the combination unit in 16mm work, you can still do a fine job; but take every opportunity to master the Moviola, as insurance against your future work. We use the combination unit for syncing voice tracks to picture and laying in sound effects. The viewer is used for locating specific takes among a mass of material and breaking out music takes from a mass. We prefer the Moviola for rhythmic editing of picture, music and effects cuing, and cutting voice tracks, but virtually all of our laying in of tracks is done on the table.

The sound reader is a device consisting of an amplifier-speaker, a volume control, and a means of picking up optical and/or magnetic sound from film. The standard model is made by Precision Laboratories (Fig. 8.30). Models that read both left to right and right to left are available and only slightly more expensive than the standard left to right model. The Model 600RL is for optical only, 700 for magnetic only, and 800RL for optical and magnetic. Our usual advice holds: Get the combination for versatility. As you know, readers can be used as the amplifier-speaker system for magnetic sound heads placed on the synchronizer. All readers are easily threaded by using common sense. Moviola also puts out a sound reader (SRM) magnetic only, (SRB) optical only (and SRC for both) (Fig. 8.43 A–D). The Precision readers will handle 16mm and 35mm;

with the Moviola readers, you must specify the models that will handle both 16mm and 35mm. Soundtracks run on a reader, or on the synchronizer with pick-up heads, can be moved back and forth carefully for accurate location of a sound, a most useful function. For high-speed or continuous operation, rewinds are used. Although the reader or sound-synchronizer is the better place for locating specific sounds, the Moviola or sound dubber is preferable for judging sound quality, particularly if you lack a synchronous drive motor on the synchronizer. Hand power on rewinds is not the best way to attempt to run sound at synchronous speed. Your main consideration in buying a reader should be its use in relationship to other units in combination. If you are going to work off of sound heads on a synchronizer, a tape reader amplifier is cheaper and will do the job. If you are going to use a combination unit like the Projectola-Magniola, you will obtain a reader as part of the unit. Readers should come with earphone jacks so you can work with complete concentration, undisturbed by and not disturbing the other people around you.

Fig. 8–43d Moviola Sound Reader Model SRB, optical sound only with amplifier/speaker

Splicers

There are two general categories of splicers: *tape* and *cement* (the latter usually are "hot splicers"). Each come in the various gauges or combinations of them. There is one further distinction: There are both *diagonal* and *straight cut* splicers. Straight cut are used for picture splicing, diagonal for sound.

TAPE SPLICERS

The function of the tape splicer is the making of a temporary splice. Tape splices can be quickly made and easily taken apart. Taped on the *base side only*, tape splices, usually diagonal, are always used for sound editing. For splicing of the picture work print, the tape splicer has almost completely replaced the cement splicer, and we certainly have always worked this way. Naturally, only straight across splices will be used for picture splicing. Some editors initially splice only the emulsion side of a work print; we splice both sides as soon as the film is reasonably "set." With only one side spliced the film will "hinge" as it passes through the drive mechanism of projection machines, and, considering the repeated projections the work print will go through, the double splice is a lot more secure, even if it takes a few moments more.

The major drawback of the tape splice is that it is not invisible. A properly made (and this is important) tape splice will run through projection machines smoothly, and it is probably even stronger in the long run than hot splices, which have been known to come apart on occasion, usually important ones. When each tape splice passes through the projection machine, the film goes slightly out of focus and the edge of the tape can actually be seen. This is not a deterrent to using tape splices for a work print, and one becomes so used to it that it is virtually unnoticeable, particularly on a Moviola. When projected on a large screen, it becomes a bit more obvious but this really is not a sufficient reason for

Fig. 8-44b Rivas-Cunningham Perforated Tape Splicer, 16mm straight-across using transparent tape for splicing picture

Fig. 8-44c Rivas-Cunningham Perforated Tape Splicer, 16mm diagonal using opaque tape for splicing sound

Fig. 8-44a Rivas-Cunningham Perforated Tape Splicer, 35mm diagonal using opaque tape for splicing sound

Fig. 8-45 Hollywood Film Company Perforated Tape Splicer, 35mm straight-across using transparent tape for splicing picture

giving up the advantages of this form of splicing of your work print. It is a good reason for not using tape splices on release prints.

Splicing tape (Permacel and Mylar are the two brands we use) can be *clear (transparent)* for film splicing or *opaque* for sound film splicing. The clear is a bit thinner, which makes up for the two thicknesses used in the straight across picture splice, so one should always use the opaque for sound editing. Both clear and opaque come *perforated* and *non-perforated,* depending on the type of splicer to be used, and there are single- and double-perf varieties for 16mm. Perforated tape is quite expensive—five times the cost of non-perf—and this is one pretty good argument for using the type of splicer that uses non-perf tape. These splicers perforate the tape themselves to exactly match the film sprocket holes. (Sixteen millimeter splicers must be made to handle both single- and double-perf film; in effect this means they work single-perf, since a double-perf operation would punch holes in the unsprocketed side of the single sprocket film when placed on the splicer.)

PERFORATED TAPE SPLICER We use both the Rivas Cunningham Splicer (recognizable by its black steel base) (Fig. 8.44 A–C), and a similar machine made by Hollywood Film Company (Fig. 8.45); both are excellent. Each has 16mm and 35mm types, and both of these are available in straight across and diagonal models. All of these use perforated tape, either clear or opaque.

These splicers are quite simple to operate, but the splice should always be made carefully (Fig. 46 A–D). If the tape and film perfora-

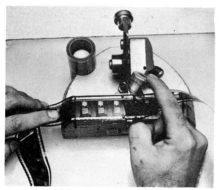

Fig. 8-46a Film to be seated across registration pins by downward flip of tape-tearer lever

Fig. 8-46b Cutting film with knife blade

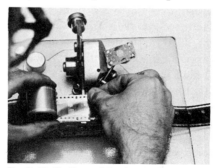

Fig. 8-46c Seating splicing tape across film sprocket holes and registration pins

tions do not match properly, the film can jam on a projecting machine and will then usually break. The roll of tape rests on a *spindle* on the back of the splicer. Film to be cut is laid across the *registration pins* and seated properly on them by flipping down the tape tearer lever. Then the *knife blade* is lowered sharply, slicing the film. (Too hard a blow will damage the knife blade, so use just enough force to cut the film cleanly.) The tape end from the roll is laid across the film with the roll held in the left hand, located just over the middle four (two in 16mm) registration pins and then the tape tearer is flipped down with the right hand, seating the tape firmly on the film, over the pins. If the tape has been held correctly initially, the lever will seat it properly, with both sets of sprocket holes aligned. Now the tearing lever is held down with the right hand and the tape torn off against the saw-tooth edge of the lever which faces your left. (Some splicers tear easily from top to bottom, some bottom to top. Check this carefully on the first splice.) Now smooth out any air bubbles trapped between the tape and film. If the other side of the film is to be spliced, turn the film over and repeat the process (with 35mm). With 16mm single sprocket film the single row of registration pins would puncture the non-perf side if you merely turned the film toward you. Turn the film end-for-end as you flip it to properly engage the pins.

There is one simple little error which will nag you in the cutting room unless you give a bit of thought to it. It is very easy in splicing film to splice together one shot with the emulsion up, the other with it down, thus reversing the image. This happens because it is difficult to tell the emulsion from the base when you are working rapidly. It is actually necessary to hold the film up to the light at an angle to spot the emulsion side, and this takes time. There are three simple ways to tell the two sides apart. If you have had the 16mm print edgenumbered, the yellow serial numbers will be on the base side; so if you look down and see numbers on one side of the splice and not the other, you are set up wrong. With 35mm, the latent image numbers are harder to see and

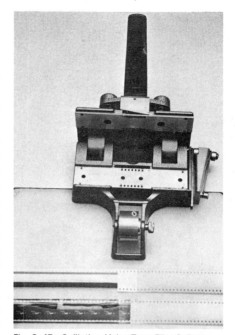

Fig. 8–47a Guillotine Mylar Tape Film Splicer, 35mm, capable of straight and diagonal splice with transparent and opaque tape

Fig. 8–46d Using tearing lever to tear off tape

Fig. 8–47b Guillotine Mylar Tape Film Splicer, 16mm, capable of straight and diagonal splice with transparent and opaque tape

Fig. 8–48 Hollywood Film Company Non-perforated Tape Splicer, straight splice only

Fig. 8–49 Splicing blocks, 35mm and 16mm

so less useful. There is also a curl to film—in toward the emulsion side—which can be spotted, particularly in 35mm. Another simple method is to touch the film with your lips or tongue; the emulsion side is sticky; just a touch of moisture will do.

THE GUILLOTINE SPLICER Supposedly introduced into the American film-making establishment by the technicians who worked on *Cleopatra* in Rome (you will recall that they had an excess of time for technical experimentation during the making of that much-discussed production), this is an excellent splicer (Fig. 8.47 A–B) for two reasons: One, it uses the much cheaper non-perf tape; and two, one splicer can make both a straight and a diagonal splice. We must confess that while we use these (especially for 16mm picture editing) and find them fast and efficient, they do not always successfully clear out the perforations nor the edge of the tape on the sides of the film. The film will run satisfactorily forward on the Moviola, but will jam while reversing; it simply will not run on a projector properly. One way of getting around this infamous backward-jamming tendency of the Moviola is to open the gate while reversing and just leave the film engaged by the two sprocket wheels on either side of the gate. Projecting a film with these splices is a nightmare; seventy-five percent of them will jam in the projector gate. We keep a razor blade handy to trim the sides of the tape from the film. Before projecting, check each splice carefully to see if the perforations are fully cleared of tape or if the tape has just "hinged" through. If so, trim the hinges before projection. It may take a couple of hours, but it's better than stumbling into the projection room for an important screening with a print that looses its loop and flutters all over the screen at every cut. The Guillotine, in contrast to the indestructible perforated tape splicer, must be serviced regularly.

On this splicer the cut is made at the righthand side of the splicer with either the *diagonal cutting* or *straight cutting guillotine blade* and the film is then moved to the middle of the splicer for taping. This splicer also has registration pins. The roll of non-perf tape rolls off away from you from a center roll and is laid across the top of the film at right angles. If you are careful to stick both ends of the tape on the splicer's cross bars, either side of the film, it will cut cleanly. Lower the hinged top of the splicer by the handle and punch the handle down; this will perforate the tape and cut it off. Then turn the film over if a second-side splice is required. (The same provision mentioned in connection with the previous splicer holds with 16mm single-perf film: you must turn it end-for-end while flipping it.)

Hollywood Film Company also makes non-perforated tape splicers (Fig. 8.48) which they call *Repair Splicers;* also an *Automatic Tape Splicer.* We have found the Guillotine Splicer useful, but you might check out the Hollywood Film Company type also.

One further suggestion on splicing in general. After the machine has made the splice, always use your fingers to rub the tape down firmly on the film (get all air bubbles out from under the tape) so that the tape is really firmly seated; if you do this initially the splice will hold forever.

THE SPLICING BLOCK   The principle disadvantage to this perforated-tape-using splicer is its slowness of operation, for the section of tape to be used for each splice must be cut by hand (Fig. 8.49). It is a sturdy and indestructible splicer which costs very little. A razor blade is used to cut the film. It is of questionable value in the advanced professional cutting room requiring fast volume work. If it is all you can afford, you can certainly make do with it in assembling a work print. Available in 16mm and 35mm versions, it can cut picture (straight across) or sound (diagonal).

To sum up: The cheapest effective splicer is the splicing block. The best sound splicer is the Rivas-Cunningham–HFC perforated tape splicer. The best 16mm picture splicer, having the advantage of low-cost tape but the disadvantage of requiring fairly frequent service, is the Guillotine. For 35mm picture, the Guillotine has some operating deficiencies, but is inexpensive to operate because of the tape. If you can afford only one splicer to do both sound (diagonal) and picture (straight across) cutting, the Guillotine is the answer, particularly in 16mm.

Hollywood Film Company and Maier-Hancock make excellent table model hot splicers (See Fig. 13.6). Also check the Stancocine and Harwald models. These use cement for welding the film together into a permanent, comparatively invisible splice which must be used for release prints and negative splicing; but such splicing is a waste of time for work print slicing. Hollywood Film makes a combination 8mm and 16mm, a 70mm, a combination 35mm and 70mm, a combination 16mm, 35mm, 70mm, and a combination 16mm and 35mm. Maier-Hancock makes a 16/35 and an 8/16 combination. They both operate similarly.

THE GRISWOLD SPLICER   This is a *cement*, but not a *hot*, splicer (Fig. 8.50). It is far from ideal, and we would not recommend its use for splicing original material, but it is a useful, inexpensive piece of equipment for the beginner. Available in 8mm–16mm and 35mm versions, it is a picture (straight cut) splicer. An enormous number of Griswolds have been sold; they are found in many projection booths.

HOT SPLICERS   A basic difference between the tape splice and the cement splice is that in the tape splice *(butt splice)* the ends of the two pieces of film to be joined abut each other, while in the cement splice *(lap splice)* a small portion of the film overlaps. The film cement is used to partly dissolve the base (the emulsion must be first scraped off the portion of film which overlaps) so that the result is literally a weld. This process works better if the splice is warm when it is made, hence the "hot" splicer, which is best kept plugged in all day (some in frequent use are kept plugged in by the week), since it takes some time to properly warm up.

Hot splicers are also available in foot-operated models (Bell & Howell models are sometimes available "used" from F&B/Ceco, and HFC makes a model). Once fairly common, they are used less often today, usually by veteran editors for large-volume work.

CEMENT SPLICERS

Fig. 8–50 Griswold Splicer, 35mm

Fig. 8-51 Hollywood Film Company bin

Film Bins

Fig. 8-52 Moviola Film bin

Fig. 8-53 F & B/Ceco film barrell

The actual operation of the hot splicer will be covered in Chapter 13, pages 477–479. Its main use is in splicing negative (or camera original), and release prints.

One additional point to remember in the cutting room. When splicing 16mm, in order to gain sufficient material to make the necessary overlap, a portion of the next adjoining frame must be used; that is, you *lose a frame* with each splice. You must keep this in mind when you are editing your work print. Do not start with the very first (nor end with the last) frame of a shot, particularly following a *flash frame* or frame with *light flare* on it. Always cut off the first three or four frames as a matter of course. Likewise, if you are going to use succeeding portions of a shot in separate scenes of your film, you cannot expect to use the adjoining frames at the cut since at least one extra frame at each end will be lost when the negative is spliced. Again, chopping off a few frames as a matter of course before using a succeeding portion of a shot will avoid this problem.

Film bins are made from steel or sturdy composition material, can be circular or rectangular, and are equipped with a *cloth liner* which fits over the top edge and completely fills the bin (Fig. 8.51). The liner is important in keeping the bin clean, and this is necessary since quite often the film lies on the bottom of the bin. (The film bin should never be treated as a waste basket; therefore, the investment in a *waste basket* is an important step in setting up a cutting room. Not only should trash and cigarettes (!) be kept out of the bin but also discarded pieces of splicing tape, which will stick to any film in the bin, and small pieces of film which are obviously to be thrown away.) The liner should be replaced periodically. We keep a couple of bins without racks just for discarded film; particularly in sound editing, quite a large amount of discarded film can accumulate, and it would quickly overflow an ordinary wastebasket. Scrap film rolled up on a flange before throwing it away takes up far less room in a trash barrel.

A principal use for the film bin is in cataloguing film. For this purpose the bins come equipped with *racks* with rows of *pins* or *hooks* sticking out from each side (Fig. 8.52). Some racks are double-tiered and so can hold twice as much film; these are recommended. The hook or straight pin type are equally useful; however, check to see that 16mm sprocket holes slip easily over the pin. If they must be pushed down on the pin with effort this will cause you a lot of wasted time in getting the film on and off the pins.

When you start to break out film, (Fig. 8.53), take a strip of masking tape and stick it across the rack above the pins. Now you can label the takes on each pin without writing on the film itself; this will be much easier to read quickly, in locating the wanted take. When you lift off the head of a take from its pin, often the end of the take is snarled in the mass of material in the bottom of the bin. Pull the take out carefully or the film will break; if it does, you will have difficulty locating the broken portion. About all you can do is to take every other take in the bin, a few at a time and pull them out hand-over-hand and put the ends in other bins placed next to the original bin. (Their heads can be left on the pins in the original bin.) When they have all been pulled out, the broken-off portion should be the only thing left in the bin.

A piece of masking tape should be placed over the end of each pin when it is loaded with takes as they have a way of dropping off into the bin from time to time. When leaving a bin overnight, hold the takes on with a rubber band stretched across the row of pins. Whenever you finish a work print you will have left-over material still hanging in the bin. You may not want to roll it up and store it until later when you finish the negative matching, in case changes are made. If this is so, take a few minutes to check each bin as outlined above; there might just be a marvelous forgotten shot on the bottom of one of the bins, and you should check this before the picture is locked in.

To avoid the problem of tangling in the bin, it is suggested that you roll any long takes up on a flange, label them and catalogue them in separate *film cans* or *boxes*, using the bin only for comparatively short takes.

Hollywood Film Company, Moviola and F&B/Ceco all make film bins.

Fig. 8-55 Plastic reel and case

Film Cans, Boxes and Fiber Cases

With the replacement of the highly explosive nitrate base film by today's safety film—acetate base—the ubiquitous film can has begun to disappear from the cutting room. Cardboard boxes and fiber cases (the cases are also excellent for carrying or shipping) have appeared in the cutting room (along with cigarettes) as the great danger of a flash fire has vanished. The fiber cases have carrying handles and are excellent for crosstown travel. Single reel sizes are useful for release prints, while multireel sizes are excellent for carrying the number of reels one needs for a sound mix (Fig. 8.54 A&B).

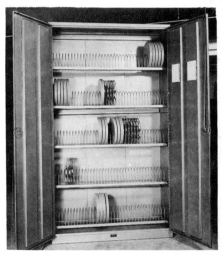
Fig. 8-56a Hollywood Film Company Film Cabinet with dividers

Fig. 8-54a Goldberg 35mm four-reel metal shipping case for 2000-foot reels

Fig. 8-54b Fibre shipping cases and cardboard film boxes

Fig. 8-56b Hollywood Film Company rack sections

Fig. 8–57 Editing room with wall racks for storage of catalogued film on reels

There is an excellent new plastic reel which comes in its own case—which can be imprinted with the name of the film and its producer—into which it locks (Fig. 8.55). These are fine for release prints, particularly when you print a large number.

Boxes and cans are always useful to have around the cutting room for storage and cataloguing of film. We never throw one away.

Storage Racks and Cabinets

These are an important item of equipment in all professional cutting rooms and some form might be considered from the start if you are setting up your own. A film cabinet (Fig. 8.56 A–C) offers a bit more protection than open racks, but racks are quicker to get at. Specify whether you want shelves or *cross bars;* the latter allow reels to be stacked on end. You can also get a model with separators, but these are not necessary. We use racks with cross bars but without separators because we sometimes use the cross bars as shelves, laying the reels or boxes sideways on them, and sometimes as cross bars with the reels on end. Also, we mix 16mm with 35mm reels, and the separators tend to commit you to one or the other. Cabinets have the advantage of being lockable.

You can also obtain *rack sections* with separators for either 16mm or 35mm in any length desired; they can be placed on shelves or tables.

Hollywood Film Company makes something called a Vault Can Rack which stores horizontally. Although not as flexible as the standard racks, it does offer a well-organized way of storing large quantities of material. F&B/Ceco also carries racks and cabinets.

We have all of our racks fastened to the wall near the top, to prevent them from tipping over (Fig. 8.57).

Miscellaneous Equipment

The following items, in their way, are also quite important. We have already discussed *acetone,* used for cleaning equipment, usually by applying it with cotton swabs. Emulsion has a way of accumulating on the heads and gates of Moviolas and readers, and splicers and synchronizers can get gummed up too. A regular program of cleaning is important, particularly sound heads, which will not function well with this accumulation, and the gates of Moviolas, where film and sound film will jam up. There are also standard types of *film cleaner; Webril Wipes* are excellent for hand cleaning; they are disposable. A *cleaning velvet* should also be kept on hand for cleaning film and sound tracks before screenings and mixes. In a pinch, a white cotton editing glove can be used, by running the film on a rewind between two gloved fingers.

Razor blades and *scissors* are useful for trimming splices and cutting the dailies. A *dispenser* which will hold two rolls of *masking tape* is necessary; the tape can come in a variety of colors, which is useful in cataloguing. If several productions are in the house, one color tape can be used for each production. Or, you might use one color for out-takes and another for trims on the same production to keep them easily recognizable. *Editing gloves* are a necessity for negative work, and some editors use them for regular cutting room work too. You will want a supply of *indelible markers* (these are to be used for marking start marks and labeling the leaders of reels where it is important that the marking not rub off) and *grease pencils* (also called *china marking pencils*) for marks which can be rubbed off. Grease pencils come in a variety of colors; dark red is excellent for transparent film or white leader, since it shows up well (the type of 35mm sound film called *stripe* is transparent, and white leader is used to label the heads and tails of picture and sound tracks for mixing and the lab). On the other hand, white shows up much better against *full base* sound film or the picture. There is also an orange grease pencil, which is the best all-around color as it shows up against both light and dark backgrounds.

Leader is used in the cutting room for marking the heads and tails of reels (clear or white leader) and for filling in portions of soundtracks where there is no sound and hence no need to run the more expensive sound film. Clear leader should also be used for *slugging* (filling in) portions of the picture where for some reason the dailies are missing. Clear leader is fairly expensive, so for soundtrack fill we use discarded release prints purchased from laboratories that have found them inadequate for releasing. You can also use worn-out release prints, purchased from distributors, but these are less satisfactory since they may have damaged sprockets or rips in the film. Special leader is used for negative matching (see pages 480–481).

A *magnifying glass* is useful for closely examining individual frames of a film without having to project them. We always keep a supply of *yellow legal-size pads* on hand for notes and cue sheets, and a *clip board* is useful to keep the pads on. Since you are often working in the dark (it is easier to see the image on a Moviola in the dark) an *illuminated clip board* is handy. *Director's chairs* are a good-looking and inexpensive chair to have around a cutting room, in addition to the high *editing chairs* which you need for working at the table or the Moviola. A clamp-on *extension lamp* is useful on the editing table. This way you can do cutting while the Moviola is running without moving back and forth to turn the overhead light on and off. The *overhead light* in an editing room should be a good one obviously.

When you are marking dissolves, fades, or titles on your film, you are marking off lengths, usually in regular numbers of frames (8, 12, 16, 24, or 32) and it is laborious to count them off each time. A scale can be made from a piece of white leader of the appropriate gauge by marking off the most-used frame lengths on it. We've mentioned the conversion of film footage from 16mm to 35mm and/or to seconds; while we do warn against mathematical error, and recommend the simple method of having multiple footage counters in each gauge on synchronizers and editing machines* or using the very useful *film stopwatch*, a device such as the Ready-Eddy will give you a handy conversion method.

Lastly, a *degausser*, or *demagnetizer*, should be kept around and used regularly. Splicer blades and scissors for cutting rooms are supposedly made of unmagnetizable metal, but they should be degaussed. The one drawback of magnetic sound film is its susceptibility to magnetization. If a cut is made in sound film with magnetized scissors or splicer, a "pop" will be noticeable when the cut passes the playback head. Other forms of magnetization can show up as noise and distortion on the tracks.

THE PROCEDURE OF FILM EDITING

Projector Screening of the Dailies

The cutting room procedure we shall outline is essentially that of the subject film rather than that of the dramatic film, basically concerned with telling a story and dominated by scenes with sync dialogue. It is the subject film with which the beginning film-maker is most likely to deal, and in many ways it is the film in which he will find the widest range of creative opportunity. The principles learned in these films will be applied throughout the entire range of film-making. The first stage of editing should be a projector screening. You will be entering a period of time in which the work print will be seen in comparatively small size on the Moviola or the viewer, so you will need to get a preliminary look at the film on a good-sized screen. Watch particularly for focus and small details that will be difficult to see on a small viewer. Seat yourself comfortably and at a time when you can devote undivided and uninterrupted attention to the screening.

The director and editor will certainly be present, and if there is a producer and a client involved, they will most likely want to attend. Some feel that it is a bit risky to let a client unfamiliar with the practice of film-making see the unedited dailies, and we have known producers who will have their editor prepare a selected version of the dailies and even a rough assemblage of some of the material expressly for a client screening. This is a matter for the individual to determine according to his own estimate of the client, with the deciding factor being the client's film experience. The viewing of the mass of unselected material can be a bewildering experience to the uninitiated. Even with an excellent *shooting ratio* the amount of usable footage may be much less than one-fifth of the material to be viewed, which means you will be looking at a lot of errors and excess footage, as well as the body of usable material.

If you are working in 35mm, you will most likely have to rent a

---

*There is a very simple way of converting 16mm footage to 35mm (or vice versa). Get a synchronizer with both a 35mm and 16mm footage counter mounted on it and set both to zero. Then run forward until the footage you are seeking appears; just reading off the footage on the other counter will give you a to-the-frame reading with no chance of a mathematical error. This is particularly useful if you must run through several reels and translate a series of numbers into another footage. The stopwatch with parallel 16mm, 35mm and seconds marked off is useful for under-a-minute converting, but gets a bit confusing beyond that.

screening room. Labs usually have such facilities; try to get them to let you screen your material without extra charge. For 16mm projection, if you do not have a projector as part of the cutting room equipment, you can usually borrow or rent one. Our strong recommendation is that you take plenty of time to absorb your material at this stage, running it over a number of times. If you want a "film-making absolute," here is one: You cannot edit until you know your material, really know it. The essence of editing is the selection and rearrangement of this mass of available material into a meaningful, rhythmic form, and the editor must at any given moment in his work be able to draw upon *all* his material for the "right" shot. He simply cannot afford to be choosing from less than all the material, particularly when he is assembling a comparatively free-form section with little specific guidance from a script. It can perhaps be said that, within such a sequence, for every shot there is one other shot which is its perfect mate; this "other shot" lies buried somewhere in a morass of material, but it need not be buried in an unreachable portion of the editor's mind. The answer lies in the original absorption of the material and an efficient system for cataloguing it. We will offer you a workable system for categorizing, assembling, and cataloguing your material. You need not adhere strictly to such a system; however, particularly as a beginning film editor, do not fool yourself into thinking that a "system" will restrict your creativity. You will have plenty of time for that later; if you know your material and can put your finger on it.

Shooting Script and Camera Reports: Sequential Editing

The advisability of using a shooting script and keeping detailed camera reports was brought out in the coverage of filming. Some productions prepare an *editor's script* in addition at this stage of work. However, if you are working independently as an editor on someone else's production, you may not have control over this. Due to the director's preference, or the conditions under which he has worked, the dailies may arrive in the editor's hands without any slating or relationship to a script; there may not even be a script. In some cases, the final form of the film may have been left to evolve from the work in the cutting room.°

If such is the case, it is quite important that the director work closely with the editor, at the projector screening, and during the *breakout* and *cataloguing* of material, since only the director knows fully the intention he has had for each shot. In this situation, the director's intent serves the purpose of the shooting script–camera reports in guiding the editor's organization of the material. Ideally, the editor should make a *shot-by-shot list* (including inclusive edgenumbers); at the least, he might make an *outline* of the film. The essence of the cataloguing system is the breaking down of the material into groupings of shots which form *sequences;* by listing these sequences the editor can sit down with the director and arrange them into the proper order, and this will create the basic form of the film. This consideration of the material as a series of sequences is the secret of controlling your material. You can first arrange

°We edited a short, *Miss Smile*, produced by Mattco Associates and directed by Richard Matt for Paramount Pictures. The subject was a "Miss Smile Beauty Contest" held at Cypress Gardens, Florida. The film was shot by two cameramen with no more instructions than to cover the several days of the contest as fully and interestingly as possible and to use a variety of camera angles. When the dailies arrived we screened them and broke the shots down, cataloguing them in groups of activities. From the material that was available, an idea for a film began to take shape. An opening sequence (an open-car procession on a highway with the girls waving happily) was chosen and an opening shot (a close-up of the flashing light on the police car leading the procession) with visual impact used to start things off. A number of activities were grouped as "the girls having fun"; some activities (a luncheon) were not used in themselves but supplied good close-ups of the girls for a montage of close-up faces and extreme-close-up smiles. A large amount of material of the girls being taught to water ski and rearrange the sequences in the right filmic order, and then proceed through the film sequence by sequence, dealing with the shots of each sequence in turn. You may find that you wish to draw upon a shot catalogued in another sequence to complete the one you're working on; this is the reason for the need to know all of your material. But at any one time, you are essentially working on one sequence.

If you have a fairly detailed script, but are lacking camera reports, your assemblage will be strongly guided by the script, including the obvious fact that the minimum length of a particular shot or group of shots will be determined by the amount of time necessary to fit the narration in. *The script serves as your outline of sequences.* This is probably the usual way that most sponsored films or instructional films are done, since it is necessary for the sponsor to see a copy of the script in approving the project. It is important to distinguish between a true *shooting script* or an *editor's script,* (Fig. 8.58), and a *narration script,* which merely tells you the commentary of the film, without guiding you in a filmic consideration of the sequence of images, as do the others. Thus a film shot to a narration script becomes a series of images, more or less well chosen to support the narration. This becomes a basic contradiction of the form of film (this subject is dealt with more thoroughly in Chapter 10); nevertheless, you may be faced professionally with this situation many times. It is important in such a case that you keep some flexibility, trying to choose your film images with an awareness of their own power and not merely as subservient images to the script. In time the narration itself may evolve filmically as the visual images have their influence upon it. Of course all this is contingent upon film images of sufficient quality to perform this job having been supplied to you.

If, on the other hand, you have a true shooting script or an editor's script this would imply that the form of the film has been determined in a filmic way. Such scripts will provide you detailed information as to your sequences, and in many cases to the order of shots within the sequence. You will be wise if you retain some flexibility in this situation also, since the shots actually on hand may have turned out better or worse than the script intended. Film-making is often a process of making the most of what you have. Still, working from a shooting script or an editor's script is the way to work. It must guide you in your breaking out and categorizing (grouping into sequences), and you may assemble the film by following the script in detail. Such scripts usually contain a suggested narration, and this will affect your minimum length of shot and guide you in your choice of images as you edit. Each shot will be slated to match the numbers of the script, so identification of each shot is a simple matter.

We have only to discuss the additional advantage to the editor of *camera reports.* The camera reports provide a record of how the shooting actually proceeded. Since no film is shot in the same order in which it will be assembled, the camera reports will show you the exact order in which the material was shot (and hence where to find it) and offer some idea of what the director thought of its quality at the time of shooting.

yielded a number of shots of the girls falling off or in various stages of difficulty, so this sequence was treated humorously. Some excellent underwater shots of the girls swimming and some poolside material were grouped into a "Busby Berkeley" sequence. Since the cameramen had not covered the actual announcement of the winners as fully as we might have wished, this sequence was played down; another ending had to be found. There was some excellent footage of a luau party with the girls dancing enthusiastically. There was a long shot of the girls in grass skirts walking in line along the beach, the late afternoon sun warming the shot. At the end, as the girls moved past the camera, the cameraman had tilted down to the sand, where their bare footprints were still visible along the water's edge. This was actually a shot of the girls heading *for* the party; but by placing it *following* the dancing, at the end of the picture, the afternoon sun became the early morning sun, and the shot made quite an acceptable ending. We had no way of knowing when this party had actually been held; but by placing it as the film's final sequence we were able to make an exciting filmic ending, certainly the best one available from the material that had been shot. The entire film was built from the footage we had on hand, with no guidance from any sort of script. When we had completed the editing, we wrote a light narration *to the picture,* comments on the visual images as they occurred; and so the script, when it finally appeared, came from the visual film. The film form itself came from the material, shaped by a sense of what would work filmicly.

DATE   PAGE

IRELAND ON THE GO

                PICTURE   SOUND

(NOTE: Numbers in parentheses refer to
Mattco Roll Numbers)

        FADE IN

        PARAMOUNT LOGO

        DISSOLVE TO

1.   EXTERIORS - BUNRATTY CASTLE   EFX - TRUMPETS BLOWING, as if an
                                          important declaration is about to be made.
      - Open on view through trees with
        flowers in FG - (5-A)

      - Bunratty Castle, stream in FG (1) CONTINUE TRUMPETS

      - Same, closer (1)

        DISSOLVE TO

2.   INTERIOR - MAIN HALL -
      BUNRATTY

      MAN in distance at table (M-2)

3.   INTERIOR BUNRATTY - CLOSER   STOP TRUMPETS JUST BEFORE MAN
                                          LOOKS UP
      on man at table. He gets up, walks MAN FROM BUNRATTY - SYNC: "Noble
      around and speaks. (M-2, J)
                                          Lords and Gracious Ladies, I bid you welcome.

                                          In fact, in the ancient Gaelic language of

                                          my country, 'Cead Mile Failte" - one

                                          hundred thousand welcomes! A land of

                                          tradition and beauty awaits your pleasure.

Fig. 8-58 Editor's Script

On some films you might not wish to go through all the material and break out every take, instead choosing to start by breaking out only the material to be assembled first. Here the camera reports are invaluable. One can determine where, within the number of reels on hand, the material is, run down to it quickly on a viewer, and pull the shots needed. However, if you can break out the entire film at once, this is our recommendation. If there is a large quantity of unusable material—*out-takes*—these can be rolled up and stored. This procedure cuts down the total amount of material with which you must deal, making it far easier to keep the usable material under control.

The information the camera reports give as to the director's opinion of the material at the time of shooting should not be followed slavishly; it is a lot easier to decide how the shot has turned out when you can actually see it. Of course, obvious fluffs were apparent at the time and are so noted, but we have often seen the director himself choose the next-to-last take of a shot when he sees them in the cutting room, even though he felt at the time that the shot was inadequate and chose to make another. Seeing it on the screen, he can reverse himself.

Perhaps we can sum up by saying that detailed camera reports, while useful, are not essential. A shooting script or, particularly an editor's script, is very important and a great help to the editor in breaking out, cataloguing and assembling. A narration script is a poor substitute for a true shooting script, but can help in guiding the editor, provided he is wary of the pitfalls of this kind of script. Lastly, if no script or shot record is available, the editor must work closely with the director in the examination and identification of the material, determine the form of the film from what is there, and assemble the film under the director's guidance as to its final form.

Organization of the Dailies into Sequences

Fig. 8–59 Cutting room set-up for breaking out of dailies

Fig. 8–60 Shot sequence hung on wall

You can break out your material on a Moviola or a viewer. If you are not facing an enormous quantity of material, you might choose to use the Moviola, which we prefer (Fig. 8.59). Although it is slower work, the image is better and the opportunity to study the shots once more at sync speed is an advantage. A good combination viewer-synchronizer arrangement having its own synchronous drive motor would be a close second choice. We set up a *drafting table*, which is small and portable, next to the Moviola. On it are kept a yellow pad and pencil, grease pencils, scissors, and masking tape. Close to the picture head is a film bin, with masking tape along the pins so that the shots can be catalogued as they are grouped on the pins. Script and camera reports, if available, are placed on the drafting table also.

Your material will be divided into *out-takes* (outs), and *usable takes*. At this stage, out-takes should be obvious out-takes; if there are two similar takes that are difficult to decide upon, hang them both. You will be better able to decide when you see them later in relation to the shots before and after, when you are ready to cut the shot into the picture. You should eliminate obvious technical flaws (out-of-focus, light flares), incomplete takes, and, if you have several takes of one shot, all but the two best takes. Choose one color masking tape for your outs and a separate film can to keep them in. Label each out-take (or group of outs, if there are several) of one shot with the scene number, or description if there is no number. The *slate* on the shot will guide you, or the director if there is no slate. Roll them up with the flange, either on the rewind or the end of the Moviola, and put them in their can. This labeling is important, because it is quite likely that you will end up using several of the out-takes when you start assembling. Store them *heads out*.

Take your usable take(s) and hang it on the first pin of the film bin (See Fig. 8.53). If you have analyzed the picture, ideally by the editor's script or by making up an outline from the projector screening and narration script with the help of the director, you have a good idea of the sequences of the film. You will probably need at least two bins, each having two sides, each side with two rows of pins for hanging. Naturally you can give some thought to keeping scenes which will be consecutive in the assembly on the same hanging area of the bin. Label the tape next to the pin with the shot number or name. If you have takes that are quite long, roll them up on the flange, mark them with another color tape—to distinguish them from the outs—label them and place them in a separate labeled can.

Often a particular scene is made up of several shots, each with its several takes. It is not necessary to hang each shot of a sequence on a separate pin. This is more than a question of saving space. This is not the time for handling the detailed cutting of a scene and you will find it difficult to remember each shot in detail when the time comes. At this stage, simply group the material from each sequence on one pin. Or, you might use one pin for the master shot, another for the intercuts. If you have a major sequence of twenty or thirty shots, try to break this down into subsequences and assign a pin for each of them. When the time for assembly comes, take the shots of a sequence, run them separately on the Moviola, perhaps giving them a simple label in grease pencil, and hang them on the wall (Fig. 8.60). Then go to lunch, or at least sit down in a comfortable chair and perhaps talk with the director. The shots will begin to arrange themselves as you cut the scene in your mind. When you return to the cutting room, the scene goes together the way it should.

Fig. 8–61a Locating clap board hit on dailies, sync sound take

Fig. 8–61b Locating clap board hit on sync sound track

SCENES WITH SYNC SOUND

Scenes with sync sound, (Fig. 8.61 A–D), should be handled separately; select a third can for them. Here the consideration as to your usable take involves both the visual and sound portions of the shot. Each slate will now involve the use of a *clapboard*. Put the picture in the viewer and locate the frame in which the clapper hits together directly under the lens. (This procedure can be done on the Moviola too.) Place the sound take in the sound reader. (The sound take will be voice slated to match the slate board.) Run the take down until you hear the sound of the clapper; mark this. On a major production, a coding (edgenumbering) system is used to keep the sound and picture takes matchable. If you are dealing with a limited number of takes, you can code them yourself in the cutting room. Take the sound and picture takes and place them side by side in the synchronizer with the start marks of each in alignment. Label the start marks identically, say "A." Then run down a few feet and mark an identical A–1 on parallel frames of each take. Proceed through A–2, A–3, etc. until the end of the take. The purpose of this is to allow you to cut out portions of the picture take to use in the work print and still be able to match them exactly with their corresponding sound, after the slate has been removed. Once you have cut off the clap, you have no way of getting back into sync without the coding; it is not difficult to restore sync if it is a few frames off, but it becomes an almost impossible job if you are trying to locate the sync with no idea of where

Fig. 8–61c Marking corresponding sync code numbers of picture and voice track

Fig. 8–61d Storing and labeling of sync voice scenes after breaking out

the corresponding sound is. Roll and label both the sound and picture and place them in their can.

You will proceed through the dailies until you have hung all your usable MOS° takes—or rolled the long ones in their own can—and placed all of the sound takes, with their soundtracks, in their can. The can with the outs can be placed on a shelf where you can reach them if needed later.

A SHOT-BY-SHOT LIST

A "textbook" view of editing would most likely suggest that the editor maintain a detailed shot-by-shot list, with a general description and the inclusive edgenumbers of the shot which would establish its length. On a major production, a feature, or a high budgeted short, where a great deal of footage has been shot, such a list is essential in maintaining some sort of control over the material. One discovers that the process of editing requires a frequent returning to trims and outs—discarded material. A shooting ratio of 5 to 1 is attainable on some types of well-planned productions. It has been said that directors such as John Ford and Alfred Hitchcock shoot at a 1:1 ratio, an obvious exaggeration which pays tribute to their pre-planning and great ability to visualize the complete film in the conceptual stage. But some of the notable films of Flaherty were, by their nature, shot at an extraordinary ratio, as are the cinema verité films of Drew-Leacock-Pennebaker. It is said that the magnificent chariot race sequence from the silent *Ben Hur,* directed by the brilliant second-unit director B. Reaves Eason, was edited by Lloyd Nosler from some 200,000 feet of film. The completed sequence ran for 750 feet in the film; that is a ratio of 267 to 1! We have worked on a number of travel shorts shot at a 20:1 ratio, and unquestionably this had much to do with the high quality of these films, since for every foot of film in the picture 19 had been discarded! With such large volumes of material the shot list can be indispensable.

For a production involving a limited amount of material, we cannot insist on the necessity of the shot list. Quite frankly, any film on which we laboriously made up one, it was so little used as to be a considerable waste of time. On all of the films on which we did not make one, there were several times when we would have given anything to have one! Nevertheless, it takes a considerable amount of time and there are other ways to control your material when the amount is within reason.°°

As for *trims,* rolling them up immediately may make it difficult to locate a particular one later, something that happens constantly in the course of editing. Use a pin in a separate film bin for the trims of each day's work; if you place the trims on the pin in order as they are cut, you will end up with the day's work in the exact order of the cuts in the picture. Make a note on the shooting script of the inclusive numbers of the sequences in each day's cutting. If you need to locate a trim, note the edgenumber of the portion of the shot cut into the picture—a convenient place to note it is on the viewplate of the moviola using a grease pencil; it can easily be rubbed off when you have found the trim—and check

*Shots without sound are labelled MOS on camera reports; MOS stands for "mit-out sound," naturally.

**On the first film I edited, we rolled every single shot, dutifully wrote a description down on a list with the inclusive edgenumbers, and put it away in a film can with a small piece of paper describing the shot held to it by a rubber band. It took two of us several days to do this. Each film can held one sequence from the film. When it came time to assemble, the label on each shot was meaningless; we had to look at every shot again in the context of the sequence to be edited. The shot-by-shot list was used a total of four times in attempting to locate misplaced shots. Both practices expended time greatly out of proportion to their usefulness.

your shooting script for the day you hung that trim. Then you have only to thumb through that day's trims on their pin until you spot the edge-number you are looking for. It is a lot easier to spot the code number than to laboriously hold each shot (especially in 16mm) up to the light to check the image, particularly if there are several similar shots. When you have completed editing—this means after the sound mix, as changes are constantly being made—roll up each day's trims as a unit, label, and place in a trim can. Even if you need to find a shot later, you can unroll that day's trims and check them.

Assembling the Work Print

You have the option here of assembling at the Moviola or at the editing table using the viewer; an excellent method is to make use of both, the viewer for locating your shot and the Moviola on which to assemble.° You will be using a tape splicer and butt splice (transparent tape on both sides). If you want to see your work immediately, splice as you go along. Taping one side only takes less time and the splices can be backed later. This is a bit laborious, so you might choose to stick the shots together on the reel with masking tape; you or your assistant can splice them together at the end of the day. Then you can run the previous day's work first thing in the morning to see where you stand before starting in on the next sequences.

THE THREE STAGES OF EDITING

A basic decision is whether you want to initially make a rough assembly of the shots in the proper order or whether you want to attempt a "tight" cut fairly close to the final cutting. Remember that cutting is a matter of (1) selection, (2) assembly, and (3) determining the film's tempo. The question is whether to attempt all three simultaneously or in separate stages of work. We recommend separate stages.

The film novice might think that a 5 to 1 ratio would mean five out-takes for every usable shot. Actually a truer figure would be one length of usable shot to one length of outs, to four lengths of trims. This means that your unusable footage is more a matter of the head and tail trims left over when you have pulled out the length of the shot you are actually to use. It is the nature of subject films in particular that the cameraman must shoot long and allow the editor to select the life of the shot.

As important as it is for the editor to find filmicly interesting entrance and exit points to the shot, his basic concern is with finding the "life" of the shot. This may be a simple matter of choosing the one section from a lengthy shot of traffic in which some interesting cars pass by, or it may involve the choice of one beautifully evocative glance or smile lasting a split second and occurring almost inadvertently within a mass of material. In one of our films we had a lengthy shot of two girls standing at a New York sidewalk hot-dog stand. Long into the shot was one moment in which a lovely cloud of steam leaped out as the man reached in for a hot dog to serve the girls. Everything else in the shot was pretty much the same all the way through; but this little cloud of

*Many editors prefer to assemble the film on the cutting table; I have always used the Moviola, doubling back into the scene each time to establish the cutting rhythm before making each new cut. The chosen point is marked with grease pencil and the film backed up so that the film can reach the splicer on the adjoining cutting table. I deal with a sequence at a time, letting the edited film spill into the canvas bag behind the Moviola. When each sequence is complete, it is rolled and labelled and placed in order on the cutting table rack and a note is made of the opening and the closing images of the scene. When all sequences are complete, following another consideration of their potential order, which may change at various times during the editing process, the sequences are assembled on the cutting table. Now the film as a whole must be run several times to see how it flows. Sequences can be shortened, lengthened, combined, or rearranged at this time.

steam was the "life" of this shot, and we never fail to notice it when we look at the film. It should be pointed out that the film-maker should not confuse the picturesque for the cinematic in choosing his material (or, for that matter, in filming it). Even such first-rate film-makers as Welles, Hitchcock, Carol Reed, and Stanley Kubrick sometimes forget this distinction.

The cameraman presents the editor with a thirty-foot shot of passing traffic; the editor first looks through the shot until he finds a filmicly interesting point, perhaps a truck passing directly in front of the camera, which will make a *good entrance* into the shot and will cut well against the end of the preceding shot. His *determination of a good exit point* may be made in several ways: He may choose a similarly interesting and effective portion of the shot to exit on. Or, he may watch the action of the shot and leave in the pause at the completion of an action. In fact, one of the most disturbing cuts is one which allows an incipient action to start for a few frames and then abruptly leaves it. Or, he may cut on a flow of action that leads with grace and rhythm into the next shot. However, it takes more than a few frames for the flow of action to begin and pull us with it. Or, he may cut metrically (some continuous actions allow this), the cut dictated not so much by the shot content as by the tempo set up by the succession of cuts preceding. This is determined by backing up the work print on the Moviola and running it at sync speed. You will immediately feel the rhythm which will set up a quite powerful *"expectation of cut."* ° One then jams down the brake on the Moviola at the right second, takes his foot off the pedal, marks the frame with a grease pencil where he will make his cut. There is one other possibility and it is the least desirable filmicly. The editor may arbitrarily cut continuous shots at a length which allows him to include the portion of narration accompanying that shot. Naturally, this is a determination of the minimum length of the shot—you might very well choose to go on longer to one of the filmicly truer cutting points. To sum up this basic tenet of editing: One chooses an appropriate filmic entrance for the shot, includes the filmic "life" of the shot, and then chooses the exit point in a variety of ways, conforming as closely as possible to the rhythm of the film. One simple rule to remember, which pretty nearly always applies: Never cut when the subject's eyes are closed or the mouth open. Think about it. °°

You now see the advantage of assembling on the Moviola and using its synchronous speed to find your exit point. But since you are running the film through the gate, you run into a problem when you want to locate the entrance point on your next shot. Here is the value of the viewer (we sometimes use a second Moviola) which allows you to view the new material without taking the assembled material out of the Moviola each time.

The above method would imply that you are performing the three editing stages of selection, assembly, and tempo simultaneously. Is there a way of separating them and still following this technique?

Yes, by using the viewer to locate your opening, then placing the shot on the Moviola and choosing an approximate exit point that may make

*Since our innate sense of rhythm is powerfully connected with our auditory sense, the film-maker might well take steps to transfer his sensing of the film's rhythm from visual to auditory channels. I often hum music to a scene I am running on the Moviola to determine the cutting pattern, and sometimes, even when not specifically "cutting to music," place a suitable piece of music on the Moviola just to help in judging tempo. Even if not using a tune, counting the cuts out loud helps. One can also listen for the sound of the splices thwicking through the gate of the projection machine. This has always reminded me of Charlie Chaplin, Jr.'s telling in *My Father, Charlie Chaplin* how his father acted to the rhythm of the motor of the silent film camera. I had always felt Chaplin must have used music to perform his beautifully "choreographed" performances to, but it was evidently the rhythm of the camera itself that determined the inner rhythm of the Tramp.

**Such editing considerations discussed in Chapter 7 —cutting on form, cutting on idea, cutting on image position—will be brought into play at this time.

the shot longer than it will finally be. By doing this you narrow down your material and make a properly ordered assembly which you can run at your leisure to determine your final cutting tempo. Some recommend that you screen on a projector, in the belief that the size-of-image difference between projector and Moviola affects the cutting tempo. We like to do the initial running on the Moviola, making cuts which appear certain and leave any questionable ones until later. Several projector screenings at a time, when you are relaxed and attentive, and your certainty on these cuts will come about naturally. Do not rush into these final cuts; note them in your mind as you screen. After four or five screenings, you will be sure of them and your final cut will go smoothly and effortlessly.

There is one obvious disadvantage to this method. Not knowing for certain the *exit point* of each shot removes one of the considerations for the *entrance point* of the next shot, as for example in positional matching. Creative editing must take this into consideration, to gain imaginative matchings and rhythmic flow from shot to shot. Still, there is nothing to prevent you from rearranging your initial assemblage after screening it, or even drawing from shots not included in this first assemblage, or in knowing the exit point from the start. Here your overall absorption of the material and your organization (now where the devil is that shot!!) of it is the key. The fact remains that this is an effective way of getting the tedious mechanical necessities of selection out of the way so you can edit creatively with a personal excitement and involvement in the filmic rhythm, and this is the way you should edit.

Optical Transitions

Having established the idea of the film as a series of sequences, let us think for a minute of the way one gets from sequence to sequence. Many times, particularly in contemporary film-making, a direct cut is the most effective transition. It is certainly the first alternative to consider. If the nature of the shot beginning the incoming sequence is such that the spectator knows with immediate clarity where he is (intelligent use of music can aid in this) the direct cut might be best. If the transition is not clear, or if you need a different feeling than that generated by the direct cut, you should consider one of several optical transitions (Fig. 8.62).

There are a number of optical devices for proceeding from scene to scene; their aesthetic application has been discussed in the previous chapter. We are now considering the practical technique for handling these in the cutting room, not the question of where they are filmicly appropriate.

DISSOLVE

As you know, this is a simultaneous fading in of the incoming shot and a fading out of the outgoing shot over a specified number of frames. In the printing of the answer and release prints from the negative (or camera original), the two shots will lie parallel to each other on the A- and B-Rolls (see pages 472 and 473) through their entire length. This is im-

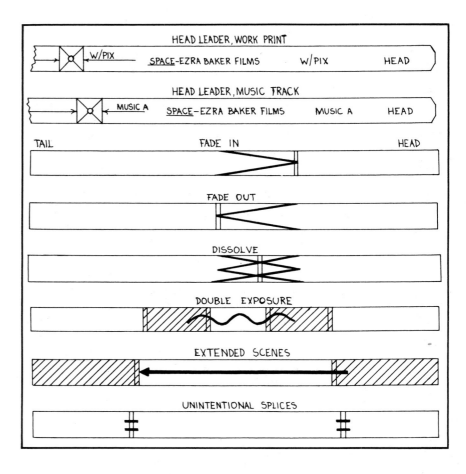

Fig. 8–62 Editor's marks for work print

practical on the work print without overlapping the film, so we cut each shot in the center of the dissolve and butt splice them. Thus in a 24-frame dissolve, the work print will have the first 12 frames of the outgoing shot's dissolve-out and the last 12 frames of the incoming shot's dissolve-in. (The 12 frames refers to a 24-frame dissolve; it is always half.) This is appropriate, since the change from shot to shot in the work print comes at the point where the incoming shot dominates in the actual dissolve. It is important that you ensure that those 12 frames which you have trimmed off each shot that you have cut in are available on the camera original. That means that you cannot start your butt splice marking the center of the dissolve at the very first frame of the entire shot, but must start at least 12 frames in. (Just to confuse you, it is actually 15 frames that we recommend; see page 304.) And, of course, it must end at least 12 (15) frames from the end of the full shot.

To ensure your having this material available in the original, you should physically cut off the other half of the dissolve for each shot, tape the trims together, and put them in a film can for *dissolve trims;* when you finish the work print, you should have a pair of these dissolve trims for every dissolve. This will prevent your having the negative matcher informing you that he doesn't have the original material to handle your dissolve. If this happens at the head of the shot, for example, he will have to pull up the shot to get the necessary frames; and obviously this will cause a different portion of the shot to appear on the screen and a different frame to end the shot. This in MOS shots might put an unwanted portion of the shot on the screen; in sync sound shots, it would throw off the sync in the release print.

Sometimes dissolves are added as a second thought to a cut made originally as a straight cut. You must look through the trims for the half of the dissolve length to make your dissolve trim. If you happen to have made the original cut right from the head of the shot, you will not be able to dissolve and so will have to move in the required amount on the shot to begin your dissolve. Don't depend on your memory; find the trim.

The dissolve is marked on the work print with its appropriate marking in grease pencil (see Fig. 8.62).

FADE

There is no overlap in a fade. Simply splice in a piece of blank leader of the required number of frames you wish to be dark between the two shots. Then mark the fade-out and fade-in on the shots with grease pencil (Fig. 8.62).

WIPE

You may refer to our chart of the wide variety of wipes available (see page 335. They are still used occasionally today. They represent an overlapping transition from scene to scene, although the images are never supered over each other. Cut the shots together at mid-point of the wipe; then mark the wipe appropriately. Since these are fairly uncommon, check with the negative matcher and the lab on how to mark them. As with titles, the dailies of the wipe can be supplied you by the optical house; you can then cut this into the work print, supplying the original to the negative matcher to conform.

DOUBLE EXPOSURE AND SUPERIMPOSITIONS

Use the basic shot of the double exposure at the start and the finish. Then cut in a short segment of the superimposed shot at the point where it enters over the basic background shot and another short segment where it leaves. Mark this appropriately (Fig. 8.62). Be sure there is an edgenumber on each segment of the shot.

EXTENDED SCENE

If you have to slug a scene in extending it (this will happen if you can't locate the actual trim), you must mark it properly so that the negative matcher knows what the slug represents. This is particularly important if there is a different shot on each side of the slug, for he has no way of knowing where the actual cut within the slug is to come. If the cut occurs within the slug, mark this point by running the arrows up to the point from each side and draw a line across the leader at this point corresponding to the splice between the shots, (See Fig. 12.1A).

UNINTENTIONAL SPLICES

Sometimes you make a cut in error, or a trim is added back onto a shot. In such a case, it is very important that you mark the unintentional cut so that the negative matcher does not cut the original by mistake (Fig. 8.62). If he does, he will lose a frame in the middle of the negative of the shot which will cause a ruinous jump.

LOSING A FRAME

This is a frequently used and much misunderstood expression. It refers to the fact that when the 16mm is hot spliced a portion of the next frame is lost. To overlap the splice, the narrow frame line of 16mm is not sufficient, so a portion of the actual adjoining frame is used to make the splice. Therefore, one "loses a frame." Some think that this means you actually lose one frame in the cumulative length of the film with each cut. So in a film with 200 splices, you would end up 200 frames (8⅓ seconds) short! Obviously this is impossible as a 2-frame deviation would be noticeable in a picture with sync sound!

What actually happens is that the negative matcher takes the extra needed frame on each side of the cut from the adjoining frame of the original (represented by the out-take of the shot in the work print). Therefore, no shot in the work print should start at the exact next frame following a slate or flash frame. We handle this by automatically clipping off the first three and last three frames of every shot before cutting it in. (And that's what our "15 frame" reference on page 302 meant.) Naturally, the same rule applies if you are to use two directly adjoining segments of one shot in different portions of the film. You cannot use the exact adjoining frames on either side of the cut, since one frame will be needed for each cut's hot splice in the original. Again, chopping off three frames automatically will handle this.

Assembling the Work Print

Whether guided by our shooting script or by our own outline, we are to proceed through the rough cut, assembling the picture sequence by sequence. Making a rough assembly implies that we shall be primarily concerned with a continuity, rather than a final rhythm, for this rhythm can only be determined when we have an opportunity of running the completed rough cut and absorbing ourselves in its assembled, coherent material. We may deal with some sequences with sync dialogue even in a subject film. We shall treat the syncing of this sound within the scene itself, scene by scene, rather than running a continuous sync dialogue track from the beginning of the picture to the end. Once a particular scene has been correctly synced, we shall roll up the sound and picture, placing them in our sync sound storage film can. Later, when the work print has been fine cut, we shall assemble our series of individual sync sound sequences, spaced by leader, into the complete sync voice track.

Some of the sequences, with or without sound, may be made up of only one shot; some may be several minutes in length, composed of literally a hundred shots. But each time, we shall work on the sequence, and then concern ourselves with the transition from it to the next succeeding sequence.

Categories of Shots

To proceed further with the practice of editing we must make some sort of division of our material into categories, for there will be some difficulties in the handling of each type of shot, representing variations in our basic approach. We shall suggest thirteen categories into which the material may fall, as a means of discussing the particular way each category is handled. This is an arbitrary organization and it is certainly not necessary to think rigidly of shots falling into these particular categories. The categories are meant to cover the range of material to be found in the typical subject film. However, as you proceed further into film-making these same categories, with some modification, will apply to other kinds of films as well, including the story film, dramatic or comic.

1. Shots with Sync Dialogue
    A. One shot making up the entire sequence
    B. One master shot with several intercuts
        1) No intercuts having sync dialogue
        2) Some or all intercuts having sync dialogue
    C. Two master shots of the sequence, each from a different camera position
        1) Two shots made simultaneously by two cameras sharing a common voice track
        2) Two shots made consecutively, each shot having its own sync voice track of essentially the same content
    D. Multiple master shots of the sequence, each from a different camera position
        1) All shots made simultaneously by different cameras sharing a common sync voice track
        2) The shots made consecutively, each shot having its own sync voice track of essentially the same content
2. Shots without Sync Dialogue (MOS)
    A. One shot making up the entire sequence
    B. One master shot, with intercuts, making up the sequence
    C. A variety of shots making up the sequence
    D. A large number of shots to be freely edited in making a montage sequence
3. Animation Sequences with and without Sync Dialogue

Sync dialogue scenes are frequently found in subject films; interviews are often carried out with a variety of experts "in the field." Sometimes the

SHOTS WITH SYNC DIALOGUE

A. One Shot Making Up the Entire Sequence.

scene is quite short, and one "master"° shot covers it in its entirety. In breaking out, you have chosen the best take, placing it and its separate soundtrack in the sound take can or box. Since the sound and picture have been coded to each other, you can leave the sound in the can at this point. The actual handling of the sound will be done when the work print has been assembled and you are assembling the sync voice track.

Locate the point on the picture at which the voice begins. Your basic cutting point for the entrance of the shot will be a few frames in front of this sound start. The same applies to the exit point of the shot—a few frames after the voice ends. Naturally, if you are to dissolve in or out, you will allow enough footage for your *dissolve trims,* and it is suggested that you set your dissolve so that the voice begins at the center of the dissolve. In a 24-frame dissolve you would cut off a 12-frame dissolve trim counting backward from the frame before the voice starts, splice the shot into the work print, and then mark off the dissolve with your grease pencil, 12 frames on the outgoing shot preceding and 12 frames at the head of the incoming sound shot. The same procedure is followed, in reverse, at the end of the shot. This center-of-dissolve rule is not inflexible; it is suggested as a safe starting point. It is not easy to gauge the effect of a dissolve from a work print. After you have seen a few dissolves rendered optically in your release prints, you may choose to vary your voice entrance point a few frames either way to suit yourself.

B. One Master Shot with Several Intercuts

1) NO INTERCUTS HAVING SYNC DIALOGUE   This is a good basic variation of the sync dialogue shot and should be used if the scene is fairly long. A sequence of a public speaker to be intercut with audience reaction shots would fall into this category. In sync dialogue scenes, your cutting point is almost invariably determined by the voice track. Just as the rhythm of previous cuts sets up an expectation of cut in MOS sequences, the rhythm of speech sets up the expectation of cut in sync dialogue sequences. If at all possible, the cut should be made at the end of a sentence or phrase, and at least in the pause between words. Never ignore the importance of speech rhythm in determining the pattern of cutting. The cut punctuates the rhythm of the line preceding, and the positioning of the incoming line is in turn strongly influenced by the cutting tempo.

One obvious point in cutting sync dialogue sequences is that you need only be concerned with sync if the shot is of the person speaking at that moment (and then only if his lips are visible). When non-speaking persons or objects are visible, the sound can be "borrowed" from synchronous shots. This is the beauty of double-system sound, enabling you to handle the voice and picture as separate entities in the cutting room, cutting them at different points.

As a basic example, if we have a shot of a man speaking and we wish to cut away to a girl listening, then return to see the end of the man's speech, we need only cut the picture, not the voice track. The voice track will continue running over the shot of the girl; that is, we "borrow" the voice from the shot of the man. Even if we took the shot of a listening girl in China and the shot of the talking man in France, we

*Throughout this chapter we use the term *"master shot"* in a particular sense. The term is sometimes used to mean a shot which includes all elements of a scene, all the way through. In other words, in a scene in which three people are talking, the master would cover all three, all the way through. This is a kind of "establishing shot." We mean by master shot a more general thing, *a shot which continues for the entire length of the scene,* but which may not include all elements. For example, if we are handling a scene in which a teacher lectures to a group of students, we might have one shot of his entire speech, several shots of him in detail, several shots of the teacher with the students also visible, and a number of shots of the students alone, some of them close-ups. The "master shot" in this case is the shot of the entire speech, even though it obviously does not include all elements of the scene. Nevertheless, it is the reference print for our editing.

could cut them in this way and obtain the illusion of the girl's listening presence; the "borrowed" sound completes the illusion of continuity.

The basic aesthetic reason for cutting within the sync voice sequence is to place on the screen shots made from a variety of camera positions, each having validity at a particular moment. This would usually mean a shot of the speaker, but would also certainly include interesting and revealing shots of listeners. A second, practical reason for cutting is to eliminate a technically imperfect portion of a shot, even though the portion is aesthetically preferable or in order to make a deletion in the picture or soundtrack. The former is self-evident; an awkward move of the camera or error of speech would cause us to cut to the alternate, error-free shot. The latter case, the making of a deletion in the voice track, is an interesting and useful practice on which we should spend a few minutes. It will also serve to present our basic technique for cutting sync voice and picture.

Let's take a scene involving a public address to an audience in which we must make deletions in the speech. The scene has hopefully been covered by at least two cameras. One has been on the speaker throughout, in a good basic "master" shot from the front, close enough so that we can match his lips to the sound. The shot is slated and a clapboard has been used to tie it to its accompanying sound take. This track contains the entire speech, with applause at various points. It has been sound coded to the picture, so we can easily match the two at any point along their length. The second camera has taken wild shots—MOS—from a variety of interesting angles. We have shots of the speaker from behind, at the side, and from the back of the audience; in none of these can we see his lips clearly enough to detect sync. We also have a variety of shots of the audience: long shots of the entire group, medium shots of portions of the audience, close-ups of individuals, including shots of the audience applauding. We will naturally want to cut in a variety of angles of the speaker and a number of reaction shots of the audience to keep the picture alive and varied and to reassure us of the scene's geography. However, these cuts will serve a further important function.

Invariably such a speech must have deletions made in it, to remove errors, objectionable material, or unimportant portions, or simply to shorten the speech to an acceptable filmic length. If we had only the master shot and simply cut out a portion of picture to match the removed portion of sound, we would produce a jump cut—the position of the speaker would suddenly "jump." If his hands had been resting on the podium just before the cut and are now gesticulating fervently before him, the sudden leap will be noticeable and distracting in the traditionally edited film. The obvious answer is to cut-away, either to a shot of the audience, or to another view of the speaker in which his hands and lips are not visible. This cut-away will bridge the two shots; we will simply assume that he moved his hands during the time we could not see him. Our sound cut can then be made at any time during the cut-away. If we are careful to match the rhythm of his actual pauses with this artificial pause, the cut will be unnoticeable, visually and audially.

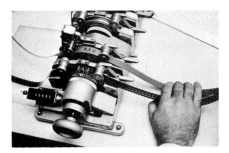

Fig. 8-63a Editing sync sound sequences

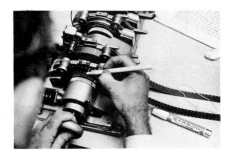

Fig. 8-63b Marking pause after last usable sentence

Fig. 8-63c Track and picture marked for cutting

Fig. 8-63d Portions of picture and sound track to be joined

Fig. 8-63e Portions of picture and sound track joined

There are several obvious variations to this basic technique. You can go to the cut-away at the exact moment you cut the sound, let the shot run for the first phrase of the "pulled up" sound, and then return to the speaker. Or, you could cut-away a phrase before the sound cut, returning to the pulled up shot and the pulled up sound at the same time. A third possibility would be to cut-away the phrase before, make the sound cut, and then remain with the picture cut-away for another phrase before returning to the pulled up picture. (And, of course, you could use several different cut-aways in succession.) The results will be the same: an unnoticeable cut. A useful variation is to wait until the speaker pauses for applause, cut naturally to the applauding crowd, and then return to the speaker as he is about to begin a new section of the speech. Of course this new section can actually have been pulled up from further on, with the actual succeeding portion removed. Your sound cut can come just as the applause dies down, removing the unwanted portion of the speech, pulling the section you wish to present up to the cut. Now that the basic principle is established, you will wish to know how the cutting is actually performed and, in particular, how we keep the track matched to the picture (Fig. 8.63 A–E).

The secret lies in the sound coding. Set up your picture in the first gang of your synchronizer with a means of viewing it. Set up your sound-track in the second gang equipped with magnetic pick-up and sync it to the picture by the sound codes. This means that corresponding codes will appear simultaneously on the two gangs, exactly parallel to each other. Let's take the example of cutting from the speaker to the audience just as we make our sound cut, returning to the speaker after one phrase over the cut-away.

Listen on your soundtrack for the pause following the last usable sentence; mark this point for cutting on both picture and soundtrack. Now roll ahead and listen for the pause preceding the portion of speech you wish to proceed to; locate and mark this pause on both sound and picture also. Leave sufficient room between the end of the outgoing and start of the incoming speech so that there is a natural pause, comparable to the speaker's usual pattern. Now roll back to the first pair of marks and make your cut, removing the portions of both tracks between the two marks. Label these trims as to scene, and place in a trim can for sound takes. If you look at your picture and soundtrack, you will observe that the sound coding skips forward at the point you have cut, let's say from A–19 to A–28, meaning you have removed portion A–20 through A–27.

What you have done is matched picture to the voice track at the expense of a jump cut; eliminating the jump is simple. Using your sound reader, move forward from the cut to the end of the first phrase of the pulled up sound and mark the pause. Measure the distance from the cut to the pause; let's say it is two feet, 6 frames. Now select a suitable cut-away that you can cut at exactly two feet, 6 frames. Mark this length exactly and cut it, hanging the trims to the shot. Now take your picture track and splice the head of this shot to be intercut at the point where the picture is spliced (the jump cut). Remove the two foot, 6 frame portion of picture and substitute the same length cut-away, splicing it to the running shot at the end. Place the master shot trim in the sound take trim can. If you run the two tracks through the synchronizer you will now note that the codes match up to A–19; however, at the point where the sound jumps to A–28, the MOS picture, which is the cut-away, is uncoded. At the end of the cut-away, the picture code begins again at A–30, (A–28 and A–29 having been removed and the cut-away substituted) exactly in parallel sync with the sound codes.

Obviously there is no need to actually make the jump cut splice in the picture. Instead, you could proceed directly to cutting in the cut-away shot, matching to your codes. In practice, however, cut-aways are usually added at a later stage of work. Adapting this technique to the variations of intercutting is just a matter of common sense from here on.

You now will understand why we are constantly subjected during television news interviews to shots of semi-interested interviewers nodding with no discernible relationship to the speaker, hands writing mysteriously on note pads, batteries of cameras, and the backs of speakers' heads. These are cut-aways used to bridge necessary deletions made in the speaker's material. Of course these banal examples, made under the pressure of daily deadlines, should not discourage you from using this technique with intelligence and creativity. Used properly, this method can not only make deletions unnoticeable but can add variety, interest, and life to the film.

2) SOME OR ALL OF INTERCUTS HAVING SYNC DIALOGUE   A bit more complex is the sync sound sequence involving intercuts having their own sync sound; the editor must handle the intercuts, each with its own sync soundtrack, using the sound coding to match them properly. Since the shots have been made consecutively, each voice track is synced only to its own particular picture. Even if the speaker has repeated his lines exactly from shot to shot, we could not intercut picture and stay on the original soundtrack and still remain in sync. This would imply that we would always cut the picture and track at exactly the same point, but there are actually several options open to us.

The possibilities can be covered by seven basic variations (Fig. 8.64):

(1) We can cut from the first speaker to the second at the exact moment that the first speaker stops and the second begins talking.

(2) We can cut to the second speaker before the first finishes speaking, observing the second speaker's reaction and then watching him begin to talk.

(3) We can remain on the first speaker after he finishes, watch his reaction as the second speaker begins, and then cut to the second speaker while he is talking.

(4) We can remain on the first speaker while the second makes a brief off-camera remark, watching the first speaker begin again on camera.

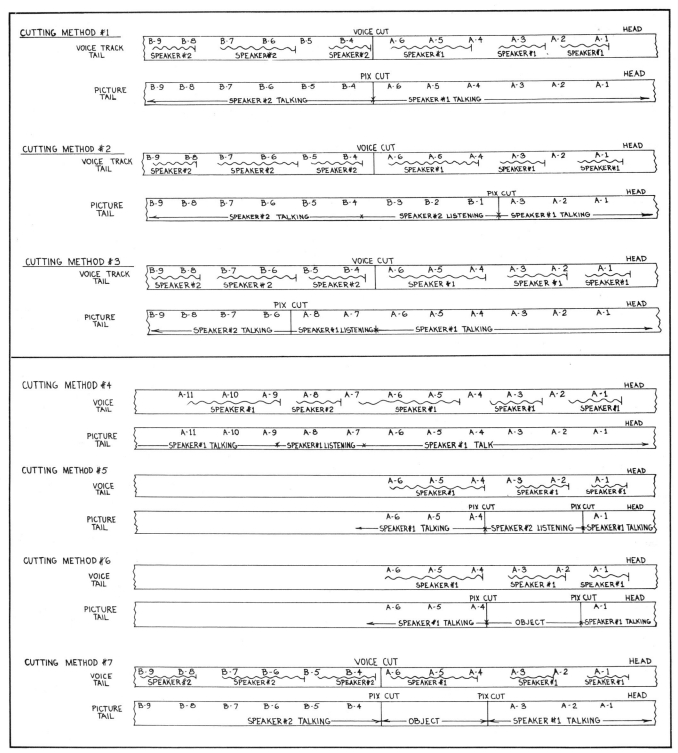

Fig. 8–64 Cutting shots with sync dialogue: seven basic variations

(5) We can cut to the second speaker during the time that the first speaker is talking in order to pick up a particularly appropriate reaction, cutting back to the first speaker while he is still talking.

(6) We can cut away to some other subject, either a person or an object, while the first speaker is on camera, returning to the same person.

(7) We can cut away to another subject while the first speaker is on camera, returning to the second speaker.

Methods 5, 6, and 7 involve the use of intercuts without sync sound, so the soundtrack of the master shot can continue to run. Method 4 also allows us to remain with the master-shot soundtrack since we hear but never see the second speaker. (If we have shot his brief speech as an intercut, we simply discard the shot and its soundtrack in favor of the master shot.) Method 1 clearly involves cutting from one shot to another, and, since we cut between speeches, we can cut the voice track at this exact point. This is a simple technique if you use the sound coding to match picture and voice (see Fig. 8.64, cutting method #1).

Methods 2 and 3 involve something more complex, since we are choosing not to cut the picture between speeches. The obvious question is: *When are we to cut the accompanying voice tracks?* With method 2, we are cutting visually to the second speaker before his speech begins. However, we shall *not* cut to the soundtrack of this new shot at this point, since it would involve joining portions of two different sound takes of the first speaker's voice. Quality can vary between different sound takes, so the match might be noticeable. It makes much more sense in this case to hold off our sound cut until the pause between speakers, "borrowing" the voice from the first shot for the opening portion of the second. Since the speaker is not actually on camera, we are free to do this; the reaction in the second shot will almost certainly fit the speech appropriately (see Fig. 8.64, cutting method #2).

The procedure to follow is quite logical. Our picture is cut first. Picture and voice track are, of course, lined up in exact sync on the synchronizer. We search for a pause in the voice one phrase before the point where the first speaker ends and the second begins; this point is marked on the picture's parallel frame. The picture is to be cut here but its voice track will be allowed to run. You now know where you wish to leave the outgoing shot but not where to cut into the incoming shot. This is a matter of simple arithmetic. Measure the distance from the marked point where you are to cut the outgoing shot to the end of the speaker's line; let's say it is exactly three feet. Now take the incoming shot and measure *back* three feet from the point at which this second speaker begins talking; since you have shot your intercuts with the off-camera actor reading his cue line for just this purpose, you are able to do this. Cut the incoming shot into the outgoing shot; you will be cutting each one three feet from the marked pause. Now run the completed picture down to the marked pause; this is the point where you wish to change from the first shot's voice track to the second's. Simply match up the second voice track to its picture with the codes; at the point where

Fig. 8–65a Master shot with sync intercuts:
teacher leading group discussion
is basic establishing shot

Fig. 8–65b c d and e Successive shots of the Speakers

Fig. 8–65f Typical cut-away

the second voice track overlaps the pause, cut it and splice to the first voice track.

Let's run the picture and track back and see what we have (see Fig. 8.64, cutting method #2). We see the first speaker talking; then the picture of the second speaker (listening) appears, although the first voice track continues to run with the first speaker's voice. This continues for three feet. At this point there is a cut in the voice track—the second voice track now begins—and we see the second speaker begin to speak on camera. As for our sound codes, they will match up to the point of the picture cut (A–1 to A–3) and after the point of the sound cut (B–4 to B–9); in between they will not match since we are running the first shot's voice track with the second shot.

In method 3, a cut in which we remain on the first speaker, cutting to the second one phrase after he begins, the procedure is the reverse. We make the voice cut first in the pause between speakers, and make the picture cut in the next between-phrase pause. Common sense will tell you how to execute this, since the principles are the same (see Fig. 8.64, cutting method #3).

Of course we have limited this consideration to the use of shots of just two men, probably point-of-view shots. In practice, most scenes of this sort would begin with an establishing shot of the two men, cut in closer to a waist-high shot of the two, and then proceed into the alternation of over-the-shoulder shots. At some time during the sequence we might well return to a two-shot, or cut to some other person or object. Still, the basic principles are the same: Cutting picture and voice in the pauses and borrowing the sound from other shots when the person on camera is not speaking. By using the variety of cuts that are possible we not only keep the cutting varied but we enable the camera to be in the right place at the right time, instead of simply sticking it into the face of the speaker every time he opens his mouth. These methods are suggested for the purpose of opening up your thinking to the infinite number of possibilities available to you in handling a simple scene such as this. You should now begin to watch dialogue scenes in films with this in mind. Such classic scenes as varied as the Marlon Brando–Rod Steiger taxi ride in *On the Waterfront* and those in your nightly television series can be examined to see just how they have made use of these possibilities. Watch especially to see how the tempo of the scene is affected by the cutting; watch fast-paced comedy to see how the cutting keeps the rhythm driving forward, as each cut comes a split second after the line preceding it, the line following the cut coming a split second after the cut.

Let's conclude this study of master-shot and sync dialogue intercuts with a typical scene (Fig. 8.65 A–F). A teacher is seen with a group of children. She makes an opening statement, followed by comments from the members of the group sitting around a table, and then makes a closing statement.

We might be tempted to shoot this sequence in a single shot (see page 305) but the chance of being able to move the camera smoothly from the teacher to the children and back is rather small. Nor would such shots all be done from the most respectively advantageous position. A more workable way is to shoot a master shot with sync intercuts. We set up the camera on the teacher and shoot a master shot, holding on her as the children speak to catch her reaction and then recording her final summation. Now we shift the camera position to a favorable set-up for the first child. The teacher reads her cuing line so that if we wish we will be able to use our cutting method 2, cutting to the second speaker in advance of her speaking. We both record and film this cue line (the camera, of course, is on the second speaker, the child) but all we are after is the filmed reaction preceding the speech on camera. When the speaker finishes, we keep the camera on her, and have the third speaker read his first phrase, giving us the opportunity if we choose of using cutting method 3, remaining on the speaker for a phrase of the next speaker. We then move the camera to the set-up for the third speaker and repeat the procedure. Finally, we might have our people repeat the entire scene and shoot wild takes MOS; these might consist of shots of the children listening, close-ups of hands drawing—anything that we might use as intercuts to add life to the scene.

Now we cut the scene. Let's begin on the teacher, using the master shot with its accompanying soundtrack. Perhaps we still cut directly to the second speaker in the pause between the teacher's line and hers (cutting method 1). Now we remain on the second speaker as the third begins to talk (cutting method 3), having observed a particularly interesting reaction as she turns to face the new speaker. During his speech we cut-away to the third child (cutting method 6), returning to the speaking child. We then choose cutting method 2, returning to the teacher a phrase before the third speaker finishes, catching the final nod of the teacher and watching her begin her summation. Naturally we follow our usual method for keeping the respective voice tracks in sync, guided always by our sound codes. After we run the scene it may occur to us that one of the phrases used by the teacher should be removed. We make this deletion in the soundtrack and picture, covering the picture jump by cutting away to a shot of a child's hands drawing. For this intercut we could have used either the MOS shots we have made for this purpose or unused portions of the master shot or intercuts, treating them as MOS shots.

This just opens the door to the possibilities in a simple scene, but it becomes obvious that the beginning editor can have a good deal of pleasure in cutting even a basic scene such as this, and can really go a long way toward making it something more than a cut-and-dried sequence one can find in every fifth-rate subject film. The key is in knowing the possibilities, planning for them in the shooting, and then using your imagination in taking advantage of what you have. And let's add, in having a good basic equipment set-up so you can do the work smoothly and efficiently.

1) TWO SHOTS MADE SIMULTANEOUSLY BY TWO CAMERAS SHARING A

C. Two Master Shots of the Sequence, Each from a Different Camera Position

COMMON VOICE TRACK   Again our use of the term "master shot" refers to the making of a shot including the entire sequence from beginning to end, but not necessarily of all the people involved in the sequence. In a subject film such a scene might be an interview between two people; in a story film, any two-person scene. The important change from our technique with the single master is that we are no longer shooting *portions* of the scene to intercut, but are each time shooting the *entire scene* from start to finish with a separate camera set-up for each person.

In this version we have the luxury of using two cameras simultaneously, which is ideal if the budget allows. Since they share a common voice track we need not cut the voice track at all; we will again use it as a guide to the spacing of phrases and hence to the exact moment to make our cuts from shot to shot. Again our seven methods of handling these cuts are open to us.

Since we now are dealing with two running shots and must make a decision as to which is the better shot to include in the work print at any given moment, the ideal machine on which to work is one of the two-viewer synchronizers we described earlier (see page 281). You can run the two pictures through together, study what is available to you at a given moment in each shot, thinking in terms of your seven basic cutting methods. When you have selected the approximate point where you wish to change pictures, use the sound pick-up head to spot the exact between-phrase point where you will make the cut. Then back off and splice the shots.° The director will often utilize a zoom lens on his cameras to render the three basic positions of long shot, medium shot, and close-up (Fig. 8.66). At prearranged points, the camera will quickly zoom to the specified position, holding it until the next shift, then zooming to a new position. These zooms will not be included in the edited film; they are merely for the purpose of getting into a new position. Therefore, the zooms will always be planned at a time when that camera is making the less important shot, allowing the editor to use the other camera's shot; and, of course, only one camera can be zooming at any one time. This means that instead of just cutting back and forth between two standard over-the-shoulder shots, the editor can cut from a long shot of speaker A, to a medium shot of speaker B, to a close-up of speaker A, to a close-up of speaker B, etc. This must be carefully pre-planned by the director according to the script; it gives him variety within the scene and the chance to use the camera interpretively to emphasize the portions of speech he wishes emphasized.

2) TWO SHOTS MADE CONSECUTIVELY, EACH SHOT HAVING ITS OWN SYNC VOICE TRACK OF ESSENTIALLY THE SAME CONTENT   This is a more likely method of handling the same two-person sequence, since budget considerations so often dictate the use of one camera. The camera is used to film the entire scene from one set-up favoring the first speaker, then moved to a new set-up favoring the second. The shots will best be handled on the two-viewer synchronizer, but now two pick-up heads must be used to handle the two soundtracks. Our seven cutting methods are again open to us, but now we are once again concerned with actual cuts

*Begin with Camera #1 on the A gang, Camera #2 on the B; if you choose to begin the scene with the shot from Camera #1, the A gang becomes the work print, the B gang, the trims. Move forward in the synchronizer until you reach the point at which you wish to change from Camera #1 to Camera #2; cross the #2 shot from the B to the A and splice it to the outgoing #1 shot. Cross the continuing but unusable portion of the #1 shot from the A to the B and splice it to the head trim of the #2 shot. As you continue you now have Camera #1 on the B, Camera #2 on the A; however, A is still the work print and B the trims. At the next cutting point, the procedure is reversed; the Camera #1 shot which is to be used is crossed from the B back to the A and the unusable tail trim to #2 is crossed back to the B and both are spliced in. When you finish, both gangs will contain alternating portions from the two cameras in chronological sequence; the A gang will be the assembled work print for the scene, while the B gang will be the assembled trims.

Fig. 8–66a Interview sequence covered by two cameras simultaneously: camera position 1–basic photo represents long shot; marked portions represent medium and close shots

Fig. 8–66b Camera position 2–basic photo represents long shot; marked portions represent medium and close shots

in the voice track and the use of the sound coding to line up each sound take with its respective shot. Of course, it is not with separate intercut takes, but portions of the master that we are dealing.

1) ALL SHOTS MADE SIMULTANEOUSLY BY DIFFERENT CAMERAS SHARING A COMMON SYNC VOICE TRACK   Again the common voice track requires no cuts to be made in the sound, using it as a guide to the exact picture

D. Multiple Master Shots of the Sequence, Each from a Different Camera Position

cutting point. If we are using multiple masters, chances are that one is a true master shot, that is, it not only runs from start to finish but it serves as a basic coverage of all of the people involved, with the other "masters" representing varying close-ups of part of the scene while running all the way through the sequence. The cameras may move at different times from close-up to medium shot to long shot. Again, we can make use of the variety of cuts open to us.

There is an excellent description of this sytem in use in the filming by Henry Freulich of the television series "Mothers-in-Law," in the December 1967, issue of *American Cinematographer*. This three-camera method of filming a TV show before a guest audience was also used by Robert DeGrasse on "The Danny Thomas Show," "The Dick Van Dyke Show," and "Good Morning World," by William Cline for "He and She" and by Maury Gertsman for "The Lucy Show." By acting before a live studio audience, the performers gained needed rapport, and using "laugh tracks" for the shows was avoided. By using three cameras, the director was sure of there always being a good interesting shot to cut to, instead of being stuck with the impossibly static result a single camera would have given. Freulich mentions the obvious importance of lighting simultaneously for all three cameras and states that his basic set-up involved an "A" camera on the left covering action in close-up with a 75mm or 100mm lens; a "B" camera in the center for the master scene, with a 35mm or 40mm lens; and on the right the "C" camera, also in close-up with a 75mm or 100mm lens. Naturally the left camera shoots close-ups on the right side, the right camera on the left (see Fig. 8.67).

2) SHOTS MADE CONSECUTIVELY, EACH HAVING ITS OWN SYNC VOICE TRACK OF ESSENTIALLY THE SAME CONTENT   This logical substitute for the simultaneous three-camera set-up ends our discussion of sync sound shots. Having the additional variables of separate soundtracks for each full-length shot adds an additional complexity to your work, but once again the basic principles of sync voice editing are involved. The considerations of budget could result in your having to use a single camera in subsequent shots, shooting the entire scene over from different points of view. Still, the use of the full-length take for each set-up seems preferable to the partial shot to be intercut, if you can afford the additional stock and lab costs.

**SHOTS WITHOUT SYNC DIALOGUE (MOS)
A. One Shot Making Up
the Entire Sequence**

We will now begin consideration of sequences containing no sync dialogue. Our primary concern in editing such sequences will be with the visual image; however, if a copy of the narration is available at this stage, either as a narration script or part of the shooting or editor's script, keep it handy and take it into consideration. In many cases your initial choice of shot length in the subject film is arbitrary; by reading the narration for that shot aloud at a moderate pace, you can determine the length of shot to use for your rough assembly. Cut the rough cut long; remember that you will waste time looking for the hung trim

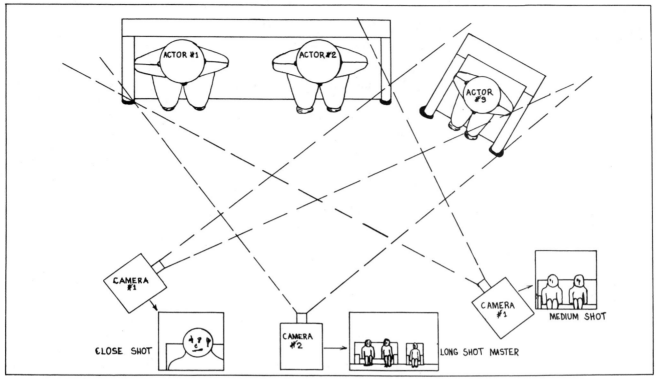

Fig. 8-67 Multiple master shots of a sequence made simultaneously from three camera positions: the variation in scale in the three shots is accomplished by the use of different lenses, not by difference in camera placement

needed to lengthen a shot and that it is generally a good deal easier to shorten shots than to lengthen them.

Our first type of MOS sequence is the simplest to handle—the sequence made up of a single shot. This is not uncommon in such subject films as industrials, travelogues, and instructional films. We quite often find that such a one-shot sequence is shot to back up a line of narration or to illustrate a particular point in the script. If the sequence is short enough, one shot may be sufficient.

We recently completed work on a short subject *Man's Love Affair with Wheels*, produced by the Mario Ghio Production Group and distributed by Paramount Pictures to publicize their feature film, *Those Daring Young Men in Their Jaunty Jalopies*. Part of the film covers the actual location shooting of the feature and a number of shots from the feature are included in it. The remainder of the film consists of a series of single-shot sequences on the subject of automobiles, specifically shot to back a humorous narration. At one point, we are introduced to a number of the stars in the film in a succession of such one-shot sequences. Each shot is complete in itself and consists of the actor performing some amusing action around one of the old-fashioned racing cars used in the feature.

In assembling the rough cut, each sequence was examined in turn and the best take chosen. In the initial assembly, a fairly long portion of the shot was chosen, containing an action complete in itself, that is, having a distinct beginning and ending point at which we could cut. Although the cameraman has been guided by the shooting script in seeking out these shots, the editor is given some leeway in assembling the sequences in a particular order, so he can give consideration to which shots cut together well; the narration was then rewritten to cover these changes. In this particular series of shots, the narration was consistently shorter than the shot, so the length of shot could be determined by our pacing of the picture. As so often happens when viewing a rough cut, shots which seem to be cut perfectly appear to drag, and trims can be made at the head and tail of many shots. One of these sequences supplies an excellent example of a basic editing principle.

An actor is shown climbing out of the sun roof of a car. As initially cut in, the shot showed him unsuccessfully trying the door, deciding to climb out, climbing, getting down from the hood, and finally, standing in mock triumph at the side of the car. Yet there was no reason for the action to be shown in its entirety; our final cut began with the actor already in the act of climbing out the top of the car. The spectator accepts the beginning of a continuous action at an obvious mid-point. The shot, instead of hanging interminably at the start, jumped forward into the important, filmicly valid action, maintaining the light, fast pace of this film.

We often find ourselves dealing with a shot of a car moving into, across, and out of a frame, (Fig. 8.68 A–F). It is perfectly acceptable to pick up the shot at a point where the car is already well into the frame, perhaps a third of the way in, and the shot can be cut well before the car leaves the frame (see Cutting on the Completion of an Action, Chapter 7). If you wait until the car clears the frame (this is quite easy to study on the Moviola, since you can stop on individual frames), the frame will "die." If you cut while the car still fills at least the last fifth of the frame, the shot's action will flow naturally onto the next shot and further the pace of the film. By following this rule in reverse, and allowing the car to both enter and clear the frame, one can consciously and effectively slow down the pace of the film. Typically, this editing "rule" works both ways, enabling the editor to achieve the desired tempo.

B. One Master Shot, with Intercuts, Making Up the Sequence

Unless it is absolutely certain that the full emotion and meaning of a sequence can be conveyed with only one shot, it is preferable that several shots be used to build the sequence. In a subject film, this is almost a certainty if the sequence is to be longer than a few seconds. Some directors feel that any shot of longer than three or four seconds will inevitably lose the spectator's interest in an action sequence. This is an obvious exaggeration—the statement ignores the fact that the particular content of a shot may hold the audience's attention well beyond any arbitrary time limit°—but it reveals the film-maker's instinctive awareness of the importance of a variety of camera angles and good pacing to the film. You will remember from your discussion of editing aesthetics that the cut must be used with discretion in the dramatic scene; since it implies emphasis it must be used where emphasis is intended. In action se-

*There is a shot in the climactic scene of *The Boston Strangler* which seems to run around four minutes, and *Breathless* contains a shot running two minutes and thirty-six seconds.

quences, the use of a wide variety of camera set-ups with quick cutting is essential. The competent director will supply his editor with shots from a variety of camera angles, including shots of the particular elements of the scene he will want to emphasize. He will also take pains to include material for cut-aways—almost neutral details of the scene which can be used to bridge shots otherwise difficult to match. (An example of this is given on page 312.)

Many film aestheticians deplore the fact that the dramatic story film, with its synchronized sound tracks, has taken the creative determination of the form of film from the hands of the editor. This is to some degree true, and it is primarily in the subject film that the editor still has the power to build the film creatively—in the full sense of that word. Such opportunity will be found in working in this and the next two subcategories—each dealing with multiple-shot MOS sequences.

A sequence which might be handled in this way is a scene of children playing on a jungle gym (Fig. 8.69 A–F). Our master shot is made from a set-up chosen to give us an overall impression of the activity; it is shot as a complete sequence, showing the action performed in its entirety. The important question, then, is how best to shoot the intercuts.

There is a technique which we consider at best an expedient substitute for the right method, but which is sometimes forced upon the director by limitations of time and space. The cameraman maintains the camera in the same set-up from which the master was photographed and uses a zoom lens to move in on the details of action as the subjects are called upon to repeat the action in its entirety. Close-ups and medium shots are made from the same camera angle. Frankly, this method is a classic misuse of the zoom lens. While you do achieve a variation of scale between the images of the detail shots and those of the master, the angle of relation of camera to subject is the same; also, the shots suffer from the characteristic lack of depth-of-field of the zoom lens shot. You have not fully utilized the potential variety of camera set-ups in detailing important portions of the action from the most advantageous position, some of which might not even be visible from the one basic camera position.

If at all possible, the detail shots to be intercut should be shot from new camera set-ups, each one carefully chosen as the best possible for filming that particular detail. This is not only the proper use of camera potential, it is the way to ensure superior editing of the sequence. However, which ever method is followed, the editor's task remains essentially the same.

Unless the form of the film specifically exempts him from this, the editor's job will be to match the shots available into an illusion of continuity. Since the shots have all been made at the same time, we are assured of such important considerations of continuity as similar lighting, the same clothing worn, loose objects on the set in the same position. Since the participants in the sequence are repeating their actions within a short time, they will be able to closely approximate their movements

Fig. 8–68a b c d e f These frames from a single shot of a car passing a stationary camera illustrate the options the editor has in beginning and ending the shot

Fig. 8–69a b c d e f The cameraman has elected to move his camera into new relationship to the subjects after shooting the basic establishing shots A and D from the front and with a straight forward relationship to subject

in the master. This will greatly aid us in cutting from one shot to another at points in which the subject's positions match from shot to shot. This is a consideration only when we cut from the master to a close shot of a detail of the action clearly visible in the master (or vice versa), or when we cut between two views of the same portion of the action. For example, if we cut from the master to one child who is clearly visible in the master, we must be certain that the basic action and body position of the child match in each shot. The editor looks for points in each shot in which such matches are evident. If the next cut is to a close detail of the same child—his hands, say—consideration of a match of the simultaneously present material must be given. However, if the next cut is to a second child, there is no question of matching; we can begin the shot of the second child at whatever point we find filmicly suitable. If that shot is in turn followed by a return to the master, then it is the second child whom we must match to the master; the position of the first child in the master is irrelevant to the match.

If it is impossible to find a match of simultaneous elements at the place where we must make a cut, the cut-away—those neutral details of the scene, such as a nearby tree, a passing bird, or an extreme facial close-up—should be inserted between the mismatched elements. This eliminates the jump cut. The beauty of the *neutral intercut* is that it always matches, or rather, appears to.

You will remember that there are a number of ways to maintain an illusion of continuity in the cut; i.e., cutting between actions just as the person begins to move, or cutting to a radically different camera angle from which it is impossible for the eye to detect the mismatch. This is the obvious advantage of using different camera set-ups which provide such variety of angle. These will cut beautifully and effortlessly with the master and give you a really exciting involvement in the action of the children. The editor will now have maximum control over the scene's tempo.

Your cutting tempo and the original camera positions will be greatly determined by the particular tempo of the action filmed; if the activity is serene or frantic, rapid or ponderous, your cutting must reflect this.

The master shot need not necessarily be used as the classic "establishing shot" at the very first shot of the sequence. Sometimes a close detail shot—or several in succession—can hook the spectator, so intriguing him that the wish to know what is happening arises within him, and is then answered by the cut to the master shot (see Impact Cut, Disorientation Cut, Chapter 7). It is more strongly justified psychologically that the intriguing detail will lead one to want to know the overall view than that the "establishing shot" will so intrigue that one will wish to know more detail about what is happening. We have always had the same feeling about the use of the zoom. It is psychologically far better to start close in on the intriguing, momentarily disorienting detail and then to pull back, revealing what the spectator badly wants to know, than to give everything away and then drift in slowly on the detail (Fig. 8.70). The movement from the overall picture to the detail badly needs the dramatic emphasis of the direct cut.°

There are times within the scene when it may be important to return to the overall master to reestablish the scene's geography. We recently cut a sequence in a film which began with a long shot of a forester moving into a forest of huge towering trees; we soon moved in to a series of close shots of him moving through the brush and measuring a tree. When we cut back to the long shot, we were once again breathtakingly reminded of his relationship to the enormous forest, which dwarfed the man, a feeling we inevitably lost in the detail shots.

Such a sequence is quite similar to the "B" sequence described above. There may be some sort of establishing shot, yet there has been felt no need to tie the entire sequence together with the overall master shot. Instead, the sequence is filmed as a series of separate shots. This requires essentially the same editing procedure as does the previous category, with the obvious difference that we need not pay homage to the master shot throughout the scene, the filmic continuity having no relationship to the order of shooting. Our continuity is freer, although it must be based on a logical continuity, usually suggested by the material itself.

We cut a typical sequence of this sort in an Ezra Baker film for IBM, *The Day Off*. The sequence involved a large television console being carried across a yard and into a house by the purchaser and a delivery man. Naturally there was a logical spatial progression from the delivery van to the house, but the sequence had been so well shot, with a wide variety of camera set-ups, that we had a great deal of freedom in assembling the section. The neutral detail shot in this case was a marvelously useful close-up of the ubiquitous tool carrier hanging from the TV man's belt, which gave us the cut-away for the one spot where we could not supply the illusion of continuity. With this fine variety of shots, we were able to cut the sequence to the exact length we wanted—a filmicly appropriate timing, a good deal faster than the literal time the action would have taken—and to give it a tempo and mood that perfectly fitted the scene. There simply was no need in this sequence for the overall master, and the director had wisely dispensed with it in favor of the variety of short sequential shots which worked so effectively.

With this category we have reached the apex of creative editing. Of course, the logic of the scene imposes a certain chronology upon the editor, but there is enormous opportunity for creative variation within this chronology. For example, in the classic cavalry charge discussed in Chapter 7, there is an obvious necessity to begin with the horses moving slowly at the far end of the valley and proceed logically through the gradual build of the force of the charge. It would be inappropriate to suddenly cut to a roaring cannon at the start of the sequence; but, once the point has been reached at which the cannons do explode into action, we have enormous freedom in the way we intercut the cannons' firing, the gun crews' frantic efforts, horses going down, riders toppling, dirt

C. A Variety of Shots Making Up the Sequence

Fig. 8–70 If we begin on the close shot of the boy we gain a great deal by the pull-back which now reveals him in a perilous position

D. A Large Number of Shots To Be Freely Edited in Making a Montage Sequence

*Remember the marvelous shot in *How To Murder Your Wife* which begins on a construction worker perched high on a beam reading a newspaper comic strip then pulls back to reveal Jack Lemmon, the cartoonist, sitting on his terrace—the worker now barely visible far in the background, a tiny figure in a small space under Lemmon's arm. The film overuses the zoom lens, but the specific uses are invariably well-done (often pull-backs) and accomplished with élan.

leaping under explosions, horses flashing by, and close-ups of the frantic faces of the men involved. The order in which these shots are cut—and the initial selection of the portion of the shot which is to be used—is in the hands of the editor. For that matter, so is the order of shots in the sequential build to the first moment of cannon fire, as we cut from the waiting gun crews, to the trotting horses, to the cannons themselves, to the riders, to the guns, to the horses breaking into a gallop, to quick, poignant details of the waiting men—a nervous smile, a sweating hand, a quick biting of lip—to the rushing charge and finally to the smashing climax of the sequence—"Fire!"—the cannon's explosion, and the first exploding shell among the racing horses.

In addition to the examples detailed in Chapter 7, we must mention the superb example of the charge of the French knights of Olivier's *Henry V*. The evocation of suspense and the creation of smashing excitement in such sequences is the work of the editor, and he can find no more exciting material to edit and no more challenging sequence to create.* It is hard to think of anything more essential to the cinema than a great chase sequence—and this is the editor's domain.

In the subject film, montage sequences are often used to great advantage. The shooting script simply states that a certain sequence will consist of a montage; the editor is handed a mass of material, and his work begins.

Remembering our statement on the importance of making a logical continuity appropriate to the subject, the director must be consulted as to the sequential order of the material. We edited a typical sequence of this type covering the process of paper-making, from the arrival of logs at the plant on railroad cars through the crushing and chipping of the wood, the chemical production of pulp, and the variety of steps that result in the actual making of paper. Naturally, the director had to establish the actual order in which the various actions took place, and this was the guide to the hanging of the shots by subsequences and the arranging of a coherent outline. Once this had been done, there was a great deal of creative freedom in the choice of shot succession.

At several points the director tempered this with specific requests, sometimes of a particular shot he wished included, sometimes in consideration of scalar relationship of shots to each other; a specific request was made for the gradual filmic emerging of the paper until the sequence climaxed with shots of the huge white sheets rolling off powerful machines. But perhaps 80% of the choice of portion of shot and the choice and timing of the cuts lay inevitably with the editor.

Of course, a montage can take many forms, not only the fire and excitement of the cavalry charge and the detailed precision of the industrial sequence, but the fun of a fast-moving dance sequence. We cut such a sequence in the previously mentioned *Miss Smile*, produced by Richard Matt for Paramount Pictures. What is interesting in this sequence is the fact that the music to which the girls appear to be dancing was composed long after the film had been shot. We must give away something of the cutter's trade secrets by pointing out that with one or two

*It is said that the invitational press audience leaped to its feet cheering at the showing of the silent version of *Ben Hur* during the climax of the chariot race, and at the first screening of *Henry V*, the climax of the charge of the French knights.

key attentions to detail the editor can skillfully cut *any* fast moving action to *any* fast moving music and get an excellent illusion of actual matching of action to sound. The eye (and the wish) supplies the match. Of course, if the editor knows the music's tempo when he is cutting the picture he can create some effective juxtapositions between the sound and visual images, a form of metric cutting determined by the musical beat.

We must mention one other use of the montage common to sponsored films, the "product montage." This is exactly what the name implies and can be a useful means of showing in a short time the great variety of products made by a particular manufacturer. Unfortunately such sequences all too often become "cataloguing" sequences, the products shot with little filmic imagination, with little consideration of their relationship to one another, and little awareness of the variety of imaginative camera angles and movements that can be used to give the sequence filmic life. If the director and cameraman have not done their job, there is little that the editor can do to the cataloguing sequence. A consultation is important beforehand to ensure that the material can be made into a valid montage.

One of the major regrets in writing this book is our inability to include material on animation, but it simply is not within the scope of the film primer. We must mention that animation sequences are often to be found in subject films, particularly industrial, educational, and instructional films. If you are fortunate in being near a city in which animation houses are found, you may seek their help in preparing certain sequences which can best be handled in this way. Animation can take the form of cartoons, actual "moving figures" with or without sync voice. It can involve the use of charts and drawings, perhaps with movement of some of the lettering or drawing on the charts, or it can mean the still-picture-camera-in-motion technique. At this time our concern cannot be with the execution of this material, but must be with the specifics of the editor's handling of it after it has been presented to him.

ANIMATION SEQUENCES WITH AND WITHOUT SYNC DIALOGUE

We will discuss first the *animation with sync sound* sequence. This will be supplied to the editor with a sync voice track (sync voice animation is always drawn *to* the previously recorded and edited voice track, not the other way around). The editor will treat this as he did the category "A" under sync sound sequences (see page 305), simply cutting the picture into the film in correct sequential order and rolling up and storing the matched sound track until it comes time to assemble the entire sync dialogue track.

As for *animation without sync dialogue,* the important thing to remember is that it will be supplied to the editor as a sequence, even a group of sequences, with the material already joined together—since this is the way it is shot on the animation cameras, even including dissolves or other optical transitions between scenes. Should the editor wish to shorten a scene or even to remove a scene involving a dissolve, he can cut the dissolve out of the film, making a direct cut to the next shot (Fig. 8.71). Should a new dissolve be desired, he can mark that on the film for the lab to do. (Normally the lab does not put in the animation dissolves since they are already in the original, executed by the animation house.) Remember to leave the necessary dissolve trim between the last frame of the new dissolve and the old dissolve. In other words, if one is putting in a 24-frame dissolve, it is not enough to start it 12 frames ahead of the old dissolve, snipping the old dissolve off at that point. The dissolve must begin a full 24 frames ahead of the old dissolve at least; then the 12-frame trim can be cut off and the splice made at that point with the dissolve marked on the film in grease pencil for the negative matcher. Be sure that any such editing of animation sequences is appropriate and will match the narration; since animation is done to exact frame counts, you must be certain that your change is justified.

THE FINE CUT

You have now worked through the entire work print, assembling the sequences in the proper order as you complete them. It is, however, a *rough cut,* so there is some important work ahead of you. Now is the time for a relaxed, attentive run-through on the projector, if possible several times in one day. You will begin to notice cuts you will want to correct, some merely by snipping a few frames, others where the cut simply does not work and must be changed. Often the sponsor or director may issue an order for a specific length of running time, and the picture must almost arbitrarily be cut to this. Never struggle against such a request;

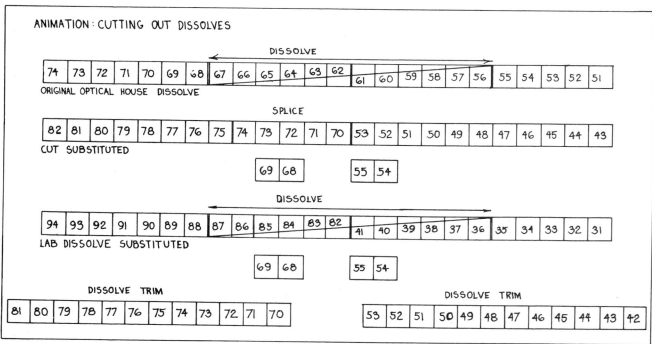

Fig. 8–71

no matter how much you are in love with your own work, it is impossible for a film not to benefit from cutting down. I have known directors, desperate to remove a few minutes from a film, to order six frames taken out at every splice in the picture—arbitrary and a bit extreme, but you get the idea. Check your narration against the picture by reading it aloud; changes may have to be made here too. Do not be afraid to rearrange sequences; no one has the ability to see everything the first time he assembles a picture. Do not live with your errors; get rid of them.

Fig. 8–72a Head marking for work print and sync voice track: film title, producer, type of track, "head"

Once you have arrived at a fine cut of the picture, you will wish to sync up each separate voice take so that they can be run as a continuous track with the complete picture (Fig. 8.72 A–D). This is a simple job, since you have marked a sync point at the head of each sound take and rolled them up in your film can set aside for sync sound material; these sync points will match specific frames marked on your work print. Place the work print on the first gang of a synchronizer and prepare a roll of blank leader for the second gang. The head will be labeled with the name of production, producer, the words "Sync Voice," and, at the very start of the leader, "Head." As a further precaution, should the head of the leader break off, write the term "Sync Voice" next to the actual start mark on the tracks. Start picture and voice tracks on the start marks, in sync, with synchronizer on "zero." Now roll forward leader and picture in sync until you reach the first sync point marked on the work print. Cut in the appropriate sound take on the parallel frame on the leader running on the B gang. Roll forward through the synchronizer and, when the take runs out, splice the leader onto the end. Now continue to roll forward until you come to the next sync point on the print; cut in the matching voice take. Proceed similarly through the last take.

It is a customary practice to run leader from the point at which the last sync sound take ends to the final footage of the picture. There is a double purpose served by the extra leader. At least fifty feet (35mm) of leader should be added at the end of any "last sound take," whether music, effects, or voice, in order to ensure that the re-recording dubbers (and, for that matter, your Moviola) will be able to play the sound smoothly, without a "wow," right to the end. (Another means of ensuring this is to use a split reel with a large core of 3 inches in diameter rather than a small one of 2 inches.) The second reason for using the leader extension—this time all the way to the end of the picture—is to allow the re-recordist at the end of the mix the option of backing up with all his tracks "in sync" to locate a previously-passed point in the film. If tracks which end part way through the picture are allowed to run out at that point, it becomes necessary to return to the picture start to line up all tracks again, proceeding down through the picture to the desired point (see Chapter 12).

Once you have assembled the entire sync voice track, run it on a Moviola with the picture; you can now make your final adjustments at the beginning and end of each sync sound sequence to get just the right

THE SYNC VOICE TRACK

Fig. 8–72b Marking of start marks

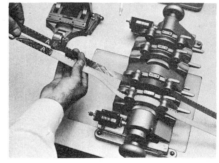

Fig. 8–72c Sync voice sequence "A" has been cut in; marked frames on pix and voice track match so sequence is in sync

Fig. 8–72d Sync voice sequence "A" has ended and leader has been spliced onto tracks; at appropriate point sync voice sequence "B" has been cut in in sync

timing; remember that there is an interrelation between the voice and picture tempos that must be considered. You now have a complete fine cut.

When you have determined the length and position of the titles, mark them appropriately on the work print with grease pencil as a guide to the negative matcher. Some editors prefer to have the optical house run a print of any required optical effects or titles from the negative they have created; if so, then you will cut the print into the work print at the points you have marked.

CHAPTER 9

OPTICALS AND TITLES

One of the film-maker's prime allies in the making of his film can be the optical house and its optical printer. The optical printer, by modifying the shot taken by the production camera, will allow the film-maker to do on film things which are impossible to do in any other way. Some of these can be done by other processes but not with the same quality of results.

The optical printer was relatively slow in coming to film; it arrived shortly before the talkies. The impetus for its development was the need for a way of making fades and dissolves after the shooting stage of production was completed and the need for a better way than the method current at that time of making a fade chemically. Until the printer was designed, the film-maker could make a fade-out by slowly closing the shutter of the camera, and a fade-in by slowly opening the camera's shutter. A dissolve was made by first executing a fade-out, then rewinding the film to a designated position and shooting the next shot by slowly opening the shutter and fading in the scene. The rewound portion of the film would contain a double exposure, and thus the dissolve.

This was, at the very least, an unsatisfactory method of achieving effects. What could the film-maker do if, in the editing process, he decided he wanted the effect on another shot? The answer to the question, of course, was nothing. Then some lab technician discovered that he could make a chemical fade by applying a chemical that would gradually eat away the emulsion as more and more of the chemical was applied to a piece of developed negative. However, when a dissolve was desired, the camera method was the only recourse until the optical printer.

The earliest printers were custom-built by each studio or laboratory in its own workshops. It was not until 1943 that a standardized optical printer was placed on the market. This printer was the Acme-Dunn Optical Printer which had been designed and constructed for the U.S. Armed Forces Photographic Units. The emergence of the standardized printer stimulated and widened the use of optical effects, for now they could be available to every film producer. The only limitations on the use of such effects were the limitations imposed by the film-maker's imagination and budget. Special optical effects houses began to emerge using the standardized equipment that was available to anyone. The later development of better duplicating films, better lenses, better processing techniques, and more skilled technicians served to stimulate the use of the printer and increase its creative and economic values.

The optical printer is a complex piece of rephotographing machinery, but basically it is composed of a camera and a projector mounted on a lathe bed facing each other. The projector is threaded with a piece of film containing the image photographed during production, either the original or an exact copy. This piece of film generally contains a positive image of very fine grain and reduced contrast characteristics—when working in 35mm a "fine grain" (see page 485) is made, while the original is generally used in 16mm reversal. The projector (called a "tailgate") is similar to a stripped-down camera—no lens, no viewfinder, no side door, no light-tight magazine—with the intermittent movement left intact. This intermittent movement, however, is one of high precision. The movement of the tailgate and the camera head are interlocked so that both turn together at the same speed. A high-intensity lamp housing is an essential addition to the stripped-down camera, so that the aperture of the tailgate is backlighted to project the image of the film moving past this aperture.

The camera, also high precision, is on the other side of the lathe bed, on which it is capable of sliding back and forth. The lens of the camera is mounted separately on a slide to facilitate its movement and is connected to the camera by means of a long bellows. Naturally this camera carries unexposed film. The tailgate and the camera head move at the same speed, the camera takes a picture of each frame of the film running through the projection head. A variety of optical effects can be accomplished by manipulating such things as the lens position, the focus, and the shutter of the camera head. The printer can be adapted from 35mm to 16mm, or vice versa, in a matter of seconds.

In order to indicate to the reader the importance of the printer in the making of films and the enormous scope to the use of the printer, here is a list of a few of the more common effects that are executed on the optical printer:

1. TRANSITIONAL EFFECTS Transitions are used to indicate a change in time or place between scenes. The fade, the dissolve, the ripple dissolve, the wipe, the out-of-focus dissolve, the zoom dissolve, the flip, the spin in and out, and the kaleidoscope are only a few of the many, and only the more typical, examples utilized.

2. SUPERIMPOSURE This effect involves the printing of the images from two or more pieces of film so that they are overlapped onto one piece of film. This is the process employed when the titles are printed over a background of still or moving images. The effect is also used in montages, double exposure, strobe effects, adding weather elements like rain, snow, or fog to a scene.

3. CHANGES IN THE SIZE OR POSITION OF THE IMAGE This effect is employed to obtain a close angle for additional editing material, to do away with unwanted areas in a shot, to reduce the size of a shot to be used in multiple screen techniques.

4. CHANGES IN THE ACTION SPEED The speed of the action of a shot can be speeded up or slowed down in multiples of the basic speed at which the film was exposed by skipping or repeating the frames of an action when printing. The jerky, speeded-up motion of silent movies can be duplicated in this way. The frame can also be held in a freeze so that the action can be stopped.

5. SPLIT SCREEN This effect is utilized to divide the scene into multiple images, to print a scene in which one actor plays a dual role in the same scene, to give the effect that a person is in the same scene with a dangerous animal. A familiar use is in science fiction films in which actors are pursued by giant insects.

6. INTRODUCTION OF MOTION The motion of an airplane, a boat, an automobile, etc. is added to an interior shot of the particular vehicle. Zoom effects, pans, and a sense of the violent shaking or jarring of an explosion or a violent impact are other examples of the motions that can be added to a shot.

7. MANIPULATION OF THE PHOTOGRAPHIC AND/OR COLOR QUALITY OF A SHOT This can be achieved by adding or reducing the filtering, diffusion, contrast, matting, etc. to create a new scene or to match one scene to another.

The optical printer has myriad uses available to the film-maker. One of its most important is the doctoring or salvaging of materials that might otherwise be useless. Many times the film-maker can find himself with material that is of no use because of some mechanical or human error during the production phase. Retakes may be prohibitively expensive, so the film-maker must rely, when possible, on the optical printer to save him. A friend recently completed shooting outside of the United States, and when his film had been processed, he looked at the dailies and discovered that a sunshade was showing along the top edge of the frame of an important shot. To reshoot the take was impossible, but all was saved by having the shot blown up slightly to do away with the unwanted upper edge. A sun flare on the film can also be eliminated in this way. This is only a simple case of the many ingenious applications of the optical printer open to the film-maker to salvage what would otherwise be a catastrophic situation.

The optical printer is also used in the reduction from 35mm original to 16mm prints, or in the blowing up from 16mm to 35mm. Blowing up 16mm is a very important function of the optical printer. Although there is some graininess due to the change in image size, the recent development of new lenses, film stocks, and liquid gate printing have done much to improve the overall quality of the blown-up print. *Endless Summer* is an example of a feature film which, by its nature, had to be shot in 16mm, and was successfully blown up to 35mm for distribution. The same is true for portions of *Faces*.

A so-called "pan and scan" operation has been developed with the optical printer so that films produced in wide screen can be converted to standard proportions (1.33 to 1) for use on television. In this operation the composition of each individual scene is scanned and the area of central interest is selected as a direct cut or a "pan" across the frame as this central area moves in the scene. Conversely, an adaptation of this technique plus a blow-up stage has been devised so that films produced in 35mm can be expanded to wide-screen proportions (2.2 to 1 in 70mm). A recent example of this is *Gone With the Wind* which was recently re-released in 70mm.

WORKING WITH THE OPTICAL HOUSE

Whether or not the optical house serves as a vital member of the production team is dependent upon whether this organization is included in the film-maker's pre-planning. Going off "half-cocked" can only decrease the effectiveness of the final results. Pre-planning offers no danger to your creative freedom. It merely decreases the pressure by decreasing the number of inane and unnecessary interruptions in the production of your film.

Do not delude yourself into thinking that your problems will end when the lights and camera have been put away. Strangely enough, many film-makers never take into consideration the swarm of problems that can descend on them when they move on to the optical house to secure their contribution—a swarm that can be reduced and even obliterated by consulting this organization before the film-maker has even begun to film. An idea in your head may seem simple and easy to execute, but in practice may be just the opposite. Stories abound about the advertising agency producer who conceived a brilliant idea only to find, after he had filmed his idea, that the necessary optical effects would cost a small fortune to execute or that these optical effects necessitated the film being shot in a different way.

Making such a mistake is not only foolish, it is unnecessary. Make a trip to the optical house before you begin production and talk with their *lay-out man*. Discuss with him your film and the optical effects you will require. The lay-out man can be a valuable ally. He can tell you whether your ideas concerning the effects are feasible or not. If not, he may be able to suggest substitutes which are just as effective. This consultation is a must if you are planning on complex optical effects. The fee for such a consultation is negligible in light of the importance that it can have on the successful outcome of your project. Take advantage of the knowledge and experience of this organization, for in the long run the optical house may save you money. They will know the best ways, the short-cuts, the pitfalls of which you must be aware. Opticals prices are fairly standardized, so the optical house must be highly competitive if it is to survive. Its ability to compete is determined by its honesty and the quality of its work. The optical house should provide you with the easiest way to achieve your desired results; it is to their advantage to do your assignment as quickly and as efficiently as possible.

On the other hand, do not be afraid to question the lay-out man's conclusions. Do not hesitate to ask why your desired effects cannot be done, or why they will cost X amount of dollars, or why they must be shot in a particular way, or why another effect will be more feasible. Make sure the lay-out man has a valid reason for his conclusions. Be true to your own creative intuition and do not let him put you off of your idea without first questioning his results. Many film-makers lack a thorough knowledge of opticals and how they are achieved, and because of uncertainties bred by their lack of knowledge, they tend to accept the word of the lay-out man as gospel. The lay-out man may not have understood your explanation of the effect you wished to achieve, or your questioning may trigger another idea that will allow him to produce what you want. It is also true that your job may require a great deal of work and will thus tie up his equipment longer than he wishes for the money your project will bring in to the firm. This is a highly competitive business, and survival is also dependent upon the quantity of work an optical house can produce. If the technician supports his contention, you will have to rethink your idea. But if he cannot, chances are that he does not want to get involved in a complex job that does not justify a sufficient monetary reimbursement for the time that will be necessary. If this is the case, go to another optical house.

If your film idea will require only standard effects, a consultation may not be necessary; but you should make arrangements with an optical house, before shooting, to handle your project. Get your project on their schedule, particularly if you are going to require rush work from them. Possibly these arrangements can be made at the same time you are gathering figures for your budget, if you know your schedule and approximately what effects you will require. At the same time you make these arrangements, it might be wise to double-check what they will require of your materials in order to successfully execute the desired effects.

At the time of your consultation with the optical house, either you or your editor should check with them concerning the marking of the work print. If markings are used that can be interpreted wrongly, the mistake can cost a great deal of money. This is one of the major reasons problems can develop at the optical house.

When the time arrives for you to submit the necessary materials to the optical house for the execution of your order, you will need to provide them with the *original footage* involved in the effects, the *marked work print*, and *thorough instructions*. If it is at all feasible, you should deliver these materials by hand so that you can go over the desired effects and your instructions with the lay-out man. This will minimize the chances for error. The optical house will then time your original, make changes in the density and color balance, and prepare a "fine grain" or precision interpositive in color if they will not be printing from the original. If your film is 16mm reversal, the density and color balance will be ascertained and corrected during the printing, because the actual effects will be printed from the original. The lay-out man will have made up a lay-out sheet which goes to the technician operating the optical printer. This lay-out sheet will include complete instructions as to the effect, the necessary filtering required, and the footage numbers where the changes and the effects are to be executed.

Do not be disappointed or disgruntled if the results you hoped for are not forthcoming the first time the optical house tries to create your effects. There will probably be no trouble if you have only sought from them a series of standard effects and titles. But if your project involves complex optical effects, it may take two or three attempts before you will be satisfied. Do not accept the job until you are satisfied. Frequently the trouble is not with the optical house, but rather is with the film-maker. Perhaps he has not made himself completely clear, or has not marked the work print correctly, or has not originally shot the scenes properly. There are a number of variables which can cause problems.

You will undoubtedly find, if you are producing in 16mm, that there is a quality difference in the print between the optical footage provided by the optical house and the original footage. When opticals are printed from 16mm stock, the resulting print begins to "pull apart"—there is a graininess and a desaturation of the color. Until very recently nothing could be done to prevent this; it was a characteristic of the film stock. Eastman Kodak, however, has recently developed a new print stock that should do much to eliminate this quality breakdown. However, the quality problem will continue to exist until the use of this new stock is standard. The film-maker can help in offsetting this quality reduction by shooting the material that will be used in the optical effects with prime lenses whenever possible and by properly lighting and exposing the camera original. Using a zoom lens or having to push the film will only accentuate the quality breakdown.

If the film-maker is concerned by the quality breakdown that occurs with 16mm, he may wish to produce such standard effects as fades, dissolves, superimposed titles, and composite images—e.g., double exposures—in the lab. Whenever possible, he should have the fades and dissolves executed by the laboratory by cutting his original into A–B rolls. The other effects can also be accomplished by the lab by placing the materials on "C," "D," etc. rolls. The effects will have better quality because there will be no generation loss as with opticals. However, a fair amount of danger is prevalent in this method because of the necessity for more runs through the printer to accommodate the additional rolls, and the cost will more than likely be higher. Producers of television commercials, in order to maintain a consistent grain and color quality, will often have the entire commercial printed optically. But such a practice is prohibitively expensive for a film of any duration.

One final word: When you are producing in 16mm, be sure to specify to the optical house the emulsion position—"A"-Wind or "B"-Wind—you will require of your opticals so that they can be cut in with the original when you are conforming the camera original to the work print.

MAKING OPTICAL EFFECTS

Working with the optical printer is a far more complex process than is indicated in the simplified explanation found at the beginning of this chapter. The complex process of optical printing is beyond the scope of this book, for the wealth of material is sufficient for a separate treatise—several of which are presently available—and is too complex and technical to be covered in a single chapter. Since our primary aim is to impart to the film-maker his role in each stage of the production of his film, the preceding material should serve as his guide to obtaining optical effects. The following is a simplified explanation as to the process of creating the more commonly used standard optical effects.

FADE   A fade is created by placing the positive print (the original in 16mm reversal) of the entire shot in which the fade is to occur in the projection head of the optical printer. The camera head is adjusted so that the registration and aspect ratio of the frames of its unexposed film are identical with those of the positive print in the projector. In other words, the camera will print 1:1. If the effect is to be a fade-out, the projection and camera heads will be run electrically interlocked so that each frame of the print is exposed on the camera's film. At the pre-marked frame when the fade-out is to begin, the shutter of the camera head will be closed a predetermined number of degrees for each frame of the fade-out until, at the completion of the last frame of the fade, the shutter of the camera will be completely closed. A fade-in begins with the shutter closed, and it is opened frame by frame a predetermined number of degrees until the shutter has reached, by the completion of the last frame of the fade-in, the desired degree of opening—the total degree of shutter opening being 170°.

DISSOLVE   When a dissolve is executed, the scene that is to fade out is run through the projector and a fade-out is carried out in the manner indicated above. The shutter remains closed at the end of the fade-out and the film in the camera is backed up to the beginning of the previous fade-out. The new scene is placed in the projection head and a fade-in is executed by the above method. The stages of the fade-out and fade-in are executed one frame at a time. The degrees of the shutter opening of the scene fading in are the subtracted number of degrees of the scene fading out so that brilliant or dark flashes are eliminated and the dissolve lighting is steady. The degrees of the shutter openings of the outgoing and incoming scene will always add up to 170°, thus assuring the steady lighting.

Frames of Dissolve	Fade-Out	Fade-In
1st	170°	0°
2nd	160°	10°
3rd	150°	20°
4th	140°	30°
etc. to end	etc. to 0°	etc. to 170°

RIPPLE DISSOLVE   A ripple dissolve is carried out in the same manner as a regular dissolve, except that a piece of ripple glass is inserted to cause the ripple effect, and the scenes can be maintained in sharp or soft focus. However, if the ripple dissolve is to be effective, it should be longer than a normal dissolve.

FREEZE FRAME   The entire shot in which the freeze frame occurs must be optically printed. For example, if you desire a freeze frame on the last frame of a shot 10 feet in length, the entire 10 feet must be optically printed. The positive image is placed in the projector and the camera records, at a 1:1 ratio, each frame of the shot. At the frame where the freeze is to occur, the projection head is stopped, and the camera head continues to record that frame for the required length of the effect.

WIPES   Wipe effects are obtained with the use of a traveling matte. The stages of the wipe movement are drawn and photographed on an animation stand. This photographed movement is made up of shifting areas of black and transparent film (Fig. 9.1). If a hard edge is desired, the matte is threaded in contact with the scenes involved in the wipe into the projection head and both are recorded by the camera head. The wipe effect can also be executed by placing the traveling matte in a special wipe head which is a second projector that is placed nearer to the camera. The position of the special wipe head in relation to the lens of the camera head can vary, thus affecting the softness of the wipe effect. The special wipe head is generally run by hand. This projector also has an open back so the scene running through the main tailgate can pass through to the camera.

DOUBLE EXPOSURE   To create a double exposure, one of the scenes involved in the double image is placed in the projection head and then exposed on the camera's film by running the two heads interlocked together. If the scene is to contain a fade-in and/or a fade-out, these are executed in the printing. At the end of this printing, the shutter of the camera is closed and the camera's film is run back to the designated place where the double exposure is to occur. The second scene involved in the effect is then placed in the projection head and is also printed onto the camera's film with any required fades. It is possible to double expose at varying degrees depending upon the scenes involved and the effect desired. When the camera's film is processed, the scene will contain the two images and any fades.

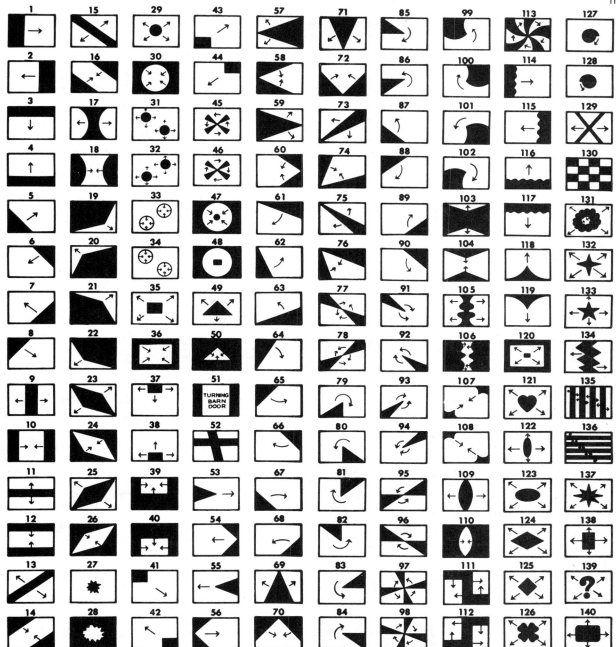

Fig. 9–1 140 different wipes that are available

REVERSED IMAGE Sometimes, during filming, a film-maker will cross the imaginary line and get a mismatch in screen direction. So for this, or some other, reason, he may need to reverse the image he has recorded. This can be accomplished in the laboratory by contact printing base to emulsion, but the results will be a soft-focused image. The best procedure is to have the reversed image printed optically. The positive image is flipped over when it is placed in the projection head. The camera head is then focused on this reversed image, and as a result the print obtained will be in sharp focus.

BLOW-UP   When a film-maker wishes to change the composition of a shot or eliminate some unwanted area near the edge of the frame, he can do this by blowing up the desired portion of the frame. The camera head is moved closer to the projection head until the desired area fills the frame of the camera. The camera's lens is focused to the new image, and the print is made by running the interlocked camera and projector.

CHANGING THE SPEED OF THE ACTION   The camera and projection heads are set at equal size—1:1. The action sequence that is to be slowed down is placed on the projector, but the camera records the action by repeating every frame twice or by recording three frames for every two of the projected frames. When this action is later run on a projector, the added frames will slow it down. If the desired alteration is to speed up the action, the camera *skip-prints* or prints every other frame, for example, so that when the resulting scene is later projected, the action is faster. It is possible to achieve some interesting optical effects through variations of this process of optical printing.

TITLES   The film-maker provides the optical house with the information to be used in the opening and closing titles, or any other titles or printed material which might occur within the film, plus the length of each title. A fairly standard procedure for determining the length of each title is to time it with a stopwatch by reading through the material that will be included in the title, then counting to five and stopping the watch. This watch reading is the length of time for that title. For example: Start the watch. Read the title's material—JOE JONES, Editor, JOHN SMITH, Camera, TOM BROWN, Music—count: one, two three, four, five. Stop the watch. This material takes approximately ten seconds. Translated into footage, that would be 6 feet of 16mm footage or 15 feet of 35mm footage. The film-maker must also inform the optical house as to whether he wishes the titles to fade-on and -off, dissolve on and off, or "pop" on and off. Again a relatively standard practice is to utilize a 24-frame fade-in and a 24-frame fade-out, for a total of 48 extra frames to the earlier 6 feet of 16mm footage (15 feet for 35mm). His title should now fade-in, be visible for the necessary ten seconds for reading, and fade-out.

If these titles are to be superimposed over background shots, he must also provide the originals of these shots (Fig. 9.2). The film-maker then selects from samples supplied to him the style of printing and the color he desires and furnishes the optical house with the instructions as to how he wishes the titles to be laid out. He must always submit his material on paper and check his spelling carefully. The titles are then made up and this art work is photographed to the needed length on the animation stand on high contrast stock—white titles over a black background. The exposed stock is then developed and a negative image

Fig. 9–2a Supered titles over a running shot

Fig. 9–2b Supered titles over a running shot: note action has progressed

Fig. 9–2c Main title: use of multiple-image format allows presentation of title material with maximum of clarity

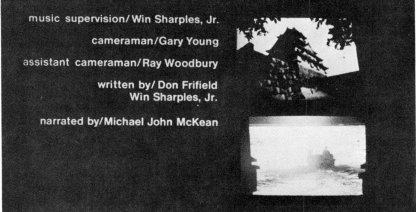

Fig. 9–2d First of four end credits

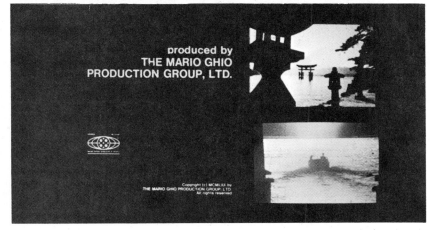

Fig. 9–2e Fourth of four end credits

results—black titles on clear film. A positive, high-contrast print is struck from the negative, and the optical house has both a positive and negative image of the titles. If the titles are to be in white—the most common—the positive image serves as the burn-in of the titles, and the negative image, as the matte. If a drop-shadow is required, the positive image and the negative image are threaded offset on the optical printer with the negative image and the background scene first running together on the printer and the white title or positive image double exposed in a separate run. White titles with a drop-shadow are the most readable, although we have used red, yellow, and green titles when the backgrounds were such that these colors would be visible. However, color titles require the use of a black matte when they are to be superimposed over a background scene and are thus more expensive. White is the television standard.

In order to determine the best placement of the superimposed title over the background, the camera of the animation stand is converted into a projector by adding a prism to the camera's movement and a lamp housing that projects a beam of light through the prism. The latest models of the animation stand have this feature built-in. A frame of the background shot is then projected onto the copy table and a tracing of the action is made. The title lay-out is next determined by fitting the titles onto the traced image. In this way the most effective placement is ascertained; the choice of color in the titles to contrast with the color of the background can then be selected before a print is made.

The material is then run through the optical printer, and the titles, background, and desired optical effects are printed onto the camera head's film.

CHAPTER 10

THE AUDIAL IMAGE: THE AESTHETICS OF FILM SOUND

Since October 6, 1929, a great many of the fervent fans of the cinema have mourned the tragic death of the "film as art," a promising youth throttled by the avaricious brothers Warner. This date, of course, marks the occasion on which Warner Brothers' *The Jazz Singer* burst upon the awareness of the film industry and the film-going public of America and the world. *The Jazz Singer* was not a total sound film as we know them today, but rather a "film with sound," containing sequences of lip-synchronized singing by Al Jolson as well as several dialogue scenes. Nor was it the first of its genre, for several studios, notably Fox and Warner Brothers, had been experimenting for some time with the making of "sound" films.* Nor, for that matter, was *The Jazz Singer* a particularly *good* film! But what it *was* is far more important than what it was not. *The Jazz Singer* was a stunning entertainment experience which captured fully the imagination of the movie-going public, leaving them forever thirsting for more. That the moguls of the movies unthinkingly tram-

*The premiere on August 6, 1926, of Warner Brothers' *Don Juan*, starring John Barrymore, using the Western Electric-developed Vitaphone (sound-on-disc synchronized with film) system to provide an accompanying orchestral score, the feature accompanied by operatic short subjects and a filmed speech by movie censorship czar Will Hayes, was another significant date. Walt Disney was at this time at work on the third episode of a series based upon a newly-created cartoon character. Disney quickly shelved the two completed films and converted the third into the first sound cartoon. *Steamboat Willie*, starring Mickey Mouse, was released to the enthusiastic public on September 19, 1928. Fox Film Corp. made the first public showings of their Movietone (a sound-on-film-system) Newsreels in January, 1927, and discontinued the making of silent pictures in March, 1929, seven months before *The Jazz Singer* premiere.

pled into the dust of southern California much that was great in the silent film, in their frantic stampede to slake this thirst, is a matter of history. Overnight the movie industry, or "The Industry," as it is fondly and familiarly termed at Academy Award ceremonies, was faced with the dramatic realization that sound would forever remain an integral part of film-making, for the mere presence of sound—any sound—could virtually guarantee the success of a film.

The first stage in the sound revolution consisted of a variety of desperate attempts to transform films in various stages of completion into "films with sound," usually by adding a few sounds to certain selected reels. The next stage represented a self-destructive weeding out of countless experienced members of the film-making community who were replaced at every level of production by theater-trained technicians, brought in to take advantage of their familiarity with the spoken word. These imported experts had little understanding of the essential nature of film, something that the un-literary, often inarticulate silent film-makers whom they replaced had instinctively grasped. While carrying out their appointed tasks with supreme technical competence, they swung the film away from its accustomed paths. But had the silent film really achieved the pinnacle of artistic achievement for the film?

To begin with, there is a good deal of evidence that the film pioneers themselves saw the lack of sound as a detriment to, rather than a strength of, the cinema. Described as maintaining that "sound came not to destroy but to fulfill the testament of cinema,"[1] André Bazin points out that all of the early inventors of cinema "in their imaginations . . . saw the cinema as a total and complete representation of reality; they saw in a trice the reconstruction of a perfect illusion of the outside world in sound, color, and relief . . . there was not a single inventor who did not try to combine sound and relief with animation of the image."[2] Edison, for example, having invented the phonograph, stated that he saw this invention as only a part of a concept that involved moving pictures in conjunction with his recorded sound. The inventors of the early motion picture cameras and projectors turned immediately to attempts to include sound as a vital portion of their films. Knowing the public's eager expectation for the film as the agent for the most perfect reproduction of reality, we can understand that sound, as an additional element of actuality, would have been sought as a part of the film experience from the start.

And what of the famed silent films? Were they the ultimate achievement one could hope for from the film?

> Directors of imagination performed feats of technical ingenuity to imply by means of visual action or suggestion what would normally be directly conveyed by words. . . . Characterization was reduced to terms of observation. . . . What was most noticeable about the silent film was its otherworldliness, its dream quality, its elemental simplicity in terms of comedy, farce, melodrama, tragedy.[3]

If you have had the opportunity of objectively viewing a number of silent films in comparison with the films of today, you will find it difficult to think of "the silents" as the highest attainment of film art. Certainly there are individual masterworks (if you still are of a mind that the silents have never been topped, take a look at some of the *ordinary* films of that era!), but the genre as a whole must be considered as an example of ingenious and imaginative overcoming of severe limitations. A game of charades can be great fun, but it is not likely to produce articulate eloquence or subtlety of expression. The silents represent an imperfect way-station along the path toward complete fulfillment of the art of film.°

The history of film sound must begin with the first film, for the cinema pioneers, searching from the beginning for a means of marrying sound with picture, made use of music to fill the void during the earliest public performance of their films. The use of music had been long established in the theater. From the time of ancient Greek drama, with its accompanying percussion and flute, through the medieval drama, commedia dell' arte, Elizabethan drama and the drama of the Renaissance, on through the nineteenth century with its opera and vaudeville, the history of the theater reveals a parallel history of the development of musical accompaniment. By the time films were born, the tradition had been well established for the use of music for the furthering of identification of character and communication of emotion.

Manvell and Huntley, in their useful work, *The Technique of Film Music*, refer to a paper on "Music to Stage Plays," written in 1910 by Norman O'Neill, the outstanding stage composer of the day; it might well serve as the instruction to a contemporary film composer:

> The musical accompaniment to a speech should steal in and steal out so quietly that the audience is not more aware of it than they are of some subtle change in the stage lighting. . . . I do not wish to give you the impression that in music for the stage melody has no place. On the contrary, no successful incidental music (or any other for that matter) can be devoid of melody and thematic material. I only feel that clearly defined tunes in conjunction with the dialogue are out of place. When a running accompaniment of music is required for a long stretch of dialogue, the exact time of each speech, the pauses, entrances, and exits, must all be carefully measured.[4]

In this climate of acceptance for accompanying music, and with an instinctive awareness of the demands of the film experience, attempts were made to fill the awful vacuum of silence—or its alternative, the rattling projector and the rustling of feet, the coughing and whispering of the audience. As early as 1900, the intriguingly titled film *Little Tich and His Big Boots* was produced with an accompanying "score" on a phonograph record, and the famed Lumière Brothers used piano accompaniment at their first public screenings in the Grand Café on the Boulevard des Capucines, December, 28, 1895.

A SHORT HISTORY OF FILM SOUND

*It is interesting to apply this same reasoning to the absence of color, another element sought from the start by the early film-makers and an obvious ingredient necessary for the close approximation of actuality. The fact is that the absence of color does not severely limit our grasp of basic emotions, ideas, dramatic situations, and character; there are many who feel, rather, that the use of the black-and-white film heightens the presentation of emotion and drama, contributing a powerful and effective stylization to the film form. There are certain films which are, simply, black-and-white—Olivier's *Hamlet* and the great American films of the Bogart era like *Key Largo*, *The Maltese Falcon*, and *Casablanca*; or *Citizen Kane*, *Strangers on a Train*, and *The Big Sleep*, for example. Even such classic adventure films as *Stagecoach*, *The Airforce*, and *Red River*, and comedies like *Bringing Up Baby*, *Mr. Smith Goes to Washington*, *The Great Dictator*, and *The Miracle of Morgan's Creek* seem perfectly suited to black-and-white. As for the necessity for color in the approximation of reality, the generation which grew up, as we did, on the films of the forties, accepted black-and-white as the natural order of things filmic, for color was then an imperfect process which automatically created a sense of unreality about the film. With today's superior color film and highly developed techniques for using it, we have come close to a "natural" color. It will be interesting to see how the present generation of youngsters, who will have experienced a virtually 100% color film and television era, will develop. It is unlikely that they will share our feelings toward black-and-white films as the "realistic" cinema.

Although, initially, light music unrelated to the content of the film was played simply as a "filler," it was not long before the pianist—or conductor of the small orchestra—took to following the action of the screen rather closely, playing certain selections appropriate to the material appearing on the screen. In 1908, Charles Pathé's company, Le Film d'Art, invited Camille Saint-Saens to compose a score for their first film, *L'Assassinat du Duc de Guise*. In 1909 there appeared the first "Suggestions for Music," issued as a guide to the accompanying of Edison's films, and even machines for providing various sound effects for film performances were on the market. The musicians soon had available to them various mood music publications, including those prepared for Sam Fox by J. S. Zamecnik and Guiseppe Becce's "Kinobibliothek," both presenting a variety of music catalogued according to mood, style, and character. At this time the conventions of film music which have carried to the present appear; we note the categories "love scene," "funeral march," "plaintive music," "love tragedy," "remorse," "agitated hurry," "shadowed!," "allegro agitato," and "mysterioso #1" (for "horror, stealth, conspiracy, treachery"). There is, in fact, little difference between the categories in today's "mood music" catalogue of recorded film background music and those used for the silent film.

There were also available for a number of films specific music cue sheets listing suggested appropriate selections, scene by scene, in many cases pieces from the classical repertoire. Liszt, whose music thundered over the fierce conflicts of the Emperor Ming and Flash Gordon in the Saturday afternoon serials of our youth, seems to have been a born "film composer," his music eagerly seized upon from the start.

Soon it became an established practice for the producers of important films to send out with them an entire original score. *Birth of a Nation* (March, 1915) was the first film accompanied by a full orchestral score, the joint work of Griffith himself and Joseph Carl Briel. (The "love theme" of The Little Colonel and Elsie was later to become well-known as the signature to the radio program "Amos and Andy.") There were famous scores during this period by Edmund Meisel for Eisenstein's *Potemkin,* Arthur Honegger for Abel Gance's *La Roue,* Darius Milhaud for Marcel l'Herbier's *L'Inhumaine,* and Dimitri Shostakovitch for *The New Babylon.* Eventually we find original scores performed by full orchestras touring with major films to the important cities in the United States.

When the breakthrough came, making it possible for the film's sound to be locked in perfect and perpetual "sync" to the picture—remember that accompanying scores on phonograph discs had been used for some time previously—it was greeted with mixed emotions by filmmakers, who particularly and prophetically feared not *sound* but the *"100% talkie."* Film entered the Age of the Technician, and creativity took second place to technical competence. For a time, the enormous difficulties involved in making sound films with inadequate equipment stood in the way of the artistic development of the film. Yet, although the first true sound film produced in America—*The Lights of New York*

(1929)—was an undistinguished work, the first efforts of the British and the French—Hitchcock's *Blackmail* (1929) and René Clair's *Sous les Toits de Paris* (1930)—were excellent films.° When one realizes the conditions under which such films were made, it is extraordinary that anything at all was accomplished.

Picture a sound stage during the 1930s: The actors take their places on the set, surrounded by a vast corps of studio technicians; the set is bathed in a broiling pool of light. Before them sits the director and, to his side, enclosed in "the black box" to stifle its noise, is the camera with its operator. This unfortunate gentleman will be pulled fainting from the black box following each take, for the temperature inside will reach 120 degrees. To one side, the orchestra waits in anticipation of the conductor's downbeat. Beyond, behind a long table loaded with the paraphernalia of the sound effects department, sit the "effects" men. Before them stands their own conductor, his feet wrapped and padded for soundless movement, prepared to dash back and forth like a frantic wraith to cue each man at the appropriate time. The director calls for quiet, and the hushed army poises expectantly, then, on cue, the vast, cumbersome machine lumbers forward, the swooning cameraman grinding away, the actors emoting for their very lives, the orchestra puffing, hammering, and sawing vehemently away, and the effects chief racing back and forth, now pointing to the "rain man," now the "wind," now the "horses' hooves," and then, in a rapid flash, the "gunshot man," until the enormous apparatus grinds to a halt of hopeful desperation. Imagine what happened if one man on that set sneezed in the middle of a take! What was lacking at this time was one absurdly simple device that is a part of every recording studio today—an interlock system. But still, they made films, and with methods that make even this description seem like space technology.

With the perfection of the interlock system it became possible for multiple soundtracks to be combined, properly balanced with each other and with the film's visual images. Virtually all film sound today is double-system, meaning that we handle the sound as a separate entity from the visual portion of the film, a practice granting maximum control over both audial and visual elements in the cutting room, where the picture and each of the individual components of the sound is edited separately.

Just as it was inevitable for the film industry to turn to the legitimate stage, where technicians competent in dealing with the spoken word existed, so was it certain that the industry would hungrily raid the music conservatories to obtain the needed talent for film music composition. One wonders if Hollywood could have survived the thirties and forties without the Budapest Conservatory. Of course the film composer quickly learned to make his music generally self-effacing and unobtrusive, but the dominant form remains, to this day, symphonic in style and Wagnerian in approach.

It is with Wagner that we associate the *leitmotiv*, or leading motif. Wagner's "music dramas," rather than mere displays of musical

*The early history of the sound film is spotted with imaginative attempts to utilize sound as one of the cinema's attributes in creating *moving* pictures, rather than in making the static "talkies" being ground out by the hundreds at the same time. Victor Fleming's *The Virginian* (1929), Clair's *Le Million* (1931) and *A Nous La Liberté* (1931), Von Sternberg's *Morocco* (1930) and *The Blue Angel* (1930), Hawks' *The Dawn Patrol* (1930), Lewis Milestone's *All Quiet on the Western Front* (1930) and Edward Cline's *Million Dollars Legs* (1932) can be viewed today in this context. It was René Clair, of course, who said "If there is an aesthetics of the cinema. . . . It can be summarized in one word: 'Movement'."

virtuosity, were attempts to use the power of music to most effectively communicate the powerful emotions, character relationships, and conflicts of the drama. In that sense, Wagner was a dramatist who employed music, rather than an opera composer. The technique of the leitmotiv involved the assigning of characteristic themes to the various characters in the drama, and then the developing and interweaving of these themes as the characters themselves developed and interacted. Thus the music serves as a nonverbal guide to the spectator's emotions, leading him to the deeply experienced, frequently nonarticulated feelings and insights desired of him by the dramatist. Obviously such a technique would be seized upon by the film-maker as beautifully suited to his purpose.

There are countless examples of fine work in this genre—although, ironically, by its very nature, this self-effacing form escapes our notice when it most fully succeeds in its purpose. Once again, television, through its one extraordinary contribution to American contemporary culture, the Extremely Late Movie, can give the student of the film an excellent opportunity for observing and learning. As an admittedly personal favorite, Miklos Rozsa's score for George Sidney's wonderfully warm and romantic film, *Young Bess*, is a classic of this type and well worth studying. Rozsa typically uses the main title music for his overture, following a brief opening fanfare with the stirring regal theme of the future Queen Elizabeth, and then introducing the moving love theme, its second statement broad and sweeping. The third important theme, a little nursery song, is then suggested by the overture, but its development is left to the ensuing scene where it will appear as *actual music,* sung by the participants. The Queen Elizabeth theme will be used only twice more within the film; the two other themes will appear repeatedly, in various guises, each appearance subtly varied to convey the specific mood of the particular scene it is backing. The credits end and the music resolves into background anticipation as a maid is seen hurrying upstairs; the music stops abruptly and points effectively the first line of dialogue: "Queen before the dawn breaks."

Bess's loyal servants, Mrs. Ashley and Mr. Parry, now begin to talk of the time that has gone before, of the ups and downs of her young life as the daughter of the all-powerful Henry VIII and the executed and discredited Anne Boleyn. The little child's tune comes naturally to their lips, "Here we go up, up, up . . . up to the sky so high." This theme will return each time young Bess's fortune turns with Henry's changing wives and she is shunted back and forth between the warmth and excitement of the court and the grey drab exile of Hatfield House ("Here we go down, down, down . . . bumpity bump, good-bye."). Mrs. Ashley quietly sings the song once more, unaccompanied by any background orchestra, then speaks the words as the tune is picked up in a low string accompaniment in the background music. The music and Mrs. Ashley's words suddenly resolve into the strong spoken words of Henry himself, "Here we go up, up, up . . . ", as he lifts the baby Elizabeth high over his head. The framing scene has ended and we are plunged into the story.

Through this scene a countermelody version of the child's theme is carried in the background music by a chamber orchestra, at once maintaining the story line and reassuring us of the period (16th century) of the film. The scene ends ominously with Henry caressing the throat of the lovely Anne Boleyn, dissolving through to Anne kneeling at the executioner's block, the music evolving into muffled execution drums. The brief scene ends abruptly on a cannon shot which startles the drums into silence and the cry of a baby—the motherless Bess. We see for the first time the carriage bearing Bess from the court to Hatfield, the music telling us, "Here we go down, down, down . . . bumpity bump, good-bye."

An important moment in the film—Bess's first meeting with the man she will love, Admiral Tom Seymour—is entirely unaccompanied until the end, when the music builds to back the warm release of emotion, soaring over the triumphant return of the carriage to the court at Tom's bidding. When Bess is introduced to the warm and friendly Katherine, Tom's secret love and Henry's Queen, a lovely new oboe theme backs the scene, perfectly expressing its gentle mood, ("How shall we see you, a younger sister, a daughter . . . ?").

Two delightful forays through the palace halls by the young Prince Edward, Bess's half brother, are backed by a spirited child's processional with oboe, chamber strings, and children's brass, warm, playful, and humorous. Like so much of the music of the film, the piece evokes the period perfectly without having to slavishly adhere to the restrictive musical form of the time.

When Bess hurries to Tom's room following the death of the King, the love theme is heard fully for the first time within the story, moving and yet bittersweet, anticipating both her future love and its ultimate loss. Later, when she begins to talk to others of Tom, revealing her deep love for the first time ("He's the finest man in England"), dreaming of the future when he shall have one day, "my ships, my flag, my love," the same theme, now soaring, backs the scene. Later, when she learns that Tom has always loved her friend, Katherine, the bittersweet note of the music is more appropriate.

Bess and Tom sail together on one of his great ships ("You and I and England") and the theme of Queen Elizabeth is heard for the first time since its brief statement in the overture, ringing out over the sea. It resolves into the warmth of the love theme ("I'd give my admiral ships") but then, when his words quietly anticipate what will come ("Who knows where I'll be when you set out to beat the Spaniards?"), the sadness within the theme gently foreshadows his death.

In a number of scenes—an unseen minstrel singing and playing, a harpsichord playing in an adjoining room, a court dance played by a chamber orchestra we do not see—the music closely approximates the style of the film's era. The music is in each case actual, a part of the scene, yet it is not localized. The general fidelity of the music to the mood and style of the film throughout and particularly during these moments sets the period of the film as much as do the costumes and decor; yet the music is never limited by this. Rosza writes with his full range of ability, using when appropriate contemporary instruments and harmonies without violating the sense of the times.

Katherine has married Tom after Henry's death and finds she must send Bess away because of the strength of their shared love for Tom. Katherine grows ill. In a scene in which Tom sits beside her bed, holding her in his arms, they talk of Bess ("You're not the first man to be in love with two women at the same time"); the music backs this scene extremely well in a minor modal theme, sweet, but at times quite serious, almost grim. Katherine is dying.

Elizabeth returns to Hatfield to find a strange new governess and steward; the music tells us immediately that something is wrong. Tom's brother, Ned, holds the regency, and he and his bitter wife, Ann, fear the strength the popular Tom would gain through an alliance with a future Queen of England. Tom's days are numbered and even Bess's life hangs in the balance. She and Tom have been apart for long months. She lies alone in bed one night, the love theme heard behind the scene quietly, unresolved. The music stirs into expectation at a knock; a dark silhouette appears and a low tremolo note is heard in anticipation. A new version of the love theme begins in the full strings as Bess moves quickly toward Tom, resolves into the familiar version, quiet for a moment, then soaring as he holds her in his arms. Later, it is almost dawn. "I have friends, we'll put up a fight," Tom tells her, the strings making a simple statement behind. "When shall I see you again?" "Perhaps never." "We planned to sail the seven seas . . . ." The theme once again soars but the edge of strength is gone from it and it sounds in a strange, new minor way over their last kiss.

When Elizabeth is led before the council of inquisitors, a low, almost subliminal beat of the by now familiar execution drum is heard. At Seymour's execution, the distant drums and lonely cannon shot are used effectively one more time as Bess and young King Edward struggle too late to write a countermanding order to save Tom. Bess puts the boy to bed, the scene backed by sweet, sad music; as she leaves his room, the love theme enters for the last time, bittersweet but strangely sweeping and then almost chilling, sending the hair on the back of one's neck rising. Ned's frightened wife, Ann, stands watching as the huge shadow of Bess is thrown against the palace wall, foreshadowing the future Queen.

The film returns to the framing story, the servants still bustling about; a fanfare is heard from the street. Once again Mrs. Ashley and Mr. Parry sing the little tune, dancing a simple quadrille, as the noise of the crowd grows outside. Elizabeth enters, for the first time as a Queen, and the child's tune is given a stirring Elgarian rendering, resolving perfectly and wonderfully into the Queen Elizabeth theme, the roars of her people now rolling up to the balcony as Bess turns to them as Queen. The music modulates and lifts us along with it, soaring as the camera moves in on the serene and regal face of the young Queen. The score ends on the fanfare of trumpet and drums which began the film.

To sum up, the music consistently and effectively leads the spectator into the desired response to the characters, their emotions and inter-actions; it does so without ever intruding or distracting, yet it is delight-ful to listen to when we do become aware of it. The music has a quality of its own, as music, yet it is an accompanying score first and foremost. We might well enjoy it for its own sake, yet it is at its best as an integral part of the film. It is a first-rate job by a man who knows how to write film music.

There is one cautionary note we must strike in dealing with the leit-motiv film score. From the time when film-makers first looked forward with mixed emotions to the coming of sound, many of those who best appreciated the nature of the film cautioned against the use of duplicat-ing sound. They saw in sound an effective *counterpoint* to the visual image, elevating its communicative power over the spectator by present-ing an oblique facet of what the visual image had already eloquently stated. It was René Clair who pointed out that there was no need for the sound of clapping when one could actually see hands coming together, a useful insight into this contrapuntal aspect of sound. Such men per-ceived, in the terms applied by Bertolt Brecht's composer-collaborator Hanns Eisler, that when a scene of emotion "A" was backed by music of emotion "A" the result must inevitably be "A" and "A" alone. However, when scene "A" was backed by music "B," the results could, wonder-fully, be "C." The Brecht-Weill song "Pirate Jenny" is a fine example of this, as are many of the songs of Richard Rodgers with Larry Hart and Oscar Hammerstein, perhaps most particularly "In Our Little Den of Iniquity" and "You've Got To Be Carefully Taught."

Two of today's outstanding film-makers, Stanley Kubrick and Feder-ico Fellini, have made fascinating attempts (particularly in *2001: A Space Odyssey* and *8½*) in the use of contrapuntal music, and we shall discuss them further. This technique does not have the almost universal applica-bility of the basic technique of the reinforcing theme, but it is an impor-tant aspect of film music, and, in the right place, supremely effective.

One further influence in film music must be mentioned—the influence of jazz, which has brought with it at long, long last the em-ployment of some of our fine Negro composers and some of the best of American contemporary music. For years jazz in films was associated with crime, late night city streets, Harlem, and/or nightclubs, and its use in any other setting was inconceivable. This peculiar prejudice was an obvious result of film music's dependence upon the stereotyped and in-stantly recognizable theme. In the last ten years this has been tremen-dously changed, with the significant landmark figures in this revolution-ary new use of the music of the Negro being, somewhat ironically, Elmer Bernstein *(Man With a Golden Arm)*, Henry Mancini (television's "Peter Gunn"), and Johnny Mandel.

There are a number of reasons for this welcome change, which has had its effect in the areas of television commercials, industrial films, and Hollywood features, as well as in the hip, low-budgeted films of today. Not the least important influence is the college background of so many of the men who are today moving into decision-making positions in the film industry. Brought up on jazz as an "acceptable" form, attending jazz concerts on the campus and at Carnegie Hall, familiar with the rich influence of classical forms on the jazz of men like Dave Brubeck, these men find nothing unusual about the climate of jazz in a contemporary film. Therefore they seek it out as a valid contemporary form for subjects for which its use was undreamed of only a few years ago. Today's social and moral revolution, by opening the doors to heretofore forbidden subjects, has increased the number of films for which jazz is particularly appropriate. The small number of men utilized in the performance of jazz lowers the cost of recording the film score, as does the improvisatory nature of jazz composition, and this factor undoubtedly has had a good deal to do with the turning to jazz by the young film-maker. The success of their iconoclastic films has been a further powerful influence upon their contemporaries.

The film producer, always eager for the "hit song" as a part of his score, has turned lately to the modern beat music of the *Downbeat* and *Billboard* "charts," finding both performers and composers in tune with the times and with the youthful, hip audience which increasingly dominates theater attendance. Initially used, like jazz, only when it specifically matched the subject of the film, as in the superb *A Hard Day's Night,* such music now enriches films which deal generally with contemporary youth—*Easy Rider* and *The Graduate*—and films which are contemporary in style—*Casino Royale, Barbarella, Midnight Cowboy.* Such music is seldom duplicative of the scene's emotions—much of Simon and Garfunkel's music used behind *The Graduate* had been written before the film was made—but it offers a rich source of contrapuntal backing. None of the lyric references in "Mrs. Robinson" were drawn from specific events in *The Graduate,* but the song, with its superbly if gratuitously evocative reference to the passing of our national pastime from the era of Joe Dimaggio to the era of Joe Pepitone, is hauntingly and obliquely appropriate.

AESTHETICS OF FILM SOUND

More than inadequate facilities has stood in the way of the full realization of the sound film; to this day there persists a chronic failure on the part of many film-makers to grasp the fundamental nature of the film, and the precise and proper relationship of sound to it. Certainly the advent of sound was viewed with what would seem to have been justifiable suspicion. As early as 1928, the Russian film-makers Eisenstein, Pudovkin, and Alexandrov issued a *Joint Statement on Sound Film,* "in which dim apprehensions alternated with constructive suggestions."[5] In the same year René Clair revealed his deep misgivings as to the effect of sound on cinema and many perceptive critics and film-makers echoed these sentiments. They were, of course, correct in recognizing that the improper use of sound could destroy the essence of the film, for film is a visual medium.

But what of the proper use of sound? Only if the sound image is properly subjugated to the visual image, only if the visuals take the lead, can the form of film survive and properly flourish. How this is to be accomplished is our present concern. Film sound is composed of the elements of dialogue, sound effects, and music. Inextricably interwoven in aesthetics and practice, they will here be considered separately.

Dialogue

Why are words so destructive to the film? Perhaps, on the simplest level, it is a matter of our being able to concentrate upon only one thing at a time. When we play music in the background as we work we are very dimly, if at all, aware of its presence; when an occasional flourish calls our attention to the music, when it becomes more than a "presence," we lose our concentration on the work at hand. To have two people (children!) talking to you at once is infuriating. We might fool ourselves into thinking that such generalizations are true only if we are dealing with two similar objects of attention, and that since visual and audial images are quite different they can somehow exist side by side, in some sort of uneasy truce. Quite the contrary is true. Words are symbols of experience; the word triggers in the mind of the viewer a certain image associated with that experience. This image must almost inevitably find itself in conflict with the visual image presented by the film. Sounds other than words, on the other hand, seem to trigger an unvoiced feeling about an experience; they appeal to our psyche, not to our intelligence. Thus they are in far less direct conflict with the film's visual images, as we shall discuss later at length. Since we must, in effect, translate words into images, going directly to the image bypasses one step. The film-maker, dealing properly in the visual image, runs less of a risk of "losing something in translation," something the maker of words cannot avoid.

Further, people are wary of speech, ironically so uncommunicative; words are all too frequently used as a subterfuge to camouflage our true emotions and intentions. One strong current of artistic effort represents an attempt to bridge the gap between us and our childhood, sensing that the child sees things as they really are while the adult perceives the world through an opaque shield of learned and expected preconceptions. The film image is seen as the pied piper to lead us back to the innocence of childhood.

VISUAL VERSUS VERBAL IMAGES

It is absolutely essential that the visual images, the photographic reality of film, dominate verbal images in order for the film to be true to its basic aesthetics. In the words of Siegfried Kracauer, "All the successful attempts at an integration of the spoken word have one characteristic in common: they play down dialogue with a view to reinstating the visuals."[6] Kracauer notes that in films in which the dialogue takes the lead

it is inevitable that out of the spoken words definite patterns of meaning and images should arise. . . . Evoked through language, these patterns assume a reality of their own, a self-sufficient mental reality which, once established in the film, interferes with the photographic reality to which the camera aspires. The significance of verbal argumentation, verbal poetry, threatens to drown the significance of the accompanying pictures, reducing them to shadowy illustrations.[7]

Even in an attempt to balance visual and sound images, the all-important visual suffers, at best, a neutralization. Kracauer correctly cites Olivier's *Hamlet* as a unique and remarkable attempt at striking an uneasy balance between verbal and visual. Tempered by Olivier's superb film sense, *Hamlet* is nevertheless an attempt to present with loving care Shakespearean dialogue on the screen, not a film adapted from Shakespeare. While a bold and imaginative effort and a stunning experience, it is not an entirely successful film.

To function properly, the dialogue of the film must be deemphasized, portrayed in natural, life-like speech and reduced in quantity. "The medium calls for verbal statements which grow out of the flow of pictorial communications instead of determining their course."[8] The speech should be nonpoetic, nonliterary, natural, light and quick, "thrown away," casual and true to life. When a character speaks, our concern must be not upon the ideas and content of the words, but upon what the speaker reveals of himself, his dreams and desires, his character and his actions. There is a fine example of this in *Cat Ballou*.

A gunfighter has been summoned to town as a "hired gun" to defend the helpless heroine and her father from threatening killers. Instead of the expected larger-than-life-size hero, he appears as a grotesque and drunken parody of a gunfighter, hopelessly inadequate to his task. Fighting a desperate hangover, he tries without success to put a bullet within the small target his employers have hung for him (or, at the very least, somewhere within the barn wall on which the target is hung). After begging a drink, he again turns agonizingly to the task, desperately pointing the wavering gun with both hands at the distant target. Then, wonderfully, the drink takes hold! He suddenly begins to emerge as something more than the wasted shadow of a once-great gunman. Our hope springs eternal; perhaps he will succeed after all! At this point, the gunfighter begins to talk, or more accurately to orate on his past glories. We are completely unaware of what he is saying; as a matter of fact, so marvelous is his physical performance throughout the film that, with the exception of one moment in which he expresses his love for the young heroine and a twice-repeated hopeful "I'll drink to that," followed by a sullen turning away when he is ignored, it is impossible to remember *anything* he has said throughout the entire picture. At this moment we are enthralled by the visual image, by this fascinating revelation of the man, and by the action: Will he be able to hit the target? The actor instinctively plays this to the hilt, teasing us at one point by suddenly stopping in mid-speech, taking careful aim for an excruciatingly long moment, then suddenly breaking off without firing, rambling and roaring on! We are still totally unaware of what he is saying, fascinated by the scene's essence: the wavering gun and the unused target. When he finally fires (naturally drilling two precise and perfect holes in the target) it is in an unexpected and sudden aside, flowing perfectly out of the action and capping the scene beautifully.°

Much of the work falling within the scope of this book has dealt with what we have called the "subject" film, which will, in a majority of cases, be narrated. Actually many narrated subject films utilize controlled sections of sync dialogue, but these usually form a minor percentage of the whole. The great majority of these films are entirely narrated by some invisible person. Let us define sound which is not a part of the world presented on the screen as *commentative sound;*°° this is sound heard only by the audience, not by the characters in the film, "sound whose source is neither visible on the screen nor has been implied to be present in the action," and which includes background music and narration. Sound which is part of the world of the film we may call *actual sound;* it is heard by the film's participants and includes most sound effects, dialogue, and music emanating from specific sources within the setting, such as a radio or a performing orchestra.

The dominance of the visual images by commentative narration is no less damaging to the film than dominance by actual speech, and any film-maker who is to enter the area of the sponsored film must be aware of this potential danger. The sponsored subject film usually stems from a script which is in no way a shooting script; rather than being a cinematically oriented guide to the visual images to be assembled, it is a literary effort, probably written for the purpose of extolling the virtues of the product and hence flattering to the client himself. The fact that these "scripts" are often written by the client's representative and not by film-makers hardly helps this situation. What such a film often becomes is a "catalogue" film, a succession of hopelessly unrelated images, bound together with little sense of filmic form, following slavishly the form of the "script." This same script is then narrated to the result and synced exactly to the duplicative visual images. In Kracauer's description, "the imagery amounts to a halfway comprehensible continuity: then the commentator, as if jealous of the pictures' ability to make themselves understood without his assistance may nevertheless overwhelm them with explanations and elaborations."[9]

This is not a film; it is the antithesis of film, a collection of colored slides run behind a lecture and a deep failure of responsibility on the part of the pseudo-film-maker who has produced it. But there is an alternative: to immediately set about translating this well-meaning attempt into a true shooting script. Then, after completing the work print, the director must assist in the preparation of a complemental narrative script. For example,

a contrapuntal relation between subdued commentary and a veritable flow of visuals materializes in a limited number of documentaries, mainly from England and Nazi Germany. In these films, which, perhaps, owe something to the English bent for understatement and/or the German sense of polyphonic instrumentation, the narrator does

*This principle of visual emphasis over the words might give us an explanation of the phenomenon of the obvious superiority of subtitled films over dubbed films. With the actors speaking in a foreign tongue, visual ascendancy is assured. Our full concentration is on the pantomine action on the screen, our eyes playing rapidly over the printed titles and then returning immediately to the screen above. But in the same film, dubbed, the inevitable less-than-right quality of the dubbing draws our attention hypnotically to the dialogue, assuring its dominance.

**These terms originate with Karel Reisz.

not simply introduce or complement the visuals but comments upon them obliquely. It is as if he himself sat in the audience and occasionally felt prompted to voice an aside—some slant on the picture he watches. Far from disrupting the pictorial continuity, his casual remarks open up avenues of thought which, for being unsuspected, may well increase our sensitivity to the multiple meanings of the imagery.[10]

SYNCHRONIZATION OF SOUND AND VISUAL IMAGES

Kracauer introduces us to four terms which will prove useful in our consideration of the aspects of film sound and will aid us in systematizing this subject: synchronism and asynchronism, parallelism and counterpoint. An understanding of these terms will demonstrate the various options open to us in the handling of film sound images in relationship to visual images.°

Synchronism is a situation in which sounds and images are synchronous on the screen as they would be in real life, as in the picture of a dog barking. *Asynchronism* is a situation in which "sounds and images which do not occur simultaneously in reality are nevertheless made to coincide on the screen," as when the dog's bark is heard over a shot of a forest.[11] *Parallelism* refers to a situation in which the words and images are conveying the same meaning. *Counterpoint* denotes a state in which the meaning of sound and visual images differs.

In any given film situation in which we consider the relationship of sound image to visual image, we shall assess both the physical and meaningful synchronization. *Physical synchronization*—i.e., the physical proximity of the image—deals with synchronism and asynchronism. *Meaningful synchronization* deals with parallelism and counterpoint. Note, however, that parallelism and counterpoint may be elements in either synchronous *or* asynchronous situations.

Synchronism is seeing a person speaking on the screen and hearing his words simultaneously. This would be a basic example of synchronism-parallelism if the words and actions conveyed the same essential meaning. Synchronism-counterpoint would occur if the images contradicted what was being said, or bore on other matters, causing us to explore in our minds a variety of possible associated meanings. We might see by his visible behavior, for example, that a boasting person was really frightened. In this case the meaning of the scene would be a product of the difference between the visual and sound images.

A basic example of asynchronism would be hearing a person speak and seeing something else, perhaps the person to whom he is speaking or another object in the room. Another type of asynchronism (the example originates with Pudovkin) occurs when, hearing a cry for help, we look out of a window and see a street filled with moving traffic but fail to take in the traffic noises because we hear only the cry that first caught our attention.°° A third type of asynchronism is represented by commentative sound such as the voice of a narrator or background film music. We might have examples of asynchronism-parallelism—no contradiction between meaning—or of asynchronism-counterpoint—a contradiction of

*For a complete and detailed exposition of his theories, we strongly recommend Kracauer's excellent book *Theory of Film*, and suggest particularly the chapters on "Dialogue and Sound" and "Music."

**This example, by the way, illustrates the "selective editing of sound" that we unconsciously practice in real life. Alexander Dean's *Directing the Play* tells of the director who hung a microphone out the stage window to record background traffic noise for his play, but found he had an unintelligible mass of confused noise when he played back the tape. He then had to carefully select and score the exact sounds which he wanted to create this background properly. This is the way most film sound is scored.

meaning or new areas of meaning opened up. We will see a variety of examples of the various possibilities in the respective areas of dialogue, sound effects, and music.

There is one more important point to be made here. These various aspects of synchronization are simply techniques and they may be used for effective as well as ineffective cinema. The heart of the matter lies in avoiding the basic ascendency of dialogue over the visual. Most critics have ignored this principle and have seen the solution to lie simply in the proper handling of the synchronization of the dialogue. The *Statement of 1928*, for example, declared: "Only a contrapuntal use of sound in relation to the visual montage piece will afford a new potentiality of montage development and perfection," and Pudovkin, among others, praised above all the asynchronous and contrapuntal as being the closest to the rendering of reality. But Kracauer correctly points out that "what accounts for the cinematic quality . . . is not so much their [sound image] truth to our experience of reality or even to reality in a general sense as their absorption in camera-reality—visible physical existence."[12] If the spoken work predominates, then we have little choice but to choose synchronous sound, burdening the visual images and eliminating them as a source of vital communication. However, if the visuals are dominant, we can use whatever methods of synchronization are the most effective for the film's purpose. "To sum up, in the light of our proposition the ascendancy of dialogue entails problematic methods of synchronization, whereas the dominance of pictorial communication brings cinematic methods within the accomplished film director's reach."[13]

Sound Effects

The fears of the silent film-makers for the future of film were based upon a fear of "words" not "sounds," (and obviously not music, already present in actuality in the cinema performance). Eisenstein stated, "I think the 100 percent all-talking film is silly. . . . But the sound film is something more interesting. The future belongs to it."[14] Cavalcanti observed that "noise seems to by-pass the intelligence and speak to something very deep and inborn."[15] Kracauer notes that

> any familiar noise calls forth inner images of its source as well as images of activities, modes of behavior, etc., which are either customarily connected with that noise or at least related to it in the listener's recollection. In other words, localizable sounds do not as a rule touch off conceptual reasoning, language-bound thought; rather they share with unidentifiable noises the quality of bringing the material aspects of reality into focus.[16]

In contrast to the sound images of the voice, which create definite patterns of preconceived meanings, limiting the imagination and binding one to a restrictive consideration apart from the visual images, the images of natural sound free the imagination and enhance our appreciation of the visuals. There is, therefore, much less of an inherent antipathy between natural sounds and visual images.

SELECTIVITY IN SOUND EFFECTS

Let us consider the question of synchronization of effects, remembering throughout that we need not here greatly concern ourselves with the problem of verbal image ascendancy. The use of effects in a film is inevitably highly selective; most sound effects are created separately and added to the sound track in the cutting room. Some effects are a residual product of the voice track (footsteps, pages turning, breathing, furniture creaking) but this source is limited, since a large percentage of film dialogue including virtually all location dialogue, is dubbed at a later stage in a recording studio. Our purpose with sound effects is to create a satisfactory filmic reality with the use of selective sounds, and not a verisimilitude which burdens us with superfluous sound images. Certainly sound effects add a dimension of reality and locale to the film. Effects are vital in creating a sense of life in the film, and as is well stated by Kracauer above, they add a further dimension by dealing with our inner depths, by-passing our intelligence to create evocative emotions and associations within us.

We can see a variety of synchronization possibilities of varying effectiveness. First, we can have a situation of synchronism-parallelism, in which the spectator actually sees the creator of the sound as he hears it and in which the meaning of the sound image is identical with that of the visual image. A dog barking on camera, hands clapping visibly as we hear the sound, the roar of a train as it speeds by us on the screen are examples. René Clair did raise an objection to this usage on the grounds of redundancy, of duplication; however, Kracauer is right in saying that the basic question is one of dominance, and that there is not actually an objection to parallelism per se. There is no inherent reason why the duplication of the visual image by the sound image should lessen our appreciation for the visual; and, if we saw the dog barking or the hands clapping without hearing sound, this unreal happening would in fact seriously affect the filmic reality, causing us to "break out" of our involvement.

SYNCHRONISM ALTERNATING WITH ASYNCHRONISM

However, even in life situations, a condition of synchronism alternating with asynchronism is more likely to occur. Our attention is not constantly focused upon the source of sound so that, in fact, the sound is often carried over adjacent images. We might look to see at whom the dog is barking, or who is being applauded, or simply to observe a number of aspects of the landscape as the train passes.*

What occurs in such cases in the film is something we will note further in the discussion of film music: the sound binds together these adjacent visual images just as music does when it runs continuously over several adjoining images. Montage is quite properly considered the unique and most creatively effective technique of film editing; it does have, however, one inherent drawback, with which André Bazin has dealt at some length. Bazin points out that by disconnecting elements present in a given situation through the device of treating them with

*Of course there are also many situations in life of *pure asynchronism* in which we never see the source of the sound—sirens at night, far-off factory whistles, and the dog barking and train passing in the distance.

separate shots, we run the risk of creating a suspicion in the minds of the audience that these elements are not really adjacent, and thus affecting the spectator's acceptance of the reality of the film. This would be particularly true in a situation in which we might be inclined to doubt their proximity anyway; for example the ubiquitous shot from the White-Hunter-with-restless-wife film in which the White Hunter points from in front of a dreadful palm tree process shot to a shot of alligators slithering into the water—patently another river, another place, another time, and another cameraman. Since we have reason from the start to believe that the actor is not going to risk his valuable hide among the alligators, we are likely to suspect chicanery. Bazin goes further and states that montage can never be utilized for such a situation: "When the essence of a scene demands the simultaneous presence of two or more factors in the action, montage is ruled out."[17] Bazin is perfectly aware of the power of sound run over the disconnected images of the montage—"the sound image, far less flexible than the visual image, would carry montage in the direction of realism"[18]—but he does not appear to fully appreciate its cementive potential in this instance. The obvious question is, when does the scene really "demand" the "simultaneous presence"?

In John Huston's *Roots of Heaven* there is a climactic scene involving the protagonist, Morel, and a native whom the audience knows has been assigned to kill him. Morel is an idealist striving to prevent the slaughter of the last great tribes of African elephants. Initially met with indifference and opposition, he has taken measures outside the law to effect this and has gathered around him a devoted band of followers. An African Nationalist leader has sought identification with Morel for his own cynical purposes. Having realized that Morel is only valuable to his cause either as a mythic figure ranging freely through the jungle or as a martyred hero, the Nationalist has secretly assigned one of his own followers, Joseph, to stay with Morel and to kill him if he is ever about to be captured. At this point in the film, Morel has reached the end of his rope and is approaching a village in which we expect he will indeed be captured. Joseph obviously recognizes this, and the film makes it evident that Morel suspects precisely what the native is about to do. Morel leaves the remainder of his followers, after carefully describing to them the route they must follow; he asks Joseph to accompany him to a nearby well.

The ensuing scene is treated as montage. As Morel bends down to fill his canteen at the well, Huston uses a high-angle shot to reveal Joseph behind Morel, unslinging his gun. The camera then cuts to a low-angle shot in depth from in front and below Morel and we see clearly the expression on Morel's face. In both shots the elements are "simultaneously present." Obviously the dramatic essence of the scene is that Morel knows he is to be shot and his behavior is of primary interest to us. At this point the director abandons the depth-of-focus shot with both principals present, and uses individual close shots. He cuts to the native in close-up, looking down past the camera; cuts back to a close-up of

Morel (native not visible); back to the rifle being raised; back to Morel, again at a low angle from in front and below; back again to Joseph; and finally, back to a lengthy shot of Morel awaiting the inevitable bullet, Joseph not visible.

Following Bazin's credo, we might consider this a shot which demands the simultaneous presence of both characters. However, what has occurred is that Joseph has begun to breathe heavily, tense with excitement. The sound of his breathing and the click of the rifle bolt carry over the shots of Morel in an example of alternating sound synchronism and asynchronism. These sounds bind the shots together, reassuring us of the continued presence of Joseph. Therefore montage, with its ability to focus upon the scene according to the "shifting emphasis of dramatic interest,"[19] has been used very effectively. The close-up of Morel's face as he awaits the bullet is excruciating, for we expect at any second to have the shattering impact of the bullet intrude horrifyingly upon the scene before us. This is much more effective than would be a shot including both figures and revealing exactly the progress of Joseph's aiming and readying the rifle. (Joseph does not fire, by the way.)

ASYNCHRONOUS SOUND EFFECTS AS A REPLACEMENT FOR THE VISUAL IMAGE

There are further intriguing possibilities for the use of asynchronous sound. "Sounds are pictures in themselves; you can use them without the supporting visual image—once the sound has been identified—to recall things without having to show them."[20] René Clair cites an excellent example of this in a scene from Harry Beaumont's *The Broadway Melody* in which the camera focuses on the face of Bessie Love watching from a window as we hear the noise of a car departing. Our dramatic interest is on her face, but the sound makes the scene explicit without having to cut away and interrupt the visual unity of the scene. "Sound has replaced the image at an opportune moment."[21]

One of the time-honored usages of asynchronous sound as a replacement for a visual image is the device of avoiding the visual portrayal of violence by showing a near-by scene while the spectator hears the sound of gun shots or beatings. This lessens the physical shock of seeing the actual violence while our imagination is allowed to portray the scene at whatever level it wishes. An excellent early example of this occurs in William Wellman's *The Public Enemy*. James Cagney and a henchman appear at an apartment to kill a man. Cagney moves forward toward the victim, seated at a piano, but the camera remains on his accomplice at the door. We hear a shot and the sound of the body falling against the keys of the piano but are not shown the actual murder. Another example is a scene from Charles Frend's *Scott of the Antarctic* in which the expedition's ponies are shot off-camera while the camera remains with the last remaining pony comforted by his master. Finally we see the collars of the dead ponies and hear the sound of the last sad shot, still from beyond our vision.°

*In Disney's *Fantasia* Mickey Mouse chops up the enchanted broom stick off-screen—we see the shadow—and the camera holds on the flailing tail of the dying dinosaur at the end of the fight. The sound (music in this case) reassures us of the presence.

SIMULTANEOUS ASYNCHRONOUS AND SYNCHRONOUS SOUND

If we may be allowed to look ahead for a moment to film music, we will consider the fact that film background music that is commentative and not actual (i.e., not emanating from a visible source on the screen) music will, of course, be asynchronous. Since there will be many cases where such asynchronous music occurs at the same time as synchronous effects, we have a situation of both asynchronous and synchronous sound occurring simultaneously. We accept this convention of film sound without hesitation.

In *Khartoum* the scene of General Gordon's heroic entrance to the besieged city is a stirring example of this. The sound track is alive with the roars of the delirious townspeople who regard Gordon as their savior—cheering and chanting "Gor-don, Gor-don" over and over. As Gordon moves into the hysterical crowd surging around him, the music begins a stirring rendition of Frank Cordell's "Gordon theme" which builds to a sweeping climax, greatly aiding our emotional identification with the scene and carrying us along on its crest. Obviously the townspeople and Gordon do not hear the music; they do hear the cheers. We, the audience, accept the hearing of both, pleased that we are involved in this stirring moment.

A classic instance of this use of sound occurs at the charge of the French knights during Olivier's superb battle sequence in *Henry V*. At the beginning we hear only the occasional clink of armor, the stamp of hooves, the snort of a horse. Then the rolling charge begins, accompanied by the dull thunder of hoofbeats, thus far an example of synchronous, actual sound. Then asynchronous, commentative music begins to swell, equaling, dominating, and finally wiping out the realistic sound of the charge. The camera cuts first to the waiting English longbowmen behind their row of sharpened stakes; then to Henry's sword, raised to signal the bowmen; then to the battle charge (camera point-of-view of the bowmen from behind the stakes); back to the bowmen; then back to Henry as the sword flashes down. Throughout this, there has been no synchronous sound, only the rolling, rising drive of the music, until finally we see the English archers loose the first huge flight of arrows in a superb soft roar—probably the single most effective dramatic sound effect ever used in a film.

Let us note one last interesting and contrasting example. In a short sponsored film we made, a travelogue, a succession of characteristic asynchronous commentative musical selections was used—a modern-beat piece for the New York scenes, light jazz for the hotel, moving jazz for the trip to the airport, cool and relaxing Brubeckian jazz for the flight, a cheerful bossa nova for the landing in South America. In the next sequence our tourists wandered through the streets and market places of Lima. Here we used a piece of native Peruvian music recorded on location at the time of filming. At the same time we ran synchronous sound effects over the scene giving a sense of activity and bustle. This sound had the effect of making the music also seem synchronous, as though the characters in the pictures might actually be hearing it. We continued to match our music and effects more specifically to the content of the scene, matching the visit to the Presidential Palace and its "changing of the guard" with a South American march and the faint sounds of military commands and marching feet. Using this technique, a visit to a bullring might be matched with the characteristic music and crowd noises of the bullfight, and a scene of a native dance could be matched to a suitable folk dance and excited crowd murmurs and applause. The sense of locale and actuality adds an important dimension to such a film.

CONTRAPUNTAL SOUND

Thus far we have discussed sounds which essentially *parallel* in meaning the visual images with which they have been associated, either synchronously or asynchronously. Now we must deal with the area of *contrapuntal* sound. There is a nice example of asynchronous contrapuntal sound in a contemporary cosmetic commercial. The visual images are of a pretty girl who "made the mistake of choosing a hair color no one would notice." Much to our enormous relief, she later chooses a traffic-stopping color from the sponsor, the commercial ending on the enthusiastic applause from the crowds her new-found beauty has gathered around her. However, in the beginning she hurries along unnoticed by anyone. At almost the precise instant that the narrator tells us this fact, we hear the rising sound of a siren. It is entirely asynchronous for we never see the source of the sound, although the locale implies that it is actual; it beautifully counterpoints the unnoticed girl with one of the most noticeable of sounds. It might be pointed out, additionally, that the siren catches the attention of the drowsing television viewer and adroitly holds this attention on the ensuing visuals. (Nor do we see the applauding crowds, by the way!)

There is an interesting use of alternating synchronous and asynchronous contrapuntal sound in Bryan Forbes' *Deadfall*. The sound used is that of a symphony orchestra, but it is not inaccurate to call its use here that of a sound effect. We are observing a scene in which two men enter and rob a house. The occupants are attending the concert, although their servants remain at home. As we see the two thieves about to enter, we suddenly hear the noise of tympani, which immediately gains our emotional attention. The sound continues as the scene changes, now revealing the tympanist tuning up at the concert hall. Throughout the entire sequence the orchestra proceeds through the preparation and performance of the concert, maintaining a consistent chronological sound line. The visuals, however, intercut back and forth (parallel editing) between the thieves struggling to complete their work and the actual locale of the concert hall, including the arrival and attendance of the couple being robbed. A third element is added when the servants in the house turn on the radio to listen to the same concert at home. The music is constantly alternating between synchronous—the concert hall and servant quarters—and asynchronous—the thieves at work. The music also serves as an effective counterpoint to the dramatic flow of the sequence and it constantly increases our suspense as the music proceeds, since we know that the end of the concert will result in the owners returning home. Thus the thieves are shown working against an audial clock, the style of which provides an effective counterpoint to their mood and actions.

There is a stunning scene in Rossellini's *Paisan* in which a child's cry is played asynchronously over scenes of partisans advancing stealthily through a marsh. When the sound becomes synchronous we see the child among a group of corpses. The contrapuntal effect of this lonely wail against the guerrillas and then the dead bodies is stunning.

There is a fascinating sound effect used at the end of Antonioni's *Blow-Up*. The photographer protagonist is watching a mimed tennis match (there are no visible rackets or ball) between two harlequins, being watched by a group of bizarrely costumed friends. Inevitably they mime the loss of their invisible ball and its rolling toward the photographer. He hesitates, looks for a long moment at the absolutely silent group, all poised expectantly for his ultimate joining of their charade. He suddenly reaches down with a quick smile, picks up the invisible ball and throws it back to them. The camera remains on him as he looks past us to the court; then from behind us, for the first time, the *sound* of the tennis match occurs. The camera pulls back and up to a high-angle extreme long shot of the photographer and remains fixed for a long moment. Then the image of the photographer fades quickly from the screen, leaving the empty expanse of grass to be filled by The End. Although the imaginary "sound" is associated with an invisible, and perhaps nonexistent, ball, it would seem that not only the audience but also the characters hear it.

We should devote a word or two to the subject of that most familiar of contrapuntal sound situations, "the raging storm outside while passions boil within." Although it is not difficult to dismiss such a use of sound as hackneyed in most of the examples we have witnessed, it does stand as a kind of essential example from which so many other contrapuntal sound and visual combinations arise, illustrating a situation which, if the sounds and words of the argument taking place were actually heard, would be almost inevitably banal. We are much better off in imagining what is taking place, allowing ourselves to be swept along on an emotional and nonverbal level by the soundtrack. There is a very effective use of such a device in Kazan's *On the Waterfront*. In the scene in which Terry tells his girl he has been involved in the murder of her brother, the sound of a ship's whistle drowns out the actual speech while we watch from a distance what is taking place; the visual images gain heightened importance through the avoidance of words, as they should.

ESTABLISHING THE ENVIRONMENT

It should be noted that in all these examples the use of sound images effectively relates us to the environment surrounding the people in the scene. The harbor and ships of *On the Waterfront,* the streets of Lima in our travel film, and the New York street of *Broadway Melody* are essential parts of the environment in which the story takes place and are effectively brought to life by the sound images used. David Lean and Michelangelo Antonioni are two directors who use effects superbly to establish locale. Antonioni has no peer in creating a "sound score" from effects, often using them as an effective substitute for music.

Film Music

You will recall from our brief summary of the history of film sound that from the birth of the film there had been demonstrated an awareness of the need for accompanying music whenever films were shown. A common explanation advanced is that this was for the purpose of covering the inherent noises of the audience—coughing, rustling of paper, and chewing whatever passed for popcorn in bygone days—and above all the projector, although the projector actually did not long remain in the auditorium proper. The historical precedence of incidental music in the theater obviously had established the convention of accompanying drama with music of matching mood, thus enhancing and furthering the emotions expressed. Yet what is intriguing is the fact that the initial accompanying music was not chosen for its duplication of the mood of the film but was simply music, any music, preferably popular tunes of the day. This would seem to imply something further, that there was some inherent need on the part of the spectator which every film house sought to satisfy, a need which the presence of any music could fulfill: "Its vital function was to adjust the spectator physiologically to the flow of images on the screen."[22] How does music do this?

Anyone who has ever sat through the appalling experience of watching absolutely silent films can attest to an experience well described as "the exquisite embarrassment of silence." Whenever we run silent films at home, we put on the phonograph a marvelous record of music written by Charles Chaplin for several of his films. That this music does not exactly match the films we are showing is unimportant; in a surprising number of places it does match uncannily, and where it does not, a strange kind of counterpoint is set up between the music and the visual images. However, showing the films without music creates a vague sense of uneasiness; a restless and awkward estrangement from the film replaces our usual deep involvement. We long for something to fill this awful void. The question of why music can accomplish this is intriguing.

For one thing, music satisfies us by aiding in creating a sense of filmic reality for which we long. Our daily reality is lived within an ocean of sounds, and so we are stricken by the sudden and arbitrary absence of all sound. "Life is inseparable from sound. Accordingly, the extinction of sound transforms the world into limbo—a common sensation of people abruptly stricken with deafness."[23] We are very close to believing in the reality of the film with its unique ability to capture life in motion, but we shall withhold our belief so long as these moving images pass before us in a ghostly flicker of silence. Music bestows the gift of life upon these silent figures.* However, as Kracauer aptly observes, the function of the music is not to restore these images to a full reality; rather, it is to " . . . draw the spectator into the very center of the silent images and have him experience their photographic life. Its function is to remove the need for sound, not to satisfy it."[24] The addition of music

*In many subject films, characteristic music substitutes effectively for the sound of machines and motors.

is a necessary ingredient in the creation of a filmic reality; silence stands irrevocably in the way of the spectator's acceptance of this.

Secondly, the form of music lends a form to the film, " . . . tying together a visual medium which is, by its very nature, continually in danger of falling apart."[25] Anyone who has had the opportunity of observing a number of films prior to the addition of music would be utterly convinced of this fact. Remember the instance from *Roots of Heaven*, in which sound effects achieved the effect of bringing together in a meaningful continuity disparate, though adjacent, images. Time and again we see seemingly unconnected and arbitrarily situated images in a montage, particularly in subject films, gain form and coherency through the use of music. It is obvious that the musical form, which is inevitable and proceeds logically to an anticipated end, lends a sense of form, of structure, of pattern to the disjointed film images, providing the glue for the filmic joints.

There also appears to be physiological principle at work. Kracauer cites in support of this the psychology class experiment in which a constant light appears to glow brighter when a buzzer is sounded. Through the use of music our perceptions are heightened and our receptivity increased as the ghostly images shine more brightly.

Lastly, there is a psychological reason. Man in our society is seldom tranquil; he betrays an inner restlessness which he strives constantly and with a variety of devices to control. Absorbing activity and participation in the deeply involving suspense of drama and of athletic contests are among his favorite devices. But we are supplied with constant evidence that he is often unsuccessful, and that the elusive and disquieting furies within us lie always just beneath the surface. The passerby with the transistor radio "security blanket" pressed firmly to his ear; the teenager studying with the radio blaring; the lonely housewife with the television set murmuring in another room; the businessman with his elevator, auto, and restaurant filled with some form of the ubiquitous Muzak all betray their constant concern with filling the void. Even movie houses today play unrelated but needed music while we impatiently await the film which will hopefully draw us hypnotically into its vortex for an hour or two of respite. Silence throws us back upon our own resources; music fills the void within our souls. Whenever a lone man has crossed the ocean in recent times, the newspaper writers quite correctly ignore the aspect of his physical triumph and say only, "What an achievement to have faced himself." Yet such men report that even they, pushed to their lonely limits, have begun to hallucinate, to create for themselves imaginary "Fridays" to fill the desperate void. In the film experience, music accomplishes this.

Conventions of Film Music

It must occur to us from our study of the history of film music that today's musical conventions are derived in large part from the haphazard development of practices appropriate to the silent film. These conventions were arrived at instinctively, often with great validity and effectiveness, but basically they were spontaneously evolved by well-meaning men who gave little thought to the principles they were in fact creating for future film-making generations. Many were ill-equipped to do so in any event. Nor have enough of the men who have slavishly followed these handed-down principles sought to understand, question, or challenge them. Throughout the history of film sound, outstanding participants have sought varied and imaginative ways of dealing with sound, but they have done comparatively little in affecting the general trend.

Our basically *commentative, asynchronous,* and *parallel* music is left over from silent days. Is it not in many instances a hopeless anachronism, existing long after its purpose has been fulfilled in other and better ways? Since we can often fill the aesthetic void of the silent film with actual sound effects, would this not be preferable to commentative and ever-present music? This argument is not far from the truth when it concerns itself with continuous and essentially parallel music. But let us not ignore the fact that "conventional" film music is enormously effective in countless instances. To reason that actual sound effects and the voice could always suffice is unreasonable in the light of our previous discussion. There are grave and inherent dangers in allowing the voice to dominate, and sound effects are far better used in sparse and exacting placement. A realization of the need for the presence of music in our lives, specifically in the movie-house, would tend to convince us that the void-filling and form-lending functions are the provinces of music and that neither the voice nor natural sound could fully satisfy the physiological and psychological needs of the audience. In discussing the functions of film music, further evidence will be given as to the variety of contributions of film music. What we ask is that the "traditional," the "conventional," the "tried and true" (and the tired and true) be challenged when inappropriate and replaced by film-making mavericks with fresh approaches, balancing a contrapuntal complexity of sound images and emotions against the form of film.

THE FUNCTIONS OF FILM MUSIC

First, let us consider a variety of observations by film-makers, composers, and critics on the function of film music. From this montage of theories we will perceive some consistent patterns, and will attempt to formalize these observations into a practical guide.* In 1936, Kurt London, in *Music for Films,* put forth the proposition that music for films must serve to further the "psychological advancement of the action." Further, that "it has to connect dialogue sections without friction; it has to establish association of ideas and carry on developments of thought; and, over and above all this, it has to intensify the incidence of climax and prepare for further dramatic action."[26] Ernest Lindgren, in *The Art of the Film,* essentially endorses London, adding that the music should sometimes "provide emotional relief."[27] Hanns Eisler, in *Composing for the Films,* endorses a contrapuntal approach, although he cautions that "Even in marginal cases—for instance, when the scene of a murder in a horror picture is accompanied by deliberately unconcerned music—the un-

*The majority of these observations have been drawn from John Huntley and Roger Manvell's *The Technique of Film Music;* others are quoted by Siegfried Kracauer in *Theory of Film.*

relatedness of the accompaniment must be justified by the meaning of the whole as a special kind of relationship. Structural unity must be preserved even when the music is used as a contrast."[28] Alfred Hitchcock, in an interview by Stephen Watts for *Cinema Quarterly* (1933, Vol II, No. 2), states, "The feeling of approaching climax can be suggested by the music. . . . Film music and cutting have a great deal in common. The purpose of both is to create the tempo and mood of the scene. And, just as the ideal cutting is the kind you don't notice as cutting, so with music."[29] Sir William Walton offers an excellent and detailed description:

> The value to a film of its musical score rests chiefly in the creation of mood, atmosphere, and the sense of period. . . . In a film, the visual effect is of course predominant, and the music subserves the visual sequences, providing a subtle form of punctuation—lines can seem to have been given the emphasis of italics, exclamation marks added to details of stage "business," phases of the action broken into paragraphs, and the turning of a page at a crossfade or cut can be helped by music's power to summarize the immediate past or heighten expectation of what is to come . . . music offers orchestral "color" to the mind's ear in such a way that at every stage it confirms and reinforces the color on the screen which is engaging the eye.[30]

Manvell and Huntley contribute a number of their own perceptive insights:

> Music, in fact, can become the short cut to emotion. . . . Normally film music should not become too complicated. It must enlighten, not baffle the audience (unless this is required for a deliberate dramatic effect). It must grip them, help them create the mood which is most in keeping with the needs of the film, and in doing this, it will have to stress now one, now another element in the drama. . . .
>
> Tension deliberately plays on the nerves of the audience when some climax of violence or threat is anticipated, but the moment of its release is unsure. Music can introduce the feeling of tension into a situation while the images on the screen retain their calm. . . . Music can be used to bring the emotions of the audience into sympathy with the characters on the screen, or to reveal the nature of their experience when it would not be appropriate dramatically for it to be expressed directly in speech or action. . . . The music often expresses emotions that the men cannot reveal directly through their speech or actions.[31]

Paul Rotha, in his book *Documentary Film,* states:

> The old idea that music must fulfill the function of an undercurrent to the picture, just quiet enough to prevent distraction from the screen, being faded down when the commentator speaks, and faded up again when he is finished, this is as antiquated as the type of film for which it is still used. Modern music for sound film must be an integral part of the sound script, must on occasions be allowed to dominate the picture, must on others perform merely an atmospheric function and frequently it must be intermixed with natural sound and speech.[32]

The film composer Arthur Bliss is quoted in *The Technique of Film Music:*

It is powerfully expressive. It can bring nostalgia to a landscape, drama to any hour of day or night; it can express undercurrents of human emotion, when the actors involved show little of it outwardly. It can suggest what is going to happen, it can recall what has happened; most important of all, perhaps, it can make what has turned dead and dull in a picture come alive and exciting. And yet, music must not obstinately obtrude, as at any time it can. Someone said that the best film music is that which is not consciously heard at all. There is a truth in the paradox. The music should do its work so smoothly and perfectly that it is only when you see the same picture run through in the studio without it, that you realize its irreplaceable importance.[33]

And finally, Muir Mathieson, also in *The Technique of Film Music:*

Music, having a form of its own, has ways of doing its appointed task in films with distinction judged purely as music, and with subtlety, judged as a part of the whole film. It must be accepted not as a decoration or a filler of gaps in the plaster, but as a part of the architecture.[34]

Let us suggest that music performs a number of functions for the sound film:

1. It can provide the audience with a sense of filmic reality.
2. It can provide a sense of locale; can complete the setting.
3. It can locate the film in time; establish the period and atmosphere.
4. It can provide reinforcement to the emotional content of the scene, often revealing emotion with a subtlety and complexity that cannot be portrayed by the characters. It can lead the emotions of the audience, contributing to psychological advancement of the action; it can anticipate a change in emotional content of the scene. All this can be communicated nonverbally. It can also determine the audience's relationship to the mood of the film as a whole.
5. It can, when appropriate, supply a counterpoint to the emotions and to the action of the scene; it can provide emotional relief.
6. It can lend to the separate images of the film its own musical form, providing a continuity and flow between the disparate shots and helping the cuts to jell.
7. As with film editing, it can provide the tempo of the scene, the build, the climax, and the relief.
8. It can supply the transitions—between scenes and between moods.
9. Through the use of the leitmotiv it can follow and communicate the development of character throughout a film.
10. It can provide the restive soul of the spectator with contentment, enhance his mood, and make him receptive to the film.

Let us now move on to a brief discussion of film music using our earlier established guides to film sound. In particular, let us go into some detail on the fifth function, the supplying of a counterpoint to the visual content.

Commentative music is by definition asynchronous. It can, and most frequently is, parallel, enhancing and conveying subtle particulars of, but nevertheless duplicating, the visual mood. This is perhaps the most important contribution of music to the story film and you can be assured that seeing a film before music is added to it would go a long way toward convincing you of this. In doing some music cutting on the American version of Bondarchuk's *War and Peace*, I found it necessary to sit through the projection of the final reel some ten or twelve times and to see it both with and without music. There is a moment of exquisite banality in this reel when Pierre sees Natasha after a long separation. We are shown his face in close-up, and he conveys his deep feeling by a raised eyebrow and a delicate trembling of his lip. This moment is appalling when viewed silently, but amazingly enough, even on the twelfth viewing, tired and disgusted and distracted, I found myself being emotionally moved at this moment due to the presence of the music.

There is ample evidence that such parallel, duplicative music works well. Why then do we find such frequent criticism of it? There are two reasons. One is simply the enormous number of times parallel music is used badly, to duplicate clumsily and unnecessarily the emotion portrayed in the desperate hope that the music will somehow salvage the scene. In this age of understatement we are particularly put off by such obviousness. The practice, not the principle, has given parallel music its bad name. The second reason is more important. By choosing the obvious course of using parallel music, we close the door to the more imaginative possibilities of contrapuntal music, with its complexities and crosscurrents to the actions and emotions. Still, parallel music has proven itself too often for us to dismiss it as one effective way to use music for filmic purpose.

Parallel music can duplicate the emotion of a particular visual scene or it can convey the mood of the entire picture. The zither music of Carol Reed's *The Third Man* is an excellent example of this, as well as a superb example of establishing a sense of locale. As Kracauer points out, the music is in some scenes parallel (the streets of nocturnal Vienna), while in others it relates obliquely and contrapuntally to the specific scene, while illuminating the mood and atmosphere of the film as a whole. The director of this film, Sir Carol Reed, has shown in a number of productions—*The Fallen Idol, Odd Man Out, A Kid for Two Farthings*—the evolution of a central musical idea to emphasize the general theme and mood of the film.

We have discussed earlier the music drama of Richard Wagner as contributing the important principle of the leitmotiv, a distinctive orchestral phrase characterizing a particular personality, situation, or idea within the drama, established upon the awareness of the audience and recurring again and again in various guises to point up, at that particular moment, the thought or emotion behind the drama or the situation of the character. Since it is a recurrent and recognizable variation on a theme, it also establishes a line of continuity throughout the drama. Interestingly, our emotional response increases proportionally with each repetition of the theme.

The leitmotiv technique is particularly effective when different themes are established for each important character in the film. Frank Cordell's score for *Khartoum* follows this development. The basic dramatic confrontation is between General Gordon, the representative of Great Britain and of European commerce and authority, and the Mahdi, fanatic, messianic, and leader of the native revolt in the Sudan. The opening title music states a stirring martial theme, quickly evolving into the Arabic motif of the Mahdi, and this in turn gives way to a stirring processional, à la Edward Elgar, "Gordon's theme." This theme recurs countless times in the film in a variety of moods and instrumentations, each time mirroring the particular mood and situation of Gordon. Often it is interwoven with the theme of the Mahdi. It is this same theme that evolves into the glorious processional entry of Gordon into beseiged Khartoum, described previously.

CONTRAPUNTAL MUSIC

Think back to the description given earlier of our playing the record of Chaplin's music, unsynchronized, accompanying the silent films we were projecting. The music seems to run its own course, almost as if it were telling its own version of the visual story, sometimes uncannily underscoring the emotions and actions on the screen, at other times commenting obliquely on the actions, and at still others, providing a somehow illuminating contrast. Instead of our emotions being led by the paternal hand of the director, we are given a choice from a range of feelings. Our mind plays over this field of emotion, pausing for a moment and moving on, perhaps skipping back across several feelings. Anyone who has worked at synchronizing music to film on the Moviola—discussed in detail in the next chapter—has observed how the moving of a piece of music a few seconds backward or forward can uncannily change its effect on the film. Interesting new combinations of sound and visual images occur, and a particular relationship of images that seemed unbeatable now rates a poor second. Such observations cause one to consider spatial dislocation as a simple means for achieving counterpoint, although this is really only the simplest form of counterpoint.

Add to this spatial dislocation of time the possibility of juxtaposition of mood and content. Kracauer quotes Winthrop Sargeant's observation that the

> trick of depicting murder to the accompaniment of trivial music is also to be found now and then in opera. . . . in Rigoletto and Carmen. . . . The very triviality of the music . . . indicates that the death is not a heroic one but merely the extinction of a rather pathetic human being who asked little more of life than the shimmering and inexpensive dream of happiness evoked by the melody.[35]

There is an effective and ironic juxtaposition in Stanley Kubrick's *Dr. Strangelove*, where a popular ballad rendition of "Try a Little Tenderness" is played over shots of Strategic Air Command B-52 bombers behind the main titles, and the saccharine "We'll Meet Again" is heard over the final montage of atom bomb bursts, signifying the detonation of the "doomsday machine" and the extinction of all life on this planet.

The entire musical score of Kubrick's *2001: A Space Odyssey* is composed of known pieces from the classical repertory and could be called a contrapuntal score. The essence of all of Kubrick's films—*Paths of Glory, Lolita, Dr. Strangelove, 2001*—is irony, and so contrapuntal music lends itself particularly well to his purpose. In *2001*, Kubrick follows shots of an apelike prehistoric man fumblingly evolving his first crude tools from a piece of bone with a stunning shot of a massive space ship whirling with infinite grace through distant space. We are at once stunned by the enormity of the evolutional leap forward that man has taken. But instead of backing this visual image with music that would parallel this visual statement, such as classic institutional-achievement "man conquers the heavens" music, Kubrick plays that most superbly banal of pieces, "The Beautiful Blue Danube." Throughout the entire film, whose visuals are an unending paean to the technological triumphs of man, there is not one word of dialogue which is not the essence of banality. The entire film is an ironic fugue of sound and visual image.

The sparse and effective score to David Lean's *Bridge on the River Kwai* uses counterpoint effectively. The famous scene involving "The Colonel Bogie March" is another interesting blending of actual and commentative sound. As the ragged band of British prisoners approaches the prison camp they are pulled into ranks by their colonel, in an obvious attempt to stiffen their backbones and prevent them from bowing before their conquerors. As the men form in proper marching order, they begin to whistle this spirited march. We first hear it in a realistic and ragged rendition, but as the men begin to swing along, Lean cuts from the façade the men present to dramatic detail shots of the bloody, rag-wrapped feet, and our emotional involvement steadily builds. The whistling, almost without notice, begins to be dominated by the sound of a brass marching band, playing the march in a glorious and spirited rendition. As the men swing into camp we have completely lost sight of their filth and frailty and find ourselves wrapped up in the emotion of the music. We have no sense of disturbance at the replacement of the feeble actual whistling by the commentative marching band, just as we had reacted to the similar scene in *Khartoum*.

At the end of *River Kwai* we have a brilliant use of counterpoint in actual music. At this point in the film the team of British saboteurs is laying explosive charges under the bridge, ironically built to perfection by the British prisoners of war. The prisoners, in fact, are at this moment celebrating the end of their work with an evening of amateur entertainment. Lean ignores the obvious choice of supplying us with redundant music of the traditional "mysterioso" type. Instead he uses only the realistic sound effects of the men working, water lapping, and the Japanese guard walking overhead, contrasted with the sound of the British prisoners singing and laughing. Lean not only brilliantly heightens the suspense with this device, he strongly implies the ironic theme of the entire film by contrasting the desperate activities of the commandos with the enjoyment of reveling prisoners, all of whom are British soldiers.

ACTUAL MUSIC

Actual music is, of course, music which is part of the actual scene; it is music heard by the characters in the film. Such music can be both synchronous and asynchronous—e.g., a radio in the next apartment—and it is a particularly effective way of presenting contrapuntal music. Sargeant's observation about accompanying murder with trivial music is a classic description of the use of contrapuntal music, but there is a very real question as to whether this will be accepted by the audience in commentative background music in a dramatic situation. (Kubrick's cited use of "Try A Little Tenderness" is ironic and humorous and occurs over titles, so we accept the contrivance in that situation.) However, nothing prevents us from having the character listening on the radio to a lullaby (or watching Casper the Friendly Ghost on television) at the time of the murder. The music rolling unconcernedly on—the camera might very well remain on the source of the music, leaving the actual violence off-camera—oblivious and indifferent to the brutality of the scene, will stir up powerful emotions in the spectator.

There can be mixtures of the actual and the commentative—*River Kwai*'s "Colonel Bogie March"—and what is in fact commentative but given the appearance of actual—the triumphal entry march into Khartoum is at one point localized in a small military band, although the sound, which does not change in perspective with the change of scenes, is obviously that of a large orchestra.

High Noon switches from actual to commentative in its recurrent use of "Do Not Forsake Me, Oh My Darling" throughout the film. This film offers another interesting example of the use of a theme which evokes locale—a particularly effective attribute of actual music—to provide a general conveyance of the overall mood of the film while paralleling the action and mood of certain scenes closely and specifically.

THE MUSIC PERFORMANCE VISIBLY PORTRAYED

Following our proposition that the visual image must dominate, the key to the successful film portrayal of an actual musical performance is the director's ability to subordinate the sound to the visual line. This can be accomplished in a number of ways. In most film musicals a large part of the plot is laid "back-stage"; the purpose of the performance is primarily to further the plot or to reveal character, not to portray the music per se. In fact, many numbers are shown in rehearsal, often in less than their entirety and in rehearsal sets and costumes, reinforcing this conviction. In the filming of a performing orchestra, the constant flow of varied images—close-ups of faces and hands on the instruments, medium shots of rows or clusters of instruments, shots of the conductor from the orchestra point-of-view—subordinates the music to the role of reinforcing these dominant images.

Hitchcock's *The Man Who Knew Too Much* demonstrates an intriguing use of a symphonic performance perfectly subordinated to a melodramatic plot which gains our full attention. It has been established that a hidden assassin will shoot down an important political figure in a concert audience when the orchestra reaches a predetermined point in the music. The situation is an excellent one for montage, giving Hitchcock the maximum opportunity for controlling the tempo of the scene by cutting repeatedly between the intended victim, the assassin, the orchestra, and the protagonist, racing to stop the attack. Throughout, the music rolls unconcernedly on; yet, as it nears the climactic point, the tension is almost unbearable. The performance is important only in the way it contributes to the drama.

Having developed an aesthetic consideration of the means of making film sound effective and contributive, let us enter the sound cutting room where we can put these principles into practice.

CHAPTER 11

THE SOUND CUTTING ROOM

We introduced several of the tools of the sound cutting room in Chapter 8, tools with functions in both the film and sound editing areas. They were: the Moviola, the splicer, the synchronizer, and the sound reader. Outside of the cutting room, we will make use of a sound transfer service, enabling us to "transfer" our sound from quarter-inch magnetic tape or disc to either 16mm or 35mm magnetic film, whichever we chose to work with. A tape recorder and/or record player, either in the cutting room or elsewhere, will be of use for monitoring disc and tape.

TOOLS OF THE SOUND CUTTING ROOM
SPLICER AND SPLICING TAPE

You will recall from our coverage of cutting room equipment that we shall use a diagonal splice and opaque tape for editing music and effects tracks. If we are using the perforated tape splicer° we must obtain the model which makes a diagonal splice and uses opaque tape; if using a Guillotine splicer, we will load it with opaque tape and use the diagonal cutting blade rather than the straight blade.

*Note photos of all splicers Fig. 8.44, 45, 47.

Why the *diagonal cut* when splicing sound tape? The diagonal splice will not "hinge" as will the straight-across splice, ensuring that it will run more smoothly through a Moviola or the recording studio's dubber. The hinging is caused by the fact that all sound splices are taped on the base side only, since tape covering a portion of the emulsion would affect the reproduction of the sound. This hinging can interfere with the all-important contact between the pick-up head and the tape, resulting in a *drop out* if the splice is close to the beginning or within the body of a useful sound on the track. Such splices create a motion problem when they pass through pick-up heads; the running sound film is a vibratory system and interference with its natural frequency of vibration can result in *wow* or *flutter* in the useful sound if the splice is close to it. Finally, the diagonal splice, cutting across the recorded sound, makes a cleaner intrusion into a continuously running sound, and such within-sound splicing is quite common in film sound work. If straight-across splices are used they will eventually result in audible *clicks* at the splicing point due to the interruption of the tape's magnetic field. You may get away with it for a while, but the consequences will eventually catch up with you. Since it is almost impossible to detect these clicks on the Moviola, the editor is forced to do emergency (and expensive) repair work at the sound mix, something to be avoided if at all possible.

Interestingly, a diagonal method has also been used in splicing optical sound tracks of composite prints (Fig. 11.1). This practice, known as *de-blooping*, uses a low triangle of opaque adhesive paper to lead the light picking up the sound of the optical track gradually up, over, and down the other side of the optical splice without discernible noise. If played unaltered, the splice would produce a "bloop," an audible noise, when passing the exciter lamp.

In editing voice tracks, the cut is often made some distance from the usable sound on the tape, and in many narration tracks the voice is infrequently cut into. Since a straight-across splicer is usually at hand—voice editing is often performed while the picture is still being edited—the lazy editor uses it to splice his voice tracks, particularly if they are 16mm mag film to a 16mm picture. Admittedly he may get away with it, but the practice can cause him trouble. If you must cut close to the voice—we often cut out pauses and even parts of words—common sense would dictate using a diagonal cut. Naturally, the thicker opaque tape of the straight-across splice is to be used rather than the thinner transparent tape suitable for picture splicing.

Since the Guillotine unperforated tape splicer has a dual function in being able to cut both straight and diagonally, it would seem to be a logical answer to this problem. Although we have used them for this purpose, we cannot give unqualified support to the practice. The tiny pieces of tape punched out at the sprocket holes of the film can pop up almost anywhere along the film and cause drop outs. If the machine imperfectly perforates the holes, wow, flutter, or, in the picture, a *lost*

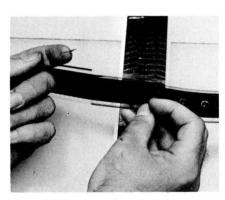

Fig. 11–1 Deblooping splice (cement) in composite print optical track

loop (page 430) may result. The clear tape adhesive has a tendency to ooze, and may foul the pick-up heads during playback.

These disadvantages—and they are real ones—must be weighed against the advantage of the dual purpose machine and its comparatively low-cost tape. We invariably use a 35mm perforated tape splicer for our music and effects editing, although we have used a Guillotine splicer for 16mm picture and voice tracks.

Quarter-inch tape is the familiar tape of tape recorders. It is comparatively inexpensive, takes little space to store, and works on portable equipment. It is possible to record synchronous sound on quarter-inch tape, a subject covered in Chapters 5 and 12. However, in the cutting room we must transfer the sound on quarter-inch tapes to a sprocketed

MAGNETIC RECORDING TAPE AND MAGNETIC FILM

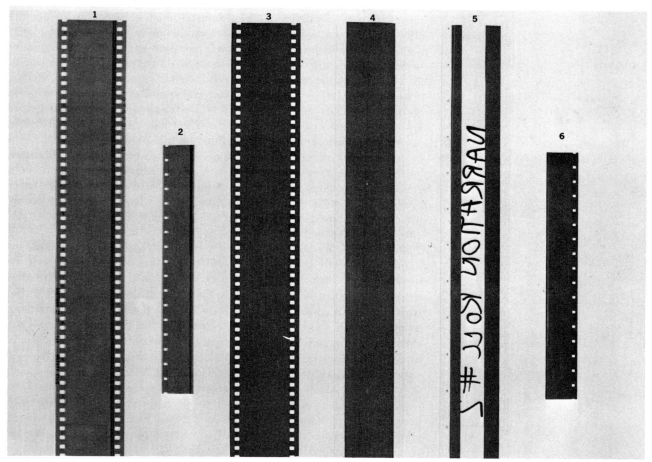

Fig. 11-2 *Magnetic and optical sound film, 16mm and 35mm* (1) 35mm Optical Sound Negative, Variable Area (2) 16mm Optical Sound Negative, Variable Area (3) 35mm Full Coat, Cellulose Acetate Base Magnetic Sound Film (4) 35mm Clear Edge, Cellulose Acetate Base Magnetic Sound Film (5) 35mm Stripe Coated, Cellulose Acetate Base Magnetic Sound Film (6) 16mm Full Coat, Cellulose Acetate Base Magnetic Sound Film

medium (using, of course, a machine with a compatible sync signal device so that the sound is reproduced at exactly the same speed at which it was originally recorded). We can then run the sprocketed magnetic film on our editing machines in sync with the picture.

Sixteen millimeter magnetic film is the cheapest sprocketed medium (Fig. 11.2). We use it most often for the voice track, particularly with a 16mm picture. The quality of sound is excellent, and so long as the equipment to be used—the sound head of the Moviola, the synchronizer, or the sound reader—will take 16mm film, it is usable. Why, then, is the more expensive 35mm magnetic film often used? Since the rate of speed at which 16mm sound film moves past the recording head is a good deal slower than the speed of 35mm, the individual notes making up the recorded music are closer together on 16mm stock, making it more difficult to cut within sound. Additionally, there is only one sprocket hole per frame of 16mm, as compared to four per 35mm frame. This means that we can divide a 35mm sound frame into quarters in splicing, allowing us to be considerably more exact. This is an important factor if we must splice within a piece of music, a sound effect or, less frequently, words, so we invariably use 35mm stock for our music and effects tracks. Sixteen millimeter stock has as good sound reproductive qualities as 35mm and therefore is acceptable for any sound in which there is to be no detailed and exact cutting, and this is often the case with voice tracks. If you expect to do a good deal of exact cutting within individual words, the voice track should also be recorded on 35mm.

Thirty-five millimeter stripe (Fig. 11.2) refers to a magnetic film that is essentially a quarter-inch stripe of sound emulsion imprinted on a celluloid, sprocketed base. It costs from $18.75 to $35 a roll (the latter price if one buys it from recording studios), but it can cost considerably less if bought used and/or containing several splices, which need not affect recording quality.

Thirty-five millimeter full base or *full coat* (Fig. 11.2) is a sprocketed 35mm stock with sound emulsion all the way across, enabling it to be used for multitrack recording. This stock is a good deal more expensive than stripe. You would be foolish to pay the extra cost for normal single-track recording where "stripe" will do the job; but full coat is sometimes available used at a comparable cost to "stripe," and there is no difference in recording quality between the two. It is a characteristic of all forms of tape and magnetic film that they can be cut and then spliced together again, or that a cut can be made at one point in the tape or film and matched to a cut at another point, without loss of quality or even detectable noise. If the cut is made within a sound running continuously, care must be taken to cut at the minute pauses available in this running sound. Nevertheless, the cut and splice properly made will result in no discernible noise.

SOUND TRANSFER SERVICE

The sound transfer service is a film service organization (frequently part of a recording studio) which has a variety of recording machines

Fig. 11-3 Sound transfer room

(dubbers) in quarter-inch, 16mm, 35mm, and sometimes half-inch and 70mm gauge (Fig. 11.3). Not every service has all types, so you would do well to first find out if they have machines capable of handling the stock required. They will *transfer* sound from one medium to another, charging at an hourly rate for the time it takes them to transfer (not for the actual time of the sound on tape) and for the stock. Since the service marks up the cost of stock for a legitimate profit, and usually sells the most expensive tape, consider buying the tape directly from the manufacturer and bringing it to the service. Check to see if the service you contemplate using allows this.

Probably the first way in which you will use the sound transfer service is in bringing them your *sync voice tracks,* or any *sound effects tracks* or *music tracks* you have recorded on location, to have them transferred to your working medium (or media, if you want to have your voice on 16mm, and your music and effects on 35mm). Later, you will *record narration* directly on quarter-inch tape, the least expensive medium. After you have eliminated the out-takes, you will have this transferred to your working medium also. Finally, if you are putting *music and effects* to the film from a *stock library* (or from material you have recorded), these sounds will almost certainly be stored on quarter-inch tape, and you will once again transfer the selected takes on to your chosen medium. One very important point: Moviolas do not have the fidelity of sound reproduction that the highly sophisticated equipment of the sound transfer service has. This is the one time to monitor your sound for quality. Since you may not be present while the service is transferring your sound, it is vitally important that you select a reliable studio to monitor the tapes. While transferring, one can monitor either the original tape or the re-recording as it is being made. The latter step

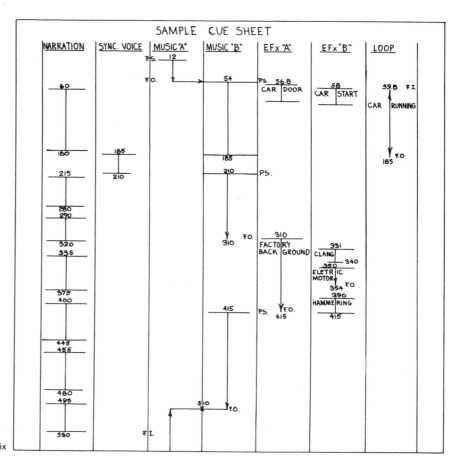

Fig. 11-4 Sample cue sheet for sound mix

is obviously necessary if you wish to detect any imperfection in the tape or fault in the re-recording procedure. You also want a transfer man who is giving your material his undivided attention. Pick a good service and tell them in clear and specific terms what you expect from them.

THE MOVIOLA AS A SOUND EDITING TOOL

We are now dealing with the practical matter of matching various sounds to picture. If we fail to maintain sync between our soundtrack and picture, the visual image will not match the sound image; we say it is "out of sync." We now use the Moviola as a tool to study the variety of ways in which we can match sound to picture, using a variety of sounds in a variety of places. If we do our work properly, we will be able to maintain sync straight through to our finished film. It is for this purpose that we utilize the Moviola (and, of course, the combination viewer-reader-synchronizer unit as a substitute Moviola).

THE CUE SHEET

As an important step before entering the cutting room to work, let us study a sample cue sheet (Fig. 11.4.). Note that it covers voice (narration and sync), music, and sound effects. The sample is the first page of a running cue sheet for a film and covers only the first few hundred feet. What we are working toward in the sound cutting room is the eventual mixing together of a multiplicity of sounds, properly balanced against each other and the picture. This *mix*, as we call it, is covered in detail in the next chapter, but it is very much our concern in the cutting room; all our work is aimed toward this. The mix will be accomplished by running each one of our separate tracks through a *dubber*, a kind of tape recorder which plays either 16mm or 35mm tracks. Each track's level of amplitude (volume) is controlled through a separate control called a "gain" or a "pot" (potentiometer) on a mixing console. Each vertical row of the cue sheet (narration, sync voice, "A" music, etc.) corresponds to a soundtrack controlled by a pot, and the vertical lines and figures—referring to 35mm feet—show the places where the sound on that track must be heard. Obviously there are overlapping sounds, so an important part of our job is to decide which sound is to dominate and to what degree. The cue sheet is rather objective in that it does not tell us the relative level each track must maintain. This will be a matter of artistic choice and, to a large extent, common sense. The voice will invariably dominate when it is present. Specific effects (explosion, door close, gun shot) come second in order of dominance, with background music and general background effects (city noises, crickets, working factory) at the bottom of the scale.

There are some interesting things to note on the sample cue sheet. The narration track is obviously cued to general sections of narration, showing us any large segments where the voice is not present, but ignoring the inevitable short gaps which occur. The *sound mixer* (also called a *re-recordist*) will set the narration track at a constant level and bring the totality of other sound down, under the narration when it occurs, and up when there is no narration, "filling the gap." Of course, we might also wish to do this to a lesser degree even in small gaps of two seconds or so. Usually the mixer does this automatically as he listens to the run-through of the mix, bringing the other-than-voice tracks up and down almost imperceptibly at these points.

The sound editor will do well to check with his specific mixer in advance of the mix as to the kind of cue sheets he will require (many recording studios will supply you with blank forms) and discover any idiosyncracies the mixer may have about particular methods of labeling cues. Most mixers will tell you to ignore any voice track pauses under two seconds, some will want every pause noted, no matter how short, and some will ignore even longer pauses. If your cue sheets do not conform to what the mixer likes to work with, he will probably start out the mix by laboriously recopying in a fine Gothic hand your unusable sheets, and you can ill afford this at $100 per hour.

The difference between narration and sync voice should be obvious to you at this time; narration is commentative sound, sync voice is actual, and, as the name tells us, is synced to match lip movements. (Of course, we may alternate asynchronous shots with those specifically synchronous, but we use the term "sync voice" to cover all of this actual speech.)

Note that the "A" music track starts at 12 feet rather than at zero. All films and their corresponding soundtracks start with eight seconds of *Academy Leader*—12 feet in 35mm, 4 feet 32 frames in 16mm, a total of 192 frames—so called because the Academy of Motion Picture Arts and Sciences has decreed this as an international universal standard.° This gives us a means of starting the picture and tracks and getting them up to sound speed before we actually see and hear them.

The music track of the sample cue sheet illustrates a system that gives a clear indication to the mixer of what he is expected to do. Whenever the line signifying the beginning or end of the music runs all the way across between the parallel vertical lines, this means that the music has a "natural" beginning or end, and hence does not need to be faded in or out by the mixer. In practice he merely opens his pot to the track at a point at which soundless leader rather than sound film is running, sets the pot at a predetermined level, and waits for the music to start "naturally." (If this occurs at the end of a music cue, he does not fade out the pot but allows the music to end "naturally.") We may also write in the margin *"natural out"* (N.O.) to reinforce the point if it occurs at the end of a piece; at the beginning, we prefer to use the commonly used term *"pre-set,"* which you can write P.S. or, if you choose, *"natural in."* When there is not a natural in or out, signify this with an arrow and the terms *"fade in"* (F.I.) or *"fade out"* (F.O.). Also, in such a case the line should not extend all the way across; you can use the half line as an arrow, guiding the mixer in the direction of the next music cue. (Note "A" music track at 54 feet.) If one cue is fading out and the other in, we have what is termed a "cross fade"—a sound dissolve—so signify it as such, a fade out and a fade in. In addition to the fade out and fade in arrows, put a cross in the middle of the line between the two tracks. (We have illustrated such a cue at 510 feet on our sample cue sheet.)

A *loop* (note last column of cue sheet) is a continuous running sound effect (running water, a storm, a machine, birds, city background) recorded on a sprocketed magnetic film which is then looped and joined together, the splice made carefully so that there is no audible change at the joint. Placed on a dubber, the loop runs continuously throughout the mix run-through with its pot closed. We open the pot, fading in the sound, running it as long as we desire, and then fade it out. (In our sample, we fade in at 59½ feet, fade out at 185 feet.) Thus we can use the loop's sound wherever we want for as long as we want, anywhere throughout the reel. Naturally, the more general the sound of a loop the better, for if it has a particular characteristic or pattern, we will begin to hear it each time it comes around on the loop.

The loop is the bane of the mixer's existence for it requires him to tie up extra machines (not to mention hands) to run them and to spend particular concentration on bringing the sound in and out on the exact cue. In obvious contrast, the specifically cut effects track practically runs itself, with only momentary attention paid on the part of the mixer, who

*Although the practice persists in calling it "Academy," the leader most commonly in use today is actually SMPTE Universal Leader, designed by the Society of Motion Picture and Television Engineers. The most important difference between this and Academy Leader is that the "count-down" leading to the picture is in seconds, not feet.

has other things to worry about during the mix. The fewer mechanical fades the mixer must make the better. If the beginning and ending of a cue can possibly be accomplished by cutting it exactly, the sound editor should do this in the cutting room, where he has plenty of time to experiment with it. The practice of coming in to a mix and "winging it" is known as "using the mix as a Moviola," and at $100 an hour it might well be avoided. Of course, if the only way the cue can be done properly is by fading or cross fading, then the mixer's job is to do this and to do it well. However, he should not be burdened by unnecessary tasks which are better taken care of in the cutting room. The ideal mix, to the sound cutter, consists of coming in with an armful of loops and "trying them out"—but not on my money, if I were the producer!

FILM TIME

Film time is reckoned in *frames,* 24 frames per second. Thirty-five millimeter film has 16 frames per foot; 16mm has 40 frames per foot. A foot and a half of 35mm film runs in one second. This makes 35mm footage quite easy to convert into seconds—it is always three to two—and is why we use it far more frequently than 16mm footage in talking about film time—and this is true even when we are dealing with a 16mm picture. In fact, soundtracks will probably be in 35mm for a 16mm picture. The *footage counter* at the mix will always be in 35mm, so it is perfectly valid to think "35" for a "16" picture.

THE CUE SHEET AT THE MIX

Let us think ahead now to the actual mechanics of the mix. Remember that we must have our separate tracks running simultaneously with the picture, from beginning to end of the reel. On our cue sheet we observe gaps in each track. For example, there is no sound on our "A" music track from 54 feet to 510 feet, yet we must keep this track running in sync so that the music cue at 510 will come in exactly on cue. Therefore, we connect these "live" portions of the track—which consist of 35mm sound film—with 35mm leader. Leader is simply some form of discarded film which has the necessary sprocket holes so that we can run it synchronously on our machines. We will later study how these sound tracks are constructed—*"laid in"* is the term used—but at this point it is important to understand how these continuously running tracks run in parallel sync.

Now let us read through and interpret our sample cue sheet. The music starts at the beginning of picture (12 feet) and runs "in the clear" for 42 feet. At this point (54 feet) we fade out our "A" music track and begin on a "B" track; the effect in the final mix will be one of continuous music. This is simply a device enabling us to make a proper changeover from one piece to another. Within 2½ feet of this music change we are to hear a car door slam; then a car starts—with the music continuing—and then the noise of a moving car begins. At 60 feet this conglomeration of sound will be lowered under the narration so that it will not "fight" it. The narration will end at 180 feet, at which time we will bring up the music and the car sound, both of which in turn end at 185 feet, the music "naturally," the car being faded out. From 185 to 210 feet there is a sync dialogue scene and no other sound. Then, at 210 feet the music starts, to be dipped again at 215 feet for the narration, brought up again to prominence at 280 feet, dipped at 290 feet, and finally faded out under narration at 310 feet. At this point a factory background will start. Since the narration ends at 320 feet, we will bring the factory noise up to prominence, noting that a specific clang of metal will punctuate the background at 331 feet. At 335 feet we dip the effects for narration; at 350 feet a motor sound enters, and at 354 feet we will fade it out, all of this occurring under the narration. Narration ends at 375 feet, and from 375 to 390 feet we have only factory background. At 390 feet we have hammering mixed with the factory noise (hammering dominating), both to be dipped at 400 feet for the narrator. At 415 feet the hammering goes out by itself, and we fade out the factory noise as the music starts naturally on the "B" track, all of this under narration. At 445 feet the music has 10 feet of prominence, dipping back under narration at 455 feet, again achieving sole prominence from 480 to 495 feet before dipping again. At 510 feet we will cross unobtrusively under narration from the "B" to the "A" music track, fading out the "B" and fading in the "A" simultaneously. The "A" continues running under narration until the music again comes up at 530 feet.

NARRATION

We gave a good deal of attention in the previous chapter to the aesthetic question of the use of words in a film. We have arrived at a stage where our picture cutting is complete. What if we require narration? How shall we proceed? Our picture has hopefully been shot and cut to a shooting or a cutting script, not a "literary effort" or a listing of a sponsor's favorite products. In any case, the director of the subject film must determine a proper narration to a film which is very rarely self-explanatory through visual images alone. We are to determine how little narration we must use. (After music has been put to the picture, the director will return to the narration and eliminate further, as he finds that music and the visual image will suffice in many areas without any reinforcement from narration.)

In dealing with the average subject film, the director must, if possible, run the picture again and again, writing a narration as a viewer of the film, commenting obliquely to illuminate aspects which the visual images suggest. If a scene needs explanation he will try to clarify what is happening, but he will not say again in words what the picture has said visually. He will avoid redundancy at all costs, never saying what can be implied.

When the script is written, we will work with the Moviola, polishing and carefully timing each section. If a particular portion of narration is difficult to fit into the corresponding visual section, we may consider lengthening the picture or, hopefully, cutting down the narration. We will carefully time the corresponding picture section and make notes on

Fig. 11–5 Dubbing session in recording studio

our script for use in the recording session so that the narrator will not read any section too slowly, making it impossible for us to fit the recording into its intended place.

Narrators will be auditioned, perhaps by having them record a portion of the script as a trial. The person having been chosen, we will invite him to the cutting room to view the picture and to practice reading against it. Perhaps he can hear some of the music selected to get a further feel of the film. Timings are set; awkward phrases corrected. Now we are ready to record. With our rehearsed narrator and our carefully timed script, we proceed to a recording studio. Of course one can record the narration on any available quarter-inch tape machine, but then one must be prepared for the possibility of extraneous noise and less-than-acceptable professional quality of reproduction. The investment in the cost of a good professional sound recording service is essential at this stage.

THE SOUND RECORDING STUDIO

The recording studio may very well be part of the same company that supplied us with our sound transfer work, and may, in fact, later perform the service of "mixing" our completed soundtracks (Figs. 11.5 and 11.6). The studio itself will consist of a room containing one or more professional quality quarter-inch tape recorders and a control panel with more sophisticated controls than the nonprofessional tape recorder possesses. There will be an adjoining booth—soundproofed and usually with a glass window—containing the microphone and a cue light which enables the director to signal the narrator. There will also be an intercom for talking to the narrator from the control panel. There will be a means for projecting film so that the director, the recordist, and usually the narrator

Fig. 11–6 Dubbing session in recording studio

can view it during the recording session. (There is generally an extra charge for recording to projection.)

We must now make a basic decision as to whether we wish to record the narration "to picture" or "wild." There would seem to be compelling arguments for having the narrator work to the picture, involving him emotionally with the film, but in practice this is seldom done. Not only is the narrator distracted by the need to watch the picture when he should be concentrating on reading, but he is also subjected to considerable tension as he struggles to complete his reading within the required time limit. Any error he makes is compounded as the next section rushes upon him without pause, and one error would ruin the entire take.

The technique of recording wild is a procedure allowing the narrator ample time to concentrate on his reading without distraction and even to make corrections as he goes. Three years ago we would have recommended this method without hesitation, but a recent development in sound studio equipment must be acknowledged. This development is the *back-up interlock system* (see page 389), which enables the recordist to halt the picture and running soundtracks, back them up in sync, and begin recording again to correct any error that has been made. In theory, this system would enable us to end our recording session with a perfect track in exact sync with the picture. Usually there is an additional charge for this system, and it requires recording directly onto 35mm magnetic film rather than quarter-inch tape. It also will probably take longer to complete the session. The main saving is in cutting room time in lining up the wild track.

The choice, particularly if a back-up system is available to you, is conditional upon the narrator. If he is a professional, experienced at this sort of work, you might very well consider recording to picture. This consideration is especially valid for radio and TV broadcasters who are trained to work live while they are watching events taking place. The professional will not be as likely to be bothered by the inherent tensions that arise from such a situation. If you are dealing with someone comparatively inexperienced in film narration, then we strongly recommend recording wild, for without question it will give you the conditions under which you will be best able to elicit the performance you want. You may then spend a bit more time in the cutting room, but that is what the cutting room is for and it is a good deal cheaper than experimenting in a recording studio. The inexperienced narrator's reading would almost certainly deteriorate as he struggles to read as you wish him to under the constant harassment of the fear that he might ruin the take.

THE RECORDING SESSION

By the start of the session, the narrator has become familiar with the work print and with the script. He has rehearsed thoroughly with the director so that the recording session is solely for the purpose of the actual recording. If for some reason the narrator is unavailable beforehand, have him meet you at the studio an hour early. Arrange with the studio for a quiet room where you can rehearse, so that when you enter the recording room (and your charges start) you will be ready to work.

The narrator takes his place in the booth, the recordist at the controls of the tape machine, the director at the recordist's side. The recordist checks the level of the narrator's voice, readies his machine, and signals that he is ready to begin. The director can give any last minute instructions to the narrator through the intercom system. The recordist will start the tape machine and will signal when to begin—usually with the term "speed," meaning that the tape is up to speed. The director may cue the narrator with the cue light, pressing the button to blink a light in the recording booth. The narrator begins to read. The director and the recordist monitor the reading, the recordist for technical acceptability, the director for quality of performance. The director also has his copy of the script before him with its notations of the length of time he wants each paragraph to take. Each paragraph should be timed with a stopwatch; most studios will have one available.

Invariably the narrator will warm to his task, and the end of the first reading is often noticeably better; there will probably be corrections the director wishes made throughout. We would suggest an approach which we think will help the director get the results he wants. When the narrator finishes his first run-through, compliment him on the reading, but point out how well he has done the last portions and suggest that he continue immediately by starting over again from the top, now that the juices are flowing. The intercom can be used for this, but perhaps stepping quickly into the booth to speak directly to him is a more personal way of dealing with the narrator. Tell him that you are "saving"—that is, not erasing—the first take, but that you are certain that he can do a really excellent reading this time. Avoid any specific criticisms even if you have a notebook full, and limit yourself to general instruction affecting overall quality, such as, "This time add the quality of enthusiasm about some of the scenes which you are describing." The entire "criticism" should not take more than thirty seconds; then duck out quickly, signal the recordist, and sit down to listen carefully. Much to your surprise, a great many of the specific errors of the first reading will disappear by themselves, and this is the best way. Obviously this is a system designed to relax and increase the confidence of the narrator, and that is precisely what it is your business to do. The fact that you have given a constructive suggestion is extremely important too. As anyone who has ever worked with actors knows, the attention paid to them while they are rehearsing or performing is a very important thing. This technique of criticism assures them of your attention and also gives them confidence in your work. Of course, it also helps if you are right, but this is your business—to be right.

If the second run-through is still deficient in a major and general way, stop the recording and enter the booth to work closely with the narrator until you have what you want. Then return to the recordist and try recording again.

If you are satisfied that the overall quality is what you want, pay careful attention to your script, time the sections in which a close match is essential, and note any errors you want corrected. When the run-through is finished you might follow this method: Compliment the narrator on an excellent job and suggest that you have a few specific lines that can be corrected. Point them out to him one at a time and move quickly to record each one in order, repeating each until it is as you want it. Of course if a discussion is needed, do not hesitate to go into the booth to work with the narrator before attempting to record.

You will have marked on your script the portions of the narration which have been done through retakes at the end of the tape (Fig. 11.7). Remember that the tape also contains in its continuity the takes which you will discard and replace with the appropriate retakes. The entire session, unless you have chosen to erase an unwanted portion, has now been recorded on quarter-inch tape. The portions you wish to use must now be transferred to the sprocketed medium you have selected for your voice track, 16mm or 35mm mag.

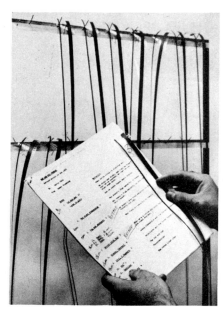

Fig. 11–7 Voice retakes hung in numerical order

THE TRANSFER AND LAYING-IN OF NARRATION

One method you might use would be to edit your quarter-inch tape first, that is, cut out the N.G. portions and replace them with the retakes. You would then be able to transfer the entire corrected recording directly to your sprocketed tape. Since quarter-inch is considerably cheaper than 35mm mag and even 16mm mag, you have every reason to keep everything you have on the quarter-inch, but cut the amount you have to transfer to a minimum. This method certainly would be acceptable, provided you were very careful to get each retake where it belongs. Let us go through an alternate method we have used, assuming we are to use 16mm mag film for our narration track. (The principle would be the same if we chose the more expensive 35mm mag.)

Request a transfer of the approved run-through and any retakes to 16mm mag. The recording studio can do this while you wait. Then take this magnetic film back to the cutting room with your script carefully marked as to which portions have been done over as retakes at the end. In the cutting room, run down to the retakes on the rewinds, using the sound reader to locate them. Then break out these retakes separately, labeling them for quick identification with a numbering system corresponding to the numbers of the paragraphs on the script. These takes can then either be hung next to the Moviola in a convenient film barrel or rolled and placed next to the machine (Fig. 11.7).

Locate the start of the narration using the sound reader or Moviola, mark it and place the reel on the supply rod of the Moviola sound head. Then place the work print on the Moviola and start a fresh roll of 16mm leader through the sound head in sync with the picture. Run down to the point at which you want the first word of narration. The placement of this and subsequent narration cues should be determined by using the brake on the Moviola, just as it was used in determining the timing of picture cuts.

Start the machine and watch the viewer to get a sense of the rhythm of the film, and as the cut passes leading into the appropriate scene, use the brake to stop the film at the point at which you feel the narration should begin. Mark the leader at this point, back up the machine and splice the previously marked start of the narration to the marked leader.

CORRECTING SYNC IN THE NARRATION TRACK

As you run forward, the narration will feed off the supply reel and take-up on the top; you will be able to listen and watch the picture. Run to the end of that cue and continue to the start of the next cue. If it starts at the proper spot, simply continue on. If the narration does not start as soon as it should, in relation to the picture, continue running until you hear the first word, stop the machine, and back it up to get the very first sound of this word exactly under the sound head. If you move the machine carefully by hand with the volume high, you will be able to pick this out without any difficulty. Mark the start and then back up the machine to the point at which you wanted this cue to actually start. Mark this point on the leader, back the Moviola to bring the point to the splicer, cut out the sound film between the two marks, and splice. Now your cue should start properly.

If your next cue starts sooner than it should, again mark the start of the voice, back up, and cut the sound film at this marked point. Splice leader to the bottom of the running film at the point where you cut, and run forward as this leader feeds into the machine. Stop and mark the leader at the place where you wish the voice to enter, back off, and cut into the leader the sound film at the point where you marked and cut it—at the sound start—before. This narration portion will be feeding off the supply reel. Should you need more exact cuing, or should a speech prove too long for its appointed section, you can take out pauses between words. Remember to mark carefully the end of sound and beginning of sound of the words on either side of the pause so you do not cut into sound. You should also be careful to maintain a sense of the natural rhythm of speech when you remove pauses. You will be amazed at how much you can shorten a paragraph or even a sentence. After a bit of practice you will be able to cut into words—shortening vowels and joining the beginning of one word to the end of another—or cut out phrases in the middle of sentences. We would recommend that you not attempt this at the start, unless you have another copy of the recorded narration handy.

REPLACING A TAKE WITH A RETAKE

Using the script at hand, you will see that you have reached a take that is to be replaced (Fig. 11.7). Run on past until you reach the first sound of the next good take; mark it and cut at this point, leaving the good take hanging below the machine on the supply reel. Back up and return to the start of the take to be discarded. Assuming this N.G. take is in proper relationship to the picture (if not, use the methods outlined above to gain this) cut out the unusable take, and cut in the good retake you have hanging in the film bin next to the Moviola. Then roll forward to the end of this take, and splice in at the right spot the following take which is, of course, hanging on the supply reel.

TIMING NARRATION WHILE LAYING IN

If you have not properly planned your narration before and during recording, there is not a great deal to be done now. But a well-planned script can be given the final delicate honing at this point. A basic consideration is the relationship of the words to the cuts of the picture. When a new scene is introduced, give careful thought to where you want the words to begin, sometimes quite close to the cut, sometimes after a considerable pause. If you plan to introduce a new scene with a dominant sound effect or an attractive piece of music, perhaps the voice cue can be held off for a few seconds to allow the other sound to establish itself. Sometimes you may wish the words to precede the image. Watch carefully when the narrator continues talking over a cut. You will find that there is a definite relationship between the rhythm of the picture cuts and the words of the narration, just as in sync dialogue, and a cut coming in the middle of a word can be disturbing. When there is a natural flow and relationship between the words and the visual images, the words are better able to blend into their proper and subordinate position rather than calling attention to themselves, as they do when they conflict with the cuts. Preferably a cut to a new scene should come between sentences or at least phrases. You would most likely not run even a commentative narration over a dissolve or fade-out. A great deal can be done at this stage, and it is enjoyable and creative work. Do not kid yourself into thinking such work can be done in an hour or two before the mix. Give yourself a full day (especially on a two-reeler) and do a first-rate job; the picture deserves it.

Even though we are dealing primarily with the subject film, a word must be said about the dubbing of dialogue (see Figs. 11.5 and 11.6). The term *dubbing* derives from the dubber, the high-performance sound reproducer handling 16mm and 35mm magnetic film, the basic machine of the recording studio. The term *dub* is used in referring to the procedure of recording sync voice to the silent work print with which we are working at this stage of film-making.

Most people have heard the term dubbing used in reference to the practice of substituting voices in a language other than that of the original picture soundtrack. The results of such dubbing offer film buffs one unique common ground for universal agreement: vehement condemnation of the practice. What is far less generally known is that a large proportion of all sync voice sequences in theatrical films—including virtually all exterior scenes—are dubbed later in recording studios, usually although not always by the actors who spoke the lines originally before the camera. This is done because of the difficulty and expense of maintaining proper conditions for the recording of these voices under typical shooting conditions, particularly on location.

You will remember that the primitive conditions of the early sound stages required the simultaneous creating of all aspects of film sound as the picture was being shot. The subsequent development of an interlock system made it possible to treat these elements separately, enabling the sound technician to run multiple tracks bearing the various elements of the film sound in perfect sync with the picture. The advent of the Italian neo-realist school of film-making following World War II gave impetus to the practice of voice dubbing. Directors such as De Sica and Rossellini made effective use of non-actors in their films. But as anyone who has ever watched a soap commercial on television has realized, it is one thing to get a non-actor to portray a role in pantomime and quite another to get him to speak lines. The Italians developed to a fine art the practice of voice dubbing, utilizing trained actors in the studio to supply the proper voices to match the superbly natural gestures of the "real" people on the screen. But, of course, this was dubbing in the original language, and this can be done so that it is undetectable to the average movie-goer.

We have mentioned one essential to voice dubbing earlier: the recording of a *scratch track* simultaneously with the shooting (see page 180). This track should be treated exactly as if you intended to use it as the actual voice track—that is, sync should be maintained and the track properly slated. However, you need not worry about extraneous noise. At the same time that you recorded your scratch track, *"presence"* recordings of the appropriate background noise should have been made; this would include both "room tone" and outdoor presence.

If you find it impossible to record a scratch track, it is essential that you keep a complete and accurate stenographic record of what has been said. You will be amazed at how lines that everyone had burned into their memory will have faded into oblivion by the time of the dubbing session six months later.

VOICE DUBBING

The preparation for the traditional dubbing session will consist of the making of *loops*, either *film* or *sound*. If you have made a scratch track, you may choose either; both techniques follow the same principle. A loop for continuous running is made of the scene to be dubbed, either of the picture, or of the scratch track, or both. In either case, at the loop's connecting splice, insert a short length of leader which will cause a brief pause before the looped scene starts again. If using a picture loop, just before the start punch two spaced holes in the leader, the same distance apart as the second is from the first frame of picture. In the case of a sound loop, use two *"beeps,"*—a high frequency tone on a piece of glue-backed quarter-inch tape which most recording studios can supply you—spaced equally up to the first voice sound. The principle is the same in either case; the beeps and the visible punch holes provide a measurable rhythm which alerts the actor to the approach of the first word he is to match.

This work will be performed in a recording studio; projection will be required if we are using picture loops. The sound loops will be played through earphones to the actor, while the director will either remain in the recording booth with another set of earphones or sit outside the booth at the recording console (Figs. 11.5 and 11.6). Outside, the recordist and the director monitor the actor's reading and the original track; if in the booth, the director simultaneously hears the reading and, through the earphones, the original scratch track. It is the director's job to determine when the two voices match and/or when the voice matches the picture. The actor watches and/or listens to several run-throughs of the loop to pick up the rhythm; he then begins to speak into the microphone upon signal that the recordist has started the tape recorder. Soon the voice will begin to match the original; it is then a matter of the director, with the help of the recordist, determining the best take. Even if the original actor is not available, dubbing a voice in the same language as the original can be done well.°

There are a number of inherent drawbacks to this traditional technique of dubbing. The creation of loops is a laborious process, and the subsequent laying-in of the new tracks is also time-consuming. There is no real way to play back the selected take, so final determination of its suitability is left until the film reaches the editing room, with the actors long dismissed. The hypnotic repetition of a rhythmic pattern tends to lure the actor into a kind of trance, and the result is often mechanical rather than free and believable. The loop's pace is unalterable; the takes often begin before the actor is ready, droning relentlessly on in its entirety while he waits for the start to come around again. If the beginning of the take is flubbed, once again the entire loop has to run its course. Nor is there any method for making split takes or for storing more than one potential acceptable take for later comparison.

The traditional technique of dubbing—like many of the complex technical procedures of film-making—presents a bewildering complexity of practices which has often overwhelmed the uninitiated. Thus the practice of dubbing has been left in the hands of a limited number of

Fig. 11–8a Magna-Tech Electronic Looping Console, which controls functions of projection, recording, and playback equipment

*Dubbing in a different language is done in the same way, except that the new voice reads an approximate translation of the speech in general sync with the film, attempting to match in particular the endings and beginning of phrases. Such work is best left to experienced professionals.

technicians who have mastered the technique. This inner circle has performed with great technical competency but with little creative innovation.

The development of the *back-up interlock system with pick-up recording* (see page 382), which has revolutionized the procedures of mixing and voice recording, has had comparable effect on dubbing. The system enables the recordist to halt the picture and any sprocketed sound tracks running synchronously with it, back up to any earlier point, and run forward again, still in perfect sync. More important, the recordist, having made an error during the run-through, may return to an earlier point of acceptable quality, move forward on "playback," and then begin to record instantaneously, even at a point at which there is continuously running sound. He accomplishes this by monitoring alternately the original material and the recording, balancing their amplitude (volume) levels before beginning to record; there is no noise implanted on the recorded track at the point at which the system begins recording, nor is there any gap in the recorded sound.

In dubbing, a three-track recording is made on full coat 35mm magnetic sound film. There is no need to loop the picture or scratch track since they and the recording medium are returned to the selected starting point by the recordist following each take. Up to three takes can be recorded on the three available channels and played back to picture for a comparison while the session is still in progress. Complete takes can be made up from portions of two or even three parallel takes. Later, a transfer can be made to 35mm mag stripe of the selected takes, and the editor can leave the session with the voice sync material perfectly matched to picture for the entire reel and ready for the final mix; there is no need to lay-in the takes back in the cutting room.

A further refinement on this method makes use of an *electronic post-synchronization system* developed by Magna-Tech Electronics of New York City, the first commercial installation being at Manhattan Sound Studios, also in New York City (Fig. 11.8 A–C). This system allows the tracks and picture to be backed up both at sync speed (90 feet per minute) or 50% faster, at 135 feet per minute. Both the start and return may be pre-set to occur automatically, a considerable saving of time which also allows the recording engineer to concentrate more on the important business at hand. The system is so accurate single words can be changed without erasing the words adjacent to them. In the event of a flubbed take, the system has a manual override, allowing the recordist to return immediately to the start where he awaits the actor's readiness.

The back-up, non-looping, system of dubbing has one obvious drawback. Looping allows the director to cluster takes involving particular actors so that all actors need not be called for every dubbing session. In films in which the same actors are heard throughout, this is not a factor. If it is a consideration, the editor should make up a series of reels for the session, grouping the work of particular actors together in specific reels. He can then reconstitute the work print in the cutting room. While stu-

Fig. 11–8b Magna-Tech Type PR–135 35mm Reversible projector, which will run release prints or spliced workprints forward or reverse

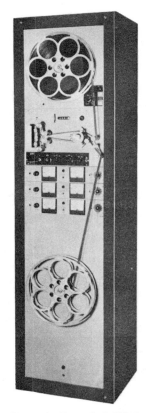

Fig. 11–8c Magna-Tech 100 Series Magnetic Reproducer operates forward or reverse

dios charge more for these back-up dubbing sessions—the time cost is greater and the stock used more expensive—there are important aesthetic gains in the actor's freedom from the repetitive loop and in the director's ability to properly select the desired take. And, the editor is spared the time-consuming practice of preparing loops and laying-in the completed takes.

Most recording studios are familiar with the technique of dubbing and will help the beginning director acquaint himself with the practice. If your budget will allow, you might call up the studio and get a quoted price for the whole service, including, if required, the preparation of loops and the directing of the session. When you have completed recording the new voice takes, they will be transferred to the sprocketed medium you have chosen for your sync voice track. If you have used the looping method, these takes will then be laid-in to picture, using the techniques we have discussed earlier in connection with the cutting of the sync track. If the post-sync system has been used, your voice track should be in sync and ready for use when you leave the studio.

SOUND EFFECTS (EFX): CUTTING ON THE SYNCHRONIZER

Subject film sound effects must be, above all, selective. Their general purpose is to provide a sense of locale and/or background and to satisfy the viewer's demand for a particular sound, the lack of which would disturb his sense of reality of the scene. Most important, a sound can be used dramatically—the snap of a twig, the flick of a switchblade knife, the thundering roll of a stampede, the complex sound fugue of a battle. We should add that in a specialized area—animated cartoons and silent movies dubbed with sound—nonrealistic and zany sound effects are used for comic effect, replacing actual, and sometimes nonexistent, sounds with exaggerated, humorous sounds.

In a realistic story film with sync dialogue the demands for detailed sound effects are greater, but we are helped by the fact that many small sounds, such as a chair creaking, footsteps, paper rustling, found in interior scenes using the original recorded tracks will be supplied by the original voice track. Most exterior sounds will have to be laid-in. In the nontheatrical subject film with commentative sound, all of our effects will be added in the cutting room. However, in such a film, we will find that our music will, in many cases, substitute for specific effects. Scenes involving factory machinery, auto motors, or motorboats can be far better served by appropriate music; the running of this sort of generalized sound can be terribly distracting after a few moments. Use effects for effect. We should also point out that an integrated score alternating portions of music and occasional specific effects with portions having full and detailed effects and no music—say a scene of heavy construction work or an amusement park—can be very effective.

Hopefully, many effects have been recorded on a quarter-inch tape machine on location. (A Nagra would be an excellent machine to use, but a lesser machine will suffice; the requirements of fidelity for effects are not as great as those for music or voice.) If not, the necessary effects can either be recorded afterwards in the appropriate places with a tape recorder, can be created in the studio, or can be purchased from film service houses specializing in libraries of sound effects.

These libraries are an excellent source for any sound you might need—and at a reasonable price. These same service houses can, with the director's guidance and approval, score and edit the complete effects job for a film. This will be an expert job by an experienced professional; we highly recommend it if your budget allows.

In many cases the sound supplied is not the actual sound portrayed on the screen; however, seeing effects in association with a visual scene lends them reality. This phenomenon is undoubtedly helped by the fact that the majority of the audience is unaware of the fact that the effects have been added in the cutting room. One word of warning on this score: The sponsor of the film very frequently is a stickler for the right sound. After all, the film is portraying things with which he is familiar, the sounds of which are ordinarily a daily part of his life. We recommend that the sponsor accompany you when you pick out the effects and give his approval of their appropriateness.

For the laying in of the effects, we shall use the Moviola, the splicer, and a quantity of leader. We will now employ the technique of laying-in on the editing table. We are carrying out the procedure of cutting our effects into a continuously running track of blank leader, but here we feel that the multiple tracks usually needed for effects work require transferring the actual laying-in to the editing table, doing only the cuing on the Moviola.

Place the picture on the Moviola, set the footage counter (35mm, the footage we will deal with at the mix) at zero, and sit down with a yellow pad. Then run forward to the first required effect. When you have located the point, stop the machine at the specific frame. This could be the first frame after a cut, in the case of a sound underlying an entire scene or the spot where the specific effect hits. Note this cue on your yellow pad. We are now building a cue sheet (Fig. 11.9). We should point out that in our experience, with the exception of certain very sharp sounds, such as gunshots, most effects are cued two frames after the picture frame in which the sound first occurs.

After noting the footage and listing the effect required, we proceed to the next effect and list it. If we have two sounds occurring simultaneously, a second, or "B," track will be necessary. We also use a "B" track and alternate our effects between it and the "A" track if the effects occur fairly close together. The mixer may have to adjust his level for different effects, and it becomes a very difficult job if the effects are too close together. If necessary, a "C" track, or even more, can be added. You will recall that a loop can be used for continuously running sound.

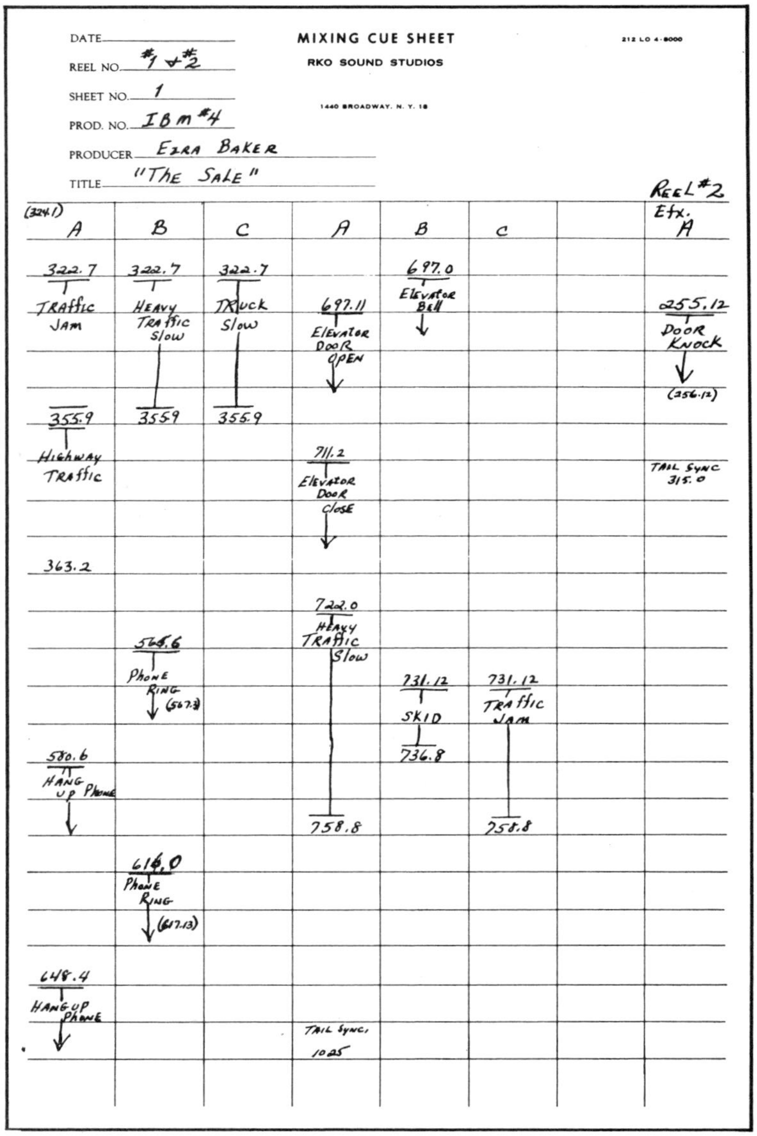

DATE _____
REEL NO. #1 & #2
SHEET NO. 1
PROD. NO. IBM #4
PRODUCER Ezra Baker
TITLE "The Sale"

MIXING CUE SHEET
RKO SOUND STUDIOS
1440 BROADWAY, N.Y. 18
212 LO 4-8000

Reel #2

(324.1) A	B	C	A	B	C		Efx. A
322.7 Traffic Jam	322.7 Heavy Traffic Slow	322.7 Truck Slow	697.11 Elevator Door Open ↓	697.0 Elevator Bell ↓			255.12 Door Knock ↓ (256.12)
355.9 Highway Traffic	355.9	355.9	711.2 Elevator Door Close ↓				Tail Sync 315.0
363.2			722.0 Heavy Traffic Slow				
	566.6 Phone Ring ↓ (567.8)			731.12 Skid	731.12 Traffic Jam		
580.6 Hang Up Phone ↓				736.8			
			758.8		258.8		
	616.0 Phone Ring ↓ (617.13)						
648.4 Hang Up Phone ↓			Tail Sync, 1025				

Fig. 11-9 Sound effects cue sheet

If one has a scene in which a number of sounds of one type, requiring a particular sound level setting, alternate irregularly with sounds requiring another setting, we should group the similar sounds on one track, rather than adhering strictly to the alternation principle; our purpose is to make the mixer's job as easy as possible.

We can now take our list of required effects and determine which we have on hand and which we need to obtain. If we must obtain some, a field trip or visit to the effects library is in order. The effects must then be transferred to the sprocketed medium we have selected for our tracks. (The library will supply them on magnetic film if you wish.) When you return to the cutting room, the effects must be *broken out*. This means running the tracks either on the Moviola or with rewinds on a sound reader, identifying each sound—a list of the order in which they were recorded or transferred is invaluable—and marking its start. Then each sound should be rolled up and placed in a rack on the table, ready to be cut into the tracks as we proceed to the procedure of laying in the effects.

Once the picture is cued, we move to the cutting table (Fig. 11.10). The necessary number of tracks are set up with running leader feeding from supply reels on the lefthand rewind through the synchronizer (where start marks are marked on each track) and on to the take-up reel on the righthand rewind. Since we are handling multiple reels the take-up reels on the right (not the left, which must turn freely and separately) must be clamped together with the spring clamp provided with rewinds and spaced apart with the appropriate spacers. The rewind is then turned and the tracks move forward with the footage counter of the rewind moving. When we reach the listed footage on the counter, we stop and mark the leader with a grease pencil, back the track off, and cut in the appropriate effect at the mark. Then we proceed to the next effect, each time checking to be sure that the effect is cut into the particular track that the cue sheet stipulates; if you make an error, it will cause the mixer to bring up the volume of the wrong track at the mix and much valuable time will be lost. Once all the effects are cut in, we place the tracks on the Moviola and run the effects against picture. If everything checks out, we are ready for the music.

LAYING IN EFFECTS

Fig. 11-10 Laying in effects

MUSIC

The stated aim of this book is to guide the beginning film-maker through the various stages in the making of a film, showing how he may perform many of the functions himself. When not specifically able to carry out the work, he will be prepared to deal professionally with the expert who will actually perform it. With this in mind, we will here discuss the director's task through a full range of participation and responsibility for the film's music. At one end of the scale is the *original score*. Here the function of the director is to choose the right composer and to guide him as to his, the director's, feelings about his film and what he expects from the score. The next possibility is the *improvised score,* and in such a case the director would provide much more exact and detailed information, perhaps even "directing" the recording session. Then there is the *music library score,* in which a skilled professional offers selections (and later performs the task of cutting them to picture), working closely with the director in the choice of music, offering him the opportunity of approving each piece well before the final mix. Finally, we will cover in detail how the *director* might perform his work if he himself were actually doing the job of a music editor, both selecting and editing all selections required for the film. We must first weigh the relative merits of these four ways of putting music to the film.

Fig. 11-11 Recording session (courtesy National Recording Studios, Inc.)

The Original Score

We assume that if we can get the right man to compose our score, find the musicians and the studio to record it properly—and can afford the cost of all this—then the original score, composed specifically for our film, is what we all strive for. Such a score gives the film unity, and a subtlety of expression not possible with the library score. Further, such a score more effectively subordinates itself, when necessary, to the words; the chance for us to choose precisely the right style of music is greater, for we are not limited to what is available, but only by our imaginations, and can, in the true sense of the word, be "original." But this is true only if the right people are available. To use an original score merely because your maiden aunt can render it on her out-of-tune piano for you to record on your $29.95 tape recorder is not exactly what we have in mind. Actually, in an initial film effort, the chances of having just the right person to do your score are rather small. Many beginning films are made by people with some connection with a school, and there is always someone lurking deep in the abyss of the music department, waiting to pounce upon your film with his preconceptions and his musicology notes tucked under his arm. Beware the composer who is eager to score your film in the authentic manner of Frescobaldi with an orchestra of shawms, rebecs, krumhorns, sackbuts, and lutes—particularly if it is a film on "Lumbering Operations in the Great Northwest." Nor does being a competent composer guarantee success in the writing of music for the film. There is some justification in working with a beginning film composer; you might have an opportunity of working with someone of proven brilliance in his field who will develop along with you into a fine film composer and who, even as a beginner, might offer imagination and talent that would lead the film beyond your expectations. However, balanced against the chance of the inexperienced composer damaging the film, the odds are not with you.

If you are in the fortunate position of being able to use an experienced screen composer, you must consider two points. The first is simply whether or not you will be able to fully impress upon him your aim in the film and whether he will be able to carry this out. Remember, you will not really know what the score will sound like until you are in the recording studio—by then fully committed financially—and you will not know how the score will actually work until you run your interlock screening just prior to the mix. By then the chance of turning back is rather small. Of course you can judge your composer's "rightness" by listening to examples of his work and by hearing his ideas on your film, but neither presents you with any real certainty as to the final results. The second point to consider is cost.

COPYRIGHT

For an original film score to be properly handled you must have some knowledge of copyright considerations. You cannot simply take a piece of music off a record, for, to begin with, the music may be copyrighted, meaning it is owned by someone whose permission is needed in order to use it. Sometimes, upon payment of an appropriate fee, one can obtain the rights to a particular piece of music.° Of course, there may be no copyright on the music if it is sufficiently old—a Mozart symphony, for example. Sometimes, particularly in the case of folksongs, only a certain arrangement or set of lyrics is copyrighted; this can also be checked. A surprising number of songs that one might assume one is free to use are actually copyrighted, including such standards as "The Daring Young Man on the Flying Trapeze," "Happy Birthday," "Sailing, Sailing," and many Sousa marches. We use the term P.D., meaning "in the public domain," when music is no longer under copyright. Some tunes are copyrighted only in foreign countries; in such a case, if the film is to be distributed only in the United States, the piece could be used without paying a fee. You are making a mistake if you use a copyrighted piece on the blithe assumption that the film will never be shown to anyone in public. The idea of doing a film with no intention of public performance is foolish, and if such a performance should become possible you would be faced with the necessity of redoing the score and the mix, and making new prints from new optical negatives. The sensible thing is to do it right from the start. If the piece you want is unobtainable, use another one that is.

Assuming that the rights to the music are obtained, there still remains the performance by the musicians and the rules of the American Federation of Musicians to consider. If you are dealing with a recording, you would first have to contact the publisher and producer of the record to obtain their permission and notice of fee. You might find it necessary to pay the appropriate film music fees to the musicians involved in the original recording. Film music is recorded at minimum three-hour sessions, at a cost of approximately $53 per man for documentaries and industrials, $76 for TV films, and double for the conductor, the contractor, and any man who performs on more than one instrument. A leader is required for a group of any size (if you hire a single musician, he becomes the leader and hence is paid double), and a contractor for any group of ten or more. The contractor can be one of the performers; in such a case you need only pay one additional fee to make up the "double," since he will be paid the normal fee for performing. The cost for a single three-hour documentary or industrial film session for a ten-man group with no doubling would then be $742.

The uninitiated are sometimes surprised at the cost. The musician's work can be used over and over again for many years during the film's distribution period without the musician receiving any further payment; in a sense, the musician's performance is in competition with his future work. The fee may seem large in proportion to some other film costs and to the time spent in the session, but it is quite small when compared to the potential millions of people who may attend the film performance.

This scale applies to professional musicians who are members of the American Federation of Musicians; it does not preclude the possibility of using a performance by amateur musicians—a high school band concert,

THE AMERICAN FEDERATION OF MUSICIANS

Musicians	10 × $53 =	$ 530
Leader	1 × 106 =	106
Contractor	1 × 106 =	106**
		$ 742

*The National Music Publishers Association, 460 Park Ave., New York, New York 10022, will inform you as to whether a piece of music is copyrighted and in what countries. They can also obtain from the copyright owner information as to the required fee, which is affected by the particular use to which you wish to put the music.

**$53 if he is already paid as a musician.

a native African dance—provided their permission is given. If the amateur performance is appropriate to the film—a story of a high school or a study of an African village—one might very well use such music throughout. It is a questionable practice merely as a means of circumventing the union rules protecting the livelihood of professional musicians. One must also ask whether the performance by an amateur group will really be first-rate. As in so many facets of film-making, you are entitled to professional work when you pay a professional to perform it.

Let us set up some basic guidelines as to the cost for an original score. We have shown above the cost of musicians for a three-hour session (perhaps fifteen minutes of film music can be recorded in a three-hour session). We would have the additional cost of the recording studio, approximately $75 per hour ($225), plus the cost of tape, transfer, and editing (approximately $100): a rough total of $325. Assuming the same ten men, contractor, and conductor, we have a total of around $750 per session for the musicians. (This figure includes the present base rate for industrial or documentary films, plus the required 5 percent union retirement fund payment.) A fair fee for a composer might be $100 per minute of music (15 × $100 = $1,500) with the costs of arranging ($800) and copying ($325) additional. Add to this another $50 for transfer to 35mm mag stock. Assuming we have an editing room and can lay-in the music ourselves, we have the following costs for fifteen minutes of recorded music, originally composed and arranged, and performed by ten men: $3,750.

Needless to say, it is vital that the conductor be able to finish the fifteen minutes of music within the three-hour period to avoid the additional cost of overtime for the studio and musicians, who receive a minimum of one hour's pay even if only a few minutes more are needed to finish. If these costs can be met within your budget, and you are satisfied as to your ability to get what you want from the composer, you may well attempt an original score. If not, there are other courses open.

Musicians	750
Studio	325
Composer	1,500
Arranger	800
Copyist	325
Transfer	50
TOTAL	$3,750

The Improvised Score

There are several ways in which this type of score might be done. Perhaps the simplest is to have one musician (a guitarist or pianist) study the film and then improvise a simple score as the film is projected for him in a recording studio; or, you might decide to use a small combo (e.g., guitar, flute, and percussion). Bring to your musicians rather detailed timings of the sections of the film requiring music. You might have a composer sketch in the basic form of the music and use a small jazz combo of five to six men to improvise on his ideas and fill in the outline of the music. In any case, your costs for composing, arranging and copying will be a good deal less; and, although you must still abide by the union requirements if professionals are used, the use of a small number of men naturally lowers your cost further. Another advantage is that you, as a director, will be able to work closely in the actual forming of the music and you will have opportunities of changing it while work is in progress. Of course it is still essential that you choose the very best people and work closely with them so that they thoroughly absorb and understand the film prior to the actual recording session.

One reservation must be offered. This method should not be thought of as a device to circumvent the composer and arranger, placing too great a burden on the performing musicians. One must be certain that the musicians understand what they will be required to do, and that they are both willing and capable of accomplishing it. If you have the right people, such an improvised score can be very effective, and a score over which you can have a great deal of influence, thus assuring its rightness for your film.

THE MUSIC LIBRARY SCORE

There are a number of film music library houses in New York City and other large cities with film centers. Often they provide sound effects libraries as well and have trained personnel to perform the functions of effects, music, and picture editing. Cutting rooms are available, and many producers simply go directly to such houses when their shooting is completed, finishing all phases of cutting on the premises, obtaining whatever help they need from the staff editors. At one end of the scale, a director might rent a cutting room for a period of time at a rate presently of around $100 per week with all necessary editing equipment, purchasing the sound effects and music he might need from the house. He might also choose to have his editing work performed by the house.

For one reel a rough guideline might be: $1,000 for editing picture, $500 for a music library score selected and edited, and $300 for a complete sound effects job. Particularly for the beginning director, the use of such a service can give a really professional finish to his film. We would recommend particularly using fully such a service if the beginner is making a sponsored film, or one that he wishes to distribute theatrically. If the film is being made for personal or academic purposes, the director might wish to cut his own picture and voice, following the techniques we have outlined before. He might then turn the music and effects work over to a professional sound editor. The sound editor's work will continue through the mix, which he attends, and his presence will prove invaluable there also. There are compelling reasons for the beginning director to follow this course. Now, what can we expect of the music available from the film music library?

THE MUSIC LIBRARY

Obviously, using library music will be a good deal less expensive than an original score; it can be done far more quickly; pieces performed by any size orchestra and by any number of different groups can be used; and, the director has the opportunity of making his selections after hearing the music played on a Moviola together with the voice track and picture. These are extremely strong arguments for using library music. But what is the music like?

Even up to 1965, the music available in libraries was limited, both in quantity and in style. One could do quite a good job on travelogues and industrial films, but even here you tended to hear the same music in a number of different films. Producers who make a large number of films complained of the constant use of the same pieces. To do a first-rate job on films in a modern style or a true dry documentary style was almost impossible. The sounds which we all associate with the travelogues of the 1940s and '50s became a cliché of the music library business and many producers were frightened away from the track score. Today, this is simply not true.

Enormous quantities of music of every description are available, scored in a modern way. The old sound of massed strings has been replaced by woodwinds and small combos, even single instruments. Bossa Nova, "Tijuana Brass Sound," "hip" Baroque, music on the twelve-tone system, modern beat, and a great quantity of various forms of jazz are readily available. Excellent documentary music can be found, and, most important, music with a contemporary sound to fit all of the standard film music categories. Today there is a quantity of music closely resembling that written for theatrical films, consisting more of "cues" rather than adhering to the old rigid style of library music. Most important is the fact that more and more clients are requesting modern scores, and their taste has had a considerable influence on the evolution of library music.

Library music is music composed for this specific purpose and recorded in Europe. Sometimes it is written for a particular film, but most often it is written to fit a certain category (Fig. 11.12). What makes possible the use of library music is the fact that film music is basically self-effacing, and that, to the inattentive ear, all film music sounds alike. Once the film-maker begins to pay close attention to music in his work, he will observe enormous differences in both style and content. The film audience does not pay such close attention however, for it is not the purpose of the music to attract attention to itself. Music to a great degree takes on the characteristics of the scene it backs, making it possible to use library music and to use many of the same pieces repeatedly and effectively in different films.

We do not imply that each scene in a film requires the same kind of music. The practice of scoring a film from library music requires the breaking down of the film into scenes, assigning each scene a category, then finding the music to fit that category. Of course, a certain kind of cliché is involved in the use of the category system but creativity enters when we see the infinite variety of categories. To ascertain that a scene requires scenic music is not difficult, but what subtle variation of scenic music? We can have panoramic, oceanic, bleak, a feeling of woodlands, mountains, or babbling brook, various national characteristics, mysterious, and countless other variations on the scenic theme. A piece of music exists to fit each sub-category. Any number of libraries are available from which the music editor can draw, and his great advantage is to be able to draw from all of the large number of catalogues at his disposal.

You can be supplied mediocre track scores and brilliant ones. Seek out a music editor, screen your picture with him, and talk to him about

INDEX

List of all records in this supplement by category

	Page		Page
ACCORDION SOLOS	8	ENGLISH HORN	19
ADVENTURE	8	FANFARES	19
AFRICAN	8	FASHION PARADES	19
AIRPLANE, AIRPORT, Etc.	8	FEAR	20
AMERICAN	8	FIFE AND DRUM	20
ANIMAL or BIRD LIFE	8	FIRE	20
ARABIAN	8	FLUTE	20
AUTOMOBILE	8	FOG	20
BAION	9	FOLK or COUNTRY DANCES	20
BALLET MUSIC	9	FOXTROT	20
BAL MUSETTE	9	FRENCH	21
BASS	9	FUNEREAL	21
BANJO	9	GAELIC	21
BASSOON	9	GAVOTTE	21
BEGUINE	9	GERMAN, AUSTRIAN	21
BELLS	9	GONG	21
BLUES	9	GREECE	21
BONGO	9	GUITAR	21
BOSSA NOVA	9	GYPSY	22
BRASS	9	HARMONICA	23
BRASS BAND	9	HARP	23
BRIGHT and FAST MOVING	10	HARPSICHORD	23
BURLESQUE	11	HAWAIIAN	23
CALYPSO	11	HEBREW	23
CARROUSEL	12	HONKY TONK – SILENT MOVIES	24
CARTOON	12	HORN	24
CELESTE	12	HORNPIPE	24
CELTIC	12	HORSE RACE, TRACK MEET	24
CEREMONIAL	12	HUNGARIAN	24
CHA-CHA	12	INDIA	24
CHARLESTON	12	INDUSTRIAL ACTIVITY	24
CHASE MUSIC	12	IRISH	26
CHILDREN & COMEDY	12	ITALIAN	26
CHRISTMAS	13	JAZZ, SWING, BOP, BOOGIE	26
CIRCUS	13	JIG	30
CLARINET	13	JUNGLE MUSIC	30
CLASSICAL	13	LANDSCAPE	30
COMEDY	13	LATIN-AMERICAN	31
CONCERTINA	14	LIGHT OCCASIONS	31
COUNTRY DANCES	14	LINKS AND BRIDGES	33
CURTAINS	14	LULLABY	35
CYMBALS	14	MAMBO	35
CYMBALOM	14	MANDOLIN	35
DANCE MUSIC, CABARET	14	MARCHES	35
DESOLATION	15	MARIMBA	36
DIXIELAND	15	MENACE	36
DOCUMENTARY	16	MEXICAN	36
DRAMATICS	16	MILITARY INVASION, WAR	36
DRUMS, PERCUSSION	17	MINUET	37
DUTCH	18	MURDER MYSTERY, (DRAMATIC JAZZ)	37
ECCENTRIC	18	MUSIC BOX	38
EERIE	18	MUSICAL SAW	38
EFFECTS	19	MYSTERIOUS, GHOSTLY, EERIE,Etc.	38
ELECTRIC ORGAN	19	MYSTERY COMIC MUSIC	39
ELECTRONIC SOUNDS	19	NEAR EAST	39
ENGLISH	19	NEUTRAL	39
ETHEREAL	19	NEWSREEL	39

I N D E X   Continued on Page 6

Fig. 11–12a Motion picture music library catalogues

it. Listen to some ideas he might have for some of the selections. You will find that working with him in building a score for your film can be an exciting and creative effort, involving you with very close control over the score of your film, and the full opportunity to experiment and polish until it is exactly what you want.

We have stated that a fourth method of doing your film music work is to perform the function of music editor yourself. Obviously, we recommend using a professional music editor to work with the director. We shall, however, give a detailed description of the work of the music editor as a method of showing the director the considerations and techniques which affect the scoring of a picture. Hopefully, he will not have to perform all these tasks himself, but his understanding of them will contribute to working effectively with the music editor. We will deal with the subject of scoring from the viewpoint of the music library score, but many of the principles are also pertinent in the consideration of the original score composed specifically for the film.

Scoring the Picture

Most film composers and music editors express a desire to begin working on the film in the script stage, and there are many ways in which such consultation can help the film. A director with some prior knowledge of the music for the film might move in a different direction, particularly in a subject film. A scene, for example, might be shot to the feeling and

6

I N D E X

List of all records in this supplement by category

	Page		Page
NEW ZEALAND, AUSTRALIAN	39	STREET SCENE	49
NOCTURNE	39	STRING QUARTET	50
NOSTALGIC, POIGNANT, WISTFUL	39	STRINGS	50
NOVELTY	40	SUSPENSE	50
OBOE	40	SWISS	51
OPENINGS AND CLOSINGS	40	SYMPHONIC	51
ORGAN, Church	41	TANGO	51
ORIENTAL, NEAR EAST	41	TENSION	51
OUTER SPACE, SCIENCE FICTION	42	THEATRICAL	51
OVERTURES	42	THEREMIN, MUSICAL SAW	51
PANORAMIC	42	TIJUANA BRASS	51
PASTORAL, SCENIC	42	TIME SEQUENCE	51
PERIOD PIECES	43	TRAGIC	52
PIANO SOLO	44	TRAIN MUSIC	52
PIZZICATO	45	TRAVELOGUE	52
POLKA	45	TRIUMPHANT	52
PSYCHIATRIC	45	TROMBONE	52
RAPID MOVEMENT	45	TROPICAL ATMOSPHERE	52
REGAL, ROYALTY	45	TRUMPET	52
RELIGIOUS	45	TUBA	52
RHUMBA	46	TWIST	52
ROCK AND ROLL	46	TYMPANI	53
ROMANTIC	47	UNDERWATER	53
RUSSIAN	47	VIBRAPHONE	53
SAMBA	47	VIOLIN	53
SAXOPHONE	48	VOCAL	53
SCHOTTISCHE	48	WALTZ	53
SCIENTIFIC EXPERIMENTS	48	WEDDING	54
SCOTTISH	48	WEIRD	54
SEA MOODS, NAUTICAL	48	WESTERN	54
SLAVONIC	49	WEST INDIAN, CARIBBEAN	54
SOCIAL GATHERING, GLAMOROUS	49	WINTER SCENE	54
"SOFT SHOE" STYLE	49	WOODWIND ENSEMBLE	54
SPANISH	49	XYLOPHONE	55
SPORTS EVENTS, NEWSREELS, Etc.	49	ZITHER	55
STINGS	49		
STORM MUSIC	49		

NUMERICAL LISTS

Numerical lists of record catalogs in this supplement.

KEITH PROWSE RECORDS (KPM numbers)---------Starts on Page 56
CONROY RECORDS (BM numbers)--------------Starts on Page 90
VIDEO MOODS RECORDS (EA numbers)----------Starts on Page 102
IMPRESS RECORDS (IA numbers)--------------Starts on Page 104
JW THEME MUSIC (JW numbers)--------------Starts on Page 107
HARMONIC RECORDS (CBL numbers)-----------Starts on Page 112
HARROSE RECORDS (HM numbers)-------------Starts on Page 117
FDH MOOD MUSIC (FDH numbers)-------------Starts on Page 119
RUTHANNE RECORDS (RA numbers)------------Starts on Page 122

Fig. 11-12b Classification of musical moods

82

KPM   Emil Ascher, Inc. RECORDED BACKGROUND & MOOD MUSIC   KPM

Numerical List.   KPM Record Catalog. Publisher:Keith Prowse Music,Ltd. (ASCAP)

12" LONG PLAYING RECORDS

Mood Modern

KPM/LP 1001 A1 RHYTHM N' HEAT   (J.Hawksworth) 4:24 -   B1 NIGHTCAP   (H.Wright)   1:52
            2 THE EYELASH   (J.Hawksworth) 1:58 -   2 BLUE ORGANZA   (H.Wright)   1:54
            3 BEAT TO BEGIN   (J.Hawksworth) 1:03 -   3 NIMBLE NUMBER   (H.Wright)   1:38
            4 THE HIP SHAKER   (J.Hawksworth) 2:38 -   4 DRY MARTINI   (H.Wright)   2:13
            5 LATIN GEAR   (J.Hawksworth) 1:48 -   5 COOL COMFORT   (G.Alderson) 2:58
            6 BEAT STREET   (J.Hawksworth) 1:40 -   6 DIAMOND   (D.Mason)   1:36
            7 BROW BEATER   (J.Hawksworth) 2:50 -   7 TOPAZ   (J.Waring)   1:20
                                                          (8) CHUNKY (J.Hawksworth)   2:30
                                                          9 FRANTIC FRACAS (J.Hawksworth) 0:54

Sounds of S.Dale

KPM/LP 1002 A1 QUITE CONTRARY   (S.Dale) 1:45   B1 MIDSUMMER LOVE (S.Dale) 2:21
            2 THE HELL RAISERS (S.Dale) 2:17   2 LAZY AUTUMN   (S.Dale) 2:28
            3 SLIPSTREAM A & B (S.Dale) 2:08   3 WALK AND TALK (S.Dale) 2:25
            4 LATE NIGHT LONDON (S.Dale) 2:11   4 DREAM FANTASY (S.Dale) 2:13
            5 KINKY BOOTS   (S.Dale) 2:50   5 TAKE A GOOSIE GANDER(S.Dale) 2:15
            6 THE PACEMAKER   (S.Dale) 1:47   (6) SPIDERS WEB   (S.Dale) 1:46
            7 CUBAN RIOT   (S.Dale) 1:46   (7) WALK IN A NIGHTMARE (S.Dale) 3:01

Baroque

KPM/LP 1003 A1 PRELUDE AND FUGUE NO.16 (J.S.Bach/A.Migiani) 3:44
            2 PRELUDE NO.24   (J.S.Bach/A.Migiani) 3:42
            3 PRELUDE AND FUGUE NO.17 (J.S.Bach   2:52
            4 PRELUDE AND FUGUE No.12 (J.S.Bach/A.Migiani) 5:15
            5 PRELUDE AND FUGUE No.12 (J.S.Bach/A.Migiani) 3:48
            B1 PETIT PRELUDE NO.6   (J.S.Bach/A.Migiani) 2:55
            2 PRELUDE AND FUGUE NO.20 (J.S.Bach/A.Migiani) 5:10
            3 PETIT PRELUDE NO.3   (J.S.Bach/A.Migiani) 3:18
            4 PRELUDE AND FUGUE NO.8 (J.S.Bach/A.Migiani) 7:06

Sacred Music

KPM/LP 1005 A1 THE CALM SPIRIT   (W.Merrick Farran)   2:50
            2 FOUR HYMNS   (W.Merrick Farran)
               a. I Sing Of Him   1:24 - c. He That Loves   1:03
               b. In That Heaven I Will Meet Them 1:03 - d. Processional   1:20
            3 INTRODUCTION AND PRELUDE (W.Merrick Farran) 3:50
            4 PIETA   (W.Merrick Farran) 2:11
            5 ALWAYS MUST WE PRAISE HIM(W.Merrick Farran) 2:36
            6 THE REFLECTIVE HOUR   (W.Merrick Farran) 2:33
            7 SOLEMN AIR   (W.Merrick Farran) 3:16
            8 TOCCATA   (W.Merrick Farran) 2:02
            B1 THE CHURCH IN TAUNTON VALE (W.Merrick Farran)3:19
            2 THE DESERTED ABBEY   (W.Merrick Farran)2:32
            3 MOTET AND CHANT   (W.Merrick Farran)3:57
            4 SALVATION ARMY   (W.Merrick Farran) 1:56
            5 HEBREW AIR   (W.Merrick Farran) 3:13
            6 FROM THE PONTUS   (W.Merrick Farran) 1:56
            7 THE CHILDRENS HYMN   (W.Merrick Farran) 1:41
            8 CORPUS CHRISTI   (W.Merrick Farran) 2:12
            9 GOD HAVE MERCY   (W.Merrick Farran) 2:22
            10 GOD HAVE GLORY   (W.Merrick Farran) 1:59

Light Industrial

KPM/LP 1006 A1 PENTUET   (L.Ashmore) 2:31   *SINGLE*
            2 SIMPLE PLEASURES(L.Ashmore) 1:17
            3 TIJUANA TAP DANCE (L.Ashmore) 2:09
            4 PRIVATE FRINGE GOES TO WAR(L.Ashmore) 1:38
            5 RATTLETRAP   (L.Ashmore)
               A. - 0:45 - B. - 0:11 - C. - 0:15
            6 PATTERN OF PISTONS (L.Ashmore)2:09
            7 PLATFORM ONE (L.Ashmore)   1:02
            8 MILITARY PICKLE (L. Ashmore)
            9 ENDLESS BELTS (L.Ashmore)A. - 0:54 - B. - 0:40 - C. - 0:10
                                                           1:12

Fig. 11-12c Sample page from Emil
Ascher catalogue

tempo of a particular piece of music—the music could actually be played
on a quarter-inch tape recorder on the shooting site—and certainly the
editing can be particularly influenced by the music. Some initial work,
such as historical research and the development of themes for the characters in the case of story films can be accomplished by the composer
while the film is being shot and edited. Nevertheless, it is the almost
universal practice to bring in the music man at the rough-cut stage.

A number of considerations face the composer (or music editor) and
the director. Probably first is the question of basic style, which is a matter of the feel of the music: is it to be modern, romantic, astringent. With

a composer involved, the question of proper style is usually determined by the director when he makes his initial choice of composer. Certainly many writers are adaptable, and Hollywood composers do an incredible variety of films.° But generally today, and particularly with the less-experienced film composer, the man determines the music. To define style verbally is difficult. Essentially, the music must "feel right" with the picture, and not be lush when the film visuals are sparse and bleak. It must not violate the sense of the film's locale or time period. The music may stem from a different source and consist of integral sounds, e.g., Simon and Garfunkel's music for *The Graduate,* and yet capture the

Fig. 11–12d Sample page from KPM catalogue

CATALOGUE LAYOUT

1. CLASSIFIED SECTION. Recordings are listed numerically under their various Mood Classifications as set out below. Details are given of KPM Record Number, Title Composer and Timing together with a brief description of the music and a cross reference to other Mood Classifications to facilitate fast and accurate selection. Record numbers with three digits refer to 78 RPM issues, and those with four digits to the '1000 series' 33 LP issues.

2. KPM '1000 SERIES' LONG PLAYING RECORDS. The individual titles on the LP's will be found in the classified and alphabetical sections. However, this section of LP's listed numerically is included as each LP contains music of a generically similar type. Reference to the titles of the LP's and the general descriptions in this section may often pin-point one LP containing a choice of material of the type required.

3. ALPHABETICAL SECTION. Titles are listed in alphabetical sections together with KPM Record Number, Composer and Timing.

MOOD CLASSIFICATIONS

A	Activity — movement
B	Children — animals — animation
C	Comedy — satire — eccentric
D 1	Dramatic action, chase, flight
D 2	Static — suspense — mystery — eerie
D 3	Drama — emotion — light
E	Elemental atmosphere (Earth, Fire, etc. — Forces of Nature — Space music)
F	Fanfare
G	Grandiose — majestic — imposing
H	Happy — gay
I	Solo or featured instruments — duets etc. — percussion
J	Jazz — dance music — dance
K	Fashion
L	Light mood
M	March — galop
N	National
O	Opening — curtain — bridge — sting
P	Period
R	Romantic
S	Sad — solemn — bitter — pity — regret — dejection
T	Industry — laboratory — mechanical motion
V	Scenic — pastoral — sea
W	Waltz
X	Religious
Z	Electronic — musique concrète

*Miklos Rozsa, for example, did the music for *Jungle Book* and *The Thief of Bagdad; Spellbound* and *The Lost Weekend; Brute Force* and *The Naked City; Quo Vadis, Ivanhoe, Julius Caesar, Young Bess, Ben Hur, King of Kings,* and *El Cid!*

Number	Title	Composer	Time	Remarks	Classification
				A : ACTIVITY — MOVEMENT	
KPM.209A	Surface Caim	Derrick Mason	1.38	Neutral abstract back-ground	BLT
	Ultimatum	Derrick Mason	0.28	Neutral abstract	DLT
KPM.210B	Chain Reaction	Syd. Dale	1.35	Tense – builds in tempo to climax	D
KPM.212A	Factory Site	Edward Purkiss	2.00	Muscular mechanical descriptive	DT
	Machines in Motion	Barry Tattenhall	1.03	Purposeful mechanical movement to big end	GT
KPM.212B	Assembly Line	Edward Purkiss	1.39	Grotesque mechanical back-ground	CDT
KPM.212B	Mechanisation	Raymond Jones	1.12	Scenes of industry and manufacture	LT
KPM.213A	Boffin House	Edward Purkiss	1.53	Fragmentary serious/comic descriptive	CDT
	Wheels and Spindels	Raymond Jones	1.15	Revolving machinery	BT
KPM.213B	Power Station	George Behar	1.50	Heavy industrious and military	DGMPTV
KPM.214A	Steel Shop	George Behar	1.55	Broad muscular, hurried activity	DGMPTV
	French Meadows	Raymond Jones	1.20	Charming provincial pastoral – French undertones	BHLNVX
KPM.215A	Village Fete	King Palmer	1.10	Bright – gay	BCHLP
	Village School	King Plamer	1.00	Pleasant – light – children	BHLV
	Village Inn	King Palmer	1.00	Jovial	BCHLP
KPM.216B	Strictly for Pleasure	Ronnie Aldrich	1.55	Lively – delicate	BHL
KPM.217B	Hungarian Suite	George Behar			
	Storm and Stress		1.20	Distress at sea	DENTV
KPM.218B	Hungarian Suite	George Behar			
	Budapest Street Scenes		2.30	Hurried activity – festive scenes and traditional gypsy violins	HJLNT
KPM.219B	Hungarian Suite	George Behar			
	Hungarian Festival		1.47	Frenzied gypsy dance	DHJN
KPM.220A	Trumpets and Tequila	Syd. Dale	2.05	Tijuana brass style – bright	BCHJNL
KPM.220B	Mexican Highway	Syd. Dale	2.39	Tijuana brass style – bright	CJLN
KPM.225B	Christmas Bells	Johnny Hawksworth	0.36	Novelty paraphrase of 'Jingle Bells'	BCHLX
KPM.226A	Power Drive	Johnny Pearson			
	A.		0.15	Highly dramatic documentary opening morse figures	DFGT
	B.		1.00	Big pounding action – documentary	DGT
	Power Drive - Complete	Johnny Pearson	2.00	Composite documentary theme	DFGT
KPM.226B	Power Drive	Johnny Pearson			
	C.		0.30	Long version of 'A'	DFGT
	D.		0.30	Alternate version	DFGT
	Searching 1b	Johnny Pearson	0.46	Neutral descriptive with movements	BLOT
KPM.227A	Power Pack 1	Syd. Dale	1.00	Strident dramatic – documentary action	DJT
	Power Pack 2		1.00	As No.1 with alto sax improvisation	DIJLT
	Power Pack 3		1.00	Strident montage	DJOT
KPM.227B	Rat Trap	Syd. Dale	1.37	Tense dramatic back-ground	DJ
KPM.228A	Impending Danger	Syd. Dale	2.10	Tense dramatic back-ground military drum figure	DM
KPM.229A	Square Bash	Syd. Dale	2.15	Novelty march	BCHMT
	Fun Show	Syd. Dale	0.30	Comedy theme	BCH
KPM.229B	Mr. Pickwick	Syd. Dale	1.52	Jovial tuba feature	BCHILP
	Trombones Take A Slide	Syd. Dale	1.40	Lighthearted Trombone feature	BCHIL
KPM.230A	Top of the Morning	Syd. Dale	1.55	Cheerful – rhythmic	BCHIJL
KPM.230B	Disc A Go Go	Syd. Dale	2.35	Light rhythmic – orchestral	BHJKLR
KPM.231A	Stage Struck	Jack Parnell	2.15	Variety show opener	CHJ
	Stage Struck Link	Jack Parnell	0.08	Variety show link	CHJO
KPM.231B	Aces to Open	Syd. Dale	1.35	Variety show opener	CHJ
	Fan Fair	Bill Martin/Phil Coulter	1.25	Modern rhythmic fanfare	BFHJL
KPM.232	Spy By Night	David Lindup	2.45	Medium tempo dramatic theme – uptempo middle section	DEG

Fig. 11–12e Classification of musical moods in KPM catalogue

feeling of the film as perfectly as a score specifically composed for it.

In the case of the library score, a vast choice of possible styles is available. Theoretically, any professional music editor can do work in any style, but here again we find areas of particular competence and enthusiasm. The wise director will do some sizing-up of his man here also. Of course, since the music to be used can actually be played for auditioning, the right style can be chosen easily by the director himself.

The trick with library music—put together from many sources perhaps, often performed and recorded by a number of different orchestras, and composed by many different composers—is to form an integral score. Sometimes we use music from only one composer to achieve this, but usually this integration is a matter of setting the style with the first important choices and then maintaining it throughout, discarding any piece that breaks the continuity of style.

FUNCTIONS OF FILM MUSIC

ESTABLISHING FILMIC REALITY The importance of this function dictates that music be used whenever possible in the narrated subject film. We will remember, however, that we need not fill every second of the film, for the presence of sound effects and/or voice also supplies this sense of reality. In practice, most nontheatrical subject films are one hundred percent music. Once you have begun using music in a film, stopping its use is quite noticeable. You must, therefore, have a reason for not using music and you must apply this reasoning consistently throughout the film, thus setting up the music conventions of that particular film. The audience will accept these conventions if you are consistent, and if they are meaningful. We will later deal separately with the all-important practical question of determining where the music is to be present.

Cut	TITLE	COMPOSER	Timing	Children/Animals	Christmas/Religious	Comedy/Humorous	Dance/Jazz	Documentary/Ceremonial	Dramatic/Tragic	Fanfare	Fashion	Industrial/Mechanical	Lt. & Modern Mov't	Links/Bridges/Curtains	Lullaby	Marches/Sports	Mystery/Suspense	National/Travel	Neutral	Nostalgic	Novelty	Oriental	Pastorale/Scenic	Period Pieces	Romantic	Sea	Solo	Space	Title (Open, Close)	Your Remarks
SF 1010A																														
1	INDUSTRIAL REVOLUTION	Mario Nascimbene																												
	(a) Comptometer		0:47						•			•		•			•				•								•	
	(b) Building Robots		0:32						•			•		•			•				•								•	
	(c) Electro-Dynamics		1:00						•			•		•			•				•								•	
	(d) Compression		0:32	•					•			•		•			•				•									
2	ORIENTAL SUITE	Mario Nascimbene																												
	(a) Far East Pastorale		2:00						•									•	•	•		•	•			•			•	
	(b) Tilling the Soil		0:57	•								•						•	•			•	•			•				
	(c) South Wind from Asia		0:56														•	•			•	•	•			•			•	
3	MEDITERRANEAN PORTRAIT	Mario Nascimbene																												
	(a) Mandolinata		1:11	•	•						•		•					•		•			•		•	•			•	
	(b) Neapolitan Serenade		0:58															•		•	•		•		•	•			•	
	(c) Courtship on Capri		2:27						•								•	•		•			•		•					
4	WALTZETTE	Mario Nascimbene	2:41				•				•							•		•	•		•		•				•	
5	PICTURESQUE COUNTRYSIDE	Mario Nascimbene																												
	(a) Donkey Trot		0:30	•			•						•	•					•	•			•						•	
	(b) Rustic Festival		1:15						•								•	•		•			•							
6	THE SHEPHERDESS AND HER FLOCK	Mario Nascimbene	1:16																•	•	•		•							
7	SIESTA IN SARDINIA	Mario Nascimbene	1:10														•	•	•				•		•	•			•	
8	FLORENTINE SUNSET	Mario Nascimbene	1:42												•				•	•			•		•	•			•	
SF 1010B																														
1	PAGAN RITES	Mario Nascimbene																												
	(a) Sacrifice to the Sun God		0:47		•			•	•								•											•	•	
	(b) The Priests' Chant		1:07		•			•	•								•					•						•	•	
2	TOT'S MARCH	Mario Nascimbene	0:45	•	•								•			•			•	•	•									
3	GOIN' TO CHICAGO STOMP	Mario Nascimbene	0:47				•						•							•	•									
4	SWINGIN' AT THE ASTOR	Mario Nascimbene	0:44				•						•							•	•									
5	ROCK DREAM	Mario Nascimbene	2:10				•						•								•									
6	THE BOB CAT'S BOOGIE	Mario Nascimbene	2:29				•						•							•	•									
7	SADNESS IN 4/4 TIME	Mario Nascimbene	1:36				•		•				•						•	•					•					
8	UNDER THE COCONUT TREE, CHA CHA	Mario Nascimbene	2:16				•						•					•		•	•					•			•	
9	BRIEF DISCUSSIONS	Mario Nascimbene																												
	(a) Harpsichord and Bass		0:37										•	•						•			•							
	(b) Clarinet, Harpsichord and Bass		0:30										•	•						•			•							
	(c) Tom Tom and Clarinet		0:43										•	•						•			•							

Fig. 11–12f Sample page from Sam Fox Film Rights, Inc. catalogue

PROVIDING A SENSE OF LOCALE   This consideration is in some ways related to the choice of musical style and certainly to the use of nationalistic or regional music. For travel films the music library can provide a wide range of authentic music for any country; also, the film's director may bring back music tapes from his location filming. Used together with sound effects, such music can do a great deal in making the locale of a foreign land come alive. The same is true for films dealing with a region of the United States—the Ozarks, the Southwest, the New England coast—where simple guitar or harmonica pieces will evoke the desired feeling perfectly. Do not ignore the way music can set the locale of a cocktail lounge, a street parade, a campfire, an amusement park, a tenement alley. Music for establishing locale may in many cases be actual music, and, for at least part of the time, synchronous. Many times, however, it can create the illusion of being actual without the source actually being seen. (Remember the barroom scene of *High Noon* with the invisible honky-tonk piano playing in the background.) Frequently the footage brought into the cutting room does not supply the picture of the supposed source, but the skillful use of appropriate music, particularly mixed with live effects, will supply an uncanny sense of reality.

Something to keep in mind in scoring is the potential use of actual music. Joseph von Sternberg's famous film *The Blue Angel,* for example, derived its entire score, with the exception of the main title music and the final music cue, from actual music.

ESTABLISHING A TIME PERIOD AND ATMOSPHERE   In the subject film, this function usually becomes a consideration in an historical section, probably dealing with the way things used to be done by this industry or in this country. If we are using a light jazz score to illustrate the up-to-date, electronically-run factory, it would be wrong to continue this same music over scenes of the 1890s factory that we are showing for contrast. Due in part to their exposure to the conventions of film background music, our audience can be assumed to have some familiarity with music associated with various historical periods and to be able to identify it. The same observation made concerning music that acquires its specific character from the scene against which it is played holds true here. Essentially the music need not be historically accurate so long as it conveys a sense of the times. In practice, a feeling of past times often comes from a quaintness, a lack of modern sophistication, a simplicity in the music.

In theatrical films with a dramatic story set in a specific time, the sense of period must be right. Yet one can be slavishly restrictive in adhering to an academically accurate form of music. Films set in Roman times are supplied by our film composers with a music that sounds grand and barbaric; we accept its essential rightness, even when it is portrayed as actual music within the film. Yet this music is frequently played on the most modern of instruments, ones totally unknown to the Romans. The fact is that we have no idea of what "Roman" music sounded like, since the system of music notation had not yet been developed. Until the day arrives when some whistling Roman steps from a time machine, his head brimming with the latest hits of the day, we are consigned to the Budapest Conservatory's version of "Roman music." In such films, the choice of music becomes a pragmatic question of whether or not it works.

The music for Shakespearean films creates a particular problem. We are faced with a choice of using music of the period of the play—which might be Roman, Greek, or thirteenth-century England—using music of the Elizabethan period when the play was written and first performed, or of using contemporary music. If you are familiar with William Walton's scores for Olivier's Shakespearean films—*Henry V. Hamlet, Richard III*—you will note that Walton was primarily concerned in writing music in his own idiom which would not shatter our belief in the sense of period. The grandeur and the vitality of the time is what the music portrays; it does not attempt to duplicate the music that might have been playing in the streets. Polonius' advice holds true: "To thine own self be true and thou canst not then be false to any man." Manvell and Huntley quote an interesting observation by Miklos Rozsa, who composed, as we have mentioned, a number of historical scores.

> When utmost stylistic care is taken in the production of a period piece, and thorough research is made for historical facts . . . I think that the musical score should not destroy this unity by introducing stylistically a completely foreign element. It has to be stylized, as the very nature of dramatic music excludes the verbatim usage of music of periods which were utterly undramatic; but with the melodic, rhythmic and harmonic elements of the past, the modern composer can create a dramatic language of his own, which fits the style of the screen drama.[1]

Rozsa goes on further to remind us that Mendelssohn set the example for this by composing in his own individual style the incidental music for *A Midsummer Night's Dream*, now accepted by all, but bearing little relationship to the actual time of the drama or of its writing.

EMOTIONAL UNDERSCORING *It can provide reinforcement to the emotional content of the scene, often revealing emotion in a subtlety and complexity that cannot be portrayed by the characters. It can lead the emotions of the audience, contributing to the psychological advancement of the action; it can anticipate a change in emotional content of the scene.* We are all familiar with these aspects of film music, but let us spend some time in examining the specifics. The nature of good stage and screen acting dictates that the performer not "demonstrate" emotion. Even when the actor is experiencing a genuine emotion, the revelation of this emotion might not be consistent with the character in that situation (a humiliated man would strive to put up a front, a frightened man might "whistle in the dark").

Perhaps we might have a scene in which a happy and confident man is soon to have his mood shattered. Take the example of two lovers clasped in each other's arms, lost to any sense of the world outside, while the woman's husband is nearing the house in which they are hidden. No possible technique can be used that will allow the actors themselves to demonstrate their anticipation of the climactic moment when the characters will confront each other. But cinematically we can cut once to the approaching husband, begin music on a rising ominous note, and then return to the lovers, with the camera dwelling occasionally on the door through which we expect the husband to enter, the music reminding us of the impending danger.

In Hitchcock's *The Birds*, the heroine has left a crowded school room and is sitting on a bench outside the school; we continue to hear the children singing inside. Suddenly a large black bird alights on the jungle gym behind the girl, unseen by her. Hitchcock cuts away and then cuts back to the gym several times, the number of birds leaping each time. Our concern grows with each increase, for we are reminded throughout the scene of the presence of the unseen children through the sound of their voices. We combine the visual image of the birds with the audial image of the children, anticipating the horrifying moment when the children will leave the school to be attacked by the birds. The scene reaches its climax when Hitchcock first follows the flight of a single bird over to a telephone wire, where a huge flock is suddenly revealed, then pans slowly back to the jungle gym, now suddenly, shockingly black with birds. At last, the heroine turns, sees them and rushes into the school to warn the children.

In conveying the mood of the film as a whole, the very first notes of the musical score for a comedy set the entire tone and allows us to sit back in joyful anticipation of the pleasure to come. And, so does the opening music to a mystery or an heroic drama set the stage emotionally for us.

AS A COUNTERPOINT TO THE SCENE *It can, when appropriate, supply a counterpoint to the emotions and to the action of the scene; it can provide emotional relief.* This is a fascinating subject, and one we have covered in some detail in the chapter on sound aesthetics. At this time let us remind you that one should always consider the possibility of running the music against the grain of the film, creating an interweaving and counterpointing juxtaposition of sound and visual images. Yet the effectiveness of this must be felt, not intellectualized; beware the rationalized "explanation" of any such use of music. Any practice can be somehow justified, no matter how foolish. If the music does not feel right, then it does not work.

GIVING FORM TO THE MONTAGE *It can lend to the montage its own musical form, providing a continuity and flow between the disparate shots, helping the cuts to "work."* You will be amazed the first time you put music behind a montage scene and observe the natural flow the music has lent the separate shots and the form, inevitability, and cohesiveness the scene has gained. A word of caution: Choose the right style, mood and tempo for a scene without slavish adherence to any rhythmic pattern in the scene. You want the general filmic rhythm and tempo, not the specific ones of a particular machine or athletic act. The music may prove to have an uncanny affinity for the scene, as our eyes and ears combine to relate the visual and sound images to each other. I have cut to music countless scenes of action sports, moving machinery, dancing, general activity, chases, and fights and continually observe how the music fits the scene with uncanny, unplanned synchronization to the cuts and individual actions. With perhaps the exception of marching and similar activities in which we recognize a measured, precise beat, we do not really know where to expect the individual beat to fall. It can be on the upstroke, the downstroke, in the middle, or fractionally before the end of the visual stroke. So the basic act of juxtaposing similarly tempoed rhythms in sound and visuals will make the two seem synchronous.

SETTING THE TEMPO *It can provide the tempo of the scene, the build, the climax, the relief.* The choice of music for this purpose is again a matter of feel, but we should caution that the varying tempo of a piece of music is a vitally important consideration in choosing it for a particular scene. When the music matches the picture in its changes and variations, it has a decided emotional effect on the viewer. We can lead our audience to the precise emotional moments of build, climax, and relief; lift their hearts; chill them; drop them exhausted and stunned. The music must acknowledge a definite sense of the tempo of the cutting, as well as the tempo of the action within the scene.

AS A BRIDGE *It can supply the transitions between scenes and between moods.* The term "bridge" is used in referring to music which supplies a transition between scenes. In the conventional film, the cue starts under the last word of dialogue and continues up to the next spoken word, bridging what may be a fade-out/fade-in which would "die" without the presence of music. When we are to change from a scene of one specific mood to another scene of another mood, music will supply the transition. In working with stock library music, we might seek a piece with this mood change inherent in its form, or we might make a skillful change at the scene transition from one piece to another, using methods we are to consider in this chapter. In contemporary films, the sound optical often replaces the conventional method of transition.

THE LEITMOTIV *Through the use of the leitmotiv it can follow the development of character throughout the film and communicate this.* The selection of a specific theme for a character is often possible even in using library music. We can then use a number of variations on this theme throughout the film. Naturally this theme can apply to people or even to the subject of the film, perhaps a country. I once used a suite called "Colossus," part of a film music library, throughout a feature film on the history of Africa. The main title section of the suite provided us with our theme, supplying the feeling of expanse and grandeur that we desired. Throughout the film other variations of this theme were used—panoramic, light scenic, humorous, dramatic—and finally a specifically written end title piece. Of course a good deal of other music was utilized in the film, including authentic African native music, but the recurrent use of the portions of this suite with its recognizable theme gave a coherence to the entire library score.

SOOTHING THE AUDIENCE *It can provide the restless spectator with contentment, enhance his mood and make him receptive to the film.* This function might appear to be simply a side result of the film score, but a specific point should be made here. Apart from all other functions of film music, something in its mere presence makes the audience accept the film more fully. The logical conclusion to this observation is that sometimes, particularly in the nontheatrical subject film, we might do well to consider the "pleasantness" of the music as an important criterion. We can become so deeply involved in matching the period, mood, tempo, and locale of sound to the picture that we ignore the essential of choosing music which lifts the spirits of the audience and conditions them to receptivity.

The late Ernie Kovacs used a delightful joke on his television shows. Three actors in gorilla suits appeared performing on musical instruments, billed as "The Nairobi Trio." The joke was inanely simple, consisting of one gorilla rapping his drum sticks on the head of the other at appropriate points in the music, the humor rising from the controlled incongruity of the scene. It has always been my contention that the enjoyment of this skit came in large part from the accompanying music, a delightful little tune called "Solfeggio." Just to sit and listen to the music was always a pleasure, and this in turn made the entire skit a pleasure. Interestingly, the same tune is used behind the excellent Colt 45 Malt Liquor commercials—"amidst the commonplace occurrences of life" —which are done in pantomime. The music performs the same function in making them quite delightful to watch and to listen to.

In "dry" instructional films which have an almost continual narration, one might be tempted to avoid using music, but that would be ignoring the opportunity of providing a climate that would make the text more palatable. Such music should be used merely as a background "presence," as unobtrusive as possible, and at a very low volume.° Still, its mere presence is immensely important. There is a school of thought that believes that unless the words are presented starkly, totally without "interference" from any other sound, they will not be absorbed; the opposite is true. Of course the words will invariably dominate the music when they perform this commentative function as part of the subject film, but the audience's receptivity to them is very much affected by the accompanying music. (This observation would seem to be a contradiction of our oft-expressed feeling that the visuals must dominate over the word. The fact is, in most sponsored films it *is* the words that dominate. Hopefully, they will not cover the film throughout but will be designed to work *with* the visual images; still, we must acknowledge the fact that when the narration is communicating facts, it must be heard and, hopefully, remembered. This is the nature of such films in which the visual images are often mere illustrations to a lecture. If such is the purpose of the "film," then it is the director's job to further that purpose, and music can do that if it contributes to the communication of the ideas expressed in the film by increasing spectator receptivity.

*To carry any film sound *too low*, at a point where it is naggingly audible but frustratingly unidentifiable, is disturbing to the spectator. Such sound is far more distracting than sound that is a bit too loud. The low sound hooks the spectator's attention the way a speech defect in a speaker does, making it impossible to concentrate on the important material.

There is increasing evidence that music which simply enhances the mood is being used, with varying degrees of success, in the scores for theatrical feature films. Scores such as Neal Hefti's for *The Odd Couple* and *How to Murder Your Wife*, Burt Bachrach's for *Casino Royale* and *Butch Cassidy*, and Henry Mancini's for *Breakfast at Tiffany's* and *Operation Petticoat* are not the traditional duplicative and conforming score. Much like the music for *The Graduate*, mentioned earlier, the music rolls along on its own course, almost as if written for another context. This is not a contrived counterpoint; the impression is almost that the music has a mind of its own and is there merely for our enjoyment. These scores work with varying degrees of success, dependent upon whether their general mood is right for the picture. Mancini's music seems most effective when it happens to match the setting, as in scenes in Mother's Bar in the "Peter Gunn" TV series in which it appears as actual music. But his music can be annoyingly out of key at other times. A case in point occurs in *The Great Race* in which the rapid pace of the climactic "silent movie" automobile chase is shatteringly interrupted to allow for the singing of the lovely, but totally inappropriate, song "Sweetheart Tree." *
We can learn from the makers of television commercials the great value of background music which makes our viewing a little more pleasant.

RELATIONSHIP TO EFFECTS

We have mentioned the need to relate the music and sound effects to each other as well as to the picture. Often both aspects of sound editing can be performed by the same editor. If not, it is essential that the two men who perform these functions work closely. There is an interesting film worth studying based on the Zuyder Zee land reclamation project in The Netherlands, *New Earth*, by Joris Ivens, with music composed by Hanns Eisler. The basic convention of the score is to accompany machinery by effects, and men, by music. It is a classic example of the integrated "sound" score, utilizing music or effects (or both) when appropriate to the picture.

USING THE ESTABLISHED PIECE OF MUSIC

Since the days of silent film music, we have been bombarded with warnings against the use of familiar "established" music:

> The disadvantages of using established music in dramatic films are several. The chief disadvantage is that it has an artistic vitality independent of the film. Its familiarity to the public has already made it a breeding ground for emotional responses which may or may not help the particular atmosphere or situation in the film.[2]

Yet throughout the history of film music we have a number of examples of such usage. Recently, Kubrick's *2001: A Space Odyssey* and Fellini's *8½* have used established pieces in ironic counterpoint to the visual images of the film, deliberately capitalizing on precisely that "breeding ground for emotional responses" for effect. An obvious note of caution: Since the public brings into the theater an infinite variety of preconceptions to this music we have little actual control over the spectator's re-

*Obviously, Mancini's purpose was to supply the film with a "hit song," an assignment at which he and Burt Bachrach have been stunningly and repeatedly successful. It is director Blake Edwards who must bear the responsibility for the particular placement of this song. However, the score of the recent Peter Gunn feature is Mancini's responsibility.

sponse and a difficulty in predicting any consistency of this response. We gave the example earlier of Kubrick using the "Beautiful Blue Danube" over the soaring accomplishment of the space ship, supposedly to counter the example of man's impressive achievement in technology with an implication that his advancement in other areas has been not nearly as impressive. But this can only work if the spectator thinks "The Blue Danube" is banal and probably only if he is willing to expend the effort on the intellectualization that must take place. If "The Beautiful Blue Danube" was played at your wedding and you danced gloriously until 3 A.M. with your spirits lifted on joyous wings of song, your response to this music would be somewhat different.

An outstanding example of the use of established music occurs in the film *Elvira Madigan* which makes repeated use of a Mozart piano concerto, much as *Brief Encounter* utilized the Rachmaninoff Second Piano Concerto as a recurring theme. Although there was a good deal of critical comment on the effectiveness of this music in both films, I think the jury is still out. As Huntley and Manvell correctly note, a principle disadvantage of using such music is the difficulty of finding a portion to correctly fit the picture's individual scenes—and, we might add, in getting a proper beginning and ending to it at the right time and place.*

We might consider as a separate category the use of established music in a film which is cut—or animated, as in the case of the Hubleys' charming Tijuana Brass cartoon—to a specific piece whose form then determines the form of the film. This principle is behind Disney's *Fantasia*. The obvious problem is that people may find it difficult to accept your particular interpretation of the music since, as we have pointed out, they usually have their own preconceptions. If they are willing to accept your interpretation, which may be a valid and entertaining one, then this can be an effective way of making a particular kind of film. However we must assume that the director has found a way to master the difficult problem of subordinating the musical images to those of the film. If the images merely duplicate various aspects of the music, the result may be charming, but it will not be a true film.

Relationship between Music and Voice

Frank Lewin, in his excellent paper, "The Sound Track in Non-theatrical Motion Pictures," published in the *SMPTE Journal* and available from them in reprint form, states the case very well.

When [the music] has to do its work in conjunction with a voice track other considerations must be observed. The meaning of the narration then becomes paramount, sometimes to the exclusion of the picture. Often the voice will utilize the image as illustrations to an abstract idea, or the picture acts as no more than a springboard for the script. If, for example, the screen shows scenes of animated industrial activity while the narrator talks in broad terms of the history of the company, it would be irritating to hear music which only suggests the bustling men and machines. . . . Music should not say one thing while the voice tries to say another.[3]

*One interesting note on that score: As a sound editor I was appalled at the clumsy way in which the selections from the Mozart concerto used in *Elvira Madigan* trailed out with no sense of resolve to the music, in a way that seemed to me terribly awkward and attention-getting. Yet quite obviously the vast majority of the audience was unaffected by this. Evidently the fact that the attention of most members of the film audience is not on the specific form of the music makes much of the film-maker's usual consideration to technical detail superfluous.

Now this cinematic blasphemy neatly contradicts the basic point we have been pounding at throughout the sound chapters—the subordination of the sound to the visual. Can we justify this observation at this point? Whether or not the sponsored film with its specific and detailed message is a "true" film, aesthetically speaking, is not, however, really the issue at this time. The film-maker will many times find himself with an entire film containing a number of vitally important messages to communicate in words. After all, most sponsored films are made for this reason and to think that the sponsor will stand for any form of distraction from his beloved words is, to put it mildly, a bit naïve. In such a film—and they may well form the majority of films you make in your life—you must give constant and proper consideration to the narration as well as to the visual images in your selection and editing of music for the film.

There are a number of ways in which the sound technician can affect the music-voice balance. To begin with, we never run music behind lip-sync sequences in the subject film. The music either ends just before the speech begins, punctuating it nicely; or, as an alternative, trails out unnoticeably under the first word or two. The music will then enter quickly at the end of the particular speech to pick up the film and move it forward, acting as a transitional aid at this point. If there are scenes of very short length between lip-sync sequences, one is likely to get a choppy effect if the music is brought in each time and then taken out as the next speech begins. A sound effect, perhaps just a background presence that fits the bridging scene, will perform the same function as music in keeping the track alive until the voice picks up again.

We can also affect the voice-music relationship by intelligent juxtaposing of the two. If possible, one should avoid any simultaneous change of the music and voice, as this can distract the viewer. Rarely do we want our narration to hit exactly on the cut; usually it is delayed for several frames, or even a few seconds. This can give our music, if it does begin on the cut, a chance to establish itself, and the music can then be brought down unobtrusively for the period of voice dominance. This is almost the inviolable rule in the case of a marked change of scene.

Many times in a subject film the "catalogue sequence"—a succession of film images—is presented with rather sparse identifying narration which fills little of the elapsed time. Music can do an effective job of filling the gap between portions of narration at such a point, also lending the disparate images form and vitality. One should be wary of splitting thoughts unintelligibly where a continuous sentence is broken up and spaced against a matching picture. The audience will accept a considerable delay in comparison with normal speech since the narrator is obviously cuing his speech to the picture, but one must still maintain some sense of continuity. This continuity is further supplied by the accompanying music and sound effects, even with the most sparse and sporadic narration. The music supplies the cement of sentences in the narration much as conjunctives do in everyday speech.

Cuing the Picture

If the film is not to contain one hundred percent music—more typical of story than subject films—your basic task, and the acknowledged first consideration of every film composer and music editor is to determine which sections need music and which do not. One consideration can guide you at this time: Does the scene hold up without music? If the emotion is unclear or the scene does not seem to hold our attention, music should be tried. Many times one simply feels a need for music—or perhaps more accurately, one feels the lack of it—and even senses the precise place it should start. In most dramatic scenes with lip-sync dialogue, music will be instinctively avoided unless a specific need is felt. In scenes of a narrator directly facing the camera and speaking, music will almost never be used. Do not make the error of trying to bury the fumbling amateur reading under music in such a case; it will only hurt. If the film is a subject film, we may very well run music throughout. If not, or if we are to alternate it with effects in a "sound score," all this must be consistently planned throughout.

Our next task is to break the film down into scenes labeled as to subject, corresponding to the categories of music: scenic, chase, dramatic, romantic, industrial, etc. Remember, these are only convenient categories to help us locate our music from the library catalogues or to help us to compose music to fit the particular scenes. The real measure of their creative use is in the subtle variations within categories to precisely fit the setting and mood of the particular scene. You might wish to actually make an outline of the film, listing the scenes in order. After a certain amount of practice, you will be able to catalogue the film automatically, another aspect of film-making in which a well-developed memory is useful.

The third consideration is where to change the type of music being used. The mechanics of this subject will be covered in the next section, but some thought can be given to it here. Obviously, your basic change comes at the point where the visual scene changes character, but there are technical considerations which can affect this. Sometimes a change of music should be made unobtrusively under narration whose beginning may follow the picture change by several seconds. Sometimes the music change should be quite dramatic, as in a move to a different locale; sometimes it should be unnoticeable and just "happen" without our being aware of the change until the character of the new music has absorbed us. Sometimes the music should "bang-in" immediately after a spoken line, sometimes it should enter only after a considerable delay, and sometimes the music may actually change unobtrusively under the last fragments of sound of the last spoken word. Since we might wish to bury the change in the music under narration, we must consider if this is feasible. Often there is a delay before the narration comes in following a picture change, so we must consider whether we can afford to wait for this or if it is essential that the music change character directly on the cut. For example, if we are going from Holland to Spain in a travelogue and the music is to have a national character, we probably must cut the music to picture change.

We have now determined where we want music, where each musical piece will change into another, and what type of music is required for each section. With a sense of the overall style and purpose of the film we can proceed. The following is a method evolved through the scoring of a number of films; it is an individual method and as such must be adapted to fit the particular abilities of the practitioner.

Scoring the Film on the Moviola from a Stock Library

We use the term "scoring" to refer to the choosing of the music and the matching of it to the picture. "Cutting" or "editing" refers to the actual work of making the individual pieces the required length and eliminating any unwanted portion of the take. "Laying-in" refers to the actual practice of building the music tracks by alternating the takes of music on magnetic film with leader. We shall work on the making of a cue sheet as we proceed. The illustration (Fig. 11.13) shows the cue sheet in three stages of our work. The first will be that which results when we have finished scoring on the Moviola; the second is the end result of our cutting the music; while the third is the sheet we will bring with us to the mix, following the laying in.

Fig. 11–13 Three stages of music cue sheet

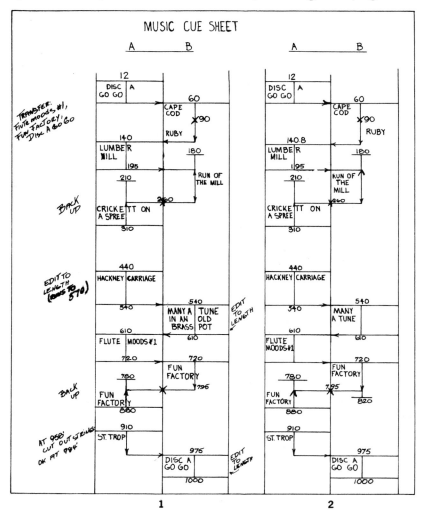

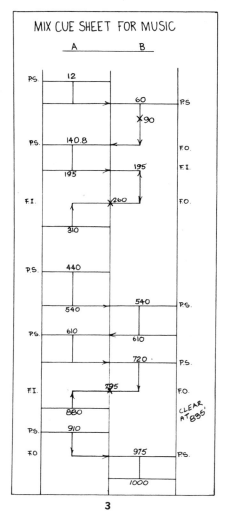

The vitally important first step in scoring is for the sound editor to run the film as many times as possible until he has absorbed it thoroughly. The first run-through might well be in the company of the director, who will explain his aims for the film in general, the audience he expects to reach, the intent of certain specific scenes which might not be clear at this stage but which the music will clarify, and his own ideas of what he expects from the music. The editor will also sound him out on his general taste in music and what he expects his audience's taste to be. All this will help to narrow down the possibilities for music and guide the editor in his search. Huntley and Manvell quote screen composer Roman Vlad's statement: "The real creator of a film, in my opinion, is the director; I always try to compose the music which he would were he a composer."[4] This applies equally well to the responsibility of the sound editor.

When the editor is confident that he has absorbed the film (this word is used deliberately rather than "understood," for much of the technique of scoring a film should be a matter of emotion), he should spend as much as a day by himself selecting music. He may draw from a number of library sources; the music may be stored on disc, quarter-inch or 35mm magnetic film. Careful notes are made and some tentative selections picked. Then the director returns for the next session with the editor.

The editor now auditions his choices. Rather than starting chronologically, he might begin with some general selections. As the general choices are made, either the director or the editor may recognize that a particular piece fits well in a specific scene; this too is noted. Soon the editor has a clear picture of what the score will be like; he has, in effect, narrowed his vast composite library down to a workable number of pieces of a consistent type, a "miniature library" suitable for this specific film. At this stage it is primarily the music editor's job to score the picture. The director is there to approve of the music.

The appropriate tapes and discs are assembled. As many pieces as possible are obtained on 35mm mag, for this enables them to be run on the Moviola in exact sync with the picture. If they are only available on quarter-inch or disc, then a tape recorder or record player on which to play them in approximate sync should be on hand. (We have a record player wired directly into the Moviola sound system.) The film and voice track are placed on the Moviola; if you do not have the voice track, a script should be kept at hand. The film is now run down to the first cue. We now play the specific pieces of music against the picture and voice track to find the right piece for each section that will require music. (The idea of where to use music and what music to use may change at this stage, for we are no longer dealing with the theoretical but with the practical question of whether the music "works.") We are to determine if the music "fits," and there are two meanings to this term. We are concerned not only with its fitting the spirit and mood of the film, but also with the actual matching of the piece at the proper length to fit the picture. Music editing is a science of taste and of changes. We must determine *where the music goes, what kind of music it shall be, how we will start and end* each piece, and *how we will get from one piece to another.*

There are four possibilities that can face us, once a particular piece of stock music has been chosen for a scene: the music can be too long, too short, just the right length, or it can match in general length but not always in specific content. It is a matter of matching music and scene where required; the editor must know when to let well enough alone. Sometimes it is far better to let the piece run, even if not all of the matches of music accent to picture are exact and specific, than to mutilate the music with innumerable cuts.° To sync one or two key hits to the picture or match one dramatic change in mood or tempo in the music to a similar change in the scene may be enough within one piece of music. Most of the major changes of scene in the picture will be covered by a change to an entirely different piece of music. However, it is quite important to avoid using a section of an otherwise excellent piece of music that suddenly goes out of key with the picture (it might contain a flowery and romantic string section that lasts for a short time before the piece returns to its original mood, for example). Once the correct piece has been chosen, music scoring involves knowing when to quit the piece; in other words, to know when it no longer works.

Remember that we will invariably lay-in the music on two separate music tracks which we will call "A" Music and "B" Music. This will be necessary if we wish to cross-fade from one track to another at a music change. It is also necessary to permit the sound mixer to compensate for differences in level or equalization between two adjoining pieces in the score. And, occasionally, it is necessary to permit us to play two tracks simultaneously, as, for example, a percussion track superimposed over an instrumental track for dramatic effect.

There will be five possible ways in which we can make our change from one piece of music to another. (1) One piece can end naturally and the other begin naturally; (2) the first piece can be faded out while the incoming piece begins naturally; (3) the first piece can end naturally while the incoming piece is faded in; (4) the first piece can be faded out while we fade in the incoming piece (cross-fade); and (5) we can cut the incoming piece directly into the first piece on the same track. The first four ways require a change to another track; the fifth method involves staying on the running track.

We will now proceed through a hypothetical film, choosing music and building a cue sheet. We shall deal with examples of each type of change and will present examples of the variety of ways the music's length will require adjustment to correctly match the picture. At this point in our work, we will not mechanically cut the piece to exact length; this will come when we edit the music. We are, at the *cuing stage,* interested in finding the right piece for each section of the picture, cuing its start, and then deciding where and how we shall make a change to the next piece. You·will note our detailed sample cue sheet. On it is covered each type of music change you might have occasion to

*Music with a recognizable cadence and familiar form such as a march is very difficult to cut unobtrusively.

use, as well as the different kinds of editing you might be required to do within the individual piece. If you refer back to this sheet continually as you read this section, you will not only find the complex material easier to grasp, but you will gain a more thorough understanding of the building of your music tracks, for the cue sheet is a diagram of these tracks.

Our first cue begins at 12 feet, following the Academy (Universal) leader, at the first frame of picture. We have chosen a piece called "Disc à Go-Go"; we place a 35mm magnetic copy on the sound head and run it down in sync to picture. It is an example of a piece that fits perfectly, for we find it ending precisely at 60 feet, the point at which we want our next number to start. This is an example of change (1), a "natural in and out"; there will thus be no need to edit "Disc a Go-Go." We roll the 35mm take back up on a flange and place it on the editing table rack, ready to be laid-in.

We chose for our second piece "Cape Cod." We start it on the machine and it matches picture very well; at 90 feet we wish to change directly to another piece, "Ruby," to match a change in picture content. "Cape Cod" has hit on a strong beat at the beginning of a new phrase of music at precisely 90 feet, and this is a situation that lends itself readily to a direct music cut. Additionally, we know the two pieces to be similar in instrumentation, recorded and transferred at the same time, so there should be no need to make changes in level or equalization in mixing from one piece to another. This will be an example of change (5), a direct cut on the same track. We set "Cape Cod" and "Ruby" aside for editing later.

At 140 feet we wish to start a new piece, "Lumber Mill." At this footage "Ruby" has also hit on a distinct beat, so we know we can make an effective change to the incoming piece. But "Lumber Mill" is rather different in character from "Ruby," so we shall wish to start it on the "A" track, and we note this on our cue sheet. When we lay it in we will pre-set "Lumber Mill" at the precise point we wish it to start, matching the beat on "Ruby," but on the "A" track. As a "pre-set," the first note of "Lumber Mill" will start at this footage, 140 feet. This is an example of music change (2), fade-out and natural in. At the mix, the re-recordist will simply close the "B" track at this point as the "A" takes over. The effect, if skillfully done—and if we have matched the start of "Lumber Mill" exactly with the appropriate beat of "Ruby"—will be of one continuous piece of music. Let us pause for a minute and discuss the selecting of the appropriate beat.

SELECTING THE CUTTING BEAT

We are looking for an appropriate place to leave the running piece of music as close as possible to the point where a change in the picture demands a change in the music. "As close as possible" implies that the exact point will be determined by the music rather than the picture, even though the need for a change is, of course, dictated by the change in the visual image or the narration. What we are seeking in the running piece is a beat of the music, preferably with a strong accent, and, if possible, the first beat after the completion of a phrase in the music. If we must interrupt a phrase because it will not be complete until some seconds into the next scene, we will try to choose at least the first beat of a measure to cut on. If even this is impossible, a third beat is preferable to a second or fourth beat. Such strict adherence to the beat is appropriate to a piece with a strong and detectable cadence; in arhythmic music, such as free-form jazz, we need be less strict. For our purposes, let us assume that the piece requires exact adherence to the beat.

We are trying to match the two pieces of music involved so that the effect is of one continuous piece of music, but with a change in character at the appropriate footage in the film, or very close to it. Rather than cutting the second piece directly into the first piece on the same track—as we did with "Ruby" and "Cape Cod" at 70 feet—we will in this example place the new piece on the opposite track, and accomplish the change by switching to the other track at the mix, closing the track bearing the first piece.

We do this because it is far easier to make an effective change between dissimilar pieces of music by cross-fading than by direct cutting. So long as the beat matches and the content of visual image has required a change, the spectator will accept a faded music change, even if the pieces are quite dissimilar in style, key, and instrumentation. Additionally, should we find it expedient during the mix to make the change a few seconds later, this option is still open to us; it would not be so if we made a direct cut.

To locate the appropriate beat nearest the picture change, we *tap the track.* To do this, take a white grease pencil and run the sound take back about twenty feet on the Moviola. Run forward, and as the machine reaches speed, begin to tap the track sharply next to the pickup head to the beat of the music, just as it passes through the Moviola gate. This will leave a mark on the track that shows us where the beat falls (Fig. 11.14 A–C). Continue to tap until past the point where you wish to change. Stop, and back up the Moviola to the mark nearest to the desired change point. If this beat fits the stated requirements (see above), then this will be our point at which to change to the other track. Moving the Moviola by hand, locate the *exact start of sound* on the track (it should be a few sprockets before the mark made by the tapping), and note this exact figure on the cue sheet; it is the precise spot at which we shall pre-set the incoming piece on the other track.

If these changes are made under narration or dialogue, they will certainly be unnoticeable, for the music will be subordinated to the words at such a point. Unfortunately, many times we leave transitions in the visual scene without sound, retarding the narration cue a few seconds into the new scene specifically to allow the new visual image and the music a chance to establish themselves. Although we advocate holding the music change a few frames if necessary to match the nearest effective beat, it is often not possible to hold off the change for the several seconds needed to enable the change to fit under the next voice cue. The test of whether this delay would be feasible would be how great the

Fig. 11–14a Tapping track running at sound speed on Moviola

change in music must be. If the change is radical—a pastoral scene changing to that of a steel mill, a scene in Mexico to a scene in Sweden —the music change must be made as close as possible to the picture change. If the change is more subtle—one scenic countryside to another— we can probably afford to wait for the voice to come in before changing the music. It should be pointed out that a change from a soft to a loud piece of music is invariably easier than the reverse. Now let us continue on with our scoring.

The next piece, "Lumber Mill," matches the scene well and, luckily, ends at 195 feet, the point we have chosen for our next change in music. Having the piece end naturally will give a sense of resolve to the scene and pave the way for a distinct change of scene; it will be particularly appropriate for a scene change covered by a dissolve or fade-out/fade-in.

We start our next piece, "Run of the Mill," at 195 feet, but notice that the first few feet of musical introduction is out of key with the picture. There is a suitable phrase 15 feet into the piece where we could easily fade into the music, for there is a short pause just preceding the beginning of this phrase. We back up the Moviola to 180 feet, and start "Run of the Mill" at that footage but with the pot on that sound head closed, fading in at 195 feet; this works nicely so we proceed to the next cue. The change at 195 feet was an example of our change (3), fade-in and natural out.

At 260 feet, the point of our next change, we repeat the procedure followed at 140 feet, locating the outgoing beat on "Run of the Mill." "Cricket on a Spree" is started at 260 feet; however, when we reach the point at which we wish the music to end (310 feet), the selected piece is still running. We take the magnetic film out of the Moviola and unwind it to the end, placing the end in the sound head so that the last note will finish at exactly 310 feet. We then carefully run the Moviola backward until we reach the head of the piece, which will be somewhere before 260 feet. We note this footage—210 feet—on our cue sheet. This means that the piece was originally fifty feet too long for our purpose. By starting the music at this point we will insure its ending at 310 feet. We have *"backed up"* this musical selection. We have now only to run down on the Moviola and check the cross-fade (change 4) to see if it works. Hopefully this point will be hidden under dialogue, for the chance of getting an exact phrase and/or beat match between pieces is small. In our example this does occur, and so we proceed to our next cue at 440 feet. (Of course, had the beats not matched, we might have adjusted either of the pieces a few frames to achieve this.) The musicless film between 310 and 440 feet (130 feet or 86⅔ seconds) might typically contain a sync dialogue sequence or effects-only sequence.

For our next cue, we settle on a piece called "Hackney Carriage," which fits well until the end, where we discover that the music, instead of ending at 540 feet, runs to 570 feet. We determine that a fade-out of the music will not work at 540 feet and that we wish the music to come to a natural end at this point. We put the piece aside and note on our

Fig. 11–14b Marks made on 35mm mag film (stripe) by tapping track

Fig. 11–14c The track in the "B" gang of the synchronizer has been tapped and the exact start of sound marked to its right

cue sheet that it is 30 feet too long. When we finish scoring we will cut this piece to the exact length we need by removing a thirty foot portion. The change at 540 feet will then be an example of change (1), natural out, natural in.

We start "Many a Tune Played in An Old Brass Pot" at 540 feet; it too works well, but it is considerably longer than the 70 feet we need. We set this aside with the note that we must also edit this piece to length.

We start "Flute Moods No. 1" at 610 feet, but it runs out at 700 feet, twenty feet too soon, for we wish our change to occur at 720 feet. This too is set aside with the note on our cue sheet to make another transfer of this piece from the quarter-inch tape master. We will then use a twenty-foot phrase from this material to lengthen the original the necessary twenty feet to reach 720 feet.

At 720 feet (another change 1) we start "Fun Factory," which is excellent but much too short, ending at 820 feet for a change we want at 880 feet. We would rather continue using this piece, however, since it fits the continuing picture well. Since we must add some 60 feet to the piece we shall use a second method of lengthening a piece. We shall obtain a second identical take of the piece and start it 60 feet later than the first take starts, 780 feet instead of 720 feet, and naturally on the other ("A") track. This gives us the first take alone on the "B" track from 720 feet to 780 feet, the two takes parallel on both tracks from 780 to 820 feet, and the "A" Track alone from 820 to 880 feet. This means we can cross-fade from the "B" to the "A" anywhere between 780 to 820 feet. After we have laid-in the tracks, we will play them on the Moviola to picture and voice, picking a suitable place to cross under dialogue. We make a note on our cue sheet to get a second take of "Fun Factory" transferred and proceed to the next cue. The change from "B" to "A" track will, of course, be a change (4), cross-fade.

At 910 feet (no music between 880 and 910 feet) we start "St. Trop," which works perfectly except for a rather lush section at 958 feet (48 feet into the piece) which is out of key with the picture. We note this on our cue sheet and set the piece aside for editing.

At 975 feet, we determine to fade out of "St. Trop" and pre-set our end title piece (change 2). For this end music we will use a second take of our opening piece, "Disc à Go-Go." Since at the start it ran from 12 feet to 60 feet (48 feet long) and our final cue is to run from 975 feet to 1,000 feet (25 feet) we know that we must shorten this second take by 23 feet. We make a note to transfer a second take of this piece and to edit it to a length of 25 feet.

We will now obtain additional transfers of "Fun Factory," "Disc à Go-Go," and "Flute Moods," and, taking the picture and voice track off the machine, sit down to edit to the correct length, "Hackney Carriage," "Many a Tune," "Flute Moods No. 1," "St. Trop," and "Disc à Go-Go," and to cut together "Ruby" and "Cape Cod." It should be noted that we have not stressed the obvious fact that, in many cases, we might normally try several choices of music against picture before the right one is chosen. Also note that we have dealt in regular footages whereas in reality many of them would be fractional, e.g., 140.7, 195.3, 443.13, etc. The total time taken for a professional to accomplish the scoring of this hypothetical one-reel film would be at least three to five hours.

Editing the Music

This phase of work certainly can be accomplished by the editor without the director present, for it is a mechanical procedure.

MUSIC CUTTING

We are at this point familiar with certain basic techniques, having already used the "track tapping" technique to locate a beat. We now must learn the technique of cutting a 35mm music take.° There are certain criteria we shall look for in determining our cutting point; these same criteria have also been applied in determining points in the music where we can fade out to another track (page 417). We will look for a sharp accent or impact in the music on a definite beat, preferably the first beat of a measure, but on a third beat if no first beat is available at the point where we need it. Hopefully this beat will come at the beginning of a musical phrase or section. If the piece has a rigid and detectable cadence, these stated criteria are particularly important, but all need not be present to make a cut work. If the piece is arhythmic or rhythmically inactive we have much more leeway in cutting, but we should still look for some definite accent. We will in each case cut into the slight sound pause that precedes the accent. Even if there is a low continuing sound underneath this cut, the accent of the new beat coming in will cover this. Not only can we cut directly into 35mm mag (and 16mm mag) film without causing any detectable click in the track, but we can later reconstitute the cut, putting the pieces back together, still without causing any detectable noise.

There is another type of cut possible in some cases: cutting within a tone or chord. (It is possible in voice editing to cut within vowel sounds, done for the purpose of shortening recorded words.) In such a case it is essential that the sound level matches on each side of the cut. This is the more difficult kind of cut to make; it is easier to find an accent, using this to help make the cut work, than it is to judge the precise matching of sound level needed in a continuous tone cut. Additionally, it is almost impossible to later reconstitute such a cut without there being a click on the track, so it is difficult to correct an error if you do judge wrong on the level on your first try. Such a cut is a last resort if the cut-on-accent cannot possibly be made.

The purpose of the music cut is to substitute a beat in an incoming piece of music for the anticipated beat in a running piece of music, creating the illusion of one continuous piece. This incoming piece may actually be a new piece of music, or it may be merely another portion of the running piece, but the effect will be the same: the sense of a continuous piece of music, as if no cut had been made.

The so-called "running" piece of music is placed on the Moviola

°Remember that we advocate using 35mm magnetic sound film rather than 16mm because it is far better for editing.

and run to the point at which the cut is to be made. We use the method of tapping the track with a grease pencil to locate the beat nearest to the point, then, moving the Moviola by hand, the exact start of sound is found and marked.* The cut will be made in the sound gap a sprocket or two before this mark, which of course locates the anticipated beat of the running piece (Fig. 11.15). We now locate the point on the incoming piece which we wish to join to the running piece at the marked point, locating the beat on the incoming piece as we did before and marking it. If we are cutting to the first note of the incoming piece, we simply mark this exactly, cutting away all excess film before it. We then return to the marked beat on the running piece, cutting it with the splicer just before the mark, having turned the film *base side up;* the process is repeated with the incoming piece. It is extremely important that the cuts be as close as possible to the start of sound we have marked without actually intruding on the sound. If we intrude on the sound, an audible click will occur on the track; if we cut too far from the sound, the silent space will be equally noticeable. Now let us begin work on the pieces of music which require editing before they are to be laid-in to our music tracks for our film.

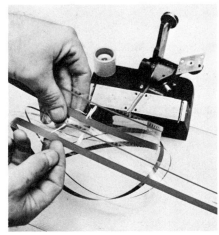

Fig. 11-15 35mm mag film with recorded music marked for cutting

EDITING TO LENGTH

Our first job will be the joining of "Cape Cod" and "Ruby." Our cue sheet shows that "Cape Cod" is to run from 60 to 90 feet, a length of 30 feet; at this point "Ruby" joins it and continues to 140 feet, fading out under "Lumber Mill." We place "Cape Cod" on the Moviola, set the footage counter at zero, and run down 30 feet. At this point we locate the nearest cuttable point, remembering our criteria for choosing such a point.

We find this cuttable point by tapping the beats with our grease pencil, finding the nearest beat to 30 feet. If it meets our criteria, we mark it for cutting. The take is placed on the splicer and the first note of "Ruby," properly trimmed, is spliced directly to "Cape Cod." If you properly label the trim (Fig. 11.16) you will be able to reconstitute the piece later and use it again. In checking over your work it is best to use the exact footages you will be dealing with in the film rather than to try to compute them; this avoids a chance of an error in arithmetic. Therefore, set the footage counter at 60 feet and run the music. Listen carefully to the cut from "Cape Cod" to "Ruby" at 90 feet to see if it works; and then listen to "Ruby" at 140 feet to see if a beat hits properly to allow us to fade out under "Lumber Mill." In this case, we discover that the beat we want comes 8 frames after 140 feet. We therefore choose to change the footage at which "Lumber Mill" is to start to 140.8. Note this change on the second cue sheet. When we run the laid-in tracks to picture later, we can see if this will work to picture and narration.

We now will begin work on "Hackney Carriage," which is 30 feet too long according to our cue sheet. We run the piece on the Moviola until we hear a good cuttable point, a strong impact at the start of a phrase. We note the footage at that point and run 30 feet farther; if

Fig. 11-16 Coding of music trims

*Locating the exact start of sound is easier to do on a sound reader; Moviola makes a special attachment called a Search Head which makes this task a good deal easier on the Moviola. However in our experience, these are not often found on available Moviolas.

there is a similar cuttable point at this footage, we have selected a 30 foot section that we can lift from the piece. Mark this second cuttable point, back up to the first point and mark it also. Then cut and splice the two together, removing the thirty foot segment between these marks; label the trim at each cut and store in the trim can. Again, check this piece to the exact picture footage; set the Moviola footage counter at 440 feet and run it past the splice, checking it as you pass. If the piece ends at 540 feet as it should we can proceed to the next piece.

"Many a Tune" must also be shortened, but in this case it is considerably longer than the footage we want, so another variation of the shortening process must be used. First take the last 50 feet or so of the piece and run it. Choose the last complete musical phrase of the piece and mark the impact note at its beginning for cutting. Then measure from this point to the end. Let us say that the phrase is 25 feet. "Many a Tune" starts at 540 feet and should end at 610 feet; a 25 foot ending, therefore, would have to start at 585 feet. Set the footage counter at 540 feet and run down to 585 feet, using the usual procedure for locating a suitable cutting point. If there is one, then we can cut in our 25 foot ending at that point, back up, listen, check the cut, and then proceed to 610 feet to check overall length. Should there not be a suitable cutting point (remember that dialogue or narration over this point will disguise a less-than-perfect cut) then we must return to the end of the piece, pick another start to the end section, measure its new length and repeat our entire procedure.

"Flute Mood No. 1" presents us with a new problem—lengthening a piece; it is 20 feet too short. We have transferred a second take of "Flute Mood"; place it on the Moviola and locate a cuttable point at the start of a music phrase. Note how far this point is from the start of the piece. Run 20 feet farther and check for a second cuttable point which completes a 20 foot phrase. We will cut this 20 foot section into the first take of "Flute Mood" at the same distance from the start at which the phrase occurred. The effect will be of this particular phrase repeating itself for 20 feet, the music then continuing as written. This might be disturbing if the phrase is a particularly noticeable one, so this factor should be taken into account, particularly if there is no voice over this section (music "in the clear").

"St. Trop" is an example of a piece containing an objectionable passage. Our note says this occurs at 958 feet. We start the take at 910 feet and run to 958 feet, mark the cutting point of the anticipated beat, then proceed to the end of the objectionable phrase and mark the first beat of the next (usable) portion. We cut these two points together as before, checking both the cut and the beat at the fading-out point of the piece at 975 feet.

Our final cut will be for the purpose of reducing a second take of "Disc à Go-Go" from its actual length of 48 feet to the required 25 feet occurring between 975 and 1,000 feet. We can use either method for shortening, the important thing being the removal of 23 feet from the middle of the piece, giving us sufficient room after the cut for our end

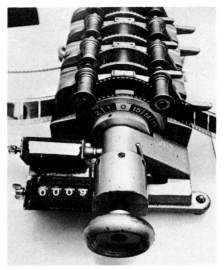

Fig. 11-17 Laying in "beep" at nine foot point of "A" music track

Laying-in the "A" and "B" Music Tracks

Fig. 11-18 Marking of laying-in point of first piece of music at twelve feet

*Since the leader is already emulsion down— and this is absolutely essential— turning it over will place it base down, emulsion up.

title music to run in the clear. There is one other way we could handle this problem: Place the end of the take at 1,000 feet and back it up to 975 feet. If there is a suitable starting point at this footage, we might choose to fade in on this piece. Since we have a fade-out on the "A" track, it would change our type of change here from type 2 (fade-out and natural in) to 4 (cross-fade).

We have now arrived at the final cutting room procedure, the laying-in of the music tracks. Once again, continual reference to our cue sheet (Fig. 11.13) is recommended.

We first set up the cue sheet on the cutting table for our reference; a two-gang 35mm synchronizer will be used. All of the 35mm music takes will be assembled on the cutting table rack. On the lefthand rewind, we place two supply reels with 35mm leader. Feed this leader off the supply reels, through the synchronizer, and on to the take-up reels on the right-hand rewind. The leader must be *base-up;* should the emulsion side be up, it will flake off in recording machines and clog the heads. We will label the head of each track in indelible marker: Head—Music Mag "A" (or "B")—Name of the film—Name of the producer. Clamp and space the two take-up reels on the righthand rewind. Now we mark with indelible pencil a start mark on each track, labeling each at this point also as to "A" or "B" music track (Fig. 8.62). Run the tracks forward to the 9 foot point and add a "beep" to the "A" track (Fig. 11.17). This is usually a piece of quarter-inch tape with adhesive backing, containing a tone which will produce an audible beep when it runs through any sound head on which the tracks are played. The purpose of this sound is to assure us that the track is in proper alignment with the picture at the mix. We have always placed the beep at 9 feet (35mm), exactly 3 feet above the first frame of picture. This sound will, of course, be reproduced on the *optical sound negative* to be made from the result of the sound mix, giving the matcher a means of correctly lining up the optical sound negative with the picture negative for printing the composite. Always let the matcher know at what footage you have placed the beep, as practice differs among labs.

At 12 feet, on the "A" track we will cut in our first cue (Fig. 11.18). We run the leader through the synchronizer by winding the righthand rewind until the footage counter reads 12 feet and the figure zero is at the top of the sprocket wheel and thus directly under the leader. We will make our 12 foot mark directly over the righthand side line of the "0" frame; then the tracks are backed up so that this mark will be placed to the left of the synchronizer, between it and the supply rewind. Now we take our first piece, "Disc à Go-Go," placing it on top of the marked leader so that the start mark on the piece matches exactly the mark made on the leader. Cut the piece just before the start of sound, being careful not to cut into the sound itself.

Now proceed to splice in the first take of music (Fig. 11.19). Turn over (emulsion down) the music take and the leader,° held carefully together with the start mark of the music matching the 12 foot mark on the leader. Stripe is transparent and thus better than full-coat in such a situation. Place the pieces down over the splicer's alignment pins with the music start mark just to the left of the diagonal groove in the base into which the knife blade will fall. Bring the blade down, cutting through both pieces of magnetic film. If you have placed the music track on top of the leader you will naturally be looking down at the leader, now cut into two pieces. Lift off the splicer the lefthand piece of leader; it is, of course, the end of the leader feeding off the supply reel on the lefthand rewind, and should remain there until needed again. You will now see that the leader is coming off the righthand take-up reel, through the synchronizer's "A" gang—we always use the gang toward the editor for the "A" track and label from front to back "A," "B," "C," etc.—and on to the splicer. At the diagonal groove of the splicer the music track begins, and, of course, the two pieces match cleanly. Place the end of the splicing tape over this cut, and tear it off with the splicer's tearing lever. Smooth out the bubbles in the tape, lift off the splice, and remove and throw away the few frames of beginning trim left over from the music sound film on the right side of the splicer. You have now joined "Disc à Go-Go" to the running leader on "A" track at 12 feet. You may either hold the wound-up take of this piece in your left hand or place it over the shaft of the lefthand rewind, in either case feeding it smoothly into the synchronizer as you take up on the righthand rewind. You will now have a "B" track consisting of leader and an "A" track consisting of 35mm mag film, both running forward through the synchronizer.

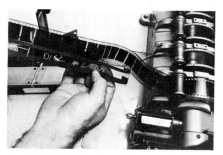

Fig. 11–19 Matching first piece of music to marked laying-in point

At 60 feet you will mark the "B" track leader and cut in "Cape Cod" (with "Ruby" spliced to it) just as you cut in "Disc à Go-Go" earlier. However, at this point "Disc à Go-Go" is running out on the "A" track. Before it runs through the synchronizer (if it does you will lose sync and have to rewind the tracks to zero and start over), take the leader that is hanging on the lefthand rewind and splice it to the end of "Disc à Go-Go." We always mark the end of a piece with a characteristic mark denoting the last usable portion of sound (Fig. 11.20). The take should be cut off just after this mark so that there is no extraneous noise left on the track that might be heard during our mix. Thus from 60 to 140.8 feet we will have a "B" music track of 35mm mag film and an "A" consisting of leader, as you can see from the cue sheet.

When we reach 140.8 feet, we cut in "Lumber Mill" on the "A." But what should we do about the "B" track, which is no longer playing after 140 feet? There will be no need to cut off "Ruby" at the exact point at which it must be faded out. Rather, let it continue to run, serving as the "leader" at this point. There are three reasons for this: (1) We might change our mind at the mix and wish to make our music change later, perhaps at 150 feet; if "Ruby" is still running we can simply make a cross-fade from the "B" to the "A" at that time. (2) We may be able to avoid cutting our music take, which is always preferable should we wish to use it in the future. (3) We avoid using an unnecessary amount

Fig. 11–20 Cutting in leader to end of running piece of music

of leader for a purpose that the 35mm mag film is perfectly capable of serving.

We now proceed to 180 feet, "Lumber Mill" still running on the "A" track. Since "Run of the Mill" does not start playing at the cut-in point—the cue sheet shows it to be faded-in at 195 feet—we may cut it in directly to "Ruby" at 180 feet. We will mark "Ruby" at 180 feet on the synchronizer, just as if it were leader, which in fact is precisely the purpose it is serving here. Then we back the tracks off to the left, place the start mark of "Run of the Mill" on top of the mark on "Ruby," turn them over and place them on the splicer. We then mark the cutting point of "Ruby" to identify the trim. When we lift up the trim (the tail end of "Ruby"), after having spliced "Run of the Mill" onto the head of "Ruby," we will roll up the film and place it in our trim can, just as we have done earlier with the trims from the pieces we edited prior to laying-in (Fig. 11.16). We then splice the leader from the supply reel onto the tail of "Lumber Mill" at 195 feet and continue. At 210 feet, we will cut in the start of "Cricket on a Spree" on the "A" track. As we continue we note that both tracks are again 35mm mag sound film, not leader.

When we reach 260 feet, we will again let our piece that is to be faded-out (in this case "Run of the Mill" on the "B" track) continue to run inaudibly, parallel to the audible piece, "Cricket on a Spree." Let us say that it is an extremely long take to illustrate one further cutting principle. At 310 feet, we cut leader onto the tail of "Cricket" on the "A" track, running the leader on to 440 feet where "Hackney Carriage" is cut in, "Run of the Mill" continuing as "leader" on the "B" track. Finally we reach 530 feet, 10 feet before "Many a Tune" is to enter on the "B" track. At this point we will cut in a section of leader, marking and storing the trim to "Run of the Mill" in our trim can. There is a simple reason for doing this. We have marked for a pre-set at 540 feet; if the previous take is running and we open the "B" track, we will hear its sound mixed with the sound of the piece on the "A" track that we actually wish to hear. So we need a short, soundless section of leader, to enable the re-recordist at the mix to pre-set this track a few seconds before the actual music change. This will allow him to devote his full attention to the "A" track at the point of change (or to an effects or a voice track, if necessary). If we consistently follow the rule of leaving at least 10 feet before a pre-set we will never have the embarrassment (not to mention unnecessary cost) of ruining the mix by opening up a track with music on it at the wrong time. You will note that at 820 feet "Fun Factory" has run out on the "B" track; we have noted this fact by telling the re-recordist on the mix cue sheet that the track is clear at 835 feet. Of course, even if we had forgotten to note that, he would know he could safely open the track at 965 feet for the 975 feet pre-set. Our other music takes are cut in routinely at 610 feet ("A"), 720 feet ("B"), 780 feet ("A"), 910 feet ("A"), and 975 feet ("B"). Note that for the first time there will be leader running on both tracks from 880 feet to 910 feet, for there will be no music during this thirty feet (twenty seconds).

We will continue to run "St. Trop" down to the end of the picture.

At 1,000 feet, at the end of "Disc à Go-Go," we will add 50 feet of leader to the "B" track (if there is more film left on "St. Trop" we can just let it run the 50 feet), running both tracks 50 feet past the end of picture. This is done in the event that we use an interlock system at the mix (see next chapter) and wish to back up the picture and tracks in sync after reaching the end of the reel. Another reason for the leader is to prevent a wow, or audible waver, in the last piece of music, caused by the dubber pulling the tape off the supply reel, the torque increasing greatly as the film reaches the end of the reel. The use of a 3-inch plastic core for your sound track instead of the more common 2-inch core will also prevent wow, but the 50 feet of leader is still a good idea.

CHECKING THE TRACKS ON THE MOVIOLA

At the end of the leader we will again mark carefully: Tail—Music Mag "A" (or "B"), Name of picture, Name of producer—with indelible pencil. Then we rewind the tracks onto split reels and cores. The Moviola is loaded with picture, voice track, and "A" and "B" music (this is why we use a three-sound-head Moviola), and the music is checked to picture and voice, paying particular attention to the cuts and changes. This is a miniature mix on the Moviola. A great deal can be checked out this way (and many corrections can be made in the cutting room, where we have the time to accomplish this work properly); it is an important step in our film sound work. But we must not fool ourselves into thinking that a Moviola sound system can approach the fidelity of reproduction of a dubber in a mix studio. It is, therefore, strongly recommended that you book time for an *interlock screening* at the recording studio at least one full day before the mix. You may need a half hour, or even an hour if your picture is longer than ten minutes, to be absolutely certain that your tracks are right. This procedure will be described in the next chapter.

One further suggestion: Use earphones with the Moviola when you run your tracks to picture. The earphones screen out extraneous noises including the racket of the Moviola itself and help your concentration; by bypassing the small speaker of the Moviola they give you a truer picture of the quality of the music.

As a last point it should be mentioned that if you have a responsibility to a producer or sponsor on your film, he should be brought back in to monitor the tracks with picture and voice, possibly on the Moviola and certainly at the interlock. This way you can make any necessary changes he may request. If he wishes to attend the mix, and this is a courtesy he should be offered, you must make it quite clear that no changes can be made in the actual music, voice, or effects at that time. Only level and balance can be controlled at the mix. To attempt to do much else will be extremely costly, and is simply not the province of the mix. When we have accomplished everything to our satisfaction in the sound cutting room, we proceed to the sound studio for our final sound work, the mix.

CHAPTER 12

THE
SOUND MIX

Have you considered the degree of accuracy involved in film sound work? We have observed in the sound cutting room that a variation of 2 frames from sync will be detectable in sync voice or in effects with a sharp and specific attack. There are 24 frames per second, sixty seconds in a minute, or *1,440 frames per minute.* In a ten minute film there are therefore 14,400 frames and in a thirty minute film, 43,200! Yet an error of two frames is noticeable. So in a thirty minute motion picture we are allowed a margin of error of one in 43,200! And this is precisely the degree of accuracy we depend upon day after day from the professional sound studio—and, we might add, from our own work in the sound cutting room.

A good mix is the essential climax of a good sound job; a poor mix can destroy the very best sound work. Yet, the mix is only a bringing together, a creative balancing of elements which have been selected and carefully matched to picture in the sound cutting room. If these elements have been poorly handled in the cutting room, if they have been badly chosen initially, or if they have been reproduced inadequately, your chances for a first-rate mix—and a first-rate film—are small.° The sto-

°We have worked on or observed a considerable number of low-budget features (under $200,000) and, without exception, their least successful aspect, technically and aesthetically, was sound.

ries are legend of directors stumbling into the mix ten minutes late, laden with a few scratched records and some sound effects loops, a narrator in tow, only to emerge two hours later with a work of genius somehow sprung full-blown from the brow of the re-recordist. Well, don't bet on it.

In most New York sound studios a mix costs over $100 an hour; this would tend to make it a less-than-ideal place in which to experiment. The re-recordist (mixer) can improve the quality of your voice tracks, but presenting him with a sow's ear will probably result in his returning you the same. He can do a great deal to make music changes involving a cross between tracks undetectable, but only if the tracks have been properly edited beforehand. The essence of the mix is the achievement of balance; the re-recordist is the juggler. It is quite enough to ask him to keep the whirling plates in the air without also asking him to construct the plates by assembling shattered pieces and gluing them together (*and* asking him to maintain an amusing conversation with his audience all the while).

PREPARATION
PRE-MIX CUTTING ROOM PROCEDURES

Assuming your work has been properly completed in the cutting room, there are some further steps to be taken to prepare for the mix. The work print should be gone over carefully, all splices checked and any excess tape trimmed with a razor blade. If any sprocket holes are obscured by the tape the splice should be remade. To do this properly the old tape should be removed—a razor blade is usually needed to pry up the edge of the tape—and a new splice made; projectors cannot handle splices reinforced by several thicknesses of tape. Any damaged sprockets should also be repaired with splicing tape. If a short section of the film is badly damaged, it can be *slugged*, which means replacing the section of film with a carefully measured piece of blank leader of exact to-the-sprocket length. Whether within the area to be slugged there is a cut from one shot to another or the shot is continuous, this must be carefully noted on the leader with an indelible pencil for the later information of the negative matcher (Figure 12.1A). If single-perf 16mm leader is used, you must be careful to place the sprocket holes on the correct side so that they will engage the sprockets of the projector. This would mean placing them on the lefthand side of the editor when facing the film with its *emulsion* side up. This way the film will run properly on both a moviola and a projector. The film may be run a number of times during the interlock and the final mix, and a breakage at the recording studio can result in an expensive delay. Remember that 16mm projection wind is the opposite—*base out* on the reel—from Moviola wind; bring your print to the mix wound properly.

Even if care is taken, it is possible that the film will "lose its loop" and flutter unintelligibly on the screen during projection. The loop in the film between the gate and one of the sprocket wheels has tightened due to the failure of the film to pass properly through the gate. The projectionist can restore this quickly enough, but there is no guarantee

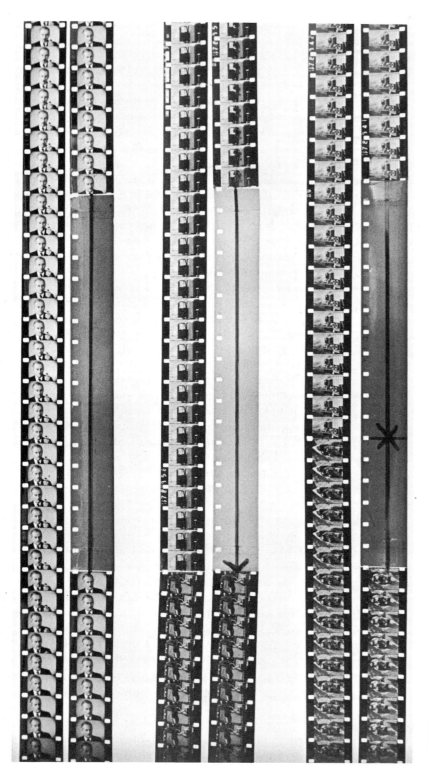

Fig. 12–1a Slugging: left-hand film of each pair
shows undamaged workprint; right-hand film
shows same portion slugged and
marked appropriately

that the loop will be exactly as it was when the film was started and hence that the picture and sound tracks will remain in perfect sync. Many directors will have a *reversal print,* a black-and-white dupe, struck from the work print and will use this to project at the mix. Since the reversal print is free from splices, it will project without slippage and maintain sync. (By doing this the director can release the work print to the negative matcher, who can thus begin his work simultaneously with that of the music editor. When the mix is completed, the picture negative is already matched and ready for the optical sound negative, and this can result in a saving of three to five days in completing the answer print.) Although I personally have a strong preference to working with the cleaner, sharper work print *in color*—this can have a considerable effect on your emotional involvement with the film—there are compelling reasons for the use of a reversal print. There are obvious advantages in seeing the film on a large screen in order to check sync detail, but the editor must learn to accomplish as much exact syncing as possible on the synchronizer in the cutting room beforehand.

Another important pre-mix procedure is cleaning the tracks (the picture should be cleaned, too), referred to as *gloving* or *velveting,* depending upon whether a white cotton editing glove or a piece of velvet, kept for that purpose, is used (Fig. 12.1B). The track is placed on the rewinds and held down on the cutting table at mid-point, with the cloth both under and over the film. Steady pressure is applied with the left hand while the film is wound with the right. Any dust on the tracks will accumulate on the cloth.° Any grease pencil marks on sound tracks would be removed at this time. The correct labeling of the tracks, both head and tail, is important, including the placing of an additional identification next to the start mark. Loops will be correctly identified, and if the loop is on full-coat magnetic film, an arrow should show which way the loop must be threaded on the dubber. We suggest taking your sound tracks on cores, providing the mix studio has split reels to handle them.

Proper cue sheets will be prepared for the mix. A call to the re-recordist ahead of time can establish his particular requirements, which probably will mean a composite cue sheet of all the tracks: voice, music, and effects. The studio usually has its own cue sheet forms which can be supplied to you. Some re-recordists prefer to make up their own sheets from the ones you supply. If such is the case make your sheets legible and try to arrive early for the mix, as it may take some time to copy them and it would be preferable that this not be done during the mix proper—at your expense. The studio must be told exactly what elements you are bringing, so that they can have the proper equipment ready for you. This means telling the number and type (16mm or 35mm) of tracks, including loops, and whether the picture is 16mm or 35mm.

Fig. 12–1b Velveting track

BOOKING MIX TIME

°For magnetic tracks, *Freon TF* solvent is recommended. For the picture, *Webril Wipes,* 8″ × 8″ cotton squares lightly moistened in film cleaner are excellent. The *Speedrol Film Cleaner* is a small machine worth the investment if you are handling a large number of films; its cleaning area is automatically moistened from a bottle of film cleaner, several brands of which are available.

You will be required to book the amount of time you believe you will need and will have to pay for this time whether you use it or not, so you cannot overestimate. Most studios will allow you a maximum half-hour *bumper*—time directly following your booked time during which the studio will not book any other client. You will be charged for this bumper time only if you use it. They may, however, book the time directly following the bumper, so you cannot count on running over your allotted time beyond the bumper. An estimate of one hour per reel for an average subject film is a fair one for a mix, but should be considered *a minimum*. This is naturally based on the assumption that you will come prepared for the mix and not waste time correcting cutting room errors at the sound studio. Most mix studios have a cutting room on hand for emergency repairs and last-minute adjustments, but keep in mind that you will be working under the pressure of time, expensive time, probably without a Moviola and possibly in competition with someone who is working in studio "B" and is trying desperately to correct *his* tracks at the same time.

It is important to book sufficient time for the mix. If you should run over your booked time, the studio will allow you to continue (and charge you for it, of course), providing no one else has booked the time. If you are fighting a deadline, you may very well wish to stay until you are done, but you cannot expect the studio to delay other clients from entering the room at the time they have booked. As your deadline approaches and tension increases, the chances for error on the part of the re-recordist increase. You must also consider the fact that the studio personnel must take a lunch break, and that most studios go on overtime at six o'clock, with the rates rising proportionately.

The basic rules, then, are: Book a safe amount of mix time, consult prior to the mix with the re-recordist as to his requirements, enter the mix properly and thoroughly prepared. The best way to ensure the latter is to have an interlock screening beforehand.

THE INTERLOCK SCREENING

The interlock screening is a run-through of all of the sound components of the mix in sync with the picture. Any mix starts with an interlock screening, for that is what the first mix run-through amounts to. What is here recommended is booking this initial run-through a sufficient time in advance of the mix to allow any needed corrections to be made in your own cutting room. (One full day is recommended for an experienced editor, more for a novice.)

Where should the interlock take place? There are rentable facilities which can run sound tracks in sync with picture for a fee of under $50 per hour. Seldom do they have enough equipment to carry the full number of tracks that a complete sound job will require, and, more important, you will have to serve as your own technician on the mixing console, as only a projectionist is provided. Such a facility is useful as a less expensive way of checking a limited number of tracks on fairly good equipment and a large screen (and a good place to invite the client or producer to approve the work), but it has its limits. We advocate an interlock at the sound studio to be used for the mix and with the re-

recordist who will actually perform the mix. This way the initial session will serve as a practice run-through and enable the man who is to perform the mix to make any suggestions he might have for final preparation on your part. The studio might consider granting you a reduced rate for an interlock, provided you have already booked the mix there. At any rate, it is worth asking them. Even if you pay the full price normally required for a mix, the studio interlock is well worth it to you, and your budget estimates should provide for such from the start.

Since the interlock will be performed by the same personnel and on the same equipment as the mix, we will not describe it in detail separately but will proceed directly to the consideration of the mix, its equipment and personnel.

SOUND STUDIO PERSONNEL
DUBBER ROOM: THE MACHINE MAN

When you arrive at the studio, you will go directly to the *dubber*, or *machine*, *room* (Fig. 12.2). You will find one or two men there who will take your tracks and place them on the required dubbers. Arriving a half hour early should give you enough time to prepare properly, enabling you to enter the mix session relaxed and confident. Spend a few minutes in the dubber room to ensure the proper identification of your tracks. The machine man will be responsible for rewinding and setting again all of your soundtracks at the end of each run-through. The skill and efficiency of the machine man can help greatly at the mix in keeping

Fig. 12–2 Dubber room (patch panel to the left)

your mix time within reasonable limits. If he seems more interested in talking to his girlfriend on the phone or in reading a book—and we speak from specific experience in these matters—do not hesitate to point out to the re-recordist that you are not paying $100 an hour for half-hearted service. He will usually take immediate steps to see that you get the service you are paying for. Be sure to get this straightened out before the session is over and you have been billed for it. If there are delays in your mix due to faulty equipment, discuss this also with the re-recordist. Most studios will be fair enough not to charge you for their mistakes. However, it should be pointed out that the re-recordist is legitimately entitled to human error in performing his work, and this you must pay for, unless he is exceptionally at fault. In such a case, he will almost certainly tell you that he is not charging you for the full elapsed time and will undoubtedly do everything he can to get you the studio time you need to complete your film. And, let it be said once more for certain emphasis, you must pay for the time necessary to correct your own mistakes at the mix.

TRANSFER MAN

Usually a separate transfer room will adjoin the dubber room, run by a man whose job it is to transfer sound from one medium to another. If you have used this facility for your transfers at an earlier stage of your work on the film, you are already familiar with the room and its personnel (see Fig. 11.3). Used for sound transfer are dubbers not utilized for a mix or recording session. The transfer man will perform for you an important function. After the mix, it will be his job to transfer the mix results from magnetic to optical sound, for the end result of a film mix will be an appropriate gauge *optical sound negative* used by the lab in making composite prints of the film. The transfer man should and must carefully monitor this transfer, listening to the transferred material as it is being recorded. The re-recordist and the sound editor are seldom present when this takes place, so the end result of your entire sound job is in this man's hands, and he should be undistracted by other jobs.

The optical negative that he is creating is, like any negative, subject to variations toward light and dark. While it is true that a successful positive print can be made from a negative either side of perfect, in practice most labs do not pay proper attention to this factor, particularly in 16mm work—at least in our experience. They tend to print from the negative as though it were a perfect balance—and, therefore, it had better be! Make your requirements clear in a pleasant but unmistakable way.

PROJECTIONIST

Having satisfied yourself that your tracks are in capable hands, you will deliver the work print to the projectionist. He will work in a booth overlooking the mixing studio and has equipment for projecting 35mm and 16mm. He also has a variety of lenses and can adjust the masking of the screen in the studio for wide screen. This simply requires informing the projectionist of what you need. Occasionally during the mix the film may frame improperly (the division line between frames will appear on the screen); an alert projectionist will correct this almost instantaneously. A sleepy (or literary) projectionist will be told to "frame it properly" by the re-recordist, who can communicate directly with the dubber room and the projection booth via an intercom on his console. Incorrect focus will be corrected in the same way.

ENGINEER

Although you will have little direct dealing with them, it should be mentioned that recording studios have men on their staff whose duty it is to maintain the equipment in top-flight order and to constantly develop and install new equipment. It goes without saying that we must have absolute faith in the equipment in the recording studio. Should you later discover that inadequate equipment has caused you to receive less than what you require from the recording studio, you are certainly entitled to an adjustment on your bill. Yet such an adjustment is meaningless compared to the loss to you of time and money, including reprinting the composite print of your film. It makes far more sense to invest in a mix at a first-rate studio and to get a professional job. As always in film work, the cut-rate will cost you money in the long run.

THE RE-RECORDIST (SOUND MIXER)

The mixer is the absolutely indispensible member of the team in the recording studio. On his skill and experience depends the successful completion of the sound work of your film. His function is, of course, to execute your wishes, and a good mixer will strive to determine them. But it is equally the job of the sound editor and director to work toward creating a climate in which the mixer can do his best work. Further, we must acknowledge that the professional mixer will have performed literally thousands of mixes and is in some ways better able than the film's director to make judgments concerning film sound, particularly technical judgments. Perhaps the best way to describe the relationship between director, sound editor, and mixer at the mix is that the mixer should be responsible for such technical judgments while the sound editor, as the director's representative, is responsible for artistic ones. Naturally, this does not exclude the possibility of each helping the other in his particular area. The editor must pay close attention at every point during the mix and not depend on the mixer to do his job for him, and it is his job to state precisely what he wants, to offer suggestions for improvement, and to approve the result. The director seldom intervenes during the working stage; when the run-through is complete he will then approve the result or request changes.

SOUND STUDIO EQUIPMENT
THE DUBBER ROOM (MACHINE ROOM)

The basic equipment of the machine room is the *dubber*, also called a re-recording or playback machine. There will be dubbers capable of handling both 16mm and 35mm magnetic sound tracks, and there must be a large number to enable the studio to carry on all its functions, including several simultaneous recording and mix sessions. Some recording studios may contain only one recording–mixing studio, but others may have several (Reeves in New York City has nine and has fifty-six machines in the dubber room), and they may all be in operation at the same time. Usually a quarter-inch tape machine or two are in the actual mix-recording studio, next to the recording console, but all of the 16mm and 35mm machines are grouped in the machine room. The machine room will contain one *recording* dubber (a sprocketed 16mm or 35mm recorder) for each separate studio and a large number of *playback* dubbers, both 16mm and 35mm. The fact that these may be used interchangeably by all of the separate mix-recording studios which share this common machine room necessitates announcing to the sound studio beforehand what kind of tracks you are bringing, and thus what kind of dubbers will be required. Any of these machines may be interlocked so that they may be started simultaneously and run in perfect sync with the required projector in any mix studio. In a sense, the sound studio functions as a giant Moviola, with the dubbers as sound heads and the studio projector as the picture head. Like the Moviola, the sound studio system requires a control panel; this is the *mixing console.*

Often this studio serves the dual purpose the name implies, although sometimes a studio is built exclusively for mixing or for recording. In this case we are considering its mixing function, having dealt previously with its use as a recording studio (Figs. 11.5 and 11.6). High at the back of the room is the glass window of the projection booth and at the front, the screen (Fig. 12.3 B). There are usually a number of chairs so that the variety of people who attend mixes may sit in front of the console to observe, hopefully quietly. (The sound editor sits behind the console at the side of the mixer.) Directly below the projection screen is a large footage counter which starts in sync with the picture and tracks and tells us the exact footage at any point of the run-through. This enables the mixer to determine, in reference to the supplied cue sheet, where to cue in the various sound elements. The quarter-inch tape machines in the mix studio may also be run in sync with the dubbers and projector. However, they will be used not for playback purposes, but only to record, all of our component tracks having been brought to the mix on a sprocketed medium. (There is one exception to this: Some studios have facilities for running quarter-inch tape loops; this is feasible for the obvious reason that loops are continuously running sound elements not requiring exact sync.)

The mixing console, or re-recording console, is the most essential equipment of the mix (Fig. 12.3A). It is a control panel with separate channels (as many as sixteen) into which can be patched (plugged in) each of the playback dubbers running our sound tracks and loops. The console then is patched into the appropriate recording dubber(s) we require. For each channel on the console there is an *attenuator,* or *gain*

THE MIXING-RECORDING STUDIO OR RE-RECORDING THEATER

F. 12–3a Mixer and sound editor at
console in mix studio

Fig. 12–3b Mix studio facing projection
screen from behind console

*The term attenuator refers to the fact that the sound
comes in at maximum level and is then "attenuated,"
or limited, down to the point of maximum attenuation,
zero.

control, commonly referred to as a "pot," from potentiometer.° The pot, which can be a slide or a knob, is used for varying the level of output from the dubbers. Additionally, on each channel is usually an on-off switch, and a re-recording equalizer with three control switches for the purpose of adding or subtracting, respectively, high, medium, or low frequencies to the sound on that particular track. There are also devices which allow us to add echo or reverberation to a track, and electrical filters, both band-pass and high- and low-pass filters (Fig. 12.4,) which can be set to subtract sharply or gradually unwanted frequencies from the track. When a pot is opened, the sound track it controls (playing on a dubber in the machine room) will be fed through a recording bus to the recording dubber and/or quarter-inch tape machine and will at the same time be monitored through the speaker system of the mix studio. When two or more pots are opened at the same time, their respective soundtracks will be simultaneously recorded and will each play through the studio speaker. Naturally they can be balanced against each other by the degree to which each pot is opened (and the sound attenuated), and this balancing is the essence of the mix.

The console also contains a V-U meter, or volume units indicator, sometimes referred to as a volume indicator, or V-I meter. This registers the subjective loudness of sound and is an average power measuring device rather than an indicator of peak intensity. The V-U meter is graduated in decibels, abbreviated db, logarithmic units of gain and loss in level. If a sound is ten times as powerful as another, it is referred to as having a level of 10 db in relationship to the first sound; a sound one hundred times as powerful as the first sound would be said to be 20 db stronger, and a sound one thousand times more powerful would be 30 db stronger, and so on. (A sound 60 db stronger would be one million times more powerful than its comparative sound!)

While the V-U meter makes no attempt to monitor the peak level of the signal, this is the task of the oscilloscope or a comparable device such as a neon lamp display, one or the other of which is to be found on the mixing console and which records the image of the sound waves as they occur in the studio system. By monitoring the V-U meter and the oscilloscope, the re-recordist is able to make the most efficient use of the track and to avoid the two opposing dangers of re-recording: the presence during playback of audible noise on the track recorded at too low a level and the distortion to be found in the track recorded at too high a level.

THE PROJECTION BOOTH

The equipment of the projection booth consists of 35mm and 16mm projectors and a small cutting table on which to rewind and, if necessary, repair the film. There is a projectionist on duty, whose job it is to thread up the picture on the appropriate projector at the start mark. He then signals the mixer that the picture is ready. When the mixer has received such a signal both from the machine man in the dubber room and the projectionist, he will start the dubbers, the recorder(s), and the projector simultaneously and in sync by pushing a button on the console.

THE CUTTING ROOM

There is one additional room to take note of, the cutting room. It will contain the usual cutting table, a sound reader, synchronizers, and splicers, but not always a Moviola. It is a good idea to check this room and its equipment before the mix starts, as it may not be identical to your own. Let us hope you will not need to use it, but if you do, it will be at a time when you want to work quickly and efficiently. If something requires correcting following a run-through, leave the mix room and pick up the picture (if needed) from the projectionist and the necessary track or tracks from the dubber room, taking them to the cutting room. The mixer can alert the machine man and projectionist to the fact that you will need these components and they will have them ready for you.

When you have completed your work, return the components and go back to the mix. If you face something with which you anticipate difficulty, the mixer might be able to help you in the cutting room. If there are other people present at the mix, ask the mixer quietly to accompany you, and move with whatever composure you can summon. The film professional can be measured by his ability to quickly and efficiently correct his errors (and those of others). And part of this ability is to go about your work as if you know what you are doing. Bringing along to the mix trims to your sound tracks, original quarter-inch tapes, and a few additional sound effects which you think you might need is not a bad idea.

THE BACK-UP SYSTEM WITH PICK-UP RECORDING

There is a device which can make your mix infinitely easier, provided the studio has such a system (see page 389). The back-up system allows the mixer to stop the picture and tracks simultaneously, including the sprocketed magnetic film on which the mix is being recorded, back up all these components, and then start forward again, still in perfect sync. The system is unique in that it enables the mixer to begin to record while continuous sound is running. No matter how many times one stops and backs up to begin recording a section over again, the end result will be a continuous track with no discernible breaks in the sound.

Before we had this system, it was necessary to make the entire mix of from ten to twenty minutes in one continuous take, and one error negated the entire mix. As you can imagine, the tension increased as the final point approached, and there was an excellent chance for a single, ruinous error during the last few seconds. Without the back-up system, it was necessary to use several run-throughs to rehearse the mix, and there was a great deal of importance in the mixer's noting and carefully remembering each cue.

When a back-up system is available, it is recommended that it be used. Not having one does not, of course, mean that an excellent mix cannot be accomplished; this has been done for years and is still being done daily. But such a system can be a great help to the mixer and another example of the technical innovations which seem to arrive on the film scene almost daily, making it possible to do the job a little bit better, a little bit faster.

Using this system necessitates the studio running a 35mm magnetic sound film on the recorder (see next section), since a sprocketed medium must be used to be able to back up and go forward in sync. You should specify that you do not wish to buy this tape after the mix (assuming you have no specific need for it) and request the product of the mix on quarter-inch tape and the appropriate gauge optical track. The studio may state that they must invest in this tape which you use, and it is true that they must tie up a certain amount of stock in doing this; but the fact is that they can eventually use this tape over repeatedly, and in our opinion you should not be required to pay for it. Check this when booking the mix.°

When sound is being re-recorded, we have the option of listening either to the original tracks or the newly recorded tape. Obviously it is preferable to listen to the re-recorded track, since this allows us to hear our actual results. If there is an imperfection in the tape, for example, this would result in a *drop out*, a break in the recorded sound, and we would naturally want to detect this the moment it occurs. Dirt on the track or equipment failure can also cause an imperfect recording. It is the nature of the back-up system with pick-up recording that our pick-up of the re-recorded sound will be retarded slightly, since we must wait until the sound is on the tape before we monitor it. This delay will be approximately 3 frames on a 35mm recording, 6 on 16mm. The result will be to make the sound appear out of sync with the picture. The simple way of correcting this is to have the projectionist retard the start of the picture the appropriate number of frames, thus restoring apparent sync during the mix.

In an article in *Machinery* of January 1917, a reference was made to a "stripe of powdered iron to be painted on a motion picture film to provide synchronous sound."°° Although it would be some thirty years before commercial use would be made of this principle, the article had other significance, for it concerned the Telegraphone, a dictation machine which recorded magnetically on a .010-inch wire. The Telegraphone was the invention of Valdemar Poulsen, a Danish engineer who first demonstrated the principle of magnetic recording—"a picture in magnetism"—in 1900; it was sold commercially in the United States for several years but could not compete with the existing cylinder recorders.

The Telegraphone made use of a *DC bias*, a steady current combined with the varying current of the signal to be recorded. If bias is not used during recording the signal is distorted when it nears the zero level. Unfortunately, there is one basic objection to the use of DC bias: Even when there is no useful signal, the wire (or tape) is still recorded, and hence magnetized. Since a magnetized wire (or tape) is noisier than an unmagnetized one, ground noise is increased and a poorer signal-to-noise ratio results.

In 1921, the work of W. L. Carlson and G. W. Carpenter established the fact that a high frequency current could be substituted for the DC current applied to the recording head. If the frequency chosen is supersonic and hence too high to be recorded on the tape, the tape is left in an unmagnetized condition when no useful signal is being recorded. Thus the positive results of DC bias are achieved without the corresponding increase in ground noise. This technique, in use in magnetic recording today, is referred to as *supersonic bias* or *AC bias*.

There were also inherent problems in the use of wire as the record-

LISTENING TO PLAYBACK

STOCK, MAGNETIC AND OPTICAL, AND THE PRODUCTS OF THE MIX
MAGNETIC TAPE RECORDING

*Not every sound studio feels that the back-up system is the ultimate device for re-recording. One argument against it is its requirement that the mix be recorded on 35mm stock. Since 35mm magnetic film is subject to imperfections (drop out, for example), the re-recordist must pay careful attention to the results during the mix, and it is not always possible under mix conditions to distinguish between trouble resulting from the inherent flaws in the tape and problems in the tracks which are being mixed. This system may well be an interim process, ultimately to be replaced by equipment in the developmental stage today and utilizing computers to "remember" the cues which the mixer wishes to repeat in later run-throughs.

**Quoted in an article by S. J. Begun, "Recent developments in the field of magnetic recording," *Journal of the Society of Motion Picture Engineers*, 48, 1–13, January 1947.

ing medium. In order for the wire to be fine enough to record effectively (around .004 inch in diameter), it becomes too thin to handle, easily broken and tangled. Splicing is virtually impossible. It is impossible to prevent the wire from rotating during winding, causing a different portion of the wire to come in contact with the reproducing head than that which has been in contact with the recording head with a resultant loss of high frequency response. A recorded portion of the wire lying next to another portion when wound on the reel causes an echo of the recorded signal to *print through* to the adjacent portion; this can be quite audible during playback. It is necessary to run the wire at extremely high speed in order to get an acceptable high frequency response. It is impossible to effectively control the speed at which the wire is run, resulting in considerable variance in the length of time of subsequent playbacks and variations from the original in the frequency (pitch) of the recorded sound.[1]

In the early 1930s, engineers in the Bell Telephone Laboratories developed a substitute for wire, a one-eighth inch steel ribbon, but the major development in this area was to come from Germany. Although wire recording was used with some degree of success in the United States during World War II, the first machines of truly professional quality seen here were those brought back by our occupation forces from Germany, where they had been used extensively in broadcast work. Also brought into the country at the same time was a new recording medium: magnetic tape. "In cleanness of reproduction, low ground noise, and volume range, the German system set a new high standard."[2]

Development of magnetic coatings on paper and other bases had been begun in Germany around 1928.[3] The Germans discovered a way of finely grinding magnetic metallic particles into powder and then bonding them onto paper tape. Thus a thin, flexible, continuously running permanent magnet was produced, one that could be magnetized differently all along its length.[4] The magnetic tape in use today consists of this finely ground ferromagnetic powder° plus a lubricant and a liquid binder coated on a ribbon of plastic (tape) or celluloid (film). The more finely ground these particles are, the higher the frequency response (range of recordable frequencies) of the tape or film.

The continuously running magnet has a high retentivity, defined as the ability to retain the magnetism induced in it. The signal to be recorded is passed through a soft magnet of low retentivity (able to gain and lose magnetism easily), a magnet coil wound on an iron core. When the tape is drawn past the poles of the soft magnet (the recording head), the varying currents are recorded as varying degrees of magnetism, forming a "picture in magnetism," an audio wave pattern in tiny magnets—the powdered metallic particles. To then reproduce this "picture" from the tape, the tape is drawn past the poles of a similar magnet (a pick-up, or reproducing, head); these magnetic impulses generate a varying voltage in the coil. This voltage is then amplified and passed into a speaker or recorder, from which emanate the audible sound waves.[5] [6]

Present machines in professional use stem from the German devel-

°The magnetic iron oxide may be either black (Fe_3O_4) or brown (Fe_2O_3) commonly called "red." The black oxide is chemically produced while the red oxide is in turn produced by heat-treating the black. While the frequency response of the black oxide is slightly better, it is a good deal harder to erase than the red. Hence it is little-used professionally.

opments in magnetic recording rather than from our own earlier work with wire. Years of developmental research have brought the American machines and recording material up to their present high standards; Minnesota Mining and Manufacturing Co. was among the first in this country to produce tape of acceptable quality and their magnetic tape and film continues to be widely used. Today polyester or acetate backing has replaced the stretched vinyl used by the Germans in the nineteen-forties and oxide is available in a variety of types (e.g. low noise oxide, high output oxide, low print-through oxide).

As you know, we use a variety of forms of magnetic tape and film (Fig. 11.2). When the oxide is bonded to a plastic ribbon without sprockets, we may have *eighth-inch* (used in the increasingly popular cassette tape recorders), *quarter-inch* (the more familiar form of magnetic tape), or *half-inch* tape (utilized in some recording studios for multiple-track recording). This tape is available on either a *polyester* or an *acetate* backing and in varying thicknesses (.50 mil and .65 mil are standard thin backings, 1.0 or 1.5 are standard thick backings). In general, the cellulose acetate backing is preferred in recording and editing work because the tape, if subject to sudden tension, will break without stretching. A break can be spliced without any detectible noise or distortion of the usable sound, but a stretch in the tape can result in uncorrectable distortion. The acetate backing tape is also more economical, so is to be preferred in work in which there is considerable waste in the editing procedure. Once the editing is completed, the sound may be transferred to polyester-backed tape for permanent storage. Its greater strength on thin backings,° long lasting qualities, and superior ability to resist drying out and/or absorbing moisture recommend it for this purpose.

MAGNETIC TAPE AND FILM STOCK

Bonded to a sprocketed cellulose acetate base film, there is *16mm magnetic film* (both single- and double-perforated), *17.5mm magnetic film,* (available single-perforated only), and *35mm magnetic film* (available double-perforated only). Thirty-five millimeter is available in *full coat, clear edge,* and *stripe coated* (stripe), which has a 300 mil recording track and a 100 mil balance stripe on the opposite edge. (The balance stripe is for purposes of even winding in rolls.) Full coat can be used for multiple-track recordings (usually three tracks in film sound work), either in the same or in opposite directions. Thus a one-thousand foot roll of 35mm full coat can store three thousand feet of sound material. Clear edge is a form of full coat, with the additional advantage of increased visibility of edgenumbers. Stripe can only record one soundtrack but it has the advantage of being less expensive, offers the possibility of marking the clear center area, and ease in viewing through the base when two films are handled together for editing. Sound film is available in standard, high output, and low noise oxide from Minnesota Mining and Manufacturing Co. (Scotch Magnetic Film), which also manufactures splicing tape and unsprocketed magnetic tapes. Reeves Soundcraft and Audio Devices are other major suppliers of magnetic sound film.

°Thin base tape is generally not used in professional sound work, due to its comparative fragility and because of its greater susceptibility to *print through* (page 445).

Prior to the availability of magnetic tape, all film sound was recorded photographically, a subject to be treated next. There are enormous advantages in using magnetic tape and film in our sound work up to the final composite print of the film, which uses, of course, an optical sound track.°

The frequency response of magnetic tape and film is almost unlimited, going far beyond the audible spectrum. Tape in present use can record from twenty cycles per second (abbreviated "cps" or, more recently, "Hz") up to twenty-two kilocycles (thousand cycles) per second. The audible spectrum is theoretically twenty cycles to twenty kilocycles, although the average human ear, dependent upon age and sex, can actually only distinguish from twenty cycles to perhaps fifteen kilocycles. Video tape in use today must record from zero to 4½ megacycles to reproduce pictures of broadcast quality for television. When we realize that 4½ megacycles is 4.5 *million* cycles, the potential of magnetic tape becomes apparent. The intensity range of magnetic tape is also considerably greater.°°

The signal to noise ratio of magnetic tape and film is also superior to that of optical sound, the magnetic tape/film volume range being approximately 64 to 72 db, the optical volume range some 40–50 db. In practice this means that we are far better able to keep unwanted ground noise below audibility while monitoring the useful sound on the magnetic tape.

Magnetic tape and film is easily erasable, and thus can be used over again, enabling us to correct errors or even to erase the entire tape when we are through with the sound recorded on it, to use it for an entirely new purpose.

With magnetic tape and film we have the advantage of immediate playback, enabling us to monitor our recording as soon as we have completed it. With direct photographic recording it was necessary to send the tracks out to a lab to be developed before playback; thus sound could not be properly judged until at least a day after it had been recorded. There were occasional surprises in the days of all-optical film sound when the tracks were played back the next day! Now if a take is poor, the recordist knows immediately and can retake the sound while the orchestra, singers, or actors are still on the spot.

The compactness and portability of magnetic recording equipment, particularly the equipment most recently developed, is an important advantage also, as is the fact that work with magnetic tape can be performed in daylight. The stock is also comparatively cheaper and takes less storage space.

Initially, technicians familiar with the photographic track were disturbed by the prospect of editing the invisible magnetogram of the magnetic track, having grown dependent upon the visible modulations of the *variable-area optical soundtrack*. The sound editor today, however, is completely at home with the editing of magnetic sound, which can be performed much more quickly with tape splices than could the editing of photographic soundtracks using a cement splicer. He finds no diffi-

---

*There are also some composite prints using magnetic sound tracks. One example is the tracks imprinted on 8mm and 16mm film, enabling the home movie enthusiast to record his own soundtracks directly on his film with certain projectors containing recording heads as a part of the system. Another example is the multiple-channel magnetic striping printed on several of the wide-screen film forms, (Fig. 8.4). For example, Cinemascope release prints may contain four magnetic sound tracks, as do those of Technirama and Panavision. Todd-AO, Super Panavision 70, Cinemascope 55, and M.G.M. 65 release prints may contain six magnetic soundtracks (two outside the sprocket holes on either side, one inside the sprocket holes on either side). Two forms, Cinerama and Ultra Panavision 70, may carry their sound on a separate 35mm magnetic film containing seven soundtracks. Such forms allow multi-channel stereo to be played through localized speakers in the movie theater. Magnetic sound on a composite print is superior to optical sound. There are, however, major reasons why magnetic sound has not completely replaced optical sound on release prints: the vulnerability of magnetic sound to inadvertent erasure and the susceptibility of the magnetic particles to flaking from the base to which they are bonded.

**In contrast, optical tracks have a limited frequency response and volume range. Motion picture photographic soundtracks can record as low as fifty cps and as high as ten kps, losing approximately one half octave at both the top and bottom of the audible spectrum. This is a practical, not a theoretical range, and, in voice recording, could be termed high-fidelity.

culty in locating the invisible modulations with a sound reader or Moviola. An experienced tape editor can edit quarter-inch tape to the degree of being able to remove and replace individual notes within the recording of an orchestra, and a sound editor can perform editing miracles with 35mm sound film.

One of the few inherent drawbacks in the use of magnetic sound tape is its susceptibility to *print through*. This is the tendency for the magnetization of one portion of the tape to be partially transferred to that portion which lies next to it when the material is wound on a reel, a problem first noted in sound recording with wire (page 442). The level is invariably quite low, although it can become audible, particularly when there is no other disguising sound on the track. The higher the recording level, the more likely for print-through to occur, so peak distortion during recording should be kept to 2 percent. Keeping the storage temperature of the material below 75° F. is of major importance in preventing print-through (never leave recorded tape in a glove compartment of a closed car left in the sun) and the relative humidity in a tape storage area should be kept between 40 to 60 percent. The use of low print-through tape, which has a thick base and a more resistant oxide formula, is advised. Since "post-echo" is usually masked by the useful recorded signal it is less troublesome than "pre-echo"; for this reason, tapes should be left "tails out" after recording (most print-through occurs within a short time of the recording). A weak magnetic field applied to the recorded tape will contribute to print-through, so tapes must be shielded from such an occurrence. Print-through is an unbiased recording.

QUARTER-INCH TAPE SPEEDS

As you may know, there is a range of speeds (expressed in inches-per-second) available for quarter-inch tape. These range from 1¾ (the speed of cassette tape), through 3¾, 7½, 15, and 30 i.p.s. The faster the speed the higher the frequency response of the tape. Also, it is far easier to edit tape recorded at a faster speed, as the individual sounds are more spread out, enabling us to cut between them (one of the reasons that we use 35mm mag in preference to 16mm mag in music editing). Thirty i.p.s. has been used infrequently; it presents difficulties in maintaining head contact. Fifteen i.p.s. is the usual speed for professional film sound recording. Naturally, the faster the speed, the more tape is needed to record a given amount of music (twice as much tape at 15 i.p.s. as at 7½ i.p.s., while 30 i.p.s. requires four times the amount needed at 7½ i.p.s.). Therefore we always use the slowest possible speed that will give us professional quality, as a matter of economy. We consider 15 i.p.s. the slowest possible speed for music and voice recording of professional caliber, while 7½ i.p.s. will suffice for sound effects recording.°

CHOICE OF MAGNETIC STOCK

The end product of the mix will usually be an optical sound negative in the appropriate gauge—16mm or 35mm—required for your film. However, the immediate results of the mix will be recorded on magnetic stock and

*The new Nagra IV tape recorder performs professional quality at 7½ i.p.s., even for voice and music work.

only later transferred to optical. In addition to the basic master recording of the mix, you should consider obtaining a *protection tape* copy and a *music-and-effects track*, commonly called an *m&e*. Sometimes the protection tape will be made simultaneously with the full mix, at other times it will be transferred afterward from the master recording. The m&e may be made simultaneously with the full mix (a minus-dialogue m&e), or it may be made during a separate run-through, either before or after the full track mix. You have several options as to the magnetic stock to use for each of these results of the mix. The question of which tape to use will be decided by its suitability to your purpose and its cost, for all of the stock available can reproduce sound more than adequately.

THIRTY-FIVE MILLIMETER MAGNETIC SOUND FILM: STRIPE AND FULL COAT

Since 35mm film is sprocketed, it is often used to make the master recording of the mix, for it will run in perfect sync throughout. Should the back-up system with pick-up recording be utilized, a sprocketed tape *must* be used, for there is no way in which quarter-inch tape can be backed up in sync with other tracks and picture. If full coat is used, a three-track recording can be made simultaneously on the same tape; with stripe, only one track can be recorded. Scotch Magnetic Films' Full Coat No. 315 is perhaps the most thoroughly trustworthy 35mm stock.

SIXTEEN MILLIMETER MAGNETIC SOUND FILM

Although a sprocketed medium, 16mm mag is not generally used for master recording purposes at the mix, even if the original component tracks and/or the picture itself are 16mm.

HALF-INCH MAGNETIC SOUND TAPE

While similar to quarter-inch tape in that it is unsprocketed and therefore cannot be backed up in sync, the extra width of half-inch tape makes it suitable for multiple-track recording. It is presently used more in the area of music recording—contemporary "pop" music utilizes extraordinary numbers of multiple tracks. Its multiple-track potential makes it a less-expensive substitute for full base 35mm mag in certain situations where you do not require sync back-up.

QUARTER-INCH MAGNETIC SOUND TAPE

So long as a sync signal (see Chapter 5) is used with quarter-inch tape, it can be run in perfect sync with the picture and component sound tracks and used to record the results of any mix made in one continuous run-through. Any subsequent transfer, to another quarter-inch tape or to a sprocketed medium, can also be accomplished in perfect sync so long as a sync tone system is used. The only disadvantage to quarter-inch are the ones we have stated: its unsuitability for use with the back-up system and for running on a Moviola. On the other hand, quarter-inch tape is considerably cheaper than any 35mm mag film, easy to edit, less susceptible to inherent flaws, and takes up a good deal less room for storage.

THE MASTER RECORDING OF THE MIX

Although you will wish to use 35mm stock for your master recording, you need not necessarily purchase the tape, preferring to take with you a quarter-inch copy—which is considerably cheaper—as well as the inevitable optical sound negative. Simply inform the mixer that you do not wish to purchase the 35mm stock; usually the studio will store the copy for a period of time, notifying you at the end of this time that they intend to erase it (to use again) and that you have the option at that time of buying it if you wish. There probably will be no need for this.

THE PROTECTION TAPE

Quarter-inch tape with a sync signal is entirely suitable for a protection tape of the mix. If at all possible, it should be recorded simultaneously with the mix, to save cost and to avoid another sound generation. However, if the back-up system has been used for the actual recording as well as for rehearsal, then the quarter-inch tape will have to be transferred after the mix. Considering the small cost of a protection tape, you should always purchase one, even if the 35mm master is bought. Should anything happen to the master, you are covered.

THE M&E

The quarter-inch tape with a sync signal is also perfectly suitable for a music-and-effects track. This is precisely what its name says, a recording of the music and effects without the voice tracks. It is used to make foreign versions of the film and also to enable you to make a new version of the film with changes in the voice track without the necessity of a complete new mix. The m&e track can be made with a separate run-through of the music-and-effects components, or it can be made simultaneously with the recording of the mix. This latter type of m&e is referred to as a *minus-dialogue m&e.* It is made by patching all of the soundtracks into one recording dubber while all of the music-and-effects tracks, but *not* the voice tracks, are patched into a second recorder. Thus the mix and the m&e are recorded simultaneously on different recorders. The advantage to this method is that a separate run-through is not required and the m&e is made without losing a further generation. The disadvantage is that such an m&e will have in it the same dips in level that the mixer makes each time the voice occurs during the mix, even though no voice has been recorded on that track. Since a foreign translation, or a future corrected voice track might not necessarily match exactly the original voice track, these dips in the m&e might not be always appropriate. If you have the time, a separate run-through to make the m&e is advisable.°

It is extremely important to make an m&e, particularly if there is any possible chance that a foreign version might be made in the future. If not, the entire procedure of the mix must be repeated, including all of the sound editing work leading up to the mix, unless all the separate component tracks are stored against this eventuality. It is really well worth the small cost of making an m&e.

There is an alternative which will serve the same purpose as the quarter-inch m&e. Since 35mm full coat has emulsion all the way across, it is possible to record three parallel tracks on the tape. You could use one for music, one for effects, and one for voice; or perhaps one could be a music-and-effects track, one the voice, and one the mix. The cost of full coat would be more than the separate quarter-inch tapes which

*We have been advised that some recording studios (Townsend Production Service in New York City) can and do produce simultaneous minus-dialogue m&e's without dips. If you require this, check to see if the recording studio you contemplate using has the equipment set-up to enable them to do this.

would be used, but the advantages are that the 35mm full coat can be played directly on a Moviola in sync with the picture and that the picture can be mixed directly from it in the future. (If quarter-inch tape is used, it would be necessary to transfer from the quarter-inch protection and/or m&e tapes to a sprocketed medium before either running on a Moviola or mixing.) So if you are fairly certain of needing the tape for either purpose, you should consider using the 35mm full coat.

CORRECTING ERRORS AFTER THE MIX WITH THE M&E

At the time of the mix, when everything seems to have been done to perfection, it is impossible to imagine that any change might later be desired. It is amazing how many times that second-guessing actually does occur. In the making of sponsored films, there is invariably some member of the client's firm who does not see the film until after its completion and then suddenly has changes to recommend. Sometimes a technical error in the narration slips by those who are supposed to check such things and is finally noticed in the answer print. When the composite is screened (and when the sound is heard for the first time as optical sound, on the imperfect system of the projector) the results may not sound as they were expected to. A request may be made to replace portions of the narration; sometimes major script changes may be made, or the narrator replaced. One or more pieces of music or certain effects may have to be replaced. Errors in negative matching can throw effects out of sync. Perhaps the most frequent error occurring is incorrect balance, as a key effect is discovered to be lost or an important phrase in the narration is found to be inaudible.

Frankly, there is no excuse for these things happening, but they do happen, and frequently. It is the first responsibility of the sound editor-mixer team to see that this sort of thing is avoided; it is their second responsibility to see that it be corrected with as little expense and as quickly and efficiently as possible.

To avoid such errors it is essential first that the script be carefully studied and approved in advance by someone competent to do so and that the interlock and/or the mix be attended by this person or someone else with approval authority. In a sponsored film, this means someone representing the client. Should changes be later requested by the client he will most likely offer to pay for them, since his representative approved of the mix. This will mean a new mix, additional editing, a new optical negative and new prints. The film-maker should always offer to make any corrections desired, but it is his right to be paid for them if they are not his fault. If they are his fault, he should make them quickly and without protest—and pay the bill.

If there are errors to correct, either the m&e or separate mixed music and mixed effects tracks recorded on full coat stock will be extremely useful.

If the change involved is a matter of adjustment of balance between the voice and other sound elements, one has only to run the m&e against the voice track in making the new mix. This can probably be done in one run-through, without the practice run-through needed when multiple tracks are run for the first time. If there are changes to be made in the voice track, reediting and possibly re-recording may be required. If the same narrator is to record the changes, the same recording studio should be used; the original voice tape should be brought to the session so that the recordist and narrator can as closely as possible approximate their original work. A "B" voice track can be used for the new portions, so the mixer can set appropriate levels for each portion—"new" and "old." No matter how well this is done, there will be some difference in quality. This will normally be undetectable, provided that there is sufficient space between the new and the old portions. For this reason the narrator should re-do the entire paragraph involved, even if only a word or a sentence is to be changed, so that the newly-recorded paragraph will be spaced apart from the old material. Particularly if there is background music, the change should be unnoticeable. Obviously a new narrator means a new recording and editing of the track; this can then be run with the original m&e at the new mix.

If the problem is improper balance between the effects and the music, separate tracks of each must usually be used. However, the mixer might advise you that he can bring up the level of one particular effect by using the m&e and running a separate track with the effect on it. At the appropriate moment he opens the new track and adds the extra level of the effect to the original re-recording.

If you wish to substitute a new piece of music or a new effect, it will normally be necessary to return to your original components and re-mix from scratch. (If you are substituting a single piece of music it is possible to run the new piece separately and to cross from the m&e to the new music track and back to the m&e at the appropriate points, but this becomes quite complex if there are effects in the original recording during the replaced piece; if you contemplate this, check with an experienced mixer or sound editor to see if he thinks it is feasible.) If the original tracks are in your hands—the mix studio will deliver them to whomever you stipulate—hang on to them; if the sound editing service has them, be certain that they (and the cue sheets!) are kept intact until the answer print has been approved and accepted. This is not in any way a complete list of the possible errors that may occur. Our purpose is merely to acquaint the film-maker with the fact that errors can happen and that making an m&e (or separate mixed music and mixed effects tracks) and keeping the original components on hand are an important insurance for the future.

THE OPTICAL SOUND NEGATIVE

The ultimate need is for some means of placing our sound on the composite print of the film. Just as the picture is printed from a negative, the soundtrack portion of the composite print is printed from an optical sound negative. Immediately after the mix, at your request, the studio will transfer and develop the appropriate gauge optical sound negative. As we have stated, your entire sound job is now in the hands of the transfer man, and a poor job will negate all of your effort. It is vital that he monitor your transfer as he performs it, giving it his undivided attention, particularly in preparing a 16mm optical negative.

If the film is 35mm, you will require a 35mm optical sound negative. Whatever the original stock of the picture, whether black-and-white or color and whether it is to be printed from the original negative, a dupe negative (black-and-white) or an interpositive (color), the same 35mm sound negative will do the job. If you plan a 16mm reduction version of the 35mm film, or if your film is 16mm originally, you will require a 16mm optical sound negative. There are two types: "A"-wind and "B"-wind. It is the nature of 16mm film that it requires a different wind for prints from original and from internegative. This means that if you are planning to strike one answer print from your original, then to go to internegative and strike all subsequent release prints from this, you will need both "A"- and "B"-wind optical sound negatives.

There is one way in which you might avoid this double expense, which might be important in a long film. You can order the "A"-wind only, printing your answer print from this in a reversed position, which makes it operate as a "B"-wind. Since you will be printing through the celluloid base of the negative the sound will be less than perfect, but it will be more than adequate for purposes of checking sync and general sound quality—and this is what the answer print is for. Then you may use the "A"-wind normally for the subsequent prints from internegative, etc.°

OPTICAL (PHOTOGRAPHIC) RECORDING

As Spottiswoode points out, the principle of optical sound is basically an adaptation of picture recording methods to the soundtrack. From the earliest days of the cinema attempts had been made to match sound on recording discs to a projected picture; exact sync was, however, difficult to obtain, as any variations in speed between the record player and projector, or an accidental jarring of the record, would throw the sound and picture out of sync. (The short playing time of records was also a disadvantage, and the sound was of inferior quality.) Obviously the ideal system would require printing the soundtrack alongside the images on the same piece of film, thus automatically maintaining exact sync throughout the entire length of the picture. But how to do this?

The principle on which picture projection works involves the use of areas of varying density (degrees of opaqueness). The projector lamp throws a bright beam of light through an image containing areas of varying density, the amount of light penetrating the film depending upon the degree of density in that area. (If the particular area of the image is opaque, a shadow is thrown upon the screen; if the area is transparent, a bright area appears on the screen.) We may say that the film's areas of varying density modulate the beam of the projector lamp to produce an image on the screen. This is precisely the principle on which the photographic sound system is based.

An exciter lamp throws a narrow beam of light into the cathode of

*The above would seem to imply that "A"-wind is used with prints from internegative and "B"-wind used for prints from reversal original. While this is generally true, there are a number of complicating factors involved in this complex subject. We advise the reader to check with his chosen lab as to their (and his) requirements in order to be able to inform the sound studio as to the type of wind desired and the print stock required, including the manufacturer and type number. The optical negative should be developed at the lab specified by the re-recordist (they are transferred at the sound studio but usually developed elsewhere).

a photocell, setting up an electric current in the tube in proportion to the intensity of the light. A picture of sound waves printed on film is interspersed between the lamp and photocell and the varying image of the sound modulates the light beam, thus setting up a correspondingly varying electric current in the photocell. The output of this photocell is then magnified by means of an audio amplifier to operate a loudspeaker.

If we think of the sound images on the film as a series of obstacles to the exciter lamp beam, the faster that these obstacles pass by the light beam, interrupting its path to the photocell, the higher will be the frequency (pitch) of the sound created in the audio amplifier by the electric current in the cell. If fifty obstacles pass by in one second, a 50-cycle tone is created; if five hundred, a 500-cycle tone. It would be possible to vary the speed at which the obstacles interrupt the light beam by varying the speed at which the film on which the images are printed moved, or by varying the distance between the images themselves. It is this latter method which photographic film sound uses, for the film must move past the lamp at a precise and constant speed.* The introduction of optical sound necessitated a change from the varying projection speeds in use with silent films (sixteen fps was the average speed at which the film was shot). A speed of twenty-four fps was chosen for the Western Electric sound-on-film system. It was Western Electric which provided both the Fox-Movietone and the Warner Brothers Vitaphone systems. The Movietone system was sound-on-film; the Vitaphone system offered both sound-on-disc (used in Warner Brothers' *Don Juan* in 1926 and their *The Jazz Singer* in 1927) and sound-on-film, the method which triumphed within a few years.

Before the introduction of magnetic sound recording there were two basic methods of photographic sound recording in general use: the *variable density* system, associated with Western Electric, and the *variable area* system, associated with RCA. Each system offers a different method for modulating the light beam from the exciter lamp as it passes through the film on its way to the photocell. In the variable density system, the soundtrack printed along one edge of the film consists of a series of parallel lines at a right angle to the path of the film. These lines, of uniform width, vary in thickness and hence present to the light an image ranging from pure black to perfect transparency, with every shade of grey between. Variable density tracks are produced by using a light valve, (see Fig. 8.4).

Variable area tracks, also printed along the edge of the film, resemble the cross-section of a jagged mountain range, an actual picture of the wave shapes of the electric currents and hence of the sound. The amount of light let through this system is dependent upon the varying silhouette of the waves, which is completely transparent on a field of black. Variable area tracks are produced with a reflecting galvanometer, (see Fig. 8.4).[7][8]

Although both systems were in general use, there would appear to have been a number of advantages to the variable area system. The variable density system requires more exacting laboratory standards and

*You will recall that the optical track is advanced ahead of the picture to avoid the intermittent action of the film gate at the moment of sound pick-up.

hence its sound quality suffers more from inferior lab work. The variable area system is easily convertible to different types of track: standard bilateral, push-pull Class A, push-pull Class B, and Class B direct positive types are used for varying purposes, principally the reduction of distortion and elimination of ground noise from the track. The variable area system is also less susceptible to ground noise resulting from the graininess of the film.

Visual inspection of the variable areas silhouette is easier (it was consequently easier to edit in pre-magnetic sound days) and it is much easier to monitor the results of the galvanometer than those of the light valve during recording.[9] At any rate, although some labs are still able to process variable density negatives (Deluxe in New York, for example), all photographic film sound on composite prints today is variable area.

The interested reader is referred to three excellent, detailed works on photographic film sound: Edward W. Kellogg's "The ABC of Photographic Sound Recording" and "History of Sound Motion Pictures," both available from the Society of Motion Picture and Television Engineers, and Chapter Ten of Raymond Spottiswoode's *Film and Its Techniques,* University of California Press. All three works are somewhat out of date—they date from 1945, 1955, and 1959, respectively—but they offer a fascinating picture of this important aspect of film-making.

THE PURPOSE OF THE MIX

We have described the process of the mix as a balancing of sound against sound, and of sound against visual image. This would imply that the sound passes through this process unaltered, but this would ignore a vitally important aspect of the mix. We must strive to make our sound—voice, music, sound effects—more meaningfully intelligible, more communicable to the spectator.

Basically, we are attempting to keep our sound free from noise or distortion which might make it distracting, unrecognizable, inaudible, or inexact. However, since the end product of our work, the optical soundtrack, has less range than does the human ear, we are concerned not with the exact duplication of actual sound, but with an aesthetically valid resemblance, a reproduction of sound which will satisfy the spectator's desire for "reality" while maintaining professional standards of clarity and intelligibility. Essentially this is the job of the re-recordist; he is well-trained for it, and he has the equipment with which to accomplish it. But we, as editors and directors, can affect this work.

The process of the mix resembles the proverbial iceberg; a certain portion of the mix is always "above the surface," evident to all as it is performed. Yet a great deal can remain hidden and quite mysterious to all but the mixer himself. The processes need not be understood in all their technical complexity for us to perform our work as editors and directors; yet, by knowing for what the mixer is striving, and the means at his disposal for achieving this, we are in a position to strongly influence the results of the mix. The editor must not expect the re-recordist to initiate all steps toward this end, for the editor too has a responsibility in this area.

We shall now proceed to define the aspects of noise and distortion we must eliminate and to acquaint the film-maker with the basic tools available to the mixer to accomplish this. We shall first cover the area of *noise elimination.* Of first importance is the initial recording and transfer of the sound, the proper performance of which will enable us to avoid noise on the tracks; we must then consider the means available at the mix to eliminate such noise if it is present.

Our second area of concern is that of *distortion.* Again, we are initially concerned with the avoidance of distortion in recording and transfer. But distortion can also result from the process of the mix itself, sometimes purposefully. Therefore, we must learn to utilize *purposeful distortion* and to avoid inadvertent distortion which can affect the clarity and intelligibility of the sound.

Purposeful distortion can take two forms. We may distort sound to change its character (a voice can be filtered to give it the characteristic of a voice heard over a telephone, a loudspeaker, or a radio) or to make it more readily communicable (we will emphasize the portion of the voice that is carried within the range of the optical sound track, deemphasizing the portion normally outside the track's range). To begin, let us discuss the properties of sound which are meaningful in our film sound work.

THE PROPERTIES OF SOUND

Sound is a basic and indefinable psychic sensation, aroused by vibrations of a certain character, received through the ear and the bones surrounding the ear, which are transmitted to the hearer through liquids, solids, and gases. Sound is also defined as the wave motion which gives rise to the sensation of sound, and which originates in the periodic vibration of waves, strings, vocal chords, reeds, diaphragms, moving columns of air, etc., as well as in the aperiodic vibration of many other structures.[10]

Sound has four characteristics with which we shall deal in the recording studio: frequency, intensity, phase, and power. *Frequency,* or *pitch,* is measured by the rate of vibrations (a complete vibration is called a *cycle*) and is expressed in the number of complete vibrations per second. The larger the number of vibrations per second, the higher the pitch. When the sound wave motion in air has a frequency which lies between 20 and 20,000 cycles per second, theoretically it produces a sensation of sound in the human ear and is referred to as occurring in the *audible spectrum.* Actually, the exact limits of the audible spectrum depend upon the individual's age and sex; in today's world the ear is so bombarded with sound that the average ear limits itself protectively to a practical upper limit somewhere between 12,000 and 20,000 cycles. Sounds above the audible spectrum are called supersonic (dogs can hear sounds up to 40,000 cycles, hence the dog-whistle inaudible to human beings, and bats can hear sounds up to 75,000 cycles); those below the audible spectrum are called subsonic.

While magnetic tape and film can easily record the full range of the audible spectrum, optical film sound is comparatively limited, ranging from 50 or 60 to 10,000 cycles in 35mm optical, and from 80 to 8000 or more cycles in 16mm optical (some say only 5,000 cycles!). The implication of this is obvious: There will be many sounds at each end of the audible range which, while capable of being recorded on magnetic tape, cannot be reproduced on the film's optical track. Therefore concern with these sounds will be useless to the final film. We will devote particular attention to the area of emphasis, of from 1,500 to 3,000 cycles, to strive to communicate best the sounds within these frequencies. The electrical filters described as part of the equipment of the mixing console will be set so as to limit the unwanted frequencies outside the limits of the audible spectrum.

Intensity is defined as the measure of the displacement of sound waves about a mean position, and has to do with volume. By placing your hand close by the cone of a loudspeaker, you can actually feel the motion, or *amplitude* (discernible volume), which will be transmitted in turn to the molecules of air. These molecules oscillate around a middle position, passing on the sound wave much as the shock wave is passed along the hanging steel balls in the currently popular desk toy. (When the ball at one end is swung against the other four balls hanging motionless, only the ball at the far end swings out, the shock having been passed imperceptibly through the others.) The greater the intensity of the sound, the larger the amplitude and the more violently the air is displaced. The train of sound waves will consist of an alternate series of compressions and expansions (condensations and rarefactions) radiating out from the source in a sphere of concentric shells.[11] We shall be vitally concerned with intensity in our film sound work. Recording at too little amplitude will result during playback and transfer in an increase in the audibility of the inherent ground noise on the tape or film; recording—or re-recording—at too great an amplitude will result in distortion and "a volume compression effect which removes the accent, the artistic touch."[12]

The third characteristic of sound with which we are concerned is *phase*. Let us say that a succession of sound waves, consisting of this series of alternating condensations and rarefactions, is directed toward a solid surface. Much of the sound will be reflected back toward the source. These waves will then pass through each other traveling in opposite directions. There will be areas, called *nodes,* in which an outgoing condensation will coincide with an incoming rarefaction. Since the same air molecules cannot at the same time be condensed and rarefied (compressed and expanded) they will, in fact, remain stationary and there will be no audible sound at this point. When two sound waves cancel each other out in this manner they are said to be 180 degrees out of phase. When their respective condensations and rarefactions coincide, so that the energy of the two waves is additive, they are said to be in phase. Phase is not normally a concern in re-recording; it is a factor in recording, where microphones are spoken of as being "in phase."

The fourth variable quality of sound we refer to as *power*. We can increase the power content of a sound without increasing amplitude, or discernible volume. This is done, as we shall see shortly, by means of compression, a technique of increasing the frequency response in the vicinity of 2,000 cycles to more than that of those frequencies outside of the intelligibility range. All of the frequencies remain the same, but their amplitude relationship is changed in favor of the frequencies which will be useful to us. By increasing the power of a sound it is made more penetrating in competition with other sounds—without, however, raising the volume. This is of particular importance in dealing with the film's voice tracks.

Most sound is made up of a complex mass of waves superimposed on one another. The basic sound wave is surrounded by a mass of harmonics, other waves which enrich, color and lend special quality to it. If we reproduce sound through inadequate equipment (and we are all familiar with the extreme of this, the tiny transistor radio) many of these complex waves will be distorted and even entirely eliminated, reducing what might have been a marvelous complexity of sound to an unintelligible mess. It is the marvel of sound reproduction that the complexity of a symphony orchestra, a massed chorus, the "Battle of Borodino," or the precise and delicate twitter of a bird can all be rendered first as a magnetographic picture on sound tape, then as an optical picture on the film itself, and finally reconstituted in the motion picture theater in a satisfactory rendering of this original sound.

NOISE ELIMINATION

You will recall from our discussion of the mixing console (page 439) that the recordist is concerned with avoiding a recording made at too low a level. There is intrinsic noise—called *ground noise*—present on both magnetic and optical sound tracks. This noise can be caused by dirt, scratches, and imperfections in the track. It can also result from electronic hum from faulty equipment or unwanted magnetic pick-up in the microphone during initial recording. This noise is usually undetectable; however, when the track is *unmodulated*—no useful sound present—the noise can become audible. One of the major advantages in using magnetic tape and film is its high signal to noise ratio of approximately 64 to 72 db. Since there is a large gap between the level of useful sound and the level of the ground noise, our job of keeping this noise inaudible is made that much easier.

However, should we record initially at too low a level, it will become necessary to increase the gain during playback, a practice which results in the ground noise becoming audible. If on the other hand the recording is made at too high a level we run the risk of distorting the sound. The ability to strike exactly the right balance between these extremes can be acquired only with experience, but we can offer some beginning guidelines.

SOME SOUND RECORDING GUIDELINES

Recording machines such as the Nagra contain a volume indicator, a rapid-acting combination of the V-U meter and the peak-indicating device discussed earlier (page 439). We have mentioned, in connection with print-through, a figure of two percent distortion which is the commonly accepted figure for professional recording (home recording allows three percent). If the recordist monitors his volume indicator carefully, he can limit peaks of sound in the three percent distortion area to rare occurrences, and peaks in the one and two percent area to a comparatively few times. In general, it is necessary to record within a twelve to twenty-one db margin over zero level to get a two percent distortion figure. Recording ten db under normal level should cause no noise problems during playback. Even twenty db under occasionally is satisfactory if these sounds are ones which can be left at this level during playback; obviously the ground noise problem occurs only when it is necessary to push the tracks in playback. If these sounds are not necessary for making the track intelligible they may be left at their low level. If sound is recorded at thirty db under normal, there will invariably be major noise problems in playback.

As a general rule, the recordist should avoid "riding the pot" during recording. He should use a rehearsal—no matter how inconvenient this may be to the performers and other technicians, the recordist should insist on it—to set his overall level on the basis of the loudest sound to be recorded, keeping this within the permissible distortion area. (Of course, if the take requires the recording of both a whisper and a scream, he can not avoid adjusting the gain during the recording; in the majority of recordings, the subject can maintain a uniform voice level.) If at all possible when recording effects, the recordist might make three takes: one at his selected level, one slightly above, and one slightly below, much as a photographer uses exposures above and below his estimated correct one to bracket the target; however, in voice recording, if a selected level appears to work, the recordist should stick to it while in that location. Monitoring the take with earphones is advised and we suggest that on-the-spot playbacks be made in a location different from that of the actual recording. If the site has contributed any reverberation or room acoustics to the recording it will be impossible to detect this if the playback is made in the identical area.

Selecting the right recorder, microphone, and stock is important. The Nagra cannot be praised too highly, particularly for location sound, and the Ampex products are also first-rate. For any motion picture recording other than music in the studio, Scotch brand 111 or 131 (low print-through) quarter-inch tape or the equivalent are excellent. As an all-purpose microphone, suitable in more varied locations than any other, cardoid mikes are to be preferred to omni-directional or highly directional types. RCA, Shure, and Electro-voice all make mikes specifically intended for film and TV boom use.

Should we find it necessary to mix with tracks which have been improperly recorded initially, there are some steps which can be taken at the mix to reduce noise. One technique is to use the electrical filters which are a part of the console's equipment to eliminate certain unwanted frequencies of sound, thus cutting off the noise if it lies within these frequencies. This can be done only if such elimination does not interfere with the quality of the useful sound on the track, dependent upon the noise to be eliminated lying at the extremes of the useful spectrum, outside the range of film optical sound. The high-pass filter is used to cut out frequencies beneath its level, the low-pass above it. For example, if there is a hum on the track at 120 cycles, by setting a high-pass filter we can cut off all frequencies below this point and entirely eliminate the unwanted sound. A low-pass filter is used at a mix similarly to eliminate disc or optical noise from tracks. However, it should be noted that *all* frequencies beyond the cut-off point are eliminated, and there is a point at which the loss of frequencies within the intelligibility range would begin to affect the quality of the sound. If the unwanted noise is in the middle of the intelligibility range we dare not eliminate these frequencies. We must repeat that there is really only one way to avoid this problem and that is to see that the original reproduction and/or recording of the sound is performed without errors. Unfortunately, in practice, a mix seldom takes place without the re-recordist's being obliged to put into play some facet of his ability to correct deficiencies in the soundtracks. Let us examine briefly the various electrical filters available to the mixer.

ELECTRICAL FILTERS

A *high-pass filter* has a transmission band extending from its cutoff frequency up to infinite frequency. A 100-cycle high-pass filter would pass all frequencies above 100 cycles. A *low-pass filter* has a transmission band extending from zero frequency up to its cutoff frequency. A 6,000 cycle low-pass filter would pass all frequencies below 6,000 cycles. A *band-pass filter* has a transmission band between two cutoff frequencies (neither of which is zero or infinite), attenuating frequencies both above and below its band. A *band-elimination filter* has an attenuation band between two cutoff frequencies (neither of which is zero or infinite), attenuating all frequencies within this band. A *sharply tuned filter* has a narrow transmission or attenuation band with a sharp cutoff on either side. A *broadly tuned filter* has a wide transmission or attenuation band with a gradual cutoff on either side. Both the sharply tuned filter and the broadly tuned filter have a single peak, representing an area of maximum transmission or attenuation. The accompanying illustration (Fig. 12.4) will aid in understanding these filters.[13]

We can also use a device called a *dynamic noise suppressor* which can be set up in the appropriate channel of the mixing console. This device automatically shuts off the track where there are no modulations, opening it up again where modulations occur. Background music can also serve the purpose of masking ground noise, which is invariably noticed when it occurs in spaces void of all other sound. At any rate, the most important thing for the sound editor to remember is that he must take every possible care to see that his tracks have been recorded properly at the start; failing this, a professional re-recordist can do a great deal at the mix to correct these errors, with, of course, an attendant increase of time and cost.

When the product of the mix is to be transferred to an optical sound track a *noise-reduction amplifier* is used to get the maximum signal-to-noise ratio on the optical track. This device works similarly to the dynamic noise suppressor in that it reduces the pick-up of sound in unmodulated areas.

There is one further precaution we can take to ensure that our tracks will come to the mix in proper condition, and that is to avoid unnecessary additional generations. The transfer of sound from one medium to another is referred to as a *generation*, and it is to be expected that sound will go through several generations in the course of normal sound work. However, any defects in the track will be cumulative with each generation. In addition to the previously discussed ground noise there is present in recorded tracks *intermodulation distortion* and both may increase by some 2 percent with each generation. Additionally present is the *violin effect*, the chatter of the tape as it passes over the head during recording. All of these are present from the start, but they begin to intrude only when their effect accumulates over a number of generations.

Let us consider a piece of stock library music used for a music track. Initially recorded in a studio on a master tape, it is transferred to a submaster quarter-inch (second generation) and supplied to a library. We transfer this to 35mm mag (third generation). The fourth generation would be the product of the mix, recorded on magnetic tape, and the fifth, the optical negative. The soundtrack on the composite print would then be at least the sixth generation. Obviously this number of generations is to be expected, but it certainly must be considered in avoiding additional generations. For example, a pre-mix of the music at the mix, or the procedure of mixing to an initially pre-mixed music-and-effects track would add one extra generation. So would the making of a second take of music from our 35mm copy instead of returning to the original quarter-inch, while working in the sound cutting room, so these steps must be carefully weighed against the resulting cumulative effects of noise and distortion on the track.

Fig. 12–4 Electrical filters (A) high-pass filter (B) low-pass filter (C) band-pass filter (D) sharply tuned filter (E) broadly tuned filter

An understanding of the distortion of sound, the means of avoiding it, and the devices at the mixer's call which can help correct it will be needed to complete our understanding of the work of the re-recordist. Sound is subject to distortion of both frequency and amplitude. Let's begin with frequency distortion.

ELIMINATION OF DISTORTION

FREQUENCY DISTORTION   This refers to a condition in which the frequencies in the output of a system emerge with relative amplitudes different from those they possessed in the input to that system. Since the range of optical sound will be 50 or 60 to 10,000 cycles for 35mm optical and 80 to 8,000 for 16mm optical, this limits our consideration to the sound within this area; it is quite important that we do not lose any of these included frequencies. If you have a record player with treble and bass controls, you have some idea of frequency distortion. If you turn the bass control past its normal setting, you hear the low frequencies almost entirely. Voices sound much deeper, the music loses its brilliance, musical instruments are difficult to tell apart. If you reverse the process and turn the treble control too far, the voices are now high, thin, and brittle, the music sounds tinny and lacks body. By overapplying the bass control, we have eliminated the high frequencies; by the same overuse of the treble control we have cut out low frequencies. Proper re-recording will avoid frequency distortion.

However, at times we may choose to deliberately alter frequency response; this is referred to as *recording equalization,* or *frequency modification.* A particular band of frequencies may be emphasized to give a special effect, e.g., a voice supposedly coming over a telephone or loudspeaker, or to compensate for losses of frequency in another part of the sound reproductive system, such as in a 16mm projector. These effects are obtained with the use of the filters and equalizers which are part of the equipment of the mixing console.

EQUALIZERS   *Compression* is a means of making a sound more communicable, without changing frequency or increasing overall amplitude, by changing the amplitude relationship of the sound. The mixer will use his console's re-recording equalizers to increase the frequency response within the intelligibility range. These mid-range equalizers are mounted on the console and are available, as are high-range and low-range equalizers, for each channel and hence each soundtrack. This is a particularly effective device for making the voice track more penetrating in competition with the other soundtracks, a familiar problem in mixing and one that cannot always be overcome simply by playing the voice louder. It is the nature of the human ear's perception of sound that mid-range frequencies respond less dramatically than either high or low frequencies to changes in gain or volume (it is for this reason that hi-fi equipment increases automatically the treble and bass frequencies when the overall volume is decreased). Equalization is a means of increasing the mid-range frequencies between approximately 1,500 and 3,500 cps to restore the naturalness of the voice, thus contributing to its audibility and intelligibility. Thus the volume units are raised without raising the peaks. Basically this is a matter of "accentuate the positive, eliminate the negative"; we dispose of what we don't need to enhance what we do. Compression is a device to increase the power of sound by altering its normal range of amplitude to purposefully produce a form of dynamic distortion.

AMPLITUDE DISTORTION   Amplitude distortion occurs when the shape of the original sound wave is altered in its passage through the electrical system. The wave form of most sound resembles the cross-section of a mountain range with irregular jagged peaks and valleys. Sound can be broken down into fundamental sine waves and their harmonic overtones. The sine wave is the simplest form of sound wave; it is produced by the vibration of a single string or reed. Most musical instruments are meant to produce more complicated vibrations. These accompanying harmonics will all be exact multiples of the frequency of the fundamental sine wave. If the fundamental has a frequency of 300 cps, the second harmonic will be 600, the third 900, and so on.

It is the relative strength of the different harmonics which gives individual voices and musical instruments their special character. Let us say that two musical instruments each have fundamental notes of 440 cps. Each will then have harmonics at 880 cps, 1,760, 3,520 and so on. What will distinguish the two instruments is that one might have richer harmonics at the second harmonic and the other in the third harmonic. If our system cuts off the higher overtones, it will be difficult to distinguish between these instruments. (This is the result we get when we emphasize too heavily the bass control.)

Sometimes the system itself produces frequencies which do not occur in the original signal; these are called distortion products and may be spurious harmonics or intermodulation products, distortions of the shape of the fundamental curve, making it either flat-bottomed or flat-topped. When we record at too great a volume we create this form of amplitude distortion. We say that we have *overloaded;* a harsh, fuzzy, "breaking up" of sound occurs, which is jarring to the ear, like the buzzing sound of piano strings when an object is laid upon them. (The same effect can be readily achieved by tuning the gain too high on a radio or record player.) Most of these harmonic distortions occur in the higher frequencies. The term derives from the fact that the system, supposed to produce a single frequency, instead produces others harmonically related to it. It is such distortion that the recordist strives to avoid by keeping his recording level sufficiently low.

Another form of distortion resulting from the production of spurious harmonics is *intermodulation distortion.* This results when tones of different frequencies are fed into an overloaded system, modulating each other and creating sum-and-difference tones, frequencies corresponding to the sums and differences of the input frequencies. If these frequencies are not harmoniously related to the desired frequencies an unpleasant, harsh dissonance results. Intermodulation distortion affects complex sounds but usually not the sounds of single instruments.[14]

Bias current can also have a distortion effect in magnetic recording, insufficient bias current invariably resulting in severe distortion. It is necessary to have the bias frequency at least five times the frequency of the highest tone to be reproduced, and so a bias frequency of between 80 and 100 kc is used. Plastic base tape is less susceptible to this form of distortion, one reason for its universal use.

In interesting contrast to the previously discussed ground noise, noticeable on unmodulated tracks, is *modulation noise* or behind-signal noise, which the ear experiences as distortion and which occurs only when there is a signal present. This noise varies with the signal and is modulated by it, hence its name. It is sometimes audible as a fuzzy edge or hoarse background to a tone. Its precise causes are subject to debate, but it is believed that the use of plastic base tape and the consequent smooth bottom surface to its coating where it comes in contact with the base, together with the use of first-rate recording equipment (the Nagra is excellent, in this respect) will eliminate modulation noise.[15]

We now enter into the vitally important final stages of our sound work, and indeed of our total film. The mix is more than a final retouching of our earlier work; it is the goal of our sound work up to this point and the determinant of its success. Much of the artistic work of film sound is involved with choice—choice of the right sound and of the right place for it, choice of how many sounds are to be heard, of their relationship and the balance between them. The craft and the art of film sound—the work of the cutting room, the recording, and the transfer of sound—are all conditioned by the mix. It is wrong to think of the mix as a magical means of correcting a cumulative string of errors throughout our work. The essence of a mix is balance; a great mix is a delicate balancing of the complex varieties of sound against the flow of visual images, resulting in the rhythmic and purposeful unity that is a film. To properly perform this function the mixer must be allowed the utmost opportunity to concentrate on this task. We have said that we would wish to avoid distracting the juggler in the midst of his balancing. We would also think twice about requiring the pilot of a jet airliner to repair the radar equipment and serve coffee to the passengers while carrying on a scintillating conversation, all during an instrument landing in a heavy snow storm.

In Chapter 11, a good deal of consideration was given to the preparation of the tracks and the cue sheets so that the mix could be performed properly. Now that you have some understanding of the equipment of the mix and the way it functions, let us reconsider briefly the area of pre-mix preparation. You will discover, as we continue, reasons for the practices advanced in the last chapter, and further techniques for the sound cutting room will be suggested at this time in relation to the mix, its personnel, and equipment. To properly study and absorb the work of film sound these chapters must be fully understood as a unit.

The mix is the process of combining a number of separate but si-

THE SOUND MIX—STEPS IN PREPARATION

multaneous soundtracks into one properly balanced track, synchronous with the picture. It involves the mixer's selecting sounds from each of these separate tracks, controlling their volume, and, to some degree, determining where they will begin and where they will end. (In practice, the actual points for beginning and ending the sounds have been determined beforehand by the director and sound editor, so the mixer is primarily concerned with effecting the sound changes smoothly and unobstrusively; occasionally he may vary the entrance or exit point to accomplish this, subject to the sound editor's approval.) With the purpose of the mix in mind we will proceed through the actual procedure, giving careful consideration to the sound editor's job. Of course, in mose cases the director is also present at the mix (it is unthinkable for the sound editor not to be present!), and it is true that he has the final say over all elements of the film; still the sound editor is really the man in control of the mix. He must anticipate what the director wants, and, balancing this against what he knows of the work he has performed previously and of what the mixer can accomplish, guide the mix to a successful conclusion. The sound editor is the only person who can perform this function. Only he can bind together these three elements, for only he of the three men—mixer, editor, director—is intimately involved in each area. The director is usually not to be expected to know fully the practices of the mix, for he attends comparatively few. The mixer is not to be expected to know precisely the director's aims, for he has not been working on this film with him over a period of weeks. And only the editor knows exactly how he has gone about preparing his soundtracks for the mix. The importance of the role of the sound editor at the mix cannot be exaggerated.

We will assume that our suggested preparations for the mix have been followed, including an interlock screening at the re-recording studio, run by the mixer who is actually to perform the mix. Corrections have been made by the editor on the basis of this interlock, based on his own observations, suggestions by the mixer, and requests by the film's director. The film is, therefore, not an unknown quantity to the mixer, and the beginning of an effective working arrangement between these three men has been formed. Everything that the editor can possibly do has been done to free the mixer from technical problems and the correction of errors, thus allowing him to concentrate on the aesthetic considerations of the mix. The realities of film-making determine that the mix must be the best possible job in the shortest possible time. As we prepare to mix, a careful consideration of the situation before us shows us certain inevitable practices that must be followed and must have been prepared for.

PRE-MIX PROCEDURES

We have observed in the cutting room that multiple tracks are used for the purpose of separating simultaneous sounds in order to properly balance them at the mix. (If, for example, we record an interview with a factory technician while machines are running in the background, we are "locked in" to the particular balance between voice and machine that we record. If, at the mix, we raise the volume of the voice, the machine sound also becomes louder. However, if we initially record the voice alone, with no background noise, and then record the factory noise separately for our effects tracks, we can maintain the voice at a clear and audible level while varying the machine noise as we desire, even eliminating it altogether.) This division of the sound elements into many separate components is a guiding rule of preparation for the mix, affecting both the original recording of the sound elements and their editing and assembly in the cutting room. However, common sense tells us that if each of these tracks is to be controlled on a separate pot by the mixer, we must take precautions to keep his effective control of these many pots within the limits of his physical abilities. The variety of sounds on the many tracks are seldom recorded in such a way that all of the tracks can be played throughout the mix at a constant level; they must be brought up and down repeatedly to set each sound at the desired level. (The one exception is the voice track, which should be capable of being played at a constant level.) Frequently, one track must be faded out and another brought in simultaneously. The object behind our method of laying out the soundtracks, then, is to avoid as much as possible more simultaneous actions that the mixer can perform with two hands, and to give the mixer ample time to pre-set his tracks so that the sounds can enter automatically at the desired level. This means leaving sufficient space between the sounds on the track, noting them accurately (including on which track they are and of what the sound consists) on the cue sheets, and giving the mixer sufficient time to rehearse and make his own notes on the cue sheets.°

The question of leaving the mixer sufficient space between sounds generally applies to the effects tracks, particularly in a case where what appears to be one effect is actually made up of a combination of several sounds occurring within the space of a few seconds. Even if we could jam these sounds into two tracks in alternation, we might leave the mixer a situation in which he would have to juggle the level of the two tracks between each effect. It would be a much more workable situation if enough tracks were used to allow one for each effect. Then the mixer could pre-set each track at the level he wanted during rehearsal, letting them run automatically during the re-recording. He could then re-set the tracks for the next effect when he finds a few moments as the mix continues.

Another help to the mixer is the editor's ensuring that there are no unwanted sounds before or after the useful sounds on the tracks. Most of such noises on music tracks are detectable but it is sometimes difficult to tell extraneous sounds from the sound effects, particularly on a Moviola. Most voice tracks contain throat clearings, paper rustling, and other by-products of the recording session, and these too are almost impossible to detect on a Moviola. The interlock screening is a good place to listen for any such noises which may have been overlooked, carefully noting the footages at which they occur for later removal in the cutting room.

*You will now understand the beauty for rehearsal purposes of the back-up interlock system available at some mix studios. If the mixer has a question about a particular sound, he can stop the system, back up, and run it over as many times as he needs until he has his levels set and the precise point to make his change determined. He then can note this on his sheets and move on to the next difficult cue. There is some question as to whether the back-up system should be used for the final re-recording, the argument against it being that the mixer loses the flow of rhythm and continuity so essential to the mix. Obviously this is a matter of personal taste and temperament, but it should be pointed out that we have personally performed hundreds of mixes using this system for the final re-recording as well as for rehearsal. There should be no argument as to its value as a rehearsal mechanism.

If at all possible, you should try to avoid giving the mixer a fade-in or -out on one track at the same time that he must cross-fade between two other tracks. This is simply a matter of common sense, since the mixer needs one hand for each pot. If two music tracks must be cross-faded, then an effect occurring at that same point should be cut off at exactly the point of entrance or exit. The effects track can then be allowed to run by itself. For particularly complex sound mixes, a second re-recordist is sometimes assigned; often an experienced sound editor may offer to handle one or more pots at a sticky spot.°

There is a practice which can be followed when there are too many sounds for the mixer to handle simultaneously: a *pre-mix* of part of the soundtracks. This means a preliminary partial mix, combining the separate music tracks or effects tracks into one. Then the mixer has only one track to control, which he runs along with the remaining unmixed tracks at the final mix. This pre-mix results in an additional generation, which must be considered in the case of music tracks, but is much less crucial in the case of effects. More important, a pre-mix commits you to the levels set at that time; you can change the balance between the pre-mixed track and the other unmixed tracks but not between the elements combined in the pre-mix. So it's not advisable to pre-mix if you can avoid it, as it takes away one element of control from the final mix.

Sometimes a fade-in or -out can be put into a track when the sound is initially transferred, sparing the mixer the need to do this at the mix. Once again you must consider the advantage gained against the disadvantage of committing yourself long before the final mix to a specific unchangeable fading point. No matter how experienced the sound editor may be, it is just not possible to determine how to handle each individual sound until they are all heard in relationship to each other and to the picture at the time of the mix.

Some sounds must start or end on an exact frame, while others require a gradual fading. The sound of a brook, birds in a forest, or rain, for example, particularly if they occur at a picture dissolve, can properly be left to the mixer to fade in or out.°°

If, however, the sound must begin or end on an exact frame, it is not realistic to expect the mixer to accomplish this. Such situations occur when the picture cuts back and forth between different viewpoints with a continuously running sound. Examples of this would be cuts from exterior to interior of airplanes, cuts from an interior to exterior of a house while a radio is playing, or cuts from close-up to long shot of a running machine. The inexperienced sound editor delights in bringing this sort of sound situation into the mix on one continuously running track, expecting the mixer to magically change the level and character of the sound at the exact frame of picture. Properly, a different sound for each perspective should be recorded and then cut onto separate tracks. The start and ending of each sound should be cut on the exact frame desired for its beginning or end. The mixer can then pre-set each track at different levels and the proper sound change will occur automatically and to-the-frame.°°° If for some reason it is impossible to record a different

*In some studios such offers of assistance may be politely refused, either because of shop rules or the re-recordist's personal way of working.

**At the great majority of mixes, the work print is used; therefore there will be no actual dissolves or fades but merely the editor's grease pencil marks designating them. This makes it rather difficult to sense how these optical effects will work in the completed film, in particular in relation to the sound. For some time we always began music or effects in the center of a dissolve, which, in a work print, seems right. After seeing the picture in completed form, you begin to realize that the picture demands that the sound change sooner than the mid-point, at the moment that the new image begins to register. In a 48-frame dissolve, 8 or 12 frames in is the spot, rather than 24.

***There is an unusually detailed example of this in Stanley Kubrick's film, *2001: A Space Odyssey*. During a scene in which a scientist lectures a group of his colleagues, the camera changes point-of-view a number of times. At each cut, the sound changes in relationship to the camera's distance from the speaker. The effect is quite unusual, and, in fact, draws attention to itself, for we are unaccustomed to this exact matching of sound and picture. The effect is to create a kind of subjective camera, or more accurately, a subjective tape recorder. Normally the guiding rule is to change sound perspective only when to not do so would disturb the audience, a practice followed by Kubrick in the war room sequences in *Dr. Strangelove*.

sound for each change in perspective, we can still gain some sense of change at the mix, providing the sounds are laid-in on separate tracks. A change in level or change of equalization between tracks will produce the desired effect. In the case of alternating scenes in a telephone conversation—where one voice is heard alternately synchronously and asynchronously, someone speaking into a phone then another man listening to him on the phone—we would cut the synchronous portions all on one track, and the asynchronous ones on another. Then by using a filter on the asynchronous track, the quality of the voice would be caused to change at each picture cut, giving the illusion of a "telephone voice." Of course, the mixer would be able to pre-set each track at the desired level and equalization and let them run. Such changes in character of the voice can even occur between words of a sentence, so long as there is sufficient space between words to allow us to cut.

For this same reason, if a soundtrack is to contain more than one narrator, or if portions of sync sound occur along with narration, these should be laid-in on separate "voice" tracks. Then the mixer can set one proper level for each track and maintain it through the mix without juggling levels constantly. Each voice, particularly if they have been recorded at different times and places, may require an entirely different equalization and level setting. The same procedure should be followed if it has been necessary for the narrator to re-record portions of the narration at a later date.

Sometimes it is necessary to make a music change at a point where the piece does not readily lend itself to this. Only experience can tell you what sort of music change a mixer is able to make perfectly by cross-fading even though an editor cannot render it by a direct cut. We can generalize by saying that there are many music changes which are impossible in direct, same-track cutting, but which can be beautifully performed by the mixer, providing the tracks are laid-in in the proper relationship to one another; essentially a matter of keeping the musical beats parallel between the two tracks.

MIX CUE SHEETS

The mixer will work from composite cue sheets, containing the following information:

1 The footage at which each sound starts, and the way it is to start (that is, faded or direct)
2 How long the sound is to run
3 The footage at which each sound ends, and the way it is to end
4 The level at which the sound is to start
5 Where the track is clear of sound (in case the mixer wishes to pre-set the track)
6 The identity of the sound

On a composite cue sheet (see Fig. 11.4), the soundtracks will be rendered in vertical columns, parallel to each other and usually reading from left to right; NARRATION, SYNC VOICE, MUSIC (A & B), EFFECTS (A, B, C, etc.), LOOPS. You are familiar with our recommended method for rendering the beginnings and endings of sounds, with the exact footage listed and the proper note specifying pre-sets, natural ins or outs, or fades-in or -out. In practice, exact, to-the-frame cues should be rounded off to half foot figures for the mixer. As we have stated, mixes are performed to 35mm footages, even if the film is 16mm. A method for converting 16mm footages to 35mm has been discussed.

The level of a sound is usually determined by the mixer during rehearsal and noted by him on the cue sheet. The sound editor is responsible only for noting major information of this sort, such as a warning to keep a particularly loud sound down or to bring up a music cue which he knows will hit unimpeded by voice and wants to establish strongly at the start. It is a good idea to position sound effects in spaces in the voice track rather than let them fall indiscriminately. The mixer will set his voice tracks to run at a constant level and vary his other soundtracks to obtain a proper balance with the voice tracks, with the obvious intention of keeping the voice audible and intelligible. Avoiding conflict between other important sounds and the voice by proper positioning will allow these key sounds to be played at full level at the mix. If they must occur simultaneously with voice, the mixer has no choice but to hold their level well below that of the voice tracks.

The mixer will use the cue sheet footages of the voice track as a cue to bringing up or down the other sounds. All other-than-voice sound forms a kind of muted background when the voice is running; when the voice ceases, the mixer skillfully brings up these other tracks (properly balanced in relationship to each other, naturally) to fill the void; he brings them down again in anticipation of the incoming voice, following the cue sheets. Most mixers would not do this for short gaps in a voice track, so you would normally not list pauses in the voice of only one or two seconds. The simplest way to make up a voice cue sheet is to run the voice track on a Moviola; while one man reads off the footages from the counter a second can list them for the cue sheet.

Most mix studios today have a *cue light system.* This is a warning light situated near the projection screen in the mix studio and triggered by the running voice track. The light goes on a second or two before the voice is heard and goes out a second or so before it is to end, enabling the mixer to bring the tracks up and down automatically. If the studio has such a system, and you wish to use it, it will not be necessary to list voice cues on your sheet. However, we recommend that it be done anyway, as many mixers find it easier and faster to work from a voice cue sheet.

We must note at what points the track is clear of all sound to enable the mixer to open the pot on that track in advance of the pre-set sound, letting it hit automatically. As we have mentioned, our method is to always leave a consistent space of at least ten feet, unless this is for some reason impossible, and if so, then to note this fact on the sheet. If the track is to be faded in, then such a note is naturally unnecessary.

The identification of sound does not extend to supplying the title of each piece of music or name of each speaker, but it should include the identification of each sound effect. The usual practice is to identify the sound actually used; that is, if we are using a tree crash as a substitute for an iceberg breaking, a ricochet for a cartoon character racing off, or a slide whistle for an object falling we will identify the former in each case. Since the mixer can see what the sound is supposed to represent, the information as to what is actually being used is more useful.

General notes as to a particular piece of music will be given if it affects the way the mixer will handle it. An example might be a piece of music that is supposed to be actual music within the film and so will be handled differently from the other music. The same applies to a portion of the voice track requiring special treatment, such as a phone voice to be filtered, or if there is a change in voices which occurs on a running track. Such tracks would require the use of filters or changes in equalization and the mixer must be alerted to this.

THE SOUND MIX—PROCEDURE

As the mix begins, the spectators take seats in the chairs provided for them in front of the console, while the sound editor, director, and often the picture editor are seated behind the console, next to the mixer. The mixer places the cue sheets in front of him so that he can refer to them constantly, in relationship to the picture and the footage counter. The sound editor should also sit where he can see the cue sheets, and probably will want to keep his own working cue sheets handy for reference. The mixer receives "ready" signals from the machine man and projectionist, then pushes the button that starts all tracks running synchronously with the picture. Should anything go wrong in the mechanical running of the tracks, the mixer will quickly be signaled by the machine man. If a "runaway" occurs, he will stop while the tracks are set up again and then begin over. If a track breaks, the sound editor will be expected to go to the machine room and repair it, and the same applies to the picture breaking, although many projectionists will perform this service themselves.

Frank Lewin gives an excellent description of what we should expect the climate of the mix to be and how the mixer will begin his work.

A mixer is a human being—a fact often overlooked by people at the re-recording session. The strain to which he is subjected is frequently greater than it seems advisable to burden a human being with . . . the human element in a mix is so closely related to what the finished print sounds like that it should not be neglected.

It is patently unfair to expect the first run-through of a reel to come up to the expectations of director, editors and others who have spent the preceding weeks or months in intimate contact with their creation. They know—or think they know—what the track is supposed to do and should sound like—the mixer has to feel his way and must find out through trial and error. The less said after the first run-through by all concerned, except the mixer asking questions, the better. He is assimilating and trying to integrate a complex assemblage of sounds; he hears many things which he would like to balance out or correct, if he is given enough time; he appreciates a few moments to make notes, repatch connections, and generally sort out what is important on the sound tracks from what is secondary.

The re-recording engineer has a further function—often felt, seldom expressed. He must perform a role similar to that of a host at a social gathering, and depending on how many clients and clients' clients, and clients' clients' representatives there are assembled in the studio, this role is correspondingly onerous—all this on top of doing the technical job required of him.[16]

It is strongly recommended, as Lewin suggests, that the first run-through be a time for the mixer to familiarize himself with the tracks and cue sheet. He should not be distracted from his concentration on them in any way, and it goes without saying that any conversation in the studio should cease absolutely as the run-through starts. Since this run is for familiarization, one should not expect a polished performance from the mixer, and to require this would, in fact, prevent him accomplishing the true purpose of the run-through: the setting of levels, equalizations, and noting of specific cues. On the other hand, frequently a client is present at the mix, hearing the sound for the first time, and his first impression is important. Seldom do nonfilm-makers understand fully the function of the mix; they can become quite alarmed at their initial hearing. Of course it will be explained to them that this is a rough run-through, but people unfamiliar with film techniques seldom are able to visualize the final product when observing its first stages. It is our opinion, therefore, that the mixer has some responsibility when a client is present, in presenting from the start a semblance of the final mix. If it is unavoidable that the client be present, you should let the mixer know this ahead of time, and tell him frankly what you require in this respect. The sound editor can help a good deal by quietly warning the mixer when cues are coming up, since he is watching the cue sheets at a time that the mixer is busy taking notes and setting levels. If the client must be present, he will have been informed as to what can and cannot be changed at the mix. He should not expect the substitution of new sounds for sounds already chosen and brought to the mix. A given sound can be played or eliminated, its level in relation to other sounds can be varied, and to some degree its beginning and ending can be varied; but that is about all. The client should know that to request anything else at this time will necessitate stopping the mix and probably canceling and rescheduling it for a later date. He should be prepared to accept this delay—and to pay for it.

If a back-up interlock system is used, one run-through is enough, as the mixer will be able to go back over any troublesome cues. If not, the mixer will determine how many rehearsals are needed before he starts to re-record. The sound editor and director are expected to give approval to the mixer's work in rehearsal and to state their aims to him so that he can carry them out. If the tracks must be readjusted, the sound editor will do this in the studio's cutting room, following the procedure we have discussed earlier in this chapter.

If you have decided to make a music-and-effects track, you must decide whether a minus-dialogue m&e will do (see page 448). If so, this can be made simultaneously with the recording of the mix. If not, you will probably wish to make the m&e first, then the full mix. If you wish to use the m&e as a sort of pre-mix, remember the earlier warnings about committing yourself before the final stage of the mix and the additional generation it will cost you. The best procedure is to set the m&e aside and start from scratch for the final mix.

Again, you must decide whether you wish to use a back-up system (if available) for the final mix or just for rehearsal.

If there is time left when the mix is completed, suggest the mixer play back the mixed track to picture so that you can all sit, relaxed and attentive, to watch and listen once more before giving your final approval. With the back-up interlock system, one ruinous error that would otherwise necessitate redoing the entire track can be corrected easily and the rest of the mix saved. After a satisfactory mix, you might wish to suggest that the mixer "save it" but try again. This means that the mixer will not erase what he has (on the assumption that he may not be able to improve on it), but will make another attempt. Normally, he might be expected to erase any unsuccessful attempt and use the same tape for his next try, although many mixers save all but the most obviously useless takes.

It is easy under the pressures of the clock (and the clock means money at a mix) to lower your standards in harried desperation. Yet, although another hour of mix time costs some $100, an inadequate sound mix will be heard every time you run the picture for the rest of your life.

CHAPTER 13

PRINTING THE IMAGE: THE ANSWER PRINT

The work print is edited; the sounds are mixed and transferred to an optical negative; the opticals and titles are prepared. Now it is time to return to the laboratory for the final steps in the production of a film. At various times we have said that the laboratory can be a most helpful associate in film production, but it is necessary that you understand the functions to be carried out by the lab and what is required of you in the preparation of your material if the lab is to provide you with high quality results.

Before you can return to the laboratory, one vital editorial function must first be executed—matching the camera original to the edited work print (also called conforming the original). Some film-makers prefer to keep the camera original uncut; they have a dupe negative or a master positive struck from the original, and this is cut to match the work print. This, of course, is costly and beyond the budget of many, and such a procedure is unnecessary unless you insist on keeping the camera original intact. Producers of commercials for television, for example, prefer not to cut the original because they can use the exposed footage to make commercials of different lengths and styles from the same footage. For our discussion, however, the term "original" will be used since the procedure would be the same with a dupe negative or master positive and since most film-makers do cut their original.

Although negative-matching can be accomplished by you or your editor, we feel that less problems will result if a "disinterested" party is secured for the job. Many film-makers have cut their own original to match the work print; it is certainly not a difficult task. But it can be trying on one's nerves, knowing that every time the scissors bite into the original you are making an irreparable cut in the original. A disinterested party, hired to carry out this vital but basically mundane task, is less likely to make mistakes because he is not worrying about making errors. As you will shortly see, the task of negative matching is not creative; it requires only good eyesight for reading edgenumbers and a knowledge of the process. If you are located in any area where a considerable amount of film production is carried out, you should have little difficulty finding a professional who will take on the job—many cutters make a living matching negatives.

CONFORMING THE ORIGINAL

Your first determination will be the method of conforming you will follow. You have basically three choices as to how to match the original with the work print: 1) single strand; 2) A-B rolls; and 3) zero cut.

SINGLE STRAND   The single strand method is possible when it is not necessary for the laboratory to effect dissolves or fades in the printing or, in 16mm, when the film-maker is not concerned with making invisible splices. The original is cut to match the work print exactly, both being a single strand.

A-B ROLLS   The A-B method is best suited for reversal master material or master positives. Following this method, the original is cut into two separate rolls to match the work print. In this way fades, dissolves, or composite images (e.g., double exposures) can be achieved on the contact printer. Alternate shots are placed on an "A" roll and a "B" roll with opaque leader between each shot on each of the rolls, maintaining synchronization. Starting with roll "A," the first shot is placed on this roll while opaque leader to match the length of the shot is placed on roll "B." The second shot is then placed on "B," and opaque leader on roll "A." This "checkerboarding"* is followed for the entire film.

In 16mm, the checkerboarding technique provides invisible splices that otherwise would appear as a quick flash when a cut passed by the projector's lamp (Fig. 13.1). This is not a problem in 35mm, due to the wider frame line, but the A-B roll method can be used with this gauge of film to achieve fades and dissolves and will be required if shots of one foot or less are in the film. In 35mm, the checkerboard technique of 16mm is modified. The only time that the cutter changes rolls is when he must cut in a fade, dissolve, or some composite image. If the first four shots of a film are straight cuts, but there is to be a dissolve from the fourth to the fifth, the first four shots would be spliced together on the "A" roll with black opaque leader on the "B" roll, and the fifth

* "Checkerboarding" is the term for this procedure in Great Britain. When they use the term "A & B rolling" they mean running consecutive shots on the roll when there is a direct cut, alternating rolls only when there is a fade or dissolve.

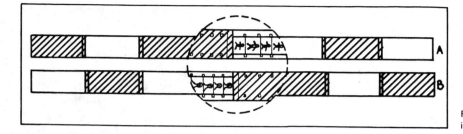

Fig. 13–1 A-B technique for making
invisible splices (Jack Fischer)

shot would be spliced to the black leader on the "B" roll with the proper overlap of the fourth and fifth shots. The sixth shot and so forth, until another dissolve, fade, or some other effect is necessary, are spliced together on the "B" roll. This procedure is followed throughout the rest of the film.

One final word about A-B matching. Should your film contain montage effects, double exposures, or superimposed titles, etc., that you wish printed by the lab rather than going to an optical house, it will be necessary for you to prepare "C," "D," etc. rolls. If you prepare these extra rolls which contain the additional material for your desired effects, the laboratory can print these effects onto your composite print. However, these extra rolls are not recommended. Such effects can be expensive and dangerous because of the necessity for another run through the printer. Laboratories prefer that the printing rolls be held to a minimum.

ZERO CUT   This is another method of concealing the splice line of 16mm film. The original is divided into A-B rolls, but the scenes to be cut together are overlapped at least two frames (Fig. 13.2). Zero-cut rolls must be printed on a printer that is equipped with a shutter that rapidly opens and closes. The shutter closes at the desired last frame of the outgoing shot and, on the second printing roll, opens at the desired first frame of the incoming shot. The cuts from shot to shot on the print will appear as approximately one-frame dissolves unless printed on a contact step printer. This can be very objectionable to many viewers, especially in 16mm. Zero cutting is more costly, and not all laboratories are equipped to print zero-cut rolls.

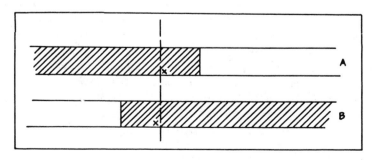

Fig. 13–2 Zero cut overlap (Jack Fischer)

The Step-by-Step Matching Procedures

The first thing you must do is to thoroughly clean the editing table. Clear away anything that will not be needed in the matching and see that the area is as clean as possible. Getting dust or any foreign matter on the original can destroy any prints that must be printed from it. Place a lintless towel over the table top; this towel will also protect the original from any scratches that might occur should the original be drawn across the bare table top. Have several pairs of inexpensive lintless white cotton editing gloves which should be worn anytime that you are handling the original. Remember, protection of the original is the word-of-the-day.

Place the edited work print on the left rewind with a take-up reel on the right rewind and run through the work print from beginning to end, making a written record of the first and last edgenumbers of each shot. A jeweler's loupe (eyepiece) can be most helpful in reading the edgenumbers. Once the list of numbers is finished, you can begin to pull the original takes, identifying them from the list of edgenumbers you have compiled. Pull the entire take from camera-start to camera-stop, and place these takes in sequence on a take-up reel by taping the ends of the shots together with a small piece of half-inch masking tape. Some people suggest placing the pulled shots in a film bin in the same manner followed when breaking out the work print. We do not recommend this, for an original take can be scratched by the other strips when it is pulled from the barrel. If you use parts of one take in several places in the edited film, insert the entire take on the roll the first time that it is to be used, and for any subsequent uses tape a short piece of white leader to the taped-together pieces of original with the edgenumbers needed written on the leader. Never project or view the original on a viewer or Moviola because this can cause irreparable damage to the original film. Upon completion of the sequencing of the original, test your synchronizer to make certain that it does not scratch the film or injure the perforation holes.

SINGLE STRAND

If you are planning to cut the original in a single strand, place the edited work print and the sequenced original in the left rewind with the work print in the first track of the synchronizer and the original in the second track. Wind the work print to the first shot and the first edgenumber of that shot. Find the matching number on the original and place it in the synchronizer opposite the work print's number. Now wind back to the start of the scene on the work print, and mark the same point on the original by placing an "x" with a *scribe* on each side of the perforation hole. Be careful to make the scribe marks outside of the picture area. Some recommend the use of a grease pencil to make the marks, but we feel that this is inadvisable since some of the crayon mark may remain on the original after the splice has been made. Using a pair of scissors, cut the original, making certain that you leave one frame beyond the scribe marks for the splice. Now wind through to the last edgenumber of the take on the work print. The corresponding edgenumber on the original should be directly opposite. Continue on to the end of the take on the work print, mark and cut the original in the same way that you did at the head of the scene. Do not forget to leave the necessary extra frame for the splice. Now repeat the procedure for the head of the next shot on the work print. The head of the second original shot can now be spliced to the tail of the first shot. Again check the edgenumbers and the splice to make certain that they correspond with the numbers and splice of the work print. Continue this process to the completion of the film. Following this procedure, you should have, upon completion of the matching, original material that conforms exactly to the edgenumbers and splices of the work print.

Should you find that you have a take that is too short and falls between edgenumbers so that you have no edgenumbers to match, you will have to match the action of the work print with the original. Any optical duplicate material that you get from the optical house will also be devoid of any edgenumbers and will have to be matched according to action. This practice holds true whether you are cutting single strand, A-B, or zero.

A-B ROLLS

In making up A-B rolls you will also place the work print and sequenced original on the left rewind. The work print will be placed in the first track of the synchronizer, the "A" roll will be in the second track, and the "B" roll, in the third (Fig. 13.3). The edgenumbers of the proper shots and the placement of the splices are located and synchronized in the same way as in the single strand technique, except that in this process the original takes are not spliced together. The first shot of the film is placed in the second track of the synchronizer—the track reserved for the "A" roll—and its edgenumbers are matched with those of the work print. Into the third track, the "B" roll, is placed double-perforated black leader, unless some or all of the original is single-perforated film. If the original contains any single-perforated film, single-perforated leader is used to prevent any later damage to the original. The perforations of the leader should, of course, be on the same edge as those of the original film. To ensure that this leader is opaque, the Association of Cinema Laboratories suggests that you secure from the laboratory black leader that has been made by fully exposing a positive stock and developing it in a positive bath to a minimum visual density of 3.00. When the location of the head and tail splice of the scene on the "A" roll is marked with the scribe, the same should be done on the black leader. Then, as usual, the shot and the leader are cut with scissors, leaving enough frames on each for the splice. The second shot is then marked and cut, but this shot is spliced to the tail of the black leader of the "B" roll, and black leader is spliced to the tail of the first shot on the "A" roll. This same procedure is followed for each successive shot that is a straight cut in the work print—the third shot on the "A," the fourth on the "B" roll, and so on.

Since the A-B roll method is used to achieve fades and dissolves

Fig. 13–3 Synchronizer containing workprint in first track, "A" roll in second track, "B" roll in third track (Mel Wittenstein)

when the original is printed, these dissolves and fades must be cut into the rolls in a slightly different way. When a dissolve is indicated on the work print, there must be an overlap of the two shots involved in the effect. A 48-frame overlap is considered standard when preparing A-B rolls for dissolves. This does not mean that the length of the actual dissolve will be restricted to 48 frames. If you desire a dissolve longer than 48 frames, overlap the scenes in the A-B rolls the desired length. Dissolves shorter than 48 frames should be prepared with a 48-frame overlap, but instructions indicating the desired length must be given to the lab. Many laboratories offer dissolves of 16, 24, 32, 48, 64, and 96 frames in length. But check with your lab before you incorporate anything but a standard 48-frame dissolve. The ACL suggests that if the film-maker is preparing A-B rolls of negative material, eight additional frames be added to the overlap of each scene in the dissolve if they are available.

When the work print was edited, the editor should have determined that he had the necessary 48 frames—or whatever the length of the dissolve—on the tail and head of the two shots involved in the effect. However, he will have included only half of the frames in the actual work print, so the splice of the two shots will occur in the center of the dissolve. When cutting the original, you must cut the tail of the outgoing shot and the head of the incoming shot the necessary 48 frames—or whatever—overlap. If you match the two shots exactly to the work print, you will be short 24 frames for your dissolve. Find, mark, and cut to the proper length the outgoing shot of the dissolve and attach its head to the black leader and run it through to its end and attach it to the black leader. Now roll back to where the second shot is to be cut in. Splice its head to the black leader. The two scenes should now be overlapped 48 frames—if you are using a standard dissolve—unless you or your editor goofed. It is always best to doublecheck the lengths of the two shots before you do any cutting of the original. Next wind to the center of the dissolve which will be opposite the splice between the two shots in the work print. This center should be marked on both the "A" and "B" roll by scribing an "x" on the frame of each roll opposite the splice on the work print—the center of the effect. These "x's" should be made on the emulsion side of the film outside the picture area. By placing these marks the dissolve overlap can be easily checked (Fig. 13.4).

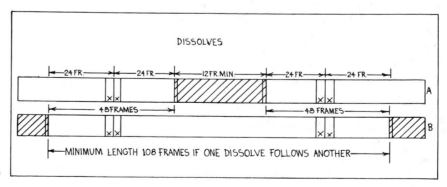

Fig. 13–4 Method of cutting in a dissolve (Jack Fischer)

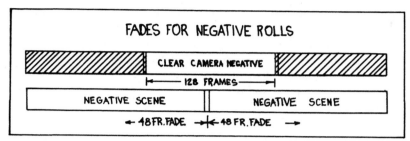

Fig. 13–5 Fades for negative A-B rolls (Jack Fischer)

When a fade-out is followed by a fade-in, and you are preparing A-B rolls from reversal original, the ACL recommends that the fade-in scene be carried across to the other roll without an overlap. Therefore, the procedure followed is the same as that used in a straight cut. But instructions must be given to the lab so that the fades will be printed in at the desired place and for the desired length. The length of the fades has been determined by the editor when cutting the work print, and the necessary length of the shots has been included in the work print. You need only match the two shots to the work print, and cut them into the rolls following the standard procedure. Make a note of the length of each fade which is marked on the work print and its footage location on the reel. The footage location will have to be determined after the leaders have been attached to the two rolls. This is the information you will pass on to the lab.

Fades on negative A-B rolls are prepared differently (Fig. 13.5). The fade-out and fade-in shots are placed on the same roll. Clear camera negative, which has been prepared by developing exposed raw stock of the same type that was used in the production of the film, must be cut in on the opposite roll in the area where the fade-out and fade-in will occur. Some laboratories insist that an additional 16 frames of clear leader be added before the opaque leader begins for each fade-out and each fade-in. The length of the fade-in, another 48 frames for the fade-out, plus 32 extra frames for a total of 128 frames of clear leader is to be cut in. The best procedure to follow when preparing negative rolls is to consult with the lab for their recommendations. Do not prepare the rolls without the lab's vital assistance. The standard fade, like the dissolve, is 48 frames, but they are also available at some labs in lengths of 16, 24, 32, 48, 64, and 96 frames.

ZERO CUT

We suggest that before employing the zero cut you consult your laboratory. They may not be equipped to handle the zero cut. Basically, the procedure is the same as in the making of A-B rolls, except that there is a four-frame overlap at the head and tail of each shot.

Splicing

Before making any splices of original film, check the lateral and longitudinal alignment of the *hot splicer* (always use an asymmetrical splicer that is electrically heated when splicing original film). Make several test

Fig. 13–6a Making a hot splice: tail on right side of splicer

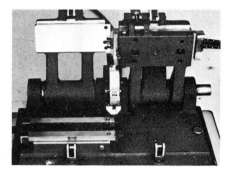

Fig. 13–6b Right side hinged up and head in place on left side of splicer

Fig. 13–6c Scraping the emulsion

Fig. 13–6d Applying the cement

Fig. 13–7 Prepared head leaders (Jack Fischer)

splices to check the depth and width of the scraped area to make sure the overlap of the splice is correct. One of the cuts—when working in 16mm—should be made on the frame line and the other cut in the picture area when you are preparing A-B rolls.

Splice the original with the utmost care. Place the tail of the preceding shot—except in A-B rolling when the black leader is always placed on the right side of the splicer (see page 479)—into the right side of the splicer so that the perforation hole of the film is seated over the registration pin (one on each side in a 16mm splicer, two in a 35mm splicer) and the marked splice line—the scribed "x's"—is positioned where the splice is to be made (Fig. 13.6 A–F). Clamp the hinged top down, then release the lever that holds the top and bottom halves of the vise on the right side, and lift the right side up on its hinges. Place the head of the next shot into the lefthand side of the splicer so that the film is also seated over the registration pin with the splice line marked with the two "x's" falling where the splice will be made. Bend down the extra frame that has been left beyond the splice marks and scrape the emulsion from the film. Remember that the emulsion side of the film must be up. You can check to see which side of the film is the emulsion side by following any of the methods suggested earlier (see Chapter 6). Next, apply the cement, but use only enough to insure a good splice. If you use too little, the splice will not hold, and if you use too much, the cement can seep onto the emulsion of the frame of the picture. Now drop down the right side of the splicer that you earlier raised out of the way, and lock it. This will cut at the correct place the two pieces of film to be spliced together, joining the two pieces together. Keep the pieces locked together no less than ten to fifteen seconds. Then lift the tops of each side of the splicer, gently rub any excess cement off with a gloved finger (one reason you will need several pair since they tend to get dirty very quickly), and lift the film out. Be sure that the splice is thoroughly dry, test it, and then wind it onto the take-up reel. Never wind a wet splice onto the roll for it could mark the next layer of film. And never handle anything but the edge of the film—this is a practice to follow anytime

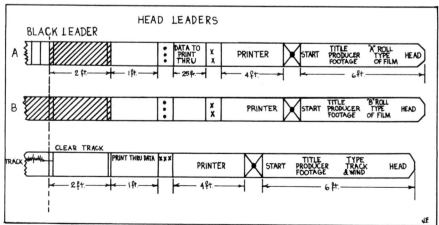

that you handle original film. Remember also that the cement in the splicer bottle will generally deteriorate in a few hours due to evaporation and should be periodically replenished.

When splicing 16mm film into A-B rolls to achieve an invisible splice, the scene should always be placed in the splicer so that it is on the left side where the scraping occurs. Never scrape the black leader, for that will, by destroying its opaqueness, create a visible splice. After you have spliced the head of the shot to the black leader, you will note that it will be necessary to turn the shot around when splicing the tail so that the shot and not the leader is placed in the left side of the splicer where it can be scraped. This can be confusing the first time you make up A-B rolls. Some cutters splice together all of the joints involving the head of the shot and tape the tail to the leader with masking tape. Upon the completion of the reel, they reverse the take-up reel to the left rewind and splice all of the tail joints. Following this procedure they do not have to turn the shot around. In following either of these methods, one edge of the splice should be on the frame line of the picture, and the other edge, which normally would fall in the picture area, should now fall in the black leader.

When the A-B rolls have all been spliced together, run back to the beginning, and then slowly run through, checking the synchronization from the beginning to the end with the work print.

Fig. 13–6e Splicer closed

Fig. 13–6f Splice completed (Mel Wittenstein)

Preparing 16mm Leaders
HEAD LEADERS

First, cut a piece of double-perforated leader (Fig. 13.7) that is approximately 12 feet long for the beginning section of the head leader and splice to it a piece of about 2½ feet in length of double-perforated black leader. If you wish to use the SMPTE Universal Leader (9, 8, 7, 6, etc.), use it in place of the black leader. Use positive Universal Leader for positive original film and negative for negative original film. The Universal Leader may be obtained from your laboratory. When preparing A-B rolls, use the Universal Leader as part of the "B" roll leader so that the first picture will occur on the "A" roll. If any of the original is single-perforated film, use single-perforated leader. If you are preparing leader for negative original, use transparent clear leader in place of the black leader. And if you are preparing leader for A-B rolls, prepare one of these leaders for each roll. For the soundtrack you will need to cut a piece of single-perforated white leader that is approximately 12 feet long and splice to it a 2½ foot piece of clear leader. Now place each of these leaders in the synchronizer with its counter set at "0" frames, so that the splices are opposite one another with the white leader on the right. Next, turn the synchronizer knob clockwise and measure exactly 2 feet into the black and clear leader, then make a crayon mark at this frame on each piece of leader. These marks will indicate to you where the splices should occur when the leaders are attached to the film and sound track rolls. You must now turn the synchronizer counterclockwise and wind back to the original splices. Now measure one foot, "0" frames forward into the white leader. This frame will be your point of *editorial*, or even, sync. This frame is marked by placing three small "x's" lengthwise in the frame of the soundtrack leader in the sound area of the track so that it will print through to the composite print, and three round dots are placed across the leader in the frame of the white leader of the picture rolls. From now on, when the frames with the dots in the picture leader are opposite the "x's" in the sound track, the rolls are in editorial sync.

However, remember that in projecting a 16mm sound film, the soundtrack must be advanced 26 frames (35mm requires a 20-frame advance) because the optical sound reproducing head of the projector is a distance of 26 frames in front of the light aperture.

To establish the *projection* (advanced) *sync* marks—also called printer sync, printing sync, and married sync in England—on the picture rolls, the white leader of the picture rolls is moved forward in the synchronizer 26 frames. The frame next to the editorial sync mark is counted as the first frame, and the 26th frame is then marked as the projection sync. This 26th frame is marked with two large "x's" going across the frame in the picture area. There now should be 25 blank frames between the editorial sync marks and the projection sync marks on the two leaders—two, of course, only if you are preparing for A-B rolls. Now the track must be removed from the synchronizer and advanced so that the sync mark on the track leader (the frame with the three small "x's") is opposite the projection sync marks just placed on the picture leader. Place the track leader in the synchronizer and relock it. At this point the track is now in its advanced position. Once the track is in this advanced position, turn the synchronizer knob counterclockwise until the picture and soundtrack leaders are rolled another four feet, "0" frames, toward the head of their white leader, and the corresponding frames of each roll's leader are then marked with the printer start marks. These marks should be made by boxing off the frame with an ink line, placing a large "X" covering the entire frame inside the box and punching a hole in the middle of the frame. Finally measure off 6 feet, "0" frames, more toward the head of the white leader and cut off the excess at the heads of each white leader.

Now the leader must be identified. Place the white leaders across the table in front of you with the end of the white leader on your right and the emulsion side up. All identification should be marked on the emulsion side of the leader with India ink. Place the word "head" at the end of each piece of white leader. To the left of this word, write the type of film and the roll identification—e.g., "original Ektachrome ECO," "A-roll." On the left of this material, write the title of the film, the producer's name, and the footage. Use the footage numbers that will be ascertained by measuring from the head printer start mark to the tail printer start mark. Do not expect your lab bill to exactly reflect this footage figure, for to this measurement must be added the footage needed for the head and tail printer thread-up. These same markings will be placed on each picture leader, the only difference being the roll identification when preparing A-B leader.

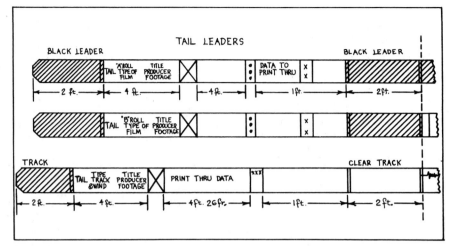

Fig. 13–8 Prepared tail leaders (Jack Fischer)

The soundtrack leader should have "head" placed in the same position as on the picture leader. Then the type of track should be recorded—e.g., "negative B-wind." The title, the producer's name, and footage should also be placed on the track leader.

The ACL suggests that all of the printer start marks be identified by writing in large letters the word "PRINTER" to the left of the start mark frame, and the word "START" on its right. Place the information to be printed through on the composite print, such as the name of the film, the producer's name, and the running time, in the 25 frames between the editorial sync mark and the projection sync mark on one of the leaders. If you are using SMPTE Universal Leader with A-B rolls, the material should be placed on the leader for the "A" roll.

TAIL LEADERS

Splice a 2½ foot piece of black leader (clear for negative rolls; Fig. 13.8), which in this case will be the beginning section of the leader, to a 10 foot piece of white leader. The black and the white leader should be the same type as used in the head leaders. Make a tail leader for each roll of picture. The soundtrack leader should consist of a 2½ foot piece of single-perforated clear leader spliced to a 10 foot piece of single-perforated white leader. Place the leaders in the synchronizer with its counter set at zero, emulsion side up, with the splice marks opposite one another and with the heads of the black leader and the clear leader which will later be spliced to the picture and soundtrack rolls on your right. (Again make certain when using single-perforated leader that the perforations are on the same edge as those on the picture or track.) Turn the synchronizer knob counterclockwise and move forward into the black leader for two feet, "0" frames, and make a crayon mark in the black picture leader and the clear track leader. These marks will indicate where the leaders are to be spliced to the tails of the picture and track rolls. Turn clockwise back to the splices in the leader where again the synchronizer counter reads "0" feet, "0" frames. Then measure into the white leader exactly one foot by turning the synchronizer knob clockwise. Place the same editorial sync marks that you placed on the head leader in this frame—three dots across the picture leader and three "x's" lengthwise on the track leader. Next turn the synchronizer knob counterclockwise and move the picture leader or leaders forward 26 frames toward the black leader with the first frame next to the editorial sync mark counted as frame number one. On the 26th frame place the two large "x's" across the picture area to designate the projection sync mark. Again there should be 25 blank frames between the editorial sync and projection sync marks.

As with the head track leader, remove the tail leader of the sound-track from the synchronizer and place the frame with the small "x's" opposite the two large "x's" of the picture leader so that the rolls are in projection sync, and relock the synchronizer.

With the picture leader and track leader locked in projection sync in the synchronizer, turn the synchronizer knob clockwise and measure 4 feet, "0" frames, from the editorial sync mark of the picture leader toward the tail of all of the leaders. The frame at the end of this 4 foot measurement will be the position of your tail printer sync marks. This frame should be marked on each leader in an identical manner to the head leaders—boxed-in frame and large 'X"—but do not punch a hole in the frame center or write the words "printer start." Finally, again turn the knob clockwise and measure four more feet toward the tail of the white leader and mark each leader with a crayon mark. Remove the leaders from the synchronizer, and splice a 2 foot piece of black leader to each of the tail leaders at the crayon mark you just made.

SPLICING THE LEADERS TO THE ROLLS

Place the picture roll or rolls and the soundtrack at editorial sync (even) in the synchronizer with the emulsion side up. Turn the synchronizer to a point a few frames in advance of the first picture or sound, whichever comes first. Place a mark on each roll at this frame and splice the head leaders to each roll at this mark. Be sure that the leader identified as "A" roll is spliced to the picture roll with the first picture. If you have used the SMPTE Universal Leader, it should have been spliced to the "B" roll leader. The "A" roll should contain the print-through data in the 25 frames between editorial and projection sync.

Now roll to the end of the film, proceeding to the last frame of picture or sound, whichever occurs last. Roll on a few frames past this frame, and place a mark on all of the rolls. Splice the tail leaders on these marks.

Final Preparations for the Lab

Full instructions to the laboratory should always accompany your film to the lab. These instructions should designate in complete detail all special effects you wish the laboratory to carry out and any special exposures.

Place the rolls in the synchronizer so that the "printer start" marks of the head leaders are in synchronization, and set the synchronizer to read "0" feet and "0" frames. This printer start mark will serve as the reference point for your cue sheet. Now roll the film through the synchronizer. You will be able to make a final check of the matching and, at the same time, prepare your *cue sheet,* which will indicate the position and length of dissolves and fades and any other information with which you feel the lab should be supplied. Use the footage and frame count that registers on the synchronizer as your cues.

While you are engaged in the process of matching the original and the work print, it is wise to keep all of your original trims taped together on a separate reel. When you have completed the matching task, take them off this reel, roll them up, and store them in a safe, cool, dry place until the release print is completed.

MAKING THE PRINTS

The film-maker is now ready to proceed to the laboratory where the final steps will be taken in the completion of his film. The matched original and the optical soundtrack negative will be taken to the laboratory with the cue sheet that he has prepared. In order to get the best service from the laboratory, your original should be properly prepared and ready for printing. The splices should be strong, having been made only with fresh cement. The leaders should be clearly marked and properly identified. The lab should be told if the track has been placed in editorial or printer sync. When dealing with 16mm, you must also submit the proper wind of optical sound negative for the job you are requesting; you may be required to submit both an "A"-wind and a "B"-wind. Your instructions should be clear and complete with the proper nomenclature used. You should determine from the lab the amount of time necessary to accomplish each of the laboratory processes. Make reasonable delivery demands from the laboratory, for your film is not the only one being processed by the lab. If you will require rush work, notify the lab in advance so that they can prepare their schedule to handle your film. Expect delays. They may not happen, but if they do, you and your client will not be disappointed then.

The rolls of film should be submitted on darkroom cores and wrapped in lintless paper or plastic bags. Place the wrapped film into cans; the cans should be taped across the top and bottom, never on the edge. The can should be labeled, identifying its contents—type of film, footage, and production title. The laboratory may ask you to submit the edited work print with the original. It can be of help to the timer.

Before you receive the first print from the original—the answer print—for your approval, the original will have to be carefully graded by the *timer.* Each density change and color balance will have to be worked out by him to ensure that each shot matches in density and color tone the one that precedes it. If you wish specific scenes printed in a particular way—day for night scenes, a certain color hue, etc.—be sure to include this information in your cue sheet to guide the timer when he is preparing the instructions for the printer.

If your film has been produced in 16mm, you will have to be concerned with a factor that still confuses the oldest professional—"A"-wind and "B"-wind (see page 450). Your answer print will be printed on a contact printer; therefore the original and the print stock will be threaded onto the printer emulsion to emulsion. The finished print will always be the opposite emulsion position from the original printing material; if the printing material is "B"-wind, the print will be "A"-wind. It is necessary for you to know the emulsion position of both your track and your picture.° In certain printing processes you may need to supply the laboratory with both an "A"-wind and a "B"-wind of your soundtrack. For example, let us say that your original picture is 16mm color reversal stock, which is "B"-wind. You submit this to the laboratory with a "B"-wind negative soundtrack. A composite answer print is struck from these materials for your approval. You approve the answer print and instruct the laboratory to make an internegative of the picture from which your release prints will be struck—a wise decision when several prints are required. This internegative will now have an "A"-wind emulsion position; therefore, you will also have to submit to the lab an "A"-wind negative of the sound track which will be used in striking the composite prints from the internegative. Hence, you will have to supply the lab with both an "A"-wind and a "B"-wind of your soundtrack. The laboratory can print from your "B"-wind soundtrack base to emulsion, thus doing away with the need for the extra copy of the track, the "A"-wind. However, the soundtrack of your release prints will contain a loss of high-frequency responses. On the other hand, if your film is as long as thirty minutes, you plan to strike prints from an internegative, and you do not feel that you need perfect sound for your answer print, the lab can print from the "A"-wind soundtrack, needed for the internegative, base to emulsion for this answer print. This would spare you the cost of the "B"-wind track needed only for the answer print.

Here is a list from the *ACL Handbook* of some of the picture printing materials, the proper track winds, and the emulsion positions of the prints you will receive.

Printing Material	Track	Print
B/W		
Original negative	B-wind negative	Positive—A-wind
Internegative from original reversal	A-wind negative	Positive—B-wind
Dupe negative from a master positive	B-wind negative	Positive—A-wind
Original reversal	B-wind positive	Reversal—A-wind
Color		
Original negative	B-wind negative	Positive—A-wind
Original reversal	B-wind negative	Reversal—B-wind
Reversal master from original reversal	A-wind negative	Reversal—B-wind
Internegative from original reversal	A-wind negative	Positive—B-wind
Dupe negative from a master positive	B-wind negative	Positive—A-wind

*Although the use of the terms "A"-wind and "B"-wind is erroneous when applied to these films—actually the terms apply only to raw stock—the usage is so universal that laboratories have had to acquiesce to this usage.

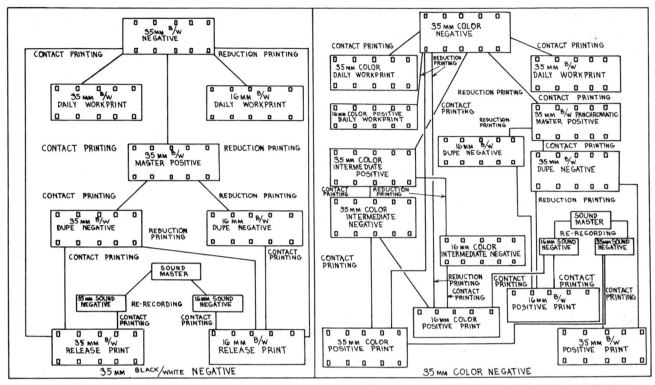

Fig. 13-9 35mm flow charts (Jack Fischer)

Protecting the Original Film

As a film-maker, your chief concern should be to protect your investment—the edited negative or camera original. You must protect yourself against damage or loss of the original. If you are planning to make any prints beyond your first answer print, it is wise to follow some protection procedure. You will, of course, need to inform the lab, since they will carry out the process.

Standard procedures exist for 35mm production since it has been the most popular film gauge for commercial production (Fig. 13.9).

When the 35mm negative is edited and the answer print made and approved, a 35mm master positive is struck from the original negative—in black-and-white this master positive is known as a "fine grain," and in color your master can be a color "interpositive" or a set of three 35mm black-and-white panchromatic separation positives. The interpositive is the most frequently used, but the separation positives are, perhaps, safer because there is no danger of dye fading. If the film-maker decides to do his release printing from the edited negative, the master positive is placed in safe storage. If, at any time, the negative begins to show signs of wear, or there is damage to the negative, a dupe negative of the damaged or worn scenes is struck from the stored master positive. If the master positive is three black-and-white separation positives, a dupe color negative is reconstructed with the use of proper filtering.

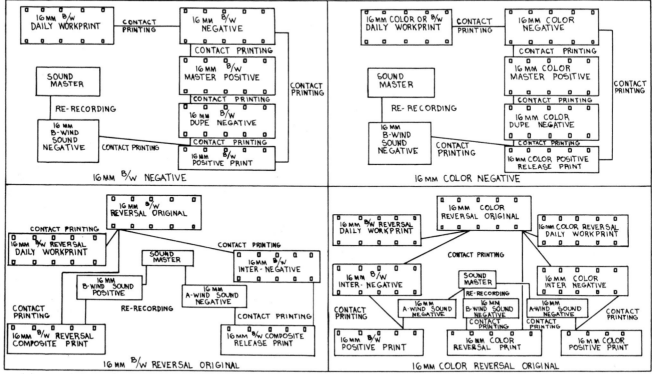

Fig. 13–10 16mm flow charts (Jack Fischer)

If the film-maker prefers to make his release prints from a dupe negative, the dupe is made from the master positive. An answer print is run from this dupe for the film-maker's approval. Then both the edited original *and* the master positive are placed in *separate* vaults for double protection.

In 16mm production the protection procedures are not as standardized (Fig. 13.10). If the film-maker's production has been shot in black-and-white reversal, he has basically two choices for release printing: 1) he can have reversal prints contact-printed from his edited original, but this offers no protection; or (2) he can have a dupe negative made and so store the original. Positive prints can then be struck from the dupe negative; they will project with the emulsion side toward the lens. This is the most common procedure followed. The prints are lower in cost, the film-maker has greater control of print quality, and his original film is protected after the dupe negative is made from it and an answer print made and approved from the dupe negative. A second method is to make a black-and-white reversal master positive from the original and then store it away. In this case, the release prints, which will be reversal positives, are made from the edited original. The film-maker can, of course, also choose to set aside the dupe negative as protection and print from the edited original.

When the original film is 16mm black-and-white or color negative, the film-maker can follow the same protection procedures designed for 35mm negative. However, the quality of 16mm prints from a 16mm master positive or an interpositive will not be as satisfactory as from the original, for the prints will be high in grain characteristics. Prints can also be made from the edited camera negative or from a dupe negative made from the camera negative. If the film-maker decides to print from the camera negative, he can protect himself by making first a master positive of it that is placed in storage. Should he prefer to print from a dupe negative, he must first have master positives made from the original scenes to be used. The master positives are then matched to the edited work print, and a dupe negative is then printed from this edited positive. The original is protected, but the quality of his prints is reduced.

Finally, what is the procedure when the camera original is color reversal? The film-maker has three choices. First, he can edit his camera original and have reversal color prints made from this, but this offers him no protection. Second, he can make a 16mm color master print of the edited original and run his prints from this master. And third, he can have an internegative made from the edited original and have positive color prints made from this dupe negative. Obviously, choices two and three are the only ones that offer him any protection.

If you are unsure as to which procedure to follow, the best advice that can be given is to consult the lab. Explain to them the uses that will be made of your film, and they can advise you as to the best procedure to follow. One fact that you should remember: Every time that there is an intermediate step between the original and the release print, an answer print or trial print must be made and approved by you. This is, of course, an added expense that must be considered in your budget. The cost of an answer print is approximately double the cost of a release print. Still, this cost can be small compared to the loss of your original without this added protection.

The Answer Print

When you have deposited your edited original, the optical sound negative, and your instructions with the laboratory, the lab will go to work to fill your order. They will assign a timer to the film. As indicated earlier, his job will be to go over the entire film shot by shot and prepare instructions for the printer so that the variations in density in the exposure of each shot are smoothed out, resulting in a well-balanced print. If your film is in color, the timer has the additional task of determining how the color of the print can be smoothed and balanced. The development of the *color analyzer* has done much to improve the quality of color control. This machine programs color adjustments on a tape which is then inserted into the printer.

The printing material then goes to the printer who works in what is referred to as "the darkroom." The printer will first run roll "A" of your printing material (if you have prepared A-B rolls) through the printer.

Any fades and the first part of the dissolve will be made in their proper place. The printed stock is then rewound, and roll "B" is then put on the printer also in contact with the printing stock. This time the fades on the second roll and the other halves of the dissolves are made in their proper places. If you have utilized a roll "C" for any double exposures, titles, etc., the printed stock is again rewound, and this roll is printed. For the final step, the printed stock is again rewound, and this time the soundtrack is added by once again running the print through the printer. Some labs, however, print the soundtrack by beginning at the tail. Some printers will also print the sound and the picture on a single pass and thus eliminate the necessity for rewinding. The black-and-white printer will make the density changes programmed by the timer. A color printer will make the density changes and also make color corrections by changing the mix of the color densities.

The exposed print stock is now sent to the processing department where it is developed, fixed, and dried. Throughout this stage the quality control people will be keeping a sharp eye on the photographic and color quality of the film coming out of the developing machine. At the completion of this stage, the answer print is ready for your screening with the timer.

SCREENING THE ANSWER PRINT

You will have to make arrangements with the laboratory for a time convenient for both you and the timer, and at a time when one of the laboratory's screening rooms is available, in order to view the answer print. It is important that this screening be with the timer. You will wish to go over the results with him, and the best time to do this is when you are both viewing the print.

There are a number of factors to look for during this screening. If the film is in black-and-white, you should pay particular attention to the density of each shot and the balance between the shots that come before and after. Unless you included in your instructions any effects you may have been striving for by manipulating the density, the timer will have attempted to get the best general photographic results. Not long ago in editing a film of ours, we discovered that we needed a transition shot, something that would signify early morning. We remembered a shot which we had previously placed in the out-takes because it had been underexposed. In the dailies, the shot appeared as a pale sky, with a building silhouetted against the sky. We pulled this "mistake" shot and used it as the needed transition shot, supplying the sound of birds chirping to complete the illusion. When we sent the original and cue sheet to the lab we neglected to include this information on the cue sheet. Later, when we screened the answer print, we found that the timer had "pushed" the shot, "correcting" it and making it totally unacceptable. This, of course, had to be corrected in the release prints.

You must also check particularly the synchronization of the track and picture. If there is some mistake, it must be corrected at this point. Watch particularly for "out-of-sync" sound effects and voice. Check the print for scratches or dirt. If you detect a scratch on the print, check through and determine whether it is on the print or on the original. If it is on the print, you should be able to see it when you hold the print under a strong light. Should there be no visible scratches on the print, check the original. If it is on the celluloid side of the film, you can have it polished or waxed out. But if the scratch is on the emulsion side, nothing can be done. Small black or white spots on the print mean there is dirt, either on the print or on the original. Dirt on a reversal original will print as black spots, and on a negative original, as white spots. Dirt on the print can be cleaned off by placing a suitable solvent such as Freon 113 or inhibited methylchloroform on an antistatic cloth and passing the cloth along both sides of the film—gently. The laboratory will have to clean the negative.

If your film is in color, you must also be concerned with the color quality of the print and the color balance from shot to shot. Seeing color is an educated sense that must be cultivated through experience, not by reading about it. But a knowledge of some basic facts may help in the education.

We have already told you that no color process is capable of reproducing all colors accurately, so you will need some sort of guide when viewing the print. The color of the skin is one that everyone will recognize so use it as your guide when screening the print for color quality and balance.

Most people are aware of the color theory of pigment—the primaries and complementaries and what can be accomplished by mixing them—but many people are not aware that the color primaries and complementaries of light are different. Basically, white light is composed of three primary colors: red, blue, and green. The complementary colors of light are cyan, yellow, and magenta. (In conjunction with color film these complementaries are often referred to as subtractive primaries.) The complementary color of red is cyan, a mixture of blue and green. Blue's complement is yellow, a mixture of red and green, and the complement of green is magenta, a mixture of red and blue. An important point to remember, therefore, is that any time you change one color you affect the others. If you add cyan to the scene, you take out the red, and so the scene is bluer and greener. On the other hand, if you add red, you take out the cyan, and so the blue and green in the scene are reduced. It is through the manipulation of these primaries and complementaries that the timer attempts to smooth and balance the color of your film.

There are two methods of printing color—additive and subtractive. In the subtractive method, white light is passed through gelatin filters in order to arrive at the preferred color balance. However, gelatin filters will pass through wide bands of the spectrum, and this causes deterioration of the colors.

The additive method is most commonly used. In the additive, the white light is divided into three beams. A dichroic filter before each beam filters out everything but one primary color, leaving three color beams: one of pure red, one of pure blue, and one of pure green. If these three color beams are again mixed, the result is again white light. Each of these three color beams has a variable light vane in its path, and these vanes offer a choice of fifty different steps of intensity of each of the colors. It is possible to make up 125,000 different color combinations by varying the vanes of the three color beams! Your timer's job is the selection of the proper combinations. Needless to say, the possibility of getting the perfect balance of color for every scene is remote. The timer will often have to compromise the color balance of one scene in order to make it harmonize with the scene that comes before or after it. Rely on the timer and trust him; his color sense will probably be a great deal more acute than yours for he must periodically pass a visual color test. But, at the same time, question his answers. Make him give you reasons why he cannot do what you wish. Just as with the optical house, you should not allow him to put you off of your ideas, for you know better than the timer what you want the color in your film to accomplish. After all, his job is to provide you with what you want, if your desires are within reason.

Know the six colors—the primaries and complementaries—and use the proper terms to describe what you want. This will make the screening with the timer more productive and will provide you with the results you are seeking.

If you approve the answer print, your film will now go on its way through the protection procedure that you selected. Each time it passes through another step toward the final goal of release printing, you will be asked to screen another answer print. Look at these answer prints as critically as you did the first. Finally you will be provided with your release prints.

Storing the Originals and Masters

When your film is completed, all of your originals, negatives, masters, soundtracks, etc. should be placed in the laboratory's storage vaults for safekeeping. Their vaults contain the proper temperature and humidity controls to preserve the film. And these materials will be easily accessible to the lab for any future print orders.

It is wise for you to keep an accurate record of all of your materials in storage at the laboratory. List the materials, footage, etc., so that when you do place any future orders for prints, you have an accurate accounting to serve as a reference. The laboratory's space for the storage of inactive films is limited, so they generally recommend that you recall all work prints, out-takes, or any other materials not necessary for future print orders within thirty days.

APPENDIX I:

A LIST OF SIGNIFICANT FILMS

I never studied filmmaking. The only school for the cinema is to go to the cinema, and not to waste time studying theory in film school. The best school of cinema in the world is the Cinémathèque of Paris. And the best professor is Henri Langlois (curator of the Cinémathèque).

—Bernardo Bertolucci, *director of* Before the Revolution *and* Partner

On Fridays, our students see two films from the archives and one or two of the latest films from abroad. All the films are discussed.

—Frantisek Daniel, *Dean of the Prague Film School*

Next to the making of a film, there is no single act more important to the serious student of film-making than the viewing of films, any film, all films. There is, fortunately, an excellent source available to the student in this country; a source which can supply him with over ninety-five per cent of the significant films made since 1929, and a major portion of the important silent films. This is the 16mm film rental library system.

The cost of rental can range from $5.00 for a short (George Méliès' *Conquest of the Pole*, Audio Film Center) to $300.00 for an outstanding contemporary color feature (Arthur Penn's *Bonnie and Clyde*, Warner Brothers Non-theatrical Division), with many excellent films falling in the $25–$75.00 range. This cost would seem to suggest that the viewing of such films should be undertaken as a group project, and it is in fact, from these rental libraries that most college film courses and cinema societies draw their films.

You are advised to request desired films as far in advance of the playing date as possible, particularly during the school year. A phone call can assure you of its availability, and a confirming letter can then be sent. Instructions for return mailing are always included.

Following is a listing of the major film rental libraries; many of the New York companies have a number of regional offices, their addresses listed in the firm's catalogue. You are encouraged to write for these catalogues, requesting the list of recent additions. Many of the catalogues include detailed listings of cast and production credits and contain illustrations as well as some selected critical comments; you will find them useful in systematizing your knowledge of film history. Particularly recommended are the following:

Audio Film Center—Brandon Films. Audio's "International Catalogue" offers an outstanding collection of contemporary films, including many important films from France, Italy, Central Europe, India, and Great Britain. They have an excellent collection of the films of Keaton, Langdon, Chaplin (early films), Griffith, Fairbanks, and Busby Berkeley. Brandon's catalogue is first-rate on the Russian silent film and has a number of "classics" unavailable elsewhere.

Contemporary Films. A fine catalogue with many classics and a growing number of contemporary films. One of the finest short subjects catalogues available.

Continental 16. Excellent contemporary catalogue, particularly good in the films of Great Britain.

Film-Makers Cooperative. A major source for experimental and "underground" films, most of them unavailable elsewhere; particularly strong in short subjects.

Films Inc. A major collection of American films; their "Half Century of American Films" is an invaluable reference catalogue.

Grove Press. A fine source for provocative contemporary films, reflecting Grove Press' position in the avante garde of political and moral revolution. Excellent collection of short subjects.

Janus Films. A superbly designed and illustrated catalogue for one of the finest collections of classic films, with Bergman, Truffaut, Wajda, Renoir, and the Japanese film well-covered; special short subjects program.

Museum of Modern Art. An indispensible, well-organized catalogue of an exceptional listing of silent, experimental and documentary films, many unavailable elsewhere. Many short subjects.

United Artists 16. A large catalogue of outstanding classic and contemporary films; their catalogue "Golden Treasury of American Film (1924–1949)" is excellent.

Universal 16. A large collection of classic American films (the Universal, Warner Brothers and Paramount films of the 1930s and 40s) and some contemporary foreign films. Excellent for von Sternberg, W. C. Fields, Sturges, and horror film classics. Their "Kinetic Art" short subjects collection is outstanding.

Warner Brothers Non-theatrical Division. A comparatively new but growing list of important American films, classic and contemporary.

You may find useful the *Directory of 8mm and 16mm Feature Films Available for Rental, Sale and Lease in the United States,* published by the Educational Film Library Association, 250 West 57th St., New York City, 10019 and available for purchase from Continental 16, 241 East 34th St., New York City, 10016.

Our own list of "significant films" follows, coded as to availability from the various film rental libraries. Some films are included which are not presently available from this source; many will soon become available, while others can be seen on television or special theatrical release. The latest films will invariably become available from the rental libraries some eighteen months after their theatrical release date in the United States. Not every film on the list is a master work; some are included because they represent milestones in film history (*Becky Sharp* and *Easy Rider*), some because they are outstanding examples of their genre (*The Bride of Frankenstein* and *Triumph of the Will*), some because they offer an excellent source for the study of a particular technique (*Young Bess* and Curtiz' *The Charge of the Light Brigade*), and some because they are delightful (*The Court Jester* and *The Scarlet Pimpernel*). It should be understood that the coverage of foreign films is dependent upon their release in the United States.

An attempt has been made to list outstanding short subjects available for rental. Such a list cannot do justice to the entire range of shorts, but we believe it a necessary beginning in acknowledging this important area of creative film-making. Shorts are perhaps the single most important training ground for young film-makers today, and an increasing number of first-rate films is being turned out by our university film system. Many times the early work of an established feature film-maker is available (Lester's *The Running, Jumping and Standing Still Film*, Godard's *All The Boys Are Called Patrick*, Polanski's *Two Men and a Wardrobe* and *Mammals*, Antonioni's *N.U.*, Reisz' *We Are The Lambeth Boys*, Richardson's *Mamma Don't Allow*, and Anderson's *O Dreamland* and *Every Day Except Christmas*). A program consisting of a short subject and a feature by the same director might offer an interesting study of the evolving technique of the film-maker. And don't forget the superb *Road Runner Cartoons*, spiritual descendants of the great silent films of Laurel and Hardy, Chaplin, and Keaton, and the finest examples of sustained and brilliantly paced comedy the cinema has ever produced.

16MM FILM RENTAL COMPANIES

AUD
Audio Film Center
34 MacQuesten Pkwy. S.
Mount Vernon, N.Y. 10550
914 664–5051

BRA
Brandon Films
34 MacQuesten Pkwy. S.
Mount Vernon, N.Y. 10550
914 664–5051

CFS
Creative Film Society
14558 Valerio St.
Van Nuys, Calif. 91405
213 786-8277

CIN
Cinema Ventures
133 W. 14th St.
N.Y., N.Y. 10011
212 533-8740

COL
Columbia Cinemateque
711 5th Avenue
New York City 10022
212 751–4400

CON
Contemporary Films
McGraw-Hill Book Company
Princeton Road
Hightstown, N.J. 08520
212 971–3333
609 448–1700

494

COO
Cooper's
Classic Film Rental Service
Northgate Shopping Center
Eaton, Ohio 45320

COS
Continental 16
241 East 34th St.
New York City 10016
212 683-6300

DBF
Don Bosco Films
148 Main St.
New Rochelle, N.Y. 10802

EMB
Embassay Pictures Corp
1301 Ave of the Americas
New York City 10019
212 956-5500

EMG
Em Gee Film Library
4931 Gloria Ave.
Encino, Calif. 91316
213 981-5506

FCE
Film Classic Exchange
1926 S. Vermont Ave.
Los Angeles, Calif. 90007
213 731-3854

FMC
Film-Makers Cooperative
175 Lexington Ave.
New York City 10016
212

FNC
Films Inc.
35-01 Queens Blvd.
New York City 11101
212 937-1110

GRO
Grove Press Film Division
214 Mercer St.
New York City 10003
212 677-2400

HCW
Hurlock Cine World
13 Arcadia Rd.
Old Greenwich Conn.
203 637-4319

ICS
Institutional Cinema Service
29 E. 10th St.
New York City 10003
212 673-3990

JAN
Janus Films
745 5th Ave.
New York City 10022
212 PL3-7100

L-P
Leacock-Pennebaker
56 W. 45th St.
N.Y., N.Y. 10036
212 986-7020

MIN
Minot Films
Minot Bldg.
Milbridge, Maine 04658

MMA
Museum of Modern Art
Dept. of Film
11 East 53d St.
New York City 10019
212 956-6100

MOD
Modern Sound Pictures
1410 Howard St.
Omaha, Nebraska 68102
402 341-8476

ROA
Roa's Films
1696 N. Astor St.
Milwaukee, Wisc. 53202
414 271-0861

STA
Standard Film Service
14710 W. Warren Ave.
Dearborn, Mich. 48126
313 581-2250

TFC
The Film Center
915 12th St. NW
Washington, D.C. 20005
202 393-1205

TWF
Trans-World Films
332 S. Michigan Ave.
Chicago, Ill. 60604
312 922-1530

TWY
Twyman Films
329 Salem Ave.
Dayton, Ohio 45401
513 222-4014

UAS
United Artist 16
729 7th Ave.
New York City 10019
212 245-6000

UNI
Universal 16
221 Park Ave. S.
New York City 10003
212 777-6600

WIL
Wiloughby-Peerless
110 W. 32nd St.
New York City 10001
212 564-1600

WSA
Warner Brothers
Non-Theatrical Division
666 5th Ave.
New York City 10019
212 246-1000

SIGNIFICANT FILMS, 1894–1970

1894–1920   RENTAL SOURCE

FRANCE

Films of the Lumières (1895–96)   MMA
  Includes *Boat Leaving the Harbor, Feeding the Baby, Workers Leaving the Lumière Factory, Teasing the Gardner, Floods at Lyon*, etc.

Films of Méliès (1899–1912)   MMA
  Includes *The Conjuror, A Trip to the Moon, The Palace of the Arabian Nights, The Conquest of the Pole, The Doctor's Secret*

Films of Ferdinand Zecca (1906–07)   MMA
  Includes *Scenes of Convict Life, Fun After the Wedding, The Runaway Horse, Rebellion, Mutiny in Odessa, Whence Does He Come?*

The Film d'Art (1908–12)   MMA
  The Assassination of the Duc de Guise, Queen Elizabeth (with Sarah Bernhardt)

J'Accuse (1919) Abel Gance

GERMANY

The Student of Prague (1913) Stellan Rye   AUD
Homunculus (1916) Otto Rippert
The Cabinet of Dr. Caligari (1919) Robert Wiene   AUD,BRA,CON,EMG,MMA
Madame DuBarry (1919) Ernst Lubitsch   MMA
Anna Boleyn (1920) Ernst Lubitsch
From Morn To Midnight (1920) Karl Heinz Martin
The Golem: How He Came Into The World (1920) Paul Wegener   EMG,MMA
  and Carl Boese
Sumurun (1920) Ernst Lubitsch

GREAT BRITAIN

The Beginning of the British Film (1901–11) Includes *Rescued By Rover, Funeral of Queen Victoria, The Airship Destroyer, Tatters: A Tale of the Slums*   MMA

ITALY

Quo Vadis? (1912) Enrico Guazzoni   MMA
Cabiria (1913) Piero Fosco   MMA
Salammbo (1914) Giovanni Petrone   AUD,EMG

RUSSIA

Father Sergius (1918) Yakov Protazanov   BRA,MMA

SCANDINAVIA

Swedish Cinema Classics (1913–24)   MMA
  Includes excerpts from *Ingeborg Holm, Terje Vigen, The Outlaw and His Wife, Jerusalem, The Phantom Chariot, The Treasure of Arne, Erotikon, The Story of Gösta Berling*

Leaves From Satan's Book (1919–21) Carl-Theodor Dreyer   MMA
The Treasure of Arne (1919) Mauritz Stiller   EMG,MMA
The Phantom Chariot (1920) Victor Sjöström   MMA

UNITED STATES

MMA	Films of the 1890's (1894–1899)
	Includes *Execution of Mary Queen of Scots* & *Chinese Laundry* (Edison Kinetoscope), *Dickson Experimental Sound Film, The Irwin-Rice Kiss* & *Burning Stable* (Edison)
MMA	Films of Edwin S. Porter (1903–07)
	Includes *The Life of An American Fireman, The Great Train Robbery, The Dream of a Rarebit Fiend, Rescued From An Eagle's Nest, Uncle Tom's Cabin*
MMA	Films of D. W. Griffith for Biograph (1909–12)
	Includes *The Lonely Villa, A Corner in Wheat, The Lonedale Operator, The Musketeers of Pig Alley, The New York Hat*
MMA	Films of Mack Sennet (1911–20)
	Includes *Mabel's Dramatic Career, The Surf Girl, His Bread and Butter, Astray From the Steerage, The Clever Dummy, Comrades*
	The Squaw Man (1913) Cecil B. De Mille
MMA	The Birth of A Nation (1915) D. W. Griffith
AUD,EMG,MMA	Intolerance (1916) D. W. Griffith
MMA	The Deserter (1916) Scott Sidney (T. H. Ince)
AUD,EMG	The Pawn Shop (1916) Charles Chaplin
AUD,CON,EMG	The Rink (1916) Charles Chaplin
AUD,CON,EMG,GRO	The Immigrant (1917) Charles Chaplin
AUD,CON,EMG,GRO	Easy Street (1917) Charles Chaplin
AUD,CON,EMG,GRO	The Cure (1917) Charles Chaplin
AUD,CON,EMG	The Adventurer (1917) Charles Chaplin
	A Dog's Life (1918) Charles Chaplin
	Shoulder Arms (1918) Charles Chaplin
AUD,EMG,MMA	Broken Blossoms (1919) D. W. Griffith
UNI	Blind Husbands (1919) Erich von Stroheim
STA	The Kid (1920) Charles Chaplin
AUD,EMG,MIN,MMA,STA	Way Down East (1920) D. W. Griffith
AUD	One Week (1920) Buster Keaton and Eddie Cline

1921–30

FRANCE

MMA	Fièvre (1921) Louis Delluc
EMG,MMA	La Roue (1922) Abel Gance
MMA,EMG	The Crazy Ray (1923) René Clair
MMA,EMG	Entr'Acte (1924) René Clair
	Ballet Mécanique (1924) Fernand Léger
	Napoléon (1926) Abel Gance
CON	Nana (1926) Jean Renoir
AUD,EMG,MMA	The Italian Straw Hat (1927) René Clair
BRA,EMG,FCE	Un Chien Andalou (1928) Luis Buñuel and Salvador Dali
	Passion of Joan of Arc (1928) Carl-Theodor Dreyer
FNC	Tire au Flanc (1928) Jean Renoir
CON,EMG	The Kiss (1929) Jacques Feyder
CON	Autumn Fire (1930) Herman G. Weinberg
	(Abel Gance: Yesterday and Tomorrow) (1962) Nelly Kaplan

GERMANY

Der Müde Tod (Destiny) (1921) Fritz Lang	EMG,MMA
Shattered Fragments (1921) Lupu Pick	
Dr. Mabuse the Gambler (1922) Fritz Lang	MMA
Die Nubelungen Fritz Lang	MMA
Siegfried (1922–24)	
Kriemhild's Revenge (1923–24)	
Nosferatu (1922) F. W. Murnau	MMA
Vaninia (1922) Arthur von Gerlach	
The Ancient Law (1923) E. A. Dupont	
Sylvester (1923) Lupu Pick	
The Street (1923) Karl Grune	MMA
The Treasure (1923) G. W. Pabst	
Warning Shadows (1923) Arthur Robison	BRA,MMA
Der Letze Mann (The Last Laugh) (1924) F. W. Murnau	BRA,EMG,JAN,MMA
Waxworks (1924) Paul Leni	BRA
The Chronicle of Grieshus (1925) Arthur von Gerlach	
The Joyless Street (1925) G. W. Pabst	MMA
Tartuffe (1925) F. W. Murnau	FCE,EMG
Variety (1925) E. A. Dupont	BRA,CFS,EMG,MMA
Faust (1926) F. W. Murnau	
Metropolis (1926) Fritz Lang	BRA,COO,EMG,MMA,STA
Secrets of a Soul (1926) G. W. Pabst	
The Student of Prague (1926) Henrik Galeen	
Berlin, Symphony of a Great City (1927) Walther Ruttmann	MMA
The Love of Jeanne Ney (1927) G. W. Pabst	BRA,MMA
Tragedy of a Street (1927) Bruno Rahn	
Pandora's Box (1928) G. W. Pabst	
Spies (1928) Fritz Lang	MMA
Dairy of a Lost Girl (1929) G. W. Pabst	
The White Hell of Piz Paul (1929) Arnold Fanck and G. W. Pabst	UNI

GREAT BRITAIN

The Lodger (1926) Alfred Hitchcock	MMA
The Pleasure Garden (1926) Alfred Hitchcock	AUD

HOLLAND

Rain (1929)· Joris Ivens	MMA

RUSSIA

Strike (1925) Sergei Eisenstein	BRA,MMA
Potemkin (1925) Sergei Eisenstein	BRA,EMG,JAN,MMA
By the Law (1926) Lev Kuleshov	MMA
Mother (1926) V. I. Pudovkin	BRA,MMA
The End of St. Petersburg (1927) V. I. Pudovkin	BRA,MMA
Storm Over Asia (1928) V. I. Pudovkin	BRA,MMA
October (Ten Days That Shook The World) (1928) Sergei Eisenstein	BRA,EMG,MMA

BRA,MMA	Arsenal (1929) Alexander Dovzhenko
BRA,EMG	The Old and the New (1929) Sergei Eisenstein
BRA	The Man With the Movie Camera (1929) Dziga Vertov
BRA	Earth (1930) Alexander Dovzhenko

SCANDINAVIA

MMA	The Story of Gösta Berling (1923–24) Mauritz Stiller
CON	The Master of the House (1925) Carl-Theodor Dreyer

UNITED STATES

AUD	The Boat (1921) Buster Keaton and Eddie Cline
EMG,UNI	Foolish Wives (1921) Erich von Stroheim
EMG,MMA,STA	Tol'able David (1921) Henry King
AUD,EMG	Cops (1922) Buster Keaton and Eddie Cline
	Grandma's Boy (1922) Fred Newmeyer (Harold Lloyd)
CON,MMA,TFC	Nanook (1922) Robert Flaherty
AUD,MIN,MMS	Robin Hood (1922) Alan Dwan (Douglas Fairbanks)
AUD,MMA,STA	The Covered Wagon (1923) James Cruze
	The Pilgrim (1923) Charles Chaplin
	Safety Last (1923) Sam Taylor and Fred Newmeyer (Harold Lloyd)
	A Woman of Paris (1923) Charles Chaplin
	Girl Shy (1924) Sam Taylor and Fred Newmeyer (Harold Lloyd)
FNC	He Who Gets Slapped (1924) Victor Sjöström
FNC,MMA	The Iron Horse (1924) John Ford
AUD,MMA	Isn't Life Wonderful (1924) D. W. Griffith
MMA	The Marriage Circle (1924) Ernst Lubitsch
AUD	The Navigator (1924) Buster Keaton and Donald Crisp
FNC	The Big Parade (1925) King Vidor
BRA,EMG,JAN,STA	The Gold Rush (1925) Charles Chaplin
FNC	The Merry Widow (1925) Erich von Stroheim
	The Salvation Hunters (1925) Josef von Sternberg
	The Freshman (1925) Sam Taylor and Fred Newmeyer (Harold Lloyd)
JAN	The Black Pirate (1926) Albert Parker (Douglas Fairbanks)
AUD,EMG,MMA	Don Juan (1926) Alan Crosland
CON,STA,UAS	The General (1926) Buster Keaton and Clyde Bruckman
MMA	Moana (1926) Robert Flaherty
AUD	The Strong Man (1926) Frank Capra (Harry Langdon)
General	The Cat and the Canary (1927) Paul Leni
FNC	The Crowd (1927) King Vidor
AUD,CON,STA,UAS	The Jazz Singer (1927) Alan Crosland
DBF,FNC,MOD,TWY	The King of Kings (1927) Cecil B. De Mille
MMA	Seventh Heaven (1927) Frank Borzage
AUD	Steamboat Bill, Jr. (1927) Charles Reisner (Buster Keaton)
EMG,FNC,MMA	Sunrise (1927) F. W. Murnau
MMA	Underworld (1927) Josef von Sternberg
	Wings (1927) William Wellman
	The Circus (1928) Charles Chaplin

Docks of New York (1928) Josef von Sternberg
The Last Command (1928) Josef von Sternberg   MMA
The Man Who Laughs (1928) Paul Leni   UNI
Two Tars (1928) James Parrott (Laurel and Hardy)   AUD,EMG,GRO,MMA
Wedding March (1928) Erich von Stroheim
The Wind (1928) Victor Sjöström   FNC
You're Darn Tootin' (1928) Edgar Kennedy (Laurel and Hardy)   AUD,EMG,GRO
Big Business (1929) J. Wesley Horne (Laurel and Hardy)   AUD,EMG,GRO,MMA
Double Whoopee (1929) Lewis Foster (Laurel and Hardy)   AUD,EMG,GRO

1929–1935

CZECHOSLOVAKIA

Ecstasy (1933) Gustav Machaty   CON

FRANCE

A Propos de Nice (1929) Jean Vigo   CON
Under the Roofs of Paris (1930) René Clair   BRA
A Nous La Liberté (1931) René Clair   CON
L'Age d'Or (1931) Luis Buñuel and Salvador Dali
Le Million (1931) René Clair   BRA,MMA
L'Affaire est dans le Sac (1932) Pierre Prévert   CON
Blood of a Poet (1932) Jean Cocteau   AUD,BRA,EMG
Don Quixote (1932) G. W. Pabst
Zero for Conduct (1933) Jean Vigo   BRA
L'Atalante (1934) Jean Vigo   BRA
Carnival in Flanders (1934) Jacques Feyder   BRA
Madame Bovary (1934) Jean Renoir
Toni (1934) Jean Renoir   CON
The Crime of Monsieur Lange (1935) Jean Renoir   BRA

GERMANY

The Blue Angel (1930) Josef von Sternberg   CFS,CON,EMG,JAN
Westfront 1918 (1930) G. W. Pabst   MMA
Comradeship (1931) G. W. Pabst   BRA
M (1931) Fritz Lang   AUD,EMG,FCE,JAN,MMA
Mädchen in Uniform (1931) Leontine Sagan   CON
Salto Mortale (1931) G. W. Pabst
The Threepenny Opera (1931) G. W. Pabst   BRA
The Blue Light (1932) Leni Riefenstahl
Kuhle Wampe (Whither Germany?) (1932) Slatan Dudow   BRA
Liebelei (1932) Max Ophuls
The Testament of Dr. Mabuse (1933) Fritz Lang

GREAT BRITAIN

Blackmail (1929) Alfred Hitchcock   MMA
Ninety Degrees South (1933) Herbert Ponting   MMA
The Scarlet Pimpernel (1933) Harold Young   ICS
Granton Trawler (1934) John Grierson   CON,MMA
Man of Aran (1934) Robert Flaherty   General
Song of Ceylon (1934) Basil Wright (John Grierson)   CON,EMG,MMA

| | The Man Who Knew Too Much (1935)   Alfred Hitchcock |
| FCE,WIL | The Thirty Nine Steps (1935)   Alfred Hitchcock |

HOLLAND

| MMA | New Earth (1934)   Joris Ivens |

RUSSIA

| BRA | Frontier (1935)   Alexander Dovzhenko |

SCANDINAVIA

| AUD,EMG,FCE | Vampyr (1932)   Carl-Theodor Dreyer |

SPAIN

| EMG,MMA | Land Without Bread (1932)   Luis Buñuel |

UNITED STATES

FNC	The Broadway Melody (1929) Harry Beaumont
UNI	Applause (1929) Rouben Mamoulian
UNI	Cocoanuts (1929) Joseph Santley and Robert Florey (Marx Brothers)
UNI	Thunderbolt (1929) Josef von Sternberg
CON,UNI	All Quiet on the Western Front (1930) Lewis Milestone
AUD	The Dawn Patrol (1930) Howard Hawks
UNI	Monte Carlo (1930) Ernest Lubitsch
MMA,UNI	Morocco (1930) Josef von Sternberg
AUD,CON,STA,TWF,UAS,WIL	Little Caesar (1930) Mervyn Le Roy
UNI	An American Tragedy (1931) Josef von Sternberg
	City Lights (1931) Charles Chaplin
UNI	City Streets (1931) Rouben Mamoulian
EMG,GRO	Laughing Gravy (1931) James Hornell (Laurel and Hardy)
AUD,CON,UAS,WIL	Public Enemy (1931) William Wellman
EMG	Tabu (1931) Robert Flaherty and F. W. Murnau
MMA, UNI	Broken Lullaby (The Man I Killed) (1932) Ernest Lubitsch
FNC,MMA	The Lost Squadron (1932) George Archainbaud
MMA,UNI	Million Dollar Legs (1932) Edward Cline
AUD,EMG,GRO	The Music Box (1932) James Parrott (Laurel and Hardy)
UNI	The Mummy (1932) Karl Freund
	Scarface (1932) Howard Hawks
UNI	Shanghai Express (1932) Josef von Sternberg
FNC	Tarzan, the Ape Man (1932) W. S. Van Dyke
UNI	Trouble in Paradise (1932) Ernst Lubitsch
UNI	Design for Living (1933) Ernst Lubitsch
FNC	Dinner at Eight (1933) George Cukor
CON,MMA,UNI	Duck Soup (1933) Leo McCary (Marx Brothers)
AUD,CON,WIL	Footlight Parade (1933) Lloyd Bacon
AUD,CON,UAS,WIL	Gold Diggers of 1933 (1933) Mervyn Le Roy
UNI	I'm No Angel (1933) Wesley Ruggles (Mae West)
FNC,JAN	King Kong (1933) Merian C. Cooper and Ernest Schoedsack
UNI	S.O.S. Iceberg (1933) Tay Garnett

She Done Him Wrong (1933) Lowell Sherman (Mae West)	UNI
The Black Cat (1934) Edgar Ulmer	UNI
Crime Without Passion (1934) Charles MacArthur and Ben Hecht	UNI
It Happened One Night (1934) Frank Capra	COL,ICS
It's A Gift (1934) Norman McLeod (W. C. Fields)	UNI
The Lost Patrol (1934) John Ford	FNC
Our Daily Bread (1934) King Vidor	JAN,MMA
The Scarlet Empress (1934) Josef von Sternberg	TFC,UNI
Viva Villa (1934) Jack Conway and Howard Hawks	FNC
Becky Sharp (1935) Rouben Mamoulian	FCE,ICS
The Bride of Frankenstein (1935) James Whale	UNI
The Devil is a Woman (1935) Josef von Sternberg	MMA,UNI
Gold Diggers of 1935 (1935) Busby Berkeley	AUD,CON,UAS,WIL
The Informer (1935) John Ford	AUD,BRA,FNC,JAN
Mutiny on the Bounty (1935) Frank Lloyd	FNC
A Night at the Opera (1935) Sam Wood (Marx Brothers)	FNC
Ruggles of Red Gap (1935) Leo McCarey	MMA,UNI
Steamboat Round the Bend (1935) John Ford	FNC

1936–1940

FRANCE

The Lower Depths (1936) Jean Renoir	CON
Grand Illusion (1937) Jean Renoir	JAN
A Day in the Country (1938) Jean Renoir	CON
La Marseillaise (1938) Jean Renoir	CON
North Hotel (1938) Marcel Carné	
Quai des Brumes (Port of Shadows) (1938) Marcel Carné	CON
Le Jour se Lève (Daybreak) (1939) Marcel Carné	JAN
Rules of the Game (1939) Jean Renoir	JAN
Volpone (1939) Maurice Tourneur	CON,MMA

GERMANY

Triumph of the Will (1934–36) Leni Riefenstahl	AUD,CON,MMA
Olympia (1936–38) Leni Riefenstahl	AUD,CON,MMA

GREAT BRITAIN

Night Mail (1936) Harry Watt and Basil Wright (John Grierson)	CON,EMG,MMA
Rembrandt (1936) Alexander Korda	
Secret Agent (1936) Alfred Hitchcock	MMA
Things to Come (1936) William Cameron Menzies	ICS,TFC
The Lady Vanishes (1938) Alfred Hitchcock	JAN
North Sea (1938) Harry Watt (Alberto Cavalcanti)	MMA
Pygmalion (1938) Anthony Asquith and Leslie Howard	
Four Feathers (1939) Zoltan Korda	

RUSSIA

Alexander Nevsky (1938) Sergei Eisenstein	BRA,JAN
Shors (1939) Alexander Dovzhenko	BRA

UNITED STATES

UAS	The Charge of the Light Brigade (1936) Michael Curtiz
FNC	Fury (1936) Fritz Lang
	Modern Times (1936) Charles Chaplin
UNI	My Man Godfrey (1936) Gregory La Cava
EMG,MMA	The Plow that Broke the Plains (1936) Pare Lorentz
FNC	The Prisoner of Shark Island (1936) John Ford
FNC	Swing Time (1936) George Stevens (Fred Astaire and Ginger Rogers)
UNI	Angel (1937) Ernst Lubitsch
FNC	The Hurricane (1937) John Ford
General	Lost Horizon (1937) Frank Capra
EMG,MMA	The River (1937) Pare Lorentz
	Snow White and the Seven Dwarfs (1937) Walt Disney
BRA	Spanish Earth (1937) Joris Ivens
CON	You Only Live Once (1937) Fritz Lang
	The Adventure of Robin Hood (1938) Michael Curtiz and William
UAS	Keighley
FNC	Bringing Up Baby (1938) Howard Hawks
	Holiday (1938) George Cukor
BRA,UAS,WIL	Jezebel (1938) William Wyler
EMG,MOD,ROA,WIL	Swiss Miss (1938) John Blystone (Laurel and Hardy)
FNC	Babes in Arms (1939) Busby Berkeley
UNI	Beau Geste (1939) William Wellman
SWA,UNI	Destry Rides Again (1939) George Marshall
	Gone With the Wind (1939) Victor Fleming
FNC,JAN	Gunga Din (1939) George Stevens
AUD,CON,MOD,TWF	Mr. Smith Goes to Washington (1939) Frank Capra
FNC	Ninotchka (1939) Ernest Lubitsch
FNC	Northwest Passage (1939) King Vidor
MOD	Only Angels Have Wings (1939) Howard Hawks
AUD,CON,UAS,WIL	The Roaring Twenties (1939) Raoul Walsh
ROA	Stagecoach (1939) John Ford
UNI	Tower of London (1939) Rowland V. Lee
TFC,UNI	Union Pacific (1939) Cecil B. De Mille
FNC	Wuthering Heights (1939) William Wyler
AUD,UNI	The Bank Dick (1940) Edward Cline (W. C. Fields)
	The Wizard of Oz (1939) Victor Fleming
CON,FNC,MMA	The Grapes of Wrath (1940) John Ford
	The Great Dictator (1940) Charles Chaplin
UNI	The Great McGinty (1940) Preston Sturges
AUD	His Girl Friday (1940) Howard Hawks
UNI	Northwest Mounted Police (1940) Cecil B. De Mille
FNC	The Philadelphia Story (1940) George Cukor
EMG,MMA	Power and the Land (1940) Joris Ivens

1941–1945

CANADA

	A Little Phantasy on a 19th Century Painting (1942) Norman
CON,GRO	McLaren

FRANCE

Le Corbeau (The Raven) (1943)   Henri-Georges Clouzot

The Ladies of the Bois de Boulogne (1944)   Robert Bresson

GREAT BRITAIN

Film and Reality (1942)   Alberto Cavalcanti   CON

In Which We Serve (1942)   David Lean and Noel Coward   COS

One of Our Aircraft is Missing (1942)   Michael Powell and Emeric
   Pressburger

Desert Victory (1943)   Roy Boulting   CON,MMA,TWF,WIL

World of Plenty (1943)   Paul Rotha   CON

Blithe Spirit (1945)   David Lean

The Life and Death of Colonel Blimp (1945)   Michael Powell and   COS
   Emeric Pressburger

ITALY

Obsession (1942)   Luchino Visconti   CON

Open City (1945)   Roberto Rosselini

RUSSIAN

Ivan the Terrible (Part I) (1943)   Sergei Eisenstein   BRA,JAN

SCANDINAVIA

Day of Wrath (1943)   Carl-Theodor Dreyer   CON

Torment (1944)   Alf Sjöberg   JAN

UNITED STATES

Ball of Fire (1941)   Howard Hawks   FNC

Citizen Kane (1941)   Orson Welles   AUD,FNC,MOD,JAN

Fantasia (1941)   Walt Disney

The Lady Eve (1941)   Preston Sturges   UNI

The Little Foxes (1941)   William Wyler   FNC

How Green Was My Valley (1941)   John Ford   FNC

The Maltese Falcon (1941)   John Huston   UAS

Man Hunt (1941)   Fritz Lang   FNC

The Shanghai Gesture (1941)   Josef von Sternberg

Sullivan's Travels (1941)   Preston Sturges   MMA,UNI

Suspicion (1941)   Alfred Hitchcock   FNC

Swamp Water (1941)   Jean Renoir   FNC

Tobacco Road (1941)   Michael Curtiz   MOD,WIL,WSA

Casablanca (1942)   Michael Curtiz   UAS

The Land (1942)   Robert Flaherty   MMA

The Magnificent Ambersons (1942)   Orson Welles   FNC,JAN,MOD

Mrs. Miniver (1942)   William Wyler   FNC

The Palm Beach Story (1942)   Preston Sturges   UNI

This Gun For Hire (1942)   Frank Tuttle   TFC,UNI

To Be Or Not To Be (1942)   Ernst Lubitsch   WIL

Yankee Doodle Dandy (1942)   Michael Curtiz   UAS

Air Force (1943)   Howard Hawks   UAS,WIL

Shadow of a Doubt (1943)   Alfred Hitchcock   UNI

UAS	Arsenic and Old Lace (1944) Frank Capra
MMA	The Battle of San Pietro (1944) Major John Huston
COS,MMA	The Fighting Lady (1944) Louis de Rochemont
FNC	Gaslight (1944) George Cukor
MOD,ROA,TFC,UNI	Going My Way (1944) Leo McCarey
UNI	Hail the Conquering Hero (1944) Preston Sturges
FNC	Laura (1944) Otto Preminger
FNC	Lifeboat (1944) Alfred Hitchcock
FNC	Meet Me In St. Louis (1944) Vincente Minelli
	Miracle of Morgan's Creek (1944) Preston Sturges
	To Have and Have Not (1944) Howard Hawks
UNI	The Uninvited (1944) Lewis Allen
EMG	And Then There Were None (1945) René Clair
FNC,MOD	Isle of the Dead (1945) Mark Robson
MMA,UNI	The Lost Weekend (1945) Billy Wilder
UNI	Ministry of Fear (1945) Fritz Lang
FNC,UAS,WIL	Objective Burma (1945) Raoul Walsh
General	Spellbound (1945) Alfred Hitchcock
FNC	They Were Expendable (1945) John Ford
General	The True Glory (1945) Carol Reed and Garson Kanin
UAS	The Woman in the Window (1945) Fritz Lang

1946–1950

CANADA

CON,GRO	Fiddle-De-De (1947) Norman McClaren
CON,GRO	Begone Dull Care (1949) Norman McClaren

FRANCE

CON	Children of Paradise (1946) Marcel Carné
JAN	Beauty and the Beast (1946) Jean Cocteau and Réne Clément
	Van Gogh (1948) Alan Resnais
GRO	The Blood of the Beasts (1949) Georges Franju
JAN	Orpheus (1949) Jean Cocteau
GRO	Guernica (1950) Alain Resnais
JAN	La Ronde (1950) Max Ophuls

GREAT BRITAIN

COS	Brief Encounter (1946) David Lean
CON	Dead of Night (1946) Charles Crichton, Basil Dearden, Robert Hamer under the supervision of Alberto Cavalcanti
COS	Henry V (1946) Laurence Olivier
CON	Instruments of the Orchestra (1946) Muir Mathieson
COS	The Seventh Veil (1946) Compton Bennett
COS	Stairway to Heaven (1946) Michael Powell and Emeric Pressburger
COS	Black Narcissus (1947) Michael Powell and Emeric Pressburger
COS	Great Expectations (1947) David Lean
CON,JAN	Odd Man Out (1947) Carol Reed
CON,JAN	Oliver Twist (1947) David Lean

Hamlet (1948)   Laurence Olivier   COS
The Red Shoes (1948)   Michael Powell and Emeric Pressburger   COS
The Fallen Idol (1949)   Carol Reed   COS
Kind Hearts and Coronets (1949)   Robert Hamer   CON,JAN,TWF
Scott of the Antarctic (1949)   Charles Frend   COS
The Lavender Hill Mob (1950)   Charles Crichton   CON,JAN,TWF
Seven Days to Noon (1950)   The Boulting Brothers   COS
The Third Man (1950)   Carol Reed   COS

ITALY

Paisan (1946)   Roberto Rossellini
Shoeshine (1946)   Vittorio De Sica
The Earth Trembles (1948)   Luchino Visconti   AUD
The Miracle (1948)   Roberto Rossellini
The Bicycle Thief (1949)   Vittorio De Sica   BRA
Bitter Rice (1949)   Giuseppe de Santis
Variety Lights (1950)   Federico Fellini and Alberto Lattuada   AUD,CON
Cronach di un Amore (1950)   Michelangelo Antonioni

JAPAN

Drunken Angel (1948)   Akira Kurosawa   BRA
Stray Dog (1949)   Akira Kurosawa   BRA
Rashomon (1950)   Akira Kurosawa   JAN

RUSSIA

Ivan the Terrible (Part II) (1946)   Sergei Eisenstein   BRA,JAN

SCANDINAVIA

Rhythm of a City (1947)   Arne Sucksdorff
Summer Interlude (1950)   Ingmar Bergman   JAN

UNITED STATES

The Best Years of Our Lives (1946)   William Wyler   FNC
The Big Sleep (1946)   Howard Hawks   AUD,CON,UAS,WIL
Diary of a Chambermaid (1946)   Jean Renoir   FCE
Lady in the Lake (1946)   Robert Montgomery   FNC
My Darling Clementine (1946)   John Ford   FNC,MMA
Notorious (1946)   Alfred Hitchcock   AUD,BRA,TWF,WIL
The Stranger (1946)   Orson Welles   AUD,UAS
Body and Soul (1947)   Robert Rossen   BRA,WIL
Duel in the Sun (1947)   King Vidor   General
The Exile (1947)   Max Ophuls
Fireworks (1947)   Kenneth Anger   FMC
Mad Wednesday (1947)   Preston Sturges (Harold Lloyd)
Monsieur Verdoux (1947)   Charles Chaplin
Out of the Past (1947)   Maurice Torneur
Woman on the Beach (1947)   Jean Renoir   FNC
Force of Evil (1948)   Abraham Polonsky   WIL
Gentleman's Agreement (1948)   Elia Kazan   FNC

UAS	Key Largo (1948) John Huston
BRA	The Lady From Shanghai (1948) Orson Welles
BRA,WIL	Letter from an Unknown Woman (1948) Max Ophuls
CON	Louisiana Story (1948) Robert Flaherty
General	Macbeth (1948) Orson Welles
	The Naked City (1948) Jules Dassin
FMC	Psyche; Lysis; Charmides (1948) Gregory Markopoulos
CON	The Quiet One (1948) Sidney Meyers
UAS	Red River (1948) Howard Hawks
	Rope (1948) Alfred Hitchcock
UAS	The Treasure of the Sierra Madre (1948) John Huston
WIL	Caught (1949) Max Ophuls
General	All the King's Men (1949) Robert Rossen
FNC	Letter to Three Wives (1949) Joseph Mankiewicz
AUD,MOD	She Wore a Yellow Ribbon (1949) John Ford
WIL	White Heat (1949) Raoul Walsh
FNC	All About Eve (1950) Joseph Mankiewicz
FNC	The Asphalt Jungle (1950) John Huston
	Devil's Doorway (1950) Anthony Mann
General	Gerald McBoing Boing (1950) John Hubley
FNC,MMA	The Gunfighter (1950) Henry King
FNC	King Solomon's Mines (1950) Compton Bennett and Andrew Marton
FNC	Panic in the Streets (1950) Elia Kazan
FNC	Sunset Boulevard (1950) Billy Wilder
General	Trouble Indemnity (Mr. Magoo) (1950) John Hubley
FNC	Twelve O'Clock High (1950) Henry King
FNC	Where the Sidewalk Ends (1950) Otto Preminger
UNI	Winchester '73 (1950) Anthony Mann

1951–1955

CANADA

CON	Blinkity Blank (1955) Norman McClaren

FRANCE

BRA	Diary of a Country Priest (1951) Robert Bresson
	Le Plaisir (1951) Max Ophuls
	The River (1951) Jean Renoir
JAN	Forbidden Games (1952) René Clément
	Hôtel des Invalides (1952) Georges Franju
BRA	The Wages of Fear (1953) Georges Clouzot
WAS	Les Diaboliques (1954) Georges Clouzot
COS	Monsieur Hulot's Holiday (1954) Jacques Tati
	Rififi (1954) Jules Dassin
BRA	Lola Montes (1955) Max Ophuls
CON	Night and Fog (1955) Alain Resnais

GERMANY

	Der Verlorene (1951) Peter Lorre
HCW	The Last Bridge (1954) Helmut Kautner

The Last Ten Days (1955) G. W. Pabst   AUD

GREAT BRITAIN

Tales of Hoffman (1951) Michael Powell and Emeric Pressburger   COS
Breaking the Sound Barrier (1952) David Lean   AUD,WIL
The Importance of Being Earnest (1952) Anthony Asquith   JAN
The Man in the White Suit (1952) Alexander Mackendrick   COS,TWF
The Man Between (1953) Carol Reed   AUD,WIL
Genevieve (1954) Henry Cornelius   COS
O Dreamland (1954) Lindsay Anderson   GRO
Animal Farm (1955) John Halas & Joy Batchelor   CON
Mr. Arkadin (1955) Orson Welles   AUD,CON
Richard III (1955) Laurence Olivier

ITALY

Miracle in Milan (1951) Vittorio De Sica   AUD
The Golden Coach (1952) Jean Renoir   BRA
Umberto D (1952) Vittorio De Sica   AUD
The White Sheik (1952) Federico Fellini   AUD,CON
La Signora Senza Camelie (1952) Michelangelo Antonioni
I Vitelloni (1953) Federico Fellini   AUD
Senso (1954) Luchino Visconti   AUD
La Strada (1954) Federico Fellini   BRA
Il Bidone (1955) Federico Fellini   AUD
Le Amiche (1955) Michelangelo Antonioni

JAPAN

The Idiot (1951) Akira Kurosawa
Ikiru (1952) Akira Kurosawa   BRA
Gate of Hell (1953) Teinosuke Kinusaga   JAN,MOD,SWA,TWY
Ugetsu (1953) Kenji Mizoguchi   JAN
The Crucified Lovers (1954) Kenji Mizoguchi   CIN
The Bailiff (1954) Kenji Mizoguchi   BRA
An Inn At Osaka (1954) Heinosuke Gosho
Seven Samurai (1954) Akira Kurosawa   AUD
The Burmese Harp (1955) Kon Ichikawa   BRA
Empress Yang-Kwei-Fei (1955) Kenji Mizoguchi   CIN
I Live In Fear (Record of a Living Being) (1955) Akira Kurosawa   BRA
Saga of the Taira Clan (1955) Kenji Mizoguchi   CIN

MEXICO

Los Olvidados (The Young and the Damned) (1951) Luis Buñuel   BRA
El (1952) Luis Buñuel   BRA
Robinson Crusoe (1952) Luis Buñuel

POLAND

A Generation (1954) Andrzej Wajda   JAN

SCANDINAVIA

JAN	Miss Julie (1951) Alf Sjöberg
JAN	Monika (1952) Ingmar Bergman
General	The Great Adventure (1953) Arne Sucksdorff
CON	Sawdust and Tinsel (Naked Night) (1953) Ingmar Bergman
JAN	Ordet (1955) Carl-Theodor Dreyer
JAN	Smiles of a Summer Night (1955) Ingmar Bergman

SPAIN

JAN	Death of a Cyclist (1955) Juan A. Bardem

UNITED STATES

FNC	A Place in the Sun (1951) George Stevens
	A Streetcar Named Desire (1951) Elia Kazan
FNC	An American In Paris (1951) Vincente Minelli
FNC	Quo Vadis (1951) Mervyn Le Roy
WAS	Strangers on a Train (1951) Alfred Hitchcock
COS	The Thirteenth Letter (1951) Otto Preminger
	The African Queen (1952) John Huston
UNI	Bend of the River (1952) Anthony Mann
AUD	Clash By Night (1952) Fritz Lang
General	High Noon (1952) Fred Zinnemann
FNC	Monkey Business (1952) Howard Hawks
UAS	Moulin Rouge (1952) John Huston
FNC	The Naked Spur (1958) Anthony Mann
AUD	Rancho Notorious (1952) Fritz Lang
General	The Road Runner Cartoons (1952–1958) Chuck Jones, I. Freleng
FNC	Singin' In The Rain (1952) Stanley Donen and Gene Kelley
BRA,FNC	Viva Zapata (1952) Elia Kazan
CON	Anatahan (1953) Josef von Sternberg
FNC	The Bandwagon (1953) Vincente Minelli
	The Big Heat (1953) Fritz Lang
L-P	Daybreak Express (1953) D. A. Pennebaker
UNI	The Far Country (1953) Anthony Mann
General	From Here to Eternity (1953) Fred Zinnemann
FNC	Julius Caesar (1953) Joseph Mankiewicz
	Limelight (1953) Charles Chaplin
	The Moon Is Blue (1953) Otto Preminger
FNC	Roman Holiday (1953) William Wyler
FNC	Shane (1953) George Stevens
FNC	Young Bess (1953) George Sidney
WAS	A Star Is Born (1954) George Cukor
AUD,FMC,GRO	Desistfilm (1954) Stan Brakhage
General	Dial M For Murder (1954) Alfred Hitchcock
FNC	Johnny Guitar (1954) Nicholas Ray
FNC	Moonfleet (1954) Fritz Lang
General	On the Waterfront (1954) Elia Kazan
	Rear Window (1954) Alfred Hitchcock
BRA,JAN	Salt of the Earth (1954) Herbert Biberman

Seven Brides For Seven Brothers (1954) Stanley Donen	FNC
The Wild One (1954) Laslo Benedek	General
Bad Day At Blackrock (1955) John Sturges	FNC
The Big Knife (1955) Robert Aldrich	UAS
Blackboard Jungle (1955) Richard Brooks	FNC
Bullfight (1955) Shirley Clarke	FMC
East of Eden (1955) Elia Kazan	General
Giant (1955) George Stevens	
The Last Frontier (1955) Anthony Mann	General
The Man from Laramie (1955) Anthony Mann	General
The Man with the Golden Arm (1955) Otto Preminger	
Marty (1955) Delbert Mann	UAS
The Night of the Hunter (1955) Charles Laughton	UAS
Rebel Without A Cause (1955) Nicholas Ray	General
Third Avenue El (1955) Carson Davidson	CON
The Trouble With Harry (1955) Alfred Hitchcock	
War and Peace (1955) King Vidor	FNC

1956–1960

ARGENTINA

La Casa del Angel (End of Innocence) (1957) Leopold Torre Nilsson	AUD

CANADA

Universe (1960) National Film Board	CON

FRANCE

And God Created Woman (1956) Roger Vadim (Brigitte Bardot)	
The Red Balloon (1956) Albert Lamorisse	BRA
The Silent World (1956) Jacques-Yves Costeau	General
Gervaise (1957) René Clément	COS
Sunday In Peking (1957) Chris Marker	CON
Le Beau Serge (1958) Claude Chabrol	
The Cousins (1958) Claude Chabrol	CON
Frantic (1958) Louis Malle	AUD
The Lovers (1958) Louis Malle	CON
My Uncle (1958) Jacques Tati	CON
Black Orpheus (1959) Marcel Camus	JAN,UAS
Breathless (1959) Jean-Luc Godard	CON
The Four Hundred Blows (1959) Francois Truffaut	JAN
Hiroshima, Mon Amour (1959) Alan Resnais	AUD,CON
Picnic on the Grass (1959) Jean Renoir	CON
Dream of the Wild Horses (1960) Denis Colomb de Daunant	CON
Leda (1960) Claude Chabrol	AUD
Lola (1960) Jacques Demy	CON
Purple Noon (1960) René Clément	AUD
Shoot the Piano Player (1960) Francois Truffaut	JAN
The Testament of Orpheus (1960) Jean Cocteau	
Le Voyage de Mr. Q (1960) Don Wolfe and Claude Labarre	CON

GREAT BRITAIN

CON	Mamma Don't Allow (1956) Tony Richardson and Karel Reisz
CON	Thursday's Children (1956) Guy Brenton and Lindsay Anderson
CON	Every Day Except Christmas (1957) Lindsay Anderson
	The One That Got Away (1957) Roy Baker
UNI	A Night To Remember (1958) Roy Baker
UAS	The Horse's Mouth (1958) Ronald Neame
COS	Room At The Top (1958) Jack Clayton
CON	We Are The Lambeth Boys (1958) Karel Reisz
WSA	Look Back In Anger (1959) Tony Richardson
CON	Our Man In Havana (1959) Carol Reed
JAN	The Running, Jumping, and Standing Still Film (1959) Richard Lester
AUD	The Angry Silence (1960) Guy Green
COS	The Entertainer (1960) Tony Richardson
AUD	I'm All Right, Jack (1960) John Boulting
COS	Saturday Night and Sunday Morning (1960) Karel Reisz

GREECE

UAS	He Who Must Die (1958) Jules Dassin

HOLLAND

CON	Glass (1958) Bert Haanstra

INDIA

AUD	Pather Panchali (1956) Satyajit Ray
AUD	Aparajito (1958) Satyajit Ray
BRA	The World of Apu (1959) Satyajit Ray

ITALY

CON	Il Grido (1957) Michelangelo Antonioni
BRA	Nights of Cabiria (1956) Federico Fellini
JAN	L'Avventura (1959) Michelangelo Antonioni
AUD	La Dolce Vita (1959) Federico Fellini
COS	General Della Rovere (1960) Roberto Rossellini
UAS	La Notte (1960) Michelangelo Antonioni
AUD	Rocco And His Brothers (1960) Luchino Visconti

JAPAN

AUD	Street of Shame (1956) Kenji Mizoguchi
BRA	The Lower Depths (1957) Akira Kurosawa
BRA	Throne of Blood (1957) Akira Kurosawa
JAN	Fires on the Plain (1959) Kon Ichikawa
BRA	The Human Condition (1960) Masaki Kobayashi
BRA	The Bad Sleep Well (1960) Akira Kurosawa

MEXICO

AUD	Nazarin (1958) Luis Buñuel

POLAND

Eroica (1957)   Andrzej Munk
Man on the Track (1957)   Andrzej Munk
Kanal (1957)   Andrzej Wajda   JAN
Two Men and a Wardrobe (1957)   Roman Polanski   CON
Ashes and Diamonds (1958)   Andrzej Wajda   JAN
Dom (1958)   Waldemar Borowcyk and Jan Lenica   CON
Knights of the Teutonic Order (1960)   Aleksander Ford

RUSSIA

The Cranes Are Flying (1958)   Mikhail Kalatozov   BRA
Ballad of a Soldier (1960)   Grigori Chukhrai   AUD,JAN

SCANDINAVIA

The Seventh Seal (1956)   Ingmar Bergman   JAN
Wild Strawberries (1957)   Ingmar Bergman   JAN
The Magician (1958)   Ingmar Bergman   JAN
The Virgin Spring (1959)   Ingmar Bergman   JAN
The Flute and the Arrow (1960)   Arne Sucksdorff   AUD,JAN

SPAIN

Lazarillo (1960)   Cesar Ardavin   AUD

UNITED STATES

The Adventures of ° (1956)   John and Faith Hubley   CON,GRO
Around the World in 80 Days (1956)   Michael Anderson   UAS
Baby Doll (1956)   Elia Kazan
The Court Jester (1956)   Norman Panama and Melvin Frank (Danny FNC
   Kaye)
Invasion of the Body Snatchers (1956)   Don Siegel   HCW
The Killing (1956)   Stanley Kubrick   UAS
On The Bowery (1956)   Lionel Rogisin   CON,GRO
The Searchers (1956)   John Ford   WSA
The Ten Commandments (1956)   Cecil B. De Mille
The Bridge on the River Kwai (1957)   David Lean   General
N. Y., N. Y. (1957)   Francis Thompson   MMA
Paths of Glory (1957)   Stanley Kibrick   UAS
Sweet Smell of Success (1957)   Alexander Mackendrick   UAS
Bridges-Go-Round (1958)   Shirley Clarke   CON,FMC
The Lefthanded Gun (1958)   Arthur Penn   AUD
Roots of Heaven (1958)   John Huston   FNC
Tarnished Angels (1958)   Douglas Sirk   UNI
Touch of Evil (1958)   Orson Welles   UNI
Vertigo (1958)   Alfred Hitchcock
Anatomy of a Murder (1959)   Otto Preminger   General
Ben Hur (1959)   William Wyler
The Horse Soldiers (1959)   John Ford   UAS
North By Northwest (1959)   Alfred Hitchcock   FNC
Rio Bravo (1959)   Howard Hawks   WSA

UAS	Some Like It Hot (1959) Billy Wilder
AUD,GRO,FMC	Window Water Baby Moving (1959) Stan Brakhage
UAS	The Apartment (1960) Billy Wilder
FNC	Chance Meeting (1960) Joseph Losey
BRA	Day of the Painter (1960) Robert Davis (Ezra Baker)
UAS	Exodus (1960) Otto Preminger
CON,EMG	The Fall of the House of Usher (1960) Roger Corman
FMC	The Flower Thief (1960) Ron Rice
CON	Harvest of Shame (1960) David Lowe
FNC	Heller In Pink Tights (1960) George Cukor
UNI	Psycho (1960) Alfred Hitchcock
AUD	Shadows (1960) John Cassavetes
FNC	Sons and Lovers (1960) Jack Cardiff
BRA	The 1000 Eyes of Dr. Mabuse (1960) Fritz Lang

1961–1965

ARGENTINA

AUD	The Fall (1961) Leopoldo Torre Nilsson
AUD	Hand in the Trap (1961) Leopoldo Torre Nilsson
AUD	Summerskin (1961) Leopoldo Torre Nilsson
	The Eavesdropper (1964) Leopoldo Torre Nilsson

CANADA

CON	Very Nice, Very Nice (1961) Arthur Lipsett
CON	Free Fall (1965) Arthur Lipsett

BRAZIL

HCW	Black God, White Devil (1963) Glauber Rocha

CZECHOSLOVAKIA

AUD	The Fifth Horseman Is Fear (1964) Zbynek Brynych
AUD	Intimate Lighting (1965) Ivan Passer
AUD	Loves of a Blonde (1965) Milos Forman
AUD	The Shop On Main Street (1965) Jan Kadar and Elmar Kos

FRANCE

CON	A Woman is a Woman (1961) Jean-Luc Godard
CON	Chronicle of a Summer—Paris (1960) Edgar Morin and Jean Rouch
AUD	Cleo from 5 to 7 (1960) Agnes Varda
JAN	Jules and Jim (1961) Francois Truffaut
AUD	Last Year at Marienbad (1961) Alain Resnais
CON	An Occurrence at Owl Creek Bridge (1962) Robert Enrico
CON	Le Joli Mai (1962) Chris Marker
COL,ICS	Sundays and Cybele (1962) Serge Bourguignon
CON	A Valparaiso (1963) Joris Ivens
	The Carabiniers (1963) Jean-Luc Godard
AUD	Contempt (1963) Jean-Luc Godard
CON	The Elusive Corporal (1963) Jean Renoir

L'Immortelle (1963) Alain Robbe-Grillet	GRO
La Jetée (1963) Chris Marker	JAN
Muriel (1963) Alain Resnais	UAS
The Smile (1963) Serge Bourguignon	CON
The Married Woman (1964) Jean-Luc Godard	COL
That Man From Rio (1964) Philippe De Broca	UAS
Umbrellas of Cherbourg (1964) Jacques Demy	AUD
World Without Sun (1964) Jacques-Yves Costeau	GEN
Alphaville (1965) Jean-Luc Godard	CON
Le Bonheur (1965) Agnes Varda	JAN
Thomas L'Imposteur (1965) Georges Franju	CON
The 317th Platoon (1965) Pierre Schoendorffer	AUD
The Sleeping Car Murder (1965) Costa-Gavras	AUD

GREAT BRITAIN

The Innocents (1961) Jack Clayton	FNC
A Kind of Loving (1961) John Schlesinger	AUD
A Taste of Honey (1962) Tony Richardson	COS
The Concrete Jungle (1962) Joseph Losey	BRA
The Loneliness of the Long Distance Runner (1962) Tony Richardson	COS
Billy Liar (1963) John Schlesinger	COS
Lord of the Flies (1963) Peter Brook	COS
This Sporting Life (1963) Lindsay Anderson	COS
Tom Jones (1963) Tony Richardson	UAS
A Hard Day's Night (1964) Richard Lester	UAS
Guns At Batasi (1964) John Guillermin	FNC
The Servant (1964) Joseph Losey	AUD
Zulu (1964) Cy Endfield	AUD,CWF
Darling (1965) John Schlesinger	AUD
Help! (1965) Richard Lester	UAS
The Knack (1965) Richard Lester	UAS
Repulsion (1965) Roman Polanski	COL

HOLLAND

Seven Authors in Search of a Reader (1965) Frans Weisz	CON

HUNGARY

The Round Up (1965) Miklos Jancso	AUD

INDIA

Devi (1961) Satyajit Ray	AUD
Two Daughters (1961) Satyajit Ray	JAN
Kanchenjungha (1962) Satyajit Ray	AUD

ITALY

Accatone (1961) Pier Palo Pasolini	BRA
Divorce Italian Style (1961) Pietro Germi	AUD
Eclipse (1961) Michelangelo Antonioni	AUD

JAN	The Sound of Trumpets (1961) Ermanno Olmi
AUD	Two Women (1961) Vittorio De Sica
AUD	Mondo Cane (1962) Gualtiero Jacopetti
AUD	8½ (1962) Federico Fellini
JAN	The Fiances (1963) Ermanno Olmi
AUD	Red Desert (1964) Michelangelo Antonioni
AUD	Juliet of the Spirits (1965) Federico Fellini

JAPAN

AUD	The Island (1961) Kaneto Shindo
AUD,JAN	Yojimbo (1961) Akira Kurosawa
	Sanjuro (1962) Akira Kurosawa
AUD	Tokyo Olympiad (1964) Kon Ichikawa
CON	Woman in the Dunes (1964) Hiroshi Teshigahara
COS	Kwaidan (1965) Masaki Kibayashi
	Red Beard (1965) Akira Kurosawa

MEXICO

AUD	Simon of the Desert (1965) Luis Buñuel

POLAND

AUD	Joan of the Angels (1961) Jerzy Kawalerowicz
BRA	Knife in the Water (1961) Roman Polanski
CON	Labyrinth (1961) Jan Lenica
CON	Mammals (1962) Roman Polanski
	Passenger (1963) Andrzej Munk and Witold Lesiewicz

SCANDINAVIA

JAN	Through A Glass Darkly (1961) Ingmar Bergman
JAN	Winter Light (1962) Ingmar Bergman
JAN	491 (1963) Vilgot Sjöman
JAN	The Silence (1963) Ingmar Bergman
JAN	All These Women (1964) Ingmar Bergman
CON	Gertrud (1964) Carl-Theodor Dryeor
	Raven's End (1964) Bo Widerberg

SPAIN

AUD	Viridiana (1961) Luis Buñuel
AUD	To Die In Madrid (1965) Frederic Rossif

UNITED STATES

FNC	Breakfast at Tiffany's (1961) Blake Edwards
AUD	El Cid (1961) Anthony Mann
FNC	The Hustler (1961) Robert Rossen
FNC	One-Eyed Jacks (1961) Marlon Brando
AUD,FMC,GRO	Prelude: Dog Star Man (1961) Stan Brakhage
UAS	West Side Story (1961) Jerome Robbins and Robert Wise

David and Lisa (1962) John Perry	COS
Hatar! (1962) Howard Hawks	FNC
Lolita (1962) Stanley Kubrick	FNC
Lonely Are the Brave (1962) David Miller	CON,UNI
The Manchurian Candidate (1962) John Frankenheimer	UAS
Merrill's Marauders (1962) Samuel Fuller	
The Miracle Worker (1962) Arthur Penn	UAS
Mister Arkadin (1962) Orson Welles	CON
Ride the High Country (1962) Sam Peckinpah	FNC
What Ever Happened To Baby Jane? (1962) Robert Aldrich	General
The Birds (1963) Alfred Hitchcock	CWF,MOD,ROA,TFC,UNI
Charade (1963) Stanley Donen	CWF,UNI
Cleopatra (1963) Joseph Mankiewicz	FNC
Dr. No (1963) Terence Young	
Flaming Creatures (1963) Jack Smith	FMC
The Great Escape (1963) John Sturges	UAS
Hallelujah The Hills (1963) Adolfas Mekas	JAN
The Haunting (1963) Robert Wise	FNC
Hud (1963) Martin Ritt	FNC
Love With the Proper Stranger (1963) Robert Mulligan	FNC
Quint City U.S.A. (1963) Richard Leacock	L-P
Scorpio Rising (1963) Kenneth Anger	FMC
Soldier In The Rain (1963) Ralph Nelson	HCW
To Kill A Mockingbird (1963) Robert Mulligan	UNI
Twice A Man (1963) Gregory Markopoulos	FMC
Breathdeath (1964) Stan Vanderbeek	GRO
Campaign Manager (1964) Richard Leacock and Noel Parmentel	L-P
Dr. Strangelove (1964) Stanley Kubrick	COL
Help! My Snowman's Burning Down (1964) Carson Davidson	CON
Lilith (1964) Robert Rossen	General
Point of Order (1964) Emile dè Antonio	COS
One Potato, Two Potato (1964) Larry Peerce	CON
Sunday in New York (1964) Peter Tewksbury	FNC
To Be Alive (1964) Francis Thompson	
Baby The Rain Must Fall (1965) Robert Mulligan	General
Black Natchez (1965) Ed Pincus and David Newman	L-P
Bunny Lake Is Missing (1965) Otto Preminger	General
China (1965) Felix Greene	GRO
Dr. Zhivago (1965) David Lean	
Echoes of Silence (1965) Peter Goldman	FMC
The Ipcress File (1965) Sidney J. Furie	SWA,TFC,UNI
Major Dundee (1965) Sam Peckinpah	General
Mickey One (1965) Arthur Penn	General
Oh Dem Watermelons (1965) Robert Nelson	AUD,FMC
The Sound of Music (1965) Robert Wise	
The Spy Who Came in From the Cold (1965) Martin Ritt	FNC
Time Piece (1965) Jim Henson	CON
Zorba (1965) Michael Cacoyannis	FNC

YOGOSLAVIA

CON	Ersatz (1961) Dusan Vukotic
CON	A Visit From Space (1964) Dusan Vukotic
CON	The Wall (1965) Ante Zaninovic
CON	Elegy (1965) Nedeljko Dragic

1966–1970

BRAZIL

GRO	Land In Anguish (1967) Glauber Rocha
HCW	Antonio Das Mortes (1969) Glauber Rocha

CANADA

CON	A Place To Stand (1967) Christopher Chapman
GRO	Warrendale (1967) Allen King

CZECHOSLOVAKIA

AUD	A Report on the Party and the Guests (1966) Jan Nemec
AUD	Closely Watched Trains (1966) Jiri Menzel
	The Firemen's Ball (1967) Milos Forman
AUD	Capricious Summer (1968) Jiri Menzel
GRO	The Joke (1969) Jaromil Jires

FRANCE

CIN	Au Hasard Balthazar (1966) Robert Bresson
BRA	La Guerre est Finie (1966) Alain Resnais
COL	Masculine-Feminine (1966) Jean-Luc Godard
CIN	Mouchette (1966) Robert Bresson
	Two or Three Things I Know About Her (1966) Jean-Luc Godard
CON	Pierre Le Fou (1966) Jean-Luc Godard
CON	The Anderson Platoon (1967) Pierre Schoendorffer
HCW	Belle de Jour (1967) Luis Buñuel
L-P	La Chinoise (1967) Jean-Luc Godard
GRO	Weekend (1967) Jean-Luc Godard
	A Movie Like the Others (1968) Jean-Luc Godard
AUD	Les Biches (1968) Claude Chabrol
	One Plus One (Sympathy for the Devil) (1968) Jean-Luc Godard
GRO	Destroy, She Said (1969) Marguerite Duras
HCW	La Femme Infidele (1969) Claude Chabrol
GRO	The Man Who Lies (1969) Alain Robbe-Grillet
GRO	Pravda (1969) Jean-Luc Godard
GRO	See You At Mao (1969) Jean-Luc Godard
UAS	Stolen Kisses (1969) Francois Truffaut
L-P	The Wanderer (1969) Jean-Gabriel Albicocco
	The Wind From the East (1969) Jean-Luc Godard
	Z (1969) Costa-Gavras
	Le Boucher (1970) Claude Chabrol
	The Confession (1970) Costa-Gavras

L'Enfant Sauvage (1970)   Francois Truffaut
Mississippi Mermaid (1970)   Francois Truffaut

GERMANY

Cat and Mouse (1966) Hansjurgen Pohland	GRO
Yesterday Girl (1966) Alexander Kluge	
Young Törless (1966) Volker Schlöndorff	CON
The Artistes at the Top of the Big Top: Disoriented (1968) Alexander Kluge	
Signs of Life (1968) Werner Herzog	

GREAT BRITAIN

Blow-Up (1966) Michelangelo Antonioni	FNC
Cul-de-Sac (1966) Roman Polanski	AUD
Fahrenheit 451 (1966) Francois Truffaut	CWF,SWA,UNI
King and Country (1966) Joseph Losey	AUD
Morgan! (1966) Karel Reisz	COL
How I Won The War (1967) Richard Lester	UAS
The Charge of the Light Brigade (1968) Tony Richardson	UAS
Charlie Bubbles (1968) Albert Finney	UNI
The Bed Sitting Room (1969) Richard Lester	UAS
If . . . (1969) Lindsay Anderson	FNC
Loves of Isadora (1969) Karel Reisz	UNI
Oh What a Lovely War (1969) Richard Attenborough	FNC

HUNGARY

The Red and the White (1968) Miklos Jancso	BRA
Silence and Cry (1968) Miklos Jancso	BRA
The Winter Wind (1969) Miklos Jancso	GRO

ITALY

The Battle of Algiers (1966) Gillo Pontecorvo	AUD
A Fistful of Dollars (1966) Sergio Leone	UAS
For A Few Dollars More (1967) Sergio Leone	UAS
The Good, The Bad, and the Ugly (1967) Sergio Leone	UAS
The Damned (1969) Luchino Visconti	
Teorema (1969) Pier Paolo Pasolini	COS
Fellini Satyricon (1970) Federico Fellini	

JAPAN

Boy (1969) Nagisa Oshima	GRO

POLAND

Barrier (1966) Jerzy Skolimowski	JAN

RUSSIA

War and Peace (1968) Sergei Bondarchuk	COS

SCANDINAVIA

	Adalen '31 (1966) Bo Widerberg
AUD	Hunger (1966) Henning Carlsen
UAS	Persona (1966) Ingmar Bergman
COL	Elvira Madigan (1967) Bo Widerberg
GRO	I Am Curious (Yellow) (1967) Vilgot Sjöman
UAS	Hour of the Wolf (1968) Ingmar Bergman
GRO	I Am Curious (Blue) (1968) Vilgot Sjöman
	Doctor Glas (1969) Mai Zetterling
UAS	Shame (1969) Ingmar Bergman
	The Passion (1970) Ingmar Bergman

SENEGAL

GRO	Mandabi (1968) Ousmane Sembene

SPAIN

	Tristana (1970) Luis Buñuel

UNITED STATES

FNC	Alfie (1966) Lewis Gilbert
FMC	Castro Street (1966) Bruce Baillie
FMC,GRO,ROG	Chafed Elbows (1966) Robert Downey
FMC	The Chelsea Girls (1966) Andy Wharol
COL	The Endless Summer (1966) Bruce Brown
FNC	Flight of the Phoenix (1966) Robert Aldrich
UNI	Mirage (1966) Edward Dmytryk
	Modesty Blaise (1966) Joseph Losey
FNC	Seven Women (1966) John Ford
L-P	A Stravinsky Portrait (1966) Richard Leacock
BRA,FMC	Time of the Locust (1966) Peter Gessner
CWF,SWA,UNI	Torn Curtain (1966) Alfred Hitchcock
	The Wild Angels (1966) Roger Corman
WSA	You're A Big Boy Now (1966) Francis Ford Coppola
WSA	Bonnie and Clyde (1967) Arthur Penn
	David Holzman's Diary (1967) Jim McBride
L-P	Don't Look Back (1967) D. A. Pennebaker
FNC	El Dorado (1967) Howard Hawks
EMB	The Graduate (1967) Mike Nichols
COL	In Cold Blood (1967) Richard Brooks
	The Nude Restaurant (1967) Andy Wharol
FNC	Point Blank (1967) John Boorman
UAS	Skaterdater (1967) Noel Black
GRO	The Titicut Follies (1967) Frederick Wiseman
COS	Ulysses (1967) Joseph Strick
CON	Urbanissimo (1967) John and Faith Hubley
L-P	You're Nobody Til Somebody Loves You (1967) D. A. Pennebaker
FNC	The Boston Strangler (1968) Richard Fleischer
WSA	Bullitt (1968) Peter Yates

Candy (1968)   Christian Marquand
Chiefs (1968)   Richard Leacock and Noel Parmentel   L-P
Coogan's Bluff (1968)   Don Siegel   UNI
Faces (1968)   John Cassavetes   COS
Greetings (1968)   Briane De Palma   AUD
The Killing of Sister George (1968)   Richard Aldrich
Madigan (1968)   Don Siegel   UNI
Petulia (1968)   Richard Lester   WSA
Pretty Poison (1968)   Noel Black   FNC
Romeo and Juliet (1968)   Franco Zeffirelli
Rosemary's Baby (1968)   Roman Polanski   FNC
Targets (1968)   Peter Bogdanovitch   FNC
2001: A Space Odyssey (1968)   Stanley Kubrick
The Yellow Submarine (1968)   George Dunning
Agnes Varda's Black Panthers: A Report (1969)   Agnes Varda   GRO
Alice's Restaurant (1969)   Arthur Penn   UAS
Butch Cassiday and The Sundance Kid (1969)   George Roy Hill   FNC
Downhill Racer (1969)   Michael Ritchie   FNC
Easy Rider (1969)   Dennis Hopper
In the Year of the Pig (1969)   Emile dè Antonio   CON
Medium Cool (1969)   Haskell Wexler   FNC
Midnight Cowboy (1969)   John Schlesinger
Monterey Pop (1969)   D. A. Pennebaker   L-P
Putney Swope (1969)   Robert Downey
Salesman (1969)   The Maysles
Tell Them Willie Boy Is Here (1969)   Abraham Polonsky   UNI
The Wild Bunch (1969)   Sam Peckinpah
Catch-22 (1970)   Mike Nichols
M°A°S°H (1970)   Robert Altman
Woodstock (1970)   Michael Wadleigh
Zabriskie Point (1970)   Michelangelo Antonioni

YUGOSLAVIA

I Even Met Happy Gypsies (1967)   Aleksandar Petrovic   AUD
Love Affair, or the Case of the Missing Switchboard Operator (1967)
    Dusan Makavejev   BRA
Early Works (1968)   Zelimir Zilnik   GRO
Kaya, I'll Kill You (1968)   Vatroslav Mimica   AUD
Playing At Soldiers (1968)   Bato Cengic
Horoscope (1969)   Boro Draskovic

APPENDIX 2:
BUDGET OUTLINE

Salaries

Director
Script, including research
Director of Photography
Talent, including rehearsal, shooting, and dubbing
Crew

    Unit Manager/Asst. Director (A.D.)
    Camera Operator
    Asst. Cameraman
    Grip
    Gaffer
    Electrician(s)
    Prop Man
    Script Girl
    Wardrobe Mistress
    Make-Up
    Hairdresser
    Go-fer
    Sound Recordist
    Sound Mixer
    Boom Man

Raw Stock

Amount determined by the shooting ratio—length of film exposed
compared to proposed length of final edited film.
Must know whether 16mm or 35mm, type of stock, whether color
or black-and-white.

Shooting Expenses

Stock Shots, including search and cost
Animation
Location scouting and trip with director and camerman
Location Shooting (all items to be multiplied by number of days
needed)

    Travel
    Permits and/or Rental of site
    Food
    Miscellaneous Expenses
    Sound Costs
        Quarter-inch Tape
        Sound Equipment
    Sets
    Costumes
    Props
    Equipment Rental (by the day or by the week, which is five
times the daily rate)

Special Equipment
Underwater, aerial, process
Studio Shooting (all items to be multiplied by the number of days needed)
Essentially the same items as Location Shooting
NOTE: For both location and studio shooting, figure the number of days needed to build and strike the set in the rental cost.

Laboratory Costs

Developing the Original: same length as stock exposed in shooting
Printing the Dailies: same as or close to the amount of stock exposed
Answer Prints: Length of picture
Internegative or Interpositive: length of picture
Optical Reduction or Blow-up: Length of picture
Release Prints: length of picture
Dissolves and Fades: estimate of number needed

Post-production Fees

Editing: length of film, but computed by the reel
Include voice editing
Matching the Original: computed by the reel
Narration
Narrator
Recording: time, quarter-inch stock, 35mm or 16mm stock, transfer, editing
Music
Library or Original
Original: Composer, arrangement, copying, musicians (a minimum three-hour session, if union, at approximate rate of fifteen minutes of music per session), studio time, stock, transfer, editing. Check union rules as to required director and contractor and union scale for all musicians.
Library: fee to include music license, selection, editing, stock, transfer, mix supervision.
Sound Effects
Recorded live: recordist, stock, and equipment
Stock Library: same as music
Editing
Opticals and Titles
Dubbing
Studio time and stock
May require looping and laying-in voice after recording
Sound Mix
Studio time; stock (quarter-inch tape and 35mm); optical negative, including stock and developing; music-and-effects track, protection tape

Screening Expenditures
Projector (16mm)
Projection Studio (35mm)
Interlock

Insurance
Equipment Insurance
Negative Insurance
Faulty Stock and Camera Insurance
Cast Insurance
Producer's Liability Insurance
Props, Wardrobe, and Sets Insurance
Extra Expense Insurance
Third Party Property Damage Insurance
Rain Insurance

Producer's Fee
Fifteen percent of the total production cost

APPENDIX 3:

AMERICAN STANDARD

NOMENCLATURE FOR MOTION-PICTURE FILM USED IN STUDIOS AND PROCESSING LABORATORIES

GENERAL

Motion picture film. Motion-picture film is a thin flexible ribbon of transparent plastic having perforations and bearing one or more sensitized layers capable of producing photographic images. *Note:* The term "film" may be applied to unexposed film, to exposed but unprocessed film, and to exposed and processed film.

Raw stock. Raw stock is film which has not been exposed or processed.

Film base. Film base is the plastic material upon which a photographic emulsion is coated; namely, the support for the emulsion in photographic film. *Note:* All film base manufactured in the United States for motion-picture use since 1952 has been safety base.

Safety base. Safety base is the slow-burning film support used for motion picture films which complies with American Standard Motion-Picture Safety Film, PH22. 31–1958.

Magnetic sound film. Magnetic sound film is a film base having film perforations along one or both edges and bearing a ferromagnetic coating, either completely across the film or in stripes, the coating capable of accepting and reproducing sound records. *Note:* Unperforated materials usually are referred to as magnetic tape.

Film perforations. Film perforations are the regularly and accurately spaced holes that are punched throughout the length of motion-picture film. These holes are engaged by the teeth of various sprock-ets and pins by which the film is transported and positioned as it travels through cameras, processing machines, projectors and other film-handling machinery.

Perforation pitch. The perforation pitch is the distance from the bottom edge of one perforation to the bottom edge of the next perforation, measured along the length of the film. *Note:* Perforations are being identified currently by two-letter designations such as BH (Bell & Howell), KS (Kodak Standard), DH (Dubray-Howell) or CS (Cinema-Scope). A numeral, such as 1866, designates the pitch in ten thousandths of an inch. A designation 1R, 2R or 4R, used with films having 16mm perforations, refers to the number of rows of perforations across the narrow dimension of the film.

35mm perforation, BH-1866. The 35mm negative perforation has sharp corners, curved sides, a maximum width of 0.110 in. and a height of 0.073 in. (American Standard Dimensions for 35mm Motion-Picture Short-Pitch Negative Film, PH22.93–1953). *Note:* This perforation is used for negative and some special-purpose 35mm films.

35mm perforation, KS-1870. The 35mm positive perforation is rectangular in shape, with a width of 0.110 in., a height of 0.078 in. and a fillet in each corner with a radius of 0.020 in. (American Standard Dimensions for 35mm Motion-Picture Positive Raw Stock, PH22. 36–1954). *Note:* This perforation is used on most positive 35mm film.

35mm perforation, DH-1870. This perforation is rectangular in shape, with a height of 0.073 in., a width of 0.110 in. and a fillet in each corner with a radius of 0.013 in. (American Standard Dimensions for 35mm Motion-Picture Film, Alternate Standards for Either Positive or Negative Raw Stock, PH22.1–1953). *Note:* This perforation is used on 35mm color print film.

35mm perforation, CS-1870. This perforation is rectangular in shape, with a height of 0.073 in., a width of 0.078 in. and a fillet in each corner with a radius of 0.013 in. (American Standard Dimensions for 35mm Motion-Picture Films, CS-1870, PH22.102–1956). The outer edge of this perforation is at a different distance from the edge of the film than the other 35mm film perforations listed above. *Note:* This perforation is used mainly on color positive film.

16mm perforation. The 16mm perforation is rectangular in shape, with a height of 0.050 in., a width of 0.072 in. and a fillet in each corner with a radius of 0.010 in. It is used on the following films:

35mm motion picture film perforated 32mm, 2R-2994. This is a 35mm film with 16mm perforations so arranged that if 1½ mm were slit from each edge of the film and the film were slit down the middle, two 16mm films would result, each having one row of perforations. The perforation pitch (0.2994 in.) is normally used for negative film and some special-purpose films (American Standard Dimensions for 35mm Motion-Picture Film, Perforated 32mm, 2R-2994, PH22.73–1958).

35mm motion picture film perforated 32mm, 2R-3000. This is a 35mm film with 16mm perforations so arranged that when 1½ mm are slit from each edge of the film and the film is slit down the middle, two 16mm films result, each with one row of perforations. The perforation pitch specified is normally used for positive film and some special-purpose films.

32mm motion picture film, 2R-3000. This is a film 32mm in width which when slit down the middle results in two 16mm films each having one row of perforations (American Standard Dimensions for 32mm Motion-Picture Film, 2R-3000, PH22. 71–1957). This perforation pitch is used mainly on positive film.

32mm motion picture film, 4R-3000. This is a film 32mm in width which when slit down the middle results in two 16mm films each having two rows of perforations (American Standard Dimensions for 32mm Motion-Picture Film, 4R-3000, PH22.72–1957). This perforation pitch is normally used on positive film.

Negative image. A negative image is a photographic image in which the brightness scale is approximately inverted with respect to the brightness scale of the original subject. In color negatives the hue scale is usually, but not necessarily, complementary to the hue scale of the original subject and the brightness scale is inverted.

Positive image. A positive image is a photographic replica in which the tones of the gray scale or color values of the originally photographed subject are represented in their natural order.

Black-and-white image. A black-and-white image is an image produced on a black-and-white film.

Color image. A color image is an image produced on a color film.

Anamorphic image. An anamorphic image is an image which has been produced by an optical system having different horizontal and vertical magnifications. *Note:* Equal horizontal and vertical magnification is assumed unless the term anamorphic is applied specifically.

Aspect ratio. Aspect ratio is the ratio of width to height of a projected picture image. *Note:* This is the more common usage, although the term is also applied to photographic images and to camera, printer and projector apertures.

Synchronism. Synchronism is the relation between the picture and sound with respect either to the physical location on the film or films or to the time at which corresponding picture and sound are seen and heard.

Projection synchronism. Projection synchronism is the time relation between picture and corresponding sound in a projection print. *Note:* The sound record on a projection print is, in most cases, in advance of the corresponding picture. The displacement is specified in picture frames in the following American Standards:

Soundtrack	Standard
A 35mm Photographic	PH22.40–1957
B 16mm Photographic	PH22.41–1957
C 35mm Magnetic°	PH22.103–1957
D 16mm Magnetic	PH22.112–1958
E 8mm Magnetic	†

Editorial synchronism. Editorial synchronism is the relationship between the picture and sound film during the editorial process. *Note:* During the editorial process, the soundtrack and corresponding picture, whether on the same or separate films, are kept in alignment and not offset as for projection. Many composite release negatives are supplied in editorial synchronism.

16mm motion picture film, 1R-2994. This film is 16mm in width, perforated along one edge only (American Standard Dimensions for 16mm Motion picture film, 1R-2994, PH22. 109–1958). This perforation pitch is normally used on negative film.

*In this case, the sound is behind the corresponding picture.

†A standard is now under consideration by the SMPTE Sound Engineering Committee.

16mm motion picture film, 1R-3000. This film is 16mm in width, perforated along one edge only (American Standard Dimensions for 16mm Film, Perforated One Edge, PH22. 12–1953). This perforation pitch is normally used on positive film.

16mm motion picture film, 2R-2994. This film is 16mm in width, perforated along both edges (American Standard Dimensions for 16mm Motion-Picture Film, 2R-2994, PH22.110–1958). This perforation pitch is normally used on both black-and-white and color camera films.

16mm motion picture film, 2R-3000. This film is 16mm in width, perforated along both edges (American Standard Dimensions for 16mm Film, Perforated Two Edges, PH22.5–1953). This perforation pitch is normally used on positive film.

Photographic emulsions. A photographic emulsion consists of dispersions of light-sensitive materials in a colloidal medium, usually gelatin, carried as a thin layer on film base. *Note:* Photographic materials are usually designated as negative or positive types according to their light sensitivity (speed), or usage; negative emulsions, in general, being more sensitive than positive emulsions.

Black-and-white film. Black-and-white film carries an emulsion in which, after processing, brightness values of a scene are reproduced only in tones of the gray scale.

Color film. Color film carries one or more emulsions in which, after processing, brightness values of a scene are reproduced in terms of color scales.

Reversal film. A reversal film is one which, after an exposure, is processed by a first development, a bleach and a redevelopment to produce a positive image. If exposure is made by printing from a negative, a negative image is produced by the reversal process.

Image (photographic). An image is any photographically obtained likeness in a processed photosensitive material.

Latent image. A latent image is the invisible image registered on a photographic emulsion due to the reaction produced in the emulsion by exposure to radiant energy. *Note:* This image becomes visible after development.

Picture image. A picture image is a photographically obtained likeness of any object on photographic material.

Sound image. A sound image is a photographically obtained soundtrack or sound record.

Camera synchronism. Camera synchronism is the relation between picture and soundtrack in a composite camera original. *Note:* Camera synchronism is generally not the same as editorial synchronism. In 16mm single systems the two are normally in projection synchronism but this is not the case for most 35mm single systems (i.e., where picture and sound are recorded on the same film).

Exposure. Exposure is the process of subjecting a photographic film to suitable intensity of radiant energy for a given time in such manner that it may produce a latent image on an emulsion. *Note:* Exposure = intensity × time.

Processing. Processing is the generic term applied to the total operation necessary to produce a permanent visible image on exposed film.

Development. Development is that part of processing which makes visible the latent image of an exposed photographic emulsion.

Fixing (fixation). Fixing (fixation) is that part of processing which removes the residual sensitive silver salts from a developed film to render the developed image permanent. *Note:* During the process of fixation, films are customarily treated to preserve and harden the developed image. Adequate washing or neutralizing treatment is necessary following fixation for image permanence.

Bleaching. Bleaching is that part of processing which converts a developed silver image into a silver salt.

Printing. Printing is the operation of exposing raw stock by using the processed image of another film as the light modulator.

Contact printing. Contact printing is that method of printing in which the raw stock is held in intimate contact with the film bearing the image to be copied.

Step contact printing. Step contact printing is that method of contact printing in which the film being copied and the raw stock are advanced intermittently frame-by-frame, being exposed to the printer light only when stationary.

Continuous contact printing. Continuous contact printing is that method of contact printing by which light modulating film and the raw stock move at the same constant speed past the printing aperture.

Projection printing (optical printing). Projection printing (optical printing) is printing by projecting the image to be copied through an optical system onto the raw stock. *Note:* The printed image with respect to the projected image may be identical, an enlargement or a reduction or anamorphic image; or additional anamorphosis may be added or removed.

A and B Printing. A and B printing is a method of making composite images, such as fades, dissolves or effects, in a release printer without requiring a duplicating process. *Note:* The name comes from the fact that the films are edited into two separate rolls called A and B rolls. The sequences of pictures originally in one roll are in synchronization with opaque leader in the other roll. When these two are printed in a separate operation onto a single roll of raw stock, an opportunity is afforded for the introduction of effects and for eliminating visible splices on the screen.

Projection. Projection is the presentation of an enlarged image of the film on a screen for visual review. In addition the sound may be reproduced for aural review.

Production. Production is the general term used to describe the processes involved in making all the original material that is the basis for the finished motion picture.

Editorial process. Editorial process is the term used to describe the combining, cutting, editing and other preparation of material obtained from the original material to make the finished motion picture.

Re-recording. Re-recording is the electrical process of transferring sound records from one or more films, magnetic tapes or discs to other films, tapes or discs. *Note:* Re-recording may be used to combine different sound records into a single record to adjust the frequency-response characteristic or to adjust the relative levels between different scenes and sequences.

Release. Release is a generic term used to designate films used for or intended for general distribution and exhibition.

Release negative. A release negative is a complete negative prepared specifically for printing release prints. *Note:* A release negative may consist of separate picture and sound negatives and may be in either projection or editorial synchronism, depending upon the film-processing technique to be employed in making release prints.

Release print. A release print is a print made for general distribution and exhibition. It may be on films of 8mm, 16mm, 35mm or 70mm width. Some release prints are composed of two or more 35mm-width films which are projected simultaneously in lateral alignment.

PICTURE NEGATIVE FILM,
BLACK-AND-WHITE AND COLOR

Picture negative. A picture negative is any processed film that possesses a negative picture image of the subject or film image to which it was exposed. This term is sometimes erroneously used to refer to the raw film before processing, either with or without exposure.

Original picture negative. The original picture negative is the negative film that was exposed in a camera and processed to produce a negative image of the original subject.

Background plate negative. A background plate negative is a picture negative which is used for printing background plates.

Picture library negative. A picture library negative is a picture negative that is usually held in a film library for use in reproducing scenes which would otherwise have to be made as original material for each production.

Title negative. A title negative is a negative that is exposed to a title card or to both a title card and background.

Picture duplicate negative. A picture duplicate ("dupe") negative is a picture negative made from black-and-white, color or separation master positive films. *Note:* It may be used for making additional prints or it may be cut and edited to form a part of the picture release negative.

Internegative. An internegative film is a negative derived directly from a color reversal original film. *Note:* All other color duplicating negatives derived from other than reversal film will be known as color duplicate negatives regardless of the generation.

Picture-release negative. A picture-release negative is a cut and edited picture negative used for printing the picture portion of release prints. *Note:* It may consist of intercut original picture negatives, picture dupe negatives, etc., depending upon the choice of available material or the intended use of the release print.

Foreign picture-release negative. A foreign picture-release negative is a picture-release negative prepared specifically for printing foreign-version-release prints. *Note:* It is almost invariably a duplicate negative.

16mm picture-release negative. A 16mm picture-release negative is a picture-release negative on 16mm film prepared specifically for printing 16mm release prints.

PICTURE POSITIVE FILM,
BLACK-AND-WHITE AND COLOR

Picture print. A picture print is a processed film that possesses a positive picture image of the subject or film image to which it was exposed.

Picture daily print. A picture daily print is the first picture print made from the original picture negative for use in checking photographic quality, camera technique, actions, etc.

Picture work print. A picture work print is a positive print which usually consists of intercut picture daily prints, picture library prints, prints of dissolves, montages, titles, etc., and has synchronism constantly maintained with the corresponding sound work print.

Picture library print. A picture library print is a picture print made from a picture library negative.

Background plate (background print film). A background plate (background print film) is a picture print made specifically for use in projection background or similar process work, and is a print of a background plate negative.

Picture master positive. A picture master positive is a print usually made on a special film, for the purpose of producing picture duplicate negatives.

35mm separation positive. A 35mm separation positive is a black-and-white film with a positive image of the red, green or blue image component of a color negative. It is usually made by printing through suitable filters from a color negative onto a panchromatic black-and-white film.

35mm protection master positive. A 35mm protection master positive film is a positive film made from the final cut and edited black-and-white or color release negative. In case of damage to the release negative, a duplicate negative could be made from this protection master positive. In the case of color, this protection master positive may be a set of three black-and-white separation master positives or a color master positive.

35mm panchromatic master positive. A 35mm panchromatic master positive is a black-and-white print made on a panchromatic film from a color negative for the purpose of making a black-and-white duplicate negative.

Composite print. A composite print is a positive film having both picture and corresponding sound on the same film, which may be in editorial or projection synchronism.

Composite daily print. A composite daily print is made from an original composite negative or original sound and picture negatives, and is used for checking photography, sound quality, action, etc. It is in projection synchronism.

First trial composite print. The first trial composite is the first composite print made from the picture and sound-release negatives for the purpose of checking and correcting picture and sound quality, negative cutting and assembly, etc. It is in projection sychronism.

Second, third, etc., trial composite print. The second, third etc., trial composite print is similar to the first trial composite print, but has successive corrections incorporated as a result of viewing the previous trial composite prints.

Final trial composite. A final trial composite is a composite print, approved for release, in which all corrections found necessary in previous trial composite prints have been incorporated. *Note:* The final trial composite may be any one of the various trial composite prints, depending upon the type and extent of corrections required.

Composite master positive. A composite master positive is a composite print usually made for the purpose of producing composite or picture and sound duplicate negatives which would be used for printing release prints. *Note:* It is usually made on duplicating positive film and may be in either editorial or projection synchronism.

Foreign version release print. A foreign version release print is a composite print in projection synchronism with dialogue made specifically for the particular language involved. *Note:* Sometimes superimposed titles in a different language are used on the print. A superimposed title consists of printed words (usually transparent) overlaying the picture image.

Foreign version trial composite prints. Foreign version trial composite prints are similar to trial composite prints made during release, except that they are made for checking the release of the particular language version involved.

REVERSAL FILM,
BLACK-AND-WHITE AND COLOR
Reversal original. A reversal original is the film that is originally exposed in a camera or recorder and is processed by reversal to produce a positive image. *Note:* This positive image obtained by the reversal process is not the same as a print from a negative inasmuch as right and left are transposed; when viewed by projection on an opaque screen, the emulsion side of the print from a negative must face the light source and the emulsion side of a reversal original must face the lens in order for the screen image to have the same lateral orientation as the original scene.

Composite reversal original. A composite reversal original is a reversal original which has both picture and corresponding sound on the same film.

Reversal print. A reversal print is a reversal-type film that has been exposed to a positive film image, usually a reversal original film, and processed by the reversal process.

Reversal master print, 16mm. A reversal master print is a 16mm reversal print made specifically for use in producing other prints. *Note:* It is sometimes referred to as a first generation duplicate, prints from it then being referred to as second generation duplicates.

Reduction reversal print, 16mm. A reduction reversal print is a reversal print made on 16mm reversal film from a 35mm positive by reduction printing and development by the reversal process.

PHOTOGRAPHIC SOUND
Note: All definitions in this section will be understood to be photographic unless the term "magnetic" is used.

Photographic sound. Photographic sound is a sound record in the form of a photographic image.

Sound negative. A sound negative is any film that, after exposure and subsequent processing, produces a negative sound record on the film. This sound record requires the steps of printing and processing of a second film in order to obtain a reasonably faithful reproduction of the original sound, by the conventional scanning system. *Note:* The negative image may be obtained by exposure through a positive sound image; by direct recording; or, by the reversal process, from another sound negative.

Original sound negative. The original sound negative is the sound negative that is exposed in a film recorder and, after processing, produces a negative sound image on the film.

Sound effects negative. A sound effects negative is a sound negative upon which sound effects have been recorded. It is ordinarily held in library stock.

Music Negative. A music negative is a sound negative upon which music has been recorded. It is usually an original sound negative but may be a library negative.

Sound Cut Negative. A sound cut negative is a sound negative that is composed of sections of original sound negatives spliced in sequence. *Note:* The sound cut negative is generally in exact conformity with the sound work print and produces a single sequentially spliced negative. The print of the sound cut negative provides all, or portions of, the re-recording print.

Re-recorded negative. A re-recorded negative is a sound negative which is exposed by re-recording and, when processed, produces a negative sound track image.

Sound release negative. A sound release negative is a photographic sound negative in the form required for the final printing operation onto the release print raw stock. *Note:* The sound release negative may consist of re-recorded negatives, intercut original sound negatives, duplicate negatives of sound records, etc., depending upon the choice of available material or the intended use of the print.

Special sound release negative. A special sound release negative is a sound release negative made for the purpose of obtaining a soundtrack which has characteristics other than those obtained from the sound release negative.

Special sound release negative for use in 16mm release of 35mm pre-print material. The special sound release negative for 16mm release of 35mm original material is a photographic sound negative, either 35mm or 16mm, recorded with specific characteristics for reasonably faithful reproduction of the original sound on 16mm reproduction equipment. It may be re-recorded from a print of the 35mm sound release negative or from the 35mm re-recording print.

Special sound release negative, foreign release in English. The special sound release negative for use in English version for foreign release is re-recorded from the re-recording print, except that the dialogue track is modified to remove American colloquialisms.

Special sound release negative, foreign language version. The special sound release negative for use in foreign language version release is usually re-recorded using all of the re-recording tracks, except the dialogue track, for which is substituted a special synchronized dialogue track in the foreign language for which the release is being made.

Sound release dupe negative. A sound release dupe negative is a duplicate negative of the sound record prepared specifically for printing the soundtrack of release prints.

Sound print. A sound print is any positive obtained by printing from a sound negative, or direct positive recording, or, by the reversal process, from another sound positive. A sound print provides a reasonably faithful reproduction of the original sound through the conventional scanning system.

Sound daily print. A sound daily print is the first sound print made from the original sound negative for checking sound quality, technique, etc.

Sound work print. A sound work print is a sound print that usually consists of intercut sound daily prints, but may also include other soundtracks of sound effects or music, or both, on the same or separate films, with synchronism constantly maintained with the corresponding picture work print.

Sound effects print. A sound effects print is a sound print made from a sound effects negative, or from another sound effects print by reversal processing.

Music print. A music print is a sound print made from a music negative.

Re-recording print. A re-recording print is a sound print prepared specifically for use in re-recording to produce a re-recorded negative. *Note:* A re-recording print may be a print from a sound cut negative, a specially intercut print, or a combination of both. It usually consists of several sound records on separate films that include dialogue, sound effects, music, or any other required material. The term is used interchangeably to designate the entire group of associated films or any individual film that is part of the group.

Re-recorded print. A re-recorded print is a sound print from a re-recorded soundtrack negative.

Sound check print. A sound check print is a sound print made from the sound release negative for the purpose of checking negative cutting, printing lights, sound quality, etc. *Note:* When a sound check print is required, it is usually made prior to the first trial composite print.

Sound master positive. A sound master positive is a sound print on special film stock that is usually made from a sound release negative for the purpose of producing duplicate negatives of the sound record for release printing.

Composite print. *See under* Picture Positive Film, Black-and-White and Color.

Composite Daily Print. *See under* Picture Positive Film, Black-and-White and Color.

MAGNETIC SOUND

Magnetic sound film. *See under* General.

Full coat magnetic film. Full coat magnetic film has the magnetic coating compound applied across the film from edge to edge.

Full coat between perforations magnetic film. Full coat between perforations magnetic film has the magnetic coating compound across the film from perforation to perforation.

Magnetic striping. Magnetic striping is a process by which a magnetic coating compound is applied in the form of single or multiple stripes, having specific widths and placements, to either surface of a film base which may or may not have a photographic emulsion.

Balance stripe. A balance stripe is a magnetic coating or coating of another material that is equal in thickness to, but may be narrower than, the stripe used for recording. It is applied along the opposite edge of the film. Its primary purpose is to equalize the effective thickness of the two edges of the striped film in order to obtain uniform winding. The stripe is sometimes used for the recording of additional sound or control records.

Magnetic original. A magnetic original is the original or first sound record on a magnetic film.

Magnetic transfer. A magnetic transfer is a magnetic sound record obtained by electrical re-recording of a magnetic original onto another magnetic film.

Magnetic master. A magnetic master is a final edited or re-recorded magnetic sound record used for transfer to a magnetic release print or for transfer to a photographic sound negative to be used for manufacturing prints with photographic sound tracks.

Magoptical release print. *See under* Release Prints.

RELEASE PRINTS

Release Print. *See under* General.

Composite release print. A composite release print is a print having both picture and sound records in projection synchronism on the same film. *Note:* The sound record may be photographic, magnetic, or both.

Domestic release print. A domestic release print is a release print intended for distribution within the country where the print was manufactured and having dialogue in the language of that country. It may be a composite print or may have magnetic sound track or tracks on a separate film.

Foreign version release print. *See under* Picture Positive Film, Black-and-White and Color.

Anamorphic release print. An anamorphic release print is a release print in which the picture image is compressed laterally, requiring a deanamorphosing lens on the projector to cause objects in the projected picture to have correct proportions.

Wide-Screen release print. A wide-screen release print is a print which has no anamorphosis but, when projected, produces a screen image having an aspect ratio greater than 1.33 to 1. *Note:* Some prints are made from negatives exposed in a camera aperture having an aspect ratio of 1.33 to 1, but which have been composed for projection to yield a projected picture having an aspect ratio greater than 1.33 to 1. A wide-screen print may also be obtained from an anamorphic negative by deanamorphosing in the printing process.

Magoptical release print. A magoptical release print is a composite release print which has both magnetic and photographic (optical) sound tracks.

(Reprinted with permission)

A SELECTED BIBLIOGRAPHY

The Liveliest Art, Arthur Knight (Mentor, New York, 1959). Excellent history of the movies. Its first half is particularly useful, much more than a history; it offers many insights into the techniques of the pioneer film-makers of silent films.

The Rise of the American Film, Lewis Jacobs (Harcourt Brace, New York, 1939). A definitive work on the subject.

The Parade's Gone By, Kevin Brownlow (Knopf, New York, 1969). A marvellous homage to the silent cinema by a contemporary film-maker who loves his subject. Based on a number of interviews with the personalities of the silent film era.

The Emergence of Film Art, Lewis Jacobs (Hopkinson and Blake, New York, 1969). A thorough coverage of the important creators of the art of film.

Cinema Eye, Cinema Ear, John Russel Taylor (Hill and Wang, New York, 1964). A useful study of contemporary directors: Fellini, Antonioni, Bunuel, Bresson, Bergman, Hitchcock, Truffaut, Godard, Resnais.

The Film Director as Superstar, Jospeh Gelmis (Doubleday, New York, 1970). Enormously revealing series of interviews with contemporary directors: Downey, Warhol, Anderson, Bertolucci, Forman, Polanski, Penn, Lester, Nichols, Kubrick, etc.

The American Cinema, Andrew Sarris (E. P. Dutton, New York, 1968). A provocative work; the author's ranking of directors and films may be argued, but his enlightened love for the cinema cannot be questioned. The year-by-year list of films is invaluable, as are the complete filmographics of each director covered. Beware of inaccuracies in dates.

Picture, Lillian Ross (Rinehart & Co., New York, 1952). A penetrating, extremely funny, thoroughly enjoyable and enormously revealing look at the making of *The Red Badge of Courage* by John Huston and associates.

Film: A Montage of Theories, Edited by Richard Dyer MacCann (E. P. Dutton, New York, 1966). An excellent introduction to film aesthetics, and a basic guide to the nature of film. It supplies a number of intriguing samples from works you will wish to turn to and offers a number of articles not easily available elsewhere.

Film: An Anthology, Edited by Daniel Talbot, (Simon and Schuster, New York, 1959). The other indispensible introduction to the art of film.

Film: the Creative Process, John Howard Lawson (Hill and Wang, New York, 1967). A basic work of film aesthetics.

What is Cinema, Andre Bazin (University of California Press, Berkeley, 1967). A provocative, stimulating work on the nature of film.

Theory of Film, Siegfried Kracauer (Oxford University Press, 1960). The definitive work on film aesthetics: indispensible.

Elements of Film, Lee Bobker (Harcourt Brace, New York, 1969). An excellent introduction to film technique and aesthetics.

Novels Into Film, George Bluestone (University of California Press, Berkeley, 1951). An important work on this vital aspect of film art.

Film Form and The Film Sense, Sergei Eisenstein (Harcourt Brace, New York, 1942, 1949). An important, highly complex work by one of the most influential directors in the history of film.

Film Technique and Film Acting, V. I. Pudovkin (Lear, New York, 1954). A great director's eloquent exposition of his art. Well expressed ideas and excellent illustrative examples of the ABC's of film-making.

Film and Its Techniques, Raymond Spottiswoode (University of California Press, Berkeley, 1959). A sometimes unnecessarily technical work, but an extremely useful exposition of the techniques of film-making.

The Technique of Film Editing, Karel Reisz and Gavin Millar (Hastings House, New York, 1968). Its first half is a classic work on traditional film editing; its second section offers many valuable insights into the techniques of the contemporary film-maker.

The Technique of Film Music, John Huntley and Roger Manvell (Hastings House, New York, 1957). Excellent examples from films are offered; the best available book on this important aspect of film-making.

The American Cinematographer Manual, Joseph V. Mascelli, (American Society of Cinematographers, Hollywood, California, 1966). This is probably the greatest source book on the market for the practicing film-maker. It is rightly considered the cameraman's "bible." It contains a wealth of information, both fundamental and highly technical, on nearly every aspect of filming. Its charts and tables are invaluable and are used by veteran cameramen for as long as they work in film-making.

The American Cinematographer. A magazine published monthly by the American Society of Cinematographers. An invaluable source for the latest information on all facets of motion picture production. Reading this magazine can keep the film-maker abreast of all new developments in equipment and procedures while offering fascinating insights into the contemporary professional cinema.

NOTES

1

1. Kevin Brownlow, *The Parade's Gone By*, Knopf, New York, 1968, p. 66.

2. *Ibid.*

2

1. Joseph V. Mascelli, ed., *American Cinematographer Manual* (2d ed.; Hollywood, Calif.: American Society of Cinematographers, 1966), p. 174.

2. *Ibid.*, p. 331.

3

1. James Wong Howe, "Photographing the Big Western," *American Cinematographer*, Volume 46 (August, 1965), p. 494.

2. Herb A. Lightman, "The Photography of *The Professionals*," *American Cinematographer*, Volume 48 (February, 1967), pp. 99–100.

3. Charles G. Clarke, *Professional Cinematography* (Hollywood, Calif.: American Society of Cinematographers, 1964), pp. 53–56.

5

1. Gillo Pontecorvo, "*The Battle of Algiers*, An Adventure in Filming," *American Cinematographer*, Volume 48 (April, 1967), p. 269.

7

1. Karel Reisz and Gavin Millar, *The Technique of Film Editing*, Hastings House, New York, 1968, pp. 350–52.

2. Interview with Richard Lester, *Movie 16*, Winter 1968–69, London, p. 19.

3. Reisz and Millar, *op. cit.*, p. 228.

4. *Ibid.*, p. 227.

5. *Ibid.*, p. 215.

6. *Ibid.*, p. 216.

7. *Ibid.*, p. 216.

8. *Ibid.*, p. 90.

8

1. Kevin Brownlow, *The Parade's Gone By*, Knopf, New York, 1968, p. 31.

2. Raymond Spottiswoode, *Film and Its Technique*, Univ. of California Press, Berkeley, 1959, p. 93.

10

1. Andre Bazin, *What Is Cinema?*, Univ. of California Press, Berkeley and Los Angeles, 1967, p. 5.

2. Bazin, *op. cit.*, p.30.

3. John Huntley and Roger Manvell, *The Technique of Film Music*, Focal Press, London and New York, 1957, p. 30.

4. Huntley and Manvell, *op. cit.*, p.14.

5. Siegfried Kracauer, *Theory Of Film*, Oxford Univ. Press, New York, 1965, p. 102.

6. *Ibid.*, p. 106.

7. *Ibid.*, p. 104.

8. *Ibid.*, p. 106.

9. *Ibid.*, p. 118.

10. *Ibid.*, p. 123–24.

11. *Ibid.*, p. 112.

12. *Ibid.*, p. 116.

13. *Ibid.*, p. 116–17.

14. Dwight MacDonald, "The Soviet Cinema: 1930–1938," *Partisan Review*, July, 1938, Vol. V, no. 2:46.

15. Alberto Cavalcanti "Sound in Films," *films*, Nov., 1939, Vol. 1, no. 1:37.

16. Kracauer, *op. cit.*, p. 124.

17. Bazin, *op. cit.*, p. 50.

18. *Ibid.*, p. 33.

19. *Ibid.*, p. 24.

20. Arthur Rosenheimer, Jr., "They Make Documentaries: Number One—Robert J. Flaherty," *Film News*, April, 1946, Vol. 7, No. 6:10, p. 23.

21. René Clair, "Reflexion Faite: Notes pour servir à l'histoire de l'aet cinematographique de 1920 a 1950," Paris, 1951, p. 152.

22. Kracauer, *op. cit.*, p. 134.

23. *Ibid.*, p. 134.

24. *Ibid.*, p. 135.

25. Aaron Copland "Tip To Moviegoers," *The New York Times Magazine*, Nov. 6, 1949.

26. Kurt London, *Film Music*, London, 1936, p. 135.

27. Ernest Lendgren, *The Art of the Film*, Allen and Unwin, London, 1948, p. 146.

28. Hanns Eisler, *Composing for the Films*, Oxford University Press, New York, 1947, p. 70.

29. Stephen Watts, interview with Alfred Hitchcock, *Cinema Quarterly*, Vol. II, No. 2, 1933.

30. Huntley and Manvell, *op. cit.*, p. 78.

31. *Ibid.*, p. 61, 74, 119, 148, 144.

32. Paul Rotha, *Documentary Film*, Faber and Faber Ltd., London, 1952, p. 168.

33. Huntley and Manvell, *op. cit.*, p. 210.

34. *Ibid.*

35. Winthrop Sargeant, "Music For Murder," *The New Yorker*, Oct. 30, 1954.

11

1. John Huntley and Roger Manvell, *The Technique of Film Music*, Focal Press, London and New York, 1957, p. 113.

2. Huntley and Manvell, *op. cit.*, p. 66.

3. Frank Lewin, "The Sound Track in Nontheatrical Motion Pictures," SMPTE Journal, Vol. 68, No. 3, March 1959, p. 2.

4. Huntley and Manvell, *op. cit.*, p. 199.

12

1. C. J. LeBel, *Fundamentals of Magnetic Recording*, Audio Devices, New York, 1951, p. 6 and 7.

2. Edward W. Kellogg, "History of Sound Motion Pictures," SMPTE Journal, Vol. 64, June, July, and August, 1955, p. 38.

3. Edward W. Kellogg, *op. cit.*, p. 38.

4. Raymond Spottiswoode, *Film and Its Techniques*, Univ. of California Press, Berkeley and Los Angeles, 1959, p. 312.

5. Raymond Spottiswoode, *op. cit.*, pp. 312–313.

6. C. J. LeBel, *op. cit.*, pp. 7–8.

7. Edward W. Kellogg, "The ABC of Photographic Sound Recording," SMPE Journal, Vol. 44, No. 3, March, 1945, pp. 151–56.

8. Raymond Spottiswoode, *op. cit.*, pp. 282–287.

9. Raymond Spottiswoode, *op. cit.*, pp. 309–312.

10. Raymond Spottiswoode, *op. cit.*, p. 276.

11. Raymond Spottiswoode, *op. cit.*, p. 277.

12. C. J. LeBel, *op. cit.*, p. 25.

13. Raymond Spottiswoode, *op. cit.*, p. 421.

14. Raymond Spottiswoode, *op. cit.*, pp. 296–299.

15. C. J. LeBel, *op. cit.*, pp. 22–26.

16. Frank Lewin, "The Sound Track in Nontheatrical Motion Pictures," SMPTE Journal, Vol. 68, No. 3, March, 1959, p. 19.

INDEX

In this index, titles of motion picture films and television shows are in italics, titles of books and periodicals are in small capitals, titles of articles in periodicals are in quotation marks. Figures and charts throughout the text are indicated by italicized numerals.

540

A Primer
for Film-Making